THE FAIRCHILD ENCYCLOPEDIA OF MENSWEAR

FAIRCHILD REFERENCE

THE FAIRCHILD

Encyclopedia
of Menswear

Mary Lisa Gavenas

FAIRCHILD PUBLICATIONS, INC.
NEW YORK

Director of Sales and Acquisitions: Dana Meltzer-Berkowitz
Executive Editor: Olga T. Kontzias
Acquisitions Editor: Joseph Miranda
Associate Acquisitions Editor: Jaclyn Bergeron
Senior Development Editor: Jennifer Crane
Development Editor: Michelle Levy
Production Manager: Ginger Hillman
Production Editor: Jessica Rozler
Photo Researcher: Erin Fitzsimmons
Assistant Editor: Blake Royer

Library of Congress Catalog Card Number: 2006940798

978-1-56367-465-5

GST R 133004424

Printed in the United States of America

TP14

This book is dedicated to
Dan McGarry

Contents

Introduction

Twenty years ago, when I went to work at the *Daily News Record*, Fairchild's menswear trade paper, I had to master a whole new vocabulary. I'd worked on midsized daily newspapers and I'd studied quite a bit of costume history in college, and now none of it did me any good. At *DNR*, I had no idea what anybody was talking about.

In this world, CLOTHING no longer meant the same thing as clothes. CLOTH was no longer a synonym for fabric. GEOMETRIC had nothing to do with protractors and rulers. A BOOTMAKER hardly ever made boots (especially if he lived in London). Likewise, most of the shoes that I'd been calling OXFORDS weren't. And I found out that BESPOKE was something altogether different from MADE-TO-MEASURE.

Quirky customs abounded. The WINDSOR KNOT was named after a man who never used one. American men wore the stripes in their REPP TIES slanting in a different direction from their British brethren. A BOWLER hat was known as a COKE among the elite, who all knew to pronounce it as "cook." Here, history was roundly ignored, but fashion fables about the origin of the TUXEDO—and the BLAZER and the SPENCER JACKET and the TARTAN— were repeated as gospel.

In those days, *DNR* was a tabloid-format paper that, like *Women's Wear Daily*, its better-known sibling, came out five times a week. So I got a crash course in GRAY GOODS and LICENSING and put in my time covering the debut of designers like JOSEPH ABBOUD (when I wasn't sneaking into Macy's Santaland to cross-examine SANTA about his costume). After a year or two of that, I left Fairchild to work for more mainstream newspapers and magazines, from *The Hollywood Reporter* to *Glamour*.

When I wasn't actively writing about movie costumes or runway shows, I began researching the folklore of menswear: figuring out why CARY GRANT supposedly wore women's underpants, how HORACE GREELEY JOHNSON got to be called the "Edison of Underwear," and why going down with the ship—in the highest-possible style—was probably the best thing that ever happened to BENJAMIN GUGGENHEIM. Slowly segueing away from menswear, I covered women's runways, wrote a book about the beauty industry, and got a graduate degree in costume history.

Then, a couple of years ago, my beat switched back to menswear. This time around, I discovered that the industry in the 21st century was radically different from the industry at the end of the 1980s. Suit sales were on the rise. Makeovers for men were a staple of reality television. Magazine publishers were busily launching male style spinoffs. Rap moguls were coining additional millions from apparel labels. Millionaire movie stars retained stables of stylists. And a debate on SHIRTTAILS had just made the front page of the *New York Times*.

However, despite the spate of style bibles and makeover guides, one thing hadn't changed: There was no place to look up a word used in a catalog description, check a spelling, figure out a usage, authenticate a date, or steal a description. No way to know what of all the completely contradictory information on the Internet was the truth. If any of it was. I met the managing editor of a menswear trade who had no idea how to describe the cuffs on the shirt he was wearing. Or the difference between a COLLAR and LAPEL. Nor did he seem to care about learning, since nobody around him knew either.

The Internet had only made things worse. Looking up a topic like LEISURE SUIT and more than one Internet source would—wrongly—inform you that it's what John Travolta wore in *SATURDAY NIGHT FEVER*. Wikipedia, so good for so many things, was a disaster for fashion entries. Googling jargon like CLOTH or GEOMETRIC would net you millions of hits without getting an answer that pertains to their particular use in menswear. Nor would you discover why it's incorrect to use SEVENTH AVENUE as slang for the men's business. Or how trousers differ from slacks. Or the many, many differences between a FASHIONISTA and GARMENTO.

Here, then, are explanations of industry slang like SOFT SEW, pattern descriptions of PUPPYTOOTH and GLEN PLAID, traditional tailors' talk like POINT-TO-POINT and JEFF, a how-to on the HALF-WINDSOR knot as well as the ASCOT, contemporary terms like DU RAG and LUMBAR PACK, and technical jargon like HYGROSCOPIC and HYDROPHILIC. Because men love statistics and dates and knowing the names of things, in this book they'll also find trivia galore on the origin of the EARMUFF, the history of the ZIPPER, and the invention of VELCRO. They'll also learn why a sweater PILLS and why SUPER 120S cost more.

Because menswear has never been as designer-driven as women's wear, I've also included the outsized personalities like NUDIE and SY DEVORE alongside the undeservedly forgotten dandies like the YELLOW EARL. I've tried to make a case for rereading *ZULEIKA DOBSON* and *THE SORROWS OF YOUNG WERTHER* as clues to cultural history, as well as showing how and why *THE WILD ONE* and *CHARIOTS OF FIRE* changed the wardrobes of millions of men who never saw those movies. Finally, I've included brief bios of dozens of distinguished men, from BEAU BRUMMELL to FRANK SINATRA, who defined themselves by what they wore.

Acknowledgments

The late Richard Martin, curator of the Metropolitan Museum's Costume Institute, was the first to encourage this project.

But I have lots of other people to thank, too: Nancy Deihl at New York University; Lourdes Font at the Fashion Institute of Technology; the expert and extremely kind reference librarians at FIT, the Metropolitan Museum's Watson Library and its Irene Lewisohn Costume Reference Library; the database experts at NYU's Bobst Library; Paula A. Baxter, curator of the Wallach Art & Architecture Division at the New York Public Library; the knowledgeable staff of Horse Country Saddlery in Warrenton, Virginia; Frank Hall, Great Britain's master maker of bespoke riding clothes; Laurel Graeber, who was the first person to translate *garmento* into English for me; as well as Diana Liu of Daunt Books, author Ron Nowicki, Stéphane Houy-Tower of the Costume Institute, and research whiz Natasha Simon.

Much of the information on textiles and tailoring practices came from hundreds of interviews conducted with practicing professionals. For patiently answering so many of my questions about construction, I also need to thank patternmaking pro Gail Gondek of Miss Thimble, as well as Samer Chamsi-Pasha, chairman of Hield. For their many, many explanations of textile techniques and terminology: Désirée Koslin; "Fabric Czar" Neal Boyarsky of Beckenstein's (who generously lent most of the samples used to illustrate patterns); Firas Chamsi-Pasha and Steve Marsden of Moxon; James Sugden of Johnstons of Elgin, for his expertise on the history of patterns and weaves; Jacques Brunel and the staff of Première Vision; and Buxton Midyette and Jesse Curlee of Supima.

Finally, for patience far above and beyond the call of duty, to Olga Kontzias, Joe Miranda, Michelle Levy, and Jessica Rozler of Fairchild Books.

—MARY LISA GAVENAS
NEW YORK, 2007

Notes on Use

Here, people, places, and things are defined mainly for how they relate to menswear. Ergo, designers like CALVIN KLEIN and YOHJI YAMAMOTO are considered mostly for their men's collections. CLIP SPOT is defined as a shirt fabric even though it was used just as often in dresses. Menswear specialists like ARNYS and BROOKS BROTHERS appear, but generalists like Macy's and Bloomingdale's do not. And men from STEVE MCQUEEN to MILES DAVIS are considered chiefly in the light of what they wore and how it influenced what other men wore.

Instead of duplicating what's already accurate and easily available, I've concentrated on definitions not found elsewhere—or on clearing up areas of misinformation. Likewise, military and sports uniforms, two areas of menswear that have already been thoroughly researched and beautifully documented, are all but passed over here. ARMOR, for example, is indexed here according to the body part it protects, exactly the way it might be quoted by an apparel manufacturer or a runway designer. Ecclesiastical garments are included as much for their silhouettes as their symbolism.

This is not primarily a historical work. The bulk of the terminology is contemporary, with historical references roughly in proportion to the number of times modern readers might encounter them. Thus, only a few entries apply to the ancient world, a few more refer to medieval and Renaissance dress, dozens more to the 18th century, and hundreds to the 19th and 20th centuries.

When two or more terms are used for the same thing, I've given the definition under the more popular and more current term. Whenever possible, cross-references are indicated by small capital letters.

THE FAIRCHILD ENCYCLOPEDIA OF MENSWEAR

abaca Fiber or fabric made from the stems of the abaca plant, which also goes by the name of Manila hemp (although botanists say it is more closely related to bananas than hemp). Also grown in locales like Central America and Ecuador, abaca is indigenous to the Philippines and has been used for apparel there for hundreds of years. Tough, fibrous, and naturally resistant to moisture, abaca is often blended with PIÑA, SILK, and/or BANANA fibers to make woven fabric used in traditional Philippine garments, such as the BARONG. It is also the chief component of most of the PAPER used to make clothes and the SHANTUNG PANAMA popular for cowboy hats.

Sometimes spelled abaka. Synonyms: Manila hemp; manilla.

Abboud, Joseph Born in 1950 to a family of Lebanese heritage, Boston native Joseph Abboud began working at specialty store LOUIS BOSTON while majoring in French and English Comparative Literature at the University of Massachusetts/Boston. After a three-semester stint studying at the Sorbonne in Paris and college graduation in 1972, he spent a dozen years at Louis Boston involved in buying and merchandising. He initially left to work for Southwick, then went to POLO/RALPH LAUREN, leaving that job in the hope of starting his own menswear collection. Eventually, at age 36, he launched his label with a successful spring 1987 collection backed by Freedberg of Boston.

Initially, Abboud became noted for clothes that were tailored but comfortably constructed (e.g., the unlined, unvented spring jackets that were a prominent feature of his first collection) and for favoring earthy, neutral colors. He won CFDA awards for menswear in both 1989 and 1990 and subsequently expanded into women's wear and other businesses. In 2004, his autobiography, *Threads*, written with Ellen Stern, was published by HarperCollins.

Abercrombie & Fitch Founded in New York in 1892 by David T. Abercrombie, as a retailer of rugged, outdoor gear for men.

In 1900, a customer named Ezra Fitch asked to buy into the business and, in 1904, it officially became Abercrombie & Fitch. Shortly before the first World War, A&F began publishing a catalog and selling items for women, moving its premises to Madison Avenue in 1917.

Joseph Abboud

Famous for outfitting sportsmen from Theodore Roosevelt to Ernest Hemingway and Clark Gable, A&F was also beloved by PREPPIES, who used its sturdy hunting gear and its leather-trimmed bags for their everyday exploits. During the 1960s, A&F overexpanded and experienced a series of financial problems, then was acquired by The Limited in 1988, which successfully repositioned it as a maker of sportswear for the college-age crowd. In 1998, A&F became independent and, not long after, launched quarterly MAGALOGS photographed by Bruce Weber, which became so notorious for their nudity that the chain became the target of boycotts.

The brand continued to expand, launching its Hollister division aimed at younger teenagers in 2000, and discontinuing its racy quarterly in 2003 in favor of a fashion magazine format.

Abruzzi tailors   Refers to tailors from the Abruzzo region of Italy who are known for adhering to an unexpectedly English, SAVILE ROW style of suit; used to describe BRIONI and certain branches of CARACENI, as well as many smaller firms.

By legend, the regional style started when Abruzzo-born musician Francesco Paolo Tosti, who had settled in London in 1875 and was knighted in 1908 by EDWARD VII, began sending his old Savile Row suits home for his relations to wear, whereupon local tailors unstitched them to copy the construction methods.

academic gowns   Usually refers to the long, purposely archaic gowns worn during graduations and similar ceremonies, the cut and color of which indicate a wearer's achievements within the academic community.

The wearing of academic gowns in the United States continues a tradition traced back to British archbishop Stephen Langton in 1222, who decreed that a long, closed gown called the *cappa clausa* be worn by clergy. At Oxford and Cambridge, clerks continued to follow his decree until, over time, the tradition became secular. Caps and gowns were a regular part of student life in the United States until the Civil War, and were worn to most classes. They remained so in England until World War II. The practice was regulated by a convention at Columbia University in 1895. In 1902, the Intercollegiate Bureau of Academic Costume was founded. In 1932, under the aegis of the American Council on Education, it formally reiterated that caps and gowns should be black, and outlined the differences between the robes of a BACHELOR, MASTER, and DOCTOR (such as shape of sleeves, length of hood, and thickness of colored trim).

Colors representing areas of academic study are standardized as:

Agriculture = Maize
Architecture = Violet
Arts, Letters, Humanities = White
Business = Drab
Dentistry = Lilac
Economics = Copper
Education = Light blue
Engineering = Orange
Family and Consumer Science = Maroon
Fine Arts = Brown
Forestry = Russet
Journalism = Crimson
Law = Purple
Library Science = Lemon
Medicine = Green
Music = Pink
Nursing = Apricot
Optometry = Orchid
Oratory = Silver

Academic gowns

Osteopathy = Green
Pharmacy = Olive green
Philanthropy = Rose
Philosophy = Dark blue
Physical Education = Sage green
Public Health = Salmon pink
Science = Golden yellow
Social Work = Citron
Theology = Scarlet
Veterinary Science = Gray

During academic ceremonies in which honors are presented, cords representing those honors (e.g., a *magna cum laude* degree) may also be worn for the event only.

accessories   A fashion and retail category that encompasses practically everything *except* pants, shirts, and suits. Therefore, hats, socks, and gloves are classified as accessories, as are more decorative and peripheral items, such as ties, pocket squares, and belts.

acetate   A lustrous CELLULOSIC fiber initially made and marketed as "artificial silk." Acetate can be dry-cleaned or machine-washed, is wrinkle-resistant, and dries quickly—qualities that make it popular for lining jackets and pants.

Invented in the 19th century for use as film, cellulose acetate's use in textiles was pioneered by Swiss brothers Camille and Henri Dreyfus, and its first com-

Achkan: Jawaharlal Nehru

mercial production in the United States was in 1924 by CELANESE, the company that was once the leading producer of acetate for apparel, but got out of that business in 2005. Acetate starts from a cellulose base (usually cotton linters) and is then "acetylized," processed, and extruded. Until 1952, when the Federal Trade Commission revised its rules, the name acetate was used interchangeably with RAYON.

achkan   The style of high-collared, lapel-less, plain-front, buttoned, traditional jacket worn in South Asia (and, in the West, initially associated with Jawarharlal Nehru, the first prime minister of India); sometimes worn over a SHALWAR KAMEEZ for everyday business. Although it inspired the Western style known as the NEHRU JACKET in the 1960s, the achkan is longer than its Western imitation, often being knee-length or mid-thigh. Its dressier   usually embroidered—counterpart is the SHERWANI. Its shorter counterpart, worn with matching trousers, is the JODHPURI SUIT.

acid-washed   A treatment for DENIM that yielded light fabric with a mottled finish, which gave rise to a fad for acid-washed jeans in the 1980s. Acid washing involved the use of pumice stones soaked in chlorine, resulting in denim that was abraded as well as bleached, and spawning dozens of subcategories like "glacier" and "ice" denim.

Acqua di Parma   Created in an apothecary in Parma in 1916, this Italian COLOGNE became famous for both its sunflower-yellow packaging and its crisp scent (a blend of Sicilian citrus, lavender, rosemary, rose, and verbena). Fashionable in the 1930s, when it was supposedly worn by style setters such as CARY GRANT, the brand was successfully relaunched in the late 1990s.

acrylic A synthetic fiber used as a wool substitute or blended with wool to produce inexpensive knits, such as sweaters and socks, as well as woven material for coats, jackets, and suits. Pure acrylic is soft, machine washable, dries quickly, resists fading, and tends to stretch during dry cleaning.

Its first commercial production in the United States was in 1950 by DuPont and, during the 1950s, acrylic/cotton blends spearheaded the move to wash 'n' wear menswear—especially in dress shirts and sports shirts.

Technically, acrylic yarn can be produced by either wet or dry extrusion, and the Federal Trade Commission defines the fiber as a long-chain synthetic polymer that must be 85 to 100 percent acrylonitrile.

activewear The industry classification for clothes worn for exercise or sports activities. (Or the apparel made to imitate it.) Activewear should not be confused with SPORTSWEAR, which is a separate, and dressier, category. For example: Running shorts, track suits, and warm-up jackets are classified as activewear. Slacks, cardigans, and sports shirts are considered sportswear.

Adidas The German sneaker and activewear company identified by a trefoil logo and its distinctive triple stripe (which supposedly originated with bands of leather added to the shoes for additional support); founded near Nuremberg, Germany, by amateur athlete Adolf Dassler, who'd begun making shoes as early as 1920 (and whose brother Rudolf founded Puma). Early on, the Dasslers were among the first to realize the value of sports sponsorships and to cater to star athletes in order to get publicity for their shoes.

Restarting his business after World War II, Dassler officially began what would become the current company in 1948, taking its name from his own: "adi" from Adolf and "das" from Dassler (traditionally, the company lowercases its name). In 1954, Germany's team won soccer's World Cup while wearing Adidas. By 1960, three quarters of the track-and-field athletes in the Olympic Games were wearing Adidas shoes. In the early 1960s, the company began making soccer balls and, later in the decade, branched into apparel. In 1987, it was immortalized in HIP-HOP history with the Run-D.M.C. hit "My Adidas." After passing out of family control and incorporating in 1989, it launched several more lines. For example: In 2001, after a successful collaboration on a sneaker line called Y3, the company appointed Japanese designer YOHJI YAMAMOTO as creative director of its new Adidas Sport Style division.

In 2006, it acquired rival footwear and apparel company Reebok.

adinkra A distinctive type of printed cloth made by the Ashanti of Ghana, worn for both formal and informal occasions. Both the background color of the adinkra and the dozens of possible designs stamped on it are symbolic as well as decorative, and experienced viewers can "read" the cloth. (For example: A particular swirl pattern symbolizes rams' horns, which represent strength.) Traditionally, adinkra is prepared from strips of imported cotton; women prepare the dyes and materials, and men do the stamping, using carved calabash shells.

aesthetic dress *or* **Aestheticism** *or* **Aesthetic movement** The Aesthetic movement, in which a group of

Adinkra painting

men in the arts rebelled against the industrialism and conformity of Victorian England by purposely evoking the dress and design of earlier eras, is usually traced to formation of the pre-Raphaelite brotherhood in 1848. However, its peak of influence on menswear came during the 1870s and 1880s, when "aesthetic dress" was identified with high-profile London residents such as Anglo-Irish writer Oscar Wilde and American painter James McNeill Whistler and pilloried in the popular *Punch* cartoons drawn by George du Maurier.

Like aesthetic dress for women, which favored the abandonment of corsets and the adoption of graceful medieval-style gowns, aesthetic dress for men was purposely anachronistic. During the era of derbies, it favored large hats with dramatically deep brims. During the era of stiff collars, it favored full-sleeved, bloused shirts, topped by poetic cloaks and capes. It reintroduced knee BREECHES. It favored outrageous BOUTONNIÈRES—sunflowers were particularly recommended—and flowing ties. Yellow was a favored color for accessories, especially for gloves. Indeed, in 1881, the D'Oyly Carte Opera Company satirized such preciousness in Gilbert and Sullivan's *Patience*, with its famous reference to the "greenery-yallery, Grosvenor Gallery" (that gallery being the site of exhibitions of pre-Raphaelite painting).

Aestheticism: Oscar Wilde as the "Apostle" of the Aesthetic

OSCAR THE APOSTLE.
Puck's "Wilde" Dream of an Aesthetic Future for America.

Despite such sustained mockery, aesthetic dress officially arrived in the United States the following year, when Wilde, who had pronounced himself "Professor of Aesthetics," embarked on an extensive speaking tour for which he had outfitted himself with knee breeches, a velvet coat, blouse-like shirts, a green tie, long hair, and a lily (a favorite prop of the pre-Raphaelite painters).

Never mainstream and always more influential for women's wear than menswear, the aesthetic dress movement soon evolved, laying the foundation for the subsequent Arts and Crafts movement and the Wiener Werkstätte on one hand, and the decadence of symbolists and the *fin de siècle* dandies on the other.

Afghan coat　Usually refers to the rough, ethnic-looking coats and jackets made of SHEEPSKIN traditionally cured in urine and then treated to a little embroidery. Originally imported from Afghanistan, these were considered an essential fashion souvenir of the overland "HIPPIE trail" between Europe and India, and first became popular in the 1960s.

Afghani hat　Because several tribes and cultures coexist in Afghanistan, there is no single national dress. Perhaps best known in the West is the round, cloth hat with a rolled brim and flat top associated with Tajik tribesmen and the Northern Alliance, called the PAKOL.

aftermarket　Industry jargon for a secondary or recycled use of clothes: literally, what comes after the primary market. Thus, when used clothing is shipped to Third World countries, that becomes its "aftermarket."

aftershave　Exactly what is sounds like: A toiletry intended for application after shaving, and thus often served as a combination of skin care and light fragrance particularly in the days before elaborate skin care and shaving regimens were marketed to men. Although often referred to as a "lotion," the traditional aftershave formulation was a clear or tinted liquid containing a hefty percentage of alcohol and was usually applied by being splashed from a bottle onto a man's palms and then patted on his face. Depending on the brand, the aftershave was supposed to either soothe the skin after shaving or "brace" and invigorate it.

Although there is no industry standard for the amount of fragrance contained in an aftershave, it is generally less fragrant than a COLOGNE and carries a maximum of 3 percent essential oils or fragrance concentrate (versus 3 to 5 percent for cologne). During the 20th century, popular brands included AQUA VELVA and OLD SPICE.

afro   A hairstyle in which kinky hair is grown out (usually longer than an inch) and worn separated and lifted to its maximum fullness.

This hairstyle first achieved wide acceptance in the 1960s, as a way to play up, rather than play down, African heritage. Up until that point, the fashionable norm for most black American men involved wearing hair extremely closely cropped or with its natural curl relaxed through some kind of hairdressing or chemical processing. The afro, by contrast, was defiantly untreated and full. Within a decade or two, the trend came full circle, when in the late 1970s through the mid-1980s, it became common for white men to get perms to simulate some of the extreme curliness of black hair.

Also known as a 'fro.

afro pick   A comblike styling tool, usually with three or four long (3 to 6 inches), forklike tines, used to separate and lift hair as a way of keeping an AFRO hairstyle at its maximum fullness. Often with a decorated handle that can be seen when the comb is worn in the hair or sported on the person (e.g., in a back pocket).

After Six   An American company best known for its efforts to popularize FORMALWEAR in the 1970s and 1980s, a category that most American men previously considered the purview of the upper crust with rules prescribed by an obscure and elaborate etiquette. After Six advertised directly to the consumer and often invented its own trends in order to keep formalwear at the forefront of American fashion. For example, in the mid-1970s, it promoted a line of TUXEDOS retailing for under $100, and sold fashionably flowered and ruffled shirts as a way for a man to update the tuxedo he already owned. The company's other divisions, producing other categories of clothes, included Bert Paley, Before Six, and House of Malcolm Kenneth.

agal   Variant spelling of AQAL, the double-rolled band, usually made of goat hair and sheep's wool, used to secure the head scarf, known as the KAFIYEH or GHUTTERA, of traditional ARAB headdress. Worn over the taqiyah, or SKULLCAP, the agal rests atop the head (and is not worn across the forehead like a headband). Also spelled IQAL.

Afro: Jackson 5

aglet The name for the tip, usually metal or plastic, put at the end of a shoelace to prevent its unraveling.

Agnelli, Giovanni ("Gianni") Born in 1921 near Turin, Italian industrialist Gianni Agnelli first gained notoriety as a trendsetting playboy before taking over Fiat, the company founded by his family, in 1966.

Handsome and wealthy, Agnelli graduated from law school but never practiced (hence his newspaper nickname *L'Avvocato*—"the lawyer"). He was wounded twice during World War II, married Marella Caracciolo di Castagneto (a long-necked Neapolitan princess consistently named to international best-dressed lists) in 1953, and owned the soccer team Juventus. A favorite of gossip columnists, he was called, among other names, the "King of Italy" after his ascension to the top spot at Fiat. His documented affairs included actress Anita Ekberg and socialite Pamela Harriman, and his undocumented affairs supposedly ranged from Rita Hayworth to Jacqueline Kennedy Onassis.

His style trademarks included a year-round tan; white hair swept straight back from his forehead to play up his patrician profile; bespoke suits (in the equivalent of a trim, European size 46) made by CARACENI; the practice of buckling his wristwatch outside BARREL CUFFS (usu-ally custom sewn by shirtmaker BATTISTONI); unbuttoning the collars of button-down shirts; the habit of treating neckties as casually as kerchiefs (for example, tucking the top blade into the waistband of his trousers, skewing the knot to the side, or allowing its blades to flop outside his vest or sweater); and the adoption of driving moccasins (TOD's created its nub-soled style for him in the 1970s).

Agnelli officially retired from Fiat in 1996 and died in 2003. Upon his death, much of his wardrobe passed to grandson Lapo Elkann.

Agnès b. A brand begun by the Frenchwoman whose real name is Trouble. Born in Versailles in 1941, Agnès Trouble married early and began her fashion career, at *Elle* magazine, while still in her teens. Soon thereafter, she began freelancing for design houses, adopting the initial "B" from her first husband, Christian Bourgois. By age 19, she had two children and was trying to live on her own.

A *soixante-huitard* (i.e., an energetic participant in the cultural and political changes of Paris during the 1960s), she established her own label in 1973 and later opened her first boutique in an old butcher's shop in Les Halles just as the neighborhood was changing from the city's central market to an arts and retail enclave around the newly built Centre George Pompidou. There she began selling redyed or modified work clothes and vernacular basics alongside her original designs for men and women. Then and now, her perennials included long-sleeved T-SHIRTS with bold horizontal stripes, black leather coats and jackets, long-sleeved cotton shirts in novelty prints, and cotton suits in solid colors.

Agnès Trouble has never advertised and has always been the sole designer for everything bearing her name. One of the wealthiest fashion designers in France, she

After Six

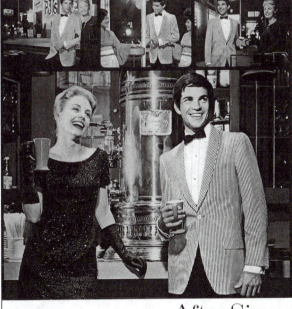

Agnès b.

operates dozens of boutiques worldwide. An avid art collector, she has had a gallery since 1984 and has dabbled in film production since 1997.

airing   Allowing air to freely circulate around apparel or fabrics, usually to prevent dampness, mildew, and/or the build-up of odor. Airing may take place either after or instead of laundering, but it is not synonymous with cleaning.

Most often, airing was conducted to prevent the damage of clothes caused by their long-term storage. (Clothes were rarely hung straight and the clothes hanger did not pass into general use until near the beginning of the 20th century.) In the days when a man's suit or greatcoat could easily weigh 5 or 10 pounds, heavy clothes, rarely cleaned and stored in damp, dark places, were prone to infestations of mold and insects, as well as to the fraying caused by folding. They also tended to absorb cooking, wood smoke, and/or gas odors. Therefore, clothes had to be taken out of storage, shaken loose, and well-aired before wearing.

In centuries when laundry was more difficult, personal linen also was often aired between washings to freshen it before the next wearing. Hence, "airing dirty linen," a phrase referring to that practice of exposure and ventilation.

alb   The ankle-length, long-sleeved white robe worn as part of priestly vestments for performance of the liturgy or other ceremonies since at least the 9th century. The alb pulls over the head and may have either a drawstring, hooded, or plain neckline. Derived from "alba," the Latin word for *white*, the alb is meant to symbolize purity and is belted by the CINCTURE and crossed by the STOLE, which is then topped by the sleeveless CHASUBLE, or (for a deacon) the sleeved DALMATICA.

albert   Although Queen Victoria gave her name to an age, her Prince Consort, Albert (as Prince Francis Charles Augustus Albert Emmanuel of Saxe-Coburg and Gotha was popularly known), gave his name to several items of menswear. Among the best known:

1. A style of man's slip-on shoe, most often a velvet slipper, with a tongue that extends upward over the instep to create a sort of flap (in a shape that recalls the pediment on a column). In the 20th and 21st centuries, worn as part of formal or semiformal dress at home: For instance, as accompaniment to a SMOKING JACKET.

2. A style of shorter watch chain popularized by Prince Albert, who favored a straight-across, pocket-to-pocket chain rather than the elaborately draped styles associated with dandies like the COUNT D'ORSAY.

3. A style of genital piercing that almost certainly had nothing to do with Victoria's consort, and involves insertion of a ring at the end of the penis.

albert cloth   Reversible, usually wool, woven cloth used for coats.

Alexander Julian   See JULIAN, ALEXANDER.

Alfred Dunhill   See DUNHILL.

alligator   Skin taken from alligator that is prized in part because it is more difficult to obtain than common cow skin and in part because of its extreme toughness and durability. Alligator can be cured to yield an extremely glossy surface with thick ridges that delineate its large, decorative scales.

Often confused with similar-looking skins, such as ALLIGATOR LIZARD (which, being a lizardskin, is lighter and far more fragile), ANTEATER (which is also much lighter and has a smaller scale), or CROCODILE (which is virtually identical except that it shows a pinprick at the top of each scale).

alligator lizard   Leather that is actually a LIZARDSKIN made from a South American species, rather than a variant on ALLIGATOR.

alligator shirts   Slang (especially when referring to PREPPY clothes) for the knit polo shirts produced by LACOSTE (and, as such, a slight misnomer, since the small emblem over the heart is actually a crocodile as a reference to tennis player René Lacoste's nickname as "the Crocodile").

aloha shirts   See HAWAIIAN SHIRTS.

alpaca   Fiber or fabric made from the hair of the alpaca, a small, domesticated llama native to the high altitudes of South America. A CAMELID, the alpaca is divided into two main types: the huacaya, and the rarer and more delicate SURI, with the latter being particularly prized for its silky, LONG-STAPLE fiber. Fine alpaca is considered a NOBLE FIBER and is thus more costly than ordinary sheep's wool. Often used undyed in its natural variations of brown, especially for sweaters.

alpargata   A rope-soled, cloth-topped slipper style; in Spanish usage, an ESPADRILLE.

alternating stripe   A pattern in which the background color stays the same, but the color of the stripes does not. Frequently used in shirts.

alternative black tie   A designation or dress code for social occasions in which a TUXEDO is the desired dress but ethnic or fashionable dress of equal formality is equally acceptable. Often interchangeable with the designation CREATIVE BLACK TIE.

American Gigolo   The 1980 movie that made superstars of American actor Richard Gere and Italian designer GIORGIO ARMANI. Written and directed by Paul Schrader, who had become an Armani customer at Maxfield's in L.A., the production had cast John Travolta, but replaced him with Gere as Los Angeles-based antihero Julian Kay ("Is giving pleasure a crime?"), a hustler whose subtly colored, softly tailored Armani wardrobe was the antithesis of the look popularly associated with prostitution and pimping. Although Alice Rush is credited with the movie's costume design, it was Armani's contribution that would influence menswear throughout the subsequent decade.

amice   The first of the traditional liturgical vestments put on by a Catholic priest as he prepares to celebrate the mass. A plain piece of cloth, which may be square or rectangular, the amice is draped over the head and shoulders and then, after the outer vestments are donned, is folded back as the priest arrives at the altar to begin mass. When he finishes and prepares to leave, he may then raise the amice again.

Amies, Hardy   Born in 1909 in London, Amies received a ROYAL WARRANT from Queen Elizabeth II in 1955. By 1958, he became one of the first of many women's wear designers to capitalize on that notoriety by selling products like ties and aftershave to men and, in 1961, to branch out to a full-fledged line of menswear. Soon thereafter, the range of his licensing agreements was rivaled only by that of PIERRE CARDIN.

As might be expected from his popularity with the women of the royal family, Amies was not known for his

American Gigolo: Richard Gere

radical fashion innovations. He also dabbled in film costume, and his credits include Stanley Donen's *Two for the Road* (1967) and Stanley Kubrick's *2001: A Space Odyssey* (1968). In his 1994 book *The Englishman's Suit* and his two memoirs (*Just So Far* and *Still Here*), Amies styled himself as an arbiter of menswear. He was knighted in 1989, retired from his business in 2001, and died in 2003.

Amish dress   Refers to the clothes proscriptions followed by the Old Order Amish, an Anabaptist sect found mostly in the United States and Canada; known as one of the PLAIN PEOPLE (along with Brethren, Hutterites, and Old Order Mennonites), the Amish use their mode of dress to symbolize separation from the world. The sect traces its name and its rejection of overtly worldly attire to its founding by Jakob Ammann (who was, ironically, a tailor) and his rift with Swiss Anabaptist bishop Hans Reist at the end of the 17th century.

The basic unit of the Amish church is the *ordnung* (equivalent to a congregation), which establishes its own rules and sets them forth in its *Regel und Ordnung*, which functions as its particularized code of conduct. Thus, while seemingly the same to the outside world, Amish attire may vary greatly from district to district. These subtle variations, imperceptible to the outsider, broadcast a man's age, marital status, and community of origin to the other Amish. For example, there may be difference from *ordnung* to *ordnung* in the width of a hat brim; some may allow zippers on pants, others may not; buttons are generally allowed on shirts, but less often on other garments.

However, there is a basic dress code: SWEATERS are forbidden, as are showy colors like red, yellow, and orange. Most clothes, except for shirts, are simple and black, without patterns, outside pockets, or ornamentation. The basic coat is called the WAMUS; its more formal counterpart is the MUTZE (worn mostly to Sunday services and usually closed via hooks and eyes), which is a split-tail, FROCK-like coat worn over a vest. Pants are uncreased and worn with plain SUSPENDERS; usually they have a button-flap closing but no fly. Unmarried men are often clean-shaven; married men wear a full beard, but not a mustache. Males wear their hair long (at least past the tops of their ears) and parted in the middle, with bangs cut across their foreheads.

A little boy gets his first flat-crowned, wide-brimmed hat when he leaves dresses behind at about age two, and thereafter all his headgear will follow a similar pattern and be either black felt or straw. Marriage attire is also plain-colored. The dead are dressed in white.

Although the Amish reject impracticality and showiness, they do not reject modernity per se. They are, for example, fond of POLYESTER for its practicality.

amulet   In historical references, the word connotes a medal, relic, scrap of fabric, or some similar object worn for religious or protective reasons, rather than pure decoration. Placement of an amulet varies according to the tradition of the wearer, and may be anywhere from the forehead or bicep to a string around the neck.

Amish dress

In contemporary references describing American or European dress, the word is more apt to be used to describe jewelry, especially tribal-style or otherwise ethnic jewelry, that is meant to look like an amulet.

analog Refers to a watch with a traditional face, including a dial, moving hands (a shorter hand for the hours, a longer hand for the minutes, and perhaps a sweep hand to indicate seconds), and numbers or markers representing 12 hours. Its opposite is digital and, in fact, the term was coined only after the appearance of digital watches, when merchants and manufacturers needed to distinguish between the two categories.

Anderson & Sheppard Considered one of the most distinguished SAVILE ROW tailoring firms; founded as Anderson & Simmons in 1906 and renamed in 1913 when Sidney Sheppard replaced the original partner; renowned for its understated line, particularly for the DRAPE front, soft shoulders, and high armholes of its jackets (a style Swedish founder Per Anderson learned working under FREDERICK SCHOLTE).

Famously close-mouthed about its clientele, A&S is nonetheless known to have been patronized by FRED ASTAIRE (who, according to legend, would do a few dance moves on the premises to judge the suit's fit), DOUGLAS FAIRBANKS JR., Averell Harriman, CALVIN KLEIN, DERRILL OSBORN, and Rudolph Valentino, and has received a royal warrant from Prince Charles. (During his two years at Anderson & Sheppard, fashion designer ALEXANDER MCQUEEN is reputed to have scrawled messages on the unseen insides of at least one jacket made for the prince.)

In 2005, A&S was forced to relocate its premises from 30 Savile Row, where it had been since 1928, to nearby Old Burlington Street, a move widely reported and direly interpreted in the international press.

Andover Shop Known as a bastion of the IVY LEAGUE LOOK, particularly during its heyday in the 1950s and early 1960s, the store was founded by Charlie Davidson on Main Street in Andover, Massachusetts, in 1949 but opened its more famous location on Holyoke Street on Harvard Square in Cambridge, Massachusetts, during the early 1950s. It was there that celebrities from MILES DAVIS to John F. Kennedy came to have their clothes custom-made under Davidson's occasionally irascible and eccentric supervision.

A friend of *Boston Globe* columnist GEORGE FRAZIER, Davidson was legendary for refusing service to anyone he didn't like the looks of and adamant in his opinions on everything from natural shoulders (for) to bow ties (against).

Anglomania 1. The fad for British fashions that began in 18th-century Paris and peaked there in the 1770s and 1780s. In his rejection of the *ancien régime*, the fashionable Frenchman also rejected what he saw as its accoutrements: elaborate suits, stiff silks, and highly embellished accessories. Instead, he embraced what he interpreted as British fashion: thick stripes; plain colors such as black, brown, or dark blue; simply woven wools; more informal attire worn in urban settings; and styles such as the FROCK COAT and REDINGOTE. Often, the most devout republican did his best to dress like an English aristocrat on a country estate.

The British influence on French menswear continued unabated until well into the reign of Napoleon, who banned the importation of British goods (although his wife Josephine was known to bootleg them for her own use) and who fostered the patronage of the French silk industry. During the restoration of the Bourbon monarchy in the early 19th century, British influence would peak again and be repeatedly revived, to greater and lesser degrees, during the following century.

2. The name given by British designer Vivienne Westwood to her line of unisex sportswear, launched in spring 1998.

angola   A reference to a plain-woven fabric used for suits; the fabric's type and fiber content vary according to when the reference is made. In earlier descriptions of men's clothes (especially before the late 18th century), "angola" is apt to be a variation of "angora," and thus a reference to mohair. Later on, it referred to a fine wool fabric that was made to resemble cashmere. Contemporary use usually indicates a wool/cotton blend.

angora   Fabric or fiber made from the hair of angora rabbits—and not to be confused with mohair, which is a totally different fiber made from the fleece of angora goats. Extremely soft and silky, true angora appears more often in clothes for infants and women than it does in menswear. When it does appear, it is apt to be a small percentage in a blend with wool, cashmere, or some similar fiber.

aniline dye   Refers to a type of dye that was "accidentally" developed for commercial use by William Perkins in 1856 as magenta or "mauvine purple" when the Englishman was only 18. Chemists had begun extracting aniline dyes 30 years before him, but it was Perkins, a student chemist hoping to duplicate quinine, who perfected the coal tar derivative as a viable dye.

Immediately popular—Perkins became a very wealthy man—anilines forever changed the way that clothes were colored. For the thousands of years before him, virtually every dye had been derived from animals, vegetables, or minerals. Anilines made intensity of color and brilliance widely available (and very fashionable for women) and therefore marvelously modern. Often blindingly bright when new, anilines remained relatively fugitive up through the 1920s, and therefore old garments dyed with anilines should never be judged by their present appearance.

anorak   A style of parka that is pulled over the head, rather than having a complete opening at the front. Primarily associated with outdoor pursuits like skiing and hiking, the anorak (like the parka) later became modish as city outerwear, especially in Europe.

Ant, Adam   The British singer, born Stuart Goddard in London in 1954, who became the poster boy for New Romantic dressing at the beginning of the 1980s. At a time when British music was still best known for punk and men's fashion was still best known for the minimalism of Giorgio Armani and Calvin Klein, the handsome, dark-haired singer adopted swashbuckling pirate and highwayman costumes. He would appear onstage with a slash of war paint decorating his high cheekbones and a silk scarf streaming from the sleeve of his tight, frogged jacket. His apogee was the 1981 release of the "Prince Charming" album containing the single "Stand and Deliver," which fortuitously coincided with the launch of MTV in the United States.

Briefly managed by Malcolm McLaren, who takes complete credit for Ant's adoption of the New Romantic image, the singer was a frequent customer of Vivienne Westwood's Worlds End shop and already a celebrity when she launched her "Pirates" collection on the catwalk in 1981.

Adam Ant

anteater　Leather made from the skin of any of several types of ant-eating mammals. Although often mistaken for ALLIGATOR, because it has a similarly-shaped scale pattern, anteater is neither as heavy nor as heavy-duty.

Anthony Eden　Slang reference to a HOMBURG hat, inspired by that style's identification with Sir Anthony Eden (1897–1977), who was often seen wearing one during his 1930s service as foreign secretary, and during his subsequent 1950s service as prime minister.

antiquing　A general reference (rather than a specific mechanical or chemical process) that indicates fabric or apparel has been purposely prematurely aged. Used most often to describe JEANS.

Antwerp Six　Refers to the Belgian fashion designers who gained notoriety in the late 1980s and early 1990s for their radically deconstructed and visibly unfinished work; so called because of their attendance at the then off-the-fashion-radar Royal Academy of Fine Arts in Antwerp during the late 1970s and early 1980s. The original six were Dirk Bikkembergs, Ann Demeulemeester, Dries Van Noten, Dirk Van Saene, Walter Von Beirendonck, and Marina Yee. However, when Yee suspended her collection, Martin Margiela soon replaced her in mentions of the movement.

Although the designers shared a similar education and aesthetic, they were neither part of a formal co-op nor a design manifesto. The reference "Antwerp Six" was coined by a fashion public relations firm who wanted to promote the young, then-unknown designers during London shows of the 1980s and found that most of the press and public could neither pronounce nor remember their names. In the context of the big shoulder pads, flashy logos, and power dressing that dominated the fashion world at the time of their debut, their work looked especially avant-garde, and occasioned comparisons to the work of Japanese designers such as Rei Kawakubo, ISSEY MIYAKE, Junya Watanabe, and YOHJI YAMAMOTO, who had similarly shaken up the fashion establishment a few years earlier.

Of the group, Demeulemeester, Margiela, and Van Noten enjoyed the biggest commercial breakouts, and their success paved the way for fellow Belgians Veronique Branquinho, Raf Simons, Wim Neels, Oliver Theyskens, A. F. Vandevorst, and Bernard Willhelm, as well as Dutchman Frits Klaarenbeek.

apache　In lowercase, the word refers to a type of early-20th-century Parisian gangster and petty criminal. The apache was so identified with rough behavior that apache dances (which often featured a man flinging his female partner around) became a staple of music hall performances in both Europe and the United States. Stereotypically, the apache would be costumed with a striped jersey, a neck kerchief, and a cigarette dangling from his lips.

Apparel Arts　An American magazine about men's fashion, founded with the Christmas 1931 issue by publisher William Hobart Weintraub and editor Arnold Gingrich; published quarterly in New York City (later becoming a monthly) with the then-outrageous cover price of $1.50. A trade magazine aimed at retailers, its initial issues included samples of actual fabrics tipped into its pages. During its heyday in the 1930s, it was one of the first publications to employ Paul Rand as an art director and its large (11 by 14 inches) format featured slick illustrations and foldouts explaining how a particular season's fabrics, patterns, and silhouettes should be coordinated. Its popularity beyond its small (7,500 circulation) trade audience has been called the impetus for Gingrich's founding of ESQUIRE as a monthly consumer magazine in 1933.

With the March 1950 issue, the title was changed to *Esquire's Apparel Arts*; from July 1956 to Spring 1958 (when it had again become quarterly), it reverted to the title *Apparel Arts*. It was subsumed into *GQ* magazine in 1958.

Apple   The clothes boutique, owned by THE BEATLES and named for their company, which opened in December 1967 at 94 Baker Street in London (and is not to be confused with their company offices at 3 Savile Row). Immediately notorious for the multistory mural painted on the outside of the building (which soon had to be painted over), the store featured work from a mostly Dutch design cooperative who had dubbed themselves "The Fool," and was intended to be, in the famous quote from Paul McCartney, "a beautiful place where you could buy beautiful things." However, chaotic management and petty theft contributed to heavy losses, McCartney's envisioned "controlled weirdness" became out of control, and the store closed at the end of July 1968.

appliqué   A textile that is "applied" to another textile with stitching or glue, usually for decorative, rather than functional, reasons. Most often the appliqué is on top of the main textile, but it can also be applied underneath where slits or some other garment construction reveals its having presence. For example: A boy's sweater with felt leaves stitched on its front would be described as appliqué decoration.

appointments class   A class in a horse show in which the rider is judged, either wholly or in part, according to the correctness and presentation of his "appointments" (meaning his riding habit and tack) according to rules set forth by the show judges or the United States Equestrian Federation.

apron   1. Jargon for the visible part of a NECKTIE that hangs down from the knot in the same way that a maid's apron hangs from her waist; more often American usage. Thus, every tie has two "aprons": the wider in front and the narrower in back. Synonym: BLADE, especially in British usage.   2. Jargon for the front section of the shoe between the toe cap and the vamp.

aqal   The double-rolled band, usually made of goat hair and sheep's wool, used to secure the head scarf, or GHUTTERA, of traditional ARAB headdress. Worn over the taqiyah, or SKULLCAP, the aqal rests atop the head and is never pulled down across the forehead.

aqua mirabilis   In the context of menswear, an early synonym for COLOGNE.

Aquascutum   The British firm, long renowned for its TRENCH COATS, founded by tailor John Emery in 1851 on Regent Street in London (which remains the address of its flagship store). Emery credited himself with inventing waterproof wool—hence the company name, which is Latin for "water shield"—and, early on, emphasized performance fabrics and durability.

The brand history encompasses both outfitting officers in the Crimean war and contributing to the kit of Edmund Hillary in his historic climb of Everest. Although its illustrious customer list included Humphrey Bogart, Winston Churchill, Greta Garbo, and CARY GRANT, Aquascutum long remained less well known than BURBERRY, the British firm also renowned for trench coats. However, in 2005, it presented its first runway show and, in 2006, underwent a major revamp aimed at making the marque more fashionable.

Aqua Velva   A brand of AFTERSHAVE launched by the Connecticut-based J.B. Williams during World War I, originally notorious for its extremely high alcohol content (causing it to be consumed by soldiers and others who had no access to more traditional beverages) and its bright blue color. Endorsed by a range of male celebrities from Lou Gehrig to LUCIUS BEEBE, the brand was promoted by the repeatedly revived jingle: "There's something about an Aqua Velva man."

Arab dress, traditional   The garments most closely identified with the traditional dress of men on the Arabian peninsula and nearby countries, include the AGAL (a double-rolled band worn on the head to secure the KAFIYEH scarf); the THOBE, a long-sleeved, full-length robe; and the BISHT, a cloaklike garment worn over the thobe.

Aran   The name for a style of densely patterned, vertically paneled, ornately CABLED knits made of heavy yarn, classically in an undyed, off-white wool known as *BAININ*.

Although identified with the folkways of the Aran Islands off the west coast of Ireland (Inishmore, Inishmaan, and Inisheer), the SWEATERS were not part of the people's traditional dress, but were a fashion that emerged in the islands during the early 20th century. No examples identifiable as the style currently associated with the term predate 1930. Previously, the islanders sported a distinctive style of heavy HOMESPUN clothes and the fishermen wore the type of dark blue GANSEYS with patterning that stopped at mid-chest, a style traditional to similar areas in the British Isles.

The sweaters' identification with the Arans came about in part because the Republic of Ireland put a strong emphasis on home-produced crafts and, in part, because a German writer "discovered" an early prototype of the sweaters during the 1930s and waxed rhapsodic about the ancient Celtic influences he supposedly found. During the 1940s, a market emerged for the style in Dublin. During the 1950s, the Irish Export Board began to aggressively promote the style.

By the 1960s, when Irish-American John Fitzgerald Kennedy was president of the United States and Ireland was enjoying a tourist boom, the style of heavy, off-white wool sweater became identified with Ireland and Irishness. It was worn by Irish musicians from the Clancy Brothers to the Chieftans, became a popular souvenir of trips to Ireland, and was frequently worn as a show of Irish heritage on St. Patrick's Day—in addition to being quoted, subverted, and reinvented by various fashion designers. (For example, in 1985, designer JEAN PAUL GAULTIER included a head-to-toe Aran ensemble in a menswear show.)

Earlier Aran-style sweaters were made in a much smaller GAUGE, which was increased to make them easier to produce. Originally, the *bainin* used to make them was a coarse wool that retained its lanolin content, giving some protection against wet weather; repeated washing made the sweaters whiter and fluffier, but also stripped the oil content that made the sweaters water-resistant. In contemporary use, many Arans are no longer made from coarse wool, but from a variety of materials including NOBLE FIBERS like CASHMERE.

The style prizes intricacy, and classic examples always include one or more patterns of elaborate vertical cabling, with virtually every area in the rest of the sweater filled with some sort of patterned stitch. Unlike its predecessor the gansey, the Aran contains virtually no plain knit stitches—except for a few that may be needed to set off the three-dimensional effect of the cables. Stitches identified with Aran knitting include: Aran diamond and trellis patterns filled with moss stitch; blackberry stitch (a textural, bobble-like repeating pattern); and cables in single, double, and even triple interlacing.

Synonym: FISHERMAN KNIT.

arcuate   In apparel, used to refer to the bow-shaped logo stitched on the back pocket of LEVI's jeans (or jeans imitating them), which first used the stitching design in 1873 and trademarked it in 1943. Subsequently, the arcuate became so identified with the Levi's brand that when World War II rationing made it infeasible to use decorative stitching, the company painted it on their jeans instead.

argyle   Refers to the pattern, more often used in knitwear than wovens, that looks somewhat like a traditional plaid skewed sideways—so that it is standing on end instead of running horizontally and vertically. The argyle consists of diamond shapes with an OVERCHECK pattern and is, therefore, always a minimum of three colors (the solid diamond, the overcheck, and the background), although it may be more, depending on whether or not the checks or overchecks alternate in color.

The name comes from the town in Western Scotland and is, like the location, sometimes spelled argyll.

Following its popularization by EDWARD VIII when he was the Prince of Wales, argyle became a menswear staple, especially for socks, PULLOVER SWEATERS, and SWEATER VESTS. After World War II, it became widely accepted in the United States, crossing from the golf market to mainstream menswear. In the early 21st century, its popularity as a pattern was revived again by Pringle, the U.K. brand, in part as a reference to the company's origins with Scottish framework knitting in the first quarter of the 19th century.

Armani, Giorgio   Born in Piacenza, in the industrial Emilia-Romagna region of northern Italy, on July 11, 1934, Italian designer Giorgio Armani became famous first for his menswear, before growing that business into a lifestyle brand that eventually encompassed everything from women's wear, jeans, and home furnishings to shoes, resorts, and chocolates. By the beginning of the 21st century, he was usually cited as the world's best-recognized, most commercially successful, and personally wealthy designer.

Having won a place to study medicine, Armani instead served in the military for two years, then quit school. Starting as its assistant window dresser, he segued into the position of assistant menswear buyer for department store La Rinascente, where he worked from 1957 to 1964. After learning the business as a buyer and merchandiser, he then went to NINO CERUTTI, where he worked as a designer on the Hitman line from 1964 through 1970. Thereafter, he freelanced and did stints at ERMENEGILDO ZEGNA and Ungaro.

Teaming up with boyfriend SERGIO GALEOTTI as his business partner, the blue-eyed, perpetually tanned designer did his first collection of menswear in 1974 and founded his company the following year. He became known first for his unconstructed jackets and for restrained color choices that little resembled the pin-

Giorgio Armani

Argyle

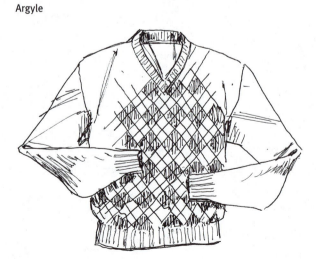

stripes and plaids favored for traditional tailoring. His style, which literally took the stuffing out of convention-al construction, also placed him at the leading edge of a move to lighten menswear—making the average suit weigh about a pound less than it had been only a few years before and only about half of what it had weighed in the previous century. In 1978, he told the trade paper *Women's Wear Daily*: "What I don't like is when Ameri-can men try to dress in a very elegant way because they don't know how. [They] look ridiculous when they try to wear a navy pinstriped suit with a satin tie. But they have a certain innate elegance when they wear sportswear."

By 1975, Armani offered a collection that applied those same principles and palette to women's wear: Hav-ing made men's tailoring softer and more feminine, he made women's clothes more restrained and masculine. Using investment money supplied by Italian manufac-turer GFT, Armani bought up the back of every issue of *L'Uomo Vogue* magazine, a move that made his company seem more prominent than it then was; partly as a result, he was soon being carried in U.S. specialty stores like Barneys in New York and Maxfield's in L.A. In 1980, his fame spread to a general audience in the United States when his clothes for Richard Gere's title character became a featured attraction of the movie American Gigolo, and, in 1982, *Time* magazine ran a cover story on "Giorgio's Gorgeous Style."

Widely favored by celebrities for his greatly understat-ed gowns and tuxedos, Armani began dressing celebrities for the Oscars and other red-carpet events during the early 1980s and, from 1988, maintained an office in Hol-lywood. He also contributed designs to theatrical per-formances and movies including 1982's *48 Hours*, 1987's *The Untouchables*, 1991's *The Object of Beauty*, 1996's *Stealing Beauty,* and the 2000 remake of Shaft.

From 1980 onward, Armani proved his business mettle by successfully signing licenses, expanding into allied fields, opening his own stores, maintaining tight control of his distribution, and acquiring established manufacturing facilities. For example: In 1980, Armani signed a license with L'Oréal, who thereafter produced his signature fragrances, which became wildly success-ful with the addition of Acqua di Gio in 1996. In 1981, he opened the first boutique for Emporio Armani, a slightly lower-priced collection and, a decade later, launched A/X Armani Exchange, a yet lower-priced line. When his partner Galeotti died in 1985, Armani surprised many with his own business acumen. By the 21st century, his empire remained solely owned—with him as president, chief executive, sole shareholder, and head designer—when most of his peers had long since sold their businesses.

In 2000, his success was certified with "Giorgio Armani," a 400-piece show filling the Guggenheim museum in New York. However, he continued to expand: In 2004, he announced a deal for Armani-themed luxury resorts; in 2005, he added a women's couture collection; and, the next year, he announced a men's tailored equiv-alent, Armani Fatto A Mano Su Misura ("hand-made to measure"). In 2007, he donated the bulk of his archives to the city of Milan; financing their upkeep in a specifi-cally designed building by architect Tadao Ando oppo-site the main Armani offices.

armor   Although the practice of wearing protective clothes for combat is ancient and has its own specialized language, the names of traditional pieces of both plate and chain mail armor continue to be borrowed for the language of fashion and be appropriated to name sports gear and workwear. Among the most common:

Abdomen = Fauld
Arms, lower or forearm = Bracer; vambrace;
    brassards or brassarts

Arms, upper =Cannon; rarebrace
Arms, outer = Splint
Back = Backplate
Buttocks = Garde-rein; culet
Chest = Breastplate
Chin and neck = Bevor
Elbow = Couter
Eyes = Visor
Feet = Sabatons; solleret
Genitals = Codpiece
Hand = Gauntlet; muffler (for chain mail)
Head = Helmet; coif (for chain mail)
Head, neck, and top of shoulders = Helm
Knee = Poleyn
Left elbow (for jousting) = Pasguard
Left hand and lower arm (for jousting) = Manifer
Legs = Chausses
Mouth = Ventail
Neck = Gorget; haute-piece
Right arm (for jousting) = Pouldermitten
Shin = Graves or greaves; schynbald
Shoulder, especially the top = Spaulder; pauldron
Shoulder, especially the armpit = Besauge
Thighs = Cuisses
Thighs, upper (over hip joint) = Tassets
Torso = Cuirass; hauberk; gambeson

armlet   1. Another name for an armband, usually made of cloth or paper, worn over the sleeve as a sign of solidarity with a cause, a badge of mourning, or some other social signifier.   2. A bracelet worn around the bicep.

armscye   Tailoring jargon for the arm's eye or armhole where a sleeve is inserted into the body of a jacket. Specifically, the armscye is the underside of the insertion.

If an armscye is high and close to the armpit than a jacket will fit tightly. If the armscye is lower down on the torso and farther away from the armpit, then the jacket will fit more loosely. Sometimes shortened to SCYE.

arm's eye   Another, more mainstream, term for ARMSCYE.

army pinks   Slang for a type of pants, originally made of wool TWILL that was not pink, but a neutral beige (albeit often with a slightly pink or yellow undertone). Part of army apparel during World War II, their sturdiness made them beloved by veterans, who wore them with civilian dress in much the same context that JEANS or KHAKI pants were later worn.

Arnys   The family-run store, tailoring firm, and men's ready-to-wear company founded in Paris in 1933, located at 14, rue des Sèvres.

   Although very much a luxury marque, from its inception Arnys followed a style of business more in keeping with its Left Bank neighborhood than its crosstown competitors like CHARVET, HERMÈS, and SULKA. Founder Jankel Grimbert had immigrated to Paris in 1898 and was a successful Right Bank tailor who located his store in the Seventh Arrondissement at the urging of his sons Léon and Albert, who had spent time in that area while studying at the Sorbonne. During the 1930s, that *quartier* was a fashionable place to live but not to shop and Arnys' corner (which intersects the rue Récamier) was still best known as the locale of Madame Récamier's legendary salon. It was only after World War II that the Saint Germain seemed like a prescient place to put a store.

   In 1947, when Swiss architect Le Corbusier, who was teaching at the Sorbonne nearby, requested a jacket that would not ride up when he lifted his arm to write on the

Arnys

blackboard, Léon Grimbert created Arnys' famous Veste Forestière, a jacket with a lapel-less collar and a specially cut armhole, modeled on a forester's traditional jacket. Following that precedent, when the third generation (brothers Jean and Michel) took over, under Jean's creative directorship Arnys became known for—in addition to its more conventional tailoring—pieces quoting workers' and soldiers' garments from earlier centuries. Among its other stylistic signatures: a seven-fold tie, which more closely resembled a 19th-century cravat than a traditional necktie; and limited editions of figured silk, used for ties and other accessories, created in-house by graphic designer Dominique Lelys.

Over the years, Arnys' list of illustrious customers included Fernando Botero, Jean Cocteau, André Gide, Ernest Hemingway, Jean Marais, François Mitterand, Philippe Noiret, Octavio Paz, Pablo Picasso, Jacques Prévert, Yves Saint Laurent, Jean-Paul Sartre, Roger Vadim, and Orson Welles.

Arrow The brand of detachable collars and dress shirts begun in 1889 by Cluett, Peabody & Co., the Troy, New York, company that itself began as Maulin & Blanchard in 1851. Abetted by the illustrator J.C. Leyendecker's invention of the Arrow Collar Man in 1905, Arrow dominated its market for decades with collar models that were generally given aspirational and/or Anglophile names (e.g., the Duncan, the Dover, the Liberty, the Spur, the Standish). However, when fashion changed and the popularity of detachable collars began to wane in the 1920s, Cluett, Peabody was notably slow to react. It did not discontinue the Arrow Collar Man advertising until 1930 and did not phase out collar production until 1937—long after the market had moved on.

In the late 20th century, the company began to market its Arrow dress shirts at slightly lower prices, selling through outlets like Sears. In the early 21st century, during a dip in the dress shirt market, Cluett, Peabody sold the Arrow brand to its longtime competitor Phillips-Van Heusen.

The Arrow Collar Man The advertising icon created by illustrator J.C. Leyendecker to advertise the detachable collars manufactured by Troy, New York–based Cluett, Peabody & Company under its Arrow brand.

Already famous for his *Saturday Evening Post* covers and commercial illustrations, Leyendecker received the commission from Arrow ad manager Charles Connolly in 1905 and would continue with the campaign through 1930. Based on the illustrator's manager and long-time companion Charles Beach, the Arrow Collar Man was a square-jawed paragon of Anglo-Saxon American manhood. Women adored him. Even though he was fictional, he received up to a thousand letters a week at the height of his popularity, which was roughly 1918 through 1920. Thanks to his influence, Arrow was selling $32 million in collars and shirts worldwide by 1918 and manufacturing 4 million a week by the 1920s. In 1923, the Arrow Collar Man inspired the Broadway musical *Helen of Troy, N.Y.*, although the fashion for detachable collars was already beginning to wane. The campaign itself lasted until 1930, when the Arrow Collar Man became a victim of changing fashion.

the Arthur See mop top.

The Arrow Collar Man

article Jargon, especially in Europe, to refer to a type of fabric. Thus, when a mill owner or tailor refers to a particular "article," he is usually referring to a specific weight and design of fabric.

artificial silk Usually refers to ACETATE OR RAYON, the then-new CELLULOSIC fibers marketed as "artificial silk" during the second quarter of the 20th century.

The Art of Hairdressing, or the Gentleman's Director Written by Alexander Stewart and published in London in 1788; a guide to the wigs, powdering practices, and hairstyles of its time.

"The Art of Wearing Clothes" The famous, novella-length essay by GEORGE FRAZIER, published as the cover story of the September 1960 issue of *ESQUIRE* magazine.

Accompanied by a lengthy "Publisher's Page" introduction by the magazine's founder Arnold Gingrich, Frazier's piece was nearly two years in the writing and marked the first time that the magazine—then considered the media's best record of all matters pertaining to menswear—had published a "best-dressed" list. In his highly opinionated and often digressive work, Frazier deified BEAU BRUMMELL, declared that women "should never be permitted to counsel men about clothes," advocated the wearing of old clothes and the following of tradition, and extolled A. J. DREXEL BIDDLE JR. as the most elegant man in America. His appended, 40-member list of the best-dressed encompassed Dean Acheson, FRED ASTAIRE, Bill Blass, MILES DAVIS, DOUGLAS FAIRBANKS JR., CARY GRANT, and (fashion editor Diana Vreeland's husband) Thomas Reed Vreeland.

ascot Neckwear that is roughly a cross between a NECKTIE and a NECK KERCHIEF; named after the British horseracing track. The ascot has two wide, usually unlined ends (both fuller and less constructed than a tie) but is narrowed (unlike a neck kerchief) and usually stitched in its center (the part that goes in the back of a man's neck when it is being worn).

In the late 19th and early 20th century when it was a relatively common style, the ascot was usually worn with a tie pin. As the century wore on, that style—using knots similar to those now used to secure a STOCK TIE—became more-or-less restricted to daytime formal dress (e.g., MORNING SUITS). The word "ascot" is also applied to neck kerchiefs worn tucked into a collar or sweater with sportswear, although purists consider this incorrect.

A-shirt Slang abbreviation for ATHLETIC SHIRT; synonym for a TANK SHIRT.

aso oke Refers to woven ceremonial fabrics of the Yoruba of Western Africa, comprising cloths such as etu (made from cotton), sanyan (made from African silk), and alaari (made from imported silk). The complex and painstaking weaving methods used to create these products meant that master weavers were accorded great prestige at the Yoruba court and that their production was also prized by collectors worldwide, as well as being a frequent source of inspiration for Afrocentric fashion design.

How to tie an ascot

Astaire, Fred   Born on May 10, 1899 in Omaha, Nebraska, as Frederick Austerlitz Jr., the future movie star made his debut in Keyport, New Jersey, in 1905 as a straight man to his big sister Adele. After success on the vaudeville circuit, the singing and dancing siblings went on to stage stardom in New York and London, arriving in the West End during the peak of influence of the Prince of Wales in the late 1920s and early 1930s.

It was there that the Anglophile Astaire developed the habit of commissioning SAVILE ROW-made suits (e.g., from ANDERSON & SHEPPARD) and custom shirts (e.g., from BEALE & INMAN or HAWES & CURTIS) and of emulating the offhand flair, pattern-mixing, and DRAPE-front jackets favored by the future EDWARD VIII and his circle. The freedom of movement inherent in that style suited Astaire's professional requirements as an actor and dancer and became part of his onstage and then his Hollywood persona.

Although meticulous about the construction, cleanliness, and fit of his clothes, he was insistent that they never look too new, and followed the British tradition of preferring his clothes to be broken in. (He was once quoted in ESQUIRE magazine as saying, "I often take a brand-new suit or hat and throw it up against the wall a few times to get that stiff, square newness out of it.") In his movies, the more formally dressed he was, the more casually he behaved, so much so that he managed to forge his fame as both a Midwestern everyman and the Hollywood's foremost proponent of WHITE TIE and tails.

Famously, he would use a necktie or scarf as a belt, claiming that his weight varied so much when rehearsing dance routines that the substitution was simply practical. Among his many other style signatures: bright socks worn with dark shoes or dark socks worn with white shoes; short pants that sometimes showed those socks; short jackets that sometimes didn't quite clear the hips; high waistbands that gave his legs a longer line; jaunty hats (perhaps to hide his baldness); tails worn so that the white vest did not extend below the jacket (also enhancing the length of his legs); casually puffed pocket squares, sweaters tied around his neck, and collar pins worn clipped to the top of his open shirt sans tie. In addition to his London sources (which included shoes made by Peal), Astaire also bought from BROOKS BROTHERS, tailor John Galuppo of Schmidt & Galuppo in Beverly Hills, and Machin in Los Angeles.

After becoming known for a series of RKO pictures costarring Ginger Rogers (beginning with 1933's *Flying Down to Rio*), he continued to make movies with partners such as Rita Hayworth, Leslie Caron, and Cyd Charisse. He made his last big movie musicals, *Funny Face* and *Silk Stockings*, in 1957 and thereafter did television specials, cameos, and guest appearances (with a

Fred Astaire

straight role in 1959's *On the Beach*). He died on June 22, 1987.

astrakhan   The pelt of a particular breed of sheep, known as a karakul, taken when the animal is as close to newborn as possible—usually under two weeks old (as opposed to the pelt of an unborn karakul, which is known as BROADTAIL). At the lamb's birth, the fur is lustrous, short, and tightly curled, becoming coarser, less curled, and lighter as the animal ages.

Synonyms: PERSIAN LAMB (used more often for women's wear, derived from the Italian description of the pelt); karakul; SWAKARA (a trademarked name for the karakul lambs raised commercially in Namibia).

In menswear, astrakhan was traditionally popular for the collars of GREATCOATS and for various styles of unbrimmed hat.

A. Sulka & Co.   See SULKA.

athletic shirt   Refers to tank-style tops, especially those used as undershirts. A popular usage in the 1930s, when sports tended to be referred to as "athletics." Predecessor of the modern T-SHIRT, it takes the "athletic" part of its name from its resemblance to early track-and-field uniforms and swimsuits. Synonym: A-SHIRT.

athletic supporter   As its name implies, refers to the undergarment worn as a support for the genitals, especially during sports. Considered a more "proper" synonym for JOCKSTRAP.

attaché case   A hard-sided case with a boxlike shape, carried by a handle; usually intended for carrying documents or other business paraphernalia. Although it can be referred to as a BRIEFCASE and may be made of any material from leather to aluminum, the term attaché case denotes reinforced sides and construction with defined corners.

aviators   A style of eyeglass FRAMES—particularly popular for sunglasses—distinguished by lenses with a teardrop shape and a straight bar (usually referred to as a sweat bar) running straight across the top of the nose piece. The first aviator sunglasses were probably the ones developed by Bausch & Lomb for U.S. military pilots. (It was, at any rate, the impetus for that company's launch of its RAY-BAN brand the following year.) The distinctive shape derives from the style's origin in flight goggles. The style that is similar to an aviator frame, but holds a rectangular as opposed to a teardrop-shaped lens, is usually referred to as a "military" frame.

Although much modified, the aviator style has rarely been out of fashion with American men. It was worn by General Douglas MacArthur during World War II and in the movie *Top Gun* in 1985.

awning stripes   Huge, vertical, BALANCED STRIPES that look like the material used for awnings and outdoor furniture. Never used to describe shirt stripes.

babouches 1. Slippers associated primarily with Morocco. Several styles go by the name (including a few with curled toes), but the best known for men has a flat shape and long, pointed, uncurled toe. 2. A style of mule-like slippers, usually made of felt and with a slightly rounded toe, worn as either slippers (on bare feet) or indoor overshoes (to preserve carpets or flooring).

bachelor's gown As regulated by the Intercollegiate Bureau of Academic Costume in the United States, the ACADEMIC DRESS appropriate for a bachelor's degree candidate or graduate is a long, full gown, falling in an unbelted, straight line. Its long, full sleeves are cut on the BIAS and end in a point. Its color is black, and it is worn with a MORTARBOARD, also black. Most often, it is worn without its hood; however, if a hood is worn, it will be 3 feet long, lined with the colors of the degree-granting institution, and trimmed with 2 inches of a color indicating the area of study.

backless vest *or* **backless waistcoat** A style of vest cut so that, when shown from underneath a jacket, it appears to be a full vest although it is actually only a vest front with a strap and a buckle across the back (where it is hidden by the jacket). In contemporary use, it appears most often in WHITE TIE formalwear. However, the idea of saving material and making the wearing of a vest less bulky and less warming dates back several centuries, and was especially popular in the 18th century, when the front length of a vest might have extended well onto a man's leg.

backlines The name for the three seams that appear on the back of a traditionally made GLOVE. Originally, the backline seams were necessary to insert the FOURCHETTES (the gussets between each finger). In contemporary gloves they are often vestigial, but should always align with the space between the fingers.

backpack A general style of bag that is supported by one or, more usually, both shoulders so that the bag hangs to the back, over the wearer's shoulder blades.

Long considered too technical for daily use, backpacks crossed over from the category of sports gear in the late 20th century, when students began using them to tote books. By the end of the century, they were accepted by the culture at large for all but the most conservative

Bachelor's gown

business engagements and formal events and were a staple in fashion lines like PRADA. In menswear, the backpack was accepted in contexts where a tote might look too much like a woman's handbag. Synonym: knapsack.

back shield Refers to the interior construction of a jacket; the portion of the INTERLINING that stays the upper back and armhole, preventing the upper back from stretching and the shoulder pad from showing through.

back-to-school Originally referred to the selling season from early August through the beginning of October; in contemporary usage may now begin after the Fourth of July.

bags Slang for a style of extremely wide trousers. See OXFORD BAGS.

bag wig A style of 18th-century wig in which the hair is pulled back into a ponytail gathered at the nape, which is then gathered into a black bag. Also called a *crapaud*.

bainin An Irish word referring to heavy, undyed sheep's wool, spun so that it retains some of its lanolin content. Best known for its use as the material of traditional, off-white ARAN-style sweaters, which grow fluffier and lighter with age and cleaning.

Baker, Robert A fashionable tailor best known for developing the region of London now called Piccadilly.

Son of a cloth seller, Baker was born in Somerset in the late 16th century, but had learned the tailoring trade and moved to London by 1600, where he became very successful at selling PICCADILLIES, the large, starched standing collars beloved by Elizabethans. Baker invested his profits in a large plot of open land, where he built himself an impressive new house. But, because of his association with the piccadilly, irreverent Londoners referred to the building as Piccadilly Hall. Baker made subsequent land deals and died a wealthy man in 1623, and the name Piccadilly passed into general usage.

bal 1. Slang for a BALMACAAN coat. 2. Reference to BALMORAL styles, especially boots (as in "BAL LACING" or "Bal look"). Usually capitalized as "Bal."

bal collar Refers to the short, turnover collar of a balmacaan-style coat, particularly one with slightly rounded collar points.

balaclava A style of knitted, close-fitting hat that pulls over the head, covering the entire head down to the base of the throat, with an opening only for the face; worn for warmth. In some

Bag wigs

OUT OF FASHION.   IN FASHION.

Publish'd as the Act directs by J. Bowen at the Golden Pallet opposite the Hay Market Piccadilly.

cases, it covers the entire face also and has only small openings for the eyes, nostrils, and mouth. Known as the "balaclava helmet" because it originated during the British army's involvement (from 1854 to 1856) in the Crimean War (particularly with the 1854 Battle of Bala-clava, famous for the charge of the Light Brigade).

Variant spelling: balaklava.

balanced jacket   In BESPOKE or MADE-TO-MEASURE tailoring, a balanced jacket is one in which the front and back lengths may have been slightly adjusted to compensate for the client's figure and posture (or lack thereof).

balanced stripe   A symmetrical pattern, indicating that the background and stripe are equal in width. Usually refers to shirt fabrics. BENGAL STRIPES are examples of balanced stripes. See color plates.

balanced weave   A symmetrical weave in which the WARP (vertical) yarns and the WEFT (horizontal) yarns are of equal weight and are equally distributed. Neither WARP-FACED nor WEFT-FACED.

baldric   A broad shoulder belt, frequently used to carry a sword; almost always slung diagonally from right shoulder to left hip.

Bal   1. Reference to a BALMORAL BOOT, especially when capitalized. 2. Jargon for a BALMACAAN, especially when lowercased.

Bal lacing   A style of lacing shoes or boots identified with the BALMORAL BOOTS designed by Prince Albert, consort of Queen Victoria. In footwear with Bal lacing, the two sides bearing the lacing eyelets seem to meet neatly in the middle and tongue beneath is not visible and, therefore, neither is the crossing of the laces.

balmacaan   Refers to a style of long (above the ankle but below the knee), loose coat. Its distinguishing feature is the RAGLAN SLEEVE seam that runs diagonally from neck to armpit. It is also single-breasted (often with a FLY front), has a short, turnover collar, and is popular for wet weather since it can be worn over bulky clothes and buttoned to the neck. Named after an estate in Scotland. In industry slang, sometimes abbreviated to "bal."

Balmoral   1. A beret-type style of brimless hat—a BONNET—named after the royal residence on the River Dee in Aberdeenshire, Scotland. The prototypical Balmoral has a soft, round top over a DICED hatband, sometimes accented by a plume on one side. Although popularized during the 19th century, the style was in existence for at least a century before PRINCE ALBERT made it fashionable. Accented with a TOORIE on top, it might be referred to as a BLUEBONNET because it was often blue. The Balmoral also gave rise to the differently shaped cap called the GLENGARRY. With a pom-pom the style is familiar as a TAM O' SHANTER. In contemporary use, the Balmoral is most often worn for Highland dancing. 2. The red and gray tartan designed by Prince Albert,

Balmacaan

Victoria's consort, during the 1850s.   3. The LOVAT-type tweed designed by Prince Albert, Victoria's consort, during the 1850s. Although its overall effect is gray, it is actually woven of navy blue, white, and red yarns.

Balmoral boots   Originally made for Prince Albert, the consort of Queen Victoria, by cobbler Joseph Sparkes Hall (who also invented the elastic-gusset boot); named for Balmoral, the royal retreat in Scotland. The Balmoral resembles an ankle-high OXFORD. Its chief characteristics are its lacing system (which does not show the tongue of the shoe and runs straight across the instep in perpendicular lines), its neat, straight toe cap, and its facings, which are neatly hidden under the vamp in the same manner as an oxford. According to legend, Albert specified the design himself because he found the close fit of the style particularly flattering to the leg.

bamboo   Fiber or fabric made from bamboo plants, usually through a process akin to the chemistry used to turn wood pulp into RAYON. Bamboo is touted in the textile market for its natural antibacterial (and therefore odor-resistant) properties as a CELLULOSIC fiber and for its ecological advantages as a "renewable resource."

banana   Fiber or fabric made from the leaves of the banana plant, prized for its toughness and resistance to rot. Woven cloth made from banana is used most often in the Philippines, where it is sometimes blended with ABACA (its botanical near-relative) or PIÑA to make traditional garments such as the BARONG.

bandana   A large, square NECK KERCHIEF, usually made of cotton and brightly colored or patterned. Associated with traditional COWBOY costume. The word comes to English from the Hindi term for TIE-DYE. Also spelled bandanna.

Although working men in other Western cultures wore neck kerchiefs, the bandana was a mainstay of American menswear from early days. Martha Washington supposedly commissioned the first one from John Hewson, a printmaker recommended by Benjamin Franklin, so that, from 1776 onward, Yankee DANDIES sported square kerchiefs showing General George Washington as a pledge of political allegiance. Printed to promote companies, candidates, and causes, they remained a bright spot in increasingly drab menswear throughout the 1800s. Red became their primary color after the Civil War, when a Rhode Island textile printer hired a Scottish dyer who specialized in TURKEY RED. On the Western frontier, they were used as handkerchiefs, headbands, bandages, slings, and dust masks. Back East, mills then churned out more prints emphasizing that cowboy connection and printed them with images of heroes like Wild Bill Hickok.

band collar *or* **banded collar**   A collar, especially on a dress shirt, that does not fold over or form points (as in its opposite, the now-common FOLD-OVER COLLAR). In the days when DETACHABLE COLLARS were popular, a banded collar was the shirt's basic style. Therefore, a shirt with a banded collar was frequently—and not always correctly—referred to as "collarless."

band cuff   Synonym for a BARREL CUFF (more common when describing women's and children's fashions). May also be called a SINGLE CUFF.

bandolier   1. Originally referred to an ammunition belt that was worn slung over one shoulder so that it hung diagonally across the chest; in contemporary use refers to any belt or strap worn so that it is slung diagonally across the chest.   2. Reference to a tie patterned with a single, wide, slanting stripe.

Bangora   A type of paperlike straw; in contemporary use, appears most often as the material of cowboy hats. Synonyms: Bandera straw; Bangkok straw.

banker's suit   Refers to a general type of suit rather than a specific style. A banker's suit is conservative in cut, traditional in material, and slightly formal in aspect. It is also associated with PINSTRIPES, called "banker's stripes" in this context. A prime example of a banker's suit: a custom-tailored, navy blue, pinstriped suit that is neither too body-conscious nor too baggy.

banyan   A category of men's DRESSING GOWN worn primarily at home during the end of the 17th century through the beginning of the 19th century. Influenced by Orientalism, banyans were often made of impressive amounts of showy silks, but their fabric could be virtually anything from printed cotton to quilted stuffs worn for warmth. Likewise, their construction varied from the voluminous to the fairly tailored and close-fitting. They were long-sleeved, generally floor-length (or at least below the knee), and worn in a variety of contexts (although never for business in town). Sometimes called Indian gowns.

barathea   1. A type of silk woven to have a crepey, textured surface; used in neckties.   2. A type of smooth wool, especially when cited as being used in uniforms of the late 19th or early 20th century.

Barbey d'Aurevilly, Jules Amédée   Born in 1808 in Normandy, the French fiction writer, journalist, and crit-ic deified the discipline of dandyism, especially in his 1843 *Du Dandysme et de Georges Brummell*, the first major work on BEAU BRUMMELL in French. Barbey praised the detachment of the dandy as an end in itself, over and above mere distinction of wardrobe—an idea that strongly influenced his friend CHARLES BAUDE-LAIRE, members of the AESTHETIC MOVEMENT, and *fin de siècle* decadents. A prolific and long-lived writer, he cast dandies in many of his books (e.g., 1874's *Les Diaboliques*) and himself dressed in eccentric patterns and colors. He died in 1889.

Barbour   The South Shields-based British outerwear and sportswear company best known for durable oiled cotton jackets (such as the "Bedale," a hip-length jacket of dark-green, waxed cotton with a brown corduroy collar, sturdy metal zipper, capacious pockets, and lining in the firm's distinctive brown, green, white, and black plaid).

One of the iconic brands of British country dress, Barbour holds multiple ROYAL WARRANTS and traces its history back to John Barbour (1849–1918), who set himself up in business in 1870 as an itinerant draper in the border country between England and Scotland. In 1894, Barbour moved to South Shields, on the British side of the border, and established a business supplying no-nonsense oilskins and other foul-weather gear to workmen, farmers, and sailors. In response to its popularity among far-flung subjects of the British empire, Barbour issued its first catalog in 1908. Although it later expanded into a range of MICROFIBERS and other modern materials, the company remained identified with its classic waxed cotton models and the refurbishments provided by its Renovations and Repair department (e.g., in 2001, the U.K. factory refurbished a 1931 jacket discovered in an attic).

bark cloth   Cloth made from the inner bark of trees. Although various cultures have invented various methods for turning tree fibers into textiles, the best known usage for apparel is TAPA, the cloth used throughout Oceania.

barleycorn   A weave pattern usually achieved by contrasting light and dark yarns so that the cloth surface has a standardized, overall pebble-like effect—supposedly resembling tiny seed kernels. One of the traditional menswear weaves, barleycorn is executed most often in wool and used for SPORTS JACKETS. See color plates.

barn jacket   General reference to a style of jacket-length, single-breasted outerwear, usually worn for work or weekend country wear (hence the "barn"). Usually made of sturdy material such as canvas, it may have a collar of corduroy or leather, and it usually features capacious side pockets. For cold weather, it may have a quilted or wool lining.

Barnes, Jhane   Born in 1954 and raised in Maryland, Barnes was a self-confessed math geek who originally planned to attend Cal Tech and become an astrophysicist but instead attended FIT and became a fashion designer. Borrowing $5,000 from a biology professor, she began her label in 1977—a year after adding an "h" to turn plain Jane to "Jhane" in order to make it seem more noteworthy and appropriate to menswear.

Aside from her trademark eyeglasses and flamboyant red hair, Barnes became known for American sportswear with distinctive textile patterns, which she designed herself. In 1980, she became both the first woman and the youngest designer to win a COTY AWARD for

menswear, and in 1981 followed with the CFDA Award and CUTTY SARK AWARD. In 1988, she pioneered the use of computers in textile designs for menswear, continuing that exploration throughout her subsequent career—becoming perhaps the first and only successful menswear designer to cite computer algorithms as an inspiration.

Barneys   The New York-based luxury retailer, founded in 1923 when founder Barney Pressman supposedly pawned the engagement ring he had given his wife in order to lease a small store space at 17th Street and Seventh Avenue in Manhattan and sell tailored clothing. By 1950, it had become so successful that Barneys claimed to employ 150 tailors making 80,000 suits a year. In 1975, Barney himself retired, leaving the company to his son Fred, who almost immediately introduced Armani and added yet more European designer labels to a merchandise mix he had pioneered the previous decade; the following year, he also added women's wear (which, by the turn of the century, had become the majority of its business). In 1991, the founder died at age 96. In 1993, with Fred's sons Gene and Robert actively involved, it opened a lavishly designed, $100 million, 230,000-square-foot store on a prime retail stretch of Madison Avenue, which put it literally in the same neighborhood as Bergdorf Goodman; at the same time, the store gained a reputa-

Barneys

tion within the industry for slow and difficult payment of its accounts and became involved in an acrimonious battle with Japanese financial partner Isetan. In 1996, Fred Pressman died and Barneys filed for bankruptcy. The following year, it closed its outpost on 17th Street and Seventh Avenue (along with branches in Houston, Dallas, and Troy, Michigan). The company exited bankruptcy in 1999, the same year that the Pressman family sold it.

However, throughout its expansion, contraction, and very public financial problems, the store managed to actually increase its reputation as an arbiter of chic: introducing new lines and gaining notoriety from the witty window dressing of Simon Doonan, who would become its creative director.

baro Slang for BARONG.

barong An upper-body garment resembling an extra-long, loose dress shirt or extremely lightweight jacket; worn for formal occasions by men in the Philippines. Contemporary barongs often sport a four-button PLACKET, a small collar, long sleeves, and impressive embroidery and/or cutwork. Most often they are made of a fine white textile, such as PIÑA. The custom of wearing a barong can be traced back to the tunic-type gar-

Barong

ments worn in precolonial days, and its collar and styles of decoration have evolved over the centuries. During the 1950s, President Ramon Magsaysay popularized the "baro" by wearing it to all formal events, and during the 1970s, President Ferdinand Marcos declared it the official national attire. Sometimes called a "barong Tagalog," which is a slang contraction of "baro ng Tagalog" roughly translating to "costume of the Tagalog people."

barrel cuff A style of shirtsleeve that ends at the wrist with a single, close-fitting cuff fastened by one or more buttons. Its fancier, doubled, cufflinked counterpart would be a FRENCH CUFF. Synonym: button cuff or button-through cuff. Other synonyms (used more often when describing women's and children's fashions) are SINGLE CUFF and BAND CUFF.

barre Literally a "bar" effect that appears as a horizontal blip or slub, usually unintentionally, in a knit or woven fabric. For example, when a multicolored or SPACE-DYED yarn is knit so that an accidental block of solid color forms, that's usually called a barre. Sometimes spelled with an accent as "barré."

barret A wide, flat, BERET-like style of cloth headwear worn in the Renaissance and most familiar from its inclusion in portraits by Holbein (e.g., Hans Holbein the Younger's *Portrait of a Member of the Wedigh Family* in 1533).

Barrett, Neil Born in Plymouth, England, in 1965 to a family involved in the tailored clothing business, Barrett studied fashion at Central Saint Martin's in London before moving to Italy to work for GUCCI. After successfully working as menswear designer for PRADA, Barrett left that company in 1999. While establishing his own

Neil Barrett

label, he scored a success in a brief freelance stint designing apparel for luggage maker Samsonite—a collection that featured witty, utilitarian travel clothes such as jackets with collars that could be inflated to form neck pillows for long plane rides. While continuing to show on the Milan runways, Barrett's other sideline stints included designing for the Italian soccer team and signing as creative director of athletic footwear brand Puma, which debuted a Barrett-designed apparel collection in January 2004.

Barrymore collar   A style of FOLD-OVER shirt collar, with extra-long COLLAR POINTS (about 4½ to 5½ inches), made famous by actor John Barrymore; not DETACHABLE, but part of the shirt. The style known as the CALIFORNIA COLLAR differs by sporting even longer points.

bar tack   Refers to stitching used to reinforce stress points, most often on JEANS. For example, on jeans a bar tack usually appears at the top and bottom of belt loops and/or other stress points that are not riveted. Also appears on the buttonholes and pocket openings of tailoring clothing. So-called because the stitches form a bar shape.

Bartlett, John   Born in 1963, raised in Cincinnati, John Bartlett got his bachelor's degree in sociology from Harvard and then headed to the London School of Economics, dropping out after spending most of his money on KING'S ROAD; whereupon he headed to FIT to study fashion design. After working for firms such as Ronaldus Shamask and WilliWear, he established his own label in 1992, gaining notoriety for the kind of edgy and erotic presentations not often seen in New York menswear shows of the time (e.g., a show that concluded with naked male models clutching strategically placed surf-

boards). Despite winning a CFDA award in 1997 and getting generally good reviews, Bartlett closed his designer line in 2002, whereupon the Catholic-reared designer headed to Southeast Asia to study Buddhism and yoga. Upon his return to New York, Barrett got back in the business, this time abetted by LICENSING deals, different lines for different markets, a job as creative director of Connecticut-based accessories brand Ghurka, and more commercially oriented runway presentations.

baseball cap   Now used to describe a general style of gored cloth cap with a tight CROWN and a medium-length front VISOR, but especially the five-panel cloth cap with a button top and its visor covered in cloth or a six-panel version with a larger visor.

Through the early 20th century, baseball players wore a variety of headgear, from brimless caps to straw hats, and hat historians trace the origin of the contemporary style to caps adopted in Brooklyn in the 1860s.

base layer   A close-fitting layer worn next to the skin, in a layering system intended to ensure efficient distribution of moisture and body heat. For cold-weather wear, especially for sports such as mountain climbing and skiing, the base layer is usually long-legged and long-sleeved in a stretchy knit construction, and made of

Barrymore collar: John Barrymore

WICKING material. It is topped, in turn, by an INSULAT-ING LAYER and a SHELL LAYER.

The term gained wide circulation among nonath-letes in the 1980s when PATAGONIA and other firms began using wicking synthetic textiles—chiefly POLYPROPYLENE—as a second skin and began market-ing what had been known as long underwear as part of a layering system.

Bashford, Wilkes   The San Francisco clothier best known as the founder and owner of WILKES BASHFORD, a specialty store based on Sutter Street.

Moving west from Cincinnati, Bashford began work-ing as a buyer for the White House, a San Francisco department store, in 1959. When it closed in 1965, he started his own store in the summer of 1966, using the tagline "menswear for the bold conservative," and pio-neering pricey imports like BRIONI. Later, he began car-rying more designer lines—most notably RALPH LAU-REN in the late 1960s and ARMANI in the 1970s—and expanded into women's wear in 1978.

Bashford underwent a very public rent battle with city government in the mid-1980s, which ended with him owing $750,000 and 1,200 hours of community service. Afterward, he (occasionally accompanied by his long-haired dachshund Freddy) remained a very visible figure in city life. During the 1990s, for example, he was famous for lunching with prominent local customers like colum-nist Herb Caen and Mayor WILLIE BROWN at Le Central.

basin cut   Refers to a type of haircut in which the hair is trimmed to uniform length, as if a bowl had been upended on the man's head and any hair hanging below that bowl's edges lopped off. Costumers and illustrators often give medieval characters this type of haircut. Syn-onyms include PUDDING BASIN CUT and BOWL CUT.

basket weave   A version of PLAIN WEAVE. In this sim-ple, symmetrical weave, two or more FILLING yarns cross over an equal number of WARP yarns (the yarns already on the loom). For example: Three filling yarns pass over three warp yarns and then pass under the next three warp yarns. When graphed, the resulting pattern always forms a perfect checkerboard. Because the yarns alter-nate—in and out, up and down—basket weaves are sometimes called "two up, two down" or "three up, three down," depending upon the number of yarns involved in the pattern. Basket weaves are often used to give an open, textured look, especially for fabrics intended for summer apparel.

Basque beret   1. The soft, brimless, pancake-shaped hat that most people now refer to simply as a BERET; tra-ditionally black. In the early 20th century, when men like the future EDWARD VIII as Prince of Wales and GERALD MURPHY made the wearing of what used to be Basque peasant wear a fashionable practice, it was referred to by both words. As it became more popular and more identi-fied with France, the term was shortened. Hence, "Basque beret" is popular in older references and cita-tions by Anglophiles.   2. A black beret banded with a thin strip of leather at the edge of its head opening; usu-ally designated as a Basque beret to distinguish that style from the differently colored berets or the styles intended for the women's market.

bass   Jargon for an area of color, particularly when dis-cussing traditional TWEEDS and tartans. For example, in a ROB ROY, a black bass alternates symmetrically with a red bass.

Bass Weejuns   The iconic style of loafers manufac-tured by the G.H. Bass & Co., the shoe company that began when George Henry Bass bought into a Maine shoe company named E.P. Packard in 1876 and, three years later, took it over and renamed it after himself.

The Weejun, which the company began to manufacture in the 1930s, was a name that came from the slang, shortened form of the shoe style then known as the NORWEGIAN, which is distinguished by a moccasin-like structure and thick seam circling the top of the forefoot. The Bass version thereafter defined the type, becoming a mainstay of collegiate and particularly PREPPY style for both sexes into the 21st century.

bast fibers   Tough, woody plant fibers. Most bast fibers end up in products like paper, rope, and matting, but a subgroup of soft bast fibers, which includes FLAX (the plant source of LINEN), HEMP, jute, and RAMIE, is used to make wearable fabric. Because these CELLULOSIC fibers have a high resistance to rotting and bacteria, some apparel manufacturers tout the fabrics made from them as "naturally antibacterial."

baste   To temporarily sew with long, loose stitches that can be easily ripped out or stitched over. For example, trouser hems may be basted in place before a fitting so that they can be checked for correct length before the final seam is sewn and pressed.

Can be done either by hand or machine, generally at a gauge of no more than six stitches to the inch.

BATA   A cooperative of stores specializing in extra-large apparel, which also runs a semiannual buying show. The acronym (spelled without periods) stands for Big and Tall Associates.

bathrobe   A robe intended to be donned after showering, swimming, or bathing, and therefore classically made of an absorbent material, such as terry cloth; always long-sleeved, its length may be anywhere from knee- to ankle-length; usually a wrap style, cinched with a sash. Its more presentable and tailored cousin, worn over pajamas et al, is the DRESSING GOWN.

batik   Refers not to a pattern, but a process. Batik is a method of patterning fabric with the use of resist dye, and although it was in use in Roman-era Egypt and is practiced in places as various as West Africa and China, it is today most associated with the islands of Indonesia—particularly Java.

Authentic batik is a labor-intensive process best done on cloth with a high-density and smooth surface (usually cotton cambric, although occasionally silk). Warm wax is applied; then the fabric is dyed. (Tiny fissures in the wax are responsible for the "crackling" or "veined" effect associated with the technique.) Then the cloth is dipped in cold water so that the wax hardens. That wax is scraped off and the pattern is laid for the next color. And so on. And so on. Until the pattern is complete.

Because real batik takes so long to make, most of the fabrics that resemble it are printed. For that reason, commercial fabrics would be properly referred to as "batik-style," "batik-influenced," or some similar usage.

Imitation batiks have been around ever since Sir Thomas Stamford Raffles ruled as governor-general of Java from 1811 to 1815. Even as he exported his own hoard of authentic batik textiles back to England, he exhorted English textile printers to create look-alike exports that could be used as TRADE CLOTH.

batiste   Supposedly named for the French weaver who first produced it in the late Middle Ages, batiste was initially used to describe a lightweight, almost sheer linen used for shirts and SMALLCLOTHES. Later, especially during the 19th century, it was produced mainly of cotton and could also be described as LAWN. Today, it is considered too lightweight for menswear.

B.A.T.M.A.N.　A semiannual trade show that specialized in extra-large apparel; the acronym stood for Big and Tall Men's Apparel Needs. After 25 years, it was discontinued in 2007.

Battistoni　Celebrated for its hand-sewn custom shirts, which have attracted clients including GIANNI AGNELLI, Cole Porter, Gore Vidal, and assorted Italian and American movie stars; founded in Rome on the Via Condotti by Guglielmo Battistoni in 1946.

battle jacket　A short, skirtless, fitted style of tailored jacket, patterned on the waist-length uniform jackets associated with General Dwight D. Eisenhower during World War II. (Not to be confused with a BOMBER JACKET or FLIGHT JACKET, which refer to styles based on outerwear.)

batwing　1. A common style of BOW TIE, in which the ends are straight and unshaped. (Its alternative number would be the THISTLE, in which the tie ends swell like thistle blooms.) Synonym: CLUB BOW TIE.　2. An extravagant style of CHAPS that flare out from the legs in great curved, winged flaps, which may be further ornamented by fringe, CONCHOS, tooling, or all of the above.

Baudelaire, Charles　Born in 1821, the French poet best known for his 1857 work *Les Fleurs du mal*, was a dandy in his time, but not of it. Although in 1842 he briefly began his Paris career as a handsome, bearded man about town in the manner of the COUNT D'ORSAY, after 1844 (when his family forcibly curtailed his expenditures), an already pronounced fondness for black progressed to obsession. For the rest of his life, he restricted himself to white shirts worn with black, which he praised as the color of negation and mourning. Likewise, although he lived among bohemians, Baudelaire affected such formality and fastidious grooming that he was nicknamed Lord BRUMMELL. A friend and correspondent of JULES BARBEY D'AUREVILLY, Baudelaire's pronouncements on the subject of dandyism in his essay "Le Peintre de la vie moderne," published in *Le Figaro* in 1863, praised makeup and other artifice, idealized the dandy as a man detached, and presented him as a hero in the fight against mediocrity, thus smoothing the way for OSCAR WILDE and the AESTHETIC MOVEMENT as well as *fin de siècle* symbolists. He died in 1867.

bay rum　Refers to a general type of men's liquid toiletry, rather than a particular brand. Still in use, it was more popular a century ago, when it appeared in most barber shops and many home dressing tables as a sort of all-purpose precursor to modern AFTERSHAVES and COLOGNES. Its spicy fragrance is created by distilling the leaves of the bay rum tree grown in

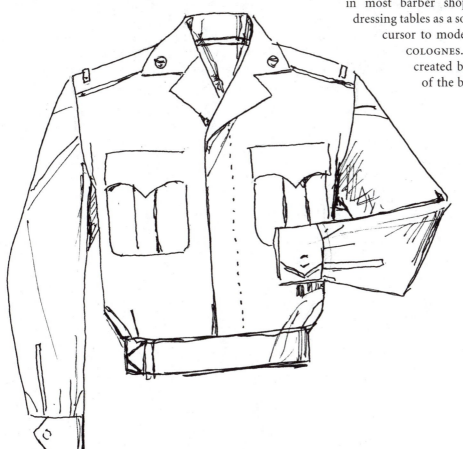

the West Indies (most brands also add some form of citrus oil). It is not a form of rum but derives its name from its original manufacture by distilling the bay leaves in white rum.

b-boy   Refers to a breakdancer, and hence is associated with HIP-HOP heritage.

BCBG   *Bon chic, bon genre.* French slang referring to the well dressed and well born, meaning the fashionable haute bourgeoisie. The closest American counterpart would be a combination of PREPPY and yuppie.

beaded stripe   Used to describe suit fabric, a beaded stripe is a type of BROKEN STRIPE that usually appears as a solid CHALK STRIPE when viewed from a slight distance but, upon close inspection, resembles a series of aligned dots.

beak   1. The VISOR of a cap. Synonyms: BILL; PEAK; visor.   2. Nineteenth-century reference to the long point of a WAISTCOAT that might be visible when worn with a TAIL COAT.

Beale & Inman   The British outfitter known for both a BESPOKE business and as a retailer of high-end brands, as well as being widely admired for remaining in its wood-paneled, original premises in London.

Founded at 131 New Bond Street in 1828 by James Beale, a specialist in hosiery, who soon went into partnership with Richard Inman. During the 19th century, its client list included kings such as Emperor Napoleon III and future kings such as EDWARD VII. Famously, after finishing *A Tale of Two Cities* in 1859, CHARLES DICKENS treated himself to an entire Beale & Inman

wardrobe before embarking on his next lecture tour of the United States. (His check for 34 pounds and 5 shillings now decorates the store.) During the 20th century, clients included Winston Churchill (who died with his bill unpaid), FRED ASTAIRE (who ordered shirts there), Tony Curtis, Jack Lemon, and Pierce Brosnan.

In 1988, its ownership passed to MOSS BROTHERS.

Bean   See L.L.BEAN.

beanie   A round skullcap with no visor or chin strap. Usually refers to one seamed and made of woven fabric, which may or may not include a fabric-coated button at its center.

The term is mostly used in an informal sense, and never to describe religious head coverings. For example, it was popular when the beanie itself was a popular part of collegiate and fraternity attire in the early 20th century; the word probably derives from American slang references, beginning around 1900, to someone's head as his "bean."

beat   An anti-fashion fashion of the 1950s, associated with the super-plain and ultra-masculine clothes of Beat writers like Jack Kerouac and Neil Cassady. Eventually, the original look of semisloppy workshirts and chinos evolved into the BEATNIK style, which was more influenced by French styles of the time.

The Beatles   From the time that Paul McCartney, John Lennon, George Harrison, and Ringo Starr signed with manager Brian Epstein in 1962 until The Beatles officially disbanded in 1970, the pop group became the decade's menswear trendsetters, popularizing fashions even when they did not initiate them.

Before Epstein, The Beatles had affected dark, ROCKER-like clothes. (Earlier still, the teenaged Lennon had been known as a TEDDY BOY and imitated his hero ELVIS PRESLEY.) But by the time of their breakthrough in the early 1960s, they were working-class exemplars of MOD style, who wore trim, collarless, PIERRE CARDIN knockoffs (in a version produced by tailor Dougie Millings that was itself later copied as "the Beatle jacket"), the much-imitated MOP-TOP hairstyle (the Beatle cut), and CHELSEA BOOTS (which inevitably came to be known as Beatle boots). In London, their style might have been considered not especially original or daring, but for the rest of the world it was both a radical reinvention of the rocker prototype made famous by ELVIS PRESLEY in the 1950s and a completely new, almost childishly youthful direction for menswear.

After achieving commercial success, all four men began to differentiate their dress and hair for performances. In private life, they pursued divergent, although often parallel, paths: All four were notable patrons of London's various trendy clothiers (e.g., TOMMY NUTTER and JOHN STEPHEN), so that, when CARNABY STREET and KING'S ROAD moved on to more camp Edwardian and Victorian styles, so did they (e.g., 1967's *Sergeant Pepper's Lonely Hearts Club Band*). Likewise, after Harrison married model Pattie Boyd, the men embraced the psychedelic revolution, and, at the end of 1967, they had opened APPLE, a clothes boutique at 94 Baker Street in London (which closed less than a year later).

After 1968, and their visit to Rishikesh in India, their style became more ethnic, with all the elements of full-on HIPPIE-dom: beards, beads, KURTAS, and the like. After disbanding, all four continued their performing career, but none had the impact on fashion of the combined group.

beatnik   A word coined by San Francisco Chronicle columnist Herb Caen in 1958 to refer to the BEAT Generation writers, artists, and hangers on congregating in the city's North Beach neighborhood. Although Jack Kerouac and other Beat writers had usually worn plain American workwear styles, the clothes that came to be identified as the beatnik look had a Gallic flavor, heavily influenced by the styles then being worn in the Saint Germain area of Paris. Men wore their hair long and their beards trimmed into GOATEES. They eschewed tailoring in favor of all-black sportswear—particularly black TURTLENECKS. In the mainstream media, the beatnik was caricatured as a young man who used jazz slang, wore a black beret, and spent his time beating bongo drums.

Beau Brummell   MGM's 1954 biopic starring Stewart Granger and Elizabeth Taylor. See BRUMMELL, BEAU.

beaver felt   A glossy felt, made from the animal's hair, much prized for hats, especially in the 1830s. (When the fashion turned abruptly toward silk hats, fur trader John Jacob Astor was forced to diversify into real estate, and thus a fashion quirk became responsible for the Astor fortune.) Synonyms: CASTOR; castor felt.

beaver finish   A glossy finish given to wool, so-called because it resembles the coat of beaver. The term gained popularity in England during the late 1800s, when

Crombie, a large Scottish mill, promoted the fabric for menswear.

bebop   See HIPSTER.

Beckenstein's Men's Fabric   The New York-based retailer and wholesaler owned and operated by Neal Boyarsky, the self-proclaimed "fabric czar." A steady supplier to Broadway and Hollywood costumers, fashion designers, and celebrities, the family-run business began before the first World War when Polish immigrant Samuel Beckenstein began collecting rags, then progressed to selling fabric from a pushcart, and eventually to establishing an Orchard Street store. After 84 years on the Lower East Side, the firm moved to the midtown GARMENT DISTRICT in 2003.

Beckham, David   Handsome and heterosexual, the un-self-conscious English soccer star was responsible for popularizing styles that were otherwise considered overly trendy or effeminate. For example, when Beckham took to wearing plunging V-necks that revealed his

David Beckham

bare chest the way a woman's dress might reveal her cleavage, they soon showed up on designer runways and—not long after—on his many, many fans. When he was photographed wearing a sweater he'd bought from Pringle (at the time a brand that had just undergone a major makeover), orders for the sweater poured in and the revamped label's immediate future was immediately assured.

Born in East London in 1975, "Becks" was a star and a style setter at Manchester United while still in his teens, inspiring the same idolatry that soccer star Bobby Moore, another working-class boy who looked great in trendy clothes, had inspired in the mid-1960s. In 1997, he began dating Victoria Adams, better known as "Posh Spice" of the Spice Girls, when that pop group was at the height of its fame. In 1999, he married her, creating a tabloid frenzy worldwide. He captained the English national team from 2000 to 2006 (approaching GIORGIO ARMANI to design the team's off-the-field uniforms and inspiring the unconstructed "Beckham Jacket" featured in subsequent runway shows). By the 21st century he had become so well known outside the soccer world that he was able to serve as the indirect subject of the 2002 movie *Bend It Like Beckham*. In 2003, the midfielder was awarded an OBE in the queen's birthday honors; that same year he also transferred to Real Madrid. In 2007, he made his much-publicized move to Los Angeles.

Beckham's taste always tended toward the extreme. Son of a hairdresser, his blond hair was variously grown long and styled into braids, pinned back with baby barrettes, or shaved to baldness. He indulged in more than the usual complement of tattoos. When he wore a GAULTIER skirt in 1998 it made headlines. A natural for endorsements, his sponsors and/or advertising contracts included ADIDAS, BRYLCREEM, GILLETTE, Pepsi, Police sunglasses, plus his own line of apparel for English department store chain Marks & Spencer and his own fragrance line.

Bedford cord   1. A sturdy, plain fabric that is "corded" or ridged (almost always vertically) but does not have the WALES or velvety surface of CORDUROY. Popular for country pursuits like hunting, shooting, and riding. 2. Reference to a pair of pants made from that material, especially in England (used in much the same way that an American might refer to "putting on his corduroys").

Beebe, Lucius   Born in 1901 to a Massachusetts family already rich with eccentrics, the man who would later become famous for inventing the term "Cafe Society," got started in the newspaper business with a job at the *Boston Telegram* after being expelled from Yale, hitting his stride in 1929 when he was hired by the *New York Herald Tribune* and was able to wear a white tie and top hat to work, and beginning his column "This New York" in 1933.

Not one to hide his light under a bushel or to use a one-dollar word when a two-dollar word would do, the 6-foot, 4-inch columnist favored ornate clothes, ornate prose, and an ornate lifestyle. He commissioned uncon-

Lucius Beebe

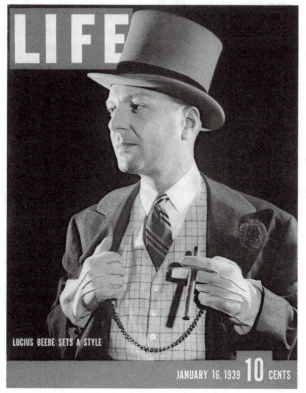

ventional custom clothes, was a connoisseur of TOP HATS, and liked to brandish a gold-headed walking stick. Reigning as America's most vocal and visible exponent of overdressing, Beebe once covered a fire while attired in a MORNING SUIT.

Obsessed with railroads and the author of multiple books on the subject, Beebe openly shared his life with Charles "Chuck" Clegg, a wealthy Texan whom he claimed to have met while wearing the Hope Diamond at a house party given by Evalyn Walsh McLean. The two traveled in their private circa 1928 Pullman car, which they had remade with Renaissance decor, complete with working fireplace, and also published a weekly newspaper. Beebe died of a heart attack in 1966.

Beerbohm, Max   Born in London in 1872, the younger half-brother of the famous actor/manager Herbert Beerbohm Tree, Sir Henry Maximilian Beerbohm first began writing about dandies in 1893, while still a student at Oxford. A friend of Aubrey Beardsley and charter member of the set who published "The Yellow Book," Beerbohm parodied the portentousness of the dandies delineated by JULES BARBEY D'AUREVILLY, CHARLES BAUDELAIRE, OSCAR WILDE, and others who had elevated the type to an antihero, and instead regarded the dandy not an exemplar of modernism but as an antique. For example, in his 1911 satirical novel *ZULEI-KA DOBSON*, its protagonist the Duke of Dorset (itself a pun on the COUNT D'ORSAY) is a dandy completely undone by a modern woman.

Fond of finery when young and infallibly well-mannered, Beerbohm lived mostly in Italy from his semiretirement in 1910 until his death in 1956.

beer jackets *and* beer suits   A custom that apparently originated among Princeton University seniors before

World War I. According to legend, in order to protect their regular clothes from heavy-duty suds, the upperclassmen donned these suits, which usually consisted of white bib-type, workers' overalls worn with a white jacket (often sporting a beer-inspired design and/or slogan on its back) and a soft, white cloth hat. After World War II, the bib overalls and hats vanished, but the jackets remained.

beetle-crushers   Heavy, dark footwear, usually synonymous with BROTHEL CREEPERS or WINKLEPICKERS. This slang was used in the 19th century for clunky boots or shoes, but, during the late 20th century, became associated with TEDDY BOY dress.

Belew, Bill   Best known as the man who put ELVIS PRESLEY in jumpsuits.

Born in 1928 in Virginia, a veteran of the Korean War, and a graduate of Parsons School of Design in New York City, Belew had previously worked on a Petula Clark television special produced by Steve Binder and was recruited by him for Elvis' NBC "Comeback Special" in 1968. In deference to the styles of the day, Belew designed a JEAN JACKET and plain-front, jeans-type pants made up in black leather (*not*, as is often reported, a jumpsuit—although the two pieces gave roughly the same silhouette).

Thereafter, the Hollywood-based Belew provided both stage costumes and a personal wardrobe for Elvis (mainly through the I.C. Costume Company) including, beginning in 1970, his many jumpsuits and their many capes. Belew also created Elvis-style signatures such as the high, Napoleonic collars (Elvis worried that his neck was too long), the riotously colored linings to dark suits, and the enormous belt buckles. At the time of "The King's" death in August of 1977,

Belew was reportedly designing a jumpsuit that would shoot laser beams.

After the demise of his best and best-known customer, Belew went on to design costumes for various television specials and series (e.g., "Mr. Belvedere" in the 1980s). From the mid-1980s onward, patterns based on his onstage and offstage clothes for Elvis were sold through Indiana-based B&K Enterprises.

Belgian Shoes   Refers to a style of slip-on shoes accented by contrasting piping and a discreet bow, sold at the midtown Manhattan shop of the same name. Begun by Henri Bendel—hence the "Belgian"—in 1956, the store sells an identical style for women and was long notorious for keeping bankers' hours. Favored by the East Coast uppercrust, Belgian Shoes have cycled in and out of more mainstream fashion (e.g., enjoying a notable vogue in the 1970s), but remain identified with a certain subset of PREPPY style.

bell-bottoms   Refers to a pants silhouette, usually jeans, with a very wide bottom hem that "bells" out below the knee. The style was part of the navy uniform (supposedly so sailors could easily roll up trousers to prevent them getting wet) and was taken up by hippies and high-fashion labels in the 1960s. Wider than BOOT-CUT. Sometimes shortened to "bells" or known as FLARES.

bell boy   Refers to the style of uniform used by hotel baggage carriers and messengers. Or to a suit following a similar silhouette. The classic "bell boy" consists of a SPENCER jacket (often double-breasted and trimmed

Bellows pocket

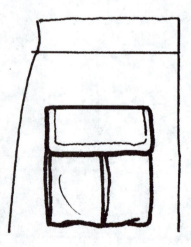

with military-looking braid or buttons), trousers (often full), and a brimless, pillbox hat (often made with a chin strap and worn at an angle).

bell hop See BELL BOY.

bellows pleat Used as a fold so that the garment appears flat from the front but has a fold of fabric at its side that allows it to expand; resembling the flat top and pleated sides of the hand bellows used on a fireplace. In menswear, most often appears on the back sides of a jacket or on a BELLOWS POCKET.

bellows pocket A pocket with a flat or gusseted front and BELLOWS PLEAT at each side where it joins the body of the garment; used for pockets meant to expand in ways that would make a patch pocket overstretched or ungainly looking.

bells Slang for BELL-BOTTOMS.

belly warmer Slang reference to a style of wide tie, usually loud and not entirely tasteful, popular in America during the 1940s and 1950s.

belt loops Narrow, vertical strips of cloth that are attached to form loops over the waistband of pants to help secure the positioning of a belt. Usually pants feature five to seven loops made of the same fabric as the rest of the pants. Not common in ready-to-wear pants before World War I, when the practice of wearing SUSPENDERS was prevalent.

belts Although belts had been worn for both practical and ornamental reasons for millennia, the practice of using them to hold up pants was not widely adopted by American men until after World War I.

Bemberg Trademarked name for woven LINING fabrics produced from CUPRO RAYON.

bench bespoke A somewhat redundant term indicating that a garment has been created from a special pattern and measurements taken for that specific purpose. (Both "bench" and "BESPOKE" when used alone have that same meaning.)

benchmade In shoemaking, the term is equivalent to "handmade." In tailoring, the term describes clothes made on premises or specifically for that shop (as opposed to work that is farmed out).

Benetton The men's and women's apparel and retail company founded by siblings Luciano, Gilbert, Carlo, and Giuliana Benetton. The brand traces its origins to the postwar era in Treviso, Italy, when Luciano convinced his younger sister Giuliana to capitalize on the brightly colored sweaters she knit and the two then sold a bicycle and accordion in order to buy a knitting machine. By 1956, they'd launched a line called Trés

Benetton: Advertisement by Oliviero Toscani

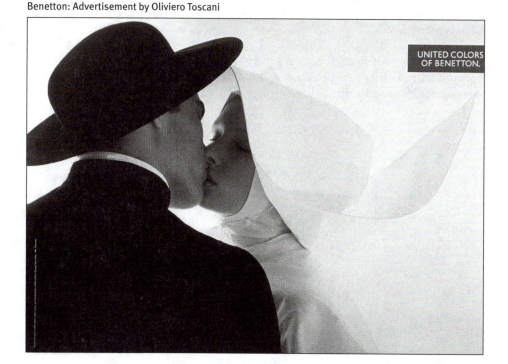

Jolie, which was rebranded with the Benetton family name in 1965. After opening boutiques near company headquarters in Ponzano Veneto in northern Italy, their international retail rollout began with a Paris boutique in 1969 and eventually expanded to over 120 countries.

Known for colorful, inexpensive sportswear, United Colors of Benetton (and its somewhat trendier offshoot, Sisley) reached their peak of popularity in the United States during the 1980s. During that time, the brand also pioneered garment-dyeing techniques and distribution strategies that would prefigure retail chains like Zara and H&M. During the 1990s, Benetton became notorious for the politically provocative advertising created by photographer Oliviero Toscani, which included photos of AIDS patients, a nun kissing a priest, and a white infant being suckled by a black woman—a campaign that concluded in 2000.

Ben Franklins   A style of undecorated, wire eyeglass frames named after those seen in popular portraits of Benjamin Franklin. The lens is small and either completely round or short and strongly horizontal. This same style may be called GRANNY GLASSES, especially when referring to the fashions of the late 1960s.

bengaline   A dressy, subtly lustrous fabric, with a corded effect that runs horizontally. In menswear, used most often for TIES or WAISTCOATS. Usually made of SILK, its etymology associates it with Bengal, the province in India from whence it was supposedly exported to Western Europe.

Bengal stripes   A two-color vertical pattern, with the background and stripe being of equal width. Refers to shirt fabrics. A Bengal stripe is broader than a PENCIL STRIPE and narrower than a CANDY STRIPE. Commonly it is done in white and one other color. Can also be described as a BALANCED STRIPE, a more generic term. Named after a fabric originally exported from Calcutta (hence the "Bengal"). Used to describe shirt fabric, but never suit fabric.

Ben Sherman   The British apparel company begun in 1963 by a man originally named Arthur Bernard Sugarman.

Born in Brighton, Sugarman took off for America as soon as he was out of his teens, married more than once, and eventually landed himself a father-in-law who ran the Santa Monica Clothing Co., a manufacturer of button-front shirts. Sugarman rechristened himself Ben Sherman, moved back to Brighton, and got into the apparel business just as the Swinging '60s were getting underway. During that decade, his shirts were worn by THE BEATLES, The Rolling Stones, The Who, and just about anybody else who sold an album in England. In 1968, he opened a shop called Millions of Shirts in Brighton, then added branches in London. Perpetually short of cash, Sherman had sold his label and headed to Australia by 1974. He died of a heart attack there in 1987, aged 62.

During the 1970s, Ben Sherman shirts became a favorite of SKINHEADS. In the 1990s, MOD and ROCKER revivals also revived the brand's cachet. By 2001, it was one of the largest casual brands in the United Kingdom, selling 5 million shirts a year and being worn by bands like Oasis and Blur. Established in the United States by 2001, Ben Sherman became identified with movies like 2001's *American Pie 2* and bands like Blink-182, Incubus, New Deal, and Sugar Ray. In 2004, it was acquired by Oxford Industries, a U.S. apparel company.

beret   The flat, pancake-shaped, brimless hat; usually made of felted material in a single piece. A style originally identified with Basque peasants (see BASQUE BERET).

Bermuda shorts   A style of not particularly short shorts that originated on the island of Bermuda and, when worn with socks long enough to cover the calves and accompanied by a dress shirt and tie, considered acceptable business attire there. (A Bermuda suit resembled a regular tropical-weight suit with the pants cut off at the knee.) Made famous worldwide by EDWARD VIII when, as Duke of Windsor, he spent WWII on Bermuda as governor of the island. Loose-fitting, they are usually done in a light color, frequently feature a pleated front, and have long since passed into the PREPPY canon. Often abbreviated to "Bermudas."

Bermuda suit   A lightweight suit substituting BERMU-DA SHORTS for full-length pants.

Bernard Weatherill   Founded in 1912, this London firm is best known for tailoring to equestrians and has held multiple ROYAL WARRANTS. Since 1969, it has shared an address with KILGOUR on SAVILE ROW.

besauge   In ARMOR, a circular piece suspended from the shoulder to protect the armpit.

besom pockets   A slit pocket distinguished by WELTED trim and no covering flap (when the material of the welt matches the material on the rest of the garment, it is said to be self-besomed). When the welting appears on both the top and bottom of the slit, the pocket is said to be double-besomed.

In menswear, particularly in jackets, the standard alternatives are PATCH POCKETS (in which the pocket is visible on the outside of the jacket) or FLAP POCKETS (slit pockets with a flap to cover the opening). In most cases, WELTED POCKET can be used as a synonym, although use of the word besom usually implies placement on a jacket or vest (as opposed to pants).

bespoke   A garment that is custom-made rather than customized. In a bespoke suit, an individual pattern is created according to the client's measurements, then sewn from material that he has chosen (hence "bespoke" to indicate that the fabric has been spoken for), and fitted on his body. A different process than MADE-TO-MEASURE.

At the beginning of the 21st century, a few of the leading London bespoke tailoring firms, in imitation of the French couture houses, began subscribing to what they called the SAVILE ROW BESPOKE CODE, which specified that a suit had to be handmade and have a minimum of 60 worker hours to qualify as bespoke.

bias   Refers to fabric that is placed sideways so that it is not aligned with grain but is instead at a 45-degree angle to both the WARP and the WEFT. More commonly used on women's wear because it makes the fabric drape differently, enhancing its natural stretch and causing it to be more clinging and close to the body. Synonym (especially in old-fashioned usage): on the cross.

bib   1. The area of a shirtfront that shows when a jacket is being worn; roughly equivalent to the compass of a baby's bib.   2. A separate garment, worn around the neck; usually to protect the clothes while eating.

Bias

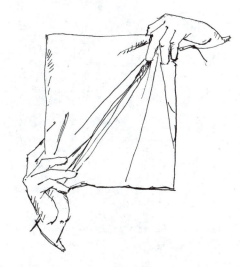

bib and band   Old-fashioned slang for shirtfront and collar, generally used in the same sense as the expression "best BIB AND TUCKER," to mean putting on your best outfit or making your best appearance.

bib and tucker   Old-fashioned slang for an outfit, generally used in the sense of "best bib and tucker" as putting on your best outfit or making your best appearance; identified more with menswear (and, if used to refer to women's wear, generally gently ironic).

bib front   1. Refers to a style of pants, such as those used for skiing or mountaineering, with fabric extending up from the waistline to cover the front of the torso (and sometimes the back and/or sides) and held up by suspenders rather than a belt. Usually worn for extra insulation during cold weather.   2. Used to describe a dress shirtfront, usually one that is made of stiffened and/or contrasting material (e.g., PIQUÉ). Unlike the stiff attached bibs that were a staple of early slapstick routines, from the mid-20th century onward the bib was stitched to the shirt: It was big enough to cover the area of the shirt that showed when the vest and jacket were

Bicorne

worn, but not so big that it chafed under suspenders or the waistband of pants. Purists consider the reference redundant, since, to them, the word "bib" refers to a shirtfront.

bib overalls   Heavy work pants with an attached "bib" or frontpiece that extends upward from the waist and over the chest to protect the shirtfront, much like a woman's apron. Most often made of denim, bib overalls were, throughout most of the 20th century, considered virtually the uniform of the American farmer. (For example: In Grant Wood's 1930 painting "American Gothic," the farmer wears denim bib overalls beneath his jacket, and many photographs of Wood, himself an Iowa farm boy, show him in bib overalls.) Unlike COVERALLS (workwear more associated with mechanics or factory jobs), "bibs" are not intended to completely protect the arms and upper body.

bibs   1. Slang for BIB OVERALLS.   2. Slang for BIB FRONT pants.

bicorne   Refers to a style of brimless hat, first popular in the 18th century, that resembles an oval chopped in two (with the straight edge crossing the forehead of its wearer); so called because it had two points.

Most fashionable at the end of the 18th and beginning of the 19th centuries, the bicorne was customarily worn with points at a right angle to the head, until, according to legend, Napoleon Bonaparte (who ordered his from Poupard in the Palais Royal), created a fashion for wearing the hat more parallel to the shoulders. When not being worn, the bicorne was flattened and carried under the arm, a bit of etiquette that inspired the manufacture of *CHAPEAU BRAS*, hats that could be carried as an accessory but not worn.

Biddle, Anthony Joseph Drexel (Jr.)　Born in 1896 into a family financially and socially well established on Philadelphia's Main Line (the first Biddle having arrived in 1681 with William Penn), the handsome, slim, and big-shouldered "Tony" Biddle had a distinguished career in public service (serving as U.S. ambassador to governments in exile during World War II and as Adjutant General of Pennsylvania), which was nonetheless eclipsed by his distinctively understated style of dress.

In 1960, he was immortalized as the most elegant man in the United States in George Frazier's famous *Esquire* magazine essay "The Art of Wearing Clothes," which enumerated the cost and construction of his wardrobe from his bespoke business suits (by H. Harris of New York and E. Tautz of London) and shirts (by Dudley Eldridge of New York) to his underwear and socks (both purchased readymade from Jacob Reed in Philadelphia). That article also ran accompanied by quotations from Biddle in which he explained that navy blue serge and charcoal gray suits offered the most versatility and that a navy blue overcoat could serve for both day and evening dress.

Biddle died in 1961.

Biella　A region in northern Italy famous for wool spinners and mills (*lanificios*). Well-known Biella firms include Angelico, Loro Piana, Luigi Botto, Trabaldo Togna, Zegna Baruffa, and Zignone.

Bijan　The Beverly Hills-based retailer and designer who became famous—even in an age of conspicuous consumption—for conspicuous consumption, specializing in items such as chinchilla-lined cashmere coats, suits with customized bulletproofing, flashy fur bedspreads, and custom revolvers, and thereby attracting customers like businessman Adnan Khashoggi, producer Aaron Spelling, singer Julio Iglesias, casino proprietor Steve Wynn, and Jordan's King Hussein.

The exuberant, Iranian-born Bijan Pakzad settled in the United States in 1971, opened for business in 1976, but hit his stride in the early 1980s when his $1 million Rodeo Drive boutique, which was open only by appointment and the implied promise that a customer intended to spend at least $2,000, seemed in sync with the high-spending ethos of the decade. Thereafter, Bijan, who starred in his own advertising, launched a line of signature fragrances (beginning with a $1,200 bottle made of Baccarat crystal), expanded into a boutique across the street from his original store, and in 1983 opened another by-appointment-only, $10 million venue on Fifth Avenue in New York City. In 1996, he added a fragrance named for basketball star Michael Jordan. In 1998, he added another venue at the Peninsula Hotel in Beverly Hills. After the market crash of the 1990s, Bijan closed his New York outpost but continued to tout himself as maker of the world's most expensive menswear.

biker jacket　See motorcycle jacket.

bikini　Because of subsequent coinages (like "monokini" for a one-piece suit), people sometimes assume that the "bi" in "bikini" is a prefix indicating a two-piece swimsuit. It's not. The bikini, which made its women's wear debut in Paris in 1946, was named for Bikini, an atoll in the Pacific that was a site of A-bomb tests. In the men's market, popular usage did not begin until a few years later, but the word has always referred to a skimpy, low-rise swimsuit, usually made of nonwoven material. It later expanded to include underpants of similar cut. In contrast to the thong, tanga, or jock, the bikini has a seat that provides coverage of the buttocks.

bill   Refers to the projecting BRIM on styles such as BASEBALL CAPS and DUCK BILL CAPS. The word bill is used more often when the brim is partial, covering only the face in a style that resembles the bill of a bird. The word brim more often indicates a projecting piece that goes completely around the head.

Synonyms: BEAK; VISOR; PEAK (more often in British usage).

billfold   Refers to a style of wallet, designed to hold paper money, that puts a premium on slimness and portability. So called because after the "bills" are placed inside, the wallet is then "folded" in half and placed in pocket. Traditionally made of leather, the billfold usually incorporates a few pockets to hold identification and credit cards but does not incorporate zippers or other hardware that might add to its bulk.

billycock   Slang reference to a BOWLER, especially in 19th-century British usage.

bin   A hat style similar to a BUCKET HAT, but with a much shallower brim. Produced by firms like KANGOL, used as an accessory in HIP-HOP fashion, and worn by musicians like LL Cool J.

bird's-eye   A traditional, woven pattern, with a small, dot pattern that supposedly looks like a bird's eye; larger than the pattern known as a PINHEAD. Not to be confused with the somewhat similar TICK WEAVE; the description is used for both wool suit fabrics and silk fabrics used for ties. Also spelled birdseye. See color plates.

bisht   A cloaklike garment worn over the THOBE in traditional ARAB DRESS.

bi-stretch   Fabric that stretches both horizontally (the WEFT) and vertically (the WARP). The majority of stretch wovens are "MONO-STRETCH," since it is much easier to make fabric that uses elastic only in the horizontal (weft) direction.

blacksmith apron   A long, sometimes near-ankle-length, apron with a skirt that wrapped completely around the body to protect it from sparks and a bib that extended upward to cover the shirtfront. Frequently made of leather (because the smiths were in proximity to hot metal and flame), but sometimes of DENIM or comparably hard-wearing fabric.

blackthorn   Refers to a type of CANE, particularly for use in the country. In the days when canes were carried for fashion as well as function, a blackthorn cane was traditional for country use with informal attire (whereas MALACCA might be more appropriate for town use). Sometimes used interchangeably with SHILLELAGH.

black tie   1. As a designation or dress code, a shorthand way of referring to the formality of the occasion; indicates that the desired dress is a TUXEDO, DINNER JACKET, or ethnic dress of equivalent formality. In contemporary practice, the more formal designation is WHITE TIE; the less formal designations are BLACK TIE OPTIONAL or BUSINESS ATTIRE; the more creative designation is ALTERNATIVE BLACK TIE. Until well after World War II, truly formal occasions automatically called for white tie or MORNING DRESS (depending upon the time of day). But, by the 1960s, most of the United States used "black tie" as a handy synonym for FORMALWEAR. 2. Reference to a tuxedo and its attendant accessories, which, in contemporary use, traditionally include: a black BOW TIE (although, from the 1990s onward, it

Billfold

became more acceptable to substitute a black, white, or silver NECKTIE); a CUMMERBUND (worn with, perhaps, a bow tie in a matching material); and a white dress shirt or tuxedo shirt (sometimes closed with STUDS instead of buttons).

black tie optional   A late-20th-century designation for social events where a TUXEDO or DINNER JACKET is not strictly required. In usual practice, a man may wear a suit (preferably black) with a dark tie or dressy accessories that distinguish his clothes in some way from the standard BUSINESS SUIT he wore to work that day.

Black Watch   Probably the best known and most popular TARTAN, developed in 1740 as a PLAID consisting of green, black, and blue, for the Royal Highland Regiment.

Thus, when the wearing of tartans was proscribed by law during 1743, the wearing of Black Watch was still legal, because it was a government and not a clan tartan. And, by the time that law was repealed in 1783, the Black Watch had become the most codified and easily identified tartan.

blade   The part of the NECKTIE that hangs from the knot, especially in British usage. Synonym: APRON, especially in the United States.

Blades   Founded in London in 1962 by Rupert Lycett Green, who located his shop first in Dover Street, then in Burlington Gardens (at the end of SAVILE ROW). Educated at Eton, Green was

not trained as a tailor. Nevertheless, he worked for ALFRED DUNHILL before opening his own shop, which made its name with slimmer-fitting suits and celebrity customers including David Hockney and Henry Herbert, the Earl of Pembroke.

blanket   Tailors' or textile makers' jargon for a large swatch of fabric showing several COLORWAYS or variations on the basic design.

blanket cloth   Textile jargon for a type of heavy, double-faced cotton with a NAP and a soft, flannelly appearance. Does not refer, as you might logically assume, to the kind of heavy woolen cloth used in traders' blankets and the coats made from them.

blanket stitch   Refers to a particular method of stitching, especially of handstitching, in which the thread loops back upon itself to form linked letter "L" shapes. The ridge thus formed by the bottom of "L" helps to prevent fraying on the fabric edge. With heavy thread stitched in a large gauge, commonly used to edge coat-weight fabrics, blankets, and other heavy woolens where a hem would prove unwieldy.

blazer   In the United States, most often describes a jacket that is navy blue with brass or gold-plated buttons;

Blazer

may be either single- or double-breasted. Worn as a SPORTS JACKET, the blazer is never matched to pants and its classic complement has always been white or gray flannel pants.

In England and other countries, where schools, teams, or regiments wear jackets described as blazers, the style is virtually always single-breasted and may be striped or in a variety of solid colors, and often carries a crest on the front pocket and a varying number of metal buttons on the cuff.

All kinds of apocryphal stories exist about the origin and naming of the blazer, and some have been repeated so often that they are accepted as fact. The best-known claims that, in 1837 when Queen Victoria was reviewing the crew of the *HMS Blazer,* she was so charmed by the dark blue coats with brass buttons sported by the crew that she ordered such jackets to be known by the name "blazer" from that day forth. Another tale claims that the word originated from the blazing color of such garments when worn as part of team uniforms. Still another claims that the style originated in the 1860s at the urging of an *HMS Blazer* captain who wanted his slovenly crew to look smart. Probably the closest to the truth is that some such garment was at some time worn on the good ship *Blazer* and that it probably originated in either the costume of the captain himself or at his urging.

In any event, by the 1920s the word was well established in its current sense and coverage of the Henley regatta mentions men wearing double-breasted navy blue models with brass buttons. By 1925, the style was well established in the States, most often as the topper to white flannel pants in a costume worn to regattas, tennis matches, and similar sports-themed events.

blazer cloth   A type of wool FLANNEL, usually navy blue; used primarily for BLAZERS.

blazer stripes   Wide, vertical stripes, like those used on school and team BLAZERS in England. Never used to describe shirt stripes.

bleeding   Refers to dye that is not COLORFAST, meaning that it is not set but runs or transfers, particularly when being laundered or when the fabric comes in contact with body moisture. For contemporary menswear, the most familiar example is MADRAS.

blends   Yarns or fabrics composed of more than one fiber. More often than not, the term implies the inclusion of SYNTHETICS. When multiple components are listed, the CHIEF VALUE goes first, then the others are listed in descending order. Thus, a blend of 51 percent cotton and 49 percent polyester would be listed as cotton/polyester blend. But a blend of 51 percent polyester and 49 percent cotton would be listed as a polyester/cotton blend.

bliaut *or* **bliaud**   The word is most commonly used for a rather fitted women's dress of the late Middle Ages (roughly 11th through 13th centuries) in Northern Europe (e.g., the costumes depicted on the cathedral in Chartres), but it can also refer to a man's costume of the same period that was worn in court settings, usually under ARMOR. A man's bliaut would have been more fitted than a tunic, had narrower sleeves, been approximately ankle-length, and had slits to accommodate striding movement of the legs.

Yet another use of the word, usually specified as a short bliaut, refers to a loose garment worn by the working classes.

blind buttonholes   Nonworking buttonholes. Typically used on the cuff buttons of less expensive jackets. (However, sometimes even the sleeve of a BESPOKE garment will have a blind top buttonhole above its WORKING BUTTONHOLES.)

bling *or* **bling-bling**   HIP-HOP slang for flashy, over-the-top jewelry. Derived from the sound of big necklaces, rings, or bracelets clanking against each other. The repeated word is the earlier usage: In the 21st century, usually shortened to a single "bling."

blocking   1. A method of sizing fabrics, primarily knits, to ensure that they meet a certain measurement. For example, when someone is constructing a hand-knit SWEATER, the individual pieces may be "blocked" before being sewn together, so that they meet the required size. Similarly, after cleaning, a sweater may be "blocked" to correct any shrinkage or stretching that has occurred during the cleaning process. In the simplest sense, the garment (or garment pieces) are dampened, laid flat to the desired dimensions, and allowed to dry.   2. A similar method of sizing a hat, usually by employing heat.   3. Short for "color blocking," literally refers to color patterned in large chunks, rather than an overall pattern like stripes.

Bling: Japanese designer/artist Nigo

block pattern   Tailors' jargon for a standard pattern (as opposed to custom or customized pattern adjusted to the measurements of a particular client).

block print   Refers to an artisanal method of printing patterns on textiles, usually by hand. In this ancient method, one "block" is carved with a design (usually from a piece of wood or gourd), then inked with dye and stamped on the cloth. A different block must be carved for every color used, and the hand-stamping process must be repeated until the patterning is complete.

Inevitably, different colors are not always aligned uniformly, or the blocks are not inked uniformly, or the blocks start to wear down—thus blurring the edges of the design. Those variables are what visually distinguish block printing from mechanized versions (such as PERROTINE printing).

blouse   A term that implies a loose, untailored shirt (as opposed to a traditional DRESS SHIRT constructed with a buttoned PLACKET and BARREL CUFFS). Ergo, styles like the COSSACK SHIRT or POET'S SHIRT may both be referred to as blouses.

blouson   Used to indicate a short jacket or shirt that is loose and unfitted through the torso, with the material gathered into its hem to form fullness around the waist; also used to describe a shirt that is worn so that it gives a similar effect. Synonym: BOMBER (for a jacket style).

blucher   A style of shoe with a lacing system that allows easy adjustment—and readjustment—to the wearer's foot (be it high-arched, wide, narrow, swollen, or whatever). A blucher, which is a variation of the basic DERBY style, positions its FACINGS on top of the shoe's VAMP (as opposed to neatly secreting them beneath a seam as an

OXFORD does). As a result, the shoe is more responsive to the lacing and its width can be altered at will.

The name derives from the Prussian field marshal Gebhard Leberecht von Blücher, who joined forces with WELLINGTON (another originator of footwear styles) to defeat Napoleon at Waterloo and who ordered boots with open, laced throats made for his army.

bluebonnet   Refers to a style of hat; see BALMORAL.

blue collar   Commonly a cultural rather than a costume designation, the term derives from the days when workmen's clothes were dyed with INDIGO, which was thought to strengthen the fabric as well as decorate it.

blue jeans   See JEANS.

board   British tailors' slang for the bench where a tailor works. Somebody who's been "on the board" has been employed as a tailor.

board shorts   Trunks used for surfing. Usually made of a sturdy woven fabric that is double-stitched. Traditional board shorts include a small pocket for board wax.

Ozwald Boateng

Boateng, Ozwald   Born in 1967, raised in north London, and the son of Ghanian immigrants, the outspoken Ozwald Boateng became known during the 1990s for suits with bold colors and body-hugging fits. As a mediagenic celebrity tailor, he also attracted attention for merging a SAVILE ROW setup with the sensibility of a fashion designer in a way not seen in London since the 1960s.

After planning to study computer science, Boateng switched to fashion at Southgate College in London, and then apprenticed himself to various tailoring firms. At age 28, he opened his own establishment on Vigo Street at the top of Savile Row—the youngest man and the first black man to do so—attracting the likes of DAVID BECKHAM, Laurence Fishburne, Jamie Foxx, and Will Smith. In 1998, his new business went bust after a falling out with his backer. Nevertheless, by 2003, when ALEXANDER MCQUEEN left the house of Givenchy, Boateng was named the designer of Givenchy's menswear; and he showed his first runway collection for that marque in 2004. In 2006, he was awarded the Order of the British Empire. That same year, his business was the subject of an eight-part reality series on American cable television called *House of Boateng*.

boater   Refers to a style of straw hat with a flat top, a shallow crown that joins the top at a right angle, and a stiff, shallow, circular brim, usually ornamented with grosgrain or other ribbon band with a flattened bow.

The style was worn by women and children as early as the 1860s, but was not widely accepted menswear until almost 20 years later. As might be suspected, it takes its name from its initial association with boating and was strictly summer headgear. (After the first quarter of the

Boaters

20th century, best remembered as a standard costume of barbershop quartets.) Related entry: HARROW HAT.

boating mocs　A style of shoes—of which Sperry TOP-SIDERS are the best known example—that generally have soles made of white rubber (or some similar material that will not scuff a boat deck), SIPING on the bottom for increased traction on slippery decks and docks, and a MOCCASIN-style top. Also worn by PREPPIES as part of casual attire.

boatneck　A wide, strongly horizontal neck opening, like those seen on sailors' jerseys. The opening of a boatneck is usually wider than that of a CREWNECK, does not have RIBBING, and has a much shallower dip—barely accommodating the Adam's apple—so that it gives the impression of slit in the fabric.

body lining　Tailors' jargon for what most people would refer to as a jacket's LINING; the layer of fabric visible on the interior of a garment. Used to distinguish between the visible lining and the INTERLINING.

bodysuit　A top that is constructed like an abbreviated, close-fitting JUMPSUIT or COVERALL, like a combination of shirt and underpants, or an updated COMBINATION or UNION SUIT; usually pants are then worn over the bottom portion. Most often made of knit or stretch fabric. For everyday apparel, more popular for women's wear.

boiler suit　A utilitarian JUMPSUIT or COVERALL, usually in British usage. A more generic reference to the SIREN SUIT, especially as worn by Winston Churchill during World War II.

bolero　A style of short vest or jacket with a rounded front; usually collarless and always worn open. The bolero always ends at or above the waist, and although it may be trimmed with buttons or other closures, they are vestigial. Copied from Spanish costume and named after the Spanish dance known as the bolero; quoted more often in women's fashion.

bolo tie　A NECKTIE created from a length of cord (almost always leather) rather than a strip of silk or other fabric; closed with jewelry-like slide clasp (as opposed to being knotted) and usually featuring decorative metal tips. According to legend, the first bolo was created in the 1940s when Arizona silversmith Victor Cedarstaff was out riding and his hat blew off. Not wanting to lose his silver hatband buckle, he put the hatband and its buckle around his neck. Later he added silver tips to the cord, named it after the bolos used by gauchos, and patented his new accessory, which has been associated with Western wear ever since (the state of Arizona made it official neckwear in 1971).

Not to be confused with a STRING TIE (which is also a length of cord but tied in a bow), or a BOOTLACE or PLANTATION TIE (which are narrow strips but also tied in a bow). Synonym: bola tie.

bolt　A unit of uncut cloth that represents the way fabric is sold to most consumers, especially for cotton shirting, wool suiting, or denim. In the standard bolt, about 50 to 100 yards of fabric—depending, in part, upon the thickness of the fabric—are doubled over and wrapped around a thick, rectangular piece of cardboard. (By con-

Bolero

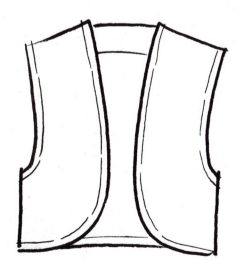

trast, silk, lace, and similarly delicate fabrics may be wrapped in a single width around a long tube).

bombachas   The loose, baggy pants identified with the working GAUCHO in South America; worn tucked into boots. Not to be confused with the fashion known as gaucho pants, a cropped, full-legged style associated with women's fashion.

bomber   Refers to a general style of long-sleeved, zip-front jacket cropped to waist length, its chief characteristic being an untailored, BLOUSON fit that does *not* hug the torso. The bomber usually has ribbing at its collar, cuffs, and hem, and may or may not include pockets. In contemporary use, the bomber is a silhouette that can be adapted to any weight of material and any season, although it remains more associated with activewear and has yet to make the transition to business attire.

The style and its name derive from the jackets worn by bomber crews, especially during World War II; its predecessor was the flight jacket. Synonym: BLOUSON.

bondage pants   Taken from fetish wear, the bondage pants worn for fashion reasons sport buckles down the back of the leg so that locomotion is limited; the more authentic fetish pants also have "bum flaps" in the back.

Popularized by the PUNK movement of the 1970s, especially by VIVIENNE WESTWOOD and Malcolm McLaren in their shop called SEX on the King's Road in London.

bonehead   Slang for a style of dress that began in the late 1970s as a blend of SKINHEAD and PUNK, primarily in Britain. A bonehead might wear narrow jeans, T-shirts, suspenders draped over his hips (instead of his shoulders), and heavy workboots.

bonnet   When applied to menswear, a bonnet is a general category describing any hat without a BRIM or BILL. (And, although its most familiar contemporary usage is for a baby's bonnet, it is not exclusive to women and children and, indeed, has a different meaning in women's wear.)

The current English word derives from the Scottish word for a brimless hat, hence its use in the styles such as GLENGARRY BONNET or BLUEBONNET.

Bonnie and Clyde   Arthur Penn's 1967 movie starring Faye Dunaway as Bonnie Parker and Warren Beatty as Clyde Barrow, her partner in crime. In this highly romanticized version of the Depression-era outlaws' tale, Theadora Van Runkle's Oscar-nominated costume designs put Dunaway in fetching berets and POORBOY sweaters and the young and handsome Beatty in snappy FEDORAS, pinstriped suits, and SPECTATOR shoes, thereby inspiring magazine editorial aplenty and creating nationwide fads for early 1930s fashions.

Bonnie and Clyde

book An old-fashioned, industry measurement of yarn. Thirty SKEINS equal one book. Thirty books equal one BALE.

Boone, Pat Born in 1934 in Jacksonville, Florida, singer Pat Boone rose to prominence during the 1950s (when he racked up most of his Top Forty hits) as the all-American, clean-cut alternative to ELVIS PRESLEY. His trademarks: white BUCK shoes, immaculately groomed hair, neat clothes, and a wholesome smile.

boot cut Refers to pants that flare slightly at the bottom of the leg—supposedly so they can be worn comfortably over boots. Boot-cut pants or jeans are not as exaggerated or wide as FLARES or BELL-BOTTOMS.

boot hooks Devices, used in pairs, for the purpose of pulling on boots, especially riding boots and other snug, knee-high styles. Often collapsible, the boot hook has a handle with a long, wide, blunted metal hook attached (somewhat resembling the hoof pick used on a horse). The hooks are placed on tabs sewn on the inside top of the boots and then used to pull; once the boots are on, the metal slides out. Synonym: BOOT PULLS.

Pat Boone

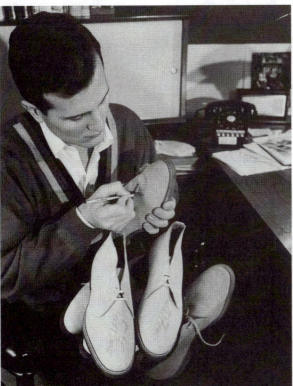

boot hose 1. Refers to a type of sock with decorated tops, particularly those worn by 17th-century CAVALIERS who allowed the tops to be visible when boots were being worn. 2. Long, usually knee-high socks worn, usually with breeches, under riding boots.

boot jack A device, usually wooden, to aid in the removal of pull-on styles of mid-calf or knee-high boots (such as riding boots). In most boot jacks, the heel of the booted foot is placed in a V-shaped indentation in the jack, while the other foot steps on top of the jack to lever the boot off.

bootlace tie Slang, usually British, for a string tie looped in a bow, rather than being knotted like a traditional necktie; especially associated with TEDDY BOY fashion. Often misidentified as a BOLO TIE. Synonym: SHOESTRING TIE.

bootmaker More often, especially in British slang, refers to a shoemaker rather than someone who makes only boots.

boot pulls Synonym for BOOT HOOKS.

boots A boot is distinguished from a shoe mainly by its length, which extends at least to the ankle or covers it. For example: When the style of footwear known as a plain OXFORD curves under the ankle, it remains a shoe; when it ventures 2 or 3 inches higher, it becomes a BALMORAL boot; the two being virtually identical in every aspect except the added height (and the extra three pairs of eyelets needed to accommodate it).

boot tops A strip of leather that looks like a sort of cuff for knee-high boots; in contemporary use, an important part of FOXHUNTING ATTIRE (and in horse show classes that take their cues from it). The color and use of boot tops are prescribed according to the wearer's rank in the hunt and the rest of his attire. For example, for a formal, full-dress hunt a man would probably wear white breeches and black boots with brown tops.

boot-tree   A device, usually wooden, inserted into a boot so that it retains its shape when not being worn. In contrast to a SHOE TREE, a boot tree has an additional, shin-shaped component that expands to fill the leg of boot, thereby preventing it from sagging.

boro   From the Japanese word for "rags," used to refer to patched or mended textiles—particularly those of humble origin. During the late 20th century, the aesthetic that found beauty in boro influenced Japanese-born designers like Rei Kawakubo who, in turn, influenced other designers as well as a general movement in Western fashion to value vintage jeans and deconstructed garments.

Borsalino   Founded as men's hatmaker in Alessandria, Italy in 1857 by Giuseppe Borsalino, an Italian who had studied hat making in France. By 1875, the hat factory offered at least six dozen distinct styles and, by the time of Giuseppe's death in 1900, was producing about 750,000 hats a year. Giuseppe's son, Teresio, further consolidated the business and reached an annual production of 2 million hats by 1913.

During the 1930s, Borsalino hats—particularly its FEDORAS and an exaggerated TRILBY style—were strongly identified with gangsters. In 1970, French director Jacques Deray capitalized on that association in his film *Borsalino*, which starred Jean-Paul Belmondo and Alain Delon as crooks in 1930s Marseilles.

bosom board   An adjunct to the ironing board (similar to a SLEEVE BOARD), shaped and sized (at about a foot wide) to aid in the creation of smoothly ironed, stiff shirtfront; used particularly when starched shirtfronts were in fashion.

Boston boot   Old-fashioned slang for the style of shoe best-known in the 19th century as the CONGRESS GAITER and in the 20th and 21st centuries as the SIDE-GUSSET.

botanies   Refers to fine wools—usually MERINO—most often intended for men's apparel. Derived from Botany Bay, the original export point for Australia's wool.

boteh   The most common of several names for the PAISLEY, the distinctive, comma-shaped motif in paisley-patterned textiles. Synonym: bota.

bottle-shaped tie   A tie shaped so that, when it is being worn, it appears to taper toward the knot.

Borsalino

bottomweights   Jargon used to refer to fabric for pants. A bottomweight is heavier than a TOPWEIGHT and includes fabrics like DENIM and KHAKI. Refers to the fabric, never to the finished garment.

boubou   General term for a style of voluminous robes worn by men in Western Africa.

bouclé   1. A knit or woven fabric with a surface full of tiny loops and knots; made entirely of or with a great percentage of bouclé yarn. In menswear, it appears most often in SPORTS JACKETS and SWEATERS.   2. The fancy yarn used to make bouclé cloth; distinguished by an uneven appearance as though the yarn has twisted back upon itself, forming tiny loops like a badly tangled piece of string.

bound buttonhole   A buttonhole bordered by a thin rim of fabric (as opposed to being finished with thread in a BUTTONHOLE STITCH); resembles a WELT pocket.

bound seam   A seam edge where the cut fabric, which is normally left exposed, is covered with SEAM BINDING or similarly finished to prevent fraying and make a neater appearance.

boutonnière   A flower worn as adornment in the buttonhole of a man's jacket or coat lapel.

Costume historians Aileen Ribeiro and Valerie Cumming have written that the practice of adding a superfluous buttonhole on the lapel in order to accommodate the wearing of a boutonnière began in the 1840s. In contemporary use, the practice is now common only for semiformal or formal occasions. For example, the average American man's encounter with boutonnières may be confined to proms and weddings. Synonym: BUTTONHOLE.

bovver boots   Usually refers to the thick-soled, steel-reinforced, black DOC MARTENS boots worn by SKINHEADS, especially for fights; from the British slang usage of "bovver" as a synonym for trouble.

Bowery, Leigh   Born in 1961 in a Melbourne suburb named Sunshine, Australian Leigh Bowery achieved his fame as provocateur and performance artist after moving to London in 1980. Infamous for his regular appearances at the West End club called Taboo, Bowery treated dressing as a performance in itself, inventing transvestite costumes that would play up his multiple piercings, involve disfiguring makeup and masks, or put him on platform shoes that made him 7 feet tall. Radically vulgar yet weirdly beautiful, these appearances are credited with influencing everyone from the followers of the NEW ROMANTIC movement through singer BOY GEORGE (in his Culture Club days) to artist Damien Hirst to designer ALEXANDER MCQUEEN.

During his most notorious performance, in 1994, Bowery gave birth on stage, while his performance partner Nicola Bateman (who married him shortly before his death), wriggled out from underneath his costume, where she had been hidden by a specially constructed harness. Among his other claims to fame: designing costumes for choreographer Michael Clark, modeling in a 1989 campaign for Pepe Jeans, appearances in the editorial of *i-D* magazine, posing for nude portraits by painter Lucien Freud, and forming the art rock band Minty in 1993.

Bowery died of AIDS in 1994. In 2002, he became the subject of a full-length musical, "Taboo," with songs by his friend BOY GEORGE, who also starred as Bowery. That same year, he was also the subject of director Charles Atlas's full-length documentary, *The Legend of Leigh Bowery*.

bowl cut   Refers to a type of haircut in which the hair is trimmed to uniform length, as if a bowl had been upended on the man's head and any hair hanging below that bowl's edges cut off. Costumers and illustrators often give medieval characters this type of haircut. Synonyms include PUDDING BASIN CUT or BASIN CUT.

bowler   Usually made of dark, hard FELT, the bowler hat has a low, round, bowl-shaped CROWN and short circular BRIM that is usually slightly curled. The same style is commonly called a DERBY in the United States and was known as a BILLYCOCK or COKE (pronounced "cook") hat in England, especially during the 19th century.

According to legend, the first bowler was commissioned by William Coke II, a member of the Earl of Leicester's family (which actually hails from Norfolk), from London hatmakers James and George Lock (LOCK & CO.) in 1850 because he sought a sturdy, low-crowned hat as a more practical alternative to the then-prevalent TOP HAT. (Coke thought a lower crown was less likely to be knocked off by low-hanging branches while on horseback.) That prototype was produced by Lock's contract manufacturers, Thomas and William Bowler, who subsequently began selling the model under their own name.

A style associated with properly dressed politicians (e.g., Prime Minister Stanley Baldwin) and cinema clowns (Charlie Chaplin, Stan Laurel), the bowler continues to be worn by equestrians in both the show ring and hunt field.

bow tie   NECKWEAR intended to be tied in a bow under the chin rather than to dangle from a SLIP KNOT like a NECKTIE; most often made from silk or a material made to look like silk. Bow ties are usually sold sized to the neck of the wearer, like dress shirts (from 15½ to 17½ inches), and average about 36 to 38 inches in length when untied.

In contemporary practice, they are sold in two basic styles, depending on the shape desired in the bow. The more popular THISTLE (also known as the BUTTERFLY) has curvaceous, shaped ends that result in a bow that flares out from the knot like the wings of a butterfly. The less popular BATWING has straight ends so that, when tied, it forms a straight horizontal bow parallel to the chin. Both are tied the same way. Variations on the two basics (such as the extra-thick, puffy style sported by EDWARD VIII when Duke of Windsor and made for him

How to tie a bow tie

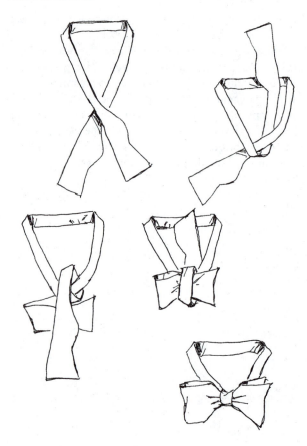

Bowler

by CHARVET) are usually effected in the shaping of the tie and not by its knot.

Although the bow tie has a closer relationship to the CRAVAT of the previous centuries than the contemporary necktie does, by the late 20th century many American men regarded it as symbol of eccentricity or affectation. Or as a symbol—the black tie and the white tie—of imposed formality.

box calf   A variety of CALFSKIN cured with chrome salts, used mostly for fine footwear and briefcases; available in both GRAINED and smooth finishes. The "box" does not refer to any pattern on the skin and is reportedly derived from either the last name of a London cobbler named Joseph Box, the logo of a famous leather firm, or the method of transporting fine skins in boxes instead of tied bundles. One, all, or none may be correct.

box cars   A generic style of thick-soled, lace-up shoes with squared toes, popular for college students during the late 1930s.

box pleat   A pleat made from making a defined symmetrical fold of material that is then flattened so that its top has a square appearance. In menswear, used most often in the back of jackets and shirts beneath a yoke; occasionally used on pants.

boxer briefs   Briefs, usually with a Y-front closure like JOCKEY SHORTS, but with legs and an inseam like BOXERS. Made of knit material, boxer briefs are not as baggy as traditional boxer shorts.

boxers   Baggy, above-the-knee underpants roughly similar in style to the boxing trunks worn by prizefighters.

Boxers

Classic boxers are made of woven cotton and have an elastic waist and button fly—as worn by Dustin Hoffman in the 1967 movie *The Graduate*.

boxing cup   A piece of rigid plastic or other reinforced material worn to protect the genitals during fights and sparring. Invention of the cup is attributed to Foul-Proof Taylor, who promoted it during the 1930s by whapping wearers in the crotch with a baseball bat to demonstrate his product's protective powers.

Boy George   Born George Alan O'Dowd in 1961, the British performer who re-created himself as Boy George became best known for his hits as a member of the group Culture Club during the 1980s and taking the NEW ROMANTIC look in a more androgynous direction. Promoted by Malcolm McLaren (at that time still heavily involved in fashion and still the partner of designer VIVIENNE WESTWOOD), George had already gone through a PUNK incarnation and become

Boy George

a regular on the London club scene dominated by LEIGH BOWERY. In his Boy George persona, he became identified with dress that quoted the garb of Hasidic Jews (long coat, high hat), smocks, and lush makeup that made him look like Elizabeth Taylor; he also bought fashion from the likes of BodyMap, Katharine Hamnett, and Westwood. In 2002, George wrote and starred in the musical *Taboo*, based on the life of Leigh Bowery, appearing in both the West End and Broadway productions as the Bowery character, while a younger actor played the Boy George part.

braces   SUSPENDERS in British usage.

braguette   French term for a CODPIECE.

braid   A narrow decorative trim, which may be either flattened or rounded like a cord, but is composed of interlaced strands that vaguely resemble braided rope; may be made from any non-hairy fiber (although for menswear, fibers that yield some sheen have proved most popular). Primarily identified with the decoration of uniforms, it has been most popular during the times when civilian men's fashion purposely imitates military styles.

Although the braid itself is nonfunctional, it may be formed into fastenings, such as button loops, FROGS, or BRANDENBURGS.

branded apparel   Jargon for clothes bearing a specific manufacturer's label—usually a well-known one. The opposite designation is UNBRANDED APPAREL, which usually indicates that the clothes were manufactured more generically.

brandenburg   1. The style of decorative fastening now better known as a FROG; usually made with BRAID; a reference used especially when describing uniforms or fashions quoting the military. Variant spellings: brandenburgh, brandenbourg.   2. Before the Napoleonic wars, used to refer to a style of long, loose coat that closed with the decorative fastenings that became known as brandenburgs.

brassard *or* **brassart**   In ARMOR, protection for the lower arm.

break   Jargon for the point at which the fabric of a garment naturally falls into a crease or bend. Thus, a tailor might refer to where the pants "break" at the knee, the sleeve breaks at the elbow, the pants hem breaks against the shoe, or the lapel breaks on the chest.

In contemporary usage, the term most often is used to describe a slight fold at the bottom of traditionally designed trousers, where the pants leg hits the instep of the foot, as in "the leg should break on the shoe." The break of a lapel is more often referred to as the ROLL LINE or BREAKLINE.

breakline   The point at which a jacket's LAPEL, which is a continuation of the main chest piece of the jacket (and not a separate, sewn-on piece like the COLLAR), folds back upon itself; the inside crease of the lapel. Synonym: bridle line; ROLL LINE.

breastplate   In ARMOR, the piece that protects the chest.

breechcloth *or* **breechclout**   A LOINCLOTH.

breeches   Refers to pants that do not fully cover the leg. A broad term indicating a type of garment (similar in use to coat or shirt), the word encompasses hundreds of historical subcategories, such as SLOPS, from the 16th century onward.

In contemporary usage, the word appears most often to describe the pants worn with knee-high boots for horseback riding.

breeching   In the days when little boys and girls were both routinely outfitted with skirts and long hair, breeching marked the time in the boy's life when he was transferred to pants (sometimes as late as age six). In the Western world, the age of "breeching" gradually became lower and lower until, by the time of World War I, the custom was virtually obsolete.

breeks   1. Archaic synonym for BREECHES.   2. Old-fashioned slang for pants with a sleek, straight line (as opposed to extremely tight or extremely baggy styles).

bricolage   In apparel, refers to the practice of reusing preexisting materials. During the 1970s, particularly identified with PUNK fashion and the practice of designers such as VIVIENNE WESTWOOD.

Brideshead Revisited   The 11-part series from Granada television in 1981, based on Evelyn Waugh's 1945 novel of life in England between the two World Wars, starring Jeremy Irons and Anthony Andrews as, respectively, narrator Charles Ryder and Lord Sebastian Flyte, with costumes by Jane Robinson. Coming at the same time as *CHARIOTS OF FIRE*, the 1981 movie with costumes by MILENA CANONERO, the series not only consolidated the stardom of Irons but revived the styles of England between the World Wars.

bridge coat   A variation of the PEACOAT, especially one that is longer (reaching to mid-thigh instead of hip-length).

bridge collection   Jargon borrowed from women's wear, usually indicating a designer's collection that is a step down in price and prestige from his or her runway collection, but a step up in price and prestige from more mass-market offerings. While bridge collections may not be the aristocrats of the fashion world, they are its haute bourgeoisie, and may appear in both specialty stores and department stores.

bridle line   See BREAKLINE.

bridle tape   A construction element, in traditional tailoring, used most often on the ROLL LINE of a lapel. Not visible when the garment is being worn.

Brideshead Revisited

briefcase   A handheld case sized for carrying legal briefs; customarily soft-sided or envelope-shaped (whereas an ATTACHÉ CASE is traditionally hard-sided); usually carried by handle or, in more contemporary versions, tucked under the arm.

briefs   Refers to a style of underpants without legs or inseam, which are abbreviated to be "briefer" than TRUNKS; usually made of knit material, with an elastic waist. They may or may not also have a Y-FRONT fly. The style became popular in the United States after 1935, when the Cooper Company introduced its JOCKEY SHORTS.

brim   The part of a hat that projects outward from its CROWN.

Brioni   The luxury Italian clothier, christened after the Croatian islands known in English as Brijuni, a resort in the Adriatic Sea off the Dalmatian Coast popular with rich Italians between the two World Wars; founded by tailor Nazareno Fonticoli and his partner businessman Gaetano Savini as the Sartoria Brioni shop on the Via Barberini in Rome in 1945. By presenting its collection on a runway in Florence in 1952, Brioni more or less invented the current Italian menswear shows. In 1954, Savini—who later appended Brioni to his surname— repeated the feat in New York, then took his show on the road by staging men's fashion shows in major American cities. During that time, the label also became famous as a sort of tailor to the stars, outfitting both Italian actors and visiting deities such as Gary Cooper and Clark Gable. In 1960, it began selling off-the-rack suits. Much later, Brioni would become famous as the Italian label that provided suits for Pierce Brosnan and Daniel Craig when each portrayed British secret agent James Bond.

Initially, Brioni made its name by drastically reducing the SHOULDER PADS and amount of fabric used in suits. Cutting close to the body, it radically simplified the line—eliminating, wherever possible, cuffs, pocket flaps, pleats, and the like. With the change in silhouette, came lighter fabrics (such as silk SHANTUNG) in a wider range of colors. Fonticoli also perfected a construction system that combined a high amount of hand finishing with quick assembly, thus giving the impression of BESPOKE at the speed and convenience of READYMADE.

The firm further expanded after 1990, when Umberto Angeloni, an economist who had married into an owning family, took over as chief executive (a position he would hold until 2006). However, the firm made it a point of pride to retain its bespoke service and continued to operate its own tailoring school.

British warm   Originally referring to the woolen GREATCOAT issued to British Army officers during World War I, this term now refers to a type of heavy, usually double-breasted, OVERCOAT with a military look, most often made of wool or a wool blend. The term gained general usage after the war, when decommissioned officers began wearing their "British warms" in civilian life.

broadcloth   1. Shirt fabric in a PLAIN WEAVE that is *not* a BALANCED WEAVE (so that it has a very slight horizontal rib).   2. A type of plainly woven wool, so called because a 15th-century English law mandated that it be made on an extra-broad loom. After weaving, it was subjected to shrinking so that the cloth became tighter and FULLED.

broadtail   The pelt of an unborn lamb from a breed of sheep known as KARAKUL. (Taken after birth, the pelt is known as ASTRAKHAN.) Taken before birth, the wool is so tightly curled and flat that it resembles crushed velvet and the skin is extremely supple and easy to sew. It also has a black color and glossy texture it loses soon after birth.

brocade A richly woven, self-patterned fabric, most often silk or a material made to look like silk, that uses contrasting textures and/or colors. Relatively heavy and relatively stiff, it was once the stuff of royalty and ecclesiastical robes. In contemporary menswear, it appears most often in DINNER JACKETS or SMOKING JACKETS.

brogan A style of sturdy, unornamented work shoe with a heavy sole (often reinforced with PEGS or HOBNAILS); reaches almost to the ankle and is sometimes referred to as a low boot. Not to be confused with the contemporary BROGUE.

Originally the brogan was a rough, homemade style worn in the Scottish Highlands. Men tramping through wet fields and streams evolved the practice of punching holes in the leather to let the water out—a practice that became known as BROGUEING and that evolved into the ornamented and distinctly different style known as the brogue.

brogue An ornamented variation on the basic styles of laced shoes, which can be either the DERBY or OXFORD. The brogue's distinctive features are its decorative punching (usually with a GIMPED edge along the curvy TOE CAP) and its heavier leather.

It may be further designated as either a semi brogue or a full brogue, the difference between the two mainly being the toe cap: A semi brogue usually follows the straight horizontal toe cap line of an oxford, whereas a full brogue has a flaring curvaceous toe cap that wings backward past the lacing and surges to a point in the shoe's center front. Although the shoe's distinctive BROGUEING was once a functional means of allowing water to escape from the shoe (see BROGAN), in contemporary use it is decorative and applied only to the outer layer of leather, leaving the foot protected by the shoe lining or underlayer.

With the addition of a KILTIE tongue and CLEATS, the brogue also forms the basis for the traditional GOLF SHOE.

brogueing The punched decoration used on leather to create full BROGUE or semi brogue styles of shoe. The practice originated in Scotland when Highlanders would punch holes in the sturdy shoes they called BROGANS so that, when they forded streams or tramped through burns, water would not remain in their shoes but would run out of the holes.

broken stripe Used to describe a pattern, usually for suit fabric, that appears as a solid CHALK-type stripe from a slight distance but, upon closer inspection, resembles a series of aligned dashes. When the breaks are very frequent and the stripe resembled dots rather than dashes, it is referred to as a BEADED STRIPE.

broken twill Refers to a TWILL weave in which the normal diagonal line of weaving has been purposely interrupted, resulting in a fabric surface that looks less regular and machine-made. Usually describes DENIM. In addition to its irregular look, broken twill is prized because the resulting fabric has less torque and therefore less of a tendency to twist when it is turned into a pants leg.

brolly Old-fashioned, British slang for an old-fashioned UMBRELLA.

bronzer A cosmetic that makes the skin looks bronzed or tan. Bronzer may be in the form of a cream, lotion, or powder, but its effect is temporary and can be washed off. A SELF-TANNER, by contrast, is a semipermanent treatment that dyes the skin, usually lasts at least two days, and is difficult to remove.

Brooks Brothers Founded in 1818 by Henry Sands Brooks as H. & D.H. Brooks & Co. at Catharine and Cherry Streets in downtown New York (now the location of the South Street Seaport), the company claims to be America's oldest clothing retailer and remains best known as a bastion of the IVY LEAGUE LOOK and purveyor of PREPPY styles. From its beginning, Brooks specialized in readymade TAILORED CLOTHING—still a relative rarity in the first half of the 19th century.

When its founder died in 1833, the company passed to his oldest son and namesake; then, in 1850, to his son's sons: Daniel, John, Edward, and Elisha. From that time, it became known as Brooks Brothers and adopted the golden fleece logo used ever since. In 1858, the store began to move to locations including Union Square and Broadway and Grand Street. In 1915, the company moved to its current address at 346 Madison Avenue, which made it convenient to the nearby Ivy League clubs as well as Manhattan's midtown business district (and later attract like-minded retailers such as PAUL STUART, CHIPP, J. PRESS, and F.R. TRIPLER to the neighborhood).

Although Brooks Brothers did not invent the BUTTON-DOWN SHIRT or many of the other iconic items associated with the store, it gave them its imprimatur; and thus formerly foreign, fancy, or otherwise unfamiliar styles found their way into the wardrobes of the store's conservative clientele. For example, when Brooks Brothers began selling SEERSUCKER SUITS in 1930, it was the seal of approval on a style that, only a decade or so

before, had been disregarded as a cheaper, less proper alternative to the linen suit. Decades later, it would make pink button-down shirts acceptable instead of effeminate and introduce wash 'n' wear shirts made of the then-new fiber called DACRON.

Many of the styles now regarded as all-American and/or preppy were, in fact, fashions that Brooks Brothers expropriated from England. For example:

• In 1890, a store executive named Francis Lloyd brought back the English fashion for silk FOULARD neckties.

• In 1896, John Brooks spotted button-down shirt collars at an English polo match and had them copied for the store.

• In 1904, the firm began importing sweaters made from the rough wool of the SHETLAND Islands.

• In 1910, it took the CAMEL'S HAIR POLO COAT sported by English players between chukkers.

• In 1920, it began selling the REPP TIE, a style associated with British regiments and clubs (although Brooks Brothers claims credit for reversing the direction of the stripes on the ties so its clients would not be mistaken for trying to pass themselves off as Brits).

• In 1920, it also introduced sportswear made of MADRAS, a fabric formerly associated with British colonies.

• In 1949, it began manufacturing socks in ARGYLE, the Scottish pattern popularized by EDWARD VIII when he was Prince of Wales, and much favored during his days as Duke of Windsor.

Post World War II, Brooks Brothers became known as the bastion of the button-down shirt and the SACK SUIT, key elements to the Ivy League look. In later decades, it was regarded as one of the definitive preppy emporia.

During its long history, the establishment's many famous customers included virtually every man on the

Brooks Brothers

best-dressed list (e.g., GIANNI AGNELLI for the button-down collars he kept unbuttoned) and practically every U.S. president: In its best-known instance of presidential patronage, Brooks Brothers produced a special black frock coat with "one country, one destiny" embroidered on its lining for Abraham Lincoln's second inaugural; it was that coat that he was wearing when he was assassinated.

The company was purchased from the founding family in 1946 by Julius Garfinckel and sold to Marks & Spencer in 1988, whereupon it started an extensive and expensive renovation of its Madison Avenue flagship. It was sold again, to Retail Brand Alliance, in 2001.

brothel creepers   British slang for a style of exaggeratedly pointy-toed shoes that became associated with TEDDY BOYS. In 1924, when EDWARD VIII, then Prince of Wales, wore a pair of tan brothel creepers on a visit to New York, Americans were scandalized because they considered such shoes too effeminate and extreme to be worn by a gentleman, much less a prince. As the 20th century progressed, brothel creepers were usually made with thick CREPE soles and were, more often than not, black. Sometimes referred to as BEETLECRUSHERS (slang dating from the 19th century) or WINKLEPICKERS.

Brown, Willie   Known for his natty dressing as well as for becoming the first African-American mayor of San Francisco (from 1996 to 2004), Willie Lewis Brown Jr. was born in 1934 in Texas and served in the California State Assembly from 1964 to 1995. A longtime customer and friend of San Francisco clothier WILKES BASHFORD, Brown favored traditionally tailored clothing in dark colors, especially by BRIONI, during his work days and indulged in more fashionable garb (an ISSEY MIYAKE jacket, a double-breasted KITON tuxedo) at other times. Early in his administration, he gained nationwide notoriety for telling his staff that casual wear and the practice of CASUAL FRIDAYS was inappropriate for City Hall. He also did various film and TV cameos (e.g., appearing as a politician in *The Godfather III*, *George of the Jungle*, and *The Princess Diaries*).

Browne, Thom   Born in 1965, Pennsylvania native Browne studied business at Notre Dame and pursued an acting career in Los Angeles before moving to New York in 1997, where he worked in a GIORGIO ARMANI showroom and then on the creative staff at Club Monaco (a sportswear brand owned by RALPH LAUREN), launching his own menswear business in 2001 with premises in Manhattan's Meatpacking District.

Willie Brown

Thom Browne

Untrained in tailoring, Browne had been fascinated by 1950s and 1960s vintage suits and explored an aesthetic that was nearly the exact opposite of the shirttails-out, LOW-RISE JEANS look trendy at that time. Instead, his designs, which the *New York Times* described as "shrunken jackets and high-water pants," focused on narrowly cut clothes in materials (suits of gray flannel, tuxedos of gray corduroy) generally disdained as NERDY—causing both detractors and admirers to cite comparisons to PEE-WEE HERMAN. His own best and most extreme exemplar, Browne was always impeccably groomed and always in pants that ended several inches above his (always bare) ankles.

In 2006, the year that he opened a store in Manhattan's TriBeCa neighborhood, signed a design deal with BROOKS BROTHERS and another with jeweler Harry Winston, and received permission from the Chambre Syndi-

cale to show in Paris. Browne also won the CFDA's award for menswear design.

Not to be confused with Tom Brown, the tailoring firm founded in Eton in the 18th century.

Brummell, Beau   1. The man most responsible for establishing austerity and understatement as the aesthetic of menswear.

Born on June 7, 1778, George Bryan Brummell was aristocratic in his taste but not his birth: The son of the prime minister's secretary, he claimed to be the grandson of a valet. Brummell attended Eton, where he gained the nickname "Buck." While still a teenager, he attracted the attention of GEORGE IV, then Prince of Wales, who commissioned him into the Tenth Hussars, where he rose to the rank of captain and often personally attended the Prince. In 1798, when his regiment was due to be posted too far from London for him to conveniently enjoy the city, Brummell resigned his post. Thereafter, he survived on a small legacy from his father, gambling, and his status as social and sartorial arbiter.

Moving to 4 Chesterfield Street in Mayfair, he became a member of the exclusive White's and Brooks' clubs. Now nicknamed "Beau," the tall and well-figured Brummell took simplicity to the extreme of severity. His trademarks included: a high collar and lightly starched cravat, both of pristine white; a buff waistcoat; buff trousers slim enough to show off beautiful legs and kept straight and unwrinkled thanks to a stirrup loop of his invention; and a CUTAWAY of blue wool snugly fitted over a trim torso.

Although styles like the cutaway had long preceded him on the London scene,

Beau Brummell

Brummell definitively rid them of any remaining association with countrified attire. Patronizing tailors with an aristocratic clientele (including Davidson, Meyer, Weston, and Schweitzer), Beau ordered coats and breeches that were ostentatiously unostentatious in their plainness of pattern and color. Perhaps only two links of his watch chain might be permitted to show. Hours were famously spent dressing and then arranging his cravat. His clothes fit perfectly. His boots glistened down to their soles (Brummell quipped that his valet Robinson used the "froth of champagne" to shine them). He scorned wigs and perfumery and wore his hair unpowdered. His personal linen was immaculate. As was his person: In an age in which bathing was still uncommon, Brummell was reputed to spend two hours a day on a toilette that involved thorough washing, tooth brushing, and shaving.

After his inevitable falling out with the Prince Regent, the "Prince of Elegance" enjoyed the patronage of the Duke of York. However, gambling debts forced him to flee to northern France in May of 1816, leaving behind his beautiful Buhl and Sèvres, which Christie auctioned within the week. In 1826, he was portrayed as the self-preoccupied character named Trebeck in Thomas Henry Lister's novel *Granby*.

Brummell never returned to England. He briefly served as a British consul in Caen, but was put in debtor's prison in 1835. Rescued from prison, the formerly fastidious Brummell was already in the end stages of the syphilis that would soon kill him and, by that point, was probably insane and incontinent. Having also grown overweight and slovenly during his long exile, he was admitted to a Caen charity hospital for the insane in 1837, and died there in 1840.

2. Although filmed on location in England, *Beau Brummell*, the 1954 drama which starred Stewart Granger as Beau, Peter Ustinov as the Prince of Wales, and Elizabeth Taylor as the Beau's supposed romantic interest, was not particularly accurate as either biography or costume history. The MGM feature was essentially a remake of *Brummell*, the 1924 movie starring John Barrymore and Mary Astor, which was itself a filmed version of the popular Clyde Fitch play, *Beau Brummell*, commissioned by actor-manager Richard Mansfield in 1889 and repeatedly revived (famously for Broadway in 1916).

3. In 2005, British actor/author Ian Kelly published a lengthy biography called *Beau Brummell: The Ultimate Dandy*, a redacted version of which was published in the United States the following year as *Beau Brummell: The Ultimate Man of Style*. In 2006 in New York, Kelly also starred as the title character in the two-man show *Beau Brummell*, written by Ron Hutchinson, which had debuted in London in 2001.

In 2006, BBC-Four also produced a multipart historical drama called *Beau Brummell: This Charming Man* with James Purefoy in the title role.

brushed finish   A FINISHING treatment that raises a NAP on fabric after it has been knit or woven.

Bryant Park   The public park at 42nd Street and the Avenue of the Americas, behind the main branch of the New York Public Library. In the late 20th century, became the main site of tents housing New York's semiannual runway shows.

Brylcreem   A man's wet-look hairdressing cream invented in Birmingham, England, in 1928 and immortalized by the American ad slogan "Brylcreem! A little dab'll do ya!" in 1949. Packaged and marketed differently in the United States and the United Kingdom, the basic product comes in a pot in England and a tube in America.

In England, sports stars were more often used to advertise the product, up to and including soccer star DAVID BECKHAM as a 1998 spokesman. During World War II, Royal Air Force pilots were nicknamed "Brylcreem boys," which inspired the 1998 film of that name.

Buchanan, Jack   Born in Helensburgh, Scotland, near Glasgow in 1891, Walter John Buchanan began his stage career in England before World War I and continued to perform on Broadway and in Hollywood as well as London's West End, throughout both the silent movie era and the talkies. Tall (6 feet, 2 inches), dapper, and possessed of a dry line delivery, he was called "the British FRED ASTAIRE" in part for his roles in light musical comedies and in part for his natty attire (Buchanan performed in TOP HAT and TAILS so often that they became a sort of uniform). His initial appearances on Broadway in the 1920s are credited with creating that era's ideal of the elegant Englishman who wore immaculate formal clothes with utter nonchalance. Now best remembered by American audiences for costarring with Astaire in 1953's *The Band Wagon*. He died in 1957.

Jack Buchanan

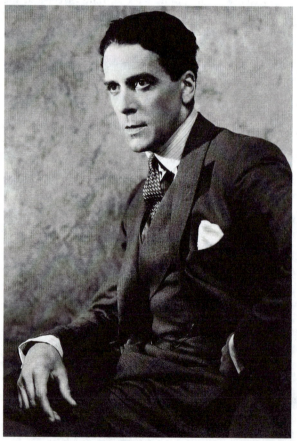

bucket bag   A style of large tote bag, with a cylindrical shape like a bucket or horse's feedbag. The top is often left loosely open or closed via a drawstring or snapped tab. Generally worn, via a long shoulder strap, across the chest or hanging from one shoulder.

bucket hat   A round fabric hat, with a circular crown piece and medium-length fabric brim of the same material; so called because it vaguely resembles an overturned bucket. Soft and easily folded, it is usually rendered in woven materials like denim, canvas, or wool. Sometimes ventilated via grommets in the sides of the crown, especially with fishing styles. Synonym: CRUSHER.

buckram   A type of plain-weave fabric made rigid by large amounts of SIZING. In menswear, buckram is used in small areas where rigidity must be added to support garment construction, or in the making of hats. It is never visible when the garment is being worn.

bucks   A style of undecorated lace-up shoes that originally took its name from a shortened form of BUCKSKIN, because they were made of that leather; now just as likely to be considered a shortened from of NUBUCK, since they are often made from nubuck cowhide; most often in a white or blond shade; always in an unwaxed, unshined leather.

Associated with slight informality (as opposed to being part of full business rig or formalwear), white bucks were a summer favorite of college boys (who varnished the soles black) as far back as the 1920s, became a classic accompaniment to the SEERSUCKER SUIT, and were also a staple of classic cruise attire. When EDWARD VIII appeared in that style on a visit to the United States while Prince of Wales, he caused a small scandal by wearing dark-brown bucks with a suit (as opposed to using them as an accessory to SPORTSWEAR).

Red rubber soles first appeared in the 1930s and passed into the PREPPY canon (where versions with uppers made of beige-colored skin are commonly called "dirty bucks"). In the 1950s, white bucks also became a trademark of singer PAT BOONE.

buckskin 1. Leather made from the skin of deer or elk, usually tanned so that its grain is not apparent and the skins have a uniform, velvety texture. 2. Clothes—usually referred to in the plural "buckskins"—devised from buckskin, especially referring to those made by Native Americans, hunters and trappers, and others associated with the American frontier.

buffalo Leather made from the skin of water buffalo (*not* from the bison known as buffalo in America).

buffalo plaid *or* **buffalo check** A symmetrical, two-color plaid that is evenly divided between red and black, forming pure red squares, pure black squares, and squares that are half red or half black. Or a check of that pattern substituting another base color for red (e.g., blue) in combination with the black. Frequently featured in hunting jackets, overshirts, flannel shirts, and other apparel made for outdoor wear.

The TARTAN with a similar pattern (usually on a smaller scale) is known as the ROB ROY.

built out *or* **built up** Jargon for areas that are padded and enhanced; especially for the shoulders of jackets that feature a strong SHOULDER PAD.

bulb toe A style in which the area of the shoe over the toes is particularly rounded and pronounced (i.e., bulbous); particularly popular in the early 20th century when the toe was used to set off pants with deep cuffs. (See BULLDOG TOE.) Synonym: freak toe.

bulla A sort of AMULET or charm worn by boy children in ancient Rome. Only freeborn males wore the bulla, which could be made of anything from precious metal to simple leather.

bull denim A twill fabric that resembles the basic DENIM used for JEANS, except that the yarns have not been dyed with INDIGO or anything else.

bulldog toe A bulbous, rounded toe in which the tip of the shoe actually flares upward (instead of tapering smoothly downward from the shoe VAMP). Popular during the first decade of the 20th century.

Bulwer-Lytton, Edward Also known as Lord Lytton, Edward George Earle Lytton Bulwer was born in 1803 and wrote *PELHAM*, a novel casting a BEAU BRUMMELL-esque dandy as its title character, in 1828. He frequented the London salon of COUNT D'ORSAY, wrote other books dealing with the fashionable life (*Paul Clifford*, *Godolphin*), then an allegorical blockbuster called *The Last Days of Pompeii*. Like D'Orsay, he is both credited and blamed with popularizing black as the predominant color for menswear (as opposed to the buff and blue worn during Brummell's time). However, as time wore on, he tired of decadence and fashion and became a rather staid Victorian (originating the phrase "the pen is mightier than the sword"). Today he is perhaps better remembered as author of the opening sentence of 1830's *Paul Clifford*: "It was a dark and stormy night." He died in 1873.

bumbag Synonym, especially in the United Kingdom, for a FANNYPACK.

bumbershoot   Old-fashioned, mostly American, slang for an old-fashioned UMBRELLA.

bunch   Jargon for a group of fabric swatches bound together like sheets of a writing tablet—specifically those shown to a tailor's customer when he is ordering a suit. Because bunches are usually grouped according to weight or design, a mill may sometimes refer to a collection as its latest bunch even if it is not talking about a specific, physical group of fabric swatches.

bundle   Traditional tailors' jargon for the pieces of a garment (usually a suit) that have been cut but not sewn together yet.

Burberry   The British brand founded in 1856 as a outfitter in Basingstoke, Hampshire by 21-year-old Thomas Burberry, who had been a draper's apprentice; best known for TRENCH COATS based on the sturdy, weatherproof GABARDINE developed for its line in 1880.

In 1891, the company moved to 30 Haymarket in London's West End, and four years later began selling the TIELOCKEN, a prototype of what would become the trench coat. In 1901, it initiated its charging-knight-on-horseback logo, whose banner reads "Prorsum" (meaning "forward"), and whose shield bears a giant letter "B." When World War I began, the War Office commissioned Burberry to revive and redact the Tielocken, which had been worn during the Boer War, and the new, improved model—distinguished mainly by the addition of EPAULETTES and brass D rings—became known as the trench coat. In 1920, it introduced its own tan, black, red, and white "Burberry" plaid as its trench coat lining, and the model was more or less set for the rest of the century. Thereafter, the firm continued to sell other apparel, but, for decades, Burberry was a wardrobe stalwart, a handy synonym for "trench coat."

In 1997, American retail executive Rose Marie Bravo, fresh from a success at Saks Fifth Avenue, was hired to revamp Burberry, which, at that point, was taking most of its profits from licensing and distribution in Asia. Although continuing to play up the Britishness of the brand and its pedigree of royal warrants, she hired Italian Roberto Menichetti as a designer and created a high-fashion line called Prorsum, complete with runway shows. By the end of the century, the Burberry plaid was appearing on bikinis and its plaid was known and pirated world over.

After Menichetti's departure in 2001, Christopher Bailey, who had worked at GUCCI, became the house designer.

Burlington Arcade   Designed by Simon Ware as a sort of indoor shopping mall and erected in 1818, London's Burlington Arcade was more or less the point of convergence for nearby SAVILE Row, Old Bond Street, and St. James' Street, attracting the dandies of the day to the area (who were known to use its upstairs premises as a trysting place). In its 19th-century incarnation, the Arcade was more concentrated on apparel and accessories businesses than its contemporary version.

Burma-Shave   The brand of brushless shaving cream that became notorious for its roadside advertising from the 1920s through the early 1960s. Using four or more billboards placed in a row, the signs would spell out promotional jingles. Example: "Are your whiskers/when you wake/tougher than/a two-bit steak?/Try/Burma-Shave."

burnoose A loose, hooded cloak that originated in North Africa, usually made of plainly woven and slightly coarse wool; identified with the Berbers but also worn by other Arabs. Its extremely full hood, which is usually pointed by a tassel, gives a graceful, draped appearance when worn down. Synonym: SELHAM.

burnsides A particularly extravagant style of SIDE-WHISKERS named after Ambrose Everett Burnside (1824–1881), who worked for a tailor before attending West Point and later rising to the rank of brigadier general in the Union Army during the Civil War, then becoming governor and senator from Rhode Island. Burnsides swoop out over the cheek so that the mustache is joined to the sideburns in a swag of facial hair that is fullest under the cheekbone. The chin is left bare.

burn test A way of testing the fiber composition of a fabric, usually by pulling loose a thread and holding it to a match to see and smell how it burns.

Experienced testers claim to distinguish between between fibers by the odor, rate of burn, and color of smoke. For example: PROTEINACIOUS fibers, such as WOOL and SILK, crisp like burnt human hair; CELLULOSIC fibers, such as LINEN and COTTON, smell like burned paper; and man-made fibers, such as POLYESTER, melt and may give off a variety of odors.

Burton An apparel and equipment brand, initially identified with snowboarding, founded by Jake Burton Carpenter in 1977 when he began making snowboards in his barn in Vermont. The brand officially expanded into apparel in 1996.

Burton's See MONTAGUE BURTON, the largest and most famous of the MULTIPLE TAILORS.

bushel In tailors' jargon, a verb meaning to repair or alter; usually applied only to tailored clothing. Alteration would be "busheling."

bushelman In tailors' jargon, a bushelman is usually someone relegated to altering other tailors' work. For instance, the tailors employed by most U.S. dry cleaners would be considered bushelmen.

bush hat Refers to the Australian style of low-crowned, wide-brimmed hat, as immortalized by the title character in 1986's *Crocodile Dundee* and 1988's *Crocodile Dundee II*.

Burma-Shave billboard

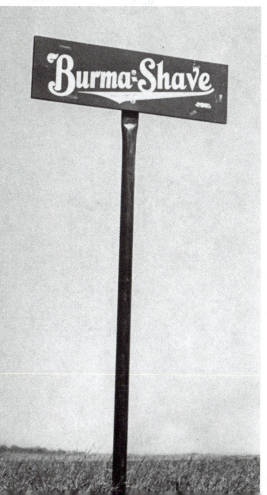

Bush hat: Paul Hogan in *Crocodile Dundee*

bush jacket See SAFARI JACKET.

business casual A designation, begun in the United States in the late 20th century, for clothes considered less formal than the full-on BUSINESS SUIT; especially associated with the practice of DRESS-DOWN FRIDAYS and the less formal business practices of companies in the tech boom of the 1990s. By specifying attire as "business casual," most companies precluded not only the wearing of the too-formal suit and tie, but the wearing of the too-informal JEANS and T-SHIRT. Most, however, accepted turtlenecks, khaki pants, sport jackets, and the like.

business suit A broad reference to a general type of suit rather than a single, specific style. A business suit is conservative and somewhat formal, and is not designed to be overtly fashionable or to otherwise draw attention to itself. By tradition, it is fully tailored and worn with a DRESS SHIRT, NECKTIE, and DRESS SHOES. Its significance as a social uniform was epitomized by the 1955 novel and 1956 movie *THE MAN IN THE GRAY FLANNEL SUIT*.

Buster Brown An enormously popular brand of children's shoes that began in 1904 as one of America's first and most successful instances of LICENSING.

In 1902, cartoonist Richard Outcault, who had invented the Yellow Kids, began a comic strip about a rich boy called Buster Brown for the New York Herald. Two years later, at the World's Fair in St. Louis, he licensed the adventures of Buster, his dog Tige, and his friend Mary Jane to almost 200 companies, including the St. Louis shoe company called Brown, founded by George Warren Brown in 1878 as Bryan, Brown & Co and renamed in 1893.

To promote its new line, Brown famously hired midgets who would be accompanied by a Boston terrier and wear a blond pageboy wig, a red suit with short pants, and saucer-brimmed red hat while touring the country impersonating Buster, a practice that would

Buster Brown

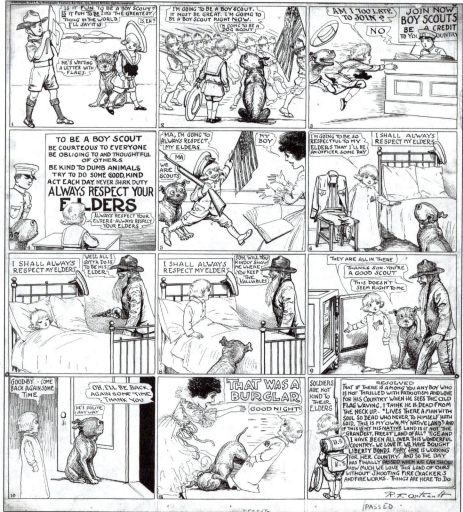

continue until 1930. In 1911, the company also began advertising in the *Saturday Evening Post.* In 1925, Universal began producing short film comedies based on Buster's adventures. The next year, the company began its radio sponsorship, which would culminate in the 1943 invention of "The Buster Brown Gang" kids' show with "Smilin' Ed" McConnell. During the early 1960s (by which time Tige was played by a boxer), television advertising promoted the shoes with the tagline: "That's my dog Tige, he lives in a shoe! I'm Buster Brown, look for me in there, too!"

Buster Brown haircut The style of pageboy haircut with bangs sported by the BUSTER BROWN comic strip character and the midgets who the company dressed as him to promote the brand of shoes.

Buster Brown suits A variation on the SAILOR SUIT, worn by young boys from the turn of the century until the Depression. Typically, what was called a Buster Brown consisted of short, knee-length pants, a loose top (which could be a sailor top, smock, or jacket worn with a round-collared blouse), and a hat worn over longish hair. Unlike the LITTLE LORD FAUNTLEROY suit, the wearing of the outfit predated its naming, since the type of suit was already popular by the time cartoonist Richard Outcault began the comic strip BUSTER BROWN in the *New York Herald* in 1902. However, calling the outfit by the name of a famous cartoon character probably made it more palatable to little boys who had to wear it.

butch Slang for an exaggeratedly male style of dress. For example, the gear of a working lumberjack, HARD HAT, or COWBOY; or the basic look of a white T-shirt worn with FIVE-POCKET JEANS and workboots. Antonym: nelly.

butterfly 1. Reference to a style of BOW TIE that flares out from the knot, imitating the silhouette of butterfly with open wings, executed with a preshaped tie also known as a THISTLE. Its opposite number, without the flare, would be a BATWING. 2. A smallish, vaguely butterfly-shaped piece of leather, usually mounted on spur straps. The butterfly fits over the center of the instep when spurs are being worn, thus preventing wear by the straps. More common in other centuries, in contemporary use it appears only occasionally with riding boots or when laced FIELD BOOTS are worn as part of a uniform.

button cover Decorative covers for shirt buttons; usually intended to be worn with FORMALWEAR and give the impression that STUDS are being worn or, at least, to give a dressier appearance to the shirt.

button cuff Synonym for a BARREL CUFF on the sleeve of a shirt (to distinguish it from the FRENCH CUFF, which closes with the aid of CUFFLINKS, SILK KNOTS, or some similar device).

button-down   Refers to a type of DRESS SHIRT with buttoning collar points, a style that originated in England at the end of the 19th century (where it was worn by polo players) and popularized in the United States by BROOKS BROTHERS (where die-hards may still refer to it as a POLO COLLAR).

The classic button-down is roomier in fit and less detailed than a JERMYN STREET-style dress shirt. For example, it has long sleeves ending in a single-button BARREL CUFF (with no GAUNTLET BUTTON), is made of cotton OXFORD CLOTH (most often in white, followed by blue, pink, yellow, or blue-and-white BALANCED STRIPES), and has a single patch pocket on the left side of the chest. It is unfitted and loose through the torso, with a full back, and a LOCKER LOOP at the center of the back yoke. The side seams are FELLED. The collar is relatively short—about 3⅜ inches—and buttons with the same size and style of white buttons featured on the front placket.

According to legend, John Brooks of Brooks Brothers was watching a polo match in England when he noticed that the players were wearing shirt collars that buttoned to the body of the shirt, supposedly to keep the shirt points from flapping in their faces as they played. Beginning in 1896, he had the style copied and produced for his own store. Over subsequent decades, the style became identified with American rather than English dress, essential to both the IVY LEAGUE LOOK and PREPPY style.

button fly   A reference to pants, usually FIVE-POCKET JEANS, that have an old-fashioned button FLY, rather than the standard ZIPPER fly. (In contemporary practice, button-fly jeans are made with five metal buttons.) Prior to the 1930s, the button fly was itself the standard.

buttonhole   1. As a slit made in material for the purpose of fastening a garment, the buttonhole was not widely adopted until the 13th century, a time when European clothes were starting their transition from draped and pinned to tailored silhouettes.   2. Reference, especially in American usage, to a BOUTONNIÈRE.

buttonhole loop   A small, discreet loop placed on the underside of a man's lapel, beneath the slit buttonhole

Button-down collar

that would accommodate a BOUTONNIÈRE; intended to secure the stem of the flower.

buttonhole stitch Refers to a particular method of stitching, especially of handstitching, in which the thread loops back upon itself to form what looks like upside-down linked, letter "T" shapes. The ridge thus formed helps to prevent fraying where the fabric has been slit to accommodate the button.

buttonhole twist Refers to a type of relatively sturdy thread used chiefly for binding buttonholes with BUTTONHOLE STITCH and for creating a THREAD SHANK to attach buttons.

buttonhook An implement used for fastening buttons—primarily those on high-buttoned shoes (which remained popular up until World War I) and even on OXFORDS (some early models of which boasted buttons). The buttonhook was generally about 7 or 8 inches long and included a long handle and a metal shank ending in a small (about a third of an inch wide), C-shaped hook.

buttoning Usually refers to the conventions attached to buttoning sports jackets, suit jackets, and vests when a man is fully dressed. For example, in contemporary practice:

• On a one-button jacket, the button is worn buttoned.
• On a two-button jacket, the top button is buttoned, but the bottom button is often left undone.
• On a three-button jacket, either the top two buttons are buttoned or the middle button alone is buttoned, but rarely the bottom one.
• On a double-breasted jacket, often only the middle button is buttoned.

• On a vest, no matter what the number of buttons, the bottom button is left undone.

button-out lining A removable lining—most often made of pile, fur, or quilted fabric—that is added to a raincoat or shell for warmth. The buttons usually follow the inside front of the garment and sometimes around the neck, but never the hem or armhole. The lining portion is made to cover the wearer's torso but usually does not extend to the sleeves, so that, when removed, it looks like a long vest. (See also ZIP-OUT LINING.)

button stance The placement of buttons on a jacket, especially of the top button. For example, a four-button suit jacket, where the top button might close a few inches below the clavicle and only show a small portion of the man's necktie, would be said to have a high stance. A particularly plunging neckline on a jacket designed with a single-button closure would be said to have a low stance. Synonym: STANCE.

button through Jargon for buttons that are not covered by a fly or flap but show through to the outside of the garment; especially on pants or tailored outerwear.

button-up 1. Slang for a DRESS SHIRT. (As opposed to "buttoned up," which is slang indicating a particular manner at attitude.) 2. Slang for a CARDIGAN.

BVD Despite many urban legends and incorrect guesses about the origin of the acronym ("boys' ventilated drawers" being among the more printable), the term actually comes from an underwear brand founded in 1876 by Bradley, Voorhees, Day in New York, which originally used initial periods when describing its wares. By the early 20th century, the acronym was already passing into American slang as a synonym for men's underwear, where it was written in uppercase letters without the periods. (In South America, the Spanish improvisation *bividi* became a synonym for a singlet undershirt.)

In the 20th century, the brand also became famous for the slogan "Next to myself, I like BVD best" and, in 1929, for signing Olympic champion star Johnny Weissmuller as celebrity spokesman for its line of bathing suits (whereupon he was discovered as the future star of 1932's *Tarzan* while modeling BVDs).

In 1976, the brand was acquired by its long-time competitor Fruit of the Loom.

bycocket   A hat style with a sloping, cone-shaped crown and a brim that is worn turned down to a point in front and turned up in the back (like a highly exaggerated, pointy-crowned antecedent of the snap-brim); worn in Western Europe in the late Middle Ages and sporadically revived thereafter. In contemporary use, best known from illustrations of Robin Hood and the Pied Piper of Hamelin. Variant spelling: bycoket.

Bycocket: Errol Flynn in *The Adventures of Robin Hood*, 1938

cabana stripes   Large, brightly colored stripes that look as though they belong on patio furniture.

cabana suit   An ensemble consisting of swim trunks worn with a coordinating (usually short-sleeved) jacket. Cabana suits often paired TERRY CLOTH with a flat, woven—sometimes *loudly*— printed fabric. Most popular in the decades following World War II.

cabbage   Traditional British tailors' slang for leftover material. When ordering a garment, the customer pays for a specified yardage. After that garment is completed, scraps are considered cabbage.

Cable Car Clothiers   Founded in 1946 in San Francisco by Charlie Pivnick as a war surplus store called Vet's Mercantile. In 1954, as military surplus sources dried up and the store began to focus more on traditional, British-style clothing, it was renamed Cable Car Clothiers. From 1970, it became known for its quarterly mail-order catalog, which eventually reached a circulation of 2 million and which helped to make the store a tourist destination. In 1972, Pivnick purchased and incorporated Robert Kirk, a San Francisco retailer founded in 1939 and also known for a focus on traditional, British-style clothing, thus allowing itself the motto "San Francisco's British Goods Store Since 1939." In 1989, it moved premises to a landmark 1911 building at One Grant Avenue (which was subsequently purchased by ARMANI), the store also experienced notorious financial reverses as a result of the move and drop-off in tourism due to the 1989 San Francisco earthquake.

cables, cabling   A method of decorating KNITWEAR that involves twisting stitches to the right or left. When executed by hand, the stitches that form the cable are

Cables

transferred to a cable needle and held in either the front or back (which determines the direction of the twist). A popular decoration for ARANS, fishermen's sweaters, and other traditional British, American, and Irish sweaters (and a feature of PREPPY style). Innumerable variations exists, among the most common: simple cables, double cables, braided cables, trellis cables, and uneven cables.

caftan   An untailored, floor-length, long-sleeved robe covering the body from the neck to the feet; identified with the dress of Western Asia. Loose and unfitted, caftans could be made of opulent materials and lined with fur. For instance, in the Ottoman empire, the caftans worn by the sultan and his courtiers were usually of extremely luxurious brocade. Variant spellings include KAFTAN (especially when referring to Russian or Ottoman costume). Unlike the DJELLABA, the caftan traditionally does not have a hood.

cagoule   A pullover style of very long, usually knee-length, ANORAK, mostly used for mountain sports and more common in Europe; not to be confused with a long PARKA, which has a complete, neck-to-hem front opening.

calceus   The shoe, which resembled a soft, ankle-high boot, worn outdoors by ancient Romans, who preserved a distinction between indoor and outdoor footwear (wearing SANDALS primarily indoors).

calendering   A fabric finish applied through pressure, heat, or both. Calendering, which usually produces a shiny or embossed effect on the fabric's surface, was most often used for suit fabrics, but fell out of favor in the mid-20th century as more and more suits were regularly dry-cleaned, a process that tended to shorten the life span of a calendered finish.

Calendar is a common misspelling.

calfskin   Leather made from the skin of an immature cow or bull, especially one that has not been weaned. In contrast to the hide of the mature animal, calfskin is finer, more supple (making it easier to cut and shape), and has an unobtrusive GRAIN that can easily be made to look smooth. The skin of the mature animal is referred to as COWHIDE.

calico   1. An inexpensive, woven fabric, usually made of cotton and usually featuring a small print on a colored background. In menswear, its use was confined mainly to workshirts, especially in the 19th century.   2. The word derives from the city of Calcutta and, in references before the early 19th century, was used to describe a more expensive and elaborately printed and figured cotton, imported from India—or fabric made to imitate it.

California collar   1. Synonym for a BARRYMORE COLLAR.   2. A style similar to a Barrymore collar, but having even longer and narrower collar points.

calot   A reference to any BEANIE style of skullcap. Sometimes used as a synonym for the ZUCCHETTO of Roman Catholic clergy. When describing European or American costume, the term is more often used for women's wear.

calvary twill   A sturdy, usually cotton, fabric popular for JODHPURS, BREECHES, or other pants intended for country wear; commonly a solid color, usually neutral (khaki, beige, taupe) or a dark, unobtrusive shade. Traditionalists do not consider it appropriate for formal or business dress.

Calvin Klein   See KLEIN, CALVIN.

cambric   A fine cotton or linen material, used for shirts. Cambric is lightweight, a PLAIN WEAVE, almost always snowy white, and differs from similar shirt fabrics in that it has a CALENDERED, slightly shiny finish. The word derives from the French town of Cambrai.

camelidae *or* **camelids**   A classification for camels and the camel-like mammals—the GUANACO, ALPACA, llama, and VICUÑA—found at high altitudes in South America. Because of their coat structure, which has a fineness and quality to rival or exceed that of the CASHMERE goat, the fashion industry considers them NOBLE FIBERS. Bactrian camels and their South American cousins are often bred so that, like sheep or goats, their coats can be harvested. Thus, their biological classification has become textile jargon.

camel's hair   The fiber taken from the coat of Bactrian camels (the two-humped, long-haired species found in Asia), and the fabric made from it. Because of its fineness and softness, hair from the underside of the animal is usually considered a NOBLE FIBER. In menswear, it is most often left in its natural range of beige shades, although it is occasionally dyed navy, charcoal, or black. It is particularly prized for sports jackets and coats—so much so that the style originally called the POLO COAT became known as the camel's hair coat.

camel's hair coat   Although beige CAMEL'S HAIR fabric is used in a variety of sports jackets and outerwear, "camel's hair coat" is most often used as a synonym for the style known as a POLO COAT.

camera bag   A style of tote bag modeled after the gear bags used by professional photographers. The camera bag is distinguished by several outside compartments that can be accessed without opening the main compartments, is rectangular or oval in shape, and is carried via a shoulder strap.

camo   Slang for CAMOUFLAGE.

camouflage   Derived from the French *camoufler* (to conceal), a print design with a purposely irregular pattern so that the person wearing the resulting fabric becomes less visible against a particular background; initially used by the military and hunters, then quoted in apparel designs making allusions to the military or hunting.

Camouflage in its contemporary form was not in wide use until World War I. Although previous fabrics and patterns were designed to blend men into the background—such as the KHAKI adapted by soldiers during the 19th century and the LOVAT and other ESTATE TWEEDS sported for shooting in Scotland—modern camouflage was born of the idea that gradation from dark to light skews perception of a surface.

Initially, the man most identified with the idea was Abbott Handerson Thayer (1849–1921), an American painter who became a self-appointed expert on the subject. Thayer devoted himself to observations of animals in the wild and expounded his theories of "protective coloration" in publications as well as letters to influential friends (including Mark Twain and Theodore Roosevelt). His theories were set forth in a 1909 book by his son Gerald called *Concealing-Coloration in the Animal Kingdom: An Exposition of the Laws of Disguise through Color and Pattern*.

During World War I, both sides applied those ideas of obliterative patterning to their men and *matériel*, although camouflage still retained its overtones of art theory. France recruited Cubists to serve as its first *camoufleurs*. Other armies drafted their own artists: By war's end, Jacques Villon, Grant Wood, Thomas Hart Benton, Oskar Schlemmer, and Arshile Gorky had all served as masters of disguise.

During the 1930s, the German military was the most aggressive in developing camouflage patterns, including its infamous "Splinter," which layered amorphous shapes on a hailstorm-style background. However, from World War II onward, it became common practice for armies to create specific camouflage patterns appropriate to their combat zones (e.g., during the Vietnam War, camouflage was commonly dark and green and used vegetation shapes; during Operation Desert Storm, it was issued in beige-colored sandstorm patterns).

Campagna, Gianni   The Sicilian-born, Caraceni-apprenticed, Milan-based custom tailor renowned for his tycoon clientele; best known, together with his son Andrea, for outfitting actor Pierce Brosnan for his title role in the 1999 remake of *The Thomas Crown Affair* (father and son make a cameo appearance in the movie as Crown's tailors). In addition to creating his soft-bodied, strong-shouldered garments for Brosnan's personal wardrobe, Campagna created bespoke suits for the likes of Ron Perelman and Henry Kravis, regularly commuting to Manhattan, where he saw clients from a suite in the Pierre Hotel. In 1999, he also launched a ready-to-wear line called Sartoria Campagna.

campaign wigs   A general category of early-18th-century wig, so-called because they were favored for wear during military campaigns and were much less elaborate than the heavy, ornately curled styles worn as part of court uniform. Most, like the Ramillies, were pigtail styles.

camp shirt   A style of loose-fitting, button-front, casual shirt, most often short-sleeved. The camp shirt may have one or two patch pockets on the chest. Usually, it is cropped and has a straight hem (as opposed to shirt-tails), since it is intended to be worn untucked and outside the trousers. The top button is left open to expose the throat, and the camp shirt is never worn with any style of tie.

canadienne   A style of heavy, unfitted outerwear, which attained a certain chic in Europe immediately after World War II, when it was famously worn by Jean-Paul Sartre.

Canali   The high-end, Italian tailored clothing label founded in 1934 by brothers Giovanni and Giacomo Canali. Controlled by successive generations of the founding family, the company expanded in the 1950s, becoming a lifestyle brand, complete with a line of accessories and a manufacturing center in Sorvino (near Milan), that was sold worldwide through other luxury retailers, as well as through Canali's own retail outlets in places like Beverly Hills and Dubai. In the 1980s, the company created a small scandal by becoming among the first of the traditional Italian tailoring firms to install a machine fabric cutter. In the following decade, it was also one of the first Italian clothing firms to aggressively expand into China. Beginning in the 1990s, Canali clothing was also featured in a number of movies including Arnold Schwarzenegger's wardrobe in 1994's *True Lies* and Val Kilmer's wardrobe in 1997's *The Saint*. Its company nickname: *la piccola rana* (the small frog).

Named for the sheepskin coats sent from Canada to keep European soldiers warm during World War I, the style evolved from basic to relatively luxurious as the century wore on. By the 1940s, it usually had a cloth body (often CORDUROY), a SHEEPSKIN collar (either real or fake), large and easily accessible pockets (either patch or set-in), and a length anywhere from just below the hip to just above the knee.

canary vest   For FOXHUNTING ATTIRE and for the horse shows and sporting events that copy its conventions, one of the regulation garments in formal attire; made of a medium-weight, plain-weave wool in a shade that is closer to butter than the bright yellow usually identified as canary.

candy stripe   A vertical pattern used to refer to shirt fabrics. A CANDY STRIPE is broader than a BENGAL STRIPE, is usually done in white and one other color (e.g., red and white), and reminds most people of a candy cane.

Cane

canapa   The Italian word for HEMP. The word sometimes appears on English-language garment labels when the manufacturer wants to indicate a specific variety of *cannabis sativa* that is grown in Italy, or when he is taking particular pains to disassociate his product from the HIPPIE overtones of hemp fiber.

cane   In contemporary use, identified with a hip-high, crook-handled stick used as an aid in locomotion; when it is carried purely as an accessory, it is often referred to as a WALKING STICK.

In previous centuries, when canes were flourished for fashion as much as function, they often lacked the crook handle. An elaborate etiquette was also attached to their use, and a large distinction was made among the materials considered appropriate for town versus country or for formal versus informal dress. Through the end of World War I, a man's evening cane might have been made of ebony banded or surmounted by silver, gold, or some other combination of precious materials; he might have had a MALACCA cane for use in town; a rattan or natural bamboo cane (especially a variety known as "whangee") for summer; a black bamboo for other times of year; a sturdy SHILLELAGH for strolls in the country; another BLACKTHORN to accessorize his tweeds; and a SHOOTING STICK for sporting events.

Length and thickness of canes also varied. For example, in the 18th century, canes were both longer (sometimes hitting a mid-chest level) and shorter (as short as 2 feet and carried as more of a SWAGGER STICK).

Canonero, Milena   Born in Turin, Italy, Mileno Canonero's first movie costume design was Stanley Kubrick's *A Clockwork Orange* (1971). She quickly built a reputation for "costume pictures," repeatedly being nominated for Academy Awards and winning them for her designs for *Barry Lyndon* (1975), CHARI-OTS OF FIRE (1981), and *Marie Antoinette* (2006). Her circa-1924 clothes for *Chariots of Fire* had enormous influence on men's fashion and inspired endless editorial layouts and retail displays, as well as a Bloomingdale's 1982 advertising campaign. At that time, she was also hired to design a line of retro-themed American clothes called Standards by Norman Hilton, which was subsequently sold in BARNEYS. Among her other credits: *The Cotton Club* (1984), *Out of Africa* (1985), work on the television series MIAMI VICE in the late 1980s, *Dick Tracy* (1990), *The Godfather: Part III* (1990), *Titus* (1999), *The Affair of the Necklace* (2001), and *Ocean's Twelve* (2004).

canvas   Jargon referring to any one of a number of woven INTERFACINGS, such as HAIR CANVAS or HYMO, especially as used in the construction of a jacket. Never visible in the finished garment. The opposite designation for menswear is usually "fusible" (as a reference to FUSIBLE INTERFACING).

canvas construction   A shorthand way of referring to the interior construction of a tailored jacket, connoting the use of CANVAS for all or part of its INTERFACING.

The use of canvas construction on the main body of a garment carries a connotation of shaping the garment (as opposed to a garment that described as DECON-STRUCTED or UNCONSTRUCTED). Because canvas is often pricier than FUSIBLE INTERFACING and generally requires handwork to secure, it also connotes a more expensive garment.

cap   Usually a general reference to a style of hat with only a visor or with no brim at all. A TOP HAT or DERBY does not qualify as a cap. A SKULLCAP and a BASEBALL CAP obviously qualify. Best summarized as: All caps are hats, but not all hats are caps.

cape button   Synonym for CLOAK BUTTON.

capote   1. A style of long, heavy, hooded coat, originated by French settlers and Métis in Canada and popular thereafter with trappers and voyageurs. The original capote was a belted wrap style made, with a minimum of waste, from striped Hudson's Bay Company blankets, and employed even the blanket fringe.   2. French reference to a condom.   3. A loose, hooded cloak worn in Western Europe from the Middle Ages onward.

capris   Refers to sporty, slim pants cropped to midcalf. Still a term associated more often with women's wear.

cap toe   A style of shoe with a horizontal seam or decoration crossing the forefoot to delineate the TOE CAP (i.e., the area of the shoe that covers the toes). In contemporary use, most often found on an otherwise-plain OXFORD. For example: A BALMORAL BOOT is technically a cap-toe style; whereas, by definition, a WINGTIP is not. See SHOE diagram.

Caraceni   The name of several related and unrelated Italian tailoring firms, the two most renowned being the Milan establishment of Ferdinando Caraceni (who died in 2004 and whose establishment on the Via San Marco was taken over by his daughter Nicoletta) and the Roman establishment founded by Domenico Caraceni in 1913, a tailor whose clientele included GIANNI AGNEL-LI, DOUGLAS FAIRBANKS JR., Prince Rainier of Monaco, King Juan Carlos of Spain, and an assortment of actors, aristocrats, and titans of industry. In the first half of the

Milena Canonero: Costume designs for *Out of Africa*

20th century, the Roman Caraceni also opened a shop in Paris, to cater to its international clientele.

In addition to the Milan tailoring firm formerly run by Ferdinando, there are at least two other Milanese Caraceni plus an assortment of lesser-known tailors with that name scattered across Italy. To further complicate matters, in 1998, the label Caraceni was legally acquired by another renowned Italian tailor, the Sicilian-born GIANNI CAMPAGNA, who had once worked at the Roman shop under the mentorship of Giovanni Caraceni and now uses the Caraceni name to make bespoke suits in Milan.

carat   A measure of the weight of gemstones (not to be confused with KARAT, a measure of the purity of gold). Five carats equal 1 gram; 100 points equal 1 carat. Derived from the ancient practice of using carob beans to measure the weight of jewelry. Usually abbreviated as "ct."

car coat   A piece of casual outerwear that is longer and less fitted than a sport coat; although it may be slim-lined, it is rarely tight at the waist, since it is supposedly intended for extending periods of sitting. The car coat covers the buttocks but stops short of mid-thigh, remaining short enough to facilitate driving and getting in and out of a car.

card case   A small, flat case sized only to carry business cards.

carded wool   A description of how the fiber was processed. Carded wool is used for thicker yarns and rougher fabrics, whereas COMBED WOOL, the alternative processing, is used to make fine yarns and light fabrics.

cardie   Slang for CARDIGAN, especially in British usage.

cardigan   A collarless SWEATER with a button- or zip-front closure from neck to waist. Although they are usually long (and may be short when done by a trendy designer), a cardigan always has sleeves; otherwise, it is a SWEATER VEST.

Originally a style of military tunic associated with James Thomas Brudenell, the seventh Earl of Cardigan (1797–1868), infamous as the leader of the ill-fated charge of the Light Brigade in 1854 during the Crimean War. In contemporary use, assumed to be a KNIT unless otherwise specified.

cardigan jacket   Jackets of leather or woven fabric that are made to resemble CARDIGAN sweaters, meaning that they do not have lapels, a shaped torso, or shaped shoulders.

Cardin, Pierre   Born in 1922 in Italy to French parents (who subsequently moved back to Saint Etienne, a city near Lyon), designer Pierre Cardin achieved commercial success with menswear, although he later became better known for his women's wear and his many, many commercial licenses (which, during the late 20th century, often numbered over 800 and were distributed in over 90 countries).

Cardin began his fashion career as a tailor's apprentice at Manby, a French clothier, at age 14. Afterward, he briefly studied architecture and worked as an accountant before landing jobs at women's wear designers Paquin, Elsa Schiaparelli, and Christian Dior. He went out on his own in 1950 and formally began the House of Cardin in 1954, also operating "Adam" and "Eve," boutiques for both genders. His first couture collection for

Pierre Cardin

women, in 1957, was a critical hit notable for its clean-lined minimalism. After a successful mass-production deal in 1959 scandalized the Chambre Syndicale (who promptly booted him out—only to reinstate him a few years later), Cardin was able to finance a menswear line in 1960.

The suits shown in that first collection, which relied upon students as models, were mostly collarless and all columnar, and the Cardin silhouette became wildly influential and much copied. In addition to its impact in the press and the favor it found with the celebrity clientele that Cardin had already developed for the ties and shirts he designed for his boutique, Cardin initiated production agreements that put his suits into stores at ready-to-wear prices. He also publicized his work abroad: pioneering the Japanese market and formally showing his menswear in London in 1965.

Quotable, marketing-savvy, with a high profile in the press (especially during his affair with French film actress Jeanne Moreau), and proud to be a businessman as well as a designer, Cardin was the first to embark on the lifestyle LICENSING that would be imitated by designers forever after. By the beginning of the 1970s, he was reputed to be the richest designer in the world. By the beginning of the 1980s, he had purchased Maxim's, the landmark restaurant built in Paris in 1893, and begun expanding its name through a worldwide licensing program.

Carhartt   The workwear company, founded by Hamilton Carhartt in Detroit in 1889. Carhartt, who had been born in New York in 1855 and grown up in southern Michigan, initially specialized in sturdy OVERALLS for railroad workers. During the 20th century, the family-run business became identified with jackets and overalls made of sand-colored DUCK, as well as DENIM work

clothes. During the late 20th century, its oversized and sturdy garments also became part of URBAN fashion.

cargo pants   A style of pants that features large CARGO POCKETS on the outseam of the pants leg—sometimes placed at mid-thigh, sometimes featuring additionally placed pockets (either cargo or patch pockets) lower on the leg; adapted from military looks, the style became fashionable for activewear and sportswear beginning in the mid-1990s.

cargo pockets   A capacious, usually BELLOWS-style, pocket; often made with a center pleat so that it expands outward to hold more.

Carnaby Street   The alley-sized street in London's West End that became known, during the 1960s, as Peacock Alley in reference to its role in the PEACOCK REVOLUTION, which saw mainstream menswear become more accepting of color and flamboyance. Located near traditional shopping streets such as Oxford Street and Regent Street, Carnaby was still a dingy, relatively low-rent district in the late 1950s when it began to attract menswear merchants like JOHN STEPHEN, a Scot who would eventually own multiple boutiques there.

A century earlier, a reference to "Carnaby boys" probably would have meant laborers in the local garment industry who were notorious for a hard night of drinking after a hard day of work.

Carnet de notes sur vêtements et villes   German-born director Wim Wenders' 1989 full-length, color documentary about Japanese designer YOHJI YAMAMOTO. In French.

carpenter's pants   Workwear, usually made of denim or undyed cotton DUCK. Worn by construction crews.

Carnaby Street

Carpenter's pants are comfortably wide-legged and have a zippered fly, two patch pockets in the back, and two jeans-style pockets in the front. They may also have one or more tool loops or additional pockets on the legs. (This term is sometimes used interchangeably with PAINTER'S PANTS, although painter's pants are traditionally made only of undyed cotton duck.)

Carpentier, Georges Born in 1894, the handsome French heavyweight boxer and onetime European champion nicknamed "the Orchid Man" was renowned for his elegant fighting style in the ring and his elegant style of dress outside it. He took up acting after his retirement from the ring in the late 1920s, then became proprietor of a popular Paris bar in 1934. He died in 1975.

carrick A style of overcoat with one or more—sometimes many more—shoulder capes. A corruption of the last name of English actor/manager David Garrick (1717–1779), the style was highly fashionable during the early 19th century. However, by the middle of that century, it was relegated to coachmen and servants.

cashmere Refers to the fiber (or the fabric made from it) sourced from the undercoat of the cashmere goat (*capra hircus laniger*); best known for its use in luxury textiles.

The goat—also known as the Kel goat, kashmir goat, and by assorted variant spellings—was originally raised in the area of South Asia now known as Kashmir on the southern part of the Himalayas (especially in the area known as Ladakh), where the high altitude and cold, dry weather encouraged the development of a silky undercoat composed of fine fibers usually ranging from 11 to 18 MICRONS in diameter. Currently, the goats are also commercially raised in China (particularly Inner Mon-

golia), Iran, and Outer Mongolia, and as a cottage industry in regions with a similar climate (e.g., parts of Montana). Because the goats do not thrive at lower altitudes and warmer climates, references to "Italian Cashmere" or "Scottish Cashmere" indicate the origin of the spun yarn or textile, not the origin of the fiber.

Cashmere is classified as a NOBLE FIBER because of its extreme fineness and prized for the warmth it yields in relation to its light weight. The yield of a single goat is relatively small, and it typically takes the fleece of several animals to produce enough fiber for a man's sweater. According to labeling regulations, a textile cannot be represented as cashmere if the average fiber is thicker than 19 microns.

cash pocket A small, usually squarish-shaped, pocket on the inside lining of a suit, jacket, or coat. Not to be confused with a TICKET POCKET, which opens to the outside, or a CHANGE POCKET or WATCH POCKET, which appears on pants or vests.

cassimere *or* **casimere** A soft, twill fabric patented in England in 1766, originally used for tailored clothing and probably intended to mimic the cashmere twills imported from India. Most often, cassimere is made of fine wool—or predominantly wool—yarn, although it may contain small amounts of cotton, silk, or other fibers. Never a synonym for CASHMERE.

cassock 1. The ankle-length, band-collared, button-front robe worn as a symbol of religious office, particularly by Roman Catholic clergy; used for everyday wear, rather than liturgical vestment. Most often black (although it can be other colors keyed to religious rank), the cassock is worn with a stiff white detachable collar and, in traditional context, with a ZUCCHETTO. Synonym:

SOUTANE. 2. A style of long jacket, similar to the JUSTA-CORPS, worn beginning in the late 17th century and continuing into the 18th century.

cast   Jargon, often used in describing the DENIM made for blue jeans, to note an overtone or undertone given to the basic color. For example, a denim might be described as having a green cast even though it is obviously blue. Often the cast is so subtle that it would not be apparent to anyone who is not either in the business or a denim connoisseur.

castor   See BEAVER FELT.

casual Fridays   The practice, begun in the late 20th century, of allowing more casual clothes to be worn to the workplace on Friday (the day when businessmen are presumably less likely to schedule client meetings and more likely to leave early). For example, a man working in an office that followed the practice of casual Fridays might wear a suit and tie on Monday through Thursday, and then wear a SPORTS SHIRT and khaki pants on Friday.

casualwear   Industry jargon for the broad category of casual clothes that includes shorts, POLO SHIRTS, and the like. Usually indicates garments that are slightly less dressy than standard SPORTSWEAR items (such as SPORTS JACKETS) and slightly more dressy than standard ACTIVEWEAR items (such as sweatshirts).

cater cap   The square-lidded cap associated with academia. More commonly used during the 19th century, especially in times and places where the cap was associated with classroom wear and not limited to ceremonial use. See MORTARBOARD.

catwalk   A synonym for RUNWAY. Ergo, a "catwalk show" or "coming down the catwalk" is synonymous with a live fashion show and presenting fashion on models rather than mannequins.

cavalier   In 17th-century England, the cavalier was an adamantly un-Puritan Royalist, who dressed to emphasize his political and personal differences from the drab ROUNDHEADS. Rather than being clean-shaven, he had meticulously groomed facial hair. He favored sumptuous rather than sober materials, added lavish, lace edges wherever possible, and wore floppy, feather-trimmed, full-brimmed hats instead of rigid COPOTAIN styles. He is associated with FALLING BAND collars, a bow-trimmed LOVE LOCK, and BREECHES that covered his knee to meet boots topped with a generous cuff.

Celanese   A brand of ACETATE marketed in the United States as "artificial silk" from the 1920s onward and, in menswear, used mostly for LININGS. Once the world's largest producer of acetate, Celanese began getting out of the textile business in 2004 and no longer produces acetate for apparel.

celluloid collar   A DETACHABLE COLLAR, in any style, made of celluloid, the easily molded and flexible nitrocellulose and camphor compound invented in 1856 (and usually associated with the composition of film).

cellulosic   A way to classify nonsynthetic fibers, usually for purposes of DRY CLEANING, dyeing, and other chemical processing. "Cellulosic" means that the fiber derives from plants. For example: COTTON and RAMIE are cellulosic materials.

The counterpart classification to indicate animal fibers is PROTEINACIOUS.

cerimonia   A category of SUITING fabric, or the CLOTH-ING made from it; worn for ceremonies such as wed-dings, christenings, and social events of similar signifi-cance. Most often in a black-on-black pattern, cerimo-nia is considered more formal than a business suit and somewhat less formal than a TUXEDO (although, when the reference is to cerimonia as a fabric, it is sometimes used in the manufacture of tuxedos). In contemporary use, popular in Italy, Spain, and Japan. In women's wear, its closest equivalent might be the little black cocktail dress.

Cerruti, Nino   Born in Italy in 1930, Nino Cerruti took over his family's textile factory and related businesses in 1950, having spent most of his teenage years apprenticed to them. In 1967, he moved to Paris and established a separate menswear apparel business, Cerruti 1881, with a boutique near the Place Madeleine. Thereafter he became widely credited with creating the concept of understated, streamlined, and very high-end clothes for men, paving the way for designers like GIORGIO ARMANI (who worked for Cerruti during the late 1960s).

Born and bred to the textile business, Cerruti designed from his deep knowledge of fabrics and his belief in saleable and wearable clothes—he was often quoted making comparisons between fashion and archi-tecture or industrial design. During the late 20th centu-ry, his thriving apparel house provided a training ground for not only Armani, but Véronique Nichanian (the longtime menswear designer for HERMÈS), Stefano Pilati (later named designer for YVES SAINT LAURENT), and women's wear designer Narciso Rodriguez.

Cerruti was also among the first menswear designers to pioneer movie placements, in addition to cultivating stars offscreen. His film career began with a few hats for 1967's BONNIE AND CLYDE and progressed to dozens of French, Italian, and American films. He outfitted actor Jack Nicholson for several films, including 1987's *The Witches of Eastwick*, as well as doing ensemble work such as 1994's *Prêt-à-Porter*.

Cerruti himself took his last runway bow in 2001, shortly after selling the remaining stock in his company to the Italian fashion conglomerate, Fin.part.

CFDA   The Council of Fashion Designers of America (which is usually abbreviated without periods) is a New York-based trade association of fashion and accessory designers for both menswear and women's wear that was chartered on December 6, 1962, to "further the position of fashion design as a recognized branch of American art and culture."

The organization traces its origin to an invitation extended by Senators Jacob Javits and Claiborne Pell to New York-based fashion publicist Eleanor Lambert to attend an October 1962 open hearing of a subcommit-tee on the arts. Realizing the advantage of an industry-wide nonprofit organization, Lambert invited designers from her wide circle of acquaintances (including Bill Blass, Norman Norell, and Pauline Trigère) to band together, and ran most early CFDA affairs from her midtown PR offices. Annual meetings were held at the Four Seasons restaurant, and annual dues were $250. Its first president was Sydney Wragge (a designer who worked with Claire McCardell), who was succeeded by Norman Norell and, in turn, Oscar de la Renta, Herbert Kaspar, and Blass.

Many costume historians also credit the CFDA with fostering a distinction between the art of design and the business of manufacturing—a difference that had pre-viously been more prominent in Paris than on Seventh Avenue. For example: In 1981, in response to members' complaints about the commercialization of the COTY

AWARDS, it sponsored its first annual awards. Like Hollywood's Academy Awards, CFDA award categories eventually came to include special tributes, humanitarian awards, and a category for "lifetime achievement" (given to the likes of Katharine Hepburn, Marlene Dietrich, and Nancy Reagan). The CFDA also sponsors scholarships, administrates trade-related events, raises money for charity, and helped to foster the COSTUME INSTITUTE at the Metropolitan Museum of Art.

chain mail   1. ARMOR made by linking rings of metal so that they create a semiflexible metal mesh. A shirt made from it is a HAUBERK. Originally known simply as mail. Synonyms: mail; *maille*.   2. Garment or jewelry construction that imitates the linking, semiflexible metal mesh of chain mail armor.

chalk   See TAILOR'S CHALK.

chalkstripe   Once used to describe a pattern of white or off-white stripes on the dark ground of cloth used for suits, the term is now used to refer to the size and style of the stripe. A chalkstripe can now be any color, but it is wider than a PINSTRIPE and narrower than a PENCIL STRIPE. Never used to describe shirt stripes. See color plates.

chambray   An inexpensive, plain-weave fabric, often made of cotton and used for workwear, such as the shirts worn with jeans. In its most common form, chambray has a light blue appearance resulting from the blend of a blue WARP and white WEFT.

chamois   1. A type of very soft leather, usually made from the inner, fleshy side of a split sheepskin (meaning that it has no grain or hair). Traditionally chamois is oil-tanned, a process that leaves it water absorbent, washable, and as flexible as fabric.   2. A fabric, usually woven, made to imitate chamois' weight and feel, often buff colored.

chandail   French for SWEATER or JERSEY. Known even to non-French speakers, especially in Canada, from the 1979 story "Le Chandail de Hockey" by Roch Carrier, which is quoted on the Canadian five-dollar bill.

Chanel   Although neither the label's originator, Coco Chanel, nor her best-known successor, KARL LAGERFELD, issued a separate menswear collection, the Paris-based women's label, owned by the Wertheimer family of France, has included men's fragrances (Cuir de Russie, Antaeus, Egoiste, Allure Homme, Technique Pour

Chain mail

Chanel

Homme, etc.) in its beauty division and, in the 21st century, often included a handful of men's looks in its ready-to-wear runway presentations.

change pocket   A term for a small pocket on pants and/or vests; often used interchangeably with WATCH POCKET—especially now that it is less common for a man to carry a pocket watch. For example, some people prefer to call the small, extra or "fifth" pocket on the right, front side of traditional JEANS a change pocket, while others call it a watch pocket.

channel quilting   Fabric that is quilted in long, equal ribs or "channels," as opposed to the more frequent checkerboard or diamond pattern. Almost always runs vertically and is confined to outerwear.

Although often misspelled as "chanel quilting," channel has absolutely nothing to do with the distinctive diamond-shaped quilting favored by Coco CHANEL, the French women's wear designer.

chapeau bras   A style of flattened, usually unwearable, hat; so called because it was designed solely to be carried under the arm (or *bras* in French). The style evolved in the 18th century when a hat was still a de rigueur complement to formal or semiformal attire, particularly at court, but where it also would have been considered a sign of extremely bad manners to keep the hat on while indoors.

chaps   A leather garment worn by riders; worn over pants or jeans to protect them from abrasion and also to enhance contact with the saddle; covering the complete leg from waist to ankle, leaving only the crotch and buttocks bared; the fastening is on the OUTSEAM of the legs, often covered by a flap.

The word, an abbreviation of the Spanish word *chaparajos*, is most associated with American cowboys, but the practice of wearing chaps spread to other horseback-riding cultures. Cowboy-style chaps, especially those worn for parades and other fancy dress, include "woolies" (in which the animal hair is left on the skin and worn hair-side-out), BATWINGS (which have a curving, winged flap on the outseam), and "shotgun" chaps (which have a straight flap).

In English riding, chaps are considered incorrect for the hunt and show ring. They are never worn over BREECHES or JODHPURS, or with knee-high riding boots. "Half chaps" cover only the lower leg, much like GAITERS.

Chariots of Fire   The 1981 Academy Award winner as Best Picture, which starred Ian Charleson, Ben Cross, and Nigel Havers as members of Britain's 1924 Olympic track team, perhaps best remembered for Vangelis's Academy Award-winning soundtrack and MILENA CANONERO's Academy Award-winning costumes (the movie also won a fourth Academy Award—for best

Chaps

screenplay). Canonero's costumes, coming at the same time as the Granada miniseries of *BRIDESHEAD REVISITED*, initiated a vogue for 1920s-style menswear and inspired many magazine editorials, retail displays, and a Bloomingdale's 1982 advertising campaign featuring the movie's actors.

Charles II   Charles Stuart (1630–1685) was the British monarch credited with inventing, around 1666, the costume that evolved into the contemporary suit. Technically, he ascended to the throne upon the execution of his father Charles I in 1649 during the Civil War. In actual fact, he was not able to take up his throne in London until the "Restoration" of 1660. Thereafter, Charles became known as the "merry monarch" and renowned for his many mistresses and his many King Charles spaniels. His reign saw the establishment of the Cavalier Parliament and the purge of the bubonic plague, followed by the Great Fire of London.

In 1666, departing from the practice of his own English predecessors and the contemporary practice of continental courts including Louis XIV's elaborate court in France, Charles declared that a costume containing a VEST be part of official court attire. Softer, longer, and more comfortable than the DOUBLET, more sober and Protestant than the beribboned styles worn in his cousin Louis XIV's court, the new style was seen as "eastern attire" after its supposed resemblance to Persian dress. It began a trend in English menswear toward stronger differentiation from the styles on the continent, which would gain momentum during the following century.

Charvet   The family-run store, tailoring firm, shirtmaker, and men's furnishings brand founded in Paris in 1838; best known as a custom shirtmaker and purveyor of luxury silk neckwear and accessories.

Founded as a shirtmaking business by Christophe Charvet (whose father had been "curator of the wardrobe" for Napoleon Bonaparte) in 1836, the company had its first fame in 1838 with the establishment of a store in a covered passage just off the rue Richelieu, which could claim to be the first of its sort in Paris (previously all shirtmakers had gone to their customers). During the 19th century, it attracted celebrities ranging from the cross-dressing novelist George Sand to painter Edouard Manet to EDWARD VII when Prince of Wales.

Eventually its customer list comprised the likes of Gustave Eiffel, Emile Zola, Marcel Proust, Claude Debussy, Jean Cocteau, W. Somerset Maugham (who used it as a setting in his 1944 novel *The Razor's Edge*), Coco Chanel (who ordered men's pajamas there), Gary Cooper, Yul Brynner, John F. Kennedy, Ronald Reagan,

Chariots of Fire: Advertisement for Bloomingdale's

Charles II

Jack Lang, Yves Saint Laurent, Catherine Deneuve, and multiple maharajas and millionaires. During the 1950s, it invented a special style of bow tie (a cross between a BATWING and a BUTTERFLY) for the Duke of Windsor in order to suit the former EDWARD VIII's predilection for puffy neckwear knots.

In the late 19th century, when the Place Vendôme became a prestigious place to shop, Charvet moved to Number 25, then, in 1920, to Number 8, Place Vendôme. In the early 1960s, when the founding family decided to get out of the business, General Charles de Gaulle (who had his own shirts custom-made there) intervened and found textile merchant Denis Colban, formerly a Charvet supplier, who took over the company in 1965. Colban expanded the ready-to-wear, came up with SILK KNOTS as a witty substitute for CUFFLINKS, and, in 1981, moved around the corner to the store's present premises at 28, Place Vendôme. When Colban *père* died in 1993, his son Jean-Claude and daughter Anne-Marie took over.

chasuble   A poncho-like, sleeveless liturgical vestment worn for the celebration of mass; worn over the ALB, its color is keyed to the liturgical calendar and it is often highly decorated.

Charvet

chatelaine   An ornamental chain that hung from the waist, to which small, useful objects were attached. For example: The chatelaine worn by a man might hold keys, seals, or smoking accessories; while the chatelaine worn by a woman might hold keys, sewing implements, or other tools associated with her household duties. The term is applied to other eras, but is especially associated with the 19th century.

chav   A sort of British counterpart to the BLING-laden lifestyle in the United States, chav was derogatory slang for behavior marked by conspicuous consumerism on the part of the working classes or nouveau riche—especially overconsumption of fashion laden with logos. For example: DAVID BECKHAM and his wife were often accused of chav behavior. Its finer points were elucidated in the 2005 book *Chav! A User's Guide to Britain's New Ruling Class* by Mia Wallace and Clint Spanner.

check   Refers to a woven pattern of regular repeated and spaced squares and/or rectangles, or a pattern printed to imitate it. A check must have at least two colors (e.g., GINGHAM, a ROB ROY, or BUFFALO CHECK), but may have more (e.g., TATTERSALL), or many, many more (e.g., an Ogilvie check or many of the other complicated TARTANS). The reference has nothing to do with either the size, shape, or color represented. A check does not contain curves or figurative patterns.

In menswear, check is the more generic term than PLAID. In other words: All plaids are checks, but not all checks are plaid. Tartans are categorized as named checks. Traditional terminology includes BASS (to refer to the background area of the pattern), SETT (to refer to the pattern itself), and OVERCHECK (to indicate a larger-format, usually simpler and more open pattern superimposed atop another, such as a WINDOWPANE).

chef's hat *or* **chef's toque**   See TOQUE.

Chelsea boots   A style of short (ankle-length), pull-on boot with elastic side gussets that was popular, especially in Britain, in the 1960s and 1970s. In the 1960s, also briefly known as BEATLE boots.

chenille   A type of yarn that sprouts short, dense hairs from all sides, so that, before being knit or woven, it looks like a caterpillar (hence its name, from the French word for caterpillar). In menswear, it usually appears as an accent in woven fabric or as a yarn for sweaters. When made into fabric, chenille's pile gives it a distinctive density of color that resembles that of other pile fabrics, such as VELVET.

chest   A horizontal measurement of girth, generally taken at the nipple line when the arms are slightly raised.

chesterfield   A style of TOPCOAT with two distinguishing factors: the presence of a velvet collar and the absence of a waist seam. Named for the sixth Earl of Chesterfield, who lived from 1805 until 1866 and popularized but probably did not invent it. A relatively dressy style, almost always worn over a suit, a chesterfield may be either single-breasted with a FLY front or double-breasted, but always has SET-IN SLEEVES and, in its 20th- and 21st-century incarnations, is relatively slim-fitting and shaped to the body.

cheviot   The coarse, springy wool made from the sheep breed of the same name.

A breed developed in the border country between England and Scotland, the cheviot was prized for its production of meat and wool in a relatively harsh climate, and that hardiness was later blamed as an indirect cause of the Highland clearances of the early 19th century, whereby Scottish peasants were driven from their land, so that acreage could be devoted to the more profitable enterprise of sheep grazing. (Unfortunately, raising cheviot did not retain its profitability either, thereby giving rise to another land use that would launch its own spate of menswear trends: leasing the land for grouse shoots, deerstalking, salmon fishing, and other sporting activities.)

The cloth called cheviot is minimally processed in order to retain the characteristics inherent in the wool and is distinctive mainly for its texture, which is rough and a bit wiry. It is not as heavy as the traditional HARRIS TWEED or DONEGAL tweed. See color plates.

chevron   Used as a synonym for HERRINGBONE, particularly if the pattern is large.

chief value   Jargon for the major component in a BLEND. When a fabric is "chief value wool," it means that it is at least 51 percent wool.

chinchilla   One of the finest and most expensive furs, valued for its extreme softness and its distinctive (usually gray) markings. In menswear, chinchilla more often appears as a NOBLE FIBER, valued for its shorn hair, which is used as a featured ingredient in fine fabrics (although it is almost never the CHIEF VALUE and tends to be added for its association with luxury).

chinos A synonym for plainly styled KHAKI pants made of sturdy—usually cotton—woven fabric. Although chinos may not always be the beige color most associated with khakis (they are often, for example, an oyster white color), they are always a neutral shade.

The term became common usage after World War II and comes from Spanish slang.

Chipp A New York-based tailoring firm founded in the 1940s by Sidney Winston and located, for the first four decades of its existence, on the midtown stretch of Madison Avenue that also harbored J. PRESS, BROOKS BROTHERS, and PAUL STUART; renowned for its boxy, soft-shouldered, IVY LEAGUE LOOK.

chiton The basic tunic-style garment worn by ancient Greeks. The chiton, which could be made of linen, wool, or silk and patterned or unpatterned depending upon the wearer's sex and status, was not tailored but draped, folded, and pinned around the body (if sewn, it was sewn only with straight seams). Its fashion and custom evolved over the centuries—for instance, the DORIC was more severe than the IONIC style—and it would have been worn under a cloak like the CHLAMYS.

chlamys A type of mantle worn in Greece and surrounding areas from ancient times through the Byzantine empire (when it evolved to more of a semicircular shape). Usually a rectangle woven from wool, it was worn pinned at the shoulder; associated with messengers, soldiers, and travelers, it is today most familiar from depictions of the god Hermes.

chooridar See CHURIDAR.

chronograph A watch that incorporates a stopwatch.

chronometer Synonym for a CHRONOGRAPH. Technically, the term is supposed to be accorded only to a chronograph that has passed a 15-day series of tests related to accuracy, under varying temperatures and in varying positions, administered by the Official Swiss Chronometer Testing Institute.

chukka boots *or* **chukker boots** Also known as DESERT BOOTS; short ankle boots, usually with only two eyelets, made of sandy-colored suede. Particularly popular from the 1960s onward, especially with a CREPE SOLE.

churidar A style of pants worn in South Asia (especially Pakistan and northern India) that may be baggy through the waist and seat but is quite tight through the lower leg (often by virtue of being cut on the BIAS); usually gathered into a drawstring waist. Variant spellings include chooridar.

Chlamys

cilice   A garment or accessory purposely worn to induce discomfort, usually for religious or other penitential reasons. For example, in the 2003 novel *The Da Vinci Code* by Dan Brown, the albino monk character, Silas, wears a cilice around his leg.

cincture   1. The belt knotted over the ALB as part of liturgical vestments. A simple cord, the cincture is traditionally associated with the virtue of chastity. It confines the loose alb, then the crossed ends of the STOLE are secured beneath it, and, finally, it is topped by the sleeveless CHASUBLE or long-sleeved DALMATICA. 2. Any belt, particularly a rope or cord belt that is knotted.

City tailors   British slang for tailoring firms located in the eastern part of London, near the "City," the traditional banking and business center; used to distinguish them from firms located on SAVILE Row.

claft   Variant spelling of KLAFT, the ancient Egyptian headdress.

clamdiggers   Pants worn as resortwear, beachwear, or in similarly informal setting; distinguished chiefly by their length (cropped to mid-calf) and their silhouette (fairly close-fitting and not baggy).

clan tartan   See TARTANS.

Clark Wallabees   The CREPE-SOLED, moccasin-type boots designed by British shoemaker Lance Clark in 1965. The style strongly resembles CHUKKA BOOTS but is even less constructed, being a NORWEGIAN-style upper attached to a thick, wedge-style heel.

classification   Jargon for a category of garments. For example: Sweaters are one classification, shirts are another.

class ring   A large ring worn to commemorate graduation from high school or, more often, college; made to resemble a signet ring. Depending on the school, it may be all metal (most often white or yellow gold) or boast a stone or intaglio. In America, particularly during the 20th century, the wearing of class rings was accepted even among conservative men who scorned the wearing of any jewelry besides a watch. Also called a SCHOOL RING. The FRATERNITY RING, a similar style worn in similar context, may be worn instead and is sometimes referred to generically as a class ring even though it commemorates membership in a fraternity rather than a graduating class. Usually worn on the fourth finger of the nondominant hand.

clicker   In the shoe business, the clicker is equivalent to the CUTTER in a tailoring business. He or she cuts the leather, traditionally with a click knife.

clip-on   A NECKTIE, usually a BOW TIE, that is pre-tied and clips on to the front of the collar. Because it saves its wearer the trouble of tying a tricky knot, the clip-on is used more often for children and is scorned by traditionalists.

clip-spot   A shirt fabric, usually made of cotton, distinguished by its construction, which leaves a short fringe of threads visible: Instead of extra threads running continuously (usually on the fabric's wrong side), they are "clipped" to the spot.
   More popular in Victorian times, when it was used for women's dresses. Synonym: clipped dobbie.

cloak   A general term applied to any loose-fitting garment worn for protection from the elements and/or concealment of the body; the term implies masking, concealment, and a certain absence of tailoring. Therefore, a cape is considered a cloak, so was a CHLAMYS; a REEFER was not.

cloak buttons   Resembling a large CUFFLINK (with which they are sometimes confused), cloak buttons were worn to fasten the front of a cloak, especially an opera cloak or cape. Sometimes called cape buttons.

clocked hose   Archaic usage; a "clock" refers to the decoration on socks or stockings, usually a figure or pattern appearing only on the outside of the leg, at or above the ankle. It never refers to an overall pattern.

clogs   An ancient form of footwear, identified with a simply constructed UPPER (which may or may not completely surround the foot) on a somewhat crude SOLE, usually an inch or more in thickness. For centuries, clogs were identified with wooden soles; then composite materials that imitated the look of wood were introduced in the late 20th century. At the same time, clogs (often more identified with women's wear) became a favorite of chefs and professional kitchen staffs.

closer   In the shoe business, the person in charge of constructing the UPPERS, after they have been cut out by the CLICKER and before they are attached to the sole by the MAKER.

cloth   In old-fashioned tailors' talk, particularly British, "cloth" was not a generic term like "fabric" but was virtually synonymous with WOOL, particularly the wool used to make a man's suit. Thus the industry's continued use of CLOTHING as a synonym reserved for tailored garments.

clothier   The term originally connoted someone who was a purveyor of cloth and made tailored clothing from it, but its usage has since expanded to include retailers who sell other products (e.g., sportswear, accessories, leathergoods) in addition to tailored clothing. LOUIS BOSTON is considered a clothier; L.L.BEAN is not.

clothing   In menswear, "clothing" is a synonym for tailored clothing and is never used interchangeably with "clothes." The word distinguishes between tailored garments, such as suits, and other garments, such as shirts and sweaters. This usage derives from the particular meaning that tailors gave to the word CLOTH as the material—usually wool—of a man's suit.

clubbing *or* **club wear**   Slang dating from the late 20th century that refers to the practice of dressing up in flashier, more fashion-conscious, and often deliberately costumey or outrageous clothes; not used to refer to FORMALWEAR or the DINNER JACKETS once associated with nightclubs. For example, the three-piece suit that was famously John Travolta's costume in 1977's *Saturday Night Fever* is an example of relatively conservative style worn for clubbing. At the other extreme: the early 1990s outfits concocted by LEIGH BOWERY.

club bow tie   Synonym for BATWING-style BOW TIE (i.e., one that does not flare out from the knot). Not to be confused with a CLUB TIE, which refers to a necktie.

club collar   A style of dress shirt collar in which the collar points are not points at all, but are rounded. Often worn with a COLLAR PIN.

club tie   Refers to a NECKTIE worn to display a man's affiliation with a particular club or other organization (such as a fraternal association); used in the same sense as wearing "the old school tie." Its particular design depends upon the organization, and therefore it may be striped, solid-colored, or patterned.

coat   In the United States, the word usually refers to outerwear. In Britain, a coat is what Americans call a "jacket," and what Americans call a "coat" would be a TOPCOAT.

coat weights   A category of heavyweight fabrics intended for OUTERWEAR. For example, 30-ounce plain-weave WOOL or 32-ounce TWEED is usually referred to as a coat weight.

cockade   An ornament, such as a rosette, most often fashioned from ribbon; usually worn on a hat to show allegiance to a particular person, place, or cause.

cocked hat   Usually refers to the three-cornered hat that most Americans know as a TRICORNE. The style originated in the late 17th century, when men began turning back the brims of their hats to better see and be seen; therefore, to "cock" a hat was to turn up its brim. (The word does not refer to COCKADE, although cockades were certainly worn on cocked hats.)

codpiece   1. The piece in ARMOR that protects the genitals, particularly for non-horsed combat.   2. A separate, usually padded, garment that covers the genitals, which began in the mid-15th century and had its fashion heyday in the 16th century. In Western Europe, the fashion for codpieces began as the longer, gownlike garments of the late Middle Ages (e.g., the HOUPPELANDE) shortened to the waist-length or hip-length DOUBLETS of the Renaissance, thus exposing the groin. By the early 16th century, codpieces became padded, elaborately decorated, and curved—a fashion that was not much loved by clergy or female monarchies. The style persisted even as doublets and jackets grew longer (and were shaped around the codpiece) but died out during the Elizabethan period.
   Synonym: *braguette*.

Cohn, Nudie   For Nuta Kotlyarenko; see NUDIE.

coke   Old-fashioned slang for a BOWLER hat, still used by LOCK & CO.; pronounced "cook." Derived from William Coke, an aristocrat who commissioned one of the first bowlers from London hatmakers Lock in the 19th century. Synonyms: BILLYCOCK; bowler.

collapsible top hat   See GIBUS or OPERA HAT.

collar   A piece surrounding the neck or neck opening. For example: A V-NECK sweater has no collar; a TURTLE-NECK has an attached collar, usually made of RIBBING designed to roll down over the neck. On a tailored garment, such as a shirt or jacket, the collar is always cut from a separate pattern piece.
   1. On a contemporary shirt, the collar may either be a STANDING COLLAR (like a BAND COLLAR or a MANDARIN COLLAR), a FOLD-OVER COLLAR (which is the most common on contemporary DRESS SHIRTS), or a FALL style (which lies flat against the shoulders).
   On the standard fold-over collar, the major parts are: the collar itself, which ends in the front in points referred

to as COLLAR POINTS; the COLLAR STAND, which is the inside band that lies against the neck and dictates the height of the fold-over; and the optional COLLAR STAYS, removable pieces slotted on the underside of each collar point to keep it from curling. A shirt collar is usually cut with the GRAIN of the fabric going from side to side. (e.g., on a striped shirt the body of the shirt will have the stripes running up and down, but they will then run side to side on the collar).

The major styles are: a "regular" fold-over collar (in which the points have only a slight separation to accommodate the buttoning and a modest NECKTIE knot); the BARRYMORE and CALIFORNIA collar (which have elongated collar points); the TAB COLLAR (which has a small cloth tab connecting the two sides of the collar in order to prop up a necktie knot); and the SPREAD COLLAR (which exaggerates the separation of the collar points, usually in order to accommodate a wider necktie knot, such as a WINDSOR knot). Dozens of named variations exist on each of these major styles,

including a few that incorporate a slight curve in the collar points.

2. On a contemporary jacket, the collar is separate from the LAPEL (which folds over from the body of the garment). Unlike the shirt collar, a jacket collar is usually cut so that its visible part, called the TOP COLLAR, is aligned with the lengthwise grain of the fabric, matching the grain line on the back of the jacket.

The line where it joins the lapel to form a NOTCH is usually called the GORGE LINE or notch line. The style that uses a gently rounded collar with no notch, which is usually reserved for TUXEDOS and DINNER JACKETS, is called a SHAWL COLLAR.

collar box   A box, usually oval or horseshoe-shaped, for the storage of the stiff, DETACHABLE COLLARS for dress shirts that enjoyed a vogue from the 1890s through the 1920s. Often made of leather and decorated as part of a dressing table set, the collar box was retained by some men for the storage of STUDS, small furnishings, and the like—long after detachable collars went out of fashion.

collar button   1. Single, studlike button worn with stiff and/or standing collars; most often made of metal. During the days of the DETACHABLE COLLAR, often rendered in precious metals. As style-setting men moved toward softer collars during and after World War I, its use gradually went out of fashion. 2. Reference to the topmost button on a dress shirt. Never used to refer to buttons on the COLLAR POINTS of a BUTTON-DOWN dress shirt.

Collars

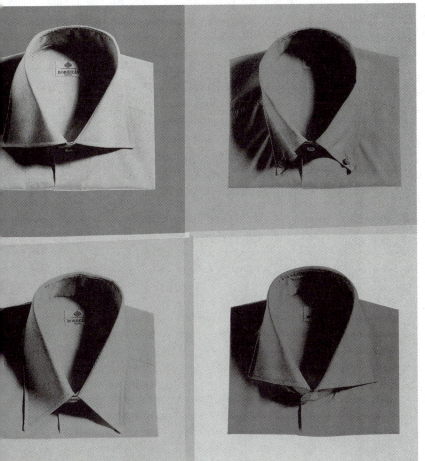

Collar City   See TROY, NEW YORK.

collar grip   A variation on the COLLAR PIN that does *not* pierce the fabric of the collar; popular during the 1920s and sporadically thereafter.

collar measurement   In the United States, DRESS SHIRTS are commonly sized according to collar and sleeve measurements enumerated in inches. To obtain the correct collar size, a man measures his neck at the bottom of his Adam's apple, pulls it snug, then inserts his index finger under the tape measure so that the final measurement allows for breathing room. Most dress shirts are sized in half-inch increments from 15 to 17 inches.

collar pin   A straight, horizontal pin worn beneath the knot of a necktie, so that the pin pierces both sides of the collar front's fabric and elevates the knot; roughly 2 inches long. Although invented earlier, as both a fashion and a piece of jewelry, the collar pin is associated with the 1920s, when soft, attached, fold-over collars replaced the stiff DETACHABLE COLLARS that had long been popular. Thereafter, it was a frequently revived fashion (and one widely quoted among men aspiring to old-fashioned dandyism).

collar points   The pointed edges of a turn-down collar on a shirt. As in: "A BUTTON-DOWN shirt is distinguished by its buttoning collar points." In contemporary use, most collar points are about 3 inches in length. Synonym: SHIRT POINTS.

collar stand   In the construction of a shirt, the piece that determines the height of the collar. See STAND.

collar stays   Small, flat pieces of plastic, flexible metal, or similar material that slide into channels sewn on the underside of a shirt collar; used to keep the collar points from curling or collapsing. Resembling shorter versions of the stays on a woman's corset, collar stays come in pairs and may be sold with the shirt. Or, conversely, they may be made of precious metal such as silver or gold and used as an occasion of inconspicuous consumption (during the 1950s, for example, playwright Moss Hart preferred monogrammed solid-gold stays). They are never visible when the shirt is worn, and are usually removed before laundering.

collection   1. Jargon for a designer or company's highest-end, most exclusive apparel offering, usually the one presented on the RUNWAY as in: "ITALO ZUCCHELLI designs the Calvin Klein collection but not the cK line." 2. Jargon referring to any themed or seasonally presented offering, be it fabric, apparel, or accessories.

The Collective   The twice-a-year men's apparel and accessories trade show that held its first edition in 1979 at the Saint Regis Hotel in New York. Known as the DESIGNERS COLLECTIVE until 1998, when it officially shortened its name.

cologne   Refers to the style and strength of fragrance that historically originated in the city of Cologne, Germany, during the 17th century as originally created by Italian perfumer Johann Maria Farina; originally known as eau de cologne or aqua mirabilis. From its creation through most of the 19th century, the word cologne automatically conjured a citrusy scent such as 4711.

    Cologne consists of essential oils dissolved in a carrier that is chiefly alcohol, usually at about 3 to 5 percent oil or fragrance concentrate. It is, therefore, not as strong as an eau de toilette (5 to 7 percent) and stronger than an AFTERSHAVE (3 percent or less) or an *EAU FRAICHE* or splash (2 percent or less).

Synonym: eau de cologne (the term does not denote a different strength or style of fragrance).

color blocking   Industry jargon for the use of color in large blocks—usually in a gridlike structure in the manner of a Piet Mondrian painting—rather than in a traditional garment decoration such as stripes or zigzags. In contemporary menswear, most frequently applied to sweaters and sports shirts.

colorfast   Fabric resistant to fading or other loss of color. Some fibers tend to be more colorfast than others: A sweater made of synthetic yarn may hold its dye well, while a cotton sweater loses color under the same conditions. Likewise, certain dyes are fast under some conditions, but not others. For example: A fabric may hold up when exposed to sunlight and then be easily damaged by machine washing.

colors   In FOXHUNTING ATTIRE, a privilege awarded to full-fledged members of a particular foxhunt. The members are then allowed to sport the hunt's chosen color on the collar of the jacket they wear on for formal hunts (some hunts also have the custom of wearing the colors on the inside flap of the jacket SKIRT).

Colours   For the apparel line, see JULIAN, ALEXANDER.

colorway   Industry jargon for the color, or combination of colors, used in a particular garment. For example, when considering a style of sweater that is being offered in red, blue, or green, a buyer may say, "I want the green colorway."

Columbia Sportswear   Known primarily for functional outdoor clothes and ski apparel, the Portland, Oregon-based company got its start when Paul and Marie Lamfrom fled Nazi Germany for the United States in 1937. The following year they purchased a company that distributed hats and renamed it for the Columbia River, which ran near Portland. Soon thereafter, they began manufacturing hats as well as distributing them.

In 1948, their daughter Gert married Neal Boyle, who joined the business and helped to expand it into apparel, and Columbia Hat Company officially became the Columbia Sportswear Company in 1960. When Neal died unexpectedly in 1970, their son Tim entered the business, and thereafter it became known for functional outdoor pieces like the Bugaboo Parka, its longtime best seller (introduced in 1986). From 1984 onward, Gert became the face of the brand in advertising that played up the supposed toughness of "Ma Boyle," (including an autobiography called *One Tough Mother: Success in Life, Business and Apple Pies,* written with Kerry Tymchuk and published in 2005). The company went public in 1998.

Columbia Sportswear: "Ma Boyle"

combed cotton   A description of how the fiber is processed; now considered somewhat old-fashioned, although once common in the description of expensive shirting fabrics. The designation implies that the short fibers have been combed to produce cotton that is better aligned, and therefore requires less twisting to turn into a yarn, making it easier to dye, softer, and more lustrous.

combed wool   A description of how the fiber is processed. Combed wool is used to make fine yarns and light fabrics, whereas CARDED WOOL, the alternative designation, is less processed and is used for thicker yarns and rougher fabrics.

combinations   Refers to old-fashioned underwear that "combines" the top and bottom in a single piece (e.g., a UNION SUIT).

comb-over   The hairstyle in which balding men grow the hair remaining on one or both sides of their head extra long so that they can comb it over the bald spot.

Combs, Sean   Born in 1969 in New York, Sean John Combs first became known as a rapper and music producer, establishing Bad Boy Worldwide Entertainment in 1993, before leveraging his financial success and per-

sonal notoriety as a dandy into his successful menswear business—the SEAN JOHN apparel line—in 1998 and becoming the CFDA Designer of the Year in 2004. Along the way, Combs regularly reinvented himself and, quite often, renamed himself to match (e.g., Puffy, Puff Daddy, P. Diddy, and Diddy). Combs was equally famous for his extravagant parties, his fondness for diamonds and fur coats, his late 1990s liaison with Jennifer Lopez, his 1999 arrest on a gun charge, and his 2004 stint on Broadway starring in *Raisin in the Sun*.

commando   1. Refers to a general, military-type style of SWEATER, usually in a dark color (army green or navy being the most common). The two most popular styles include a ribbed pullover reinforced with woven patches along the shoulders and/or other points of wear (such as the elbows and forearms); and a four- or five-button HENLEY collar.   2. As used in the phrase GO COMMANDO, a slang reference to going without underwear.

Concho belt: Nayenezgani, a Navajo deity

Sean Combs

Como The region around Lake Como in northern Italy, famous for its SILK mills and scenery.

concept store Retail jargon that emerged in the 1990s to describe stores—most famously Colette in Paris—selling a complete lifestyle concept. The prototype is a destination selling clothes, shoes, jewelry, grooming, food, magazines, and interior design items in a mix that is highly edited rather than intended to appeal to everyone. Retailers tend to reserve the reference for high-end and/or avant-garde product mixes. For example: 10 Corso Como in Milan is regarded as a concept store.

concho *or* **concha** A disk-shaped decoration, usually silver or similar metal, used to decorate apparel (e.g., CHAPS or vests) and accessories (e.g., belts) in the American Southwest; from the Spanish word for shell.

concho belt Usually refers to a style of belt, developed by Navajo craftsmen in the late 19th century, decorated with multiple heavy silver CONCHOS. The earliest styles used relatively plain conchos, often made from silver dollars, with slits in the center through which leather was threaded. Later styles became increasingly elaborate, with turquoise being added in the early 20th century.

Cone *or* **Cone Mills** Known best as a specialist in DENIM, the material of now-vintage WORKWEAR brands such as Big Red, Big Winston, Calf Skin, Stonewall, and Stronghold, as well as J.C. Penney and LEE; for several years in the 20th century, the exclusive purveyor of denim for LEVI STRAUSS.

Founded by brothers Moses and Ceasar Cone, who began making textiles in 1891 and devoted their third plant, the White Oak facility in Greensboro, North Carolina, exclusively to denim production. Cone claims that the White Oak facility, where it opened a denim museum in 1996 and archive in 2005, was the first to use a continuous INDIGO dye range and the first to weave denim on superfast, shuttleless machines. In 2004, Cone was purchased by the International Textile Group owned by Wilbur Ross.

congress gaiters Not a GAITER at all, but footwear (a low boot or medium-height shoe) constructed with an elasticized side gusset; a style pioneered by Queen Victoria's favorite cobbler, J. Sparkes Hall. Synonyms: BOSTON BOOTS; SIDE-GUSSETS.

Continental look As a reference to a style of men's dress, "Continental" is often juxtaposed against "British" or "Ivy League," particularly when talking about men's clothing in the 1950s and 1960s. Inspired by the body-conscious tradition of Italian tailoring, the Continental silhouette was tighter and closer to the torso than its British or American counterparts, and connoted slimmer pants, a more nipped-in waist, and a sleeker shoulder line.

conversationals A broad category of prints that depicts a recognizable person, place, or thing. A conversational may be as elaborate as an entire scene (e.g., a hunter firing his rifle at a deer), as representational as a *trompe l'oeil* pattern of fur, or as stylized as a diagonal stripe of five-pointed stars. Also referred to as NOVELTIES. Contrasting categories include CHECKS, GEOMETRICS, and stripes.

Converse high tops   Founded by Marquis Converse in 1908 in Malden, Massachusetts, the Boston Rubber Shoe Company added the Converse All-Star shoe for basketball to its line of rubber-soled footwear in 1917, a style made famous by former player Chuck Taylor, who joined the company in 1921. By the late 20th century, the cloth-topped, flat-soled sneakers were no longer worn on college or professional courts, outpaced by the technological innovations of other brands, but were sold as a fashion and "retro" streetwear item. In 2003, the company was acquired by one-time rival NIKE.

converter   A business that takes GRAY GOODS or fabric that has been woven or knit someplace else and then dyes, prints, embosses, or otherwise FINISHES it.

convict stripes   Synonym for the extra-wide, black-and-white, horizontal stripes also known as PRISON STRIPES.

Coolmax   A MOISTURE MANAGEMENT fiber that is a registered trademark of INVISTA, which has both capitalized (CoolMax) and lowercased the M in its official usage. Invented by DuPONT in the late 20th century, Coolmax is composed of specially structured polyester and became popular for apparel—either alone or blended with fibers such as cotton—for both activewear and sportswear.

coonskin cap   A hat made of raccoon fur, with a raccoon tail hanging from its center back. The style became a craze for little boys during the mid-1950s when *The Wonderful World of Disney* broadcast five episodes of *DAVY CROCKETT* in 1954 and 1955. As portrayed by 6-foot, 5-inch Texan actor Fess Parker, "the king of the wild frontier" wore a coonskin cap along with his BUCKSKINS. Although the frenzy for the hats soon died, Parker was back on television wearing a coonskin cap as "Daniel Boone" in the series that ran from 1964 to 1969. (Much later, when Parker retired from acting and opened a California winery and spa, he sold coonskin caps there.)

Cooper, Art   Editor-in-chief of *GQ* magazine from 1983 until shortly before his death in 2003 at age 65, New York City native Arthur Cooper attended Penn State and worked for the *Patriot News* in Harrisburg, Pennsylvania, and *Time* magazine before moving to *Newsweek*, *Penthouse*, and *Family Weekly* magazines.

While at *GQ*, he became renowned for his relationship with writers and was therefore able to take what had been a niche journal about men's fashion into a full-fledged competitor of its progenitor, *ESQUIRE*, a magazine that had long-established literary clout. Famous for loving the good life, Cooper was lunching at his favorite restaurant, the Four Seasons, when he was felled by a stroke that soon proved fatal.

cope   A type of CAPE. When describing a garment from centuries past, "cope" may include a cape with hood and/or arm openings. In contemporary use, it is a long, hoodless, open-front cape worn with liturgical vestments.

copotain   The style of round, high-crowned, medium-brimmed hat known to most schoolchildren as the PURITAN HAT. Usually made of dark felt, the copotain became popular in the mid-16th century, and was later adopted by Puritans because it became considered relatively sober and unfashionable.

Converse high tops

Corbu glasses A style of thick, black eyeglass FRAMES like those affected by Swiss architect Le Corbusier (Charles Edouard Jeanneret, 1887–1965). Popular among architects, "Corbu glasses" have simple, straight sidepieces and round, or nearly round, lenses. The influential American architect Philip Johnson, a pupil of Le Corbusier, was inspired to design a similar pair of eyeglass frames for himself in 1934, and they thereafter became his style signature.

Cordings Founded on the Strand in 1839 by John Charles Cordings, this London firm moved to Piccadilly in 1890. A specialist in kitting men for shooting parties, country pursuits, and anything that might involve rough weather (in 1871 it outfitted Sir Henry Morton Stanley for his African expedition to locate Dr. Livingston), Cordings is famous for the sturdy wool twill COVERT CLOTH it introduced in the 19th century and still sells a COVERT COAT, as well as DEERSTALKER caps, PLUS FOURS, and other British classics. It also claims the inspiration of taking TATTERSALL checks off horse blankets and putting them on shirts.

cordovan A type of leather popular for men's shoes because it is sturdy and highly resistant to water. Most cordovan leather is dark brown or black. The name comes from the Spanish city of Cordoba, once renowned for its prowess in tanning.

cords Slang for CORDUROY; usually refers to corduroy trousers.

corduroy A type of sturdy woven fabric distinguished by velvety, vertical ribs called WALES. The fabric may be further described according to the number of wales per inch: Corduroy known as FINE WALE, PIN-WALE, or NEEDLE WALE has very thin wales (usually twelve or more per inch, i.e., the width of a pin), while WIDE WALE corduroy has thicker wales (usually six or fewer per inch). Corduroy that tends to neither extreme is known as medium-wale or simply called corduroy without any modifiers. Corduroy in the form of an unribbed velour that resembles velvet is called NO-WALE.

Inexpensive and long identified as a fabric for working men, corduroy was also the costume of the artist and bohemian through the first quarter of the 20th century and played much the same role as denim in masculine sportswear and workwear.

cornrows An ancient style of braiding hair in tight rows of often elaborate patterns lying next to the skull. The tradition originated in Africa, but in the United States it persisted for generations only in the styling of children's hair. After the AFRO became fashionable in the 1960s, cornrows became the next Afro-centric hair fashion, popularized first for women by actress Cicely Tyson in the early 1970s, then reaching the men's mainstream after being adopted by entertainers like Stevie Wonder.

corrected grain Refers to leather where a grain (or pattern) has been embossed on the hide, as opposed to being processed to reveal only that hide's natural grain.

correspondents British reference to the two-color style of shoes that Americans commonly call SPECTATORS.

Cossack shirt A full, bloused style featuring a high banded collar, full sleeves with a drop (rather than set-in) shoulder, and either a side or center-front placket (which is sometimes embroidered); traditionally of at least hip-length and worn outside the wide, loose pants, then belted at the waist.

costume French reference to a man's suit; without the implication of dressing up or theatricality that the word carries in English.

Costume Institute The department of New York City's Metropolitan Museum of Art devoted to apparel. The collection, which comprises well over 75,000 pieces, concentrates on a "best of the best" approach (as opposed to an anthropological study).

Officially a curatorial department in the museum since 1959, the collection came from the Museum of Costume Art, founded by Irene Lewisohn in 1937. In 1946, plans were made to merge Lewisohn's collection with the Met's, and in 1948, fashion publicist Eleanor Lambert arranged the first "party of the year" as a fundraiser a function that continued to be an annual draw for members of New York society and the fashion industry. From 1973 through 1989, fashion editor Diana Vreeland worked at the Costume Institute, initiating its blockbuster exhibitions.

cotta A short SURPLICE, usually worn by choirboys, especially in the Anglican church.

cotton Refers to the plant or to the fiber; "cotton" by itself does not refer to a weave or a style of fabric, only to its fiber content; classified as a CELLULOSIC FIBER. The cotton used in apparel comes from two categories: *gossypium hirsutum*, the more common variety, also known as UPLAND COTTON; and *gossypium barbadense*, the less common variety, also known as LONG-STAPLE COTTON (and including varieties such as EGYPTIAN, PIMA, and SEA ISLAND).

Cotton Incorporated A Cary, North Carolina-based research and marketing company devoted to the promotion of UPLAND COTTON grown in the United States. Although Cotton Inc. works with fabric and apparel makers to promote the use of cotton (including everything from research on fiber and fabric treatments to television advertising), it does not produce or manufacture any fabric or apparel. In the 1990s, it was famous for its "Fabric of Our Lives" advertising tagline, created by Ogilvy & Mather and discontinued in 2003.

Coty Award The award officially known as the "Coty American Fashion Critics' Award" and popularly known as "the fashion Oscars," began in 1942 as a way of promoting American fashion. Sponsored by Coty, the cosmetics company, the presentation included a bronze statuette—known as a "Winnie"—designed by Malvina Hoffman. However, when the sponsoring company, which had become more mass market, launched a "Coty Awards" collection of makeup in 1979, many industry insiders felt that the prize lost its prestige. An additional blow came with the launch of the CFDA awards program in 1981 (a year when Halston and CALVIN KLEIN both declined to attend the Coty ceremony). By 1985, most top designers had stopped attending the ceremony even if they were being honored, at which point Pfizer, the parent company of Coty, pulled the plug on the financing and discontinued the awards.

coucher The evening ritual of undressing the king and preparing him for bed. Its opposite is the *LEVER* or *LEVÉE*, the morning ritual of dressing.

Council of Fashion Designers of America See CFDA.

Cotton field

counter A stiffening or reinforcement used in the construction of the SHOE, usually at the back of the heel, to shape it and keep it from collapsing. In certain styles (such as some COWBOY BOOTS), it may be on the outside of the shoe or both inside and outside counters may be used. But in dress shoes it is more often part of the shoe's unseen construction. Synonym: HEEL COUNTER.

Countess Mara The company best known as a manufacturer of pricey NECKTIES prominently displaying a CM logo surmounted by a crown. Founded as a New York tie shop in 1938 by Lucilla Mara de Vescovi, who had renamed herself Countess Mara and gone into business when, according to legend, her husband challenged her to come up with a better necktie than the one he had just bought. ("Tell a man you like his necktie and you will see his personality unfold like a flower," she reportedly once declared.) Despite the death of the "Countess" in 1968, the business continued to expand, eventually offering apparel and leathergoods, and had its heyday in the 1980s, when its logos were at their largest and it was briefly billed as the most expensive necktie in the world. The company was acquired by Randa, the parent of assorted other accessories brands, in 1997.

County Slang for the British equivalent of PREPPY style. Often used interchangeably with SLOANE, with the equivalent derogatory reference to an "Hooray Henry" as an exemplar of the type.

court shoes British usage for PUMPS, used to describe both men's and women's shoes. When the men's shoes are made with any lacing or ties, they are known as "court ties."

couture In proper usage, "couture" refers only to custom-made clothes for women. The men's equivalent is BESPOKE. (For that same reason, the word couturier has no place in menswear.) In the early 21st century, it became used as an ironic, slang reference to fashion.

coveralls Protective workwear with long sleeves and full-leg pants, intended to be worn over other clothes—literally to "cover all."

covered buttons Literally a button that is covered with the same cloth as the garment (and therefore almost always a shanked button). In menswear, covered buttons are most often used in outerwear. Not to be confused with the BUTTON COVERS worn with formal and semiformal clothes.

covert cloth A sturdy, densely woven wool twill, named for its intended wear in covert (pronounced "cover"), where a hunter may pursue game—and where more fragile fabrics might be snagged and ribboned by brambles, stray branches, and thorns. Used by the London firm of CORDINGS for its COVERT COAT. Most often in MARLED tan, followed by charcoal gray.

covert coat A style of topcoat manufactured of COVERT CLOTH by the London firm of CORDINGS, or a coat made to imitate it; a fly-front coat that falls at or above the knee and is distinguished by four rows of stitching at the bottom hem and edge of each sleeve, as well as by its sturdy fabric. The covert coat also has a welted breast pocket, two flapped front pockets plus a flapped ticket pocket, and (unlike most topcoats) a series of roomy inner pockets, including a POACHER'S POCKET. Because of its proper pronunciation as "cover," sometimes misspelled as "cover coat."

cowboy Although working 19th-century cowboys actually wore relatively drab work clothes and utilitarian boots eked out by available army cavalry gear (sometimes left over from their own service in the Civil War), a flamboyant style evolved around their culture, aided in the popular imagination by the flashy, fringed clothes in the Wild West shows of Buffalo Bill Cody and other performers, the highly decorated gear worn by TOM MIX and other Hollywood horse opera actors (up to and including Roy Rogers), and the fancy apparel favored by country-western singers, rodeo stars, and others (e.g., tailor NUDIE) who took a "Let's-see-you-top-this" approach to cowboy costume. Distinguishing elements include:

• High-heeled COWBOY BOOTS
• High-crowned COWBOY HATS with side-rolled brims
• A bright, usually oversized, BANDANA worn with everyday costume
• For more formal occasions, neckwear such as a TECK, BOLO, BOOTLACE, or silk NECK KERCHIEF in place of a regular necktie or bow tie
• Leather belts (sometimes tooled or beaded) with large, ornamental buckles
• BLUE JEANS, made of heavy DENIM
• Shirts made with both front and back YOKES, with pearl-snap closures instead of buttons, and with half-moon pockets instead of patch pockets
• Triangular, arrowhead-shaped bands of embroidery to reinforce pocket corners

Cowboy boots

• Liberal use of contrast PIPING (e.g., to trim shirt PLACKETS, pocket edges, collars)

Other common accessories include fringed GAUNTLETS or fringed and/or tooled leather CUFFS and fancy CHAPS (especially BATWING style).

Synonyms may include "western" (especially in references to garment construction, such as "western-style jacket").

cowboy boots Refers to a style of pull-on, high-heeled, mid-calf boot originally associated with working cowboys; often made with exotic leathers and/or highly decorated, especially when adapted for street or business wear.

No matter what their style of toe, cowboy boots are tight and tapered. The typical cowboy boot has a V in both its front and back, with short, visible pull straps on either side, and a line of piping that runs down the outside of the boot like the seam on the outside of a pants leg. The heel is most often around 2 inches in height and almost always UNDERSLUNG (boots worn for parades or fancy styles may have even higher heels). The sole may be steel-shanked or pegged for reinforcement—a feature that originally made it much easier for working cowboys to stand in their stirrups but also makes walking in cowboy boots relatively uncomfortable.

The lines of parallel decorative stitching over the toes are called toe wrinkles, and a more elaborative and decorative stitch pattern in the same spot is known as the medallion. The pointiest toe style is known as a needle toe or needlenose; but other toes may be a "shoe" toe or a squared toe or a squared needle toe—depending on current fashion. The pull straps at the top of each boot are sometimes called ears (oversized pull straps are called mule ears); less often, a boot may be made with pull holes that serve the same function. The band of decoration at the top of the boot is called the collar.

Although most of the traditional cowboy costume can be traced to the dress of the *vaqueros*, cowboy boots seem to come from an amalgam of sources including cavalry boots and HESSIAN BOOTS (the supposed origin of the V-cut in the front). Boots that look like antecedents of the contemporary cowboy boot seem to have appeared after the Civil War, at approximately the same time as the great cattle drives from Texas to Abilene. Historians of the style say that the toe wrinkle originated in the early 20th century, that highly decorated and customized cowboy boots were popularized by cinema cowboy TOM MIX during the 1920s and 1930s, and that pointed toes were not made until the 1940s.

Fanciful and elaborately decorated custom boots that look like rodeo wear have been popular with businessmen and politicians, particularly in Western states, since at least the mid 20th century, and have been worn by presidents from Lyndon B. Johnson to George W. Bush.

Among the best-known manufacturers: Acme, Dingo, Justin, Luchese, Nocona, Olathe, and Tony Lama.

cowboy-cut   Refers to pants, usually JEANS, with a roomy seat and high back pockets that supposedly make time in the saddle easier. May also refer to legs that are tapered at the bottom (so that fabric does not tangle in stirrups) and belt loops that are widely spaced in front (to accommodate large, championship-style buckles).

cowboy hat   Although 19th-century working cowboys wore hats with deep BRIMS (usually about 5 inches) and often with high CROWNS (from 6 to 8 inches), the creased-crown, side-rolled brim style now identified as a cowboy hat was not common until after 1900. (For instance, the sugarloaf, which had a high, uncreased crown and flat, wide brim, was a common style.) Then and now, creases, peaks, dips, and rolls develop according to region, the offerings of the manufacturer, and the taste of the wearer.

cowboy shirt   Like other COWBOY clothes, the classic shirt was designed to be both durable and highly decorative. Its distinguishing characteristics:

• A double-thickness YOKE in front (frequently in a contrasting color), usually on a shaped seam

• A shaped yoke in back (frequently in a contrasting color), also usually on a shaped seam

• A snap front (substituting pearl-snap closures for buttons), supposedly so that the shirt would open quickly if the front caught on something while the cowboy was working

• Inset pockets in a half-moon shape, often ending in arrow-shaped stitching for more decoration and reinforcement

• Cuffs (frequently in a contrasting color) that are sewn to integrate to the shirt sleeve and use snap closures

• Liberal use of contrast PIPING (e.g., to trim PLACKETS, pocket edges, collars)

cowhide   Leather made from the skin of a mature bovine, and the most common leather used in menswear because of its durability, availability, and amount of workable area. Synonyms include COWSKIN and STEER HIDE. Skins made from immature animals, particularly those not yet weaned, are referred to as CALFSKIN or KIP.

cowskin   Synonym for COWHIDE.

cravat   A general reference to decorative neckwear, particularly to that which is conventionally worn with tailored clothing. The term originated in the 17th century as "Cravate," a French reference to the Croatian soldiers who were in the habit of adorning themselves with neck cloths. It remained an identifying term for the precursors of modern NECKTIES and BOW TIES throughout the 18th and 19th centuries, and was never identified with a single pattern and specific dimensions. In contemporary use, it often signifies fuller, or more old-fashioned, neckwear (e.g., an ASCOT, a SEVEN-FOLD tie, or a formally knotted NECK KERCHIEF or STOCK TIE). Fashion copywriters also tend to use it as a highfalutin' synonym for a necktie.

Cravanette   A patented and trademarked process to make cloth water-resistant. Discovered in 1877, the Cravanette process replaced waxed or vulcanized garments and the "Cravanette Sheds Showers" label was popular for mid-priced lines through the mid-20th century.

creative black tie   A designation or dress code for social occasions in which a TUXEDO is the desired dress but ethnic dress, fashionable dress of equal formality, or some other nod to the special status of the evening is equally acceptable. Often interchangeable with the designation ALTERNATIVE BLACK TIE.

Creed   Now better known for its participation in the perfume business, the Creed tailoring dynasty began when James Creed came to London from his native Leicestershire in the second half of the 18th century and reached its apogee in the early 19th century when great-grandson Henry Creed became tailor to COUNT D'ORSAY, the preeminent dandy of his day.

According to company legend, founder James Creed drummed up piecework by frequenting the same haunts as gentlemen's valets. When he found a forgotten guinea in the pocket of a waistcoat he was sewing, Creed used the money to set himself up in business. His namesake James also became a tailor, as did grandson Henry and great-grandson Henry—the Henry who set up premises at 33 Conduit Street and attracted D'Orsay as a client. Through the D'Orsay connection, Creed made its name on the continent, attracted Emperor Napoleon III as a client, and set up premises in Paris.

creel   A woven basket with flat back and a flat, flapped top. Traditionally made for fishermen to carry their catch. Usually has leather accents (e.g., a leather shoulder strap and leather tab closure).

crepe   A light fabric with a distinctive rough, pebbly surface. Woven with a proportion of threads that are purposely overtwisted, the fabric is then dunked in water so that the crepe thread shrinks and/or releases some of its twist.

crepe sole   Not a reference to the fabric, but to thick, spongy rubber with a crinkly surface (imitating the crinkly surface of CREPE-woven fabric); popular for BUCKS and other relatively informal styles from the second quarter of the 20th century onward.

crewneck   A style of collarless, round neckline; seen most often on knits like PULLOVER sweaters and T-shirts; usually trimmed with a band of flat RIBBING.

crimp   In textile industry jargon, refers to the amount of natural waviness in an individual fiber, especially in WOOL and other fibers taken from animal fleece.

Although there are technical reasons why it does not always hold true, most of the industry sticks to the rule of the thumb that the greater the crimp, the finer the fiber; most grading systems rate wool according to the number of crimps per inch (five to eight being considered "very fine").

crin   The French word for HORSEHAIR. The favored term for describing that fiber (or fabric made from it), even in the U.S. and British markets.

crocking   When the color of a fabric rubs off on skin or other materials, it is "crocking" because the dye has not been set correctly. Reasons might include insufficient rinsing, improper application, or simply a poor match of dye to material.

crocodile   An expensive leather made from the skin of crocodiles. Like ALLIGATOR, which it closely resembles, crocodile is thick, extremely long lasting, and yields a highly decorative, glossy leather. Most of the crocodile used for shoes and other accessories is baby crocodile, since the animal can easily grow so large that its hide becomes too stiff, scarred, and brittle to work. For similar reasons, the best-quality hide is taken from the belly of the animal, because it is less likely to have scarring and damage. (To distinguish crocodile from alligator, look for a small barb near the edge of each scale—alligator skin is completely smooth.)

croquet sandal *or* **croquet shoe**   Forerunner of the tennis shoe and sneaker, the croquet sandal was a rubber-soled, canvas shoe created during the 1860s and marketed to croquet players.

crosshatch   Jargon used most often to describe the DENIM produced for JEANS; describes a weave that is purposely made to look crosshatched because the vertical (WARP) and horizontal (WEFT) yarns are irregular in size and/or shape.

crown   General term for the part of any hat that covers the head (as opposed to the BRIM, which protrudes from the crown). The crown may be either rigid (as in a BOWLER) or soft (as in a CRUSHER) or somewhere in between (as in a TRILBY). It may either exaggeratedly high (as in a TOP HAT or TEN-GALLON HAT), strangely shaped (as in a SHAKO), or simply fitted to the head (as in a SKULLCAP, which is all crown and no brim).

crow's foot   Reference, usually British, to the check pattern known as a HOUNDSTOOTH.

crushed beetles   British tailors' slang for buttonholes that are badly sewn.

crusher *or* **crush hat**   A style of soft, fabric hat with a narrow, encircling brim; similar to a BUCKET HAT, but without vents.

cuban heels   Thick shoe or, more often, boot heels, usually between 1 and 2 inches in height, which taper slightly from the shoe to the ground (at the back) but are straight, not tapered, in front (under the arch of the shoe); popular for many of the CHELSEA BOOTS worn by MODS at the beginning of the 1960s, as well as most styles of COWBOY BOOT. Synonym: UNDERSLUNG.

cuff   1. A rigid bracelet, generally a band of metal that rolls or slips on the wrist via a small opening (rather than fastening via a clasp). 2. A thick band of metal or

Cuban heel

leather, worn for ornamentation.   3. An accessory of COWBOY dress, in which large, flared cuffs (which resemble fancy GAUNTLETS without the hand covering) are worn over the wrist and are often ornamented with beading, fringe, and/or elaborate tooling.

cufflinks   Jewelry used to fasten the sleeve cuffs of DRESS SHIRTS made with FRENCH CUFFS (i.e., those that do not fasten with buttoned BARREL CUFFS).

Although examples existed as early as the 17th century, cufflinks did not come into wide use until the mid-19th century, when they began to be used as a way to relieve the darkness and uniformity of men's dress. Over the ensuing decades, fashions in cufflinks would come and go, usually reflecting the aesthetic of the time (e.g., Art Deco patterns on flat enamel links during the 1920s). Like earrings, cufflinks have many, many standard constructions; among the more popular:

• A decorative stud fastened to a toggle back (and worn so that the toggle is inside and unseen)

• Two identical or mirror-image decorative studs connected by a link or short chain

• A decorative stud attached to a straight back that pops down to form a toggle

cuffs   1. On DRESS SHIRTS, the cuff is a separate pattern piece stitched to the end of the sleeve. In contemporary use, it is usually a variation of either a BARREL CUFF, which buttons, or a FRENCH CUFF, which is a doubled cuff that closes with CUFFLINKS. Both styles have a short sleeve PLACKET (also known as a GAUNTLET) and, depending on the shirtmaker, may also have a GAUNTLET BUTTON.   2. On TROUSERS, the cuff is usually a folded-back continuation of the pants leg. Cuffs, which go in and out of fashion for business attire, generally range from 1½ to 2 inches, remaining the same depth around the leg of the pant but being canted ever so slightly in the front to allow for what, in an uncuffed pants leg, would be the break against the shoe. The general rule for depth is: The taller the man, the deeper the cuff. Synonyms (both British usage): TURN-UP; PTU.

cuirass   In ARMOR, the piece that protects the main torso; the breastplate. Because the original Roman cuirass was made of leather, much resembling a VEST or jerkin, the word is often used to imply armor providing both the back covering for the torso as well as the front.

cuisse   In ARMOR, the piece that protects the thigh.

cummerbund *or* **cumberbund**   A broad, sashlike, pleated band worn around the waist as part of SEMIFORMAL dress (e.g., with DINNER JACKETS and TUXEDOS); its decorative, pleated fabric is worn to the front and its closure is hidden in the back beneath the suit jacket. Often a bright color or pattern, sometimes in a material to match the BOW TIE being worn with it, the cummerbund is worn with its pleats facing up, where, by custom, men may secrete their ticket stubs, hat checks, and the like.

Etymologists and costume historians say that the word derives from Urdu word *kamarband* and from the practice of wearing a long, lengthwise-pleated sash among workers in South Asia. However, it should also be remembered that its use arose during an era when many court and military uniforms included sashes and ZOUAVE styles had already influenced mainstream fashion. In Western menswear, it came into fashion in the late 19th century with the wearing of dinner jackets, where it was seen as a replacement for the vest and, as such, was never worn with one—a practice continued into the 20th and 21st centuries.

cup A rigid, protective piece worn over the genitals. See BOXING CUP.

cupro Refers to the fiber or the fabric made from cotton linter. A CELLULOSIC fiber, cupro is derived from the cotton plant (as opposed to the fluffy white cotton boll used to make cotton fiber) through a process akin to the making of rayon. In menswear, its best known use is in BEMBERG, a trademarked brand of LINING fabrics.

curtain On tailored pants, the piece of fabric (most often cotton or pocketing material) that falls from the waistband to the top of the pocket insertion. The curtain, which is usually cut on the BIAS, acts to line and support the area around the waist. Not visible when the garment is worn.

custom-made In tailoring, the term is synonymous with BESPOKE, and may be somewhat redundantly referred to as "fully custom" in order to distinguish its usage from "customized," a word that means a prior pattern has been adapted to specific measurements (and is, by contrast, a synonym for MADE-TO-MEASURE). Synonyms: bespoke; custom; fully custom.

cut and sewn Exactly what it sounds like: industry jargon to refer to apparel that is cut and sewn, as opposed to being KNIT or made by some other method. Usually applied to more traditional categories of apparel, such as shirts, suits, and the like.

cutaway 1. A style of tailed coat worn, in contemporary use, only for the most formal daytime occasions; an essential component of the MORNING SUIT. In front, the cutaway curves or slants from just below the waist, descending in an unbroken line to the tails in back, the split flap of material which falls to the back of the knee. The front usually closes with a single button, but it may sport either a regular notched lapel or a peaked lapel. It differs from the tailcoat worn for evening wear by being more gracefully and less abruptly cut in front and also by its single-button closure.

Like other tailed styles, the coat traces it origin to the 18th century, when the front of the jacket was "cut away" to facilitate horseback riding, a morning activity.

2. Jargon for a suit jacket or sport coat with a particularly abrupt taper in front, so that it seems to imitate the line of a cutaway tailcoat.

cutie culture A style that originated in Japan in the third quarter of the 20th century, initially among young women. See KAWAII.

Cutler & Gross The brand of eyeglass frames and sunglasses founded by London-based optometrists Graham Cutler and Tony Gross in 1969; considered among the first firms to view eyewear as an item of fashion as much as function. Renowned for dealing in vintage frames and for eschewing large logos on their lenses and frames and also for generating unusual or vintage-inspired styles for collectors and celebrities such as Elton John.

cut-offs Refers to shorts created from long pants by cutting off the leg, with the bottom edge left unfinished. Originally, most cut-offs were made from jeans that had torn knees but a still-usable seat; therefore, the resulting shorts usually looked well-worn and the legs showed a frayed edge instead of a hem.

cutter In a traditional tailoring firm, such as the established names of SAVILE ROW, a cutter typically takes the clients' measurements, cuts the fabric and then checks the nearly finished results when the client returns for fittings. Actual sewing is done by the TAILOR.

Cutty Sark Awards   Awards for men's fashion design sponsored by the Cutty Sark brand of Scotch whisky. Initiated in 1980 in conjunction with the Men's Fashion Association (MFA), the awards were bestowed at an annual dinner in New York City and timed to coincide with the press week for men's fashion. In 1989, Cutty Sark ceded sponsorship to the Wool Bureau and they became the WOOLMARK AWARDS.

Dacron Trademarked name for a POLYESTER created by the division of DUPONT that became INVISTA. Billed as "wash and wear," Dacron was most popular for men's shirts during the mid-1950s through the 1960s, despite the fact that early Dacron material was prone to PILLING.

Although DuPont was working on the polymer that later became Dacron as early as the 1930s, the company concentrated its resources elsewhere and, as a result, ended up buying the license from British chemists who had patented it as Terylene. DuPont experimented with its new "Fiber V" in 1950 and built its first dedicated plant in Kinston, North Carolina, in 1953.

Daddy, Puff See COMBS, SEAN.

dagged edge A decorative edge in which the material is purposely shaped in a repetitive pattern—usually points or squared tabs. Although the term can and is used to describe contemporary fashion, the practice of dagging edges was more common from the Middle Ages to the 16th century.

The Daily News Record See *DNR*.

DAKS Simpson The London brand forever famous for its 1934 invention of "DAKS slacks," the patented pants with a self-supporting waistband.

Founded in 1894 by Simeon Simpson as a Whitechapel tailoring factory supplying men's clothing stores, the business expanded into women's wear in the new century, and built a state-of-the-art apparel factory in Stoke Newington in 1929. In 1932, Simpson's son Alexander, "Alec," Simpson inherited the business, expanding its ready-to-wear and coining the name DAKS (usually spelled with upper-case letters) as a cross between the words "dad" and "slacks." In 1936, the company opened a modernist, steel-beamed flagship store designed by Lazlo Moholy-Nagy and Joseph Emberton. With the success of its slacks, DAKS became one of England's largest men's apparel companies and subsequently held multiple ROYAL WARRANTS. Identified with the rise of sportswear, DAKS fostered that association with team sponsorships and pioneering use of lightweight and otherwise innovative fabrics. In the 1970s, it created the first of its signature checks.

In 1991, it was purchased by Sankyo Seiko, the Japanese company that had previously been its licensee.

Dale of Norway   Best-known for Scandinavian-style, patterned ski sweaters, made from wool of its own manufacture, spun and knit in the town of Dale. The company began when Peter Jebsen visited the village in 1872 and conceived the idea of starting a textile business there. In 1879, it began producing as Dale Fabrikker, spinning its first Heilo wool yarn in 1938, and becoming famous worldwide when it created sweaters of special design for the Norwegian team to wear in the 1956 Olympics. In 1967, it launched a ready-to-wear line and, in 1999, officially changed its name to Dale of Norway. During the last quarter of the 20th century, the company began regularly issuing sweaters of special design for important sporting events, such as the winter Olympics and the skiing world championships.

dalmatic   An outer vestment worn chiefly by deacons in Catholic ceremonies, usually decorated by two vertical stripes running the length of the garment; derived from the DALMATICA of ancient Rome.

dalmatica   A long-sleeved, closed robe that began as a sort of oversized tunic worn by residents of Dalmatia (hence the name) and popular in Rome from the 2nd century onward. Worn as an outer tunic by both sexes of the upper class during the Byzantine era, it gradually became more shaped, flaring out toward the hem, and its use continued through the Middle Ages; also the origin of the DALMATIC worn by Catholic clergy.

damask   Although the term is now used to describe a form of figured weaving done in a variety of fibers (e.g., damask linen tablecloths), the term as applied to menswear usually signifies the luxurious silk damask that was introduced to Europe in the late Middle Ages through the city of Damascus—hence its name.

In old portraits, aristocrats and men wearing ecclesiastical robes can be seen wearing damask of Arab origin. However, by the 14th century, production was well underway in Europe. Damask may be of a single color or of several colors in which the main pattern is made to contrast with the background. It differs from BROCADE by being less three-dimensional and usually less heavy.

dance belt   A type of ATHLETIC SUPPORTER worn by male dancers. Usually in black or beige elastic material, the dance belt differs slightly from the standard JOCK STRAP in that it is made to give the genitalia a rounded shape under tights, as well as providing support.

dandy   1. A term in use since the late 18th century to refer to an exaggeratedly stylish man. For example, "Yankee Doodle Dandy," originally sung by the British to mock the colonists, survives from the 1770s.

Dalmatica

Dale of Norway

Ellen Moers, author of *The Dandy* (New York: Viking Press, 1960), calls the development of the dandies a social and political phenomenon and traces their true origin to Regency England where the dandy was "a creature perfect in externals and careless of anything below the surface."

2. The name of an award conferred by the British trade magazine TAILOR & CUTTER.

"Daniel Boone"   The television series, broadcast from 1964 to 1969, in which actor Fess Parker famously wore the COONSKIN CAP that was part of his costume for the earlier DAVY CROCKETT.

dart   A method of shaping fabric, and one of the ways that Western tailoring differs from the flat-patterned or draped garments of the ancient or non-Western canon. Essentially, a dart is a seam and/or cut designed to remove fabric. Before being stitched, it often appears as a wedge or diamond shape on the flat pattern. However, after being sewn, it gives a rounded form to the fabric, making something that was once two-dimensional more three-dimensional. (An analogy might be the way cutting a circle of paper and then taping the cut turns it from a flat disk into a cone.)

In menswear, darts appear most often on tapered shirts, as seams extending down from the waistband of pants, or as vertical seams extending over the middle of the torso, where they are used to give shirts and jackets a waist indent.

dashiki   Initially identified with the radical chic of the 1960s, when the garment became a popular symbol of Black Pride (or solidarity with that movement), the word refers to a variety of loose-fitting tops derived from the menswear traditions of West Africa (e.g., Yoruba and Hausa). However, in the United States, the dashiki is most often identified as a colorful, pullover shirt—either hip-length for more informal wear or ankle-length for dressier occasions—with a decorated front neck opening. It is generally made of woven cotton or linen, has elbow-length sleeves, and a V-shaped notch cut into the center of the neck opening.

Daudet, Lucien   A *fin de siècle* French dandy once famed for an almost feminine refinement of person and today best remembered as a lover of Marcel Proust (who was provoked to fight a duel when accused of the affair). Son of the novelist Alphonse Daudet (author of *The Nabob*) and friend of Jean Cocteau, Lucien, who was born in 1883, graduated from the Academie Julian (the well-known art school), subsequently studied with James McNeil Whistler, and wrote a book called *Le Prince des Cravates*. However, his talents may have found their truest expression in his much-documented gesture of daring to wear a plum jacket ornamented by a BOUTONNIÈRE of Parma violets. He died in 1946.

Dave the Tailor   Although David K.C. Sheung was born in Taiwan in 1949, he primarily achieved fame as "Dave the Tailor" for his attempts to restore the pre-World War II reputation of SHANGHAI TAILORS as the world's best.

Born to a family that could not afford to keep him in school, at age 15, Dave was apprenticed to a Shanghai tailor who had fled to Taipei after the war. At age 27, he set up his own shop, eventually migrating to mainland China at the end of the 1990s and establishing a custom-tailoring shop in Shanghai, then another in Beijing. When his partner took the original Shanghai shop near the Portman Ritz-Carlton, Dave reestablished himself in Shanghai by buying a villa in the Xuhui District (off Wuyuan Road), a part of town still best known as the French Concession. His business became famous for its

Dashiki: Black Panther Eldridge Cleaver

unobtrusive, unexaggerated fit, excellent-quality cloth (imported from Italy and England), low prices, and a customer base concentrated among Western diplomats and businessmen.

Davidson, Charlie   Founder and proprietor of the Andover Shop in Andover and Cambridge, Massachusetts.

Davis, Miles   Born in 1926 in Alton, Illinois, to a well-off, sharply dressed dentist dad, Miles, and a mother, Cleona, who had her own wardrobe custom-made; Miles Dewey Davis III became best known as a jazz trumpeter and a clotheshorse who was constant only in his constant change of styles.

As a teenager, Davis used the money from his first gigs to buy suits at pawnshops and then make them over. By the time he left the Midwest to attend the Juilliard School, he was buying Brooks Brothers but, once in New York, soon switched to a bebop style. After a few years of that, he started buying the Ivy League look at the Andover Shop. Then came a sharp-edged Italian and continental silhouette. In 1960, he was named one of the best-dressed men in America by George Frazier's famous "The Art of Wearing Clothes" essay in Esquire. But by the time the article was published, he'd changed looks again. In the next three decades, he would go from one-buttons to Afrocentric dashikis to funk to Armani and Versace to Miyake to hip-hop.

As befit a performer who often turned his back to the audience, Davis often wore sunglasses—leaving his aviators on for the cover of "'Round About Midnight" in 1956. Famously vain about his appearance, he worked out even after suffering from diabetes, sickle cell anemia, arthritis, bursitis, a bleeding ulcer, a hernia, and multiple drug addictions. He died in 1991.

Davy Crockett   The sporadic miniseries in which 6-foot, 5-inch actor Fess Parker portrayed the "king of the wild frontier" on five episodes of *The Wonderful World of Disney* originally broadcast in 1954 and 1955. Because Crockett was costumed with a coonskin cap (complete with raccoon tail dangling down the back), the broadcast inspired a nationwide frenzy for little boys who wanted coonskin caps like their hero the "buckskin buccaneer." An estimated $1 million worth of coonskin caps were sold within one year and related crazes were created for buckskin, fringe, beaded belts, and Native American moccasins. (Parker later returned to television to portray another coonskin-capped, buckskin-wearing frontier hero in *Daniel Boone* from 1964 to 1969.)

dead stock   Unworn, "as new" apparel that is either out of production or out of fashion. For example, opening an old warehouse and finding boxes full of unsold jeans dating from the 1930s is a discovery of dead stock.

Dean, James   Born in 1931, the American actor identified with on-screen and off-screen adoption of anti-establishment, anti-fashion clothes like leather jackets, oversized greatcoats, jeans, and T-shirts. When he wore blue jeans as the angst-ridden antihero in 1955's *Rebel Without a Cause*, Dean lent them an anti-authoritarian glamour that they would enjoy for the next two decades, and helped to make them a quasi-official teen uniform. He died in 1955, but the James Dean estate later licensed

Miles Davis

his name and image for apparel—including jeans and leather jackets.

deck pants   Slang for a style of sporty pants cropped to mid-calf; used in the third quarter of the 20th century. Synonym: CLAMDIGGERS.

deck shoes   Shoes with a flat rubber sole, with a SIPED design to maintain traction on slippery wood and not leave scuff marks on the deck (e.g., TOP-SIDERS).

Early deck shoes tended to be modeled after street shoes, except that they had canvas or duck uppers and dark-colored rubber soles.

deco   Short for DECORATION. Industry jargon, especially for suit fabric, used to refer to pinstripes, checks, etc.

deconstructed   May refer to garments purposely made without certain standard construction elements of conventional, fully tailored clothing (such as lining or interfacing); or, used in the more fashionable sense, may refer to tailored pieces that are purposely made to look unfinished or finished and then taken apart again (e.g., with visible seams, ragged edges, hanging threads).

During the late 20th century the term became a popular way to describe the type of lightweight tailoring pioneered by GIORGIO ARMANI in the late 1970s and early 1980s (which would be more accurately described as

UNCONSTRUCTED, since it was conceived without the additional materials). In the early 1990s, the term was used to describe the much more radically and visibly unfinished clothes from the Belgian designers who were part of a movement called the ANTWERP SIX.

decoration   1. Industry jargon for the pattern (usually woven as opposed to printed), on cloth. Most often used to refer to stripes or checks in suit materials. Sometimes abbreviated to DECO. For example: Navy wool with a beige PINSTRIPE might be described as "navy cloth with beige deco." 2. General reference to a medal, award, badge, or similar honor.

deely-boppers   Novelty headbands, worn for parties or celebrations, that usually boast a pair of spring-mounted eyeballs—or some other equally cartoonish item—sprouting from the head like antennae.

deerstalker   The sporting style of cap made famous by its association with Sir Arthur Conan Doyle's fictional detective SHERLOCK HOLMES (who is never mentioned as wearing one in the books). Made of cloth, usually a heavy tweed, the deerstalker is a soft cap that completely covers the head, has short symmetrical visors in both the front and back, and long ear flaps that are usually kept tied above the head.

As one might guess, the deerstalker was popular among deer hunters in the 19th century. Originally, it would have been worn with a NORFOLK JACKET and/or other shooting clothes and heavy tweeds. Its association with Sherlock Holmes began when

Deely-boppers

the stories' original illustrator, Sidney Paget (himself a wearer), added it to his depictions of the detective.

Dege & Skinner   The London tailoring firm best known as a specialist in BESPOKE military dress. Founded by German immigrant Jacob Dege in 1865, the firm employed various members of the Skinner family in various capacities through the 19th and 20th centuries before being officially renamed in 2000.

denier   A way of measuring the weight of a YARN; meant to convey the density of textiles. The higher the denier number, the heavier the yarn. For example, yarn used to make pants or jackets might be 150 denier, a T-shirt might be 60, and a MICROFIBER might be less than one.

denim   1. A sturdy, TWILL fabric, most often made of COTTON, with an indigo warp and an uncolored (i.e., natural, off-white) fill; most often the material of BLUE JEANS. Most historians trace the fabric to the workmen's cloth, produced primarily for sailors, in the city of Nimes in southern France (hence *de Nimes* = denim), although similar fabrics were also woven in Italy. According to LEVI STRAUSS, the first identifiable jeans model, the "XX" made in 1873, was made of 9-ounce, XX (an indicator of

Deerstalker: Basil Rathbone in *The Adventures of Sherlock Holmes*

quality) blue denim sourced from the Amoskeag Mill in Manchester, New Hampshire.

In contemporary use, denim is woven from cotton or cotton-blend yarn that is either RINGSPUN or OPEN-END (each being favored according to the denim fashion of the time) on a huge power loom. Denim that is produced on the older, shuttle loom is narrower and referred to as SELVEDGE DENIM. The most common twill is a three-over-one construction, following a right-hand twill line and using Z-TWIST yarn—a combination of right-hand twill plus Z-twist that enhances the strength of the fabric. In contemporary use, most denim is produced in weights between 5 and 16 ounces, with most jeans falling in the 10 to 12 ounce range.

2. Jargon for the JEANS market.

de Paris, Georges   Born in 1934 in France, de Paris immigrated from Marseilles in 1960 and became a personal tailor to every American president from Lyndon B. Johnson through George W. Bush, as well as various cabinet members. Noted for his short stature, thick white hair, and habit of wearing a suit and tie at all times, de Paris maintained a shop near the White House, which sold both readymade and custom clothing.

derby   1. American reference to the BOWLER hat, a name derived from that style's popularity with the late 19th-century crowds at Epsom Downs, the racecourse where the Derby Stakes originated.   2. Jargon for a basic style of laced shoe. The derby differs from the OXFORD in two important ways: It has an "open-lacing" system, which means that the quarters are on top of the shoe's vamp—making it easier to adjust the width of the shoe; and the tongue, which lies underneath the lacing, is simply an extension of the vamp (rather than a separate piece). The style and construction known as the BLUCHER is a variation of the derby. See SHOE diagram.

desert boots Synonym for an ankle-high, suede CHUKKA BOOT. Spelled with capital letters, Desert Boot refers to the popular style of chukka boot manufactured by Clarks of England (which is simply constructed from two pieces of suede fastened with a two-eyelet lacing system). In lowercase, it is often used to refer to that general style of footwear—whether manufactured by Clarks or other companies.

Designers Collective The pre-1998 name of the twice-a-year trade show for men's clothes, shoes, jewelry, and related items; subsequently called THE COLLECTIVE.

detachable collars Invented as a laborsaving device (in what is variously reported as 1825 or 1827) by Mrs. Hannah Lord Montague of TROY, NEW YORK, who was tired of constantly laundering and replacing shirts for her husband Orlando, a blacksmith, who supposedly demanded a clean white shirt to wear each night when his day's work was done. According to legend, Mrs. Montague observed that only the shirts' collars were dirty and thereupon decided to cut them off, bind the edges, and rig a reattachment so that, thereafter, she would only have to launder collars.

Although Mrs. Montague's invention was commercially manufactured soon after and Troy subsequently earned the title of "Collar City," becoming known as the world capital of the men's dress shirt and detachable collar business, it took decades before the new detachable collars supplanted the shirt status quo. Part of a general societal trend toward readymade apparel, detachable collars really took off in 1889, when local manufacturer Cluett Peabody instituted its ARROW brand, which it advertised with illustrator J.C. LEYENDECKER's famous

Derby

ARROW COLLAR MAN in a campaign that lasted from 1905 to 1930.

By World War I, the fashion had become ubiquitous. But by the following decade, as women's wear began to bypass the corset and the floorsweeping skirt, menswear began to bypass the stiff collar, and detachable collars became associated mainly with FORMALWEAR. Arrow, the best-known manufacturer, finally phased itself out of the collar business in 1937.

Devore, Sy Born Seymour Devoretsky in Brooklyn in 1907, Sy Devore became best known as court clothier to FRANK SINATRA and other members of the RAT PACK during the late 1950s and early 1960s. But the man who gave himself the sobriquet "tailor to the stars" also dressed Desi Arnaz, Milton Berle, Nat King Cole, Tony Curtis, Jimmy Durante, Bob Hope, Rock Hudson, Sidney Poitier, and ELVIS PRESLEY, contributed menswear to his clients' movies and TV shows, and managed to make his main shop, near the Brown Derby restaurant in Hollywood, into an early 1960s tourist attraction.

After working for his father, a Russian immigrant who also ran a tailoring shop with a show biz clientele during the 1920s, Devore opened his own establishment in Manhattan in 1930. Moving to Los Angeles during World War II, he opened a store in the heart of Hollywood on Vine Street near Sunset Boulevard. A high-liver who loved throwing parties as much as attending them, Devore opened the nightclub (rumored to have mob connections) called Slapsie Maxie's in 1946, and although it was soon defunct, managed to keep many of its performers as permanent clients.

During the 1950s, Devore began evolving what became known as the Rat Pack look: a suit made of SHARKSKIN or some other sharp, slightly shiny fabric (preferably with some MOHAIR mixed into the wool), squared shoulders, square shoulders, narrow lapels, and plain-front pants with no cuffs. He also sold accessories, shirts, off-the-rack suits and did a great business in V-necks and other pullovers, especially in alpaca. (According to legend, Ella Fitzgerald once went into Devore's and ordered enough pricey sweaters to give as Christmas presents to her entire band.) Through his high-profile, often-copied clientele, Devore established an American style that owed little or nothing to English tailoring or other traditional models.

During the Rat Pack's ascendancy, when he charged upwards of $250 for a suit and reputedly grossed over $1 million a year, Devore opened branches in their stamping grounds, such as Palm Springs, the Sands Hotel in Las Vegas, and Sherman Oaks. After his death in 1966, the business continued to operate but the original Vine Street store closed in 1969. By the beginning of the 21st century, the sole outpost, run by his niece, was located in Studio City.

D&G   A slightly sportier, less expensive line from Dolce & Gabbana , the Italian design duo of Domenico Dolce and Stefano Gabbana.

dhoti   Traditional to India, where a khadi dhoti was famously worn by Mahatma Gandhi as a symbol of the swadeshi movement, the dhoti is a single piece of unseamed cloth loosely wrapped around a man's waist and between his legs. Its use is ancient and, like the sari worn by women, there are many ways of draping, folding, and tying it.

diamond   Jargon for a textile pattern, usually on a tweed; the herringbone, instead of forming the usual zigzag, reverses on itself, forming diamond patterns in the cloth.

diapered *or* **diaper pattern**   Nothing to do with baby nappies. Refers to a category of prints that are small, tightly patterned geometrics—most often in some sort of diamond pattern. More generically, diaper prints would be called geometrics or "geos."

diced   A way of describing a pattern of alternating solid checks, as on a checkerboard or chess board.

dickey *or* **dickie**   1. A small piece of apparel, usually just enough to fill in the neckline of a sweater or jacket, meant to give the illusion that a turtleneck or full shirt is being worn.   2. A removable shirtfront, especially on stiffened, bib front dress shirt.

Diddy, P.   See Combs, Sean.

dimple   The name given to the indentation formed just below the knot of a correctly knotted necktie. By tradition, the dimple should be deep and dead center. Steps to ensure that the dimple forms:
- Tightening the knot by pulling on the front apron of the tie; a loose knot will not dimple
- Pinching the tie where it's expected to dimple to encourage the indentation
- Tugging on the bottom apron of the tie while simultaneously pinching the front to help keep the indentation in place

Dinka corset   A distinctive style of beaded corset, worn for ornament rather than restraint, by the Dinka men, herders of the southern Sudan. Formed by rows of beading and edged with a fur skirt, the corset covers—but does not conceal—virtually the entire trunk and celebrates the small waist and tapering torso of the adult male.

Dhoti: Mahatma Gandhi

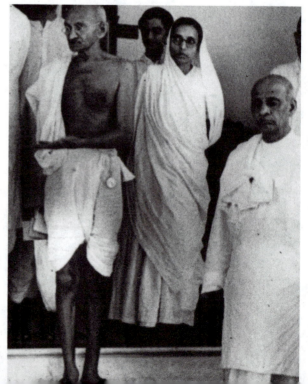

dinner jacket   1. Used as a synonym for TUXEDO.   2. A separate, tail-less jacket, worn in the context of a tuxedo but made in a material unmatched to the trousers. For instance, in summer, a man may wear a white jacket of lighter material as his dinner jacket—although he will likely follow all other tuxedo conventions, especially the black bow tie.

Dior Homme   The Christian Dior line that became the most conspicuously chic collection in men's fashion for a few years beginning in 2001, when celebrated designer HEDI SLIMANE, the former YVES SAINT LAURENT menswear designer, who was then at the height of his fame, switched to Dior. In 2007, designed duties devolved to Kris Van Assche.

dips   Jargon used to describe the DENIM produced for JEANS; a dip is the immersion in dye. The higher the number, the more expensive and labor-intensive the process and the more saturated and controlled the dye. Usually the mere presence of a dip number in the fabric's description—e.g., "15-dip denim"—is intended to connote artisanal production.

dirty denim   Denim that has been made to look worn and soiled, usually by some process of overdyeing. Popular for jeans in the early 21st century.

disposable collars   Collars, usually composed partially or completely of paper, designed to be thrown away when dirty. A process binding a cotton to paper was patented for the purpose of making collars in 1864 by George Snow, founder of the Melrose, Massachusetts-based Gibson Lee company, when, according to legend, he encountered a shortage of appropriate collar fabric during the Civil War.

Disposable collars were mostly used as a cheap and convenient variation of DETACHABLE COLLARS, and enjoyed roughly the same heyday: from the time of the Civil War until the end of the 1920s. Afterward, they were produced mainly for clerical collars, military full-dress uniform, or evening dress.

distressing   Purposely abrading, bleaching, tearing, or otherwise stressing fabric to give it a prematurely aged appearance after it has been woven but before it has been worn.

ditto   A suit in which all components (usually vest, pants, and jacket) are made from the same material. The term was most popular in the 18th and 19th centuries, when the fabrics of suit components more often complemented or contrasted.

ditty bag   Usually refers to a small bag used by servicemen to carry small personal items like grooming aids, toiletries, or a sewing kit.

diving watch   Refers to a style of oversized, exaggeratedly utilitarian wristwatch, often worn on a rubber wristband. The face of a diving watch is purposely overstated so that it can be read underwater, and the crystal is bulbous rather than slim. At the beginning of the 21st century, it became fashionable to wearing diving-type watches (e.g., those made by PANERAI) to accessorize tailored clothing.

djellaba   A long, loose robe, distinguished by its usable hood and long, full sleeves; associated primarily with Morocco. The garment's cut, length, and decoration vary according to region and the occupation of the wearer. It differs from a CAFTAN by the attachment of a hood.

DNR   *The Daily News Record*, a New York-based trade publication about the menswear industry founded by Fairchild Publications in 1892. A precursor to *Women's Wear Daily*, it is published by the same company, shares facilities, and, for many years, shared a similar format: a black-and-white tabloid newspaper published daily Monday through Friday. In 1997, it switched to three-times-a-week frequency. In 2001, it became a large-format color weekly. Industry veterans tend to preface the name with an article, referring to it as "*The* DNR."

dobby   Refers to cloth, most often for shirts, made with a small, recurring pattern due to a special type of weaving (executed on a dobby loom). A dobby is usually a small, highly stylized and/or geometric pattern that is added to give interest but not predominate the fabric. Its plural is "dobbies."

Dockers   Launched by Levi Strauss & Co. in 1986, this brand borrowed its name from a 1984 line of jeans with nautical styling that originated in Levi Strauss Argentina. The Japanese division of the company liked the name enough to borrow it for a line of casual pants done for the Asian market. The "Dockers" name then made it back to the United States, where it was applied to high-waisted, cotton twill khaki pants with a wing-and-anchor logo that read "since 1850" and implied that the pants were long the choice of longshoremen.

By 1988, the brand had expanded to include shirts, women's wear, and children's wear. In 1991, it became immortalized in an episode of *Seinfield*, and, in 1998, an episode of *The Simpsons*. From 1995 to 2005, the brand was advertised with the "Nice Pants" tagline.

Doc Martens   Officially spelled as Dr. Martens, the brand began on April Fool's Day, 1960, with workboots and went on to become identified with goths, punks, skinheads, and a variety of other anti-fashion, anti-establishment types. Its origins date to 1945 when German doctor Klaus Maertens injured his foot in a skiing accident and improvised footwear with a thick, cushioned sole made from old tires. Together with his friend Herbert Funck, they began a business called Dr. Maertens in 1959 and had their footwear manufactured in Wollaston, England, anglicizing the company name to Dr. Martens.

The company's first and still best-known model was the "1460," an ankle-high, eight-eyelet style with black leather, loud yellow stitching, steel-reinforced toe boxes, and the trademarked, wavy-edged Air-Wair soles. Synonym: bovver boots.

DNR

doctor's gown (academic) As regulated by the Intercollegiate Bureau of Academic Costume in the United States, the ACADEMIC DRESS appropriate for a doctoral degree candidate or graduate is a long, full gown, falling in an unbelted, straight line, with a wide strip of velvet running down its front and around its collar. It also has long, bell-shaped sleeves, which have three bars of velvet apiece. In the back, it sports a 4-foot-long hood lined with the colors of the institution granting the degree and edged with 5 inches of the color corresponding to the area of study.

Although black is still the most popular color for the body of the gown, doctoral robes seem to invite more liberties of design and represent more departures from the prescribed standard. For instance: Harvard uses a crimson gown with black velvet trim; the University of Chicago uses maroon with black velvet; and Yale uses blue.

dogs' ears A late-18th- and early-19th-century hairstyle in which the hair is worn long in the front and arranged so that it falls forward on either side of the face like the ears of a hound; particularly associated with the MUSCADINS of the Directoire period in France, although also adopted by the young Napoleon Bonaparte, their political antithesis.

dogskin A light leather made from dogs, popular for gloves in the 18th and 19th centuries.

dogtooth *or* **dogstooth** A synonym, usually British, for HOUNDSTOOTH check.

doeskin A woven fabric with a soft, slightly napped finish that gives it a matte appearance and a passing resemblance to soft leather. Usually slightly lighter in weight and made of finer weave than MOLESKIN, but otherwise similar in surface effect.

Dolce & Gabbana The Italian design duo of Domenico Dolce (the shorter, balding partner, born in Palermo in 1958) and Stefano Gabbana (the taller, rangier partner, born in Venice in 1962). The two met in 1980, worked in the garment industry in Milan, and then launched their own business in 1982.

Initially famous for women's wear capitalizing on sexy, Sicilian-widow styles and leopard prints, they began designing for men in 1990 and won a WOOLMARK AWARD for their menswear in 1991. Initial collections played on the Sicilian gangster prototypes—"We're Sicilian first and Italian second," Dolce has repeatedly told the press—then, in 1993, their runway designs spearheaded the revival of the rich HIPPIE look.

Fervid believers in soccer players as the modern epitome of male style, they signed an agreement in 2004 to design uniforms for A.C. Milan and then designed formal uniforms for the Italian national squad at the 2006 World Cup.

domino Derived from the Latin word for "lord" frequently used in Catholic prayer, the domino was originally a garment with a large hood worn by monks. Later the term was applied to hooded cloaks worn by both men and women and, finally, became associated with a form of disguise at masked balls, particularly in Venice.

Stefano Gabbana and Domenico Dolce

Donegal   A type of medium-weight or heavyweight TWEED woven from yarn with colored SLUBS. Originally, the term referred to cloth of that appearance made in the county of Donegal in Ireland, then to British weaving that was shipped to Donegal for finishing. Now the term is used generically. When a yarn, sweater, or other knit is described as Donegal, it indicates that it is produced from a roughly spun, nonlustrous yarn with colored slubs.

dopp kit   A small bag containing a man's shaving accessories and other toiletries, which originated in the early 20th century. Although Dopp is a trademarked name, it has been used generically for decades, especially since World War II, when soldiers used "dopp kits."

D'Orsay, Count Alfred   Born in France in 1801, Alfred Guillaume Gabriel D'Orsay inherited BEAU BRUMMELL's mantle as England's arbiter of elegance. Where Brummell espoused austerity, D'Orsay espoused opulence. When Brummell preferred quietly perfect private gatherings, D'Orsay was an outgoing creature who shone brightest in wide society. D'Orsay has been called the first modern celebrity, fodder for the tabloid press of his time.

Despite his title, D'Orsay's family line had more of the grand bourgeois than the ancient aristocrat. The son of one of Napoleon's generals, D'Orsay spent most of his time in London from 1821 onward, where he was a member of Crockford's and lived with Marguerite, Countess of Blessington, who was 12 years older and supposedly turned to novel writing after her husband's death in order to support D'Orsay, who was rumored to be the lover of her husband and was officially the husband of her step-daughter (having married Lady Harriet when Lord Blessington's daughter was aged 15 and then apparently never consummated the marriage).

A gambler, an expert horseman, a fine fencer, and an accomplished amateur artist, D'Orsay counted Lord Byron, Charles Dickens (who named a child after him), Benjamin Disraeli, and Alfred Lord Tennyson among his many friends. Thomas Carlyle called him the "Phoebus Apollo of dandyism," and his social and sartorial influence peaked during the 1830s and early 1840s.

An athletically built 6 feet, 3 inches, D'Orsay enhanced his height by wearing long, straight, skintight trousers; huge lapels; and a very high top hat. Often credited with the invention—or at least the popularization—of the PALETÔT, the silhouettes of his clothes (made by tailor HENRY CREED, among others) were more curvaceous than Brummell's and their materials more luxurious. His CRAVAT was apt to be glossy black or sky-blue satin, his colorful WAISTCOAT of similarly splendid stuff, and the long watch of massy yellow gold. His hair was auburn and as lushly curled as his whiskers. (His whiskers are, in fact, credited for inspiring the multitude of beards, mustaches, and sidewhiskers that infected the remainder of the 19th century.)

In 1849, he and Lady Blessington fled to Paris to escape creditors. She died soon after. D'Orsay died in

Count Alfred D'Orsay

1852 and is buried beside her in France. The subject of numerous biographies (e.g., *Last of the Dandies* by Nick Foulkes in 2005), a caricature of his type now appears annually on the cover of *The New Yorker* as Eustace Tilley, the dandy peering through his QUIZZING GLASS at a butterfly.

double-besomed   See BESOM.

double-breasted   Refers to a suit jacket or coat with double vertical rows of buttons that roughly align with the nipples of the body beneath; the style always crosses left over right (buttons on the left-hand side are vestigial—present for symmetry only), and the overlapping material is usually secured on the inside of the garment by means of a flat, unseen button known as a JIGGER, which ensures that the front hem hangs in a straight, even line. When used on a suit jacket or blazer, the style is customarily limited to either six matching front buttons (two rows of three each) or four buttons (two rows of two each). On TOPCOATS and the like, a greater number may be employed. The style with a single row of buttons and no overlapping fabric in front is known as SINGLE-BREASTED.

Tradition long dictated that double-breasted suit jackets and blazers be augmented by PEAK LAPELS. Likewise, traditionalists decreed that on a six-button model, only the middle right button be fastened, although on a four-button model, only the top right button or both may be used.

double cuff   Used as a synonym for a FRENCH CUFF.

double-faced   Any cloth (usually a woven) designed to have two "right" sides and no "wrong" side. In menswear the term is used most often to describe jacket fabric that has a different color or pattern on each side.

double-soled   Refers to a shoe constructed to have both an OUTSOLE (the bottom part that comes in contact with the ground) and a MIDSOLE for additional support (which is not visible—either from the inside or outside—when the shoe is being worn). Most contemporary dress shoes are double-soled.

double stripes   Exactly what it sounds like: a pattern of two PINSTRIPES, PENCIL STRIPES, or other narrow stripes in proximity. Usually refers to shirt fabrics.

doublet   Refers to the short, usually padded, garment covering the upper torso; worn by Western European men of nobility or substance during the 15th and 16th centuries. Its name supposedly derives from the "doubling" of material that characterized its construction: an inner fabric and outer fabric sandwiching the padding in between. Depending on the time and place, the padding might be engineered to enhance the man's shoulders, his belly (e.g., the PEASCOD doublet), or his chest. Sleeves were often attached separately, rather than sewn to the body of the garment.

Doucet Jeune   A menswear establishment on the rue Halévy in Paris, popular in the last quarter of the 19th century (when it also had branches in Britain and the United States), which specialized in shirts and FURNISHINGS and enjoyed much the same status that its competitor CHARVET would continue to enjoy 100 years later. Although it is often confused with the couturier Jacques Doucet, it was an unrelated business owned by a different branch of his family.

douppioni   A woven SILK with an irregular appearance incorporating long, narrow SLUBS (or a blend woven to imitate it). In menswear, it is identified with Italian suits. Also spelled doupioni or dupioni.

drag 1. The practice of men dressing as women, as in "drag queens" or "drag balls." 2. Slang for an outfit or style of clothes, especially a uniform. As in: "He put on his business suit and left the house in full work drag."

dragon robe A generic Western reference to the figured, full-length, long-sleeved robes worn as symbols of the status of the imperial Chinese Dragon Throne, especially those made during the Qing dynasty (1644 to 1911). The most elaborate and best-constructed robes were woven for the emperor, important members of his clan, and those upon whom the Son of Heaven bestowed special honor: These featured five-clawed dragons against background colors decreed by ceremony and season. Similar robes featuring four-clawed dragons could be worn by lesser relatives, officials, and members of court. Some dragon robes were also produced for a Western market as a sort of pricey souvenir of China.

Symbols on the robe were placed very specifically. The neck opening corresponded to the gate of heaven because the material world was represented by the material of the robe and the spiritual world was represented by the wearer's head. All symbols on the robe—especially on a formal, imperial robe—therefore had to be aligned in harmony with the gate of heaven, especially the 12 imperial symbols, some of which dated to the Zhou dynasty (1050 BC to 221 BC):

Axe = The power to punish. Because it can cut and sever, it symbolized the decisiveness of the good emperor in difficult situations.

Constellation = The stars—together with the other imperial symbols of the sun and moon—were symbols of enlightenment, heaven, and the universe. Usually depicted as three dots connected by lines.

Cups = Filial piety. One cup usually depicts a tiger (physical strength), while the other cup has a monkey with a long tail (cleverness).

Dragon = Yang (the male principle). A dragon changed infinitely thus symbolizing the adaptability of the good emperor. Four dragons radiated from the neck opening.

Fire = Intellectual brilliance. Because it melts metal and cooks, it symbolized the renewal of the emperor's virtue.

Fu = The power to judge.

Grain = Grain, depicted as millet, is the mainstay of life, just as the emperor is the mainstay of all things.

Moon = Yin (the female principle). The universe. Usually depicted with a hare (who is pounding the elixir of immortality) on a light blue or green disk.

Mountain = Earth. Stability. A mountain disperses clouds and rain and is therefore a symbol of the emperor's beneficence.

Pheasant = Literary refinement.

Sun = Yang (the male principle) balancing the Yin of the moon. Heaven. Intellectual enlightenment.

Waterweed = Water. Purity. Because it rises and falls with the water, it symbolizes the emperor's response to the needs of his people.

These 12 imperial symbols were arranged in concentric rings around the neck in order of importance. In the first ring, the sun and moon appeared on the shoulders, the constellation and mountain at the chest and back. In the second ring, at waist level: the fu and the axe in front, the dragon and pheasant in back. In the third ring, at knee level: the waterweed, ceremonial cups, flame, grain. The background was an overall pattern of stylized clouds, representing peace and good fortune. (By an 18th-century decree, the clouds on imperial robes were multicolored as an auspicious sign.) At the hem were diagonal bands and rounded billows symbolizing the waves of the universal ocean surrounding the earth.

Throughout the Qing dynasty, the emperor's dragon robes were produced by the royal factories as SUMPTUARY LAWS had ordered in, variously, 1652, 1748, and 1759. Nevertheless, an imperial robe from the end of the 19th century looked very different from one made in the 18th century. As the Western world literally began beating down the doors of the Forbidden City, the dragons' grace gradually disappeared. Meanwhile, more symbols than ever were piled on. Manchus had initially avoided figural imagery except for the ancient imperial emblems, but then the likes of bats and swastikas and peaches appeared alongside other symbols of luck and longevity. The twelve imperial emblems no longer seemed to be enough for the emperor: By the end of imperial production, it looked as if the Son of Heaven and his court needed all the luck they could get from any place they could get it.

drainpipes   Skinny, unpleated, straight-legged pants that are neither flared nor nipped at the ankle. Associated with TEDDY BOYS and 1950s fashion.

drape   Refers to a style of tailoring that originated in the 20th century in England, in which the body of the jacket relies on judicious draping of fabric rather than on padding and heavy CANVAS CONSTRUCTION. The drape has a strong shoulder line and is generally considered to be lighter and less stiff than alternative styles of tailoring.

Most costume historians trace the style to FREDERICK SCHOLTE, who, for four decades, was tailor to EDWARD VIII from his days as Prince of Wales through his days as the Duke of Windsor. Many also say the style arose in response to the reshaped physique of that era's clientele: men who returned from World War I with larger shoulders and leaner torsos than their Edwardian forefathers.

On SAVILE ROW, the firm most often associated with the style is ANDERSON & SHEPPARD, who famously created draped tailoring for clients such as FRED ASTAIRE. The construction is, in any case, highly suited to wool and highly unsuited to silk or the stiff materials then associated with Italian tailoring.

In America, the style became exaggerated and associated with big shoulders and a bulky chest; at its extreme, unrecognizable to Scholte, it eventually became the ZOOT SUIT, which boasted of its "drape shape." Synonym: ENGLISH DRAPE.

draper   Someone who sells textiles or apparel; unrelated to either the ENGLISH DRAPE or DRAPES. Never used to describe a tailor or tailoring firm.

drapes   A synonym, particularly in the 1930s, for the exaggerated drape of the style later and better known as the ZOOT SUIT.

drawers   Slightly old-fashioned slang reference to underpants—hence the expression "hold your drawers!" as a caution to someone who is rushing or getting overexcited.

drawstrings   Pants that close by means of a drawstring waistband, rather than a FLY or FALL; pulled on over the hips, the garment becomes easily adjustable and therefore the construction is associated with pajamas, and similarly informal and untailored apparel such as ACTIVEWEAR and beach wear.

dreadlocks   Refers to a hairstyle in which the hair is twisted—or "locked"—into purposely matted hanks, which resemble rope or felted fiber (as opposed to being combed, cut, or braided). Although the style itself is ancient, the term "dreadlocks" originated in Jamaica with the Rastafarian culture in the 20th century, and thereafter was frequently shortened to "dreads," especially after the style became fashionable in the United States during the late 20th century. Synonyms: dreads; locks.

dress-down days   A practice—most familiar from the designation of DRESS-DOWN FRIDAYS—extended to a specific day or for a specific period.

dress-down Fridays   A dress code initiated in offices and schools during the last quarter of the 20th century. On Fridays, men were allowed to "dress down" and wear more informal clothes to work instead of SUITS and NECKTIES (although many firms continued to forbid the wearing of JEANS). Also called "casual Fridays."

Dress for Success   The best-selling book by image consultant John T. Molloy; first published by Warner Books in 1975.

Aiming at men in the corporate work world and writing in a tone that brooked no argument, Molloy reduced the vagaries of fashion to a series of formulas, such as: "If your principal business associates are over 45 years old, or if you must deal frequently with people from the lower middle class (say you are a banker or a lawyer), never wear pink or pale lavender shirts, which have negative masculine associations."

His book also provided a system for shopping, explained the basics of business attire (complete with diagrams on shirt stripes and how to knot a necktie), and set forth rules on the wearing of jewelry (less is more) and the correct color for raincoats (beige). Molloy's work, which was subsequently issued in paperback, inspired countless imitators. Molloy himself later did spinoffs aimed at women, and an update for men, issued in 1988.

dressing gown   A front-closing gown or robe worn at home for undress; usually a wrap style with sash tie, similar in silhouette to the BATHROBE. Classically worn over pajamas, the dressing gown may be slightly more formal (and more presentable to non-family members) and, in contemporary use, is often more tailored and made of finer material such as silk. The garment evolved from relatively tailored in the 19th century to less structured and

Dreadlocks: Bob Marley

lighter in weight during the 20th century. In contemporary use, referred to simply as a "robe."

dressing to the left *or* **dressing to the right**   Trade jargon for the direction—left or right—that the genitalia fall inside a pair of pants. The pants on bespoke suits in particular are made to accommodate a client's preference.

dress shirt   1. In American usage, the term refers to the style of SHIRT traditionally worn with a NECKTIE and BUSINESS SUIT (and is used in much the same context as the term DRESS SHOE). In contemporary practice, the typical dress shirt has a FOLD-OVER COLLAR, SET-IN SLEEVES that are more often long than short, and a fully buttoning front made with a PLACKET construction. Its traditional materials are lightweight wovens, such as fine COTTON and SILK, and, although fashions for patterned fabrics come and go, it is most often a solid color, a DOBBY, or a vertical stripe. In addition, pricey or custom shirts, such as though made by JERMYN STREET shirtmakers, may feature a SPLIT YOKE construction in the back, as well as a small GUSSET on the side seam, which unites the front and back SHIRTTAILS.

During much of the 20th century, the dress shirt was similar to the SPORT SHIRT in construction, but remained markedly different in appearance. For example: Dress shirts tended to have lighter, finer materials in lighter colors, while sport shirts were made of MADRAS or patterned FLANNEL; dress shirts were often starched while sport shirts were softer and more casual; dress shirts more often made use of COLLAR STAYS, featured finer stitching, MOTHER-OF-PEARL buttons, and sleeve details like FRENCH CUFFS and GAUNTLET BUTTONS. By the 21st century, the categories became more blurred, as sport shirts were worn in increasingly dressier contexts and dress shirts were worn with JEANS.

However, one telling difference remained: Sizing. Dress shirts are more specifically sized, with a neck size given in half-inch increments, often followed by a sleeve length given in inches. (Dress shirts that are marked "tall" customarily add an extra inch to the sleeve length.) Sport shirts are sized more generically: small, medium, large, etc.

dress shirt sizes	sport shirt sizes
14 neck, 32 sleeve	small
14½ neck, 33 sleeve	small
15 neck, 33 sleeve	medium
15½ neck, 34 sleeve	medium
16 neck, 34 sleeve	large
16½ neck, 35 sleeve	large
17 neck, 35 sleeve	extra large
17½ neck, 35 sleeve	extra large

2. In British usage, the term dress shirt usually implies that the shirt is worn with SEMI-FORMAL or FORMALWEAR.

dress shoes   Shoes considered appropriate for wear with a BUSINESS SUIT and tie. (Not, as the phrase might imply, shoes reserved for formal occasions.) Traditionally made of a medium or dark shade of leather and more structured than casual shoes. LACE-UPS and even MONKSTRAPS are considered dress shoes; SNEAKERS and MOCCASINS are not. For construction, see SHOE diagram.

dress sword   Refers to a sword worn as part of formal military and diplomatic dress for ceremonial occasions, for example: the ceremonial épée accorded to writers who are members of the Académie française.

drill   A densely woven cloth prized for its sturdiness and cheapness and, therefore, often a component of

WORKWEAR; usually made from coarsely spun cotton, or a cotton blend.

driving gloves   GLOVES worn to enhance the grip on a steering wheel, not for warmth or protection. Driving gloves are usually made of flexible, lightweight leather, do not cover the wrist, are worn tight, and are frequently fingerless. They may also have holes placed over the knuckles (to facilitate grip) and usually close with a snap fastening.

driving moccasins *or* **driving mocs**   Light, usually slip-on, MOCCASIN-style footwear; instead of a solid sole, the leather is studded with rubber nubs on the bottom to enhance traction on pedals; the rubber pad or nubs extend also up the back of the heel to cushion the heel while it is propped against the accelerator.

drop   The difference between the CHEST measurement and WAIST measurement. Most American suits are made with a 6-inch drop, patterned on a 40-inch chest and 34-inch waist, although lines aimed at younger men may have a 7-inch drop.

drop front   A broad reference to pants made with a front flap or FALLS (as opposed to being made with a FLY. Traditional sailor's pants, for example, have a drop front. Traditional blue jeans do not.

drop seat   A flap or fall at the back over the buttocks; traditionally associated with union suits and added to facilitate toilet visits. Slang synonym: trap door.

drummer   In British tailors' slang, someone who makes TROUSERS, not jackets.

dry cleaning   A cleaning method using solvents; an invention usually attributed to either Thomas Jennings,

an American slave who patented a similar process in 1821, or to a Monsieur Jolly Bellin, a Parisian who opened a dry-cleaning business in 1825. The "dry" in dry cleaning is misleading, since it refers to cleaning without water—but not without liquids. During the first century after its invention, dry cleaning was thought to wear out clothes and was conscientiously avoided by valets and others charged with the care of fine menswear.

dry shaver   An ELECTRIC or battery-powered shaver. The first commercial model was patented and produced by JACOB SCHICK.

DTI   Abbreviation of DuPONT Textiles & Interiors, which renamed itself INVISTA in 2003, and manufactures brands including LYCRA, COOLMAX, Stainmaster, and Teflon.

duck   A sturdy, plain-woven fabric, invariably made of cotton or a blend that resembles it; sometimes used as a synonym for cotton canvas. Favored for workwear and industrial uses (most tarpaulins and sails, for example, are made of duck), the term supposedly originated in the 19th century when the imprint of a duck indicated the weight of certain sailcloths.

duck-bill cap   A hat that resembles a BASEBALL CAP, except that it has a longer and narrower BILL. Usually associated with hunting or other informal, outdoor activities. (Although it may be made of canvas, the "duck" refers to the shape of the bill, not to the fabric.)

duck boots   Usually a reference, especially in PREPPY parlance, to the rubber-bottom, leather-upper MAINE HUNTING SHOE invented by L.L.BEAN in 1911 (or to footwear made to resemble it).

duck's ass   Slang for a style in which the hair was grown long and combed back to form a ridge above the spine, so that it looked like the ridge of feathers on the rear of a duck; almost always worn in conjunction with hair that was poufed into a POMPADOUR in front. Maintenance of a perfect ridge required careful creasing with a comb and plenty of POMADE or similarly greasy hair product. Associated with GREASERS, PACHUCOS, ROCKERS, TEDDY BOYS, ZOOT SUITERS, and imitators of early ELVIS PRESLEY. Synonym: ducktail.

duende A term popularized by Boston newspaper columnist GEORGE FRAZIER, who first used it in 1963. Frazier, who also wrote the "Elements of Style" column for *ESQUIRE* magazine, used the Andalusian word to indicate an inborn amalgam of charisma, nonchalance, and élan, freely attributing it to his favorite persons, places, and things: FRED ASTAIRE, for example, had duende. As Frazier once wrote "Duende is so difficult to define, yet when it is there, it is unmistakable, inspiring our awe, quickening our memory . . ."

According to Frazier's biographer Charles Fountain (in 1984's *Another Man's Poison*), Frazier himself borrowed the term from a Kenneth Tynan article about MILES DAVIS.

duffel 1. A type of coarse, heavy fabric, originally associated by the region of that name in Belgium, near Antwerp. Today, the fabric is more commonly called duffel, while the coat associated with it is more commonly spelled duffle. 2. Slang for a DUFFEL or DUFFLE COAT.

duffle coat Refers to a style of sporty, single-breasted overcoat originally made from a single layer of coarse, heavy wool known as DUFFEL. Beloved first by sailors working along the coast of Belgium, then by the British forces in World Wars I and II, then by college students, then by the world, the duffle is distinguished by patch pockets, a pancake hood, TOGGLE closures, and an extra layer of cloth across the shoulder. It is generally knee-length or shorter. In the British regulation-issue version, it sported wooden toggles attached via jute-rope cording and a larger bucket hood, while its patch pockets had no flaps.

The brand most associated with the style is GLOVERALL. Synonyms: TOGGLE COAT; MONTGOMERY COAT.

Duke of Windsor See EDWARD VIII.

dundrearies A style of long, flowing SIDEBURNS most popular during the third quarter of the 19th century. Dundrearies were often longer and more lush than MUTTONCHOP whiskers, forming a virtual beard, except that the chin remained clean-shaven. The name derives from Lord Dundreary, a character in the 1858 *Our American Cousin* (playing at Ford's Theatre on the night Abraham Lincoln was shot in 1865). In England, the same style probably would have been called PICCADILLY WEEPERS.

dungarees Reference to heavy work clothes or, as "dungaree," to the sturdy fabric used to produce them. The term has been traced all the way back to the 18th century and a Hindi word that is usually translated with the spelling "dungri," which referred to a type of heavy, simply woven cotton favored for sails, awnings, and, later, for sailors' clothes. During the 19th century, the cloth was often dyed blue and used for sailors' WORKWEAR. From the beginning of the 20th century, it was used more generally as a synonym for COVERALLS, OVERALLS, and sturdy work pants, so that, in contemporary use, it often applies to other colors and workwear with no nautical link.

Dunhill Founded by Alfred Dunhill in 1893, when he took over his father's saddlery, the leathergoods business evolved when Dunhill opened a luxury tobacconist's shop in London's West End in 1907. The firm first gained notoriety for an expensive model of pipe that it produced in 1910 (which was distinguished by a white spot inlaid in the mouthpiece). In 1921, the shop gained its first royal warrant. In 1923, it opened its first branch in New York and introduced its lighters, which could be operated by one hand.

Founder Alfred Dunhill retired in 1928 and was succeeded by his brother and son, who added men's fragrance in 1934. Clothing was not introduced until much later.

DuPont   The chemicals company founded by French immigrant Eleuthère Iréné du Pont de Nemours in 1802 in Delaware's Brandywine Valley (near its subsequent headquarters in Wilmington), originally as a manufacturer of explosives.

During the 20th century, the company coined slogans such as "Better Things for Better Living . . . Through Chemistry" and "The Miracles of Science," developing textile applications that included NEOPRENE, NYLON, ORLON, DACRON, KEVLAR, LYCRA, COOLMAX, Thermolite, and NOMEX.

Although the company DuPont still exists as a separate entity (which still produces chemicals), as pertains to the apparel market, it is the original name for the fiber company now known as INVISTA and owned by Koch Industries.

DuPont began to separate its best-known textile brands from its other chemical applications toward the end of the 20th century and in the early 21st century grouped most of them under DuPont Textiles and Interiors, often abbreviated as DTI, which was subsequently renamed Invista and then sold off to Koch Industries. After 2003, the correct reference is Invista.

du rag   A close-fitting, nonbulky head wrap that completely covers the hair and is tight enough to be worn beneath other headwear, such as a baseball cap or football helmet; in contemporary use, made of thin, stretchy material.

The contemporary du rag originated with the tight head wraps used for decades by African American men to flatten processed hair or encourage ironed and/or waved hair to lie close to the skull. Early du rags were usually improvised from kerchiefs, rags, or women's stockings and worn mostly at night—having roughly the same social connotations as a woman's curlers. However, later in the 20th century, with the rise of hip-hop, du rags became accepted streetwear and were sold as fashion items. Variant spellings include do rag and doo-rag.

duster   A style of long, loose coat, worn over regular clothes, literally to protect them from dust; associated with driving or riding in early automobiles; often constructed from linen or a sturdy cotton.

Dutch boy cap   A style of dark, billed cap, as sported since 1907 by various incarnations of the blond boy on the logo for the Dutch Boy paint brand.

Dutch boy haircut   The blunt-edge, bobbed haircut with bangs, as sported since 1907 by various incarnations of the blond boy on the logo for the Dutch Boy paint brand.

dye lot   Yarns or lengths of cloth dyed in the same batch, usually identified by the batch number. To ensure uniformity, a garment's maker will try to match all components from the same dye lot, since intensity of color can vary from batch to batch, particularly with hand-dyed goods.

ear flaps   Flaps attached to headgear, usually a hunting or sporting hat, to protect ears from the elements. Often, as in a DEERSTALKER cap, they can be tied up or down, depending upon weather and need.

earmuffs   Two pieces of warm, protective fabric—one for each ear—connected by a slim band that runs across the top of the wearer's head. Invented by 15-year-old Chester Greenwood of Farmington, Maine, in 1873, when he made two ear-sized wire loops and asked his grandmother to sew fur scraps over them.

As he grew, Greenwood would progress to the whistling tea kettle, the mechanical mousetrap, and assorted other inventions, but earmuffs were the foundation of his fortune. He patented a refined version of his "ear-mufflers" in 1877, and thereafter built Greenwood's Ear Protector Factory, bringing prosperity to himself and his hometown by supplying World War I soldiers with ear protectors.

In 1977, Maine declared December 21 to be "Chester Greenwood Day" in his honor. However, Farmington celebrates its status as "Earmuff Capital of the World" by declaring the first Saturday in December to be "Chester Greenwood Day" and holding a parade featuring cows, cars, and police cruisers disguised as earmuffs, as well as earmuff-themed floats.

ears   Refers to the pull straps on boots, especially COW-BOY BOOTS.

Earth Shoe   A brand best known for its trademarked Negative Heel, which made the front of the shoe higher than the back, and for its wide, obliquely shaped toe (both design features in complete contradiction of customary footwear styling). Dreamed up by a Danish yoga instructor in the late 1950s, the brand became wildly popular in the 1970s, especially for its ungainly, tie-front style that looked like a cousin to the CLARK WALLABEE.

easy fit   A designation of comfort rather than high fashion. "Easy fit" refers to the silhouette and sometimes the sizing of apparel, usually of pants and especially of

Earmuffs: Patent drawing by Chester Greenwood

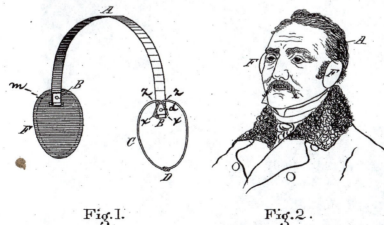

jeans. Easy fit JEANS are cut wider through the thighs and have more room through the buttocks. They may also be made with a slightly larger waist measurement or have some equivalent comfort feature, such as a waistband or fabric that incorporates stretch.

eau fraiche   A light fragrance formulation, designed to be used liberally. Although formulas vary from manufacturer to manufacturer, an *eau fraiche* is usually a maximum of 1 or 2 percent essential oils or fragrance concentrate dissolved in a carrier that is chiefly alcohol. (A COLOGNE, by contrast, is about 3 to 5 percent.) Synonym: SPLASH.

Ede & Ravenscroft   Founded in 1689 by the Shudall family, the company claims to be London's oldest still-operative tailoring firm; best known, in addition to BESPOKE and ready-to-wear men's apparel, as a specialist in court robes, coronation robes, and other ceremonial gear, as well as being the world's foremost purveyor of the wigs worn in British courts and the courts of other countries that follow their costume conventions.

Holder of multiple ROYAL WARRANTS, the firm achieved its present dominance of the world's legal wig market back in 1822, when Humphrey Ravenscroft invented the "forensic," a wig made from horsehair that did not need to be constantly repowdered and recurled.

Although it previously had premises on Chancery Lane and the City (as well as Oxford and Cambridge), the firm did not open an outlet on SAVILE Row until the beginning of the 21st century.

Edun   The apparel brand founded in 2005 by designer Rogan Gregory, Bono (lead singer of the band U2), and Bono's wife Ali Hewson. Following the slogan "trade not aid," the company was conceived as a way of producing fashionable men's and women's clothes in Third World factories.

Edward VII   Born in 1841, Albert Edward (better known as "Bertie"), was the second child of Queen Victoria and her consort PRINCE ALBERT. At age four, he set his first fashion by being seen in a SAILOR SUIT that had been created in imitation of the sailors' suits on the royal yacht. It was prophetic for a man who would again and again popularize fashions that were practical to wear, slightly theatrical or costumey in aspect, and less rigid in construction than the accepted attire.

Like his grandson EDWARD VIII (who consciously emulated

Edward VII

his style), Edward VII was a frequent patron of SAVILE ROW (HENRY POOLE was his tailor), but particularly loved quotations of traditional and ethnic costume. As Prince of Wales he brought TYROLEAN HATS and HOMBURGS to British fashion, and delighted in shooting clothes like NORFOLK JACKETS. As the inventor of the style (in 1860) that became known as the TUXEDO, his eveningwear, although staid by modern standards, was considered shockingly casual for a Prince of Wales. After finally ascending to the throne in 1902, he died in 1910.

Edward VIII *or* Edward, Prince of Wales *or* Edward, Duke of Windsor

Born in 1894, when his great-grandmother Queen Victoria was still on the throne, Prince Edward Albert Christian George Andrew Patrick David Windsor became best known for being the only English monarch to voluntarily abdicate the throne (in 1936) and being thereupon given the title Duke of Windsor; for marrying the twice-divorced American Wallis Simpson (in 1937); and for a style sense that made him, during much of the 20th century, menswear's greatest trendsetter.

After his father, George V, ascended to the throne in 1910, Edward, who was known to his intimates as "David," was made Prince of Wales in a special investiture ceremony (held partly to appease Lloyd George and other Welsh politicians) in which he was decked, much to his own dismay, in white satin and purple velvet. Tellingly, it would be the first of many occasions in which the Prince chafed against the costume and formalities imposed by what he considered to be outdated etiquette. His own flamboyance harked back to his *bon vivant* grandfather, EDWARD VII, rather than his stern and severely dressed father and, for the next quarter century, he would be in almost continuous conflict with his rigid, duty-bound, and unfashionable parents.

For example, the golden-haired prince (who affected the side-part style barbered by Charles Topper of Mayfair for the rest of his life) wore soft, relatively casual hats like the FEDORA more often than his father considered proper. He quickly adopted zipper-fly pants, which his father considered distasteful. He allowed himself to be photographed in rolled-up sleeves. He favored soft, flannel suit materials. He eschewed FROCK COATS for jackets that sometimes featured flaps on the pockets (a style then more associated with riding clothes). He disdained stiff collars and instead wore soft shirts with FOLD-OVER COLLARS. He wore trousers with TURN-UPS, colorful socks, and extra-baggy PLUS FOURS and "PLUS TWENTIES." He wore WINKLEPICKERS and brown BUCKS with his blue or gray suits.

A small, slim man (with a height reported between 5 feet, 5 inches and 5 feet, 8 inches and a 29-inch waist), the Prince adored bright colors and pattern mixing, enthusiasms reportedly inspired by his childhood

Edward VIII

admiration of the YELLOW EARL. After World War I, he traveled widely on official duties, becoming a global "Prince Charming"; when he was seen wearing a blue-and-red-striped tie from the Brigade of Guards, the entire world wanted to wear REGIMENTAL TIES. Among the other fashions that he set or popularized:

• The soft, unconstructed suit silhouette that became known as the ENGLISH DRAPE, which was said to be invented by FREDERICK SCHOLTE (his tailor from 1919 to 1959).

• Unlined suit jackets or sports jackets.

• Midnight blue TUXEDOS with black satin lapels. (The prince and his brother, then the Duke of Kent, became so associated with the style that a double-breasted, midnight-blue dinner jacket was known as a KENT.)

• Thick knots for both his NECKTIES and BOW TIES (an effect that gave rise to the WINDSOR KNOT, even though the Prince himself used a FOUR-IN-HAND on specially constructed neckwear made by firms such as HAWES & CURTIS and CHARVET).

• Cuffed trousers, worn without suspenders (usually made by FORSTER & SONS or H. Harris).

• Double-breasted jackets with a low button STANCE (made by Scholte or, after Scholte's death, by James & Son).

• The FAIR ISLE sweater, a folk style that flew to the height of fashion after the prince wore it golfing at St. Andrews in 1922.

• The PRINCE OF WALES PLAID, a check that had been invented in the 19th century, supposedly for his grandfather, but became identified with Edward VIII during his own days as prince. (He also had a favorite suit made of the Sutherland district check and several garments made of HARRIS TWEED and SHEPHERD'S CHECKS.)

• TARTANS, as both KILTS and the material of pants and suits.

• ESPADRILLES.

• TYROLEAN HATS, and other bits of traditional European costume that had also been popular with his grandfather.

Although his wife was known for the severe chic and lack of pattern in her clothes, the Duke of Windsor continued to favor plaid suits and bold resort wear until the end of his life: mixing stripes, checks, and FOULARDS, donning red corduroy pants for a day on the golf links.

During World War II, he was installed as governor of Bermuda, but after the war returned to a life centered around a chateau in Neuilly on the outskirts of Paris, with frequent trips to New York and Palm Beach to meet jet-set friends for golfing and parties. He collaborated with a ghostwriter on *A King's Story* published in 1951 and wrote *Windsor Revisited,* published in 1960, about his own wardrobe and the wardrobe of his family. Until the end of his life in 1972, he remained immaculately groomed and insisted that his suits be regularly rotated by his valet Sydney Johnson. When his suits were auctioned by Sotheby's in 1998, they became the objects of a furious bidding war between BRIONI and KITON, with Kiton proprietor Ciro Paone eventually spending a six-figure sum to acquire 11 lots.

eel *or* **eelskin**   A lightweight, not particularly sturdy, leather prized for its distinctive streaky GRAIN.

Egyptian cotton   Originally a reference to certain types of LONG-STAPLE COTTON (such as Giza cotton) cultivated in Egypt. However, since a minority of the cotton raised in Egypt is actually the prized luxury fiber, unscrupulous manufacturers use the phrase misleadingly for coarser and more common varieties of cotton that originate in Egypt.

Eisenhower jacket   A style of short, skirtless jacket ending at the waist, derived from the military jackets worn by General Dwight D. Eisenhower during World War II.

elastane Another name for SPANDEX, the polyurethane-based stretch fiber. Usually European usage.

elbow patch An oval patch—usually of leather or suede—added to the sleeve of sports jackets or other jackets where the material of the elbow would wear through with use; not used on suits. Associated with academics and country sports—particularly the tweedy chic of pipe-smoking professors and the countrified chic of Britain's upper classes—elbow patches evolved from preventative to fashion statement as, in the mid-20th century, the patches went from an item of functional repair to an item of decoration applied before the garment was bought.

electric shaver Also referred to as a DRY SHAVER. The first commercial model was patented and produced by JACOB SCHICK.

Perry Ellis

Élégant A species of late-18th-century fop primarily found in pre-Revolutionary Paris. Predecessor to the INCROYABLE and France's counterpart to the MACARONI.

elephant corduroy An especially oversized WIDE-WALE corduroy.

elephant leg pants Refers to a style of pants, trendy in the early 1970s, that were wide-legged (but did not flare in the manner of BELL-BOTTOMS) and tended to have a high waist (rather than a LOW RISE). A variation, elephant bells, did flare at the bottom—but from an already wide, "elephant," leg.

elk leather Misleadingly, the term is used by shoemakers for a certain type of leather made from cowhide. (The leather made from the skin of elks is usually BUCKSKIN.)

Ellis, Perry Born in 1940 in Portsmouth, Virginia, Perry Edwin Ellis spent most of his life on the business end of fashion before launching his own label in the late 1970s and becoming best known for his fresh and fashionable take on wholesome, all-American PREPPY clothes.

After attending William & Mary, where he majored in business, he got a master's in retailing from New York University, then moved back to Virginia to work for Miller & Rhoads, a department store chain based in Richmond, where he became a successful sportswear buyer. He next worked for John Meyer of Norwich, then for Manhattan Industries, which asked him to design and merchandise a collection called Portfolio. By 1978, Manhattan Industries backed Ellis's own women's wear and, in 1980, his own menswear. His first few collections, which fashion writers delighted in calling the "Slouch Look," concentrated on loose jackets, sweaters knit of wool so unprocessed that sometimes little twigs were still found in the yarn, and loose-fitting pants—particularly the CHINOS he loved to wear himself. His models were clean-cut and collegiate looking, as was Ellis: His trademark look included a BUTTON-DOWN shirt, KHAKI pants, a CREWNECK sweater, and a neat ponytail. Well-liked in the fashion world, Ellis served two terms as president of the CFDA before his death of AIDS-related illness in 1986.

After his death, the women's wear collection (designed for a few years by Marc Jacobs) was discontinued as unprofitable, and the company eventually evolved into the parent not only of Perry Ellis, but of a slew of other menswear brands, including Cubavera, Farah, Manhattan, and MUNSINGWEAR.

end   Jargon for an individual WARP yarn (the yarn that runs vertically on the loom). Its counterpart, the weft yarn that runs horizontally, would be a PICK. For example: Industry veterans might describe the construction and density of a fabric as "60 by 50," indicating the number of ends followed by the number of picks in a single inch of that fabric.

end on end   A type of fabric, most often used for shirts, constructed so that the WARP (i.e., the END yarn) alternates color. Typically, an end on end might alternate between blue and white yarns, giving a faintly striped or textured appearance to the final fabric.

engineered print   Refers to a print that is "engineered" to fall in a particular place on the uncut fabric, making it easier to position on the final garment. (As opposed to standard fabric printing, which REPEATS the design at more regular and symmetric intervals.) Most often, an engineered print is a large figure that will be positioned on the chest, sleeve, or back of a man's shirt. For example, when you see a sports shirt that has a huge flower printed over the right side of the chest, that's an engineered print. Sometimes called a PLACEMENT PRINT.

engineered stretch   Usually refers to fabric (such as cotton or wool) in which stretch is created during the weaving process, rather than from the inclusion of elastic fibers such as SPANDEX. Although they sound like antonyms, engineered stretch and NATURAL STRETCH are often used interchangeably.

English drape   Original name for the style of tailoring known as the DRAPE, as famously espoused by tailors from FREDERICK SCHOLTE to the firm of ANDERSON & SHEPPARD and worn by clients ranging from EDWARD VIII to FRED ASTAIRE. Synonym: LONDON CUT (as it was originally christened by *TAILOR & CUTTER*).

English-style closure   A synonym, especially in 19th-century American usage, for high-buttoning RICHMOND-STYLE closures.

enzyme wash   A treatment, usually for DENIM, in which enzymes are used to eat away the cellulose content of the cotton, resulting in fabric that is lighter in color and weight and less stiff than unprocessed denim.

epaulettes   1. From *epaule*, the French word for shoulder; refers to a shoulder ornamentation extending along the shoulder seam to the point of the shoulder. Originally featured on military clothing, epaulettes became a feature of garments like TRENCH COATS, SAFARI JACKETS, SAFARI SHIRTS, and other styles that deliberately evoked uniforms.

In contemporary civilian clothes, the epaulette is usually a strip of fabric that passes from the neckline or collar through a loop at the arm seam and back toward the collar. Its stiff, single-piece counterpart, appearing on uniforms but not on civilian dress, is called the SHOULDER BOARD.

2. A fringe or other ornamentation decorating the shoulder of a uniform.

Ermenegildo Zegna   The textile maker, apparel brand, and retail company founded by Ermenegildo Zegna in 1910 when he took over his father Angelo's textile company in Trivero, a town in the BIELLA region of northern Italy. Controlled by the Zegna family through successive generations; best known for luxury off-the-rack and made-to-measure clothing.

Although Angelo had originally been a watchmaker, he nonetheless decided to get into the local wool-weaving industry, which was enjoying a small boom in Biella at the end of the 19th century. When the youngest of Angelo's ten children, Ermenegildo (1892–1966), took over his father's mill, it was still a modest business with a mere three looms (which Ermenegildo immediately replaced). Aiming at the high end of the menswear market, the company then known as Lanificio Zegna sourced the highest grades of wool and the latest machinery until it was able to fulfill Ermenegildo's aim of rivaling the quality of cloth traditionally produced only in England. Constantly promoting his brand by advertising, Zegna had more than 1,000 employees by the 1930s, began exporting to the United States in 1938, and, before the start of World War II, had endowed Trevira with social-welfare programs and public facilities including a swimming pool and medical clinic, as well as what later became known as the "Oasi Zegna," a panoramic stretch of road planted with trees and flowering bushes.

In the 1960s, Ermenegildo began passing control of the business—by then known primarily as Ermenegildo Zegna e Figli—to his sons Aldo and Angelo, who began aiming at luxury end products as well as luxury textiles. In 1968, Zegna opened a factory for clothes production in Novara, Italy, soon followed by facilities in Spain and Switzerland. They also expanded into sportswear and accessories (the infamous yellow tie that Monica Lewinsky gave to President Bill Clinton was from Zegna), and in 1972, launched a made-to-measure business. During the 1980s, when the fourth generation of the Zegna family became involved in the business, Zegna began opening its own retail outlets (first in Paris in 1980, then in Milan in 1985), eventually growing to hundreds worldwide. However, throughout its relatively rapid expansion, the company remained vertically integrated—controlling its product and image all the way from its wool sourcing in Australia to the merchandising in its stores.

At the end of the 20th century and beginning of the 21st, Zegna continued its rapid expansion, opening more retail outlets in Asian markets (especially in China), taking over former rival Agnona (which also produced both cloth and clothing), and entering into production agreements and joint ventures with GIORGIO ARMANI (who, early in his career, had been a freelance designer for the company), Ferragamo, and Gucci, and later with designer TOM FORD (following his departure from GUCCI).

Escorial   A branded fine wool fiber made from the fleece of Mahgreb sheep and marketed by the

Ermenegildo Zegna: Namesake of the founder

Christchurch, New Zealand-based Escorial Company, which was founded in 1999 by farmers in New Zealand, Australia, and Tasmania.

Escorial is a curly, springy fiber and thus, say its advocates, better able to recover from crushing and wrinkling, as well as being more resistant to PILLING because it is less hairy.

Escorial producers proudly trace the heritage of their sheep back to the Mahgrebs kept by Spanish royalty at El Escorial northwest of Madrid from 1340 onward. From that point, they connect the breed even further back to the merinos who came to the Iberian peninsula from North Africa via the 8th-century Arab invasions.

espadrille The inexpensive, rope-soled, cloth-topped, slipper-style shoes traditionally worn in western Mediterranean countries. Previously considered peasant wear, espadrilles were elevated to the status of chic summer footwear after World War I, when they were sported by style setters like GERALD MURPHY and EDWARD VIII while Prince of Wales. Synonym, in Spanish usage: ALPARGATA.

Esquire The consumer magazine founded by Arnold Gingrich in 1933 with the subtitle "The Magazine for Men"; spurred by the success of the allied APPAREL ARTS (a quarterly trade magazine that Gingrich edited, founded in 1931); published by Hearst since 1986.

Although conceived as a quarterly, *Esquire* became a monthly after its first issue and, in its early editions, was a bastion of chest-thumping masculinity that featured big-name fiction by the likes of Theodore Dreiser and Ernest Hemingway. (During World War II, the magazine did its bit for soldiers' morale by publishing the pin-ups of Alberto Vargas.) For years, all its covers depicted the adventures of "Esky," a popeyed, mustachioed cartoon

figure seen in manly endeavors such as sailing a yacht or leaping from a lifeguard's chair.

Early, the magazine asserted itself as the last word in all matters pertaining to menswear. For example: In 1958, *Esquire* revived the *Apparel Arts* title as a supplement concentrating on fashion. (That supplement, renamed GENTLEMAN'S QUARTERLY, went on to a life of its own, becoming, after its sale to Condé Nast in 1983, a rival to its progenitor.) It employed GEORGE FRAZIER as style columnist and occasional copywriter, a collaboration that culminated in the September 1960 publication of Frazier's cover story "THE ART OF WEARING CLOTHES."

Through the 1960s the title also became a showcase for the New Journalism from writers like Norman Mailer, Gay Talese, and Tom Wolfe, as well as featuring the covers of art director George Lois (most famously Andy Warhol drowning in a can of Campbell's Soup to tout an article on the death of Pop Art). By the 1970s, however, its fortunes were in decline. After briefly becoming a biweekly, it was sold to 13-30, a publisher that repositioned the formerly macho publisher of Hemingway and Mailer as a magazine for the sensitive man. In 1986, it was sold again to Hearst Publications, which took the title closer to its original mission and began capitalizing on franchises like "Women We Love" and the annual "Dubious Achievement Awards," and instituted a British edition in 1991.

Esquire's Encyclopedia of 20th Century Men's Fashions The oversized, 709-page reference and style history written by O.E. Schoeffler and William Gale and published by McGraw-Hill in 1973. Following a format that divides apparel into chapters according to purpose, "Shooting Clothes," "Fur Coats," and so forth, the majority of the text is a sort of précis of what appeared on the magazine pages, supplemented with overviews from Fairchild's trade publications (especially for the early 20th century).

estate tweed   The practice, primarily in Scotland, of associating a patterned wool with a particular estate, where it is worn by both the gentry and the servants (making them different from clan TARTANS, which are worn by blood relatives, regardless of location). The first estate tweeds were designed and produced in the 1840s, when it became fashionable to own an estate in Scotland for shooting and fishing (especially after Queen Victoria and her consort ALBERT leased Balmoral). According to Johnstons of Elgin (which, with Ballantyne of Walkerburn, was one of the two main suppliers to the market), the very first estate tweed was the Glenfeshie, a pattern designed by General Balfour's daughter when he was renting that estate from 1834 to 1841.

Many estate tweeds contain at least one thread or stripe of a bright color like coral or hyacinth blue because this supposedly makes them a more effective camouflage than a uniformly dark pattern. Like tartans, there are hundreds of named estate tweeds, including Altnaharra, Barrisdale, North Affric, South Uist, and Wyvis. Unlike tartans, subtle variations of color may matter greatly (e.g., a dark brown is definitely not interchangeable with a light or medium brown).

Esterel, Jacques   Born in France in 1917 as Charles Henry Martin, the designer who rechristened himself as Jacques Esterel in 1945 would become best known for creating skirts for men and also by association with designer JEAN PAUL GAULTIER, the best-known of several designers who apprenticed with him.

Esterel worked as a cartoonist and an industrial designer before establishing his own fashion house in Paris in 1953, where his successes included Brigitte Bardot's famous gingham wedding dress. During the 1960s, when the trend to unisex fashion was generally interpreted as pushing women to dress more like men, Esterel pushed men to dress more like women: He designed skirted suits for men that variously resembled kilts combined with shorts, then debuted a dress for men that looked like a nightshirt.

In addition to couture and ready-to-wear design, he also took to composing musicals, songwriting, and a variety of other artistic endeavors. He died in 1974.

Eton blue   A shade that most people would call pale green; worn by teams representing the English public school, especially in the 19th century. Subsequently it was replaced by a baby blue; then, in the 21st century, traditionalists made a move to restore a pale green-blue as the representative school color.

Etro   The textile company, apparel and accessories label, and retailer founded in 1968 in Milan by Gerolamo "Gimmo" Etro as a textile design company; best-known for colorful prints—especially paisleys—and embellished menswear. As Gimmo's four children grew up, the business gradually expanded: including ties and other accessories in 1983, moving on to its first store in 1984, and from there to men's and women's fashions, shoes, home furnishings, and other ventures. Jacopo, the oldest child, headed textile design, home furnishings, and accessories; Kean became the menswear designer; Ippolito headed company finance; and Veronica became designer of the women's collection.

Gimmo Etro

exam gown   A loose, HOSPITAL GOWN-type garment, used for doctor's examinations, which may open to either the front or back and be made of sturdy washable fabric or a disposable, clothlike paper material.

exquisite   A DANDY of especially refined—or over-refined—sensibilities, particularly in Regency England (1811 to 1820), when BEAU BRUMMELL became exemplar of the type.

extremes   Old-fashioned trade jargon for styles that push the limit. For example: A 1940s retailer would have called the ZOOT SUIT an "extreme."

eyeglasses   Usually refers to clear lenses worn to correct a defect of vision—a practice that can be traced back to 13th-century Italy but may have originated in China even earlier. The lens itself may be either prescription or nonprescription and may combine corrections with a bifocal or even a trifocal lens. (For styles and materials of their settings, see FRAMES.) A slightly old-fashioned synonym: spectacles.

Tinted lenses worn for sun protection are sunglasses; clear lenses, especially if they are nonprescription, worn to protect the eye from sparks, metal shards, wood chips, etc., are usually referred to as goggles, no matter what their size. Oversized lenses, both tinted and untinted or prescription and nonprescription, are also called goggles when worn for sports.

When two lenses are worn in a style of frame that does not have side pieces, it is a PINCE-NEZ. A single lens, supported in the eye socket by squinting, is referred to as a MONOCLE. A single lens, held by a short handle, is usually called a QUIZZING GLASS.

eye ring   Anachronistic name for a MONOCLE.

eyeshade   A VISOR worn indoors.

eyewear   1. Jargon for EYEGLASSES and sunglasses, particularly when referring to the FRAME designs. As in: "That designer made a lot of money from his prescription eyewear licenses." 2. In older references, refers to types of corrective lenses that do not have a frame supported by sidearms (e.g., a PINCE-NEZ and MONOCLE).

fabrications   Jargon for fabrics.

face   The front or right side of a fabric.

facing *or* **faced**   1. The fabric, usually in a contrasting color and/or texture, used to highlight garment features such as collars, lapels, and/or cuffs. For example: A SHAWL-COLLARED dinner jacket may sport black satin facing on its collar (even though the body of the jacket is black worsted); or a SMOKING JACKET may feature quilted black-satin facings for its collar, cuffs, and pocket edges, even though the main body of the jacket is burgundy velvet.   2. On a shoe or boot, pieces on the UPPER that wrap around the top of the foot; usually the piece that contains the holes for the shoelaces.

factory seconds   Usually refers to clothes that do not pass a factory's quality control inspection, for reasons that may range from the minute to the major. Often sold in factory outlet stores.

Fairbanks, Douglas Jr.   Born in 1909 to swashbuckling silent movie heartthrob Douglas Fairbanks Sr. and his first wife Anna Beth Sully (whom Fairbanks Sr. divorced in 1920 to marry Mary Pickford), dashing Douglas Fairbanks Jr. was an American native who nevertheless became so identified with English dress and manners that almost everyone believed him to be British-born and raised (a fiction furthered by his starring in roles such as the young English soldier in 1939's *Gunga Din*). Much like his friend and colleague CARY GRANT, Fairbanks suavity came from his physical grace, great good looks, terrific nonchalance, and transatlantic accent. Fairbanks enhanced that image by affecting an Anglophile style incorporating a slim moustache, hats by LOCK, custom shirts with spread collars, ties with a Windsor-style knot, and draped suits made by ANDERSON & SHEPPARD on SAVILE Row or Stovel & Mason on nearby Old Burlington Street, and then adorning almost every suited ensemble with a carnation in his buttonhole.

In 1929, he married fellow clotheshorse Joan Crawford, whom he divorced in 1933. During World War II, he was a lieutenant-commander in the U.S. Navy but was decorated by the British government, who later bestowed an honorary knighthood upon him. For several decades beginning in the 1950s, he actually lived in London with his family. He died in New York, the city of his birth, in 2000.

Fair Isle   1. Refers to a distinctive type of patterned sweater using motifs that originated on the remote Fair Isles, off the north coast of Scotland. The motifs, which are related to geometric, Norwegian-style patterns, were originally rendered in undyed wool in various shades of brown and gray, but came to be identified with extremely colorful patterning. In the most traditional versions of Fair Isle-style knitting, two yarns are stranded throughout an entire row and are continually intertwined on the "wrong" side of the garment (an effect that creates a warm, almost double-thick, knit).

Fair Isles first came to be considered fashionable in 1922, when the Prince of Wales (the future EDWARD VIII), wore one at the Golf Club at St. Andrews.

2. In writing before 1922, may refer to a type of heavy TWEED produced in the Fair Isles.

faille   A type of woven fabric, usually silk, used in NECKWEAR; it has tiny horizontal ribs formed by heavier filling yarns and looks like GROSGRAIN but is flatter and slightly shinier.

fall *or* **falling band**   Refers to a—usually large—flat collar that "falls" over the upper shoulders—this to distinguish from the stiff, framing RUFF, one of the styles that immediately preceded it. The style and the term that describes it were most popular in England during the second quarter of the 17th century, where they can be seen in Anthony Van Dyck's portraits of the aristocracy.

fall-downs *or* **fallfront**   See FALLS.

falls   Reference, from the 18th century onward, for the flaps covering the crotch opening of pants, similar to the opening on modern sailors' pants. Falls came in as many styles and variations as the pants they were attached to, but were usually subdivided into whole falls and small falls, which simply indicated a larger flap versus a smaller flap. By the 1840s, they began to be supplanted by the modern FLY opening, especially in dressier and more tailored apparel.

false calves   Padding or prosthesis worn to make a man's leg look more shapely. False calves were made obsolete first by fashion's switch from BREECHES to longer pants at the end of the 18th century and then by fashion's switch from form-fitting PANTALOONS to looser styles after the first quarter of the 19th century.

fancy, **fancies**   Industry jargon, usually for a weave or pattern—be it striped, checked, dotted, or some combination thereof—that does not fit neatly into the standard categories.

fannypack   A small utilitarian bag, usually with one or more zippered closures, worn around the waist and outside the clothes. Fanny packs vary in size and shape from simple, half moon-shaped pockets to elaborate constructions with loops, pockets, and provision for a water bot-

Falls

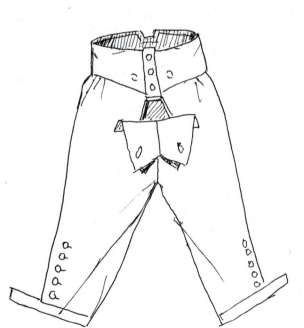

tle. Originally worn with the pocket to the back (hence the "fanny"), they became a popular part of tourist attire in the late 20th century and were worn with the pocket to the front to enhance access and prevent theft.

Slang references include MOONBAG and BUMBAG. When a fannypack is called a LUMBAR BACK, it is usually larger and worn to the back as a substitute for a small backpack during hiking or some similar sport.

fanon A short shoulder cape, worn only by the pope while he celebrates solemn mass; in use since at least the 8th century.

Fashion Institute of Technology See FIT.

fashionista Slang for someone who lives and dies by fashion. In its first usage, during the 1990s, the term referred only to women, but has since broadened to mean anyone of either sex who is passionately involved with trends. In contrast to the GARMENTO, the fashionista does usually not overly concern himself with the bottom line.

Fashion Week Jargon for the semiannual concentration of fashion shows and related events, which may be slightly more than or slightly less than a conventional seven-day week. Twice each year (in the very early spring for clothes to be worn the following fall and during the early autumn for clothes intended to be worn the following spring), the international press, models, and buyers arrive in a city and follow a schedule of intensive presentations and parties.

Each major fashion venue has its own Fashion Week, thus the industry usually speaks of New York Fashion Week, London Fashion Week, Paris Fashion Week, and Milan Fashion Week. In imitation of the more established venues, offshoots include Shanghai Fashion Week and Australia Fashion Week.

fast A dye that does not bleed or fade. See COLORFAST.

Fauntleroy See LITTLE LORD FAUNTLEROY.

fauxhawk A style that became popular in the first decade of the 21st century. Refers to short hair that is spiked with styling products in the center or is left slightly longer down the center of the head. The name is derived from and the style is intentionally reminiscent of the more radical PUNK hairstyle known as the MOHAWK.

faux turtle A close-fitting, usually RIBBED style of sweater collar that covers the entire neck but does not fold back on itself like a TURTLENECK. A turtleneck uses a double layer of material; a faux turtle only looks like it does. A similar style, usually slighter wider and lower, is called a FUNNEL NECK. Synonym: mock turtleneck.

fedora A style of brimmed felt hat with a fairly low, creased crown. Named for the 1882 play "Fédora" by Victorien Sardou, in which Sarah Bernhardt played a Russian princess dressed like a boy in a costume that included a soft felt hat. Women adopted the hat as a consciously masculine style, which later crossed over to menswear—abetted by EDWARD VIII while Prince of Wales.

felled seam The flattened, stitched-down seam, familiar to most men as the seam on the outside of their JEANS; a felled seam displays a double row of stitching and no raw edge. Usually it is created by making the seam with two wrong sides together and making the two sides of the seam allowance uneven (e.g., making one side ⅜ of an inch and the other ⅝ of an inch) and wrapping the longer around the shorter.

felt   1. Refers to fabric that is neither knit nor woven but is formed from fibers that are purposely matted together via heat, pressure, and/or water. Its construction gives it the advantage of being excellent padding or reinforcement, but the disadvantage of being not pliable or easily tailored.   2. Used as a verb, refers to the process of taking a knit or woven textile and creating a feltlike surface, usually through shrinkage; may be done either before or after the fabric is made into a garment. This is sometimes done to increase the density of the fabric and make it less porous.

Ferry, Bryan   Born in 1945, the handsome and dark-haired British performer best known as the lead singer of Roxy Music became an exemplar of suited suavity at a time in the 1970s and 1980s when his contemporaries (e.g., bandmate Brian Eno) still tended toward outrageous getups and glitter rock. A patron of celebrity tailor ANTONY PRICE, Ferry was more glam than glitter and

Bryan Ferry

became famous for his liaisons with fashion models (e.g., Jerry Hall before her marriage to Mick Jagger). Even into the 21st century, his reputation as the most dapper man in rock led to him being hired, in 2006, as the face of a Marks & Spencer menswear line.

Féruch, Gilbert   Born in Algeria in 1924, Féruch moved to Paris in 1950 and set up shop as a tailor whose clientele included PIERRE CARDIN, YVES SAINT LAURENT, and Pablo Picasso. He is usually credited with introducing suit jackets and sport coats with a NEHRU-style collar at the start of the 1960s (on a tuxedo made for mime Marcel Marceau), and thereby negating the fashionable man's need for a tie. He was also renowned as a proponent of JUMPSUITS, of tailoring created with less INTERFACING, and of longer, slimmer suit jackets.

fez   A style of stiff, conical hat with a flattened top; named after the city of Fez in Morocco, one of the places it was traditionally made. The traditional fez has no brim but sits atop of the head and is often trimmed with a tassel dangling from its center top. Its use became widely popular in the 19th century, especially in the Ottoman Empire and countries bordering it. In South Asia it became headgear identified with Muslims. And in Egypt it was part of army headgear (and even worn by royalty on formal occasions with their otherwise-Western dress). In the 20th century in America, it became identified with the costume of the Shriners, a popular fraternal association. Synonym (especially in Egypt): TARBOOSH.

fiber   The most basic component of any garment. For example: In a man's wool suit, the sourcing starts with the fiber, which is spun into yarn, which is woven into fabric. The order of production is: fiber, yarn, fabric, garment.

In contemporary fashion journalism most mistakes are made by comparing a type of fiber with a type of fabric, which is really comparing apples and oranges. For example, the runway journalist who wrote that one jacket was cotton (a fiber) but the other was corduroy (a type of fabric that was probably made from cotton).

In menswear, the most commonly used fibers include cashmere, cotton, linen, nylon, polyester, rayon, silk, and wool. These may be divided into categories by their source, such as natural versus synthetic, or by PROTEINACIOUS (animal) versus CELLULOSIC (plant). Or they may be classified by their form and length (STAPLE versus FILAMENT). Blends, usually indicated with a slash between the words (e.g., cotton/polyester), are not a fiber themselves but two or more fibers working together in a particular yarn.

2. Used as a general synonym for filament (which is actually a subcategory of fiber).

fiberfill   Refers to insulation and/or padding using any of a variety of lightweight, manmade fibers (as opposed to traditional insulation such as down). Most often used in cold-weather outdoor gear. Not visible when the garment is being worn.

fibula   Large brooch used to hold together any caped or draped fabric except a TOGA (which was always held in place by tucking or draping); often ornamental as well as functional; usually worn at the shoulder. Used for centuries in pre-Christian Greece, it remained common in Byzantine, Celtic, and medieval dress. Frequently in the form of a half circle closed by a horizontal pin. Its plural is fibulae.

field boots   Refers to a style of knee-high riding boots worn for foxhunting (especially for RATCATCHER) and for activities that emulate its dress code, such as horse shows. Field boots may be either brown or black leather but are distinguished by a BLUCHER-style construction and lacing over the instep.

Variations include styles that also have a three or more buckles running up the front of the leg (so that they can be stepped into instead of pulled on), and contemporary versions with unobtrusive back zippers and faux lacing. They are never worn with BOOT TOPS (the band or cuff of a different leather at the top of the boot).

figured silk   A patterned SILK, usually with the pattern formed as part of the weaving process.

filament   Jargon for textile fiber that is extruded or otherwise manufactured in a continuous strand (without being plied or twisted). Its counterpart is STAPLE fiber. Also referred to, somewhat redundantly, as "continuous filament."

filling *or* **fill**   Industry term for the WEFT of a fabric; so called because the WARP is put on the loom first and then the weft yarns are used to "fill" the space. For example, in DENIM or CHAMBRAY, the warp is commonly INDIGO and the filling may be white or natural.

filling-faced   Synonym for WEFT-FACED.

findings   An industry term for miscellaneous fasteners and ornamentation, such as hooks, buttons, snaps, and zippers. The term is sometimes broadened to including semifunctional and decorative trims, such as ribbing, edging, piping, facings, and linings.

finish   Refers to the surface appearance of the fabric, especially to one obtained by extra processing after its

Fibula

initial weaving. For example, a CALENDERED finish makes the fabric shiny; a BRUSHED FINISH raises the NAP, causing a slightly hairy appearance.

finishing   Jargon for almost any quality that does not derive directly from the production of the fabric. In most garment production, it refers to almost anything that happens *after* the fabric is knit or woven and *before* it's turned into apparel (or, in the case of JEANS or other apparel that may be "GARMENT-DYED" or "garment finished," even after that). The list of finishing processes includes (but is not limited to) printing, CALENDERING, distressing, embossing, FLOCKING, lamination, or application of NANOTECHNOLOGY or performance products (like antiwrinkle treatments or stain resistance). Finishing is the specialty of CONVERTERS, who are separate entities from a mill and do not actually weave or knit fabrics.

Fioravanti   Founded in 1951 by William Fioravanti, the New York custom tailoring firm, located on West 57th Street off Fifth Avenue, became best known for its "power look:" strong shoulders, a suppressed waist, and a slim-hipped, Italian fit.

Fish, Michael   The Londoner behind the label "Mr. Fish" started as a delivery boy for a menswear retailer and grew up to become a salesman at SULKA. In 1962, he launched brightly patterned shirts and ties of his own devising for shirtmakers TURNBULL & ASSER (and thereafter claimed that the convention of calling wide ties KIPPERS came from a pun on his surname). In 1966, backed by Barry Sainsbury, he opened his own boutique, which sold all manner of bright, exotic menswear. For example: The white "mini-dress" and white pants worn by Mick

Jagger during the July 1969 Rolling Stones concert in Hyde Park was a Mr. Fish purchase.

fisherman knit   Although this term can refer to any of the hard-wearing, warm sweaters (e.g., GANSEYS) favored by fishermen in the North Atlantic or environs, fashion writers most often use it as a synonym for ARAN-style knits and a reference to rough cabled designs made of undyed wool.

fisherman sandal   A style of sturdy, structured SANDAL, distinguished by a cap that covers the toe and a COUNTER that covers the heel, leaving only the sides of the foot truly exposed. The style is often made in a T-strap configuration and closed with a buckle that crosses the instep (in the manner of a woman's Mary Jane style).

fishing vest   A style known for its multiplicity of pockets, as well as a boxy, short shape that allowed ease of movement, and sturdy, no-nonsense construction; adapted for those reasons by nonsportsmen with the same requirements, such as photographers. The fishing vest was distinguished in part by its abbreviation: ending at or above the waist in order not to interfere with anglers' hip boots or waders.

FIT   The common reference, usually written in capital letters without periods, for the Fashion Institute of Technology, the branch of New York's state university system located at Seventh Avenue and 27th Street in New York City.

Established in 1944 as a post-high-school technical institution specializing in education related to fashion, textiles, and related fields (later including interior design), FIT became authorized to award Bachelor of

Arts and Bachelor of Science degrees in 1975, began a Menswear Design program in 1976, and added master's degrees in 1979. The Museum at FIT, one of America's largest permanent collections of apparel, accessories, and textiles, was founded in 1967. Its famous alumni include designers of menswear such as JHANE BARNES, JOHN BARTLETT, David Chu, CALVIN KLEIN, and Michael Kors.

fitting   The "try on" process—especially in BESPOKE tailoring—in which the garment is adjusted to the body and the pattern is made. A bespoke garment requires a minimum of one fitting, but two is customary, and three or more are not unknown.

five-fold tie   An unlined necktie that imitates the construction of the SEVEN-FOLD TIE (but uses less fabric and fewer folds).

five o'clock shadow   A slight growth of beard. Originally used to describe the slight growth visible on men who had shaved in the morning but who had such heavy beards that stubble was visible again toward the end of the day (hence the "five o'clock"). In the 1980s, when Don Johnson's character on *MIAMI VICE* and other style setters made stubble fashionable, the term was sometimes extended to include anything that was more than one day's growth but still less than a short beard.

501   See LEVI STRAUSS.

five-pocket   Describes a silhouette of pants, modeled on traditional JEANS (which have two patch pockets in the back, two inset scoop-shaped pockets in the front, plus a small coin or WATCH POCKET on the right side). Therefore, a "five-pocket jean" is somewhat traditional in style (as opposed to pleated, high-waisted jeans or other jeans made in imitation of trouser fashions). Similarly, a "five-pocket cord" would be a pair of CORDUROY pants modeled on traditional blue jeans.

While the front configuration of blue jeans has been virtually unchanged since LEVI STRAUSS began producing WAIST OVERALLS in 1873, initial models had only one pocket in the rear until 1901—thus the first jeans were actually four-pocket models.

FIT

flamed   In industry jargon, refers to a yarn that is purposely designed to vary in thickness, going from thick to thin without the addition of SLUBS or special threads.

flannel   1. Woven fabric with a soft hand and a slight NAP; usually either a PLAIN WEAVE or a simple TWILL weave. Made of wool, flannel was a favorite for suits and especially for pants. Made of cotton, flannel became a standard for workshirts and pajamas.

2. In the plural, "flannels," invariably refers to pants made of that fabric. Through the middle of the 20th century, off-white flannel pants were the preferred costume for sports activities ranging from tennis to cricket. Early on, "white flannels" also provided the traditional accompaniment to navy blue BLAZERS, especially in nautical settings (e.g., as a yachting costume or when attending a regatta). Gray flannel pants became more identified with non-summer wear and collegiate settings. They too became a traditional accompaniment to navy blue blazers, although usually in a non-nautical setting.

Therefore, whether a reference to "flannels," refers to white or gray depends on the context. For example, "the designer showed a V-necked sweater worn with old-style tennis flannels" would be a reference to the white flannels; while, in most contemporary use, "he wore his blazer and flannels" would imply gray flannels.

flap pocket   A slit pocket with a flap covering the opening (e.g., the pockets on a HACKING JACKET style); slit pockets with a flap that buttons for reasons of security or style (e.g., the back pocket on pants) are usually specified as button-flap pockets.

flares   See BELL-BOTTOMS.

flat-front pants   Jargon for pants that do not have pleats. Not used to describe jeans. Synonym: PLAIN-FRONT pants.

flat machine   Jargon for the type of sewing machine that produces a LOCK STITCH; the same type of machine used by most home sewers and what most people identify as a sewing machine.

flat weave   Jargon for a woven fabric that has no surface contours or appearance of three dimensionality. For example: MUSLIN and POPLIN would be flat weaves; CORDUROY and VELVET would not.

flax   The raw material of LINEN; name of both the plant and the BAST FIBER. Never used as the name of a fabric or cited in a blend.

flea fur   Refers to the fashion for wearing small pieces of fur around the neck (mostly during the 16th century); supposedly (although probably apocryphally) worn to distract fleas from the skin.

fleece   1. Used literally as a synonym for sheepskin, processed with its hair (i.e., "fleece") still attached to the skin.   2. As a synonym for polyester pile fabrics like the POLARFLEECE produced by Malden Mills.

flight jacket   Sporty outerwear inspired by the jackets that fighter pilots wore during World War II (which themselves were standardized over a decade earlier). A classic flight jacket is long-sleeved, hits just above the hips (to make it practical for sitting in a cockpit for extended periods), and has a full-length brass zippered front, a contrast collar, ribbing at the cuffs and waist, and two flap pockets positioned just above the waist (often with side hand slits for easy access). It is made of leather—originally horsehide in the Army Air Corps—with a fabric lining. A flight jacket may also be called a BOMBER JACKET, although "bomber" has become a more generic description and is now used to indicate the silhouette.

flip-flops A generic name for inexpensive rubber sandals that stay on only by means of a THONG between the big toe and the second toe. Derived from the sound they make as they flop against the foot.

float Jargon for yarn that "floats" across the wrong side of a fabric in what looks like long, unbound threads. Applies to both weaving and knitting. For example, looking at a sweater from the right side, you may see a pattern of widely spaced red circles; on the wrong side, the pattern is reversed and the red yarn "floats" from circle to circle in long unbroken stretches of yarn.

floating canvas Jargon to refer to a CANVAS INTERLINING that is placed by hand, rather than a FUSIBLE that is integrated into the fabric; a mark of more labor-intensive garment construction; never visible when the jacket is being worn.

flocking A process in which a VELVET look is created by applying fibers to the surface of a fabric, instead of creating them as part of the weaving process. For example, an adhesive is applied, and then the "flock" (very short fibers that are usually leftovers from other textile manufacture) is dusted on top. Found most often in trendy fabrics for shirts or pants.

floods Slang for pants that are too short, especially if they are a style not intended to be that way. For example, full-length pants that hit at or above the ankle might be called floods.

Floris The specialist in men's toiletries founded by Juan Famenias Floris in 1730 at 89 JERMYN STREET. Founded as a barber's establishment, Floris began selling fragrances not long after its opening. It supplied scent to the likes of Florence Nightingale, is the holder of multiple ROYAL WARRANTS, and was the supposed choice of fictional character James Bond (who favored No. 89).

floss 1. Unstranded SILK or very loosely stranded silk that gives the appearance of being loose fiber; used in embroideries and decoration. 2. Used as designation

Flip-flops

for embroidery floss, and therefore a synonym for thread; may be silk, cotton, or similar material.

Flusser, Alan   Known as an author and arbiter of taste as well as a designer and custom clothier.

Raised in New Jersey, Flusser commissioned his first British-made BESPOKE suits while still a student. After graduating from Temple University in 1968 with a liberal arts degree, he studied at both FIT and Parsons and worked for PHILLIPS-VAN HEUSEN and a division of PIERRE CARDIN, before opening his own luxury label in 1978. By 1985, he was concentrating on custom tailoring, although he also developed less expensive lines for retailers like Stein Mart. He won a COTY AWARD in 1984 and a CUTTY SARK AWARD in 1986. In 1987, he designed the wardrobe for Michael Douglas as corporate raider Gordon Gekko in the movie *Wall Street*.

Well-versed in the minutiae of menswear and a stickler on matters of style and presentation, Flusser also developed a complementary career as an author, contributing to magazines such as *Esquire* and *GQ*, and writing a series of well-reviewed and best-selling sartorial guides: 1981's *Making the Man*, 1985's *Clothes and the Man*, 1996's *Style and the Man*, and 2002's *Dressing the Man*.

fly   1. A fabric flap that hides the closure system of a garment, be it the zipper on a pair of trousers or the buttons on a coat front; the fly presents a smooth appearance and conceals the buttons, zippers, etc., when the garment is being worn.   2. Reference to the simple front opening for pants that allows a man access to his genitals and also allows him to take pants on and off more easily. The fly was not in wide use until the 1840s. (Before that,

pants and breeches opened by means of the FALL.) The contemporary zippered fly was not in wide use until the 1930s and after.   3. A slang approbation, as in "that's so fly," in use from the late 1980s to the turn of the century.

FMT   Abbreviation for the Federation of Merchant Tailors, the trade association to which most SAVILE ROW firms belong.

fob   May refer either to the chain that leashes a pocket watch to a garment or to a decorative ornament dangling from that chain. Commonly made of precious metal, a fob could also be leather or ribbon. By custom the watch was worn in a vest pocket and the chain or leash was secured in a buttonhole, the dangling fob, as well as being ornamental, made it easier to pull out the watch. During the late 19th century, watch fobs became a popular form of political advertisement, much like the contemporary campaign pin.

fold-over collar   In contemporary use, the most common style of shirt and jacket collar; used more often to describe shirts. In a fold-over, the collar piece is deliberately bent down to create two points on either side of the neck opening (as opposed to standing straight up on the

Alan Flusser

neck in the manner of a BAND COLLAR). In late 19th and early 20th centuries when stiff collars were still widely worn, this was an important distinction, and the fold-overs, which were more comfortable, were also considered slightly more casual (e.g., as worn by the future EDWARD VIII when Prince of Wales).

forage cap   A cloth cap with straight sides, generally worn so that the corners point front and back; folds flat into a rectangular shape. In the 20th century used in uniforms by the military and police of several Western countries, including the United States, who, when not wearing the cap on their heads, would fold it and place it through the right epaulette or over their belts. Synonyms: garrison cap; fore-and-aft cap. Similar styles: GLENGARRY CAP; NEHRU CAP.

Ford, Tom   Born in Austin in 1962 and raised in Texas until his parents moved to Santa Fe, New Mexico, when he was a teenager, Ford remains best known for his fourteen years as head designer of GUCCI—the last ten as creative director.

Ford, who moved to New York to attend New York University at the end of the 1970s, dropped out of school, enjoyed New York nightlife, and had a brief career acting in commercials before enrolling in Parsons School of Design to study interior design. After attending Parsons' Paris program, Ford graduated in 1986 and went to work for women's wear designer Cathy Hardwick. At about

the same time he met his long-time companion, Richard Buckley, an influential fashion writer who had worked for Fairchild Publications and would later become editor-in-chief of *Vogue Hommes*. In 1988, he was hired by Marc Jacobs, then at PERRY ELLIS.

In 1990, he was hired by executive Dawn Mello, then in the midst of her makeover of Gucci. In 1992, he was made the firm's design director. When Mello left for Bergdorf Goodman in 1994, Ford was made creative director and began to solidify his previously combative relationship with Gucci executive Domenico De Sole. By the following year, Ford had hit his stride, giving Gucci its first serious menswear collection and creating men's and women's looks—he was credited with initiating the 1990s fads for LOW-RISE pants and BOOT-LEG cuts—favored by both celebrities and the fashion press. At that point, Ford became a celebrity himself: almost always appearing in a dark suit with an unbuttoned shirt collar and sporting a perpetual five o'clock shadow, with his face turned three-quarters to the camera. He also became an expert at merchandising controversy and sexual innuendo: for example, the M7 fragrance campaign that showed a full-frontal male nude and the women's wear ad featuring a model with pubic hair waxed into a "G" logo.

By the end of the 1990s, Ford had definitively revived the fortunes of Gucci and, by 2000, when the company

Tom Ford

bought the YVES SAINT LAURENT ready-to-wear business, taken over that designer's Rive Gauche lines. However, after a falling out with management, both Ford and De Sole left Gucci in 2004. Ford launched his own fragrances, menswear line, and Madison Avenue store in 2007.

Forestière   In writing about menswear after the 1950s, usually a reference to the VESTE FORESTIÈRE made by ARNYS.

foretop   Synonym for a forelock or TOUPET.

formal trousers   In contemporary use, the TROUSERS worn for formal events are usually distinguished by a stripe or stripes down the side seam. The usual conventions:
   • For WHITE TIE, the pants are made of the same material as the tailcoat and sport a double stripe down the outer seam of the leg.
   • For BLACK TIE, the pants have a single stripe down the outer seam of the leg. If they are worn as part of a TUXEDO (as opposed to a DINNER JACKET of contrasting material), the material of that stripe usually matches the FACING of the tuxedo jacket.
   • For a MORNING SUIT, the pants are made of vertically striped fabric, unmatched to the coat, and have no extra stripe or decoration on the side. For an example of the traditional striped pattern, see color plates.

formalwear   Industry jargon for TUXEDOS, DINNER JACKETS, TAILS, and other CLOTHING worn to formal events. In the early 21st century (especially in Europe and Japan), it expanded to include CERIMONIA, a category of suits that were usually cut like business suits but that were, by virtue of their sometimes shiny, usually black-on-black materials, considered too dressy for daytime business attire.

Of the aforementioned categories, the least formal is cerimonia, followed by BLACK TIE. The most formal is WHITE TIE (for evening dress) and a MORNING SUIT (for daytime dress).

Forster & Son   A firm famous for supplying suit trousers to the EDWARD VIII (whose suit jackets were made by another tailor, FREDERICK SCHOLTE).

As well as accommodating his request for pockets that allowed easy access to his cigarettes, Forster & Son made his trousers according to specifications that included a high RISE, a fairly full leg, no external waistband, and an internal waistband that functioned as a stomach-flattening girdle.

fourchette   The name for the gusset between the fingers of traditionally made GLOVES; from the French word for fork. On more elaborately constructed gloves, there may also be another small gusset placed at the base of each fourchette; this is known as the QUIRK.

4711   An iconic brand of COLOGNE, best known for a traditional cologne formulation featuring citrus fruits and trace amounts of rosemary and lavender, as well as for its elaborate label and early-19th-century bottle.

The brand traces its origin to 1792, the year that Wilhem Muhlens, a resident of Cologne, Germany, received a wedding present of a formula for the astringently alcoholic, slightly citrusy concoction then generically known as aqua mirabilis or eau de cologne. During the subsequent Napoleonic wars, both eau de cologne in general and the formula that Muhlens manufactured in particular became popular with occupying French troops. (The brand's numeric name derived from the 1796 order of the French commandant to number streets: The Muhlens manufactory happened to be located in the building henceforth known as number 4711 Glockengasse.) In 1820, the company began bottling its formula in a flacon created by local distiller Peter Heinrich Molanus. The blue-and-gold label was introduced in 1839.

Celebrity customers of 4711 have included writer Johann Wolfgang von Goethe, composer Richard Wagner, and multiple members of English, Prussian, and Russian royalty.

foulard   A type of small-scale, symmetrical, nonrepresentative pattern, often printed on the SILK used for traditional NECKWEAR and DRESSING GOWNS.

Foulards are usually conservative and often have a dark ground. Common colors include gold, navy, and maroon. Common motifs include medallions, florets, or GEOMETRICS.

In references before World War I, the word usually refers to a type of medium-weight silk from which the pattern name derived.

foul-weather gear   Refers to heavy, waterproofed outerwear, especially as worn by sailors and fishermen; worn for function, rather than fashion.

four-in-hand   The slip knot that is the most traditional method of tying a NECKTIE, and of the three best-known methods (the other two being the HALF-WINDSOR KNOT and WINDSOR KNOT), the one that produces the slimmest knot and uses the least amount of tie (about 3 inches less than a Windsor).

In the second half of the 19th century, when the fashion of wearing a long necktie with a slip knot got started, "four-in-hand" referred not only to the knot but also to the

longer style of tie, differentiating it from the shorter, fuller neckwear that had been in fashion. (The term is borrowed from the four-in-hand coach, with its longer reins.) The style of knot persisted into the 21st century (and was the style favored by EDWARD VIII, who did *not* use the Windsor knot named after him when he was Duke of Windsor). In the 1990s, DERRILL OSBORN is credited with starting a fashion for FORMALWEAR accessorized with four-in-hand neckties instead of the then-customary BOW TIES.

foxhunting attire   For formal meetings of the hunt (e.g., opening day, Thanksgiving), recognized foxhunts follow a dress code based on recommendations from the Masters of Fox Hounds Association of America. Some of the suggested personal appointments:
- A scarlet FROCK COAT for the master of hounds
- A scarlet or black coat with rounded corners or a black frock coat for members of the hunt
- Sturdy, light-colored BREECHES
- A CANARY vest or TATTERSALL vest
- A top hat or a black velvet hunt cap

How to tie a four-in-hand

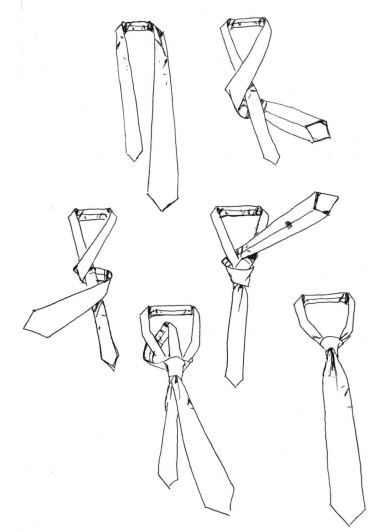

• Black boots with brown tops
• A white STOCK TIE

The separate dress code followed on less formal occasions is known as RATCATCHER.

fracque   French reference to a FROCK COAT. When ANGLOMANIA swept France in the second half of the 18th century, the fashionable began using *fracque*, the Gallicized pronunciation of frock, to refer to the style.

frames   Most often refers to all parts of EYEGLASSES or sunglasses except the actual lenses.

Commonly, the part that surrounds the lens is its frame; the piece that crosses the nose to join the two frames is the bridge (which may or may not have nose pads). The lenses at the front are joined by hinges to sidepieces, referred to as arms or temples. Most often, the arms are straight with a slight angle at the ends to keep them secured over the ears; but they may also be perfectly straight (when they are known as "librarian" style) or curved into a C-shape (also called a "cable"). In addition, the piece that runs straight across the bridge of the nose on AVIATOR and military frames is usually called the sweat bar. The style of frame that does not use arms or temple pieces is called a PINCE-NEZ.

Common materials include carbon fiber, HORN RIMS (once created from horn and now made from plastic), nylons, tinted plastics, stainless steel, titanium, and tortoiseshell (once made from actual tortoiseshell and now imitated in plastic or composite materials). Less common materials include precious metals such as gold and materials such as bone or ivory.

Common shapes and styles include aviators, BEN FRANKLINS, CORBU frames, folding frames, half glasses, military frames, RIMLESS, WAYFARERS, WIRE FRAMES, and WRAPAROUNDS. Certain styles, such as cat's-eye glasses, are rarely, if ever, worn by men.

Francis I   Born in 1494, *François 1er* was the first French monarch to deliberately establish and conscientiously maintain Paris's reputation as a fashion capital. His reign, from 1515 to his death in 1547, was the peak of the French Renaissance: Leonardo da Vinci decorated his court, the Louvre became a horde of historically important artwork, and the king's library became known for both its acquisitions and its availability to scholars. Francis made French, not Latin, the official government language and lured the top tier of Italian apparel craftsmen—weavers, jewelers, glove makers, and the like—to his court. His role in establishing Lyon as a major silk-weaving center would facilitate France's later reputation for luxury goods.

fraternity pin   A small pin, usually meant to be worn as a tie pin or lapel pin, featuring a fraternity crest, which only members are entitled to wear. (Pledges are usually given a pledge pin to serve until they are full-fledged members.) During the middle of the 20th century, the pin became especially significant when it was bestowed on a steady girlfriend, a step considered a preliminary to engagement.

fraternity ring   See CLASS RING.

Frazier, George   Born in South Boston in 1911, George Francis Frazier Jr. became best known as a Boston newspaper columnist who coined—or at least popularized—the term DUENDE; for being *Esquire* magazine's in-house arbiter of elegance as author of that magazine's "A Sense of Style" column; and also for writing the September 1960 cover story "THE ART OF WEAR-ING CLOTHES."

Frazier established himself first as a stylist, then as a writer about style. From a working-class background (his father was a fireman), Frazier attended Boston Latin and then Harvard—where he promptly flunked out. After giving it another go, he graduated in 1933. He then made his name as an impassioned jazz critic, writing for *Down Beat*, *Mademoiselle*, the *Boston Globe*, and the *Boston Herald*. Fast friends with fellow jazz fan CHARLIE DAVIDSON, Frazier had a particular fondness for pink BUTTON-DOWNS from BROOKS BROTHERS and was conscious enough of his appearance that he reportedly asked his wife to carry his cigarettes so that they did not interfere with the line of his suit. He died of lung cancer in 1974.

freak toe   Synonym for BULB TOE.

French backs   Underpants with adjustable button tabs on the waistband, so the size can be modified by the wearer.

french canvas   A type of stiffened INTERFACING, often linen; frequently employed in the front of traditionally tailored jackets.

French cleaners   Synonym for dry cleaners, since the process was invented and popularized by the French. As used by most cleaners in the United States, the term is meant to imply a more expensive establishment; however, the technique and materials remain the same whether or not the cleaners choose to designate themselves as French.

french cuff   A style of shirtsleeve that ends at the wrist with a wide, double-length cuff that folds back on itself and is fastened at the wrist by cufflinks. Its buttoned counterpart is a BARREL CUFF.

french terry   Usually made of cotton or a cotton blend, french terry is a knit fabric made with uncut loops on one or both sides. Apparel makers often use it in the same context as fleece: as a material for sweats, warm-ups, and other casualwear. The plural is "french terries." (See also TERRY CLOTH.)

fresco   A type of woven cloth much favored, particularly in the early 20th century, for spring and summer suits; usually wool. A plain weave, fresco was made of highly twisted (often three-ply) yarn, so that it had a crisp surface and created a very airy and breathable structure. Developed in Great Britain, the word "fresco" was an allusion to its supposed ease and airiness—used in the sense of "dining al fresco" rather than "fresco painting."

fribble   An 18th-century predecessor to the DANDY, MACARONI, and EXQUISITE.

frieze   A thick, heavy-duty fabric that took its name from the Dutch province of Friesland. In early references it probably indicates roughly woven wool.

'fro   Slang reference to an AFRO hairstyle.

frock coat   Refers to a style of suit jacket, which may be either single- or double-breasted, but is noted for its long skirt, which usually extends to anywhere from mid-thigh to just above the knee in both front and back, most often from a defined waist seam.

In the 18th century, the frock coat was associated with the country wear of English gentlemen and was notably looser in fit and less formal than the JUSTAUCORPS, was more often made of wool than silk, and, unlike the justaucorps, always came with a collar. Thanks to the ANGLOPHILIA that influenced French fashion, as well as England's own move toward more understated clothing, the frock coat eventually came to be worn in town. During the Victorian era, it became accepted business attire and, by the early 20th century, its original connotations had completely changed: Long gone were its implications of lighthearted informality; instead, the frock coat was a symbol of stuffiness—the ultra-correct formal attire for daytime. By the 1920s, it had been more or less supplanted in that role by the CUTAWAY. However, it continued to appear in specialist roles (e.g. as part of formal attire for FOXHUNTING).

frog, frogged, *or* **frogging**   A decorative closure, usually made of looped braid or cord. Associated with both military uniforms and Asian dress, the frog began appearing in European menswear toward the end of the 18th century and is still occasionally employed where ornament is required and extravagance is allowed (e.g., on SMOKING JACKETS and DRESSING GOWNS). Frogged garment closures—now mostly archaic—include the OLIVET and BRANDENBURG.

front shield   A term borrowed from women's wear to indicate the interior construction of a jacket; a portion of the INTERLINING that stays the front neck edge and the armhole.

fugitive dye   Dye that washes out, BLEEDS, fades, or is otherwise impermanent—either by design or accident.

fuji silk   A type of plain, relatively lightweight, woven silk fabric that wrinkles relatively easily (or synthetic made to resemble it).

full canvas   In the construction of traditional tailored clothing, refers to a jacket made all or in part with woven interfacing (classically with HAIR CANVAS). Almost always, its construction will also include SLEEVE HEADERS, SHOULDER PADS, WIGAN, PAD STITCHING, a full lining, and all the other bells and whistles associated with traditional tailoring.

full dress   Usually a synonym for the most formal attire (e.g., a MORNING SUIT for daytime wear and WHITE TIE for evening).

full-fashioned   An industry term that refers to a knit garment that is shaped—or "fashioned"—as it is being produced (as opposed to being shaped by cutting and sewing). Common examples of full-fashioning include hosiery or underwear that is shaped by the increase or decrease of knit stitches while it is still on the knitting machine.

fulling   A FINISHING process—usually for wool— designed to shrink the fabric, tighten its weave or knit, and/or raise some sort of NAP, so that it resembles FELT. The process usually involves water, heat, or both.

"Fulled" was originally the term for shrinking, as was the now-archaic term WAULKING. Over time, it became synonymous with MILLED, a process that involved heavy washing. Synonyms: milling; waulking.

Fu Manchu mustache   A style of thin or medium-weight mustache that begins as a line across the upper lip and then droops down toward the chin, extending past the corner of either lip (and in some cases off the chin). Named after a fictional villain, it became briefly modish in the 1960s when football star Joe Namath sported a modified style.

fun fur   Fake fur in a color or pattern that is not meant to look realistic.

funnel neck   A neckline, usually on a sweater, intended to evoke a TURTLENECK style. Usually a funnel neck is a bit wider and shorter than a turtleneck and does not hug the throat. Also, it never features the fold-over, or double layer of material, that distinguishes a turtleneck. A similar style, usually closer fitting, is the FAUX TURTLE.

furnishings   Retail jargon referring to almost anything that isn't actual apparel, such as neckties, ascots, belts, etc.; in older references the category was often expanded to include shirts. The usage is based on the verb "to furnish" as a synonym for "to accoutre." The category corresponds strongly to accessories but does not include shoes.

fused construction   Refers to garment construction, especially the jacket in traditional tailored clothing, that is created in whole or in part with FUSIBLE INTERFACING.

fusible interfacing   INTERFACING made of nonwoven material (as opposed to traditional CANVAS) that is created so that it can be chemically "fused" to the fabric it supports. Like its woven counterpart, fusible interfacing comes in a variety of weights. However, unlike canvas, it does not require stitching and laminates directly to the other fabric, usually through heat-setting. Generally, it is also a less expensive material than the traditional woven interfacings (such as HAIR CANVAS or HYMO). Invented at the end of the 1940s, fusible interfacing was not widely adopted in U.S. apparel production until after 1950. Then, as now, it was never visible on the finished garment.

The advantages of fusible interfacing include cheaper and more efficient garment production; it can also impart a crisper appearance. Its disadvantages, especially when fusible interfacing is poorly selected and applied, include an increased rigidity of the fabric and possible delamination during dry cleaning. Except in very high-end tailoring, the methods are not exclusive; contemporary production of ready-to-wear tailored clothing may use a combination of construction methods and materials.

"Nonwoven" is sometimes used incorrectly as a synonym for fusible interfacing. This is a misnomer since, although all fusibles are nonwoven, not all nonwoven interfacings are fusible. In industry jargon, garments constructed by such methods may be referred to as "fusibles."

fustian   1. A woven textile whose original implication was far different from its current dictionary definition of pretentious verbiage. In the 17th century, fustian was a no-nonsense material produced in England (especially in Lancashire) from imported cotton and local linen. Made by working people for other working people, it was undecorated and sturdy—a sort of all-purpose predecessor to denim.   2. In earlier, now more obscure, usage, fustian is a general name for a woven material that could refer to a variety of fiber blends (including wool).

Fu Manchu mustache: Christopher Lee

gabardine A medium-weight fabric in a simple TWILL weave; distinguished from other twills by the steepness of the twill line and the dominance of the WARP. Sturdy and versatile, gabardine is therefore prized for pants and suits. Often made of WOOL or wool blend, almost always in a solid color. Variant spelling (especially in British usage): gaberdine.

gaiter A covering for the lower leg. In contemporary use, worn for functional purposes by hikers and climbers to keep snow and dirt from entering the top of the boot; a gaiter may extend all the way from the welt of the boot (completely covering the foot) to just underneath the knee, or it may be as abbreviated as a piece of cloth covering the instep and going immediately above the ankle.

In earlier eras, abbreviated gaiters—such as SPATS—were worn for fashion as much as function. At the beginning of the 20th century, the word was also used synonymously for GALOSHES that completely covered the foot and ankle.

Galeotti, Sergio Best known as the partner of GIORGIO ARMANI and the man who encouraged that designer to start his own business.

After graduating from the University of Cararra in 1967, Galeotti was working for an architectural firm when he met Armani. In a relationship that is inevitably compared to businessman Pierre Bergé's with designer YVES SAINT LAURENT, the two first became romantic partners. In 1970, Galeotti began working as a buyer for the Larus chain of menswear stores while also functioning as the designer's agent as Armani freelanced for various labels.

In 1975, the two established their own company. (According to legend, the two had to sell their Volkswagen to help cover the $10,000 start-up costs.) As chairman of that company, Galeotti was credited with many of the unconventional business decisions that contributed to its success, such as: the founding of the lower-priced Emporio Armani line; the respite from expensive runway shows during the early 1980s; and a firm hand in dealing with retailers who wanted to carry an Armani collection.

He died in August of 1985, aged 40.

gallapava Leather made from the skin of turkeys. A sort of poor man's version of OSTRICH, it features a similarly pimply surface where the feathers have been plucked, but the grain is not as prominent and the skin is not as sturdy.

Galliano, John   Born in Gibraltar in 1960 to a Spanish mother and an English father, John Galliano studied textiles and fashion design at Central St. Martin's in London and was crowned as fashion's darling after showing his 1984 graduation collection, "Les Incroyables" (which incorporated menswear). Showing in the late 1980s in London, his signature collections for men continued to subvert standard cuts, make extensive historical quotations, and pile on styling touches usually associated with women's runway shows. However, it was as a designer of women's wear that Galliano made his primary fame, particularly after taking over as head designer at Givenchy in 1995 and then Dior in 1996. (Although he never designed for Dior Homme, a label that became fashionable after signing Hedi Slimane.)

Galliano opened a store on rue St. Honore in Paris in 2002 and in early 2004 took up menswear once again when he revived his signature line at the Paris shows in a collection that incorporated pinstriped suits with a bias cut (a hallmark of many of his women's wear designs at the time) and track suits that quoted heavily from traditional matador looks.

Even before the conversion to physical fitness that made him famously buff and fond of posing without his shirt, Galliano became known for his own costumes: notorious for taking his runway bows in everything from a feathered eagle bonnet to an astronaut's spacesuit.

John Galliano

gallows   Slang, especially in 18th- or 19th-century England, for suspenders or braces (because pants hang from them).

galluses   Straps or suspenders—usually elastic—that hold up pants. For example, the elastic inserts in the back of old-fashioned bib overalls are usually referred to as galluses. The singular is gallus.

galoshes   Protective overshoes meant to shield less sturdy and/or more expensive footwear from mud, rain, and snow. In contemporary usage, often connotes a larger, sturdier overshoe, sometimes with a buckle or other closure.

galuchat   Leather made from the skin of the stingray. Like shagreen, which it resembles, it is fairly stiff, appears more often in accessories, and has a distinctive pebbly grain.

gambeson   In armor, a padded cloth or leather jacket; worn either alone or in combination with chain mail or metal armor. Its padding later influenced the civilian styles such as the doublet.

gamp   Old-fashioned, mostly 19th-century slang for an oversized umbrella. Supposedly derived from the character Sarah Gamp in Charles Dickens' 1843–44 novel *Martin Chuzzlewit*.

Gandhi cap   An earlier name for the cloth cap now better known as the Nehru cap.

gansey   1. A style of pullover sweater, traditionally handknit in a fine gauge of five-ply wool, most often in dark blue. The style was worn on the fringes of the

British Isles: the coasts of Scotland, Cornwall, the island of Jersey, and even the pre-1930 ARAN Islands, with different areas evolving different decorations.

Ganseys were traditionally knit in the round and patterned only over the chest and upper arm. As knitting designer Alice Starmore points out in her 1993 book *Fisherman's Sweaters*, this pattern had the practical advantage of enabling the sweaters to be unraveled and reknit when the heavily used parts such as elbows and hems became worn out. However, it also had the distinct disadvantage that the pattern could not easily be sized smaller or larger and, instead, had to be computed to the individual wearer.

2. Any knitted garment, especially in Irish or English usage, but especially a pullover sweater worn for sports activities that resembles the traditional fisherman's gansey.

Garment District   The area of midtown Manhattan that was once the heart of much of the U.S. apparel industry, bounded on the north by Times Square and on the south extending roughly to West 23rd Street, going west from the Avenue of the Americas to the Jacob K. Javits Convention Center on the western edge of the island.

The area concentrates many of the city's fashion-related schools (the midtown branch of Parsons, FIT, the High School for Needle Trades), the showrooms of many major designers and mass-market manufacturers, buying offices, and the related businesses (jobbers, notions suppliers, etc.) who cater to them.

garment-dyed   Exactly what it sounds like: The garment is dyed after it is made. Used most often for jeans or trendy tops, garment dyeing allows the manufacturer to wait until the last minute to ship products in a particular color scheme. Typically, when linings, labels, and interfacing are the exact some color as the rest of the garment—even though they are made of different fabrics—it's a telltale sign that the piece has been garment-dyed.

Garment dyeing is also used to give a sort of "reverse fading" effect, so that the material under the belt loops and at the seams may be slightly lighter, where the dye hasn't soaked in as easily.

garmento   Industry jargon for an old-timer who uses lots of industry jargon. (As in the sentence: A garmento sources shirtings, suitings, and other fabrications offshore to get the best-price goods to market.) Although he usually owns or operates a fashion business, a garmento is more concerned with the bottom line than with design or arty aspects of the fashion business. The garmento's trend-conscious counterpart would be the FASHIONISTA.

gaucho   A South American cowboy whose distinctive traditional dress, like that of his American counterpart, has been highly romanticized and frequently adapted as fashion. A stereotypical gaucho outfit might include a PONCHO, worn as top layer and protection from the elements; a neck kerchief; a dark felt "gaucho hat" with wide brim and shallow, flat crown, secured under the chin by a slide fastener; a long-sleeved cotton shirt; a wide belt ornamented with silver; baggy pants, called BOMBACHAS, that can be tucked into boots; and boot-GAITERS formed by allowing the hide of a freshly skinned horse to form to the leg.

gauge   A measure of threads or stitches per inch. The higher the number, the finer the weave or knit. The lower

Garment District

the number, the rougher the weave or knit. For example, a rugged-looking, handknit sweater might have a gauge of 3 stitches per inch, while machine-knit dress socks might have a gauge of 12 or more stitches.

Gaultier, Jean Paul The designer who would be known as the "enfant terrible" of French fashion well into his middle age was born on April 24, 1952, in Arcueil, a suburb of Paris, and secured his first job at Pierre Cardin in 1970. He then assisted at Jacques Esterel (who had designed modified skirt/pants for men in the 1960s), at Jean Patou, and again at Cardin, in addition to producing small, inventive collections under his own name, finally gaining his first major sponsorship from the Japanese company Kashiyama in 1978, whereupon he began making his name in the women's wear market.

In 1984, he did his first menswear collection. The following year, he launched skirts for men, an idea he would revisit regularly in subsequent collections. The fashion press frequently described his work as "transgressive" and he regularly featured pierced, tattooed, and other alternative beauties as his runway models. His

Jean Paul Gaultier

name became familiar to an audience beyond high fashion when he designed Madonna's costumes—most notably her cone-shaped bras—for her 1990 world tour.

In 1995, he followed the successful 1993 launch of his women's fragrance line (which came packaged in a tin can) with Le Mâle, a men's fragrance featuring a bottle design that scandalized the market by including an anatomically correct bulge at the crotch. In 1997, the heretofore conservative Hermès acquired a share in his company and, in 2003, officially hired him as the designer for its women's collection. In 2003, he also launched Tout Beau Tout Propre, a "makeup for men" line.

Gaultier's personal trademarks included closely cropped, platinum-dyed hair that emphasized his round head, large ears, and prominent nose; tight, striped sailor jerseys; clunky Doc Marten-type boots; frequent wearing of kilts or jeans; and an irreverence that bordered on the punk. Collaborations included costumes for director Peter Greenaway's 1989 film *The Cook, The Thief, His Wife and Her Lover*. Fluent enough in English to be witty and quotable in that language, he was a regular host for the British-based variety program *Eurotrash* during the 1990s.

gauntlet   1. Heavy work gloves, worn for protective purposes; usually with a liberal cuff that extends onto the forearm and also protects the wrist.   2. The placket on a sleeve opening, immediately above the cuff.   3. In armor, glovelike protection for the hands. When protrusions, such as spikes, are placed over the knuckles, they are known as "gadlings."   4. A glove cuff that is particularly flared and long, in imitation of a protective gauntlet. For example, the portion of a fancy cowboy glove that extends past the wrist and is decorated with beading and long fringe is referred to as the gauntlet.

gauntlet button   In shirts, a single button and button-hole (usually horizontally placed) on the GAUNTLET—the opening directly above the cuff—is considered the sign of a better-made DRESS SHIRT, since it is considered uncouth for the skin to show through a gap in the placket when the cuffs are fastened. Synonym: PLACKET BUTTON.

gauze   A lightweight and loosely woven fabric that supposedly takes its name from the Middle Eastern city of Gaza. Most often made of cotton, the lightest-weight gauze is used in bandages and dressings. Otherwise, men encounter the fabric—in a slightly heavier version—in tops made for warm weather.

geek chic   An anti-fashion fashion, coined in the late 20th century as an ironic reference to the guy, classically a computer geek, who wore unfashionably thick (often black HORN RIM) eyeglass frames (perhaps with a bridge mended by tape or temple hinge fixed with a paper clip), pants hemmed too short (so that they fall at or above the ankle), a short-sleeved shirt (of man-made fiber) accessorized with a pocket protector, and short hair (possibly with a cowlick). In its designer incarnation, geek chic usually translated to too-tight, too-short suits.

References to computer geeks changed from negative to grudgingly positive during the years when Microsoft founder Bill Gates was repeatedly named as the richest man in the world. See also NERD.

The Gentleman's Journal   An American, tabloid-format weekly published from 1869 to 1872, under the subtitle "An Illustrated Magazine of Literature, Information and Amusement."

Gentleman's Quarterly   See *GQ*.

geometrics   Absolutely nothing to do with protractors, proofs, or geometry. In the fashion and textile industries, "geometric" connotes any print that is not pictorial. Therefore, its opposite category would be CONVERSATIONAL.

George IV   Born in 1762, British monarch George Augustus Frederick was a creature of excess: vastly overweight, obstinate in his aversion to his wife Caroline, overfond of overspending, and profligate in his patronage of his beloved design projects (such as the building of the Royal Pavilion at Brighton). As Prince of Wales, he became Prince Regent upon the illness of his father George III and the Regency Act of 1811 (although costume historians generally count the Regency period as the decade from 1810 through 1820). He ascended to the throne on the death of his father in 1820 and himself died in 1830.

In the history of menswear, George is best remembered as the patron of BEAU BRUMMELL, whom he began to befriend in the late 1790s. It may be a testament of their friendship and measure of Brummell's personal genius that Brummell was able to establish an aesthetic of elegant refusal during the reign of a slovenly prince who virtually invented the fantastical "Indian gothic" as an architectural style and who personally had a waistline over 50 inches. Even after their

George IV

inevitable falling out (caused by Brummell's ill-advised witticism about the Prince Regent's corpulence) and Brummell's subsequent flight to France in 1816, George's regency and reign remained regarded as the apogee of the English dandy.

ghillie A style of shoe that laces through loops instead of eyelets; originally from Scotland. Popularized by EDWARD VIII when he was Prince of Wales, the ghillie is lightweight and slipper-like, also worn with the KILT and used for traditional Scottish dancing.

ghillie suit A CAMOUFLAGE suit, originally used in hunting game, then identified with sniper activity; from the original Scottish use of "ghillie" to mean a gamekeeper's assistant. Synonym: SNIPER SUIT.

ghuterra *also spelled as* **ghutra**, **ghutrah**, *or* **gutra** The scarf component of tradition ARAB headdress. A large square usually made of COTTON or RAYON, the ghuterra is folded in half and the fold is worn forward, centered over the face. Its color varies according to region. For example: Kuwaiti men may favor plain white; Saudi men may wear white or white-and-red; while the black and white KAFIYEH is favored in Iraq and Jordan. The ghuterra is worn over a SKULLCAP called a taqiyah and is secured by an AQAL.

gi The traditional white or off-white loose pants, wrap-front top, and thick cloth belt worn for most martial arts, including karate and judo. According to a system invented at the end of the 19th century, different colors of belt correspond to different degrees of expertise: A beginner wears a white belt and progresses through various colors to the achievement of a black belt, with intermediary and subsequent degrees depending on the particular martial art and the dojo's own tradition. Also according to some traditions, the belt remains unwashed.

gibus Synonym for an OPERA HAT, a collapsible TOP HAT; named for Antoine Gibus, who first offered what became the most widely used type of spring mechanism hat in Paris in 1837.

Gieves The London tailoring firm that traced its founding to military tailor Meredith Gieves, setting up shop in Portsmouth in 1785, at about the same time that the Royal Navy began to standardize its officers' uniforms and also in plenty of time to dress Admiral Nelson for the Napoleonic wars and the Battle of Trafalgar. Through moves, incorporations, and partnerships, the same firm was known as Galt & Gieves in the mid-19th century. In 1914, it patented the first inflatable life-saving waistcoat. In 1974, it merged with HAWKES to become GIEVES & HAWKES and moved to 1 SAVILE ROW.

In 2003, the name was relaunched as a more fashion-oriented collection aimed at younger customers, with an entrance at 2 Savile Row, and was marketed with images of a father wearing Gieves & Hawkes next to a son wearing Gieves.

Gieves & Hawkes The SAVILE Row tailoring firm formed by the 1974 merger of GIEVES and HAWKES, which were both firms established in the 18th century and both firms with a specialty in military tailoring.

gilet The French word for WAISTCOAT.

gills Slang in the 19th century for the upright points of a man's shirt collar. Also called "shirt gills."

gimp   1. In construction of traditional tailored clothing, cord that is used to help create the buttonhole.   2. Decoration such as a braid, a sense used more often to describe women's wear or upholstery.

gimping   In references to shoes, describes the process of creating a decorative edging on leather (e.g., the DAGGED EDGE visible on BROGUES); a process done with a gimping machine.

gingham   A type of PLAIN-WEAVE fabric, most often made of COTTON or a cotton blend. In menswear, gingham is most often used for shirts and most often appears in a simple, two-color CHECK pattern. See color plates.

Girbaud, Marithé *and* **François**   The apparel label established by the French husband-and-wife design team of Marithé (born in 1942) and François (born in 1945); best known for launching successive successful JEANS styles under their own label or through licenses, which had huge influence on the worldwide denim market.

In 1964, the Girbauds, who were admirers of Americana, began importing COWBOY-style jeans to Western

François and Marithé Girbaud

House, a Paris retailer. Three years later, they began the fad for prematurely aging the jeans via industrial LAUNDERING and, in 1968, introduced their first collection in Europe. By the 1970s, they were infamous as the inventors of STONE-WASHING. In the 1980s, they pioneered purposely torn and tattered jeans.

They are also credited with launching the trend to exaggeratedly baggy and ELEPHANT-LEG jeans in the early 1980s (which would endear them to the HIP-HOP market well into the 21st century).

The Girbauds' other influential designs include a major redesign of the uniforms for Air France in the early 21st century. The couple also became known for their espousal of environmental awareness—to the extent of incorporating "living walls" into their boutiques. They opened an American showroom in 1982, but did not open their first wholly owned American store until 2003.

glen check *or* **glen plaid**   A general description referring to a family of designs; not necessarily a shortened from of GLENURQUHART. Refers to checks such as the PRINCE OF WALES, glenurquhart, or patterns that resemble them.

Because glen is the Scottish word for valley, many of the ESTATE TWEEDS, which were named for their location and built upon a glenurquhart-type pattern of squared mini and maxi checks as their background, became known as glen plaids. This group includes both the legitimate, registered patterns, such as Glenfinnan, Glenisla, Glen Orchy, and Glen Tanar, and the newly invented patterns that fashion and textile designers create to imitate that look. See color plates.

Glengarry bonnet   A style of brimless hat—known as a bonnet in Scotland—that is high and narrow and can be folded flat like a FORAGE CAP. The Glengarry is distinguished by a checked brim—properly referred to as DICED—and by ribbons in the back (which were used to adjust the hat). Popularized by the flamboyant Alasdair MacDonell, chieftain of the clan Glengarry and Sir Walter Scott's inspiration for the 1810 novel *Waverley*, the bonnet style is said to have originated from the traditional BLUEBONNET style later known as the BALMORAL, from men who preferred to wear the style puffed up on top (rather than flattened like a beret). Associated with Scottish regiments (in the 19th century it was briefly adopted by most of the British army), in contemporary use the Glengarry is worn by Highland musicians and dancers as well as occasional used with evening dress.

glenurquhart Refers to a specific black-and-white pattern with no OVERCHECK or other colors; a bold, squared plaid combining mini and maxi checks; most often confused with a PRINCE OF WALES pattern (which *does* incorporate a colored overcheck). Pronounced *glen-URK-hart*.

Originally an ESTATE TWEED commissioned by Caroline, Countess of Seafield for her land at Glen Urquhart in Scotland, the first glenurquhart was made in navy and white and was probably designed by Elizabeth Macdougall, building on a traditional black-and-white white SHEPHERD'S CHECK, and woven by a Lewiston weaver named William Fraser in about 1840. It may be generically referred to as a GLEN CHECK.

gloves A generic name for hand coverings with individual attachments to cover all or part of the fingers (whereas MITTENS only differentiate between the fingers and thumb). Gloves with differentiated fingers but no fingertip covering are called MITTS. Protective gloves used in armor, for work, or for sport are usually called GAUNTLETS.

In general, the terminology for a glove follows the terminology of the hand it covers: The "finger" covers the fingers; the "thumb" covers the thumb; the "palm" goes over the palm; the "cuff" is any part extending past the wrist. If the cuff is flared and extends to protect the wrist, that is called a "gauntlet." In traditional construction, gloves were made with a separate gusset piece between each finger, which was called the FOURCHETTE. In old-fashioned glove making, especially before the 19th century, the insertion of the fourchettes required three seams that extended onto the back of the hand, which is why today many traditional gloves still have three seams, now called BACKLINES. (And which is also why, as a mark of quality, the backlines should always be aligned with the spaces between the fingers.) In addition, older and more elaborately made gloves have another, smaller gusset, called the QUIRK, in between each finger, which falls at the base of each fourchette.

Glovemaking is ancient. Gloves have been found in Egyptian tombs, were mentioned in Homer, and were cited in *Beowulf*. However, they did not become standardized until the late Middle Ages, when they were taken up by the clergy and nobility. Thereafter, gloves became an item of fashion, with European glovemakers doubling as the first perfumers (an expertise necessitated by the fact that most leather was tanned in urine or some similarly unpleasant substance). In the court of LOUIS XIV, for example, both men and women wore gloves filled with perfumed unguents to soften their hands. Among the once-usual leathers for gloves: chicken skin, doeskin, dog skin, and the hide of unborn calves.

For related entries, see: GLOVE SIZES; GLOVERSVILLE.

Gloversville The New York town, located at the edge of the Adirondack Mountains, still known as the GLOVE-making capital of the United States. According to

Katherine Morris Lester and Bess Viola Oerke in *Accessories of Dress*, the local industry got its start in 1760, when William Jonson induced families of Scottish glovemakers to settle in the area, which was richly supplied with hemlock trees (an aid to tanning leather). By the early 19th century, the city began exporting its gloves and, by the turn of the 20th century, had cornered the market and was responsible for about 90 percent of the gloves made in the United States.

After World War II, glove production moved offshore and most of the city's glove-making factories and support industries closed their doors.

glove sizes　Glove measurements are usually taken when the hand is flattened (but not spread) on a table; the hand is then measured around the knuckles but not including the thumb. Unlike women's gloves, which still use a number system, contemporary men's gloves are usually sized small, medium, and large. (The exception being military gloves, which are sized 3, 4, 5, and 6.) Nevertheless, the "standard" glove sizes—especially those manufactured outside the United States, which tend to run small—can vary by up to an inch. The general outline:

Hand Width in Inches	Glove Size
7 to 7.5	Small
8 to 8.5	Medium
9 to 9.5	Large
10 to 10.5	Extra large
10.5 to 12	Extra, extra large

Gloverall　The English firm, founded in 1951 by Harold and Freda Morris as a vehicle for the British government to dispose of its excess World War II DUFFLE COATS and related garments. In 1954, when its source of government surplus ran out, the Morrises began to make the coats under their own label. Manufactured in Northamptonshire, the classic Gloverall coat is made of heavy wool or wool blend DUFFEL material, is knee-length, and has a PANCAKE HOOD, toggle closures, an extra layer of cloth stitched over the shoulders for warmth, and two large PATCH POCKETS.

goatee　A small beard trimmed so that it does not join sidewhiskers and does not include a MUSTACHE; so-named because it supposedly looks like the tuft of hair on the chin of a billygoat. The goatee differs from a VANDYKE, another style of chinwhiskers, in that it does not include a mustache and is usually not as shaped.

go commando　1. Slang referring to the practice of going without underwear (specifically underpants). Supposedly derived from the practice of commando forces to go without briefs during extremely hot weather and/or during battle conditions that require them to pack as few items of clothing as possible. Passed into general usage in the third quarter of the 20th century (and was used as a plot device in a 1996 episode of the popular television series *Friends*). 2. Slang reference to a young man who must be toughened up, which includes learning not to overdress.

Goethe, Johann Wolfgang　See THE SORROWS OF YOUNG WERTHER.

goggles　A category of protective eye gear, which may be worn for sports (e.g., skiing, scuba diving) or work (e.g., in laboratories). Goggles come in a variety of styles and transparent materials but, unlike most glasses, usually fit closely to the face, forming a sort of seal around the eye area, and are not worn for streetwear.

golf shoes   Refers to a style of shoes made for the golf course and based on BROGUE but featuring a decorated, long TONGUE that flaps over like a KILTIE. It is generally made of heavier, waterproof leather for wear on dewy ground and may also be an unusual color (like white) or two-toned (like a SPECTATOR). A shoe actually intended for wear on the golf course customarily is fitted with nine or eleven spikes on the sole to improve the player's stability on slippery grass.

golf umbrella   A hugely oversized UMBRELLA with a cover almost twice the area of a standard umbrella. Unlike umbrellas used in business or town settings, the cover (cloth canopy) is always brightly colored or a combination of white and some bright shade. Never black. Also, unlike more formal umbrellas, the shaft is never overdecorated or made of precious material.

gore   A piece of cloth, most often shaped like a wedge of pie, inserted into a section of the garment to add fullness.

Gore-Tex   Trademarked name for a membrane process commercially introduced by W.L. Gore & Associates in 1976, primarily to make apparel weatherproof. The Gore-Tex system touts the "breathability" of its design, in which the billions of microscopic pores per square inch in its extremely thin and flexible membrane allow water vapor from the skin to pass outward but do not allow raindrops to soak through to the skin.

Most previous weatherproofing systems for apparel—waxed cotton, rubber rain gear—formed an impermeable barrier that tended to trap sweat next to the wearer's skin.

gorge   From the French word for throat, today used as industry jargon as a quick reference to the placement of a jacket's neck opening. Depending on context, in contemporary usage the term is used to indicate one or all of the following:

1. A shortened form of GORGE SEAM—i.e., the meeting of the collar (which curves around the back of the neck) with the LAPEL (which is part of the jacket body); this usage makes it synonymous with NOTCH.

2. The set of the neck opening, especially how high or low it falls on the chest; this usage makes it synonymous with BUTTON-STANCE.

3. The actual placement and height of the collar around the throat. In this usage, a suit jacket with a high gorge obscures virtually all of the collar of the dress shirt worn beneath it. Conversely, a suit jacket with a low gorge would be one that reveals virtually all of the dress shirt collar. (In traditional menswear, the ideal is generally considered between the two extremes—with the gorge revealing a flattering margin of shirt collar.)

gorge seam   In the jacket or coat of traditional tailored clothing, the seam where the lapel—i.e., the front of the jacket body that folds back—joins the collar, a separate pattern piece. (Hence, a shawl collar, which is formed from a long, single collar, has no gorge seam.) The customary V-shaped indent where the two pieces join is referred to as the NOTCH. Synonyms: GORGE; gorge line.

Goth   A street fashion that cultivated a resemblance to vampires by emphasizing black clothes (with the occasional accent of dark purple or blood red), extremely pale skin, and black (frequently spiked) hair.

Goth began on the London club scene in the 1980s—notoriously at the Batcave, which opened in 1982, and claimed to be its birthplace—had a wide influence in the 1990s, and thereafter was revisited regularly on designer runways. Goths frequently accessorized themselves with exaggerated makeup—including black eye makeup and black nail polish—and heavy silver jewelry that referenced vampires, Celtic motifs, or medieval (i.e., Gothic) religious motifs.

GQ   The men's fashion magazine initially founded as *Gentleman's Quarterly*, a spinoff of *Esquire* magazine in 1958; later made a monthly magazine, which was sold to Condé Nast and reconfigured as *GQ* in 1983.

GQ can trace its heritage back to *Apparel Arts*, the fashion trade first published as a quarterly in 1931, which in turn inspired the publication of *Esquire*, a consumer magazine, in 1933. Initially begun as a revival of *Apparel Arts* aimed at *Esquire*'s circulation, the magazine was almost exclusively preoccupied with fashion until it was acquired by Condé Nast, a publisher that then installed Art Cooper as editor-in-chief. Cooper promptly reconfigured the magazine's coverage to include sports, literature, and all manner of matters pertaining to the good life, and, by 1993, *GQ* was outshining and outselling *Esquire*, its progenitor. Its own subsequent spinoffs—some successful and some short-lived—have included *GQ Cars* and *GQ Style*, as well as separate editions edited and published in Australia, Germany, Russia, and the United Kingdom.

Cooper's reign lasted for nearly two decades, when falling circulation and the temporary popularity of rowdy "lad" magazines like *Maxim* inspired Condé Nast to install Jim Nelson as editor-in-chief in 2003.

grain   1. In leather, refers to the distinctive pattern formed by the animal's pores, scales, and/or hair follicles. For example, CALFSKIN is prized for its relatively smooth grain, while OSTRICH is prized for the circular, pimply pattern created by its plucked feathers.

A grain finish is one in which the markings are visible (as opposed to being smoothed out). A "corrected grain" leather is a hide on which a pattern has been artificially applied.

2. In fabric, refers to the direction of the weave. When constructing a garment, pattern pieces must be allied with the grain in order for the finished garment to hang correctly.

When tailors and patternmakers speak of the grain or "lengthwise grain," they are talking about the direction of the WARP, which runs vertically. Due to the construction of woven fabric, the warp direction or lengthwise grain is the strongest, a fact that is exploited in the alignment of pattern pieces for traditional menswear.

grain suede   Synonym for NUBUCK leather.

gram weight   Used as a measure of the heft of fabric, usually as the weight of a meter. (In the English system, the equivalent is ounces per yard.)

Along with other qualities like fiber composition, weave, and design, a fabric's weight is one way of determining its suitability for certain categories of apparel. For example, SHIRTWEIGHT fabrics often have a gram weight of 150, SUITWEIGHTS may be in the 200s, BOTTOMWEIGHTS may go to 200s and 300s, and JACKETWEIGHTS and COAT WEIGHTS are generally from 250 to 400—or above—grams per meter. Fabrics with gram weights above 550 are not often produced for apparel.

granite   A type of cloth, usually wool, that has a pebbly surface affect—hence the name—almost like a wool crepe.

granny glasses   A style of undecorated, wire eyeglass frames named after the glasses associated with caricatures of little old ladies; fashionable for young men during the mid 1960s (especially after they began to be worn by John Lennon). The lens is small and is usually either completely round or strongly horizontal. The horizontal version may be called BEN FRANKLINS.

Grant, Cary   During his 75-film career, which began in 1932 and ended with his retirement in 1966, Grant embodied the *beau ideal*, even though he did not spend an untoward amount of money on clothes, sometimes wore the same piece for decades, and managed to become a fixture on *Esquire* magazine's best-dressed lists without really following fashion.

Grant was born Archibald Alexander Leach in Bristol, England, on January 18, 1904, the only child of a working-class family (an older brother having died before he was born). His father was a tailor's presser, who reportedly told his son to buy the best quality because it lasted longer; his mother put a premium on his appearance, making sure that her son's clothes were always immaculate. Coming to America in 1920, the young acrobat and would-be vaudevillian found himself aboard the same ship with his idol, the tanned and supremely fit Douglas Fairbanks Sr., who made such an impression that Grant himself stayed tanned and supremely fit until the day he died.

Arriving in New York, he began to emulate the other Brits working on Broadway, who wore formalwear and fine tailoring as casually as later generations would wear sweatsuits. Hence, in 1933's *I'm No Angel*, Grant is dressed to the nines but slouches and sticks his hands in his pockets. Forever after, Grant would treat his formal clothes informally (adopting casual poses, performing athletic stunts), and his informal clothes formally (accessorizing jerseys and workshirts with neck kerchiefs in the perfect pattern, tying them with just the right knot). Ian Fleming once said that he had a mental picture of Cary Grant in mind while writing his James Bond novels.

On-screen, Grant controlled his image by controlling his costuming. His suits, sometimes made on Savile Row (e.g., KILGOUR, FRENCH & STANBURY), do not have the exaggerated drape or shoulders so popular in the 1940s or 1950s and were fitted to ensure ease of movement, always with the high, tight armhole that Grant insisted upon. With a collar size variously reported as 17 or 17½ inches, plus the slope-shouldered build of an acrobat, the 6-foot, 1-inch Grant minimized his neck by ordering shirts with

Cary Grant

higher COLLAR STANDS, by buttoning up his pajama tops (e.g., in 1940's *The Philadelphia Story*), and by using neck kerchiefs to fill in the open throat of shirts and sweaters (e.g., 1955's *To Catch a Thief*). He thought his head was too big, so he rarely wore a hat. He hated both belts and suspenders, so he commissioned his pants to need neither. Having last changed the part in his hair for 1932's *Blonde Venus*, he didn't change it again until the day he died. When starring opposite Ingrid Bergman in 1955's *Indiscreet*, he wore an overcoat commissioned in 1933.

Grant let his hair gray gracefully and eventually go white. When he needed glasses, he wore thick black frames, which never went out of fashion because they had never been in fashion. He became infamous for adopting women's nylon panties on the grounds that they were more practical and comfortable than the underwear made for men. Although in later life his casual wear sometimes incorporated cowboy shirts and jeans (when riding with his daughter) or CAFTAN-type tops (run up by his wife Barbara Harris on her sewing machine), Grant retained his relatively conservative and minimalist style in public (commissioning some of his later suits from Quintino in Beverly Hills)—particularly for appearances made on behalf of Fabergé, the fragrance company on whose board he served. He died in 1986.

graves   In ARMOR, the pieces that protect the shins. Variant spelling: greaves.

grayers   Early-20th-century slang, usually British, for gray flannel pants, particularly as casually worn by the upper class.

gray goods   Industry jargon for textiles that have not been dyed or finished, so called because they are usually a dirty, off-white shade. Gray goods may be produced in vast quantities by one mill and then sent to a CONVERTER to be transformed into a color or pattern dictated by the fashion of the moment. Synonym: GREIGE.

grease wool   Wool that has been processed—or purposely left unprocessed—so that it retains its natural lanolin.

greaser   Pejorative slang for the style better known in Britain as the ROCKER. Sanitized into the beloved Fonzie character played by Henry Winkler on the long-running (1974–1984) sitcom *Happy Days*, the greaser worn his hair poufed in front and combed into a duck's ass in back with the aid of a product like BRYLCREEM (hence the grease), a black leather jacket, tight white T-shirt, motorcycle boots, and blue jeans.

greatcoat   Refers to any of several styles of big, bulky overcoats, such as the ULSTER, or the BRITISH WARM. (All greatcoats are overcoats, but not all overcoats are greatcoats.) Never used to describe ACTIVEWEAR styles (such an ANORAK). A greatcoat is generally a tailored style but not as lightweight, finely tailored, or close to the body as a TOPCOAT.

greaves   In ARMOR, the pieces that protect the shins. Variant spelling: graves.

Grecian Formula   The men's hair-coloring product launched in 1961 as Grecian Formula 16. A comb-in product that promised to change gray gradually—so that no one would suspect a man was dyeing his hair—it remained the dominant product in the men's market for decades. In 1987, its manufacturer, Combe Incorporated, launched Just for Men, a shampoo-in hair color.

Greek dress (ancient) See individual entries for CHALMYS, CHITON, FIBULA, PETASOS, and SANDALS.

Greek key A symmetrical border pattern that appeared on ancient Greek art and architecture and that reappeared during the 18th century as Western Europe's passion for neoclassicism progressed. This mazelike pattern resembles a pattern of endless waves lapping against each other, except that all curves are squared. Classically the width of each repeat is equal to its height.

greige Industry jargon for fabric that has been knit or woven but not dyed, printed, or otherwise FINISHED. Synonym: GRAY GOODS.

Grenfell cloth A cotton fabric popular for sports and technical gear before the invention of modern laminates and SYNTHETICS. Sturdy and closely woven, it is highly water- and wind-resistant and is still used in the production of clothes for country pursuits. Named after British explorer Sir Walter Grenfell, who wore it on expeditions.

grip *or* **gripper** A small strip of fabric, usually rubberized, on the inside of the pants waistband, where it is intended to help hold the shirt in place. Not visible from the outside. In contemporary fashion, grips never appear on custom or designer clothes.

grommet A reinforcement, usually metal or plastic, around a hole made in plastic or leather. The word refers to the reinforcement and not to the actual hole. For example, old-fashioned sneakers usually have eyelets through which to thread shoelaces, and those eyelets have grommets.

grooming credit In magazine or other editorial layouts, the person (or persons) performing hair and make-up chores gets a "grooming credit." Depending on the photographer, subject, and publication, these duties vary wildly. Sometimes elaborate hair styling and application of cosmetics may be required. At other times, the "groomer" may simply be required to comb the subject's hair. The women's equivalent is the "beauty credit" and generally reads "hair and makeup by . . ."

grosgrain A horizontally ribbed, woven fabric with a use mostly confined to the edges of menswear (e.g., hatbands, the ribbons used in medals and military decorations, lapels and stripes on pants in formalwear). In contemporary menswear, fabric that is ribbon width is usually grosgrain, and similar but wider fabric is usually FAILLE (which is slightly flatter and often shinier).

ground Refers to the basic color of a textile; used in the sense of "background." For example: "His tie showed a pattern of small yellow dogs against a navy blue ground."

grunge A style that began in the Pacific Northwest during the mid-1980s, especially among fans of grunge rock bands, who had appropriated the alienation of their predecessors, the PUNKS. When the music went nation-

Grunge: Kurt Cobain

wide in 1991, with the success of bands like Pearl Jam and Nirvana (and the particular success of grunge posterboy Kurt Cobain), so did the clothes.

At a time when high fashion was focused on conspicuous consumption and VERSACE and his supermodels ruled the runways, grunge rock fans rescued most of their clothes from thrift shops or throwaway bins. They wore WATCH CAPS indoors, along with dirty JEANS and flannel shirts tied around their waist. They had dirty, unstyled hair and sparse, untrimmed beards. Their piercings and tattoos were considered ugly and overdone, and their predilection for tatty, POLYESTER clothes baffled the garment industry. Their clothes were radically different from the HIP-HOP styles of the same time, which were exaggeratedly oversized, extremely label conscious, and scrupulously pristine.

Although the movement influenced the high end of the women's market, where *Vogue* produced issues featuring the new fashion as interpreted by designers like Marc Jacobs and worn by "waif" models like Kate Moss, the same did not happen with high-end or mainstream menswear. Its strongest crossover was in the DENIM market, where jeans had pre-made "dirty" finishes. As a separate style, it petered out following Cobain's death from a heroin overdose in 1994.

guanaco   A CAMELID native to South America. Although the guanaco's coat yields very fine fiber that easily allows it to be classified as a NOBLE FIBER, it appears in menswear less often than its other camelid cousins because the composition of its coat has very thick guard hairs, making the fine fibers underneath more difficult to harvest.

guard's coat   A pseudomilitary style of double-breasted GREATCOAT distinguished by a half belt across its back; modeled after the coats worn by the Grenadier Guards (the former regiment of EDWARD VIII and thus the most fashionable). Dark in color and designed to give a slim appearance, the guard's coat is actually quite accommodating to movement due to its construction, which incorporates a long, INVERTED PLEAT in its center back.

guard's tie   Refers to a traditional style of necktie with a REGIMENTAL STRIPE. According to costume historians, the British fashion for wearing a striped tie in the colors of one's former regiment crossed the pond when the future EDWARD VIII visited the United States as Prince of Wales in 1919. Being a former officer of the Grenadier Guards, the prince affected his regimental tie of blue and red, and thereafter the style came to be known as a guard's tie. Synonym: regimental tie.

guayabera   A style of unfitted, four-pocket, button-front shirt with a straight bottom. Made of plain, unpatterned fabric—most often cotton or a cotton blend, and most often white. The guayabera may have short sleeves or long sleeves and may be decorated with pin tucks or embroidery, but its decoration is always symmetrical and the shirt is never tight and is never worn tucked in. Traditionally, the small shirt collar is always worn open, with the topmost button unbuttoned, even at receptions and formal events; however, during the 20th century, some men started to add a TUXEDO-style bow tie for formal occasions.

According to popular lore, the guayabera was first widely adopted in Cuba during colonial times and subsequently spread throughout Latin America, where it was worn on both informal and formal occasions, functioning as both shirt and jacket. Famously, it was worn by Ernest Hemingway and Fidel Castro.

Gucci   Founded by Guccio Gucci in 1921 as a luxury leathergoods shop in Florence, by the late 20th century the brand had become as well known for its family melodrama and many lawsuits as for its luxury apparel and accessories.

When Guccio died in 1953, ownership passed to his three sons, Aldo, Vasco, and Rodolfo (but not his daughter Grimalda). During the next two decades, Aldo spearheaded the brand's international expansion and its chic among the jet set (and was turned in to the IRS for tax evasion by his own son). In the third generation, Rodolfo's son, Maurizio, became the family's highest-profile bad boy, marrying a woman named Patrizia Reggiani against his father's wishes, supposedly allying himself with the Mafia, and being tried—and acquitted—for forgery and other dodgy business deals, then splitting from Reggiani in 1985.

In 1989, fueled by a feud with Maurizio, Aldo's sons sold their shares of the company to an Anglo-American holding company called Investcorp, which brought in American retail executive Dawn Mello to turn around a brand badly in need of a makeover. In 1990, Mello imported designer TOM FORD. Meanwhile, Maurizio sold his 50 percent of the company in 1993, ending the founding family's involvement, and then was gunned down in broad daylight in 1995 (with ex-wife Reggiani later being convicted of commissioning the killing).

However, the brand was heating up again. Ford, who was getting great reviews for his women's wear, began a full-on men's collection in 1995. Up until then, Gucci trademarks had included metal horse bit decorations (first used in the 1940s), red and green SURCINGLE webbing (from pre-World War II), and linked G logos woven into fabric (from the early 1960s). Ties had first appeared in the late 1950s. Ford, who became creative director in 1995, made Gucci synonymous with sex. He oversaw a huge increase in its advertising presence, making it markedly more provocative with high-profile fashion photographers such as Mario Testino, Steven Klein, Terry Richardson, and Craig McDean.

But the brand's business troubles weren't over. In the late 1990s, Gucci became the source of a bitter battle between luxury conglomerates Louis Vuitton Moet Hennessy (better known as LVMH) and Pinault-Printemps-Redoute (better known as PPR). In 1999, the PPR faction won, and, soon thereafter, the Gucci group went on its own buying binge, acquiring (among others): YVES SAINT LAURENT's business in 1999, Balenciaga in 2001, ALEXANDER MCQUEEN and Bedat watches in 2000, and BOTTEGA VENETA in 2001. However, in a dispute with Ford, the brand lost its star designer, who said goodbye in a January 2004 runway show with professional strippers working poles placed along on the edge of the runway. That year, designer John Ray took over the men's collection and was quickly succeeded by designer Frida Giannini.

Gucci loafer   Refers to the style of slip-on shoe, or loafer, first manufactured by GUCCI in 1953; distinguished by being ornamented across its long VAMP by a metal horse's bit (an eggbutt snaffle) and, in some versions, sporting a band of SURCINGLE webbing striped in Gucci's red and green colors beneath the bit. A longtime staple of both playboy and PREPPY wardrobes (both groups traditionally wearing it without socks), the footwear was so identified with a monied and leisure class that, in 1987, author Alan Murray named his book about tax reform *Showdown at Gucci Gulch*, in reference to the loafers of the lobbyists.

Guggenheim, Benjamin   Although neither his life nor his work was particularly distinguished, playboy investor Benjamin Guggenheim secured his place in fashion history by the style in which he chose to die.

Born in 1865 in Philadelphia, he was the fifth of the seven sons of Meyer Guggenheim, who had made a fortune in mining. Married and the father of three daughters, Benjamin Guggenheim nonetheless maintained an establishment in Paris in order to pursue his other interests. In 1912, with French mistress in tow, he boarded the RMS *Titanic* to return to New York.

Because it was a Sunday evening when that ship struck an iceberg, passengers were not in the formalwear then customary for other shipboard evenings. So Guggenheim, attired in sweater and life preserver, first graciously assisted female passengers (including his mistress and her maid) to the available lifeboats, then returned his life preserver to a steward and repaired to his cabin to change into more formal attire. He reappeared in full regalia and announced "We've dressed in our best and are prepared to go down like gentlemen." He also told a steward: "Tell my wife I did my best to do my duty." Guggenheim and his valet were last seen at about 2 a.m. on April 15, 1912 in superbly correct evening dress, sitting on deck chairs with their brandy and cigars.

gum boots   Rubber boots, especially WELLINGTONS (aka "WELLIES"), especially in British usage; derived from the usage of gum as a synonym for rubber. Boots that do not also rubber uppers are properly referred to as gum-soled.

gummies   A style of shoe with a very thick crepe sole, especially in the mid-20th century.

gum shoes   RUBBERS.

gum twill   A silk TWILL, usually patterned, used for neckties, ascots, and the like. Synonym: FOULARD.

gun club check   A style of check design derived from ESTATE TWEEDS. In a classic gun club, three colors of yarn are used: a light ground color (white or off-white), a dark color (black or very dark brown), and a medium shade (reddish brown). The medium and dark colors are arranged in a symmetrical, overlapping grid pattern that resembles GINGHAM. The name derives from a U.S. gun club's 1874 order for Coigach estate tweed, which uses the same pattern. See color plates.

gun flap   A flap of fabric added to right shoulder of a jacket or coat as a way of reinforcing it against the butt of a rifle; in contemporary use, still found on traditional TRENCH COAT styles.

gusset   A piece of fabric added to an area such as a crotch or armpit to increase range of motion without straining the seam; usually not visible when the wearer is at rest. For example, ACTIVEWEAR pants may have a diamond-shaped gusset added to the crotch so that activities like leaping or stretching do not split the seam.

guv'nor   Usually an honorific form of address for the head, or "governor," of a tailoring firm.

gym bag   Generic late-20th-century reference to a functional style of large bag meant to tote gym clothes. The classic gym bag has a zipper closure and is made of material that is resistant to dirt and moisture. It often has double handles made of webbing, an additional shoulder strap so that it can be carried on the shoulder or across the chest, and it may also have a net pocket where damp clothes or sneakers can be stored while they dry out.

H&M Hennes & Mauritz, a chain of fashion retailers based in Sweden and notorious for getting the latest trends into its stores very quickly and very inexpensively. In 1947, when Erling Persson opened his first Hennes (a name that translates to "hers") store in Västeråas, it sold low-priced women's fashion in an upscale setting. Soon after, he expanded to Stockholm, acquiring a hunting and fishing retailer known as Mauritz Widforss along with its extant stock and thereby incorporating men's fashions. Subsequent stores reflected the new name and merchandise mix. By the 1960s, the chain expanded into children's and teen sizes. By the 1980s, it had expanded beyond Scandinavia. In 2000, it opened its first U.S. store on Fifth Avenue in New York City. Beginning in 2004 with KARL LAGERFELD, it initiated a series of collaborations with high-end designers and celebrities who were commissioned to do heavily promoted one-off collections for the chain.

haberdasher Originally someone who sold the ACCESSORIES and accoutrements to TAILORED CLOTHING (including shirts), but not the clothing itself. Although the word's etymology connotes a seller of small wares, in contemporary usage it usually connotes someone who sells all kinds of menswear—including tailored clothing.

habit Usually refers to apparel that follows such established conventions or is subject to such stringent dress codes that it amounts to a sort of a quasi-uniform—thus its use as "court habit" or "riding habit."

Hackett Founded in London in 1983 by Jeremy Hackett and Ashley Lloyd-Jennings (who met at the Portobello Market while searching for vintage clothes), Hackett was initially a shop on New Kings Road that handled second-hand SAVILE Row clothing. Not long after, it began offering traditional English apparel and accessories under its own label and promoting itself as the source of "essential British kit." In 1992, it opened what became its flagship store on Sloane Street.

hacking jacket A style of tailored jacket associated with horseback riding (especially with less formal riding or RATCATCHER as opposed to full foxhunt or show regalia), or the SPORTS JACKETS made in that style.

The hacking jacket is closely fitted to the body, has a high armhole to facilitate movement, and flares from the waist (which may be positioned a tad higher than it is on an ordinary jacket). Traditionally, it has a flapped breast pocket in addition to two flapped bottom pockets, known as HACKING POCKETS, positioned on a slant. It may also have a TICKET POCKET, also positioned on a slant. It always has a single vent in the back and a three- or four-button front (three buttons being most common in contemporary use) and is one of the few menswear styles where it is considered correct to wear all three buttons buttoned: It is, in fact, mandatory when wearing the jacket for riding. Both the collar and the lapel of the jacket are often made with buttonholes so that the neck of the jacket can be buttoned closed in dirty weather.

Although the style is renowned for its longish SKIRT, earlier hacking jacket styles tended to have even longer skirts. In contemporary use, the jacket is usually short enough to be worn on the street. Jackets intended to be worn for horseback riding usually have an additional waxed-cotton lining inside the back vent and more capacious pockets. Worn as part of ratcatcher turnout, they are often an earthy-toned tweed (in wool, linen, or some other fiber appropriate to the local weather).

hacking muffler   Refers to a style of looping a long scarf or MUFFLER around the throat. The scarf, usually about 6 feet long, is folded in half, and then the loose ends are threaded through the loop formed by the fold. EDWARD VIII made the style popular when he was Prince of Wales, and the mode was widely revived in the 1990s.

hacking pockets   Slanted pockets with flaps, especially on a SPORTS JACKET. Derived from the style traditionally found on HACKING JACKETS for horseback riding.

hair   Jargon for fibers made from animal hair, such as ALPACA, CAMEL'S HAIR, CASHMERE, CHINCHILLA, GUANACO, MOHAIR, ORYLAG, or VICUNA; most often the fibers that are also known as NOBLE FIBERS. Never used to refer to wool.

hair canvas   A type of woven INTERFACING made with animal hair (e.g., *CRIN* or goat hair) so that it has a firm, slightly wiry feel and can thus be employed for the effect of shaping a garment (e.g., creating the roll of a lapel). When used in a jacket front, it imparts a nice, unbroken line that can be used to subtly flatter the silhouette of the man wearing it. More pricey than most other interfacing options, it requires skill to be used to best effect, and thus remains one of the star components in the construction of traditional FULL-CANVAS clothing.

hair cloth   1. Jargon for woolen-type woven fabrics created from animal hair such as ALPACA, CHINCHILLA, or ORYLAG; most often those that are now better known as NOBLE FIBERS. Never used to refer to wool.   2. A reference to HAIR CANVAS.   3. A reference to scratchy, uncomfortable fabrics such as those that might be used for HAIR SHIRTS.

Hakama

hairline stripe About the width of a hair (which makes it skinnier than a PINSTRIPE). Often used to describe shirt fabrics; rarely used to describe suit fabrics.

hair shirt A deliberately scratchy and uncomfortable undergarment, usually made of a material like HORSE-HAIR, worn next to the skin for religious or other penitential purposes.

hakama The traditional, Japanese, ankle-length garment for the lower body, derived from samurai tradition. In contemporary use, used for martial arts, tea ceremony, and formal occasions such as weddings. The hakama has more than one variation and may resemble either a sort of split pants-skirt (*umanori*) or skirt (*gyoto hakama*), and may be fastened at the waist by several traditional methods; but it is always made with seven pleats—five in the front, two in the back—to symbolize the seven virtues of the samurai.

How to tie a half-Windsor

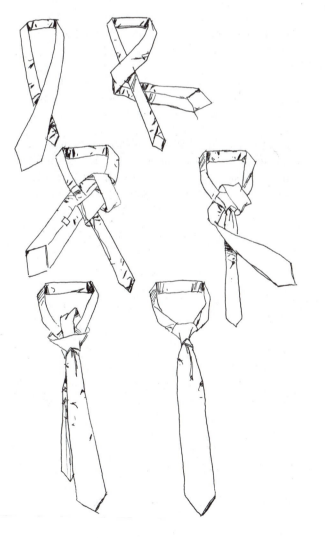

half boots A general term, more commonly used before World War I, to refer to BOOTS that do not extend all the way to the knee. A half boot usually hits mid-calf and is slightly taller than the contemporary COWBOY BOOT.

half hose Socks, especially short dress socks and especially in British usage.

half-Windsor knot Refers to a method of tying a NECKTIE so that it results in a medium-sized knot; it is, literally, an incomplete WINDSOR KNOT.

The half-Windsor results in a knot that is thicker than the traditional four-in-hand and thinner than the full Windsor.

half-zip A style of top or outerwear in which the zipper is placed front and center and does not extend all the way from the neck to the waist. Most "half-zips" actually extend no more than a quarter or a third down the front of a man's shirt or sweater—some only extend as far as the placket in a polo shirt.

halo stripe A pattern sometimes used in suit fabrics, which looks as though the center of a stripe is the same color as the background but is surrounded by another color in a "halo" or eclipse effect.

Half-zip

hand   Short for "handle." Jargon for the feel and drape of fabric. For example, a protective treatment may be praised because it doesn't change the hand of the fabric. Or a BIELLA-made wool may be touted as having "a fine Italian hand." Sometimes stated or written as "hand feel."

handcrafted   Usually indicates a garment that has been HAND-FINISHED, although the garment may or may not have been completely handmade. For example, a sweater may be labeled as "handcrafted" even though it was made on a small knitting machine (as opposed to being completely hand-knit).

hand feel   See HAND.

hand-finished   1. A garment that has been constructed chiefly by machine, usually with the decorative details done by hand. For example, a jacket's inner construction may be sewn on a machine with only the decorative stitching edging its lapels and pockets—i.e., the stitching that shows when the jacket is worn—done by hand. Similarly, a sweater may be knit on a machine and have its ribbing either knit or attached by hand.   2. Refers to a fabric finish—usually a distressed effect applied to expensive denim jeans—that is applied by hand, either before or after the garment is made. For example, a pair of "hand-finished" jeans may be sewn and then have the front of the knees sanded by hand to more accurately simulate the irregularity of long wear.

handle   See HAND.

handlebar mustache   A style of luxuriant mustache that curls up at the ends, so named in the late 19th century because it supposedly resembled the handlebars of the then-faddish bicycle.

hand-loomed   A term most often applied to knitwear as a way of implying that it is handmade, even though it is actually manufactured on a machine. For example, an ARAN-style sweater labeled "hand-loomed in Ireland" is not produced on two (or four or five knitting needles) but is instead produced on a small, old-style knitting machine that is hand-operated (a method that produces sweaters more quickly and results in a more reliable GAUGE.)

hand-rolled hem   A small, unobtrusive hem in which the fabric is literally rolled back on itself and then lightly stitched in place. Hand rolling is employed when a maker does not want to add stiffness or reinforcement to a finished edge, particularly with silk or other lightweight and pricey goods. Silk NECK KERCHIEFS or POCKET SQUARES commonly have hand-rolled hems.

handstitched   Refers to sewing of a garment with the millennia-old means of needle and thread (as opposed to the use of any machine).

hangdown shoulders   In tailors' jargon, refers to droopy, poorly constructed shoulders (usually created by the poor placement of SHOULDER PADS).

hangtag   A tag attached to a finished garment in addition to its price tag. Customarily, hangtags explain and promote special features of the garment, such as a stain-repellent fabric treatment. (According to industry wisdom, men supposedly pay more attention to information on hangtags than women.)

Hang Ten   The brand founded by surfer Duke Boyd in 1959, derived from surf slang for the trick of hanging all ten toes over the edge of the board, and known for its two-footprint logo. After joining with a Long Beach manufacturer in 1960, Hang Ten became a multimillion-dollar SURF brand best known for BOARD SHORTS; striped, surf-styled T-shirts; and other style allusions to California beach life. Boyd left the company in 1970 and rejoined it as a consultant in 1987.

hanseline   A style of DOUBLET, popular in Western Europe just before the Renaissance.

hard finish   Jargon for fabric that has no suggestion whatsoever of PILE, NAP, or three-dimensionality. For example, a SHARKSKIN suit fabric or flat shirt cotton might be described as having a hard finish; a MOLESKIN would not.

hard hat   1. The round, protective, helmetlike headgear required to be worn by construction workers, engineers, and their colleagues on job sites.   2. A style of dress distinguished by JEANS, workboots, T-SHIRTS, and plain grooming; synonymous with construction workers. A term that became popular in the last third of the 20th century.   3. In the context of horseback riding, reference to the peaked black-velvet cap worn by members of the hunt or the standard headgear for competition in horse shows.

hard press   Ironing a pattern piece or garment with heavy pressure, usually done with the intention of shaping the fabric.

hard spun   Jargon for yarn that is tightly spun so that its fibers are compacted and it results in a dense, strong material. Synonym: hard twist.

hare pocket   Synonym for a POACHER'S POCKET, usually on the inside or back of a jacket.

harness looms   As applied to menswear, the description of cloth being made on a harness loom is generally used to indicate artisanal or deliberately old-fashioned production (e.g., certain types of TWEED) and is used—not so much as a technical description of a mill's actual mechanics—but as shorthand to distinguish such weaving from mass production and to signal a cloth that is narrower in width.

Harris tweed   A type of heavy wool cloth made in the Outer Hebrides, a group of islands on the west of Scotland. Popular for outerwear and jackets, its best-known form is a two-color HERRINGBONE TWILL of off-white and near-black.

For centuries, the islanders wove TWEED for their own use. However, in the late 1840s, when the Industrial Revolution had already mechanized wool production elsewhere, the widow of the Earl of Dunmore began to promote this homespun, home-woven product to the apparel industry. Beginning in 1906, islanders began to seek trademark protection for their product to distinguish it from machine-made imitators originating on the mainland. In 1934, a 345-page judgment from the Scottish Court of Session guaranteed the current terms of the trademark.

Members of the Harris Tweed Association authenticate their product with the words "Harris Tweed" and the symbol of an orb surmounted by a Maltese cross, and stamp it on the back of the fabric every 3 yards. This trademark may or may not also include the fabric's isle of origin. Under terms of the trademark, Harris tweed must be VIRGIN WOOL produced in Scotland and spun, dyed, handwoven and finished on Barra, Benbecula, Harris, Lewis, South Uist, or other parts of the Outer Hebrides. Before a new plaid or pattern is permitted to be sold with the trademark, it must be registered and numbered by the Harris Tweed Association.

Harrow hat   A distinctive style of deep-brimmed straw BOATER worn at the English public school.

Hartmarx Corporation   The largest manufacturer of tailored clothing in the United States; parent company of brands including Hart Schaffner & Marx, Hickey-Freeman, SANSABELT, and Palm Beach.

harvard cloth   Woven fabric that is virtually identical in its use and weight to OXFORD CLOTH, except that it is a TWILL instead of a PLAIN WEAVE.

hatband   A decorative band or trim that encircles the crown of a (usually brimmed) HAT. For instance, on a modern FEDORA, the hatband may be a GROSGRAIN or satin ribbon in a color that matches the felt or other primary material of the hat. In a straw BOATER, the hatband may be bright colors, signaling a school or team association.

The hatband, which appears on the outside, should not be confused with the SWEATBAND, which is the (usually leather) band on the hat's inside.

Hathaway   A DRESS SHIRT company founded in Maine in 1837, Hathaway manufactured shirts for the Union Army during the Civil War, but gained its greatest notoriety after September 1951, when its ad campaign, "The Man in the Hathaway Shirt," debuted in *The New Yorker* magazine. Created by Ogilvy & Mather, the first ads featured middle-aged model George Wrangell as a mustachioed man of mystery wearing a Hathaway shirt and an eye patch. For four years, the Walter Mitty-esque adventures of the "Man in the Hathaway Shirt"—conducting an orchestra, painting, checking his shotgun—appeared only in *The New Yorker*, and Hathaway shirt sales tripled. In subsequent years, celebrities such as Ted Turner put on an eye patch and played the Man in the Hathaway Shirt.

By the time Hathaway closed its Waterville, Maine, plant in 2002, it claimed to be the last dress shirt factory in the United States. In 2004, the label, which had been bought by the Ike Behar company, was revived—although Hathaway shirts were no longer made in America.

hat retainer *or* **hat guard** *or* **hat leash** *or* **hat cord**   A slender cord, rarely more than 6 inches in length, which attaches the back of a hat (such as a DERBY or TOP HAT) to the back of a collar for the purpose of preventing the hat from blowing away or falling off. For example: Many foxhunting packs specify the use of hat retainers as part of riding attire.

hat sizes   A hat size is based on a measurement taken at the widest part of the head, which is generally about ½ inch above the top of the ears.

Informal and/or inexpensive hat styles, such as BASEBALL CAPS or CRUSHERS, are generally sized S, M, L or may be simply "one size fits all" (which is generally a little over 22½ inches or the big side of a medium). These sizes may run from XS to XXXL.

Metric sizes, used in mainland Europe and much of the rest of the world, simply measure the head and use the number of centimeters as the size number. Generally, these sizes run from 53 through 64 or 65.

Elsewhere though, hat sizing becomes considerably more complicated. To arrive at an American hat size, the head is measured in inches, then divided by pi (3.14159265) and rounded to the closest eighth. These sizes generally run from 6⅝ to 8⅛.

British hat sizes (which are generally used in Australia as well as the former British colonies) use a similar system that is even more complicated: The head is measured in inches, then divided by pi (3.14159265), rounded to the nearest eighth, and then an eighth is subtracted from the total (which means that a British hat size is generally ⅛ smaller than its closest American equivalent).

Unfortunately, metric sizes do not have an exact conversion to the British and American system, the closest equivalents are:

Inches	Metric	American	British	General
21	53	6⅝	6½	XS
21½	54	6¾	6⅝	S
21¾	55	6⅞	6¾	S
22	56	7	6⅞	M
22½	57	7⅛	7	M
22¾	58	7¼	7⅛	L
23	59	7⅜	7¼	L
23½	60	7½	7⅜	XL
24	61	7⅝	7½	XL
24⅜	62	7¾	7⅝	XXL
24⅞	63	7⅞	7¾	XXL
25⅛	64	8	7⅞	XXXL
25½	65	8⅛	8	XXXL

hauberk In ARMOR, a shirt made of CHAIN MAIL or scaled metal.

haversack A generic style of knapsack or backpack that is usually worn on one shoulder only.

Hawaiian shirts Best identified by their bold prints and boxy shape, the casual tops known as Hawaiian shirts first became widely worn in those islands during the 1930s (when their wear was encouraged by the custom of "Aloha Fridays"—a sort of local precursor to "casual Fridays"), although the style actually originated in the previous decade. Most costume historians trace the shirt's shape to the checked PALAKA shirts popular among plantation workers and PANIOLOS, and trace the shirt's stylized prints to the Japanese kimono cloth and the Polynesian PAREU fabrics widely available in the islands. The fashion was spread through tourism and, after World War II, a concerted effort on the part of the local government to encourage islanders to wear the shirts during festivals.

Then and now, the typical Hawaiian shirt is short-sleeved, button-front, loose through the body, and worn with its collar open and its hem (which is usually straight instead of being formed into shirttails) outside the pants. Although fashions for their fabric and prints come and go, the shirts are always boldly printed on a woven fabric, most often cotton, rayon, or silk. Common patterns include flowers (especially hibiscus), foliage (especially banana leaves or palm fronds), fruit (especially pineapples and coconuts), and island lifestyle scenes (especially hula dancers or beach landscapes). Synonym: aloha shirts.

Hawes & Curtis Founded in 1913 by Ralph Hawes and Freddie Curtis, this JERMYN STREET clothier's business was made when, nine years later, EDWARD VIII (then Prince of Wales and considered the best-dressed man in the world) became a customer. Thereafter, many stylish

Hawaiian shirt

men, from the Earl of Mountbatten to FRED ASTAIRE, followed suit.

Known primarily as a custom shirtmaker, Hawes & Curtis credits itself with inventing the SPREAD COLLAR for the prince, as a way of accommodating the knots of specially made, thickly lined neckties he favored. It also claims invention of the backless WAISTCOAT for wear with WHITE TIE and TAILS.

Hawkes, Thomas   The Stourbridge-born, London-based tailor who established his own firm in 1771; best known for suiting many of the late-18th- and early-19th-century aristocrats, including George III and GEORGE IV. Also renowned for developing a technique of hardening leather to withstand saber strokes, something considered a substantial advance in body ARMOR in the centuries prior to the invention of KEVLAR. He died in 1809, aged 64.

The firm he founded continued both its military and civil custom through the 19th and 20th centuries, moving to 1 SAVILE ROW in 1912, and merged with GIEVES to become GIEVES & HAWKES in 1974.

head banger   A fan of HEAVY METAL.

heavy metal   A music genre that can be traced back to the late 1960s, heavy metal's style evolved over subsequent decades, but its most reliable components seemed to be plunging necklines (revealing unshaven, unwaxed chests), tight pants (varying from denim to spandex to leather, depending upon the decade), big hair, and a ready adoption of makeup and ornamentation (especially chains and studs). The basic look was established during the 1970s by bands like Aerosmith, Alice Cooper, Blue Öyster Cult, and Led Zeppelin and interpreted by hundreds of successors and rivals, including Judas Priest, Kiss, Motley Crüe, and Van Halen.

Unlike PUNK or other music styles, heavy metal was never a darling of high-end designers, although it helped popularize the adoption of big hair (and an increased use of hair products), tattoos, decorated leathers, and other forms of self-decoration among male fans (known as metalheads).

heel counter   Synonym: COUNTER. See SHOE diagram.

heel stay   A small piece of fabric used to line the inside back of tailored TROUSERS. Traditionally, the heel stay is there not only to support the fabric but to prevent it from being stained by shoe polish. Not seen when the garment is being worn.

Hemming, Lindy   Born in Wales in 1948 and educated at the Royal Academy of Dramatic Arts in London, this costume designer is best known for her work on the James Bond movies, which she began designing in 1995 with *Goldeneye*. Although all previous Bonds had been suited by British tailors, Hemming gained immediate notoriety by using the Italian company BRIONI to give her Bond, Pierce Brosnan, the look of British BESPOKE, a tradition she would continue when Daniel Craig took over the role in 2006's *Casino Royale*.

Her other credits include: *Batman Begins* (2005); the Lara Croft Tomb Raider movies; *Harry Potter and the Chamber of Secrets* (2002); *Topsy-Turvy* (1999), for which she received an Academy Award; *Four Weddings and a Funeral* (1994); and *My Beautiful Laundrette* (1985).

hemp   A fiber used as a sort of poor man's LINEN for centuries, particularly for shirts. In contemporary use, the *cannabis sativa* used in high-end clothes may be referred to by its Italian name CANAPA.

henley   Refers to a style of pullover shirt or sweater with a round neck and a short, buttoned placket in front. Synonym (especially for one that resembles long underwear): WALLACE BEERY.

Hennes & Mauritz   See H&M.

Henry Poole   The family-run bespoke tailoring firm located at 15 SAVILE Row that traces its origin to the linen business set up by James Poole in 1806. During the Napoleonic wars, the firm became a military tailor. When James died in 1846, his son Henry expanded the extant premises and located the entrance on Savile Row (hence its claim to be "founder" of the Row). In 1876, the business passed to Henry's cousin, Samuel Cundey, who expanded it into the Continent. Thereafter, it was managed by succeeding generations of Cundeys.

Tailor to the great and famous, its client list has comprised Emperor Napoleon III, Winston Churchill, the Emperor of Japan, Charles Dickens, and Charles de Gaulle. In 1860, for example, it made the first suit of the style that later became known as the TUXEDO for EDWARD VII, then Prince of Wales.

Herman, Pee-wee   The cartoonish character created by actor Paul Reubens; see under PEE-WEE.

Hermès   Founded in 1837 as a saddlery and harness business by Thierry Hermès, the manufacturer and retailer now based at 24, rue du Faubourg Saint-Honoré in Paris became best known for luxury leather-goods, including its Kelly and Birkin bags for women and, for men, its distinctively patterned, hand-rolled silk twill neckties, as well as men's ready-to-wear designed by Véronique Nichanian.

Operating under the premise that its first client was the horse and its second was the rider, Hermès also continued to hand-manufacture fine tack and riding clothes, and to sponsor events, such as the prestigious Prix de Diane race at Chantilly, emphasizing its equestrian heritage. Beginning in 1987, the company also began announcing annual themes—"The Year of the Hand" (2002), "The Year of the River" (2006)—used as motifs in both merchandise and marketing.

Hermès also owns large shares of luxury companies such as JOHN LOBB shoes, Saint Louis crystal, Puiforcat silver, and the textile group Perrin.

herringbone   A symmetrical weave pattern that alternates between right-hand and left-hand TWILLS. The effect of this switching back and forth is that the twill line zigzags up and down across the fabric, so that it supposedly resembles a fish backbone—hence the "herring bone," or its old-fashioned synonym, "fishbone." The pattern can be any size, but when it is particularly large, it's usually called a CHEVRON weave instead of a herringbone.

One of the most popular weaves for menswear, herringbone is used on everything from fine shirt fabrics to

Hermès: Véronique Nichanian

denims to heavy wools, and is famously associated with Harris Tweed. Synonyms: chevron; reversed twill; zigzag. See color plates.

Hessian boots A dashing and romantic style of boot, derived from Hessian military uniforms, especially popular in the early 19th century. Hessian boots were lower on the sides and rear, rising to a summit just below the knee, from which was suspended a dangling tassel. Generally worn with tight pantaloons.

high waist A description of pants that begin at or above a man's natural waist. The opposite designation is low-rise. Hollywood waist pants are high-waisted. Hip-huggers are not.

Hilfiger, Tommy Born in Elmira, New York in 1951, designer Thomas Jacob Hilfiger became best known for clean-cut, all-American jeans and sportswear, which he himself described as "preppy with a twist."

Hilfiger's fashion career began in 1969 when the high school senior and two of his friends got together $150 and opened People's Place, a hippie-style head shop selling jeans, records, rolling papers, and related paraphernalia. He expanded to seven stores, but was forced to close in 1976 due to both economic and style changes. In 1983, he began working as a freelance designer for Jordache and, the following year, met jeans mogul Mohan Murjani, who financed a line of men's jeans. In 1985, a publicity blitz positioned Hilfiger as the fourth great American designer for men in ads listing him next to Calvin Klein, Perry Ellis, and Ralph Lauren; the campaign also made Hilfiger's vaguely flaglike, red, white, and blue logo instantly familiar.

By 1989, Hilfiger formed a new partnership and, in 1992, took his company public. At the same time, his brand also became beloved by rappers and others in the hip-hop world (e.g., Snoop Dog's 1994 appearance on "Saturday Night Live" in a Hilfiger logo shirt), and he branched into women's wear. In 1995, the CFDA named him menswear designer of the year. In 1997, he opened luxury stores in London and Beverly Hills and in 1999 did his first runway presentation in an extravaganza at Roseland Ballroom that featured a live performance by Sugar Ray, the group on the next month's cover of *Rolling Stone*. That same year, he also reinforced his company's identification with rock 'n' roll with tie-ins to Lenny Kravitz and a Rolling Stones tour. In 2000, Hilfiger's stock price plunged, and within a year or two, he had closed his luxury stores. At the beginning of the 21st century, his company became renowned for its fluctuations in management and stock prices.

In 2004, he went into business with Karl Lagerfeld and, in 2005, he also starred in a reality TV series called *The Cut*.

hip buttons Nonfunctioning buttons positioned at the back of a man's coat or jacket at waist level, usually over vents, pleats, or flaring fabric. Most common from the 17th through 19th centuries.

Tommy Hilfiger

hip-hop   A category of fashion that began with street styles worn by kids living in New York in the 1970s (hence the use of STREETWEAR, URBAN FASHION, or URBAN STREETWEAR as synonyms); initially identified with the cultural movement that included rap music, break dancing, its own argot (including fashion coinages like BLING and KICKS), and eventually encompassing its own lifestyle publications (e.g., *XXL* and *Complex*).

In popular mythology, hip-hop traces its origin to a party thrown by Jamaican immigrants Cindy Campbell and her brother DJ Kool Hercon at 1520 Sedgwick Avenue in the Bronx on August 11, 1973. Supposedly, Campbell held the party to raise money for a new back-to-school wardrobe, and her brother, who was playing music, created mixes that extended the rhythm breaks. "Break dancing" was created to match the style, with "b-boys" favoring oversized, ACTIVEWEAR styles for the freedom of movement they allowed.

As the music became more popular and more hip-hop music stars started their own brands, many of the styles initially identified as hip-hop—such as gigantically oversized T-shirts and jeans, state-of-the-art sneakers, and DU RAGS—migrated to the culture at large. By the 1980s, "urban" clothes were a staple of apparel selections in small towns and suburban malls. By the 1990s, the movement had come full circle and labels heretofore identified as hip-hop were launching their own tailored clothing lines.

Some of the mainstream labels appropriated as hip-hop fashion at various times include: ADIDAS, CONVERSE, TOMMY HILFIGER, KANGOL, and TIMBERLAND. Labels originating from—or identified with—hip-hop include: Cross Colours, Ecko, Fat Joe 560, Fubu, Lot 29, Mecca, Pelle Pelle, PHAT FARM, ROCAWEAR, SEAN JEAN, and Southpole.

hip-hugger   Pants, particularly jeans or casual styles, that have a LOW-RISE so that their waistband crosses the hipbone or below (as opposed to the navel or waist).

hippie   Although the term evolved in America in the mid-1960s, from the earlier use of HIPSTER, the hippie subculture rejected the exaggerated tailoring of the hipster and instead embraced exuberance (e.g., psychedelic, swirling prints that were supposed to evoke the visions induced by LSD and other hallucinogens) and ornamentation (e.g., long leather fringe), appropriating some of the costume conventions associated with women (e.g., long hair, fanciful decoration, flowers, and jewelry). Also in complete contrast to his immediate predecessor, the MOD, the hippie generally preferred the artisanal, the handmade, the ethnic, the "authentic," and the unfinished.

Hippie style peaked in 1967 with the "Summer of Love" in San Francisco and lasted until the end of the decade. And, although the movement emphasized individuality, it had strong identifying elements that were quoted by contemporary fashion designers of both the 1960s and the following decades, such as:

• Long hair—the longer the better—parted in the middle but otherwise ungroomed. Long sideburns and/or untrimmed mustache or beard

• Clothes incorporating elements—such as embroidery, feathers, and flower motifs—usually considered ethnic and/or feminine

• JEANS or pants with a LOW-RISE

• Homemade, multicolored TIE-DYE, especially for T-SHIRTS

• T-SHIRTS or jewelry emblazoned with a peace symbol

• T-SHIRTS, KURTAS, and tunics

• SANDALS, bare feet, or boots

• An AFGHAN COAT as a souvenir of "the hippie trail" between Europe and India

• Medallions and LOVE BEADS worn around the neck

hippie beads   Dating from the 1960s and the heyday of the HIPPIE movement, a beaded, usually handmade and ethnic-looking necklace extending to about mid-chest; sometimes worn in multiples. During the late 1960s and early 1970s, used as an accessory to everything from open, chest-baring shirts and LOW-RISE pants (as worn by JIM MORRISON) to more traditional, snappy sportswear (as worn by FRED ASTAIRE). Synonym: LOVE BEADS.

hipster   A style of dressing associated with bebop jazz and copied by its fans, from the years immediately following World War II through the early 1950s. Hipster tailoring incorporated some of the exaggeration of the ZOOT SUIT—like extra-wide shoulders and a high waist—but the jackets were much shorter and the pants were not as narrowly pegged. Hipsters were cool cats who favored styles like double-breasted suits worn with sharply creased pants and floppy SPANIEL TIES.

Not to be confused with the narrow JAZZ SUITS earlier in the 20th century.

Synonym: BEBOP.

hobnail   A type of nail with a large, slightly rounded head, pounded into the sole of work shoes or workboots, usually for the purpose of increasing traction in the days before LUG SOLES; associated with the working class.

hobo   A general term used to refer to a bag without interior structure or any rigidity. A hobo may be made from any material, but the reference derives from the tramps and vagrants who were classically depicted carrying their positions in an improvised bag made of fabric and suspended from a stick.

holiday   Refers to the selling season around Christmas time, which the industry considers to be mid-November through New Year's (although holiday items were traditionally discounted on the day after Christmas). Customarily, the holiday collection is where and when a menswear line produces its counterpart to women's party dresses.

Holland & Holland   Famous first for guns and later for shooting accoutrements, the firm was founded by Harris Holland, an accomplished sportsman who wanted his own gun business, in 1835. In 1876, the firm officially changed from H. Holland to Holland & Holland to reflect the partnership with his nephew Henry Holland. Throughout the next century, Holland & Holland patented numerous designs and received multiple royal warrants. In 1989, it was bought by the owners of Chanel, and clothes were introduced in the 1990s. These included garments (from hats and boots to socks and garters) for both shooting sport and its concomitant, country lifestyle.

Hollywood waist   A style of pants with an extra-long rise so that the waistband visibly extends above the belt. This high-waisted style originated

Hippie

in the 1930s, but had its heyday during the subsequent two decades.

homburg A style of stiff felt hat with a dented crown and shallow, slightly rolled brim, first popularized by EDWARD VII (then Prince of Wales), who began affecting one after a visit to Bad Homburg, the resort town near Frankfurt. Initially a sporty style, the homburg quickly took on connotations of formality and became a favorite of diplomats and financiers. For example: ANTHONY EDEN became British slang for a homburg because Sir Anthony Eden was so often seen wearing one during his 1930s service as foreign secretary and during subsequent public appearances (including his 1950s stint as prime minister).

homespun 1. In menswear, a general—if misleading—reference to rough TWEEDS made from irregular yarns. The tweeds may be actually produced by artisans, or they may be produced at a mill to look as if they are. Originally, the term was significant because fabrics woven by a single producer on a small loom tended to come in much narrower widths (usually 28 inches) than the textiles produced by the commercial mills. 2. In more general use, a simple—usually PLAIN-WEAVE—fabric produced on a household loom for personal use or barter; made from yarn also produced by the household (as opposed to yarn that is commercially manufactured). Used by costume historians as a designation for textiles intended primarily for personal use, especially in colonial America (e.g., Laurel Thatcher Ulrich's 2001 *The Age of Homespun: Objects and Stories in the Creation of an American Myth*). 3. Industrially produced fabrics that imitate the simple weave and slightly uneven texture characteristic of homespun.

honan Refers to a type of silk, similar to PONGEE. Originally handspun and handwoven, honan now more often refers to a midweight fabric with a simple weave that shows some surface roughness (which may include SLUBS) and is used for suits or sports jackets.

Hong Kong tailor Now a generic term for a tailor, usually Asian, who works quickly and cheaply. Derived from the multiplicity of tailors in Hong Kong who promise to copy or custom-make complete suits and deliver them within a day or two.

Not all of the tailoring firms located in Hong Kong, however, fit the derogatory stereotype. Many were originally trained by SHANGHAI TAILORS fleeing the Japanese occupation of that city and are only marginally less expensive than their European counterparts.

hoodie A shirt with an attached hood. The word was originally slang for the hooded sweatshirts worn by athletes but became applied to lighter-weight, usually knit, shirts during the 1990s.

hook-and-eye A system of fastening garments in which small, blunt hooks (usually metal) are positioned opposite small flat tabs; usually sewn on in strips.

hopsack A simply woven fabric made of thick yarns; meant to resemble burlap. In menswear, hopsack is used most often for SPORT COATS and—although it may be woven of materials ranging from linen to silk—in designs that play up its deliberate coarseness.

horn rims Refers to a style of thick eyeglass frames, usually black. Once actually made from animal horns, the style now known as horn rims has been, since the second half of the 20th century, made from plastics.

In their most basic, slightly rectangular, variation, they are a common attribute of NERD style and GEEK CHIC.

horsehair   A fiber taken from the mane—or, more usually—tail of a horse and not from its hide; used, often in conjunction with other fibers, to impart sturdiness or stiffness. For apparel, the more popular term continues to be the French word *CRIN*.

horsehide   A type of heavy leather taken from horses, but otherwise similar to COWHIDE. In contemporary menswear, appears most often in MOTORCYCLE JACKETS.

hose   Jargon for socks. Often used interchangeably with "hosiery," although some traditionalists consider hosiery to sound more feminine.

Historically, the word most often refers to the leg coverings worn with BREECHES. (Thus traditionalists, especially in England, still specify "half hose" when they refer to socks, lest anyone assume they are referring to the longer leg coverings meant to be worn with breeches.) What most costume historians regard as hose began in the Middle Ages, with garments made of woven material that was sometimes cut on the BIAS to more closely follow the contour of the leg. By the 16th century, hose began to be knitted—a transition that was virtually complete by the beginning of the 17th century.

hospital gown   A loose garment that fastens in the back usually by means of ties (thus inadvertently exposing the derriere and making it the butt of countless slapstick routines); worn by hospital patients or those undergoing medical procedures and examinations. Unshaped, it is usually knee-length with either short sleeves or cap sleeves and made of the same sort of sturdy cottonlike fabric used for SCRUBS, so that it can be subjected to hospital laundries. In its incarnation as a EXAM GOWN, it may have a wrap tie and front closure and be made of disposable materials.

houndstooth   A symmetrical, two-color check formed by the weave structure of the fabric; distinguished by its jagged edges, which are tangent twill lines that flare from the side of each square, forming an interlocking pattern (which some people see as the shape of dog's fang).

When woven in a certain scale (e.g., six yarns by six yarns) and color (black and white or brown and white), may also be used to describe the SHEPHERD'S CHECK.

Its plural is "houndstooths." Synonyms: DOGTOOTH or DOGSTOOTH (in British usage); PUPPYTOOTH (for a particularly small version); *PIED DE POULE* (in French usage); or *PIED DE COQ* (in French usage for a particularly large version). See color plates.

houpelande *or* **houppelande** *or* **houpplande**   A style of gown worn in Western Europe from the late Middle Ages until about 1500 by both men and women of nobility and/or substance. Its chief characteristics: long sleeves, construction from heavy woven material (making it highly suitable for showing off brocade or other fancy stuffs), fullness through the body, and a somewhat fitted shoulder and neckline that covered the body up to the collar bone. Otherwise, as befits a style that endured for several hundred years, the houpelande went through a variety of changes. For example: The man's garment was most often ankle-length or mid-thigh, but a mid-calf length was also worn at one point; sleeves varied from funnel-shaped to closed at the wrist; and the distribution of fullness or presence of pleating also varied according to time and place.

huaraches   A Mexican style of woven leather shoe or sandal that, from the mid-20th century onward, traditionally used old tires as the sole. Usually handmade, huaraches use thin strips of leather in a style that recalls basket weaving more than shoemaking, slip on without the aid of buckles or fasteners, and tend to completely surround the foot like a flat shoe or slipper.

Hugo Boss   The Metzingen, Germany-based apparel-making business founded by Hugo Boss in 1923. Not very successful at first, the Boss factory specialized in workwear and then added the manufacture of Nazi uniforms, a business practice that led to its censure following World War II. In 1953, it began making men's suits but did not gain a reputation as a high-end, fashion-driven line until well into the 1970s and 1980s (when Boss jackets were used on the style-setting TV show *Miami Vice*).

By 1991, when Uwe and Jochen Holy sold the company to Marzotto, tailored clothing represented half the business. At that point, Lothar Reiff became creative director and supervised the 1993 launch of the company's first fragrance, which subsequently became a successful source of revenue. In 1996, the company began the Hugo Boss Prize, a cash award made every other year to an artist in any medium; its first prize went to filmmaker and former model Matthew Barney. In 1997, it was revealed that the factory used slave labor—probably including concentration camp prisoners—during the war.

As the label became more popular and more fashion-driven, the brand began splitting into subcategories, with "Hugo" as its trendy incarnation, "Boss Black" as its most luxurious, and "Boss Green" as its sportiest and most connected to activewear (a label it promoted by sponsoring teams and athletes in multiple sports—chiefly in Europe).

hunt buttons   Special jacket buttons bearing the emblem of a particular fox hunt, a privilege accorded full-fledged members of that hunt. Usually hunt buttons are accompanied by a collar in the hunt COLORS. Hunt buttons are never worn by nonmembers or guests, no matter how distinguished.

Hush Puppies   The casual shoe brand officially launched by the Rockford, Michigan-based Wolverine in 1959, supposedly as a way of using the pigskins it had accumulated when perfecting the machine-processing of pigskin. The brand name is a play on the slang "barking dogs" to express sore, tired feet. The original Hush Puppies' styles had thick crepe soles, were constructed of pigskin suede, became best known for a sort of loafer style, and used a lovable basset hound as company logo. By the early 1960s, the company was able to claim that one out of every ten Americans owned a pair. As the '60s wore on, however, the comfy middle-class shoe fell from fashion favor, only to be revived in the retro chic movement of the early 1990s with the slogan "we invented casual."

husky sizes   A range of sizes for boys' wear, most often 8 to 20, equivalent to "chubby" sizes for girls of the same age. Husky clothes are usually proportioned to be the same length as the standard size but have a waist from 3 to 6 inches wider than the standard non-husky cut.

hydrophilic   Describes a fiber or fabric's ability to absorb water. Many natural fibers, like cotton and wool, are highly hydrophilic. In underwear, socks, or athletic apparel, a hydrophilic fabric may be prized for its ability to wick perspiration away from the skin. Its synonym is HYGROSCOPIC. Its antonym is HYDROPHOBIC.

In the fashion industry, hydrophilic is used more often to describe man-made fibers, while hygroscopic still tends to appear in descriptions of natural fibers or in European usage.

hydrophobic   Describes a fiber or fabric's ability to repel water. Many synthetic fibers are highly hydrophobic. In technical apparel, a hydrophobic fabric may be prized for its ability to keep water on the outside of the garment where it evaporates quickly. Its opposites are HYDROPHILIC or HYGROSCOPIC.

hygroscopic   Describes a fiber or fabric's tendency to absorb water. For example, certain types of wool are prized because they can absorb up to a third of their weight in water without feeling appreciably damp. Its synonym is HYDROPHILIC. Its antonym is HYDROPHOBIC.

In the fashion industry, hydrophilic is used more often to describe man-made fibers, while hygroscopic still tends to appear in descriptions of natural fibers or in European usage.

hymo   A type of plain-weave canvas INTERFACING, used in the interior construction of traditional tailored garments; typically used to make areas firm but not stiff.

ice cream suit   Slang for a white, pastel, or otherwise light-colored traditional suit, like those famously sported worn by writer Tom Wolfe.

ID bracelet   1. Short for "identification bracelet"; a metal bracelet consisting of curb links supporting a front bar about 2 inches long engraved with the wearer's name or initials; usually silver or silver-plate. The practice of American men wearing ID bracelets became popular after World War II, when they more or less brought the habit home from the service with them. Unlike other forms of jewelry, the wearing of a chunky ID bracelet was not considered effeminate, and courting customs evolved whereby a boy, especially in high school, would bestow his ID bracelet on his girlfriend. 2. A simple rubber, plastic, or metal bracelet usually worn to alert others to a wearer's allergies or medical

status (such as diabetes or a heart condition) in the event that he is unable to speak for himself. Worn for functional rather than decorative purposes. Synonyms: alert bracelet; medical alert bracelet; medical identification bracelet.

ikat *or* **double ikat**   A fabric in which the decorative pattern is formed by dyeing the threads *before* they are woven. Inevitably, this leads to a slight irregularity at the pattern's edge, which is an ikat's distinguishing mark. In a simple ikat, either the WARP (most common) or WEFT threads are dyed to form the pattern. In a double ikat, both warp and weft threads are dyed, making the pattern alignment doubly difficult.

   The word itself translates as "knot"—the most common way of gathering the threads to keep out certain colors of dye. Production can never be casual, and true ikats (as opposed to fabrics printed to resemble them) often have ritual significance, particularly in southeast Asia, where the process is done completely by hand and may easily take months to produce a single length of

Ikat

Ice cream suit: Tom Wolfe

189

cloth. The correct description for most commercially produced textiles is therefore "ikat-style" or "ikat effect."

Synonym: chiné (used to describe the equivalent Western production, e.g., the similar process as originally replicated in French silk mills and still used more often for women's wear).

inch tape A synonym for a tailor's MEASURING TAPE.

Incroyable Translated from the French as "unbelievable"; like his predecessor the *ÉLÉGANT*, the Incroyable who appeared in mid-1790s Paris dressed to shock and annoy. For example: To underscore the difference between himself and the *ancien regime*, he pronounced the word *incroyable* without an "r" so that nothing would sound the same. He was particularly noted for huge NECK CLOTHS and for exaggerating English style to the extent that it could no longer be associated with either simplicity or economy.

Indian gown If referring to a Western man's dress, particularly during the 18th century, usually a synonym for BANYAN. A reference to the robes of South Asians, not Native Americans.

indigo Refers to the plant used for its distinctive blue dye.

For thousands of years, used as magic, medicine, and cosmetic adornment, as well as mere color. Ancient Britons daubed themselves with woad (*Isatis tinctoria*, the Western European equivalent of the *Indigofera* plant varieties produced in warmer climes) before going into battle. In northern Africa men rubbed it into their skin as protection against the elements. The popularity and the politics of its cultivation caused both prosperity and famine—particularly in 19th-century India (e.g., the Indigo War of the 1860s) and other former European colonies.

Indigo provided a beautiful blue that was relatively stable, took well on both plant and animal fibers, and not only did not degrade the fabric but had the reputation of actually strengthening it. These qualities made it much favored by armies, as well as by workmen (hence the origin of the term "blue collar"). In Western tradition, it was the dye that made blue jeans blue (although, for the last century, most jeans have been dyed by artificial indigo).

Incroyables

There was, nonetheless, an art to using natural indigo. First, the dye had to be extracted from the plant, a process accomplished in preindustrial eras through fermentation or, in some cases, the use of urine. Even then, the density of the dye on the fabric could not be judged simply by eye. Undyed material entered a dye bath that was yellowish, emerged as yellow or green, and then oxidized to its eventual blue shade. Synthetic indigo was not developed until the end of the 19th century and not available in a commercially viable form until Germany produced it at the beginning of the 20th century.

inexpressibles Victorian sensibilities became so refined that it was considered vulgar to refer to any item of apparel below a man's waist. Hence, TROUSERS and BREECHES (as well as undergarments) were referred to as "inexpressibles"—a word often used ironically even during in the 19th century. Synonym: UNMENTIONABLES.

ink Slang reference to tattoos.

innerwear Industry jargon for underwear.

inseam 1. A measurement of the seam that runs on the inside of the leg, from the crotch to the hem of a pants' leg. By contrast, the OUTSEAM extends from the waist to hem on the outside of the leg, which means it is always a longer measurement. 2. A measurement of the inner seam of a sleeve, from the armpit to the cuff.

insole 1. Jargon for the interior of a SHOE's sole, the part that comes in direct contact with the foot (and not the pavement like the OUTSOLE); not visible when the shoe is being worn. Often stamped with the shoe manufacturer's name, the insole may—depending on the craftsmanship and expense involved—extend only to the arch of the foot or it may be full-length. Additionally, it may be only a thin layer of fake leather, or may be a fine leather with additional cushion to add comfort. 2. A removable piece added to the inside of the shoe for a function such as extra cushioning or support.

instep The top of the foot; the arched portion that extends from the ankle to the beginning of the toes. The portion of the shoe that covers the instep is called the VAMP.

insulation layer The heat-providing layer worn over the BASE LAYER, in a layering system intended to maximize heat and minimize weight for sports or other outdoor activity. For cold-weather sports, such as mountain climbing and skiing, the insulating layer may be wool, down, or a synthetic made to imitate either. It may be topped, in turn, by a SHELL LAYER—especially in inclement weather.

intarsia In knitwear, refers to a technique in which a pattern or different color is set in, so that it looks like an island of different yarn on its reverse side. This differs from knitting techniques like FAIR ISLE, in which two yarns are carried through the entire row, forming a double layer of yarn that shows as stranded twists of yarn on its reverse. Because intarsia forms a single layer of yarn throughout, it is lighter, more saving of yarn, and allows more whimsical, scattered design.

Intarsia: Front . . .

. . . and back

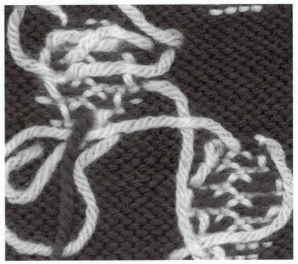

interfacing Layer of woven or nonwoven fabric used in the construction of a garment for purposes of stabilization and shaping, including:

• Prevention of stretching and distortion while the garment is being sewn

• Prevention of stretching and distortion when the garment is worn—as a guard against bulging, bagging, and rippled edges

• As a method of disguising other elements of construction (e.g., an underlayer that creates a smooth-surface effect to prevent the shoulder pad from appearing as an unsightly hump)

• As a way of creating a firmer edge—preventing ripples, sagging, or an unintended ruffling effect

• As a way of adding body to the garment, especially if the main fabric is lightweight

• As a way of sculpting the garment into a desired silhouette

In traditional tailored clothing, interfacing is commonly used in areas such as the FRONT SHIELD and BACK SHIELD of a jacket, WELT pockets, pocket flaps, COLLAR STANDS, and sleeve openings. Because it is never visible in the finished garment, it is usually sold only in white, natural (meaning an undyed, off-white or beige), or black.

Interfacing comes in FUSIBLE or nonfusible forms. The more traditional form is nonfusible, especially for tailored clothing (and indeed was the only option available until about 1950). The best-known types of nonfusible wovens, generically referred to as CANVAS, include HAIR CANVAS, HYMO, and WIGAN. Designation of tailored clothing production as half canvas or FULL CANVAS is thus a reference to its method of construction with interfacing. Fusible interfacing, which is generally bonded (i.e., "fused") to the fabric by heat, does not require stitching and is thus a faster and easier method of application.

Additional forms of interfacing do exist—such as weft insertion interfacing, nonwoven nonfusibles, and knit interfacing—but they are used much less often in the men's market and almost never in traditional tailoring.

Because of the many uses of interfacing, both fusible and nonfusible are available in various weights. Frequently, different weights are combined in the construction of a single garment, and many relatively expensive ready-to-wear tailored garments combine both fusible and nonfusible types.

When a similar layer of material is added primarily for the purposes of warmth, then the proper reference is INTERLINING.

interlining 1. Industry jargon for INTERFACING. 2. A layer interposed between the outside or shell of the garment and its lining for purposes of added warmth or to add stability to the garment's construction. It is never visible from either the inside or the outside of the garment. Interlining is never a synonym for lining.

interlock Knit fabric made on a special knitting machine that uses both short and long needles—a production method that

Interfacing visible on the jacket collar

preserves the stretchiness and "give" of knit fabric, but creates a denser cloth that is easier to sew into apparel. The resulting fabric also looks the same on both sides.

Inverness cape   A 19th-century style of cape or single-breasted loose overcoat with a shorter cape on top covering the arms past the elbow; a style that came to be associated with depictions of Sir Arthur Conan Doyle's fictional detective SHERLOCK HOLMES (although, like the DEER-STALKER CAP, it is never actually mentioned in the stories).

inverted pleat   A fold of fabric that goes in (toward the body) instead of belling out (away from the body). For example: The pleats at the waistline of most pleated pants are inverted pleats; so is the collar-to-hem pleat on the back of a GUARD'S COAT.

Invista   A division of Koch Industries, Invista is the manufacturer of fibers and fabric treatments including LYCRA, COOLMAX, Stainmaster, Teflon, and Antron. Formerly a division of DUPONT known as DuPont Textiles & Interiors, it was renamed Invista in 2003 and subsequently purchased by Koch.

iqal   Variant spelling of AGAL or AQAL, the rolled bands that form part of the traditional Arab headdress.

item   Industry jargon for a single unit. Therefore, a style may still be broken down into item numbers, and a "hot-selling item" could refer to anything from a pair of shoes to a style of belt. Often, an item may be further subdivided by stockkeeping units (see SKU).

It Happened One Night   Director Frank Capra's 1934 romantic comedy starring Claudette Colbert and CLARK GABLE as, respectively, an heiress on the run and a reporter out to get her story. Robert Kalloch's uncredited costume designs featured few changes of clothes; however, the movie became famous for its impact on the UNDERSHIRT industry. In one key scene, Gable was required to keep up witty banter while changing clothes, and when it was decided that taking off his undershirt was taking too long, the scene was filmed sans undershirt. As a result, undershirt sales dropped drastically for the next two years and undershirt makers tried to sue Columbia—establishing a precedent for the importance of product placements in movies.

Ivy League look   Refers to a particular post-World War II suit silhouette consisting of a single-breasted, unfitted jacket with a NATURAL SHOULDER and a single vent in the back. This style was markedly more relaxed and less form-fitting than its European counterparts and was worn with PLAIN-FRONT, loose, often ankle-grazing pants; associated with tailors and retailers such as BROOKS BROTHERS, CHIPP, and J. PRESS. Beginning in about 1950, most fashion magazines and retailers—most notably *ESQUIRE* magazine—began referring to it as

It Happened One Night

"American informal" because the shoulders were less BUILT OUT and the LAPELS narrower than the styles popular during World War II.

The Ivy League designation became popular after the Ivy League was formally established in 1954, although those same schools had been considered collegiate fashion leaders as early as the 19th century, particularly because they tended to attract moneyed young men from influential families.

Aside from that boxy suit silhouette, elements considered essential to the Ivy League style included BUTTON-DOWN shirts, MADRAS sportswear, blue BLAZERS, PENNY LOAFERS, CAMEL'S HAIR coats, tweed sports jackets, and the accoutrements also associated with East Coast collegiate life and PREPPY style.

Izod A brand name that originally belonged to a British tailor, who became more famous after he quit the business, and best-known from the 1930s through beginning of the 1990s as the licensor and maker of the LACOSTE "alligator" shirt.

The company that became known as Izod began in the early 20th century when apparel entrepreneur Vin Draddy bought the rights to the name of Jack Izod, a London shirtmaker whose clients had included King George VI. Thereafter, the firm remained identified primarily with tops—particularly after it signed an agreement in the 1930s with French tennis player Rene "the Crocodile" Lacoste to produce cotton PIQUÉ tops bearing the logo that became known in the United States as an alligator. Until 1981, over 80 percent of Izod Lacoste's business was in selling solid-colored "alligator" shirts—so much so that, when striped tops suddenly became fashionable, the firm's fortunes sank precipitately. After changes in management and distribution and later losing the rights to the Lacoste name and the alligator logo in the 1990s, Izod adopted a crest composed of its own name or, for its golfwear, of crossed golf clubs. In 1995, the brand was bought by PHILLIPS-VAN HEUSEN.

J. Press The CLOTHIER founded in New Haven in 1902 by Jacobi Press, best known as a bastion of the IVY LEAGUE LOOK (especially for the distinctive pocket flap on its BUTTON-DOWN shirts); bought in 1986 by Kashiyama, the U.S. branch of the Japanese apparel producer; also with stores in Washington, D.C., Cambridge, Massachusetts, and in midtown New York near BROOKS BROTHERS and PAUL STUART.

jabot A style of neckwear, particularly favored in 18th-century France, in which a piece of fine linen or lace was worn falling from the neck, filling approximately the same space and function as a contemporary necktie.

jacketings Industry jargon for fabrics intended for SPORTS JACKETS (usually heavier than either SUITINGS or BOTTOMWEIGHTS). Refers to the fabrics, never to the finished garments.

jacquard 1. A method of weaving that allows intricate patterning to be built into the weave in a time- and cost-efficient manner (as opposed to the more ancient draw loom); made possible by the loom invented by Joseph-Marie Charles Jacquard and in use since 1801. 2. Knit fabric with an integral pattern that imitates a jacquard weave.

Jack Tar suits Slang reference to SAILOR SUITS, especially in the 19th century.

Jacob the Jeweler The self-styled "king of BLING," Jacob Arabov, the proprietor of Jacob & Co. and long a favorite of rap royalty.

Jacob, who often wrote his surname as Arabo, emigrated from Uzbekistan and started his business on New York's West 47th Street in the 1980s. In the 1990s and early 21st century, he became a sort of court jeweler to Jay-Z, P. DIDDY, Pharell Williams, and other HIP-HOP stars, providing them with extravagant commissioned pieces including outrageously diamond-decked watches and other jewelry. In 2005, he moved to independent premises on East 57th Street. In 2006, he was arrested on money-laundering charges.

jammies A slang reference to pajamas, most often used by children.

Jacob the Jeweler: Playboy watch

Jams   A trademarked name that is now used generically for just-above-the-knee, loose-fitting swim trunks made from brightly printed woven material.

The trend began in Hawaii in the early 1960s when Dave Rochlen, a surfer from Santa Monica, started a company called Surf Line Hawaii and began selling the Jams he had created for himself. The name derives from their resemblance to cut-off JAMMIES, a slang reference for pajamas. Rochlen got the idea after seeing a picture of Russians strolling around a Black Sea resort in bathrobes and pajamas, and he made the first pair from sateen on sale for less than a dollar a yard.

Jaymar-Ruby   An apparel company founded in Chicago in 1915 by Jack Ruby, best known as the maker of SANS-ABELT pants, which it launched in the United States in 1957. It became part of HARTMARX CORPORATION in 1967.

jazz suit   Unlike the oversized suits with wide shoulders that would be associated with jazz music later in the 20th century (e.g., ZOOT and HIPSTER suits), the jazz suit, which surfaced after World War I and was out of fashion by the early 1920s, had a tight shoulder and was worn with short, skinny pants.

However, because the jazz suit exaggerated proportions and boasted a jacket with an extra-long SKIRT and a nipped waist, it should not be counted as completely unrelated to the subsequent jazz-inspired styles.

jean jacket   A style of short, skirtless jacket made of DENIM and constructed in a manner similar to blue JEANS. The classic jean jacket tapers toward a waistband and has a straight front yoke; a button front; a small, pointed collar; long sleeves ending in a single-button cuff; two flapped breast pockets; and two vertical hand-warmer pockets.

jeans   The style of pants that became America's most popular contribution to international fashion got its start when a Bavarian immigrant named LEVI STRAUSS began making pants for miners, "the forty-niners," who flocked to California during the gold rush of the mid-19th century. The Levi's company itself dates its invention of the blue jean to 1873, the year that San Francisco-based merchant Strauss and Reno, Nevada-based tailor Jacob Davis received U.S. Patent 139121 for their process of reinforcing pants with copper rivets.

Strauss made the first versions of what he called "waist-high overalls" from canvas, but soon began using the sturdy, INDIGO-dyed TWILL fabric known as *serge de Nimes*, named after the port in southern France, and abbreviated to DENIM in American usage. (Strauss himself used denim from the Amoskeag Mill in Manchester, New Hampshire, for the pants he patented in 1873.) Some costume historians say that because the fabric was already associated with sailors from the Italian port of Genoa, the pants became known as jeans—although that usage was not widespread until after World War II, and Levi's itself did not begin using the word until about 1960. In 1873, Strauss also added a decorative ARCUATE to the back pockets. By 1901, he had added a second back pocket to the pants, and the FIVE-POCKET model was established. Other companies imitated both the denim material and the pants' general design (especially after the company's exclusive patent expired in 1890), with jeans becoming particularly associated with COWBOYS and the American West.

However, through the first half of the 20th century, jeans were considered WORKWEAR and were widely referred to as OVERALLS. (ELVIS PRESLEY, for example, avoided them for decades because they conjured too many associations with rural poverty; he supposedly loathed his denim and CHAMBRAY wardrobe for 1957's *Loving You* and *Jailhouse Rock*.)

But, in the 1950s, that lowly status began to be exploited as an anti-fashion statement. Jeans became the acknowledged uniform of the biker (e.g., as seen on Marlon Brando in 1953's THE WILD ONE) and the teenaged rebel (e.g., JAMES DEAN in 1955's *Rebel Without a Cause*). Elvis's film appearances had made them de rigueur for the ROCKER, too. Students around the world wore them in imitation, and, by the 1960s, they were ubiquitous on college campuses.

By the 1970s, that changed again: Jeans were a fashion statement. Designers such as the GIRBAUDS were manipulating both the shape of the jeans and the appearance of the denim. DESIGNER JEANS offered by the likes of CALVIN KLEIN became an established market segment, and fads came and went for denim that was ACID-WASHED, ANTIQUED, ENZYME WASHED, STONEWASHED, or WHISKERED.

Synonyms: blue jeans; DENIMS; FIVE-POCKETS; overalls (especially in pre-World War II usage); WAIST OVERALLS (especially in pre-World War I usage).

jeep coat   World War II-era slang for MACKINAW, especially as issued by the U.S. military.

jeff   British tailors' slang for a small tailoring shop, usually a one-man operation (as opposed to SAVILE ROW houses, which customarily employ specialists for each phase of the job).

jellybag   Archaic slang for a style of knitted cap similar to an abbreviated stocking cap with an extra-large tassel at the end; worn with the tail flopped to the side of the face; popular in the early 20th century for skiing and other winter sports.

Jelt denim   A type of hard-wearing denim using tightly twisted yarns in a close weave. Made by CONE and used and advertised by LEE beginning in 1925, the 11½-ounce fabric was supposed to be as hard-wearing as 13-ounce denim.

jeri curls   A style of shiny, small, tight-to-the-skull curls, formed with the help of large amounts of hair product; associated with African-American men in the 1980s and famously worn by Michael Jackson on his 1982 *Thriller* album. For most people, the hair had to be chemically processed to release its natural curl and then reprocessed into the shape of the jeri curl, which was secured with an oily product known as an activator (hence the high shine as a hallmark of the style).

Jermyn Street   A short street in London's SW1 district that, because of its proximity to Kensington Palace (the residence of the Prince of Wales), became a favored address for makers of gentlemen's shirts (TURNBULL & ASSER), accessories (NEW & LINGWOOD), and toiletries (FLORIS). Named for Henry Jermyn, Earl of St. Albans, who developed the area in the 1660s, it was primarily residential rather than retail until the mid-18th century.

Sometimes used as a synonym for custom shirts, in the same way that SAVILE ROW is used as a synonym for custom suits. The service of many Jermyn Street firms also extended to laundering customers' shirts to their taste.

Jermyn stripes   Rather than a specific type of stripe, this is a broad reference to the style of bright, boldly striped shirt fabrics favored by custom shirtmakers located on or around JERMYN STREET in London. Therefore, Jermyn stripes may describe BENGAL STRIPES, CANDY STRIPES, or any of the traditional shirt stripes.

jetted pocket   An inserted (as opposed to a PATCH) pocket that does not have a flap to cover its opening.

jigger   In a DOUBLE-BREASTED jacket or coat, a small button attached to the inside, or "invisible," part of the crossover, so that the front aligns perfectly—without pulling on the exterior buttons or drooping at the hem.

jipijapa   Synonym for a PLANTER'S HAT, used mostly during the mid-20th century. Originally the word, which is the name of a small town in Manabi, a coastal section of Ecuador, connoted only a PANAMA hat and described the straw more than the style. By the 1930s, the usage reversed and it became identified with a deep-brimmed, shallow-crowned style.

jock   1. Shortened, slang reference to an athletic supporter for the genitals. The usage apparently dates from the late 19th century and the design of the supportive straps for "bicycle jockeys." By 1897, the Bike Athletic Company had patented a model, and, by 1902, a similar supporter was being featured in the Sears catalog.

Prior to that, similar garments called modesty girdles had been worn under bathing suits for purposes of masking manly bulges as much as for support—in much the manner of a modern DANCE BELT.

2. Shortened, slang reference to an athlete and/or to the clothes he wears, as in, "That runway collection used the theme of Jocks versus Nerds."

jockstrap   A JOCK.

Jockey Shorts   Trademarked name for briefs invented by the Cooper Company (already famous as manufacturers of the KENOSHA KLOSED KROTCH) in 1934. The name Jockey was given to the new, Y-FRONT design to emphasize its supportive pouch and its relationship to a JOCKSTRAP. Although the company has made many variations, the classic Jockey Shorts are white, made of cotton knit, have an elastic waistband, and have no legs or inseam.

Jockeys first appeared at Marshall Field's main Chicago store during January of 1935 and sold out immediately, despite debuting on the day of a fierce snowstorm. During the next three months, 30,000 pairs were sold and Cooper fielded a "Mascu-liner" airplane to fly emergency deliveries of its masculine support briefs to desperate retailers.

Also referred to generically as BRIEFS, Y-FRONTS (especially in British usage), and by slang terms like TIGHTIE WHITIES.

jodhpuri suit   In contemporary use, refers to a suit that looks like a hybrid of the South Asian ACHKAN and the Western business suit. The jodhpuri suit has a high-collared, lapel-less, plain-front jacket but is abbreviated to fall just below the buttocks and is therefore not as long

Jockey Shorts

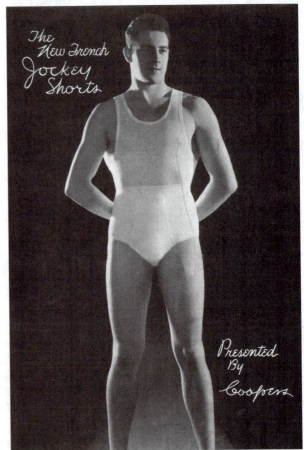

or flowing as the achkan. Like a Western business suit, it is usually worn with matching slacks.

It closely resembles the Nehru jacket styles launched in the West in the 1960s.

Contrary to the implications inherent in its name, it is not worn with jodhpurs.

jodhpurs　　Named for the city in western Rajasthan in which they originated, jodhpurs are full-length trousers distinguished by a flaring thigh, although they are closely fitting from the knee down and usually end in a tight, small cuff covering the ankle (which is often secured by an strap extending across the sole of the shoe). In the West, they became pants for horseback riding—primarily associated with English-style riding—when they were worn with hacking jackets and the ankle-high boots known as jodhpur boots. Not to be confused with riding breeches, which may have the same flared thigh, but which are not full-length and are worn with knee-high boots.

John Lobb　　Usually referred to as a "bootmaker" or "cobbler" in the upperclass slang of its customers, the establishment at 9 St. James's Street, London, traces its origin to John Lobb, a lame farm boy from Cornwall, and its official opening to 1866. Since securing Edward VII as a customer (while still Prince of Wales), the family-run firm has held multiple royal warrants and enjoyed famous customers including Prince Charles, Prince Philip, Hardy Amies, Guy Burgess, J. Paul Getty, Alfred Hitchcock, Emperor Haile Selassie, and Frank Sinatra. It opened a branch in Paris at the beginning of the 20th century. After being purchased by Hermès in the 1976, Lobb also began making limited quantities of readymade footwear that resembled its bespoke products.

johnny collar　　A style of shirt sporting a small V-neck with an attached collar—somewhat like a polo shirt with its placket permanently open; customarily used on knits.

Johnson, Horace Greeley　　Born in Canada in 1867, Johnson became known as the "Edison of underwear" for his invention of the Kenosha Klosed Krotch, the direct antecedent of Jockey Shorts.

Johnson went to work at his father's knitting mill at age 16 and moved to Kenosha, Wisconsin, to work for the Cooper Company's knitting mill in 1901. In 1909, while working for that company as a supervisor, he supposedly had a dream in which he envisioned a new crotch system for men's underwear, which would replace bulky and cumbersome drawers. He awakened his wife, Olevia, who stitched up a prototype of the overlapping front opening that, in 1910, was patented as the Kenosha Klosed Krotch.

Johnson retired early and lived off the royalties of his invention. He died in Wisconsin in 1936.

Julian, Alexander　　Born in 1948, apparel designer Alexander Julian grew up in Chapel Hill, North Carolina, where he worked in his father's clothing store, Julian's College Shop, then opened his own store, Alexander's Ambition, at age 21. In 1975, he moved to New York to start a menswear collection, winning the first of five Coty Awards in 1977.

In 1980, he launched Colours, the label for which he would be best known, and that same year received the first of three Cutty Sark Awards, quickly becoming one of the decade's most successful designers and receiving a CFDA award. Because he also designed so many of the textiles for his collections, Julian was particularly identified with the introduction of color into men's

Alexander Julian

sportswear. He also became one of the first big names in fashion to design team uniforms (notably for the National Basketball Association's Charlotte Hornets in 1990) and to outfit professional drivers such as Mario Andretti. In addition, he provided menswear for a variety of TV shows and films, acting as costume designer for 1992's *The Player* starring Tim Robbins.

Later in the 1990s, when his backers backed out of the apparel business, he lost most of his retail distribution. However, he branched into home furnishings and other areas of design and, in 2007, launched a line of sportswear called American Modern.

jumper   Slang for a PULLOVER sweater, particularly in British usage.

jumpsuit   Refers to an all-in-one garment in which the top and bottom are not separated, so that, instead of being donned separately (as in a shirt and trousers), a man puts on a single piece. Usually, the style connotes long trousers and long sleeves, with a single, center-front opening.

When used to describe fashion and civilian garments (as opposed to uniforms or purpose-specific WORK-WEAR), the term connotes a garment that is not worn over another garment (unlike the COVERALL, which has the same silhouette but may be worn over other clothes to protect them).

jusi   A sheer fabric traditional to the Philippines that uses PIÑA as the WARP and SILK, COTTON, or ABACA as the filling.

justaucorps   A style of long jacket worn by the affluent from the end of the 17th century through much of the 18th century. Long-sleeved and knee-length, the justaucorps was made without a waist seam but with a flared SKIRT. It buttoned down the front, obscuring most of the BREECHES worn beneath and sported lavish, turned back cuffs. The style definitively replaced doublets and short jackets and set up menswear for the development of the modern suit.

K

kafiyeh The scarf worn under the AGAL in traditional ARAB headdress. Its many variant spellings include keffieyh, kaffiyeh, and keffiyed.

kaftan Variant spelling of CAFTAN, often encountered in writing about Russian or Ottoman dress.

kamis A long-sleeved shirt, part of traditional dress in the Middle East; length varies according to the era and area, as does the width of its sleeves; usually slips over the head with only a partial front opening.

kamishimo The traditional formal attire of the Japanese samurai; in contemporary use worn only on ceremonial occasions. A two-part costume, the kamishimo consists of the katingu, a caped vest with distinctively flaring shoulders, and matching HAKAMA pants, which are so full that they are often mistaken for a skirt.

kangaroo A soft leather made from the Australian marsupial, favored for being stronger than similarly soft, lightweight leathers (such as CALFSKIN).

kangaroo pocket A large, single pocket placed front and center over the belly, like a kangaroo's pouch. Frequently found on ANORAKS and CAGOULES. Used more often for boys' wear.

Kangol The hat company, best known for its caps and other sporty styles, founded in the town of Cleator in Cumbria, England, by Polish immigrant Jakob Henryk

Kafiyeh

Spreiregen, who had been an importer of BERETS before he started making them himself (and supposedly invented his brand name by using "K" to stand for either silk or knit, the "ANG" to stand for angora, and the "OL" to stand for wool).

Kangol supplied berets to the British army during World War II, then during the Korean War. When peacetime ensued, Kangol diversified, creating its signature "504" flat cap style. Inspired by HIP-HOP customers asking for "kangaroo" hats, the firm adopted its kangaroo logo in the 1980s. Thereafter, Kangol became known for producing materials like "furgora" (a mixture of angora and wool) and styles as varied as the BASEBALL CAP, BIN, Lindale, PULL ON, SKULL CAP, TRILBY, and TRAPPER.

karakul   Often used interchangeably with ASTRAKHAN, refers to a breed of Central Asian sheep with a tight, curly coat and particularly to the pelt of the newborn lambs. (The pelt of the unborn lamb is referred to as BROADTAIL.)

karat   A measure of the fineness of gold (not to be confused with CARAT, a measure of the weight of gemstones). Pure gold is 24 karat, ergo 12-karat gold is half gold and half alloy metal. Usually abbreviated by a capital K, as in 24K or 12K.

kawaii   A style that became popular during the second half of the 20th century in Japan, as a sort of "anti-PUNK." Synonymous with things that were cute, round, pastel, preadolescent, and not traditionally Japanese. Initially identified with females and cartoonlike figures (such as Hello Kitty), kawaii later became more androgynous and came to encompass everything from the design of household articles to a style of handwriting. Also known as CUTIE CULTURE.

Keds   The brand introduced in 1916 by U.S. Rubber, when it was the first sports shoe to be aggressively advertised to the general population; best known for its white canvas, tie-front style modeled on an OXFORD, with a relatively flat rubber sole and a blue box logo placed on the center back of the heel.

Although it undoubtedly did not invent the word (which seems to have been in use for rubber-soled shoes as early as the end of the 19th century), Keds claims credit for popularizing the word "SNEAKER" under the aegis of its advertising agency N.W. Ayer & Son.

In 1949, it introduced a Pro-Keds line aimed at the basketball market. In 1979, both Keds and Pro-Keds were acquired by the Stride Rite Corporation.

Keezer's   The Cambridge, Massachusetts, store founded in 1895 by Max Keezer; best known for renting tuxedos to generations of Harvard men and as a resale shop where wealthy students, including John F. Kennedy, could dispose of their unwanted clothes for extra cash. Located on Harvard Square until the 1960s, when it moved to River Street near Central Square.

kennel coat   A loose, long-sleeved coat falling past the knee (but not ankle-length); usually made of coarse, undyed cotton, linen, or similarly sturdy fabric. Used, like the contemporary BARN JACKET, to protect clothes while performing kennel inspections and similar chores. The kennel coat resembled the DUSTER worn to protect clothes while driving early automobiles and was popular during roughly the same era.

Kenosha Klosed Krotch   The direct antecedent of JOCKEY SHORTS. According to legend, in 1909, HORACE GREELEY JOHNSON, an employee of the Cooper knitting mill in Kenosha, Wisconsin, awoke in the middle of the night with the brainstorm of replacing the bulky button fly with a diagonal-access opening, whereupon he awakened his wife, Olevia, who stitched up a prototype.

The finished product, the Kenosha Klosed Krotch, was patented by Johnson and his employer in 1910, earning Johnson the sobriquet "the Edison of underwear" and forever changing menswear. In 1911, the Cooper company commissioned the prominent illustrator J.C. LEYENDECKER for advertisements in *The Saturday Evening Post*, effectively creating the first national print campaign for men's underwear.

Kent   Old-fashioned slang for the double-breasted, midnight-blue TUXEDOS favored by the Duke of Kent and his brother the Prince of Wales, later EDWARD VIII.

kente cloth   The multicolored, basketweave-effect fabric composed of alternating warp- and weft-faced fabrics, produced by the Ashanti of Ghana; originally made from European silk that had been carefully unraveled for the reuse of its thread and worn by the elite of the 18th-century Ashanti court. Alternative spelling: KINTA.

Kevlar   A flame-resistant synthetic five times stronger than steel, Kevlar was patented by DUPONT employee Stephanie Kwolek in 1966. Since then, it has been used in everything from parachutes to sails, but is most often encountered in bulletproof vests or, in an extremely thin topical application, as a protective finish for WORKWEAR materials like DENIM.

keyhole buttonhole   A style of thread-bound buttonhole that resembles a keyhole turned on its side; normally appears only in machine-made buttonholes. Used primarily with SHANKED BUTTONS, the keyhole adds a semicircle to one end of the customary buttonhole slit so that, when the fastening is closed, the button supposedly does not distort the buttonhole but slides easily to the circular edge.

khadi   India's traditional handwoven cloth made from handspun yarn (most often in cotton, but occasionally in fibers such as silk, wool, or ramie); also identified with the political ideals of Mahatma Gandhi.

Khadi production in India dates back thousands of years, however, during British rule, India was forced to export its raw cotton to England, where it was turned into cloth by the highly mechanized British textile industry—and then shipped back to India for sale. As a protest against that and other economic policies, Ghandi foreswore European dress in 1921 and began wearing a DHOTI made of khadi. Himself frequently photographed with a spinning wheel, Ghandi encouraged the spinning and weaving of simple cotton khadi as a means of India's economic and spiritual revival. (For example: While in prison, future prime minister Jawaharlal Nehru wove a khadi wedding sari for his daughter Indira.) When India achieved its independence, the first national flag unfurled in New Delhi was made of khadi. During the 1950s and 1960s, it was mainly favored by politicians, but became widely fashionable again after its extensive use by costume designer Bhanu Athaiya in the 1982 movie *Gandhi*.

Although always a simple weave, it may be of any weight from heavy to diaphanous, and may be dyed any color.

khaki   1. A term applied to a variety of dull, earth-toned colors, as well as to the sturdy, unpatterned fabrics dyed in that color; originally associated with military use.

Kenosha Klosed Krotch

The etymology of "khaki" traces from Hindi back to a Persian word meaning "dust" and was originally used to indicate a dusty beige. The custom of dyeing fabric with that color is not as easy to trace, since several armies claim to have originated it by deliberately staining their once-white uniforms a dull earth shade—for the purpose of either providing camouflage or masking stains. Probably the British have the best claim, based on Sir Harry Burnett Lumsden's documented 1848 order to outfit his men on India's northwest border in khaki uniforms.

2. In the plural, "khakis," refers to a style of pants worn as sportswear, a custom begun by American GIs returning from World War II, who were still wearing the type of sturdy twill pants they had been issued in the military, such as ARMY PINKS or khakis (or among the younger men imitating them, who bought their own versions at army surplus stores). Synonym: CHINOS.

kicks   Slang, originally from HIP-HOP, for sneakers. In early 21st century, extended, usually ironically, to other types of fancy footwear.

kid mohair   The softest MOHAIR fiber, made from the fleece of ANGORA goats less than six months old. (It is prized because the coats of older goats yield coarser, less lustrous fibers.)

kidney   Slang, now archaic, for a THROAT LATCH; so called because it was often in a kidney shape.

kidney pad   Protective construction, usually a piece of padding and/or quilting in the center back over the kidneys; a standard feature of traditional MOTORCYCLE JACKETS, and sometimes quoted in styles that allude to motorcycles.

kidskin   Leather made from the skin of young goats (kids). Like CALFSKIN, favored because it usually has a finer grain than the skin of the mature animal. Usually imported from Morocco, other regions of North Africa, or Spain.

Kilgour *or* **Kilgour, French & Stanbury**   The Savile Row tailoring firm established in 1882 as A.H. Kilgour, which merged with T&F French in 1923 and, in 1937, added the name Stanbury in honor of Hungarian brothers Fred and Louis Stanbury (who had joined the firm in 1925); famous for creating the tailcoats worn by FRED ASTAIRE in the 1935 movie *Top Hat*, for suiting CARY GRANT (especially for 1959's *North by Northwest*), for costuming Rex Harrison (especially for 1964's *My Fair Lady*), and for outfitting a subcontinent's worth of maharajas.

Identified from the 1920s onward with a particularly clean-lined suit (considered not as DRAPED as, for example, ANDERSON & SHEPARD), by the late 20th century, Kilgour's basic bespoke silhouette had become a jacket with a straight, somewhat structured chest and relatively natural shoulder worn with plain-front trousers. In the United States, its name was licensed to the specialty store BARNEYS for ready-to-wear clothing from 1968 to 2001. Afterward, it signed a license with IAG (an American company that also owned OXXFORD) to manufacture READY-TO-WEAR. In the late 1990s, it had also introduced a less expensive bespoke—"straight finish"—service executed by tailors in Shanghai.

In 2003 and 2004, the firm was purchased from its previous owner, the Holland & Sherry textile group, by its managing director Hugh Holland in partnership with its design director Carlo Brandelli and retail specialist Clive Darby, undertook an extensive renovation of its premises at 8 Savile Row, and reverted to the single name Kilgour.

kilt The pleated knee-length wrap skirt made of TAR-TAN wool, worn as an emblem of Highland dress. Derived from the earlier tradition of wearing a PLAID, the patterned length of fabric that was worn wrapped around the body and belted at the waist. The contemporary form of the kilt, which was probably invented at the end of the 17th century and was codified by the end of 18th century (after the Dress Act, outlawing the wear of Highland garments, was repealed in 1782), has its pleats permanently sewn in.

The style that schoolgirls wear is properly referred to as a kilted skirt.

kiltie A style of shoe, best known from its use in kiltie loafers and old-fashioned GOLF SHOES, in which the shoe's tongue is extended so that it folds back over the VAMP, covering most of the instep with a fringed flap of leather.

kimono The untailored, open-front style of sleeved, full-length robe worn by both men and women in Japan. Especially in contemporary use, the man's version is usually conservative, relatively undecorated, and rendered in dark colors; if it is patterned, the background to the pattern is generally dark. Unlike the woman's, its underarm sleeves are generally sewn shut.

The kimono, which has no closure system but is secured by a sash or obi, is worn with its left side wrapped over the right. That wrapping is reversed only for burial.

King's Road The major shopping street in Chelsea, a neighborhood in southwest London. Once Charles II's own thoroughfare for commuting between his palaces at Whitehall and Hampton Court, King's Road changed from a relatively quiet area to a center of BEATNIK CHIC during the 1950s, especially after designer Mary Quant opened her Bazaar boutique in 1955 and the Royal Court Theatre opened in 1956. By the following decade, when "Swinging London" was in full swing, King's Road was, along with CARNABY STREET, considered a fashion focal point, famous for boutiques like Hung on You and Granny Takes a Trip. During that decade, most shops also took the then-radical step of remaining open on Saturday afternoons, a time when most traditional retailers were closed. Additionally, the area benefited from its proximity to the Chelsea Antique Market, particularly when fashion began quoting its own earlier frivolities. During the 1970s and 1980s, King's Road again became notorious as the location of the boutiques owned by VIVIENNE WESTWOOD, putting it at the center of the PUNK and NEW ROMANTIC movements.

kinran Reference to a type of rich gold brocade that probably originated in China with the Song dynasty, but later more identified with Japanese costume and ceremony.

kinta cloth An alternative spelling of KENTE CLOTH.

kip Leather taken from the hide of a young animal, usually a bovine. Sometimes used as a synonym for CALFSKIN, and sometimes used to denote an animal that is slightly older than a calf but not fully mature.

kippah A name for the SKULLCAP worn by observant Jewish men. Synonym: YARMULKE.

kipper 1. Slang, usually British, for a very wide necktie. (See FISH, MICHAEL.) 2. British tailors' slang for a seamstress.

Kilts

kissing buttons Slang for buttons that are neatly aligned so that they seem to touch, although they function independently (e.g., the WORKING BUTTONS on an expensive jacket cuff).

kiton For the garment worn in ancient Greece, see CHITON.

Kiton The high-end Italian clothing label, founded by Ciro Paone in 1968 with manufacturing headquarters in Arzano, outside Naples; best known for the deliberately expensive fabrics and determinedly labor-intensive production of its suits.

Born in 1933 into a Neapolitan family that had already been dealing in apparel textiles for four generations, Paone first began a tailoring manufacturing company called CI.PA. during the 1950s. Aiming squarely at the luxury end of the market, Paone named his next venture for the "chiton," the classic garment of the ancient Greeks, and quickly became famous for offering fabrics of almost ridiculous rarity (e.g., VICUÑA, the world's most expensive woven), as well as by describing his competitors to the trade press with statements such as "we are doing poetry, they are doing business."

Paone began expanding his business to the United States during the 1980s and launched a line of ties (specializing in SEVEN-FOLDS), gradually developing his clothing business into a lifestyle brand. He added fragrance in 1996 and shirts in 1998. (That year he also made headlines by bidding against Brioni and acquiring the bulk of the late Duke of Windsor's suits—eleven lots in total—for over $111,000 during an auction at Sotheby's.) In 2000, he added sportswear, and in 2001 founded his own tailoring school, with a two-year curriculum, to ensure that Kiton would always be supplied with properly trained tailors. After initiating its own stores in 2001 (e.g., the 2002 transformation of the former Bank of Naples in New York into a Kiton store at a cost of about $40 million), the brand continued its expansion, adding shoes in 2004.

klaft The ancient Egyptian headdress seen on King Tut's tomb and on the Sphinx. Customarily made of striped, woven fabric, the klaft combined headdress and head kerchief. Variant spelling: claft.

Klein, Calvin Born in 1942, the native New Yorker became world-famous for his minimalist aesthetic and his marketing savvy—particularly the sexually provocative advertising of his jeans and fragrance brands.

Klein's grandmother on his mother's side was an Austrian immigrant who had worked for women's wear designer Hattie Carnegie and then supported herself as a seamstress and by working in a notions store; his father, Leo, was an Hungarian immigrant. Raised near Mosholu Parkway, in the same lower-middle-class Jewish neighborhood of the Bronx as Ralph Lifshitz (who became designer RALPH LAUREN), Calvin Richard Klein attended high school in Manhattan, graduated from FIT in January

Kiton: Ciro Paone

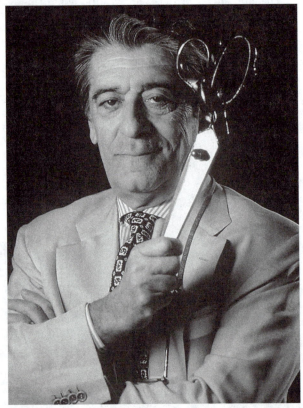

of 1963, and married Jayne Centre the following year. By 1968, he had started his own women's wear label, specializing in coats, together with business partner and childhood friend Barry Schwartz. Not long after opening a showroom in the York Hotel, the new label was discovered by an influential buyer from Bonwit Teller, and not long after that, Klein's clean-lined designs made him a darling of retailers and the fashion press, eventually winning him multiple Coty and CFDA Awards. In 1977, he announced his expansion into menswear. Later that year, he announced his designer jeans.

The 1980 television and print campaign to advertise those jeans, photographed by Richard Avedon and starring 15-year-old Brooke Shields delivering deliberate double entendres (e.g., "Want to know what gets between me and my Calvins? Nothing.") set a precedent for all the brand's subsequent campaigns: It was immaculately executed, way ahead of the curve, incredibly controversial, and reaped millions of dollars in free publicity worldwide. The 1982 launch of his men's underwear line started a similarly controversial collaboration with photographer Bruce Weber, and its images (particularly of Olympic pole vaulter Tom Hinthaus) were widely hailed—or reviled—as homoerotic.

Calvin Klein

Good-looking, 6 feet, 2 inches tall, and also extremely lean, Klein achieved a personal fame that transcended fashion. His nights partying at Studio 54 made him a regular feature of the gossip columns, as did his 1977 purchase of a house in the Pines section of Fire Island. The kidnapping of his daughter Marci in 1978 and his rescue of her made world headlines. In 1986, he married employee Kelly Rector and switched to summering in East Hampton. By 1988, he had entered drug rehab.

Despite his state-of-the-art advertising for jeans and underwear (e.g., using Kate Moss and actor Mark Wahlberg when he was still known as rapper Marky Mark) and his successful launches of fragrance franchises like Obsession, Eternity, and Escape, Klein's business—undermined by a bad bond deal—was on the brink of disaster in 1992 when he was bailed out by a huge loan from friend David Geffen. Within a year, he had rallied. Reversing his own precedent, he launched the wildly successful cK in 1993 as a unisex fragrance and promptly became the first designer to win CFDA Awards for both menswear and women's wear in the same year.

Nevertheless, at the turn of the century, Klein was advertising his willingness to sell his business, although he later took it off the block. Finally, at the end of 2002, Klein and Schwarz sold the brand to Phillips-Van Heusen. In 2003, the then 38-year-old Italo Zucchelli, who had joined the company in 2000 and previously worked for Jil Sander, took over as designer of record for the men's collection.

By the 21st century, his name, along with Giorgio Armani's, was one of the most easily recognized designer brands in the world.

knapsack   Generic reference to a backpack.

knee breeches   Refers to breeches that end under the knee, not on it; usually a description of court dress or costume, since the custom of wearing breeches at court, or on other ceremonial or diplomatic occasions, persisted long after the fashion for breeches had given way to full-length pants.

knickerbockers   A term used from the 1860s onward to describes BREECHES that end below the knee with the fabric gathered into a band; usually worn for sports.

The name derives from Washington Irving's 1809 *A History of New York*, for which he created the eccentric fictional narrator Dietrich Knickbocker. (Illustrations done by George Cruikshank in the London edition show Dutch settlers in baggy breeches and created the nickname.)

knickers   The shortened and more common reference to KNICKERBOCKERS (although, in contemporary British usage, the word is usually understood to mean women's underpants, derived from the 19th century days when women wore baggy pantalettes that looked like breeches).

Knize   A clothier established in Vienna in 1858; by the 21st century, known as much for its Knize Ten cologne and its Jugendstil premises (designed by Adolf Loos) as for its tailoring. During the 20th century, it began carrying readymade suits by other luxury labels in addition to its bespoke service, and established a reputation for custom shirtmaking, which attracted celebrity clients like Maurice Chevalier. Although the firm's other famous patrons ranged from Empress Elizabeth of Austria to conductor Georg Solti, its influence on international fashion peaked between the first and second world wars.

knit   1. Textiles formed by interlooping on needles—either by hand or machine. Machine knitting was invented at the end of the 16th century by Englishman William Lee (who, failing to find English backers for development of his invention, eventually took it to France). Machine knitting was mostly confined to the production of hosiery until the 19th century, and machine knits were not applied on a truly industrial scale until the end of that century.   2. Industry jargon for apparel that is produced by mechanical knitting, usually used to describe knit tops in order to distinguish them from the opposite category of WOVENS. As in "Because his polos were more successful than his dress shirts, the designer's knits outsold his wovens by two to one." Thicker knits (e.g., sweaters) are more often designated as KNITWEAR.

knit face *or* **knit side**   The smooth, or "right," side of a knit fabric (e.g., the kind of smooth machine-knit used in most T-shirts and polo tops); showing the V-shaped knit stitches.

knit tie   A necktie that is produced by either hand or machine knitting, usually with a squared bottom and without a lining. Considered by purists to be slightly more informal than woven silk ties.

knitwear   Industry jargon for sweaters, although the term is sometimes broadened to include any KNIT apparel.

knockoff   Any garment or accessory purposely made to imitate another—usually more expensive—variety. As

Carson Kressley (right)

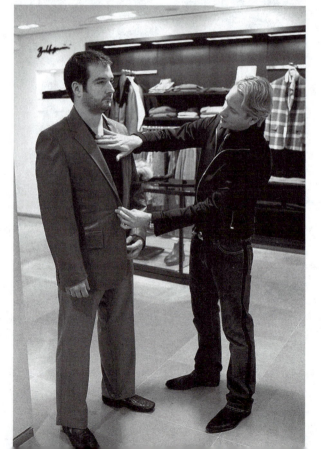

in: "That $200 polyester suit was a line-for-line knockoff of the $2,000 super 100s suit he bought at Barneys."

Kressley, Carson   Born in 1969, Carson Lee Kressley achieved national fame in 2003 with the success of the reality television program QUEER EYE FOR THE STRAIGHT GUY. As the blond, blue-eyed fashion expert on the "Fab Five" makeover team, Kressley was responsible for editing the man's wardrobe, taking him shopping for new clothes, and teaching him how to dress, but he also became notorious for his witty off-the-cuff commentary on the proceedings as well as for launching his distinctive Carson-isms—referring to clothes as "couture" and using "zhoosh" as a verb meaning "tweak"—into the national vocabulary.

Prior to the show, Kressley, who had successfully competed on the horse show circuit riding gaited horses, worked at POLO RALPH LAUREN. In 2004, he capitalized on the show's success with his own book called *Off the Cuff: The Essential Style Guide for Men*, followed by a 2005 children's book, *You're Different and That's Super*. In 2006, he also did a fashion line for QVC television.

Kuppenheimer   Established in 1878 by German immigrant and Civil War (Union Army) veteran John Kuppenheimer, the Atlanta-based Kuppenheimer Men's Clothiers achieved national prominence in 1910 when it hired German-born illustrator J.C. LEYENDECKER (fresh from his success with the ARROW COLLAR MAN) to create its adver-

tising. Not long after, it expanded to a national chain of specialty stores, selling upper-end suits of its own manufacture. In 1996, the firm filed for bankruptcy; at the time of its split-up, it owned large clothing factories in Wellston, Ohio, and Loganville, Georgia, and operated 87 stores in 18 states, including multiple stores in Chicago, Phoenix, Atlanta, Washington, D.C., Denver, and Detroit.

kurta   The long-sleeved, tunic-type shirt worn in South Asia; may be anywhere from hip-length to knee-length; usually made in lightweight, plain-weave cotton or silk. In contemporary use, made with a short, button placket extending to mid-chest; worn in the West for beach and other casual wear.

Kuski suit   Popular reference for the Kuskipuku (which translates as "coachman") suit, designed by Pentti Rinta for the Finnish firm MARIMEKKO in 1972. Its jacket looked like a cross between a NEHRU JACKET and a "riihipaita," a traditional Finnish peasant top: It had no lapels, no waist seam, and four flap pockets on its front. The matching, moderately low-rise pants had a zip fly, with a patch pocket on either side, and were worn without a belt. Supposedly, Rinta invented the prototype for his personal use, but the style quickly crossed over to a unisex fashion and became popular among architects, artists, and academics in the United States and Western Europe. It was manufactured in solid colors including white, kelly green, and black.

Kurtas

lace-ups   Technically a designation of any style of shoe with laces, but in contemporary jargon applied only to dress shoes (and to OXFORDS in particular). Although the term could describe a BROGUE, it is usually reserved for plainer styles.

Lacoste   The brand begun by and named for Jean René Lacoste (1904–1996), the handsome French tennis player who gained international celebrity by being the first non-English speaker to win the Davis Cup (during a dramatic match with Bill Tilden in 1927). Thereafter, Lacoste won the French Open, Wimbledon, and U.S. Open, becoming famed for his tenacity on the court. According to Lacoste, his resulting nickname as "the Crocodile" became general knowledge after newspapers reported on the crocodile suitcase he had won in a bet with the captain of France's Davis Cup team. Thereafter, Lacoste had the animal embroidered on his team blazer like a logo.

René Lacoste

At the end of the 1920s he was also notorious for wearing short-sleeved POLO SHIRTS on the court. In 1933, teaming with a French knitwear manufacturer, he began marketing a white, PIQUÉ knit version of that style with his crocodile logo embroidered on the chest.

For the next decades, Lacoste remained a tennis brand, also becoming a staple of collegiate and preppy fashions in the United States, where the logo had been licensed to IZOD and the distinctive polo style was called an "alligator shirt." In the 1960s, management of the brand was taken over by René's oldest son Bernard. The brand proliferated wildly in the following decades and then was revamped beginning in 1995, once again becoming more exclusive and playing to the upper end of the market. In 2000, Christophe Lemaire became its official designer. Upon Bernard's death in 2006, Bernard's brother Michel took the company reins.

ladder lacing   A style of lacing boots or shoes so that the laces seem to run horizontally, instead of crossing each other (e.g., BAL LACING).

Lagerfeld, Karl   Born into an upper-middle-class German family in a year that he says was 1938 (and most other sources put at 1933), the prolific designer nick-named "Kaiser Karl" by the fashion press influenced the men's market chiefly through his own highly mannered, widely publicized, and much-imitated modes of personal dress, after establishing himself as a designer best known for his women's wear for Chloé, CHANEL, and Fendi.

In 1983, he began a revival of Chanel that soon doubled that label's business. However, by 1989 and for a decade afterward, following the death of his close friend Jacques de Bascher, Lagerfeld became noted for wearing dark clothes, often from Japanese labels such as Matsuda and Comme des Garçons. His other mannerisms included frequent use of a folding fan, an almost constant use of dark glasses, and pulling his graying hair into a ponytail that purposely recalled the style of the Enlightenment.

After the millennium, Lagerfeld embarked upon a drastic, doctor-supervised weight loss, supposedly inspired by his admiration of HEDI SLIMANE's designs for DIOR HOMME. Thereafter, he affected a style that merged GOTH and motorcycle cultures, labels like Chrome Hearts, and custom shirts with high starched

Karl Lagerfeld

collars from Hilditch & Key—elements of which were reflected in his menswear designs. In late 2004, he sold the labels under his own name to TOMMY HILFIGER.

Lake Como   See COMO.

lambskin   1. A fine-grained, flexible, and lightweight leather, made from the cured skin of a young sheep. 2. Reference to a type of condom made from sheep intestines.

lambswool   1. Refers to unwoven, unknit wadding used in garment construction, especially for SLEEVE HEADERS and SHOULDER PADS.   2. Used as either a general or technical description for wool textiles. When used in the general sense, lambswool becomes a synonym for wool that is finer spun and less scratchy. When used in the technical sense, lambswool refers to wool sourced from sheep that are less than seven months old.

lamé   Metallic, often glittery, fabric. A broadly used term, lamé may indicate a BROCADE or some other fabric featuring a sparkling yarn, or it may be applied to a fabric that looks wholly metallic. Because of that, lamé rarely appears in traditional menswear, and then only in DINNER JACKETS and their ilk.

landhausmode   A sort of Germanic equivalent to the PREPPY of the United States or the COUNTY style of the United Kingdom; a style of dress that eschews fashion in favor of conventional garments accented by country clothes, especially traditional *TRACHT* garments, such as the LODEN COAT.

lanificio   Italian word for a wool mill. Often appears in the company name of high-end Italian firms that produce their own yarns and fabrics and then make them into apparel (e.g., Lanificio ERMENEGILDO ZEGNA, Lanificio LORO PIANA).

Lansky Brothers Men's Shop   The Memphis, Tennessee, menswear store made famous by customers such as ELVIS PRESLEY, Jerry Lee Lewis, Roy Orbison, B.B. King, and Booker T & the MG's.

Opened by brothers Bernard and Guy Lansky in 1946 as an army surplus store at 126 Beale Street, the store soon switched to the flashier fare favored by musicians migrating to its immediate neighborhood. During the 1950s, it supplied Elvis with his pink-piped suits, his hi-boy shirts, and his LAMÉ jackets (selling Elvis his first gold lamé number in 1956 for $125). Much later, the store trademarked the slogan "Clothier to the King of Rock 'n' Roll" in conjunction with the Presley estate. It also claims to have put Johnny Cash in his first black suit.

In 1981, it moved to the lobby of the Peabody Hotel and leased its original premises to the Presley estate.

Lansky Brothers Men's Shop: Elvis Presley

lanyard   A cord worn around the neck to hold a tool or case; in late 20th and early 21st centuries, refers to the cord worn around the neck for security passes and identity cards.

lapel   Part of the main body of the jacket and not cut as a separate pattern piece (which would make it a COLLAR). The lapel adjoins the collar and forms a NOTCH. The fabric folds back on itself along a ROLL LINE, forming REVERS (i.e., the portion of the lapel that is visible when the coat is being worn).

lappet   A tab of cloth with ornamental or ceremonial significance, rather than practical use. In various cultures and circumstances, lappets, usually in pairs or other multiples, may appear at the neckline, extend from a caped garment, or decorate headwear (e.g., on the back of a Catholic bishop's MITER).

laser cut   Exactly what it sounds like: textiles that have been cut by lasers instead of handheld shears (or their mechanized equivalent).

last   A form, usually wooden, used in the creation of shoes or boots.

Factory-made footwear is made on a sized, "standard last," matched according to shoe size and width (e.g., the last for an 8EE will differ from an 11C). Custom cobblers will usually carve a last according to their clients' measurements.

laundered   Nothing to do with home washing machines or local Laundromats. Usually jargon for fab-

Lapel

ric, most often DENIM, that has been through a commercial LAUNDRY.

laundry   Nothing to do with the standard washing machine. In the garment industry, a laundry is a business that specializes in FINISHING fabric—usually DENIM for JEANS—with processes such as ACID WASHING, STONE WASHING, GARMENT DYEING, and their ilk.

Lauren, Ralph   Born in 1939, native New Yorker Ralph Lifshitz founded an international apparel and retail empire based on lifestyle marketing, beginning as a menswear designer who offered romanticized renderings of English riding habits, COWBOY costume, safari gear, SAVILE Row tailoring, PREPPY sportswear, and other traditions that were richly evocative rather than specifically fashionable, and then branching out to women's wear, home furnishings, children's wear, activewear, and beauty licenses.

The man that designer KARL LAGERFELD once called "the American Gatsby-dream designer," was raised near Mosholu Parkway, in the same lower-middle-class, Jewish neighborhood of the Bronx as designer CALVIN KLEIN, and was, even when he attended DeWitt Clinton High School from 1954 to 1957, already known for a style that was IVY LEAGUE rather than trendy. In 1959, he and his brother Jerome legally changed their last name to Lauren; he also briefly studied business at City College, worked as a neckwear salesman at BROOKS BROTHERS, was drafted into the Army Reserve, and worked as sales rep for a glove manufacturer. By his early twenties, he had started to come into his own: acquiring a Morgan (the first in what would become a world-famous collection of sportscars); marketing ties for his employer; being written up in the menswear trade paper *DNR* for his personal dress sense; and meeting Ricky Anne Low-

Beer, the blue-eyed blonde whom he would marry in 1964.

By 1967, Lauren had begun selling—at the then outrageous price of $25—wide, thick silk neckties under his own brand, Polo, as a division of a manufacturer named Beau Brummell. By 1968, when those ties were a hit in Bloomingdale's, Lauren took his brand and instead went into business with suit manufacturer Norman Hilton (whom he would buy out in 1972), and by the end of the year, Polo's retro-styled suits were being featured in *DNR*. By 1970, Lauren, who had no formal training in design, patternmaking, tailoring, or any other technical aspect of the business, had won his first COTY AWARD as best menswear designer. The next year, he opened a store in Beverly Hills and branched into women's wear, starting with shirts that featured a polo player emblem embroidered on the cuff, the first major addition to a brand assortment that would eventually include Chaps,

Ralph Lauren

Club Monaco, Double RL, Lauren, Polo, Polo Jeans, Polo Sport, Purple Label, Ralph, RLX, and Rugby.

In 1974, he received extensive press coverage for his contributions to the menswear of the movie *The Great Gatsby*. In 1977, he was again hailed for the clothes worn by Diane Keaton in *Annie Hall*. Beginning from 1979, his print campaigns, especially in the advertising shot by Bruce Weber, pioneered lifestyle branding, with men and women mixed together in what looked more like movie outtakes than fashion photographs, and uninterrupted, multipage portfolios (often twenty pages at a go) that told the season's story in the purest, most controlled manner possible. In 1986, the same year that he remade the Rhinelander Mansion on upper Madison Avenue into his New York flagship, he also made the cover of *Time* magazine. Lauren, who was short, fit, tanned, and had a distinctive thatch of prematurely gray hair, had become a face to the public at large—during that era most often photographed in battered blue jeans on his Colorado ranch.

In 1992, he won his first of several CFDA Awards. In 1993, he launched Polo Sport for men, a hybrid of activewear and sportswear (followed by a women's version in 1996). In the early 1990s, after a series of financial ups and downs, the company received an influx of working capital in an investment agreement brokered by Goldman Sachs. Later, in 1997, the Ralph Lauren business had its initial public offering, becoming traded on the New York Stock Exchange under the symbol RL. In 2004, he launched Rugby, a line aimed at 18- to 25-year-olds. In 2006, things came full circle when Lauren, who had often riffed on both British style and old-time tennis whites, became the official outfitter for Wimbledon.

lawn   A lightweight, plainly woven fabric, usually made from cotton. In previous centuries, used for shirts and SMALLCLOTHES. In contemporary use, most familiar as the printed fabric (known as Tana lawn) in LIBERTY PRINTS.

leatherette   An imitation leather, which may be made of anything from polyurethane to coated woven or knit fabric.

lederhosen   The short leather pants associated with the folk costume in the mountains of Austria and Germany; usually manufactured of a sturdy, inelegant hide such as pig or cow. Considered part of the TRACHT (traditional Germanic clothes) appropriate for Oktoberfest.

The pants are always worn with a distinctive style of SUSPENDERS with a decorative horizontal band linking the two front tabs; they are also accompanied by knee socks, ankle-high boots, and either a short-sleeved shirt or a shirt with its sleeves rolled to the elbow. By custom, the pants become more shiny and more comfortable with wear and are never washed.

Lederhosen

Lee Founded in 1889 as H.D. Lee Mercantile in Salina, Kansas, by Henry David Lee (1849–1928), a Vermont-born entrepreneur who had already been a teacher and the owner of an oil-supply business, and who had moved to Kansas after a bout of tuberculosis. Initially, Lee Mercantile was a grocery business, but in 1911, Lee opened an adjunct that manufactured OVERALLS and other WORKWEAR. During the 20th century, it became best known as a competitor to LEVI's in the JEANS market, especially with Western styles.

In 1913, the firm began producing its UNION-ALL, a long-sleeved overall that was adopted as part of the World War I army uniform in 1917. That same year, it launched its ad campaign for Lee Union-Alls in the *Saturday Evening Post*. In 1920, a Lee salesman named Chester Reynolds began handing out a promotional doll nicknamed Buddy Lee, who modeled the company's workwear.

In 1924, Lee got into the jeans business big time with the introduction of its Cowboy Pants, also known as the "101," which was followed by other models named after loggers and seamen. Building on that cowboy connection, in 1941, during a cowboy convention in Kansas City, fan dancer Sally Rand ripped apart a pair of jeans and pinned them on her rodeo-champion husband, Turk Greenough, in a tighter, butt-hugging cut: Thus the "Lee Rider," thereafter the company's most popular product, was launched. In 1944, the company adopted its "Lazy S," which resembles the Levi's ARCUATE, as its back-pocket design.

During the 1950s, with the rising popularity of jeans as leisure wear, Lee introduced related apparel lines, including the 1954 "Leesures" and, in 1959, white jeans. During the 1960s, it expanded into stretch pants. In 1969, Lee was acquired by VF Corporation, an apparel conglomerate. In 1993, as part of the general segmentation of the jeans market, it split its branding, selling its Riders through MASS-MARKET channels like Wal-Mart and retaining the Lee name for mid- and higher-priced jeans.

Leeds The city in England known during the first half of the 20th century as the center of MULTIPLE TAILORING. Leeds was not only the home base of the largest multiple tailors (e.g., MONTAGUE BURTON), it also was the center for the factories that produced clothes for lower-middle-class and working men, and for the subcontractors who supplied those businesses.

left-hand twill Refers to a TWILL weave in which the diagonal runs from lower right toward the upper left. It is sometimes referred to as an S-TWILL. Its opposite is a RIGHT-HAND TWILL (a Z-TWILL).

When a left-hand twill and a right-hand twill are placed side by side, the left-hand twill will often have a more noticeable twill line. That's because, in the left-hand twill, the yarns are being woven in the direction opposite of their own twist. Because of its construction, a left-hand twill also results in a slightly softer fabric—a prime consideration in the JEANS market according to whether softer or stiffer DENIM is more prized at a particular moment.

leisure jacket A style of SPORTS JACKET, popular after World War II, that was constructed as a cross between a sports shirt and a jacket. Usually the style had an open collar that resembled a shirt collar (instead of a rolled lapel) and symmetrical patch pockets on both the chest and lower torso.

leisure suit 1. A 1970s fashion retrodicted by various names—including the "sleaze-ure suit"—due to its association with swingers, suburbanites, and disco denizens. Prototypically made of double-knit polyester, the leisure suit was a two-piece outfit with a jacket that had no lapels and resembled an overshirt, usually with patch pockets on the chest, and matching pants, sometimes in a beltless design. A leisure suit could be a solid or pattern of any color, although brown, navy, and powder blue were popular.

Classically, the leisure suit was worn with a slinky, brightly colored, and patterned polyester shirt with its top three buttons undone, shiny white patent or polyurethane loafers or boots, and a gold medallion. Roundly reviled by tailors and high-end designers, the leisure suit was nonetheless widely adopted by the middle class. Mainstream manufacturers who offered leisure suits included Palm Beach, Marc Pierce, Mavest, Ratner, and Tobias. Its peak of popularity was about 1974, when LEE advertised its powder-blue polyester leisure suit in *GQ*.

The name leisure suit derived from "leisure jacket," a popular style of sport coat in the 1940s and 1950s, which featured symmetrically placed patch pockets on the chest and often had a shirt-collar-style opening.

2. Another name for the 19th-century SACK SUIT.

leisure wear During the 1970s, industry jargon for leisure suits and their like (i.e., clothes that did not fit the traditional suit or sports jacket categories). Later used to describe even more informal categories—the equivalent of ladies' "at home" wear.

lenpur A fiber made from pulped wood, usually white pine. In the early 21st century, touted in the textile market for its then novelty, for its natural antibacterial (and therefore odor-resistant) properties as a CELLULOSIC fiber, and for its ecological advantages as a "renewable resource."

leontine A type of dressy watch chain. Usually Victorian or Edwardian usage.

lever or **levée** The morning ritual of dressing the king. Its opposite is the *coucher*, or nighttime undressing.

Levi Strauss & Co. The San Francisco-based company founded by and named after Bavarian-born Levi Strauss (1829–1902), who immigrated to New York in 1847 and then to San Francisco in 1853, where he began wholesal-

Leisure suit

ing dry goods, later including a product that would be the forerunner of JEANS.

The company itself dates the birth of the blue jean to May 20, 1873, the day that Strauss and a Reno, Nevada, tailor named Jacob Davis received U.S. Patent 139121 for their process of riveting pants at seam stress points. Initially, the pants were called WAIST OVERALLS and the specific model manufactured by Levi Strauss was the "XX," which would later become known as the "501." Made of indigo-dyed denim, it had suspender buttons (belt loops would not be added until 1922), a waist cinch (discontinued in 1942), and only one rear pocket, which was decorated with an ARCUATE.

In 1886, the company instituted its Two-Horse leather patch (replaced by card stock in the 1950s). In 1890, when its patent for riveted clothes became part of public domain, the company began numbering models and first used its "501" designation. In 1901, it added a second back pocket, establishing the five-pocket prototype that would be synonymous with jeans for the next century. In 1915, it began buying denim from CONE MILLS, which developed its famous 10-ounce, red SELVEDGE denim exclusively for Levi's in the late 1920s.

In 1936, the company added its first Red Tab to the back pocket, as a means of distinguishing itself from competitors. In 1961, it introduced its first preshrunk jeans and, in 1966, replaced the copper rivets on the back pockets with bar tacks. Toward the end of the 20th century, LS&Co. became part of a general trend in the jeans market to differentiate brands and to emphasize its authenticity, creating sub-brands such as Silver Tab, Red Tab, and Vintage.

Leyendecker, J.C.   Born in 1874 in Germany, illustrator Joseph Christian Leyendecker immigrated to Chicago with his family in 1882 and later studied art in Paris, along with his younger brother Francis, who would also become a well-known illustrator. Best known for over 300 *Saturday Evening Post* covers, beginning at the turn of the century and continuing for decades, and for creating a painted paragon of pre-World War I American manhood analogous to Charles Dana Gibson's creation of the Gibson girl. Because the *Saturday Evening Post* regularly commissioned him to do the covers for major holidays, the illustrator is famous not only for his square-jawed, clean-shaven beau ideal, but also for helping to codify the new year as a diapered baby, UNCLE SAM as a white-haired gentleman in a suit of stars and stripes, and the jolly archetype of SANTA CLAUS.

In 1905, he created "the ARROW COLLAR MAN," supposedly modeled on his agent and companion Charles Beach. In 1910, he created a campaign for KUPPENHEIMER, a manufacturer of men's clothing. In 1911, his illustrations of men wearing KENOSHA KLOSED KROTCHES became the first prominent ad campaign for men's underwear. Later advertising campaigns featuring Leyendecker men included HART, SHAFFNER & MARX clothing and Chesterfield cigarettes.

He died in July 1951 at his home in New Rochelle, New York, aged 77.

Levi's Red Tab: Red Tab 1939 and Red Tab 2007

Liberace Born in 1919 in West Allis, Wisconsin, Wladziu Valentino Liberace came into the world wearing a caul—which his Italian-Polish family interpreted as a sign of great things—and was a surviving twin whose brother died before birth. While still in diapers, he could already play the piano by ear. By age four, he had begun formal music lessons. By the time he was a teenager, he had turned pro. But from the 1950s until his death in the 1987, he was better known for the flash of his stage costumes than the facility of his piano playing: For most of his career, he earned over $5 million a year and regularly reinvested six-figure sums in costumes.

Liberace, who used a single name professionally, was the first male performer to so cheerfully and continually transgress the boundaries of good taste and so successfully reap the resulting publicity. His costume schtick began when he wore white tails to a Hollywood Bowl concert in 1952 and quickly escalated in outrageousness from gold LAMÉ jackets (he credited himself for inspiring ELVIS PRESLEY's) to a sparkling suit with piano-keyboard motifs on its collars and cuffs. Audiences adored him for it.

He not only wore capes, he wore a $300,000 fox cape with a 16-foot train. He played the piano while wearing fistfuls of rings, including one shaped like a piano and another like a candelabra. (In one of his several autobiographies, he

advised: "Don't wear one ring; wear five or six.") Well past middle age, he performed in sequined hot pants. Onstage, he wore over-the-top ensembles by Ray Acuna and Michael Travis. Offstage, he accumulated closets full of clothes by the likes of SY DEVORE. His Sherman Oaks house had a piano-shaped swimming pool, and his bedroom in Las Vegas had a ceiling that copied the Sistine Chapel's—but put his own beaming face in the center.

Liberace went to great lengths to deny any allegations of homosexuality, successfully prosecuting a case in London during the 1950s and protesting even when he became the subject of a palimony suit by former companion Scott Thorson in the early 1980s. He was also unamused by the campiness of piano player Elton John and other openly gay performers.

When he died of congestive heart failure in 1987, not long after setting box office records at Radio City Music Hall, many of his obituaries cited AIDS-related illnesses as contributing factors.

Liberace

Liberty print   For menswear, the phrase refers to any of the colorful, usually small-scale figurative prints manufactured by Liberty of London; the fabric itself, a cotton lawn called Tana lawn, originated in the second quarter of the 20th century and is reissued each season in new or revived designs and colorways. In contemporary use, it is most often employed as shirting, although Liberty prints on other fabrics, such as silk, may appear as ties or linings. See color plates.

licensing   As applied to apparel, the practice of selling the rights to an identifiable name and/or logo for its use on a garment, for either a flat fee, a percentage of the profits, or some combination thereof. Examples range from the name and image of actor JAMES DEAN (on leather jackets) to Tabasco sauce (on ties and golf shirts). The licensor is the person who allows use of the name; the licensee is the person who uses it; and the license is the agreement between them.

Lilly Pulitzer   Although better known for women's wear made in signature prints that capitalized on colors like hot pink, lime green, and bright yellow, the brand founded by Palm Beach socialite Lilly Pulitzer in the late 1950s expanded into menswear and was producing a full line of hand silk-screened sports jackets, shirts, jeans, shorts, and other resort wear—favored by PREPPIES and the Palm Beach set—by the 1970s. Lilly herself retired in 1984, although she allowed the brand to be revived in 1993.

lincoln green   A type of sturdy wool dyed a distinctive dark green, lincoln green (which refers to the fabric and not just its color) was favored for hunting and outdoor work, especially during the 19th century. It takes its name from the city in England, not the 19th-century

American president. Today, its closest equivalent would be LODEN.

linen   1. Refers to either the fiber or the fabric made from it; commonly cited as the oldest apparel textile in the world and, for millennia, one of the most common apparel textiles in Europe. A CELLULOSIC fiber, linen is sturdy, lustrous, and is easily woven and washed, but wrinkles easily and has little RECOVERY (making it a difficult material for KNITWEAR); naturally LONG-STAPLE, it is resistant to PILLING and softens and whitens with age.

Linen is created from the stalks of the FLAX plant. After harvesting, it is first subjected to "retting," a process of induced rotting that loosens the fibers and makes them easier to process. It is then "scutched" (essentially a crushing process), before being combed and, finally, spun.

In descriptions of fiber composition, the word linen is used, never flax.

2. A reference, especially before the 20th century, to a man's shirt and other personal items (e.g., nightshirts); a usage that arose because such items were customarily made from linen, but continued even when they were composed of cotton or blends.

In previous centuries, a change of linen was the equivalent of a modern shower: Medical men thought that wearing linen—because it absorbed sweat, smell, and dirt—was a way of ridding the body of impurities.

lines   Jargon for a measurement of button size in which an inch is equal to 40 lines.

linette   A type of semitransparent, PLAIN-WEAVE, extremely fine LINEN or cotton/linen mixture. Weighing even less than LAWN, BATISTE, or modern handkerchief linen, linette was featured in the showier parts of men's clothes (e.g., cuffs during the 18th century) and is no longer produced.

lining   A lightweight fabric used to protect the interior of a garment and/or to mask its seams and construction. In menswear, most often made of a smooth-surfaced material such as BEMBERG or silk. By tradition, the sleeves of a tailored jacket sport striped lining and the main body of the jacket may sport a bright or decorative lining. In tailors' jargon, the lining of a jacket is referred to as the BODY LINING, so that it is not confused with INTERLINING, which is added to the garment for construction and reinforcement and is never visible when the garment is finished.

linsey-woolsey   Archaic reference to a simply woven, coarse fabric worn mostly by farmers and workmen, chiefly in England and her cold-weather colonies before the 20th century. So called because the WARP was made of LINEN and the WEFT was made of WOOL.

liripipe   A style of soft headcovering worn from about the late 13th century onward. Resembling a wildly overgrown version of today's STOCKING CAP, the liripipe was a cap or hood with a very long—in some cases knee-length—funnel of fabric coming from its crown.

lisle   A type of cotton fabric, usually knit, known for its extreme smoothness (or materials using other fibers—such as nylon or polyester—made to resemble it). Technically, lisle refers to the yarn and its method of processing rather than to the finished material, but the men's fashion industry tends to use the terms interchangeably. Used most often in socks and underwear.

Little Lord Fauntleroy   A type of romantic, dressy suit for young boys (generally ages four to eight) inspired by Frances Hodgson Burnett's tale of *Little Lord Fauntleroy*, which first appeared as a story in *St. Nicholas* magazine in 1885 and was published as a book the following year. The illustrations by Reginald Birch and the author's descriptions of her hero, Cedric Erol, were based on the clothes that Burnett invented for her own son, Vivian. Originally, this meant a CAVALIER-style costume consisting of plumed hat, floppy lace collar, velvet knee breeches, short velvet jacket, and long, curled hair. Eventually,

Little Lord Fauntleroy poster

"I'm Very Glad I'm Going To Be An Earl"

the style encompassed large hats made of straw and suits of similar silhouette but different materials.

Antithetical as it may have been to that era's rough-and-tumble ideal of American boyhood, the popularity of the story condemned countless boys to suffer being dressed as the "brave little lad" of the Burnett book, and the fashion did not finally disappear until after World War I.

lizard Leather made from the skin of any of several species of lizard (e.g., iguana), prized for its distinctive grain (which may be ridged, scaly, and/or rectangular depending upon the species used). Prized for decoration rather than sturdiness.

L.L.Bean The Freeport, Maine-based mail-order, manufacturing, and retail company founded by Leon Leonwood Bean in 1912; established first as a specialist in men's hiking, camping, and outdoor gear, and subsequently as a purveyor of practical and simply styled flannel, wool, and corduroy casual clothes and accessories—especially of items such as BARN JACKETS, MAINE HUNTING SHOES, and canvas boat-and-tote bags that passed into the PREPPY canon.

Born in 1872 in Greenwood, Maine, Bean began hunting at age 13 and working in his brother's shoe store after graduation from commercial college. In 1911, inspired by his own experiences hunting in the Maine woods, he hit upon the idea of attaching a sturdy leather upper to a flexible, waterproof, rubber bottom. By spring of the following year, Bean had sold 100 pairs of his Maine Hunting Shoes—with 90 of them being returned as defective when the leather upper separated from the sole.

Undaunted, Bean borrowed money to make refunds, found a new supplier and reoffered the boot. He developed his mail-order list by accessing buyers of hunting licenses and soon expanded into sturdy weatherproof clothes and basic camping supplies. In 1917, he opened a showroom and, in 1920, built a store in the center of Freeport. As of 1951, Bean began keeping his store open 24 hours a day, year-round; thereafter, midnight raids on Freeport became a rite of passage for college students and other Bean customers.

In 1954, he offered women's wear; in 1993, the company expanded into children's wear. By the time Bean died in 1967, his business was one of the world's largest mail-order operations and his Freeport store was one of Maine's top tourist attractions.

Lobb See JOHN LOBB.

Lock & Co. *or* **James Lock & Co.** The London firm of hatters, located at 6 St. James' Street, that traces its origin to its founding in 1676 by Robert Davis (whose heirs married into the Lock family and adopted that name during the next generation); perhaps best known for its invention of the BOWLER.

In the store's long history, its illustrious customers have encompassed the Duke of Wellington (who wore a Lock hat during the Battle of Waterloo), Admiral Horatio Nelson (who was wearing a specially commissioned model when he was killed in the Battle of Trafalgar), DOUGLAS FAIRBANKS JR. (who once lived above the store), and celebrities including FRANK SINATRA. In the United States, often referred to as "Lock's of London."

locker loop 1. The extra loop, made of fabric, on the center back of a shirt, especially of a BUTTON-DOWN shirt (the idea being that the loop can be used to hang the garment in a locker or on a coat rack when no hanger is available). Also referred to as a "fairy hook," and a variety of other, less printable slang.   2. A loop of fabric inside the center back of pants or a jacket.

locks   Synonym for DREADLOCKS.

lock stitch   Jargon for the type of machine stitching used to sew most woven fabrics. A lock stitch uses two threads—a top and a bottom—and as one penetrates the fabric, it is "locked" in place by the other. The lock stitch is produced by a FLAT MACHINE, the type of sewing machine most familiar to both home sewers and professionals.

Its most common alternatives are: HANDSTITCH, which uses a single thread, no matter what style of stitch is being executed; and the machine-made chain stitch, which uses only one thread and creates a line of stitching resembling crochet (and tends to unravel easily once the thread is broken).

loden   A type of fabric associated with Austria, especially the mountainous region known as a the Tyrol and the clothes worn there. Originally made from the coarse, unprocessed wool of mountain sheep, loden retained its natural lanolin content, which made it highly resistant to wet weather; this was further enhanced by a tight weave and brushed surface that made the fabric wind-resistant. Typically produced in a flat, dark hunter green, although also seen in navy or dark gray.

Popularized in the 19th century, when it was worn by the future EDWARD VII during his hunting and shooting excursions as Prince of Wales and also by Emperor Franz Joseph I. The fabric again became the height of fashion in the United States and United Kingdom before World War II, when menswear became briefly besotted by all things Tyrolean.

loden coat   A style of sporty coat, associated with the LANDHAUSMODE of the upper middle classes of Germany and Austria; made of LODEN fabric and worn in much the same context as a DUFFLE COAT. Unfitted through the body and usually unlined, the coat reaches to just below the knees. Its back is made with a deep center vent that swings out from the shoulder blades; its front has a fly opening so that the buttons (which are usually made of horn) are not exposed.

Loden-Frey   The Munich retailer founded by John George Frey in 1842, best known for selling LANDHAUS-MODE to the upper middle class, especially TRACHT items such as LEDERHOSEN and LODEN COATS.

loft   A term used to describe the bounce-back of a fabric, not its height. For example, when wool quickly returns to its original position after being crushed or crumpled, it is praised for its "loft."

loincloth   A garment or cloth draped to hide the genitals, which appears—in variations—in virtually every culture, whether used exclusively as an undergarment or worn in public (by slaves, laborers, or athletes). In ancient times, commonly worn by Egyptians, Minoans, Greeks, Etruscans, and Romans before it disappeared beneath other clothes.

London cut   See ENGLISH DRAPE.

London line   Used during the early 1960s to refer to a style of suit that updated traditional English tailoring with wider lapels and other MOD references.

London shrunk   A now-old-fashioned term indicating wool or wool-blend cloth that has been preshrunk. In the days when wool was less widely preshrunk and suit materials might come from dozens of small and sometimes dodgy mills, "London shrunk" presented an industry standard.

long johns   Long underwear, especially thermal underpants with a full-length leg or a union suit with legs extending at least to mid-calf (as opposed to being cropped at mid-thigh). According to charming—but probably apocryphal—folklore, the slang originated at the end of the 1870s with the fame of boxer Big John Sullivan, a prizefighter who fought his bouts in a UNION SUIT.

long-staple cotton   Refers to a type of unspun or unwoven COTTON fiber that has longer basic STAPLE or fiber length than its more common UPLAND COTTON cousins (and generally carries a premium price to match); derived from certain varieties of *gossypium barbadense* cotton plants (generally grown in very dry regions).

In general, a LONG-STAPLE fiber (e.g., PIMA cotton) is preferred because it requires less twisting to turn into a yarn, and a yarn that is twisted fewer times is not as stiff and therefore makes fabric with a softer HAND. Popular types of long-staple cotton include pima, EGYPTIAN, and SEA ISLAND.

Lonsdale *or* **Lord Lonsdale**   See YELLOW EARL.

look book   An illustrated guide to a designer or high-end manufacturer's collection, created for the use of editors and retailers—but not for publication. A high-fashion designer's look book may simply be an outfit-by-outfit breakdown of his or her runway show, but a look book may also be an elaborately photographed and styled shoot. Or it may simply be a collection of still-life photos or sketches.

Because the looks are usually numbered, the look book allows an efficient, standardized reference to the pieces in the collection.

Loro Piana   The Italian yarn spinner, textile producer, apparel maker, fashion brand, and retailer; best known for its production of luxury goods, particularly CASHMERE.

In the 19th century, the Loro Piana family were merchants who began producing their own goods, opening their first factory in Quarona in northern Italy and becoming identified with the production of very expensive wools and cashmere yarns and cloth. It was not until the opening of its New York store in 1993 that the family again directly operated a store; this was followed by the opening of Italian stores in 1998 and a subsequent retail rollout.

In addition to producing for its own brand, the company acts as a manufacturer for other high-end designers, especially in the production of luxury knit goods.

lorum   See PALLIUM.

Loro Piana: Sergio (left) and Pier Luigi Loro Piana

Louis Boston   The high-end clothier and specialty store in Boston's Back Bay neighborhood; the store itself frequently writes the name as a single word, "Louis-Boston," and pronounces its name as "Lou-eez"; although in the 20th century it often wrote its name with a comma as "Louis, Boston," it has never interjected the word "of" in its name.

The family-run store traces its history to a pawn shop opened by Louis Pearlstein in the 19th century, which frequently dealt in clothes. In the 1920s, Pearlstein's sons Saul and Nathan began a business selling new menswear. Under the next generation, Murray Pearlstein made the store nationally famous for its introduction of high-end tailoring brands and, in 1989, moved the store into the 1863 William Preston-designed landmark building that formerly housed Bonwit Teller. The business passed to Pearlstein's daughter, Debi Greenberg, in 2003.

Louis XIV   The "Sun King" whose long reign (1643–1715) became synonymous with splendor and who did the most to establish France as Europe's capital of luxury and fashion (memorialized in the contemporary Comité Colbert, a trade organization of luxury goods purveyors named after his minister of finance). Several economic historians have theorized that the magnificence of his courts, particularly at Versailles, and the dress proscriptions he imposed on his nobles had the effect of decreasing the nobles' income and hence their ability to revolt. However, it's also certain that Louis genuinely enjoyed opulent objects and loved to dress up and dazzle his subjects. Among the many, many fashions he decreed were RED HEELS for the nobility and multiplicities of ribbons.

Born in 1638, Louis was handsome and egocentric. While Jean-Baptiste Colbert banned the importation of lace, silks, and other luxury goods, Louis fostered the use of those very materials, thereby creating a market for French-made products. In 1669, he appointed a special minister for his wardrobe.

lounge suit   The name given, particularly between World War I and World War II, to the style of suit also known as the LONDON CUT or the ENGLISH DRAPE. The lounge suit was softer in construction and had a broader shoulder than the FROCK COAT or some of the other styles that preceded it. As its name implies, it was also considered slightly less formal: A comfortable suit to be worn with unstarched shirts made with FOLD-OVER COLLARS.

The term has no connection to LOUNGEWEAR.

loungewear   Retail jargon for a category of clothes that includes robes, pajamas, and related pieces that may be decorative as well as functional. For example: The silk boxer shorts and silk robes that are popular gifts for Valentine's Day and Father's Day are classified as loungewear, and a traditional tailor may extend the designation to SMOKING JACKETS.

Louis XIV

lovat   Refers to a type of traditional tweed that creates the effect of a solid ground but is, on closer inspection, actually a mix of colors.

According to the book *Scottish Estate Tweeds* by Johnstons of Elgin, the first Lovat Mixture (the word is capitalized when referring to the original tweed rather than the general type) was woven in 1845 at the request of Lord Lovat, who wanted an estate tweed that would imitate the mottled effect of the flowers and foliage on hillside and loch shore, which he believed would create a sort of CAMOUFLAGE—in the days before that word was used—helpful for stalking and shooting. The true Lovat has an overall mid-brown effect with blue and yellow undertones, and is a mixture of (from high to low): light blue, chrome yellow, bright yellow, dark yellow-brown, and white.

love beads   Slang for a beaded necklace, especially when referring to 1960s-era fashions worn by a man; a popular accessory to NEHRU JACKETS. Synonym: HIPPIE BEADS.

love lock   Associated with the CAVALIERS of the 17th century, the love lock was a lock of hair in the front of the head that was grown longer than the rest and usually set off with a bow.

low-rise   Refers a style, such as HIP-HUGGERS, that falls below the natural WAIST. The RISE, or measure from crotch seam to the waistband, of most men's jeans is about 12 to 13 inches, while anything below 10 inches is considered a low-rise.

low shoes   Usually a reference to distinguish shoes from boots, especially in anything written before World War I; most often refers to OXFORDS.

Lowther, Hugh   The colorful fifth Earl of Lonsdale, better known as the YELLOW EARL.

lug sole   A type of thick, rubber sole for shoes—especially workboots—with exaggeratedly deep treads to increase traction.

lumbar pack   A utilitarian bag, usually with one or more zippered closures, worn around the waist and outside the clothes. Usually larger than a FANNYPACK, and worn as a substitute for a small backpack during hiking or other sports.

Lurex   Trademarked name for a type of shiny, metallic-looking yarn, or the fiber used to make it.

Lycra   Trademarked name for a type of SPANDEX, an elastic yarn composed primarily of polyurethane. Created by DuPONT (now INVISTA) in 1958.

lyocell   CELLULOSIC fiber created with a process similar to the making of RAYON (often using wood chips as its basic ingredient). A more generic name for branded fibers like TENCEL and Lenzing (which share a parent company).

Lytton, Lord   See BULWER-LYTTON, EDWARD.

M magazine   Offered as the men's counterpart to the same publisher's more successful *W* magazine for women, *M* chronicled the luxury lifestyle for men and the fashion that went with it. It began as a four-color monthly in October 1983 from Fairchild Publications and, in 1990, acquired and incorporated the business magazine, *Manhattan inc.*, briefly switching its name to *M inc.* in an effort to broaden readership and peaking at a circulation of about 220,000. Its last editor was Clay Felker, who had become a celebrity with his founding of *New York* magazine in 1968. Fairchild executive Michael Coady closed the title with its November 1992 issue, citing a poor market for luxury advertising.

M notch   A style of lapel on a man's tailored jacket that, instead of forming the customary V-shaped NOTCH where the LAPEL meets the COLLAR, is cut to form a reverse letter M. The extra cutting needed to create the fancy notch is performed on the collar portion, not on the lapel. Most fashionable in the first half of the 19th century.

mac   Originally, an abbreviated and slang reference to MACINTOSH, a type of raincoat; later used generically as a reference to any raincoat.

Macaroni   Derived from the Macaroni Club founded in London in 1764, the appellation quickly came to refer to an affected young man who exaggerated his dress to a degree considered fussy and effeminate, favoring highly formal hair, breeches, and coats in contrast to the simple and sober styles then gaining in popularity. (Perhaps the most famous Macaroni was Charles James Fox, who espoused the style and then repudiated it just as passionately.) His much-caricatured ensemble might include a tiny TRICORNE worn atop his towering hairstyle or outrageous wig; two watches worn at once; silk stockings gartered with multiple ribbons; a tight-fitting coat with

Macaroni

oversized buttons; shoes with huge, flashy buckles and red heels; and a cane dangling tassels or yet more ribbons. His French counterpart would have been the ÉLÉGANT.

To be "à la macaroni" was to be outlandish. Today, the slang survives in the verse of "Yankee Doodle Dandy" that ends with the DANDY who "stuck a feather in his cap and called it Macaroni."

macassar oil   A sweet-smelling, tropically derived oil used as a dressing for men's hair, purportedly imported from the Sulawesi port once known as Macassar. During the 19th century, men's use of macassar oil was prevalent enough to inspire the invention of the "anti-macassar," a doily placed on the back of a chair to protect upholstery from oil stains.

macclesfield   Used to describe a distinctive type of patterned necktie silk, as well as the ties made from it. The macclesfield is SELF-PATTERNED with a small, usually geometric, weave using only two colors (most often black and white, which, because of the diminutive repetitions of pattern, tends to read as a silvery gray when seen from a short distance). The name derives from a style of weaving practiced since Victorian times in the Cheshire market town of Macclesfield, a traditional center of England's silk industry during a time when the highway from Manchester to Macclesfield was called "The Silk Road."

In earlier references, when all ties with this type of pattern could be assumed to have originated in Macclesfield, the word was capitalized. In contemporary usage, when ties of that type are just as likely to have originated in China or Italy, the word is lowercased.

The macclesfield differs from the SPITALSFIELD, a patterned, multicolored necktie silk of similar origin, by having a smaller pattern and being limited to two colors.

machine-knit   The designation usually implies machine production of something that is ordinarily hand-knit or meant to resemble a hand-knit (e.g., a sweater made from relatively thick yarn); rarely used for items that have a very fine gauge or are assumed to be made on a machine (e.g., dress socks).

Historically, when machine knitting came into broad adoption for men's HOSE in the 17th century, machine work was prized for producing a smoother, smaller knit.

Confusingly, in contemporary usage, high-end apparel makers sometimes use the phrase "hand-loomed," a synonym that indicates the apparel was made on a small-sized knitting machine rather than a huge industrial model (but does not mean that a knit was made by hand).

mackinaw   1. Named after the city in Michigan, the name refers to a style of short, heavy, woolen coat that is usually double-breasted.

Invented by a British officer, Charles Roberts, who captured the city of Mackinaw during the War of 1812 and did not have enough warm coats for his men, the first mackinaws were improvised from Hudson's Bay Company blankets. Just before and during World War II, the U.S. military adapted the style for cold-weather use, and it was also known as a "jeep coat." Today, the style is most often made from thick, checked wool, especially in a red-and-black check.

No relation to the MACINTOSH.

2. Heavy woolen fabric from which a mackinaw coat might be made; similar to a Hudson's Bay Company blanket.

macintosh   1. The process of creating waterproof cloth by bonding fabric and rubber, invented and patented by Scottish chemist Charles Macintosh in 1823 as Patent Waterproof Indiarubber Cloth, after he noticed that coal tar naptha dissolved rubber. Macintosh was not the first to experiment with rubber coating of fabric, but he became its most successful promoter. By the 1830s, macintosh fabric was widely used for rainwear, despite the fact that the 19th-century versions of rubberized fabric quickly became quite smelly. (Various treatments and tricks were offered to counterattack this unfortunate quality throughout the rest of the century.) The correct spelling of the man's name, the fabric, and the resulting raincoat is Macintosh, without a "k"; although "mackintosh" has become an accepted variant when referring to the raincoat.   2. Generic reference to a raincoat (made of any material), especially in British usage; derived from the long association of the rubberized fabric with protective raingear. Often abbreviated to MAC. Variant spelling: mackintosh.   3. A popular pattern of TARTAN.

madder   1. A type of pattern, usually small-scaled and nonrepresentative. During the 1800s, these patterns were popular for women's dresses. Today they most often reappear on silks for ties and dressing gowns. Madders are distinguished from similar classifications, such as FOULARDS, by their palette: Whereas foulards commonly include gold, navy, and maroon, madders are confined to earthy colors like black, brown, mauve, sienna, off-white, or white.   2. A crimson dye derived from a European herb, or a color that resembles it.

made-to-measure—Unlike CUSTOM-MADE or BESPOKE, a made-to-measure garment is usually based on an extant sample and pattern, which is then customized according to the client's measurements. This process may be as simple as a pair of pants where the standard pattern has been altered to accommodate the client's waist and inseam measurements. Or it may be as complicated as an entire suit, including so many measurements and options that it is virtually custom-made.

Made-to-measure also differs from traditional bespoke clothing in that it is sewn by machine, whereas the finest bespoke tailoring is completely hand-constructed. Synonym: SEMI-CUSTOM.

madras   A lightweight, flat, plain-weave cotton fabric so called because it was originally produced in the area around Madras, the city in India known since 1996 as Chennai. Although solid-colored or undyed fabrics may technically be called madras, the term has become virtually synonymous with plaids. By tradition, madras was made from cotton dyed with vegetable dyes and thus gained its reputation for BLEEDING, giving a distinctive blurred effect after a few washings and softening the pattern as it aged.

Following World War I, the material found favor with American men for summertime jackets, pants, and sports shirts. After BROOKS BROTHERS began to carry it in 1920, both madras and madras patchwork became mainstays of what evolved into PREPPY style.

magalog   An advertiser-sponsored publication that is a hybrid of catalog and magazine. Magalogs are often produced when a company wants to communicate a lifestyle message in its marketing. The magalog may use magazine-type articles, feature photography, and formats combined with standard catalog information such as prices and ordering information.

MAGIC   A huge apparel trade show held twice yearly in Las Vegas. The name, which is usually spelled in uppercase letters without periods, is an acronym for the Men's Apparel Guild in California, a trade organization founded in southern California in 1933. In 1942, MAGIC held

Traditional Menswear Patterns and Fabrics

Unless otherwise indicated, all patterns are reproduced true to size.

Mille stripe

Hairline stripe

Pinstripe

Chalkstripe

Pencil stripe

Bengal stripe

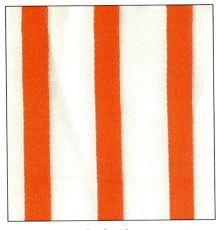

Candy stripe

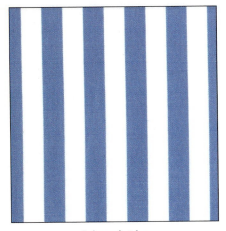

Balanced stripe

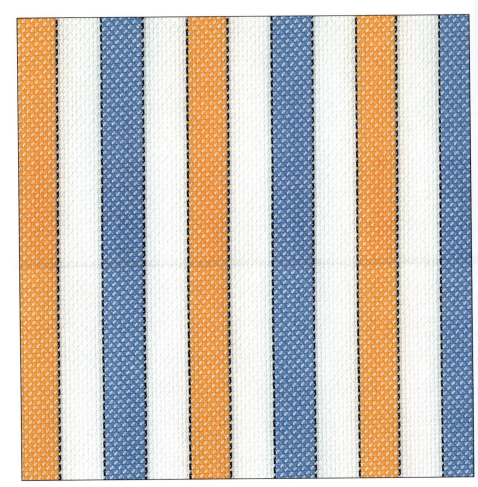

Alternating stripe

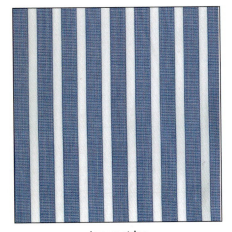

Jermyn stripe

Double stripe

Triple stripe

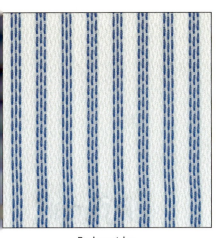

Broken stripe

Multitrack

Pincheck

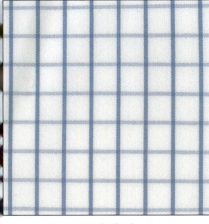

Simple check

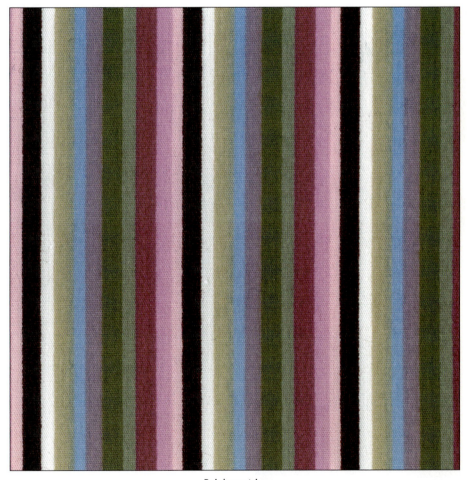

Rainbow stripe

Gingham

Ticking stripe

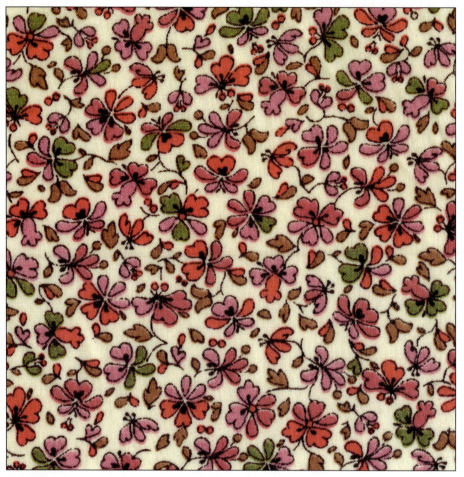
Liberty print

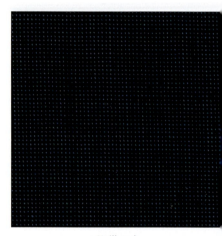
Nailhead

Pinwale corduroy

Bull denim

Right-hand twill denim

Tattersall

Gun club check

Overcheck

Black Watch tartan

Royal Stewart tartan (reduced)

Rob Roy tartan (reduced)

Cheviot

Shetland tweed (in herringbone weave)

Donegal tweed

Saxony

Broken stripe

Chalkstripe

Covert cloth

Moleskin

Casabry twill

Whipcord

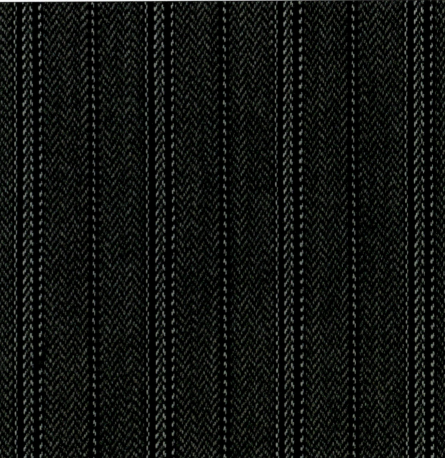

Morning stripe (enlarged)

Venetian

Sharkskin

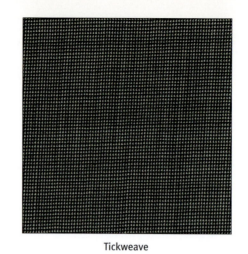

Tickweave

Birdseye

Barleycorn

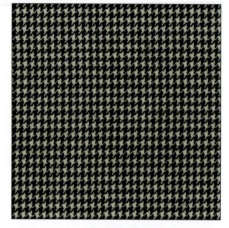

Puppytooth

Houndstooth

Herringbone

Glen check

Prince of Wales

its first "Roundup" in Palm Springs. In 1979, the shows were moved to Los Angeles. In 1989, they moved to Las Vegas. In 1995, they began to incorporate women's wear.

mail or *maille*   Chain mail; reference to armor.

Maine Hunting Shoe   The rubber-bottom, leather-upper, boot-type footwear invented by L.L.Bean in 1911, and subsequently offered by that company in a variety of boot heights and styles (lace-up, pull-on, zipper). Synonyms: Bean boot; duck boot, especially in preppy parlance.

maker   1. Although sometimes used in the same sense in tailoring, "maker" is a common reference in custom shoemaking to the person who attaches the upper to the sole (after the leather has been cut out by the clicker and assembled by the closer).   2. Slang reference to a brand or manufacturer.

malacca   Much sought after as a material for the canes and umbrella shanks used in business and formal settings; used straight or bent, full-bark or stripped. From a variety of reedy palm imported from Southeast Asia.

The Man in the Gray Flannel Suit   The 1955 novel by Sloan Wilson and the 1956 movie made from it (which starred Gregory Peck as hero Tom Rath, an ex-GI with a public relations job) used the gray flannel suit as a symbol of corporate conformity, rather than as a fashion statement. In the book, more than the film, the hero's unease at buying a Brooks Brothers suit, which he can't really afford and doesn't really want, is used to parallel the pressure he feels to conform to postwar society. The book also makes reference to the uniformity of trench coats and other items of attire among the men commuting from the suburbs to jobs in New York. The film was designed by Charles Le Maire, then the head of wardrobe at 20th Century Fox, who also costumed New York-based everyman characters in *The Girl Can't Help It* that same year and *Will Success Spoil Rock Hunter?* the following year.

mandarin collar   A style of collar with a short, standing band and no lapel; although it is supposedly associated with Chinese dress, the term is used interchangeably with Nehru collar (to describe the collar of achkans and similar styles) and other non-Western styles.

mandilion   Refers to a 16th-century style of short jacket, intended for fashion rather function; often worn flung over one shoulder, with sleeves dangling front and back.

Manic Panic   Founded by sisters Tish and Snooky Bellomo in 1977 as a boutique on St. Mark's Place in New York's East Village (supposedly in Jimi Hendrix's old crash pad) and billed as America's first punk boutique. Although the store itself eventually closed, the business survived the punk era due to the success of its proprietary cosmetics line—favored by a succession of alternative lifestyles from Goth to neo-punk—and particularly for its hair dyes, which offered colors unobtainable elsewhere (e.g., "Atomic Turquoise" and "Pretty Flamingo").

Mani-Hose   Pantyhose for men, introduced in the United States in 1970. At a pricey (for that time) $6.50 per pair, Mani-Hose were made of stretch nylon, came in several colors, featured a fly front, and were designed to be worn underneath pants (the lower leg was ribbed so that it resembled a nylon sock). They were marketed primarily toward outdoorsmen as a sort of lightweight update of long johns.

Manila hemp   A synonym for ABACA.

manilla   A synonym for ABACA.

man-made fibers   Fibers not derived from animals, vegetables, or minerals. Widely used man-made fibers include ACRYLIC, NYLON, POLYESTER, and SPANDEX. In the final product, a man-made fiber may be virtually indistinguishable from a natural fiber—for example, a well-made polyester may appear virtually identical to silk. However, man-made fibers have a very different chemical structure, which affects properties like tensile strength, abrasion resistance, and ability to absorb dye. In a BURN TEST, man-made fibers tend to melt rather than burn.

Man-Tan   Launched in 1959 by New York-based Drug Research Corporation as a shaving lotion, Man-Tan was one of the first products to contain DHA (dihydroxyacetone), the active ingredient in SELF-TANNERS.

Mao collar   Widely used as a synonym for a MANDARIN-style collar or jacket—and therefore both politically and factually incorrect.

The actual suit style favored by Mao Zedong (1893–1976) and his followers was a tailored, hip-length jacket of unpatterned material almost always made with matching pants, which was itself modeled on the type of military-inspired suit sported by Sun Yat-sen. The jacket featured a front opening that fastened with round buttons and Western-style buttonholes; two patch pockets symmetrically placed on the chest; and two patch pockets with flaps symmetrically placed over the lower abdomen. It lacked lapels and had a high, tight neckline with a small, fold-over collar that resembled a dress shirt collar in shape and size.

Mao jacket   1. A reference to the military-type suit jacket adopted by Mao Zedong and other officials of the People's Republic of China.   2. A mistaken reference to a jacket with a Nehru-style or mandarin-style collar, and therefore a misnomer.   3. A reference to the plain, padded cotton jackets worn by the Chinese during the reign of Mao Zedong.

marcella front   Refers to a particular type of fine, white, woven PIQUÉ fabric called marcella (especially in British usage), which is used for the front of dress shirts intended to be worn with FORMALWEAR. Thus, what the British and others would call a "marcella-front shirt" is usually the same thing that Americans call a "piqué-front shirt."

mariachi traditional dress   See *TRAJE DE CHARRO*.

Marimekko   The Finnish design firm, manufacturer, and retailer founded in 1951 by Armi Airaksinen Ratia (1912–1979), best known for its bold textile designs and the clothes silhouettes it invented to show them off.

Having not been accepted to its art teaching program, Ratia studied textile design at Helsinki's Institute of Industrial Arts instead. After graduation and return to her home in Karelia, she established a weaving workshop, which she was forced to close after the Russian invasion of the region in 1939. Back in Helsinki, she worked as an advertising copywriter, eventually became interested in textile printing, and began designing for Printex, a specialist in fabrics for interior design that had

Mao Zedong

been acquired by her husband Viljo in 1949. In 1951, together with a few friends, she established Marimekko to market Printex designs and, thereafter working as the firm's managing director and publicist, staged her own fashion show—one of Finland's first—so that potential apparel customers would know what to make of her strange-looking, hand-screened cottons.

Brightly colored and audaciously oversized, Marimekko's initial textile designs were considered blatantly uncommercial, and as the years passed and the company evolved, they only became more so. Ratia had been joined by designers like Maija Isola, who invented enormous abstracts that were impossible to sew into standard apparel or use in conventional interiors. It then hired Vuokko Eskolin-Nurmesniemi to create a line of like-minded clothes. When nobody knew how to market the results, Ratia opened the first Marimekko shop in 1952. When Americans couldn't imagine how to live with her in-your-eye aesthetic, she dispatched her Finnish sales force to create a Marimekko environment at the Design Research store in Cambridge, Massachusetts. By 1967, Marimekko was in 90 stores in Finland and another 140 overseas.

Marimekko's menswear freed wearers from close-fitting, confining tailoring and the convention of wearing neckties. In particular, Eskolin-Nurmesniemi's Jokapoika shirt, designed in 1956, provided men with a colorful shirt that was neither Hawaiian nor plaid, and the unisex Kuski suit, designed by Pentti Rinta in 1972, provided architects and intellectuals with their own alternative to traditional business attire. Annika Rimala's design for the Tasaraita T-shirt in the 1960s turned bold horizontal stripes into the uniform of the *haute bohème* (and preceding similar offerings by everyone from Sonia Rykiel to Agnès b.). At the company's peak in the the 1960s and early 1970s, it hired an architect to create a prototype of

affordable housing called the Marihouse, launched a harebrained scheme to market prefab saunas to the United States, and built its Herttoniemi factory in as a workers' paradise.

Following Ratia's death in 1979, her heirs sold the company to an international conglomerate in 1985, and it subsequently became a public company.

Marinella A family-owned maker of luxury goods, specializing in silk neckties; based in Naples and famed in part for the eccentric operation of its tiny flagship, which measured only about 215 square feet and opened at 6:30 a.m. most mornings.

Mark Cross A luxury leathergoods maker, founded in 1845 in Boston as a saddlery, and subsequently famed for its briefcases and wallets, with specialty stores throughout the United States—most notably on Fifth Avenue in New York.

In the 1920s, the stylish scion of its owning family, Gerald Murphy, known as a painter, a friend of F. Scott Fitzgerald, and as center of the U.S. expat community in France, moved back to the United States in the 1930s to run the store. In 1983, the brand was purchased by Cross pens, which expanded the number of stores. In 1993, it

Marimekko: Armi Ratia in a Jokapoika

was sold to the Sara Lee Corporation, which also owned Coach Leatherware; four years later, the parent company closed the stores and discontinued production.

marled   Describes a fabric—or the garment made from it—that is constructed of yarn containing strands of more than one color; more commonly describes knits. For example: In a marled yarn, a strand of beige and a strand of dark brown may be twisted together in a single yarn; a sweater is then knit from that yarn that has a slightly uneven, marled surface color—neither beige nor dark brown—resulting from that stranding. DONEGAL, heathered, or SPACE-DYED yarns create a similar surface effect through different means.

Marlboro Man   Originally a woman's brand, Marlboro cigarettes became the symbol of all-American manhood in the 1950s when Philip Morris relaunched the brand as filtered cigarettes and needed a macho image to cancel out the namby-pamby connotations of using a filter. The subsequent advertising by Leo Burnett featured sportsmen, COWBOYS, and assorted models of unquestionable masculinity engaged in suitably rugged pursuits. Briefly, the Marlboro Man became a tycoon settling in for a smoke. Then, in the 1960s, the brand began showing him only as a cowboy, often shooting its advertising with authentic cowboys. Thereafter, the macho image passed into popular culture as a shorthand reference to a type of American masculinity, especially in the gay community.

martingale   A half belt; usually refers to a belt that runs only across the back of a jacket.

mass-market   Industry designation for the low-priced retailers and/or the apparel and other products made and sold by them. Examples of mass-market retailers include chains like Wal-Mart and Target. "Volume retail" is sometimes used as a synonym.

master's gown   As regulated by the Intercollegiate Bureau of Academic Costume in the United States, the ACADEMIC DRESS appropriate for a master's degree candidate or graduate is quite similar to a BACHELOR'S GOWN in that it is a long, full gown, falling in an unbelted, straight line. It also has long, full sleeves, but instead of ending in a point, they are closed around the wrist. (Older versions may be open at the elbow as well.) Its main color is usually black, and, in the back, it sports a 42-inch-long hood lined with the colors of the institution granting the degree and edged with 3 inches of the color that represents the area of study (for a table of colors, see ACADEMIC DRESS).

matchsafe   Synonym for what the British more often called a VESTA CASE.

The Matrix   Beginning with 1999's *The Matrix* (and continuing with its two 2003 sequels, *The Matrix Reloaded* and *The Matrix Revolutions,* as well as the 2003 videogame "Enter the Matrix"), Kym Barrett's costume designs painted a picture of the future where the good guys wore sleek, dark clothes and stylish sunglasses and the bad guys were in ill-fitting suits and geeky frames. The general look of the movie was reflected in designer collections from Balenciaga, Helmut Lang, SEAN JOHN, and HEDI SLIMANE. In particular, the long, black-leather trench coat worn by Keanu Reeves as the hero Neo is credited with helping to create the sudden surge of trench coats on designer runways.

the maxi   A term that first surfaced in the late 1960s as a reference to ankle-length fashions (to contrast them with the then-prevalent "mini" lengths). Although both the word and what it symbolized were more prevalent in women's wear, the maxi did cross over to the men's market, where it was featured in fashionable, floor-grazing topcoats and sported by celebrities such as Joe Namath.

McQueen, Alexander   Born in East London in 1969 as one of six children in a working-class family, Lee Alexander McQueen remains best known for women's wear under his own label and for his late-1990s stint as a designer at Givenchy (where he was head designer of both men's and women's collections).

McQueen dropped out of school at age 16 and briefly apprenticed himself to traditional tailoring firms ANDERSON & SHEPPARD (where he claims that he scrawled nasty comments on the inside of suit jackets destined for Prince Charles) and GIEVES & HAWKES, as well as to theatrical costumers Angels & Bermans, where he was able to work on historical patterns. He then worked briefly for Koji Tatsuo and then Romeo Gigli in Milan, before returning to London in 1994 and entering the master's program in Fashion Design at Central St. Martin's College of Art and Design. Upon graduation in 1996, he became a critical darling (influential stylist Isabella Blow purchased his entire degree collection), known for theatrical fashion presentations and outrageous behavior. He received his first Best British Designer of the Year Award in 1996, the same year that he did his first collection of menswear and, despite his carefully cultivated reputation as high fashion's bad boy, was given a CFDA Award in 2003 and a CBE in

the Queen's Birthday Honors of the same year. In 2004, he was named Britain's Menswear Designer of the Year.

McQueen, Steve   Born in 1930 in the small town of Beech Grove, Indiana, Terence Steven McQueen reigned in the 1960s and 1970s as Hollywood's alpha male—its "King of Cool"—best known for his macho minimalism. Dyslexic and abused, McQueen had a horrific childhood: He never knew his father; his mother vanished for years on end; and he was raised by an uncle in rural Missouri until age 12, when his mother reappeared and took him to Los Angeles. After a stint in reform school at age 14, he drifted for a while and then spent 1947 to 1950 in the Marines. On the G.I. Bill, he studied at the Actor's Studio in New York and eventually landed stage and television parts, starring in *Wanted: Dead or Alive* from 1958 to 1961.

McQueen consistently and deliberately underdressed for his roles, which invariably focused every eye on him. In his Westerns, he tended to simple shirts and raw leather, while everyone else sported fringe and kerchiefs and fancier cowboy gear. In 1958's *The Blob* he wore a simple shirt, while everyone else was in fussy stripes or suits. In 1963's *The Great Escape*, he spent most of the movie in a ripped sweatshirt. In 1968's *Bullitt* he wore a dark turtleneck and run-of-the-mill raincoat that only made the shoulder holster he had to wear all the more disturbing. Even in his dressiest movie, 1968's *The*

Steve McQueen

Thomas Crown Affair, he practiced in his unaccustomed suits and dress shoes until he completely dominated the costumes.

Offstage McQueen epitomized the ultracool, anti-establishment rebel. He raced cars and motorcycles, owned Ferraris and Porsches, practiced martial arts, collected expensive watches, and wooed his 1972 *The Getaway* costar, Ali MacGraw, away from hit producer Robert Evans (marrying her in 1973 and divorcing her in 1978), then marrying model Barbara Minty. Only 5 feet, 9 inches, McQueen worked out religiously each day, with results that later made such workouts standard practice for actors.

In 1980, McQueen died of complications from lung cancer caused by exposure to asbestos. In the early 21st century, he again became a fashion icon, cited in descriptions of the clothes then being made fashionable by designers like THOM BROWNE and posthumously starring in ads for Tag Heuer's Monaco watch.

measuring tape   Not in wide use until the beginning of the 19th century, the thin, flexible ribbon or tape marked with quantifiable inch or centimeter measurements was a technical advance in tailoring claimed by both Britain and France. (Previously, tailors had measured their clients with systems including knotted string, strips of paper or cloth that could be marked or cut, and ROCK OF EYE.)

The measuring tape, which probably enabled a more widespread adoption of elaborately tailored clothing by the middle class, allowed accurate measurement around curves, which could then be accurately translated to a flat surface (such as the pattern of a suit fabric), thus permitting more efficient sculpting of a two-dimensional material (suit fabric) into the desired three-dimensional object (a finished suit). Synonyms: inch tape; tape measure.

mechanical stretch   Jargon for a woven fabric that achieves its stretch (usually a very small percentage) by virtue of a special weaving process, rather than by the inclusion of a stretch fiber such as SPANDEX. Usually synonymous with NATURAL STRETCH.

mélange   Literally "mixed." Jargon for yarn where the components are not smoothly blended, and two or more textures, colors, and/or types are thrown together in a single yarn.

melton   A heavyweight, unpatterned, woven wool with a slight surface nap, traditionally the favored material for jackets in riding habits, particularly those worn when foxhunting. The name derives from Melton Mowbray, the English town where it was first produced. Melton's sturdiness results in part from its production, which involves first creating a heavily milled cloth (i.e., a cloth that is compressed and, in effect, preshrunk), then raising fibers on its surface, and then cropping those fibers to a uniform length so that the surface nap is dense and uniform.

In contemporary use, melton also appears on the underside of many jacket collars, where, by tradition, it is added to aid in the collar's shaping and heft.

Men's Dress Reform Party   An English movement, founded in 1929, that urged men to imitate certain aspects of women's dress, such as lighter, brighter fabrics and less constricting tailoring. Its founders protested against the asceticism of menswear and lobbied for a return to Bryon collars, blousy tops, shorts, and sandals. Related to similar post-World War I movements in England that advocated against corsetry for women or more hygienic dress for the population in general (e.g., the Sensible Dress Society and the New Health Society). The membership of the Men's Dress Reform Society (as it was also known) was often depicted wearing shorts and was frequently characterized in the London press of the 1930s as a group of cranks who were advocating skirts for men.

Men's Fashion Association   A trade association better known by its acronym. (See entry for MFA.)

Men's Vogue   The menswear counterpart to Condé Nast's *Vogue* that launched in September of 2005 with actor George Clooney as its first cover subject and Jay Fielden as its editor-in-chief. Created under the auspices of *Vogue* editor Anna Wintour, it shares a similar format and layout with its sister publication.

Menswear magazine   A consumer magazine about men's fashion produced by Fairchild Publications and written by the staff of *DNR*, the men's apparel industry trade magazine.

Although its publisher traces the title back to 1890, the first periodical to actually appear with the name *Men's Wear* (then written as two words) did not come out until 1896.

mercer   A merchant selling fine fabrics intended for fine apparel (as opposed to coarse commodity fabrics like cotton duck or denim intended for workwear or some other utilitarian purpose). Because many mercers were associated with the selling of SILK, their customers were more female than male. Common usage in the 19th century.

mercerized   A treatment invented around 1844 by Englishman John Mercer, who did not patent the process until about 1850. Mercerization makes COTTON yarn (or a similar fiber, such as RAYON) shinier and more receptive to dye. Either before or after weaving, cotton is mercerized by being immersed in a caustic solution and then neutralized in another solution, causing the thread to permanently swell.

merino   A type of fine sheep's wool. Because they yield abundant fleece with silky, very CRIMPED WOOL (invariably under 25 MICRONS), merino breeds have been prized since the Roman empire. Although these medium-sized sheep probably originated in northern Africa and came to Europe through Spain, from the late 19th century onward much of the merino used in men's apparel has come from Australia, Tasmania, or New Zealand. For example, a 10-year-old New Zealand merino named Shrek, who evaded shearers for six years by hiding in a cave, yielded a record fleece—60 pounds, or enough for about 20 suits—when he was finally captured and shorn in 2004.

merlan   Slang reference to a wig maker or hairdresser, from the French word for whiting fish; used in the era when hair was powdered because men in that profession inevitably became covered in white powder.

mess jacket   A style that refers to the short, skirtless, tail-less jackets worn by military officers on formal occasions—the "mess" referring to an officer's mess hall, or eating place, rather than to any state of sloppiness. Dur-

Men's Vogue

Merino

ing the 1930s, there was a fad for civilians to wear mess jacket styles as DINNER JACKETS, but it ended by the beginning of World War II.

messenger bag   Refers to the style of sturdy, rectangular tote bags constructed with large flaps and shoulder straps; originally associated with New York City bicycle messengers. As made by companies including Manhattan Portage, messenger bags were of Cordura or similarly hard-wearing canvas-type fabric (usually black) and featured a vinyl lining (usually bright yellow).

Beginning in the 1980s, they began to be used by people besides messengers. By the 21st century, the style was used as a generic reference, and "messenger bags" were featured in the lines of luxury goods manufacturers like PRADA.

metrosexual   A pop culture term coined at the beginning of the 21st century to refer to men, usually heterosexual, who adopted a refinement of dress and grooming previously associated with women or gay culture.

Mexican hat   See SOMBRERO.

Mexican wedding shirt   Used as a generic reference to a GUAYABERA, a style that actually originated in Cuba.

MFA   Better known by its acronym (which is usually written without periods), the Men's Fashion Association was a trade group formed in 1955 at a convention of menswear retailers. Initially known as the American Institute of Men's and Boys' Wear, it was best known for promotions with taglines like 1956's "Dress Right—You Can't Afford Not To!" In 1969, it changed its name to the MFA and later sponsored the American Image Awards as a way of recognizing stylish politicians, celebrities,

and other public figures who did not qualify for the CUTTY SARK/Woolmark awards (the best-known fashion awards geared to the menswear industry) since they were not designers or otherwise involved in the industry. In 1993, the association expanded into women's wear and changed its name yet again, becoming the Fashion Association.

Miami Vice   A hit television series that ran on NBC from 1984 to 1989. The look created for actor Don Johnson playing vice detective Sonny Crocket is credited with sparking the 1980s crazes for T-shirts worn with unconstructed suits, loafers worn sans socks, and RAY-BAN Wayfarers, as well as for making a stubbly, unshaven face sexy during daytime. (According to legend, that character's stubble originated when Johnson came into an audition messy and unshaven, fresh from an all-night stakeout with the real Miami police.) Producer Michael Mann, who made a *Miami Vice* movie in 2006, is credited with creating the distinctive look of the show by directing the crew to contrast cool pastels with earthy neutrals. Jodie Killen, as costume designer for the series pilot and its first episodes, is credited with establishing the characters' wardrobes (which had to accommodate considerations like designer jackets roomy enough to

Messenger bag

conceal shoulder holsters), but other costume designers subsequently worked on the series, including Oscar-winner MILENA CANONERO.

microfiber   Description of a fabric that is composed of ultrafine, man-made yarns (usually POLYESTER). The prefix "micro" is used to imply that the threads are so fine that the human eye can't count them, even with the help of basic magnification. Although microfibers certainly exist that are both thicker and thinner, the standard description of a microfiber is one that yields 10 kilometers of thread per 1 kilogram of yarn. Microfibers were mostly developed by Japanese mills in the 1980s and were extremely expensive when they first appeared.

micron   A measurement used for the thickness of fibers: a millionth of a meter. For example: A fine MERINO wool may be referred to "an 18-micron wool" because it is woven of fine wool fibers only 18 microns in thickness. In general, when referring to wools or NOBLE FIBERS such as CASHMERE, the lower the micron number, the higher the price.

middy   1. A square-backed SAILOR COLLAR. 2. A shortened reference to a middy blouse (which features a sailor collar) or a child's middy suit (also known as a SAILOR SUIT). The term derives from a slang abbreviation of the word "midshipman."

middy blouse   A long-sleeved shirt, usually in plain white or navy, that slips over the head and features a square-back SAILOR COLLAR. The word blouse is used in references to both men's and women's wear.

middy suit   A child's SAILOR SUIT; used most often in 19th-century references.

midsole   Sandwiched between the INSOLE and OUTSOLE, the midsole of a boot or shoe is usually made of a material that enhances shock absorption or warmth. It is never visible—from either the inside or outside—once construction of the shoe is complete. Synonym: middle sole.

midweight   Jargon for a fabric—especially a suit fabric—that falls between the very heavy weights used for SPORTS JACKETS and coats and the lighter weights used for summer clothes; usually 11- or 12-ounce cloth. The majority of suit fabrics probably fall into this category, since it is the main material of THREE-SEASON SUITS.

Milan   Industry slang for the semiannual menswear runway shows and trade shows conducted in Milan and nearby Florence. As in the sentence: "CALVIN KLEIN shows menswear in Milan and the women's collection in New York."

military belt   A reference to the type of belt issued with uniforms. A military belt is made of webbing that is usually tipped on one end with metal. Its design is adjustable, and its buckle snaps into place instead of using punched holes.

military uniforms   Not in general use and not necessarily standardized until the 18th century. Prior to that, a soldier's dress might be—depending on his status and his place of service—simply new clothes provided by his employer, clothes provided by himself, or the equivalent of a modern uniform.

mille stripe   A finely striped fabric that looks like a solid from a short distance, because the fabric is striped almost thread by thread (actually, the stripes are usually formed by groups of two or three threads, and a true thread-by-thread stripe is known as an END ON END). Refers to shirt fabrics, never to suit fabrics. See color plates.

minet   France's mid-1960s counterpart to the MOD. Dressed in the latest London-inspired fashion and frequently found in the precincts of Le Drugstore on the Champs-Élysées, he was more angst-ridden, more affluent, and less teenybopper-ish than the YÉ-YÉ.

Missoni   The Milan-based, family-run design house begun in 1953, the same year that Yugoslavian-born Ottavio Missoni (better known as "Tai") married Italian-born Rosita; best known for its pricey, colorful knitwear. Starting with only four knitting machines, the Missonis initially executed other designers' work, but by the mid-1960s had expanded their business and assigned themselves design duties: Tai, who had run an activewear business before marrying, was in charge of textile designs, and Rosita was in charge of turning them into clothes. Tai's designs, capitalizing on zigzagging stitches that resembled bargello work or florentine embroidery, gave the company's clothes a signature look of jagged, multicolored, horizontal stripes that made them highly sought after in the 1970s and influenced the wider sportswear market—kicking off a craze for colorful, expensive men's sweaters that lasted into the 1990s. Eventually, all three of the couple's children became involved in the business, with son Luca succeeding his parents as creative director in 2003.

miter   Ceremonial headwear associated with high-ranking Catholic clergy, especially as the symbol of a bishop's office (only bishops, cardinals, and the pope are allowed its use; other clergy must have special dispensation). The miter is formed by joining two flat, matching pieces of stiffened fabric that ascend to a peak; it also has two LAPPETS hanging from its center back. Depending upon the church calendar and the clergyman's rank, the miter may be plain or richly ornamented, but its basic color is always white. Variant spelling: mitre.

mittens   Hand coverings, usually worn for warmth, which group the fingers together under one covering and the thumb under its own covering, thus leaving the wearer without the dexterity of independently operating fingers but with the use of an opposable thumb.

mitts   A style of fingerless glove, usually worn for warmth on occasions when the fingertips must be left free for the sake of dexterity. The mitt covers the palm and knuckles like a regular glove but usually stops its finger casing between the first and second joint, thus leaving the tip free (as if the ends of a normal glove have been chopped off). Most often, the term is used to refer to hand covering of knit construction and is not applied to hand coverings made of leather. For example, DRIVING GLOVES frequently leave the fingertips free but are nevertheless referred to as gloves and not as mitts.

Missoni: Ottavio and Rosita

Miu Miu   The label begun by designer Miuccia Prada (and using her nickname) with a women's wear collection in 1992, as a slightly less expensive version of Prada, aimed at a slightly younger customer. In 1998, Prada showed her first Miu Miu menswear collection for spring 1999.

Mix, Tom   Born in 1880 in Mix Run, Pennsylvania, Thomas Mix used his riding talent to become a star, first in Wild West shows and subsequently as a stunt man and then star in the silent movies, beginning in 1910. A showman through and through, Mix's many, many Westerns—and the unquestionable riding skill he displayed in them—created the popular conception of cowboy as dandy: a man in high-heeled, elaborately tooled cowboy boots; fancy belt buckles; fringed chaps; embroidered shirts with front yokes and piped trim; oversized hats; and never without his neck kerchief. Mix's career extended into the talkies, and he died in a car accident in 1940.

Miyake, Issey   Born in Hiroshima in 1938, Japanese fashion designer Issey Miyake became best known for creating clothes that blended the traditions of both East and West, as well as the avant-garde of both art and technology. A pioneer in textiles as well as in fashion design, Miyake delighted in the exploration of synthetic fibers, and often had to commission the invention of equipment in order to execute the ideas for his clothes.

Miyake first showed his fashion work in 1963 in a multimedia event he called "A Poem in Cloth and Stone," a presentation that would prove prescient for his later collaborations with visual artists. After graduation from Tokyo's Tama Art University in 1964 and moving to Paris the following year to study at the L'École de la Chambre Syndicale, he worked at Guy Laroche and Givenchy, then moved to New York in 1969 to work for Geoffrey Beene.

Moving back to Japan, he launched his first label in 1971 and began showing in Paris in 1973.

At a time when French fashion began recycling the silhouettes of other eras and other cultures for the runway, Miyake turned more and more to technology and fine art for inspiration, relentlessly reconsidering everything from seams to shapes to fibers. For example, he made several attempts to combine clothes with furniture, to create one-size-fits-all garments, and, in 1997, began research on A-POC ("a piece of cloth"), a line based on a process whereby clothes could be produced without sewing: Yarn was fed into the machine and a tube of cloth emerged that could be cut along premarked seams to create the intended garment. Soon the company extended the integration of sizing and patterning to its wovens as well, calling the garments "A-POC Inside." In 2006, the world learned that Miyake label made reversible, APC-constructed jeans; typically, this took place not at a runway presentation, but at an exhibition called "Skin and Bones: Parallel Practices in Fashion and Architecture" at the Museum of Contemporary Art in Los Angeles.

In 1986, he was featured on the cover of *Time* magazine. In 1998, a retrospective called "Issey Miyake Making Things" at the Foundation Cartier in Paris focused on his work with like-minded artists and architects. In 1999, designer Naoki Takizawa officially began designing the Miyake collection; then segued into another job within the Miyake company in 2006, when Dai Fujiwara took over as its creative director.

Issey Miyake

moc   Jargon for MOCCASIN.

moccasin   A shoe with a soft, flexible sole, frequently featuring handstitching and initially patterned after the footwear made by Native Americans; usually a SLIP-ON style. The moccasin is worn with casual wear, never with business suits or formalwear. Most often made of leather (or a leather lookalike), it may be worn as a sort of slipper indoors, or it may be a DRIVING MOC style with nubs of rubber studding the sole (e.g., TOD'S). Often abbreviated as MOC.

mock turtleneck   A high-necked style of sweater or knit shirt that is made to look like a TURTLENECK but that, instead of having a true turtleneck's fold over or roll of fabric, consists of a single layer at the neck. The neck of mock turtle (as it is sometimes called) is distinguished from a FUNNEL NECK (also a single layer of fabric) by being tighter and closer to the body. Synonym: FAUX TURTLENECK.

Mod   The youth-centered style that flourished in London, from roughly 1958 to 1966, and that established CARNABY STREET and KING'S ROAD as centers of men's fashion. The Mod style was described in Colin MacInnes's 1959 novel *Absolute Beginners*, seen in the suits worn by THE BEATLES and The Who in their early appearances, quoted by Michael Caine's clothes as the title character in 1966's *Alfie*, and evoked by Patrick Macnee's costumes as John Steed in the television series *The Avengers*.

   Their rivals were known as "Rockers," whom they battled for style supremacy—"Mods versus Rockers"—both metaphorically and physically (with the beach city of Brighton as main battleground). Mods favored scooters, while the Rockers rode motorcycles. Mods were fastidious, whereas the Rockers affected a wilder appearance. Mods favored the new suits being sold by new London tailors (e.g., the SMARTIE suit), whereas the Rockers liked their leather jackets. Mods wore Clark DESERT BOOTS and parkas and white pants. By the mid-1960s, the Mod movement was already being supplanted by the freedom and ethnicity of what would become the HIPPIE look.

Mod Gods   British, 1960s-era slang for the young men who shopped CARNABY STREET and KING'S ROAD and favored MOD fashions.

modal   Refers to a fiber, or the fabric made from it, usually created from wood chips via a RAYON-like process. When used alone, it is a generic term and lowercased. When used in conjunction with a fiber producer, it may be a trademarked name and thus uppercased. (For example, Lenzing, the Austrian company that is one of the fiber's chief producers, has trademarked the name Lenzing Modal.)

mogador   A type of woven silk with a very high thread count per inch. Synonym: Moroccan silk.

mohair   A lightweight, lustrous fiber, known for imparting shine to woven fabrics and a distinctively hairy appearance to knits. Used to make men's apparel since the days of the pharaohs, mohair is made from the fleece of Angora goats (while ANGORA is made from angora rabbits). These goats, which took their name from Anchora, a province in Turkey renowned for raising them in the Middle Ages, have hair with larger, flatter scales than sheep's wool, which accounts for the fiber's light-reflective properties and slightly slippery feel.

mohawk   A hairstyle originally associated with Native American men in the northeastern United States, who had the habit of roaching their hair into a style that left the head shaved except for a center strip running from center front to center back (with a scalplock left at its end). Sometimes they would also wear a strip of false hair made from hair, fur, or porcupine quills.

In the 1970s, PUNKS adopted the style (minus the scalplock) for its outrageousness, stiffening and straightening their hair so that it stood on end, and often dyeing it pink, blue, scarlet, or some other unnatural color. In the early 21st century, evolved into a less radical style called the FAUXHAWK, which allowed hair to grow on the sides but still evoke the mohawk.

moiré   Fabric that is finished so that it has a rippling, water-stained appearance. In menswear, moiré fabric—usually FAILLE—is encountered most often on CUMMER-BUNDS and the LAPELS of TUXEDOS and DRESSING GOWNS, as well as the accoutrements of Catholic clergy.

moisture management   Jargon for fibers or fabrics that manage perspiration through WICKING or absorption processes. Not generally used to refer to water-repellent fibers or fabrics.

moleskin   A woven fabric with a soft, suede-like surface. Often made from cotton, moleskin was and is traditionally made into pants and was a common component of English country clothes. Most often manufactured in neutral colors (e.g., grays and beiges).

Molloy, John T.   Author of *DRESS FOR SUCCESS*.

money belt   A belt created for the concealment of cash. For example, a money belt may resemble an ordi-nary belt but have slits or other secret compartments on its inside. Or it may be a pouch meant to be worn under a shirt where no one can see it.

money clip   A clip used to keep paper money neatly folded and organized inside a man's pocket. Used in place of a wallet or BILLFOLD, the money clip functions like an oversized paper clip and may be made of precious metal.

Mongolian lamb   A showy type of sheepskin with extremely long, soft, and wavy hair; off-white when undyed. In menswear, appears most often on styles meant to evoke ethnicity; a favorite in 1960s and 1970s HIPPIE styles. (Not to be confused with the dark, lustrous, and short-napped PERSIAN LAMB.) Synonym: TIBETAN LAMB.

monkstrap   Refers to a style of men's DRESS SHOES in which a strap crosses high across the instep and buckles to the outside. Sometimes the strap and buckle are functional; sometimes they are purely decorative and the shoe is essentially a SLIP-ON.

moño   The short, full tie, resembling a cropped JABOT, that accessorizes the *TRAJE DE CHARRO* worn by MARIACHI musicians.

monocle   An eyeglass with a single lens, worn fitted into the eye socket; usually attached via a ribbon or cord to the underside of a man's lapel and stored in the chest pocket of his jacket or pocket of his waistcoat when not in use. Originally developed in Germany in the 18th century, the style was long more popular there and, partly for that reason, was rarely seen after Germany's defeat in World War I (when it was widely caricatured as the preferred eyewear of the pretentious Prussian officer).

Mohawk

Unlike the two lenses of the PINCE-NEZ, which had a pinch or spring mechanism to aid in keeping them perched in place, the monocle was never the most practical eyewear and required something of a squint to use. It differed from a QUIZZING GLASS by being fitted into the eye socket, rather than held in the hand. Synonym: eye ring.

monogram   The decorative use of letters in a name; in Western menswear of the last century, the placement of a man's initials appears most often on his jewelry (cufflinks, belt buckle, signet ring, tie clip, cigarette case, watch case), his pajamas, and/or on his dress shirt.

On the shirt, a man's monogram most often appears as block capital letters embroidered in a shade of thread that contrasts with the shirt fabric (perhaps surmounted by a crown or crest if he has connections to the aristocracy) and is rarely more than an inch high. Because it is easier to personalize and more expensive, hand embroidery is considered the most desirable method of monogramming a shirt. The monogram generally appears on the left side between the fourth and fifth button, although placements vary: Some men favor the shirt pocket (or its approximate location if there is no pocket); others may prefer the cuff or a location on the lower sleeve.

mono-stretch   Fabric that stretches in one direction only: the WARP, or horizontal direction. (See also BI-STRETCH.)

montagnac   A heavy fabric, most often used in overcoats, in a simple TWILL weave with a slight napped surface; usually made of a NOBLE FIBER, such as cashmere or camel hair. The term, which became generic, originally referred to the distinctive fabrics of that description manufactured by a textile mill called Montagnac.

Montague Burton   The largest and most famous of the MULTIPLE TAILORS.

In 1900, Lithuanian immigrant and former peddler Montague Burton opened a shop in Chesterfield offering boys' and menswear for the working class. Since the range of suits available in that price range was limited, he set up a deal with a clothing factory in LEEDS that enabled him to offer his customers MADE-TO-MEASURE. By 1910, the company had its own factory.

To keep prices low and keep his factory productive, Burton pushed high volume. By the end of World War I, Burton had 40 shops, a larger, consolidated factory in Leeds on Hudson Road, and controlled virtually all fabric production. By 1929, when the company went public, he had 200 shops. By 1939, he had more than 600, employing more than 10,000 workers and taking 50,000 suit orders per week.

Burton died in 1952, and, the following year, the company's board of directors decided to exit the multiple tailoring business. Burton's then moved to a more conventional menswear retailing format.

Montague, Mrs. Hannah Lord   Lauded as the inventor of the detachable collar; a resident of TROY, NEW YORK, which later came to be known as COLLAR CITY. Although the reported date of her invention varies (most often it is given as 1825 or 1827), it was undoubtedly during the 1820s. Montague came up with the idea as a labor-saving device when she tired of constantly laundering and replacing entire shirts for her husband Orlando, when only their collars were dirty.

montecristi A type of PANAMA hat; its quality is determined by the fineness of the weave and the number of rows in its crown: the higher the number, the higher the quality (and the price tag).

Montgomery coat Reference to a DUFFLE COAT, especially in British usage, because the style was worn by Field Marshal Bernard Law Montgomery during World War II.

moonbag Slang, more often British, for a FANNYPACK.

moon boots Refers to a style of padded, flat-soled, mid-calf boots that resemble the footwear worn by astronauts during lunar landings. First popular in the 1970s, moon boots were made by several manufacturers and usually featured a high-tech fabric on the outside, insulation that obliterated the definition of the ankle and curve of the calf, and rudimentary lacing over the instep. More popular for women's wear.

mop top A hairstyle associated with THE BEATLES, especially during their breakthrough in the United States during the early 1960s. Radically unlike the ELVIS PRESLEY-inspired POMPADOUR sported by most ROCKERS of the 1950s, the shaggy, moplike style was long in both front and back, included bangs in the front, and did not depend on styling products; similar to the DUTCH BOY HAIRCUT, PRINCE VALIANT, or the cuts popular for little boys during the late 19th and early 20th centuries.

Also known to hardcore fans as the ARTHUR, from George Harrison's deadpan reply to the question "what would you call that hairstyle you're wearing?" in the 1964 movie *A Hard Day's Night*.

morning coat The tails that are worn as part of formal daywear and are part of a morning suit. Synonym: CUTAWAY.

morning stripe Refers to one of the traditional vertical stripe patterns used for the trousers worn with the MORNING SUIT of formal daytime attire. See color plates.

morning suit The most formal attire worn during daytime; equivalent to nighttime's WHITE TIE and TAILS. In contemporary practice, it is confined to a palette of black, white, and various grays and consists of:
• A dark, single-breasted CUTAWAY (black or dark gray) with either standard notched or PEAK LAPELS
• Striped gray trousers in a pattern known as MORNING STRIPE, unmatched to the coat
• A pearl-gray, white, or buff-colored vest, which may be either single-breasted or double-breasted
• A white shirt with either a regular FOLD-OVER COLLAR or a WING COLLAR
• Either a silk necktie or silk ascot in a subtle pattern of black and white or a solid gray.
• Optional accessories such as a TOP HAT and pearl-gray gloves.
Most often seen at daytime weddings (especially for male members of the wedding party), formal race meetings, and diplomatic events. Not to be misspelled or otherwise confused with attire worn for mourning.

Morrison, Jim Born in Florida in 1943, rock star James Douglas Morrison grew up with the seminomadic life of a child whose father was a naval officer, and attended Florida State University before graduating from U.C.L.A. in 1965 with a major in film. Afterward, he moved to Venice Beach, where he met Ray Manzarek and formed

The Doors, the two soon being joined by John Densmore and Robby Krieger. By 1967, with Morrison as its charismatic frontman and chief lyricist, the band was already at the top of the charts with a string of hits beginning with "Break on Through [to the Other Side]."

Like his lyrics, Morrison's style of dress combined the standard sex, drugs, and rock 'n' roll with heavy doses of shamanism and symbolist allusion. The man who called himself the Lizard King and once said "I am a Rimbaud in a leather jacket" favored a bare chest or open-to-the-navel shirts, AVIATOR sunglasses, long curly hair and extremely LOW-RISE (often leather) pants worn with large, decorative belts. Both during his lifetime and after his death, Morrison became a fashion icon: the cultural reference for a rock star's appearance.

He died in Paris in 1971 aged 27, and his gravesite in Père Lachaise became a place of pilgrimage for rock fans and others who continued to believe that mystery surrounded his death.

mortarboard   The cap with a stiff, square-shaped top famously associated with scholars and graduates, and part of the ACADEMIC DRESS prescribed for the bachelor's degree. The mortarboard consists of a skull cap with a rigid attached lid, reminiscent of an extremely thin, square book balanced on the head. It is worn so that a point of the square aligns with the center of the face, the center back of the head, and each ear. The tassel hangs from the center of the square and is always long enough to dangle at least an inch or two in front of the face. The tassel may be either black or in a color that signifies the bachelor's area of study.

By popular custom, most students wear the tassel hanging on the left side of their face. However, until the late 20th century, it was more usual for the tassel to be worn on the right before the degree was officially conferred and then flipped to the left front side at the moment of graduation. Or, alternatively, the entire class would "flip" at a designated point in the ceremony.

In previous centuries, the mortarboard and robe were considered part of academic garb and not worn exclusively at ceremonies. Historically, the style derives, like much academic costume, from medieval garb, in particular from a style worn at English universities. The Cambridge version has a soft cap, and the Oxford version's cap is stiff.

Also called a CATER CAP, especially during the 19th century.

Moschino, Franco   Born in Abbiategrasso, near Milan, in 1950, the Italian designer studied art at the Accademia di Belle Arti and worked as a sketcher for GIANNI VERSACE and GIORGIO ARMANI before taking a job at Cadette in 1976, He then launched his own women's wear label in 1983. In 1985, he did his first men's collection for the spring 1986 season. With his dadaist sensibility, Moschino delighted in upsetting the status quo.

Jim Morrison

Flamboyantly gay, he sometimes starred in his own print ads, disguised as Popeye or a transvestite, except for his recognizable crew cut hair and heavy mustache. Untrained in either tailoring or dressmaking, he worked through drawings and descriptions and delighted in visual puns (e.g., the men's shirt with extra-long sleeves that wrapped like a straitjacket and read "for fashion victims only"). After suffering from AIDS, he died at his country home outside Milan in 1994, and his partners and licensees continued the label.

Moss Brothers   The British firm originally famous for its "dress hire" business, which enabled men to rent appropriate formal and/or court attire without the bother of having to buy it. The firm's reputation for impeccable cleanliness and correctness earned it the custom of celebrities and aristocrats (e.g., the Duke of Norfolk, who hired robes for the coronation of Queen Elizabeth II in 1953).

Begun in 1851 by Moses Moses as a second-hand clothes shop in Covent Garden, its founder subsequently eliminated the "e" in his first and last names and called himself Moss Moss. The business then passed to his two sons, who officially instituted the famous "hire department" in 1897 and formally changed the name to Moss Brothers the following year. The firm maintained a thriving uniform business during World War I, and then, after the war, began emphasizing ready-to-wear. During the following decades, its wholly owned brands and franchise agreements expanded to include names such as BEALE & INMAN, Savoy Guild Taylors, HUGO BOSS, and CANALI.

mother-of-pearl   A hard, lustrous material derived from the inside of mollusk shells; in menswear, used primarily for shirt buttons. Customarily, buttons are cut from the nacreous inside shell of an oyster, abalone, or other mollusk.

For buttons, the most sought-after quality is provided by pearl oyster shells from the South Seas around Tahiti, which produce buttons that are thick, sturdy, and pure white, with no veins or other colors on either their top or underside. Synonyms: PEARL buttons; SHELL buttons.

motorcycle jacket   Refers to a distinctive style of short leather jacket, which is typically made of heavy, black leather (usually in a tough, fairly rigid quality such as COWHIDE or HORSEHIDE) and features a zippered front closure set on the diagonal, KIDNEY PADS, padded waist, EPAULETTES, a double-pleated back, sturdy metal hardware including large-tooth zippers and snaps, a snap-down collar, leather-lined cuffs and waistband, and a plain lining. The jacket may or may not also include a wide belt, but it always ends at the waist and never covers the buttocks or includes a SKIRT.

In the early 20th century, the motorcycle jacket evolved from jackets worn by the military and, after World War I, became more standardized in its interpretation by manufacturers such as Harley-Davidson and SCHOTT BROTHERS, and then by Joseph Buegeleisen, Indian, and Hercules. During the 1950s, the style became identified with opposition to the business suit and its implied lifestyle choices—particularly after the success of the 1953 movie THE WILD ONE, in which Marlon Brando wore a Schott style that thereafter was considered the exemplar of the type. In the following decades, motorcycle jackets became more common as outerwear and were quoted by fashion brands as a reference to rebellion and ruggedness.

mouton   Sheepskin, usually from a MERINO, that is close-clipped to a tight, wavy layer of hair. Most familiar in 20th- and 21st-century menswear from its use on coat collars and as trim in FLIGHT JACKETS.

mozzetta   An elbow-length cape, with an ornamental hood, allowed only to the highest ranks of Catholic clergy and worn only for ceremonial, rather than practical, purposes. Most often black, white, scarlet, or violet, its color is strictly codified according to the wearer's rank and the church calendar. It may be made of virtually any solid-colored fabric but, in contemporary use, is most often seen in silk MOIRÉ. For example, the pope wears a red mozzetta for most of the year, but a white one during Easter.

MR **magazine**   A monthly, New York-based trade magazine covering men's apparel. Its name derives from an abbreviation of *Menswear Retailing.*

Mr. Fish   See FISH, MICHAEL.

Mr. T   1. An invention of *ESQUIRE* magazine's fashion department in 1950, "Mr. T" was a silhouette meant to symbolize what was then seen as a trimmer look than the big-shouldered, DRAPED looks that had been popular right after World War II. In a boxier form, it evolved into the IVY LEAGUE silhouette.   2. The performing name of actor Laurence Taureaud (born in 1952), who first became a celebrity on the television series *The A Team* from 1983 to 1987. Known for his extreme style, Mr. T sported a MOHAWK haircut, a full beard, dozens of thick gold chains (usually atop a bare chest), and large, thick, gold hoop earrings.

mud cloth   Usually a two-color fabric with a light-and-dark patterns created by outlining designs and then filling in the background with dark, sometimes fermented, mud. In the West, the best-known mud cloth comes from Mali (especially the bogolan cloth produced in the Bamana-speaking region), or from the Dogon or Fulani tribal areas. From the 1970s onward, mud cloth began to be incorporated in U.S.- and European-made menswear and women's wear as a feature of Afrocentrism.

muff   A tube-shaped accessory, used as a handwarmer; open on either end, the muff could—depending upon the time and place—be either relatively large or barely bigger than the width of a palm. Made of fur or fabric, it sometimes contained interior pockets that enabled it to be used like a purse. Although now an accessory associated with females, the muff was widely carried by fashionable men during the 18th century.

muffetees   1. Mini MUFFS worn on the wrists like large cuffs, usually for warmth (especially in the 18th century).   2. Crude MITTENS (especially in the 19th century).

muffler   1. A thick scarf worn around the neck, primarily for warmth. A thick, woven plaid scarf worn with a topcoat would usually be described as a muffler, whereas a fringed silk FOULARD would not.   2. In ARMOR made of CHAINMAIL, the word indicates a mitten-shaped piece, usually joined to the sleeve of a HAUBERK to protect the warrior's hand.

mufti   When anyone who normally wears a uniform to work is, instead, wearing casual or civilian clothes, he is said to be "in mufti." This usage began in the 19th century to refer to British soldiers but, in more contemporary context, has been used ironically to refer to men out of their habitual work dress (e.g., businessmen wearing golf clothes).

Although the same spelling indicates a judge of Islamic law, the word does not refer to his clothes.

mukluks   A type of soft boot worn by the Inuit, usually made of a material like seal, moose, or reindeer hide. Mukluks look like a shoe with a legging attached. Lightweight, warm, and practical, mukluks feature a soft, silent sole ideal for hunters.

mullet   The short-in-front, long-in-back hairstyle that first appeared in the 1970s and reached its height of popularity in the 1980s, when it was worn by celebrities like singer Michael Bolton and tennis player Andre Agassi (and later continued to be worn by country singer Billy Ray Cyrus and baseball player Randy Johnson). After the 1980s, the style was decidedly outside the mainstream and had HEAVY METAL, country music, or redneck connotations, becoming the butt of jokes, as some mullet-wearers—even into the 21st century—refused to give it up.

multiple tailoring   Refers to the businesses established in England that offered MADE-TO-MEASURE suits for middle-class and working-class men, and flourished from the end of World War I until the end of the 1950s. Centered in Leeds, the multiple tailoring industry had its own storefronts where measurements would be taken and fabrics selected. Then, the measurements would be relayed back to the factory, where the suit could be executed promptly and cheaply. The stores remained a staunchly masculine enclave—some having additional enticements such as billiards adjoining the salesroom—and stayed open late to accommodate the working man.

Sociologists credit them for teaching men that shopping could be a masculine activity and for hastening the demise of the small, locally owned retailer on the British high street. It has been estimated that, before the start of World War II, they supplied between a third to a half of all the suits worn by British men. The largest multiple tailor was MONTAGUE BURTON, which virtually invented the industry and which, by 1939, had more than 600 shops and employed 10,000 workers to produce up to 50,000 suits per week.

multitrack stripe   A pattern mixing stripes of different "tracks" or spacing. Usually refers to shirt fabric, rarely used to describe suit fabrics. An even more generic term for a multitrack would be a "fancy." See color plates.

Munsingwear   Founded in Minnesota in 1887 as Northwestern Knitting Mills with George Munsing as its managing partner, the company specialized in men's underwear and officially became Munsingwear in 1919. Like other underwear specialists of the time (e.g., BVD), the company got into allied markets, such as activewear, after World War I. Spurred on by CEO Byron "Tubby" Reed beginning in the late 1960s, the company experienced a growth spurt with its menswear, becoming especially known for its PENGUIN golfwear during the 1970s. After Reed's retirement in 1980, the company changed ownership and management several times, dropping off the fashion radar until its eventual owner, the Perry Ellis

Mullet: Bono

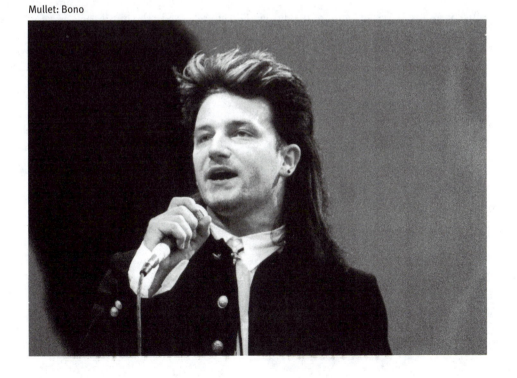

Corporation, began successfully reviving the penguin-logo golfwear and other sportswear in the early 21st century.

Murphy, Gerald   Born in Boston in 1888, scion of the family who owned the MARK CROSS leathergoods business, Gerald Clery Murphy became known for his much-envied expatriate lifestyle, his flair for dressing, and his friendships with the famous.

While attending Yale, where he was voted the best-dressed man in the class of 1912, he befriended a freshman named Cole Porter. Later, having taken up painting, he moved to France from 1921 to 1929, where Porter introduced him to the French Riviera. Murphy and his wife Sara bought a villa in Cap d'Antibes in 1923, rechristened it the Villa America, and played host to the likes of F. Scott Fitzgerald and his wife Zelda, John Dos Passos, Fernand Leger, Igor Stravinsky, and Pablo Picasso. There, Murphy, along with the future EDWARD VIII, created the fashion for wearing ESPADRILLES, striped jerseys, BERETS, and other elements of the local villagers' dress.

Prompted by the illness of one of their sons and the stock market crash, the Murphys moved to Switzerland and eventually resettled in America, where Murphy took up the reins at Mark Cross (filling his windows with anti-Nazi propaganda well before America entered the war). He died at his home on the South Fork of Long Island in 1964.

muscadin   A type of young dandy in Directoire France; so named because he supposedly favored musky cologne. Neatly groomed, reactionary, and royalist, the muscadin is usually depicted in tight BREECHES, boots, an immaculate white shirt, a tailcoat, and a BICORNE hat.

His hair is carefully arranged into a DOGS' EARS style that droops long in the front to frame his face. He carries an extra-long walking stick (handy for impromptu political arguments) and makes his headquarters around the Palais Royal.

muscle shirt   A TANK SHIRT with its armholes cut extra low, supposedly to accommodate bulging muscles.

musette bag   Refers to a style of bag that originated with the military as a sort of KNAPSACK or medium-sized BACKPACK. Constructed of heavy fabric (e.g., olive drab) without hard sides or an interior frame, the musette bag was roughly rectangular and closed with a large flap fastened via two buckles and straps; it also sported two straps that allowed it to be worn over the shoulders as a backpack or could be connected to a shoulder strap. Because they were sturdy, cheap, and easy to obtain from army surplus stores, college students adopted musette bags as book bags in the second half of the 20th century, before the transition to outdoor, hiking-style backpacks.

muslin   1. An inexpensive, usually undyed, type of woven cotton fabric.

2. The first draft of a bespoke suit, because that first attempt is usually made from muslin fabric.

After measuring the client, a tailoring firm usually drafts a first pattern on brown paper and makes it out of muslin (or may make the muslin directly and do the paper pattern later after all mistakes have been corrected); the muslin acts as a sort of trial balloon, so that any mistakes in fit can be corrected before cutting into the expensive suit fabric. Thus, when a client arrives for the first fitting of a custom garment, he is usually trying on the muslin.

mustache A general reference to wearing hair on the upper lip, distinguished throughout the history of menswear by the striking number of countries and cultures that have forbidden its wear, beginning with the ancient Egyptians, Greeks, and Romans (who identified the mustache with barbarians) and continuing through the present-day AMISH (who identify the mustache with military display).

muttonchops Very full sidewhiskers, shorter than DUNDREARIES; so called because they are shaped like a muttonchop or pork chop (with its meaty end down toward the jaw and the slim, boney end of the chop near the ear). Although associated primarily with the 19th century, the style was revived briefly in the late 1960s and early 1970s.

mutze The longer coat, resembling a FROCK COAT, worn for more formal occasions by AMISH men. The shorter coat, resembling a suit jacket, is a WAMUS and is worn for everyday and most Sundays.

N

nailhead A woven design, seen in traditional WORSTED fabrics intended for tailored clothing; small and symmetrical, so called because it resembles a dot pattern formed by nailheads. Larger than a PINHEAD; smaller than a BIRD'S-EYE. See color plates.

nainsook A type of plain, lightweight, woven cotton (or cotton blend). In menswear, its chief claim to fame was as an underwear fabric, and was famously advertised as the material of BVDs around the time of World War I.

nano technology As applied to menswear, refers to modifications of fabric on the "nano" level (i.e., smaller than the "micro" and measurable only by nanometers, which are equivalent to one-billionth of a meter). Molecular manipulation of the fabric to enhance its ability to repel stains, wick moisture, or perform some similar function were introduced in the 1990s, most notably by polymer chemist David Soane, Ph.D., who invented Nano-Care. Before that, most protective treatments involved the addition of a virtually invisible layer on top of the cloth (e.g., SCOTCHGARD).

Nantucket Reds A trademarked name referring to a distinctive style of pants made of thick, brick-colored, cotton canvas similar to that used in old-fashioned sails, which fades to a medium red then to pink with repeated laundering, exposure to the sun, and age. Sold by Murray's Toggery Shop on Nantucket Island and beloved by PREPPIES, especially in the Northeast.

nap The hairlike surface of a textile, which occurs when part of the fibers are brushed up from the underlying weave, knit, or skin. In menswear, most napped fabrics are cut so that the nap lies relatively flat, giving a sleek, smooth appearance to the surface of the cloth.

napa A soft leather cured by a special process, usually made from goat or lamb hide; named after the county in California where it was first produced. Favored for apparel and gloves because it is extremely soft and pliable. Variant spelling: nappa.

Naples tailors A general reference to a style of Italian tailoring that was supposedly lighter in weight, less

Nantucket Reds: Murray's Toggery Shop and a pair of Nantucket Red shorts

250

padded, and less constructed overall than the styles associated with tailoring in Milan or Rome—supposedly in deference to the hotter weather in Naples and the different fabrics worn by its natives.

Natick, Massachusetts Longtime site of the U.S. Department of Defense's enormous Soldier Systems Center, which combines research and support for textile and apparel design for the Army, Navy, and Coast Guard. The name of the city near Boston is often used as a synonym—especially within the textile and apparel industries—for the U.S. Army as a whole, especially when referring to the commissioning, development, and/or testing of uniforms and combat gear, as in "Natick introduced a new CAMOUFLAGE" or "Natick developed a new body armor."

natural Refers to a hairstyle without chemical straightening or processing. See AFRO.

natural fibers Fibers derived from animal, vegetable, or mineral sources. WOOL, RAMIE, and asbestos are examples of natural fibers. NYLON, POLYESTER, and ELASTANE are not.

natural shoulder In tailoring, refers to a shoulder that is not "BUILT OUT" to make a man's shoulders look wider than they actually are. Some firms interpret the term strictly, using it to indicate that the shoulder has no enhancement at all; however, most interpret a natural shoulder more loosely and may include a very lightweight SHOULDER PAD or interfacing to help the garment retain its shape.

natural stretch Industry jargon for a fabric, such as wool intended for a suit, that has been woven with a process that allows it to "give" or stretch (usually about 1 or 2 percent) without the addition of a stretch fiber such as SPANDEX. Synonym: MECHANICAL STRETCH.

neats Very small-scale prints with simple, small repeats. Neats were usually done in only one or two colors, making them cheap and extremely popular during the 19th century. In the 21st century, neats appear most often in the patterns of tie silks.

neck cloth Refers to the large pieces of fine linen or muslin, usually an immaculately laundered and snowy white, that formed the favored neck wear of the fashionable man from the late 18th through 19th centuries—particularly in England and those seeking to imitate the fashions of that country. Adjusting the neck cloth to its ultimate perfection—neither too high nor too low, neither too casual nor too sloppy—was an art identified with the Regency dandy, particularly BEAU BRUMMELL.

neck gaiter Usually worn for sports or extreme cold weather, a neck gaiter replaced a MUFFLER as a way of keeping the neck warm without the fuss of tying a length of cloth. As adopted in the late 20th century, a gaiter was often made of manmade FLEECE, popped over the head and covered the area from mid-ear to collarbone.

neck kerchief Generic reference to a square of fabric worn around the neck for either decorative or functional purposes; encompasses both the humble BANDANA worn by working COWBOYS and the fancy FOULARD knotted like an ASCOT.

neck ring See TORQUE.

necktie 1. Although it technically could refer to any NECKWEAR, in common practice the term refers to the very long strip of fabric that most people refer to simply as a "tie." In that sense, it distinguishes the standard tie from other neckwear such as the BOW TIE or ASCOT, and from alternatives such as the BOLO TIE, STRING TIE, PLANTATION TIE, or NECK KERCHIEF.

In contemporary practice, the standard tie is about 57 inches long (although that may vary anywhere from 55 to 60 inches depending on the manufacturer, the country of origin, and the particular fashion of the day). At its widest point, it may be anywhere from 2 to 5 inches (again depending on fashion), although somewhere around 4 inches is often the norm. It is most often made from silk or a material that resembles it, which is cut on the BIAS, and lined with a lighter weight of material, also cut on the bias—which helps the tie to regain its shape after being knotted and worn. This construction became standard in the 1920s. Unlined ties are generally hand-made and referred to by their construction, either SEVEN-FOLD or FIVE-FOLD.

It may be tied with any of a variety of knots, the best known being the (in order from thickest to thinnest): WINDSOR, HALF-WINDSOR, and FOUR-IN-HAND (for diagrams, see individual entries). According to convention, whatever knot is used should be taut enough to remain in place without adjustment, to arch out slightly when seen in profile (rather than drooping forlornly), and to create a slight DIMPLE in the exact center of the blade directly beneath the knot. The portion that hangs from the knot is known as the APRON (in America) or BLADE (in England).

Its usual accessories include the TIEPIN, TIE TACK, TIE BAR, or TIE CLIP—although they are worn one at a time and none is mandatory in contemporary use.

2. In references to neckwear of earlier

centuries, costume historians often use the word necktie even though the style (e.g., the huge, horizontal bows popular during the 1840s) may more closely resemble a modern bow tie.

neckwear   1. Industry jargon for the merchandise category that primarily consists of NECKTIES, BOW TIES, and ASCOTS.   2. General reference to anything worn around the neck except jewelry; in that sense often spelled as two words: neck wear.

needlecord *or* **needle-wale**   Describes a type of COR-DUROY with very small WALES, which Americans might call PINWALE, because the ribs are approximately the width of a pin. "Needlecord" is more common in British usage.

Nehru cap   The symmetrical cloth cap (resembling the FORAGE CAP of the U.S. military), worn with points front and back, identified with Jawaharlal Nehru, first prime minister of India.

When Nehru himself first adopted it, the style was known as a GANDHI CAP because Mahatma Gandhi had started the fashion as a political statement: Previously, headgear was assigned according to caste, whereas with the simple cloth cap was worn by all castes (and usually made of KHADI as a sign of solidarity against the British).

Nehru collar, Nehru jacket, Nehru suit   In the Western world, usually refers to a 1960s style that imitated the high-collared, lapel-less, plain-front jackets worn by Jawarharlal Nehru, the first prime minister of India.

Nehru jacket

In the West, most "Nehru jackets" were approximately the length of a traditional sport coat or suit jacket and worn with traditional trousers, whereas Nehru himself wore longer versions of the traditional jacket called the ACHKAN. (In contemporary usage, the style known as a Nehru suit in the West during the 1960s would probably be referred to as a JODHPURI SUIT.)

Several designers and celebrities take credit for the invention of the Nehru jacket and its popularity in the West, but Paris-based designers PIERRE CARDIN (who was showing a similar, completely collarless style early as 1960) and GILBERT FÉRUCH (who experimented with mandarin-style collars and quoted Asian tunic styles in the jackets he tailored for French celebrities) probably had the strongest claim to its invention. From 1965 to 1968, when interest in India was at its peak, the Nehru jacket was adopted as a short-hand symbol of hipness, worn by everyone from THE BEATLES to Johnny Carson, and sometimes accessorized with LOVE BEADS or (less often) medallion necklaces.

The same style is often incorrectly referred to as a MAO COLLAR, MAO JACKET, or Mao suit (although the actual style of suit worn by Mao and his associates, by contrast, has a high, fold-over collar and symmetrical pockets on the jacket front).

Synonyms: rajah collar; MANDARIN collar.

neoprene   A synthetic rubber, used most often for wet suits but occasionally incorporated into swimwear and surf styles. Invented by Wallace Hume Carothers (who also developed NYLON) in 1930 for DuPont and announced in 1931, neoprene was the first synthetic alternative to rubber to become commercially viable. During World War II, it was the only nonmetal to be classified as "most critical" to the war effort.

nep   An irregularity—like a small blip—in a yarn; usually caused by a knot, impurity, or spinning problem. Unlike the colorful nubs that distinguish DONEGAL yarns (and hence the tweeds made from them), a nep is usually considered a defect.

nerd   A 20th-century term of derision that evolved into a description of style (or lack thereof). As with GEEK CHIC, the nerd flaunts his brains rather than his body. A typical outfit might include: glasses with thick, unfashionable frames, pants that are too short and made of an unfashionable material (such as a particularly practical polyester) and are worn high and belted, a shirt buttoned to the throat (or the top button unbuttoned to reveal a white T-shirt beneath), and a pocket protector for the inevitable chest pocket of that shirt. In his dressier or business incarnation, he resembles the PEE-WEE HERMAN character.

Occasionally, to signal a style that that was not meant to look sexy, designers or stylists riff on the nerd in runway presentations or fashion editorial, usually quoting from the nerd's cluelessness about style rules rather than his actual apparel (e.g., pairing white socks with black shoes, whereas a real-life nerd would probably pick dark, polyester dress socks as his all-purpose hosiery).

nested suit   Industry jargon for a suit that is sold with the jacket and pants together on a single hanger (as opposed to SUIT SEPARATES, where pieces made to be worn together can be purchased separately).

New Edwardians   A short-lived style initiated by the London customers of high-end tailors in the years immediately following World War II. In admiring imitation of their grandfathers and great-grandfathers, the New Edwardians eschewed the DRAPE-FRONT, big-shouldered fashion of the day in favor of suits with longer, more flared SKIRTS, tighter sleeves, tighter pants legs, and longer, more styled hair. Soon copied in South London, where it was taken to an extreme that became known as the TEDDY BOY look, it was out of fashion among the uppercrust by the early 1950s.

New & Lingwood   Known since 1865 as the official outfitters to Eton College, New & Lingwood also provides men's bespoke shirts and shoes, as well as ready-made shirts, shoes, tailored clothing, sportswear, formalwear, and accessories ranging from socks to cufflinks—especially at its London branch.

Founded at its still-operating premises at 118 Eton High Street in 1865 by Elisabeth New and Samuel Lingwood (who subsequently married), the firm opened an additional shop, on Jermyn Street in London, in 1922. When that building was bombed during World War II, it moved to its present premises at the 53 Jermyn Street entrance to the Piccadilly Arcade. In 1972, it incorporated bespoke shoemakers Poulsen Skone and, later, custom shirtmakers Bowring Arundel.

Newgate knockers   In 19th-century England, virtually a synonym for the style of full SIDEWHISKERS known as PICCADILLY WEEPERS or DUNDREARIES.

Newmarket   A center of British racing since the 17th century, when it flourished under the patronage of CHARLES II (the same monarch credited with the invention of the suit), the town in Suffolk County directly north of London gave its name to a variety of men's fashions, which either originated there or borrowed the name for its automatic association with horses and English country life. For example: In the 1750s, George Washington ordered "a Newmarket GREATCOAT."

In contemporary usage, the name is still used for NEWMARKET BOOTS and is the indirect derivation of the check pattern called TATTERSALL.

Newmarket boots   Refers to a two-tone style of knee-high riding boot that combines a brown leather boot top and brown leather foot with a leg made of undyed or beige waterproofed canvas or linen. In contemporary use, the combination is often imitated in rubberized boots.

In the hunt field, they may be worn as RATCATCHER (especially in dirty weather), but are considered inappropriate in more formal situations such as the show ring or a formal meeting of hounds. The name derives from the English town famous as a horseracing center, and the style was popularized by the London firm of CORDINGS in the early 20th century.

New Romantic   Taking the grab-bag and dress-up aspect of PUNK—without its S&M or confrontationalism—New Romanticism succeeded punk as a fashion movement in 1979 and the early 1980s. New Romantic menswear capitalized on tight, FROGGED jackets, flowing POETS' SHIRTS, and other costumey elements meant to evoke PIRATES, heroes, and the INCROYABLES of a revolutionary Paris.

Its supposed birthplace: London clubs such as Billy's and Club for Heroes. Its poster boy: ADAM ANT, the handsome, dark-haired British singer who favored dressing in costumes that recalled early 19th-century naval epics. Its retail epicenter: WORLDS END, the London boutique operated by VIVIENNE WESTWOOD and Malcolm McLaren. Its canonization on the catwalk: "Pirates," Westwood's first formal fashion collection, shown in 1981.

newsboy cap   A hat with a shallow VISOR and a large, floppy CROWN (usually made of eight or so pie-wedge-shaped panels). It resembles a BASEBALL CAP with a stubbier brim and a hugely overgrown crown.

nightcap   For centuries before the word was appropriated as a synonym for the last alcoholic beverage of the evening, a "nightcap" was any headcovering worn to bed—a necessity in the days of drafty bedrooms and doctors who warned of the dire consequences of a man not keeping his brain warm. In the Western world, depending on the time and place, nightcap styles ranged from tied-under-the-chin caps similar to the ones now worn by infants to styles that resembled modern shower caps to STOCKING CAP styles.

nightshirt   A long—generally knee- or calf-length—shirt designed for sleeping. In contemporary use, nightshirts are frequently long-sleeved and usually have a button PLACKET that stops at mid-chest. In earlier centuries, a nightshirt was often full-length and followed the untailored construction of a blouse-like shirt.

If the garment is made of jersey or other knits, it is more often described as a SLEEPSHIRT and not a nightshirt. "Nightshirt" is an earlier and more general usage, usually associated with woven materials.

Nike   The world's largest sneaker and activewear brand, which grew out of Phil Knight's 1964 partnership with his former track coach Bill Bowerman at the University of Oregon. Known for its "swoosh" logo; for slogans including the 1988 "Just Do It"; for signing star athletes to multimillion-dollar endorsement deals; also credited with creating and feeding the craze, particularly among urban kids, for expensive sneakers.

Up until the newly degreed MBA Knight and former Olympic coach Bowerman began importing Onitsuka Tiger sneakers from Japan, the market for running shoes had been dominated by German brands like ADIDAS. By 1967, the Japanese company was using a heel designed by Bowerman and the original partners had incorporated their Blue Ribbon Sports company as BRS and opened a store in Eugene, Oregon. However, BRS soon had a falling out with its Japanese partners.

In 1971, a student at Portland State named Carolyn Davidson designed the "swoosh" logo for the grand sum of $35 (later supplemented with Nike stock), an employee

Nightshirt and nightcap

named Jeff Johnson had literally dreamed up the name "Nike" for the new company, and Bowerman was trying out new sole designs on his wife's waffle iron. After a falling out with its Japanese partners, BRS debuted its own shoes at a trade show, and, in 1973, local Oregon boy and international track star Steve Prefontaine became the first big-name athlete to wear the brand. In 1977, the already successful company debuted the first of many memorable T-shirt taglines: "There is no finish line." By 1978, BRS has officially changed its name to Nike and signed its first endorsement deal with tennis star John McEnroe.

In 1979, Nike introduced its first Air Sole, a then-new method of compressing air into a sole to cushion the stride. Throughout the 1980s, Nike dominated its market: signing basketball star Michael Jordan for $2.5 million in 1984; entering the sports apparel market in 1986; and acquiring traditional shoemaker Cole Haan in 1988. Into the 1990s and the 21st century, the company continued an expansion fueled by acquisitions (e.g., Hurley in 2002 and Converse in 2003), technical development (the Nike Shox soles in 2000), award-winning advertising by agency Weiden and Kennedy (1990's "Bo Knows" campaign), and alliances with star athletes (golfer Tiger Woods in 1996, basketball star LeBron James in 2003).

Nik-Nik An American label, founded in 1970 by Harold Schulman and famous for its colorful sport shirts with all-over—and often offbeat—prints. The brand was dissolved in 1977, but the name was licensed to an Italian company in 2005.

Ninja, Willi Born William Leake in 1961 in the New York borough of Queens; the dancer who became the best-known exponent of the 1980s dance style known as vogueing, establishing its style in both choreography and costumes and becoming a star of the 1990 documentary *Paris Is Burning*.

Although the DRAG balls where he initially performed had a decades-long tradition of adapting the prancing and poses of high-fashion models, Ninja aided a martial-arts element (hence his stage name) and sharp, unexpected moves.

Tall and broad-shouldered, but essentially androgynous, Ninja created fashions that were widely copied in clubs and eventually ended up on designer runways (e.g., his practice of wearing a traditional tailored suit jacket with a skirt). He himself modeled for JEAN PAUL GAULTIER and founded a 2004 modeling agency called EON (an acronym for Elements of Ninja). He died in 2006, at age 45.

noble fibers An industry term referring to a class of very fine—and usually very expensive—fibers made from animal hairs, a group that includes ALPACA, CASHMERE, GUANACO, QIVIUT, SURI, and VICUÑA. Most noble fibers are under 16 microns in diameter and are prized, in part, because they produce textiles that are silky and light yet warmer than ordinary sheep's wool (which ordinarily runs upward of 18 microns).

Nomex A brand of heat-resistant, fire-resistant nylon developed by DUPONT during the mid-20th century. Used primarily in protective apparel for the military and firefighters.

nonwovens Although the term technically means any textile that isn't woven (encompassing everything from

Nike: Swoosh logo; advertisement

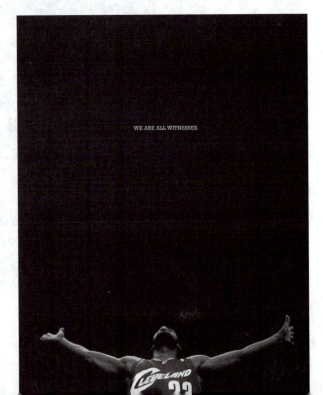

WE ARE ALL WITNESSES.

leather to felt), in apparel jargon it usually refers to knits and is used most often to refer to sweaters, T-shirts, polo shirts, and other tops. In textile jargon as applied to tailoring, the term usually refers to fabrics composed of fibers that are pressed or bonded together, such as FUSIBLE INTERFACINGS.

Norfolk jacket Known in its early incarnations as the "Norfolk shirt," the style's design is variously attributed to the Duke of Norfolk, his gamekeepers, or EDWARD VII when he was Prince of Wales. All of those stories may be apocryphal. However, it is certain that the style was worn on the Duke of Norfolk's estate and gained its great popularity during the 1860s and the remainder of the 19th century by being worn by the ebullient and sports-loving prince.

Then, as now, the Norfolk jacket is primarily distinguished by its belted waist seam (which may either be a self belt of matching fabric, or a stitched-down band that simulates a self belt). Its other characteristics are sturdy material (often a drab tweed); a squared front hem; a single-breasted, button-front opening; long sleeves; a short length that covers the buttocks but stops at the top of the leg; roomy patch pockets (originally with their openings covered by flaps); and stitched-down front straps that extend from the shoulder seam to the hem and cross the waist (as if they were stitched-down suspenders). The back construction is more varied: It may have either a similar stitched-down strap in its center, a pair of such straps, or box pleats at its side.

As originally worn with matching pants (either PLUS FOURS or trousers with turn-ups), the Norfolk jacket had, by the 1880s, become the basis of apparel for almost every kind of sport except horseback riding, spreading from shooting to cycling to general country pursuits. In the early 20th century it began to appear with unmatched trousers and became, if not the father to the contemporary sports jacket, then at least its close relative. Even into the 21st century, the style retains sporty connotations.

Norwegian A style of sporty shoe easily distinguished by its front, which, instead of arching smoothly over the foot, has a thick seam outlining the top of the foot in a construction more associated with Native American MOCCASINS. The top of the shoe is relatively flat and meets its sides, which extend about an inch up from the sole, almost at a right angle. The term is usually abbreviated to WEEJUNS in the American market.

Originally a rough, sturdy shoe made by Norwegian fishermen (hence the name), the Norwegian could be either laced or slipped on. The style was first taken up in

Norfolk Jacket

Willi Ninja

England (during EDWARD VIII's heyday as Prince of Wales, when rustic styles had a particular chic), then crossed the pond to the United States and was practically ubiquitous by the mid-1930s, becoming codified after G.H. Bass, the Maine shoe manufacturer, began offering its "Weejuns" in 1936. In that incarnation, the style retained its sturdy (as opposed to soft) leather, fairly rigid leather sole, and thick, visible stitching, and thus became the progenitor of many of the slip-on styles that people now refer to as LOAFERS.

notch   The indent formed where the LAPEL meets the COLLAR on a traditional tailored jacket or coat. The standard notch is roughly V-shaped—although the angle becomes more abrupt if the jacket has a PEAK LAPEL—and other shapes, such as a letter M, occasionally appear.

notch collar   Used as a synonym for NOTCHED LAPELS (although both are misleading, since the notch is customarily formed at the juncture of the COLLAR and LAPEL—and not one or the other). Although the notch may be literally nicked into a collar that is then attached to the body of the jacket, such invention is not considered traditional tailoring.

notched lapels   Any style of tailored jacket that contains a notch; usually cited to distinguish the model from alternatives such as the PEAK LAPEL, SHAWL COLLAR, or the banded collar of a NEHRU JACKET.

novelty prints   A broad category of prints that depicts a recognizable person, place, or thing. A synonym for CONVERSATIONALS.

no-wale   Refers to a smooth CORDUROY, made without the ribbed effect given by WALES.

nubuck   Any leather, but most often COWHIDE, that has been buffed on its grain side—the outside of the animal—so that its surface has a slight nap and somewhat resembles SUEDE. This process is known as "sueding," although true suede, by contrast, is buffed on the flesh side of the skin. Synonyms include GRAIN SUEDE.

Nudie   Best known as Nudie Cohn, Nuta Kotlyarenko was world-famous for gaudy, glitzy Western wear based on his personal motto, "It is better to be looked over than overlooked."

Born in Kiev in 1902, Nuta was smuggled out of the Ukraine during the pogroms against Jews and renamed in 1913 by an immigration official at Ellis Island who couldn't pronounce his real name. He apprenticed to a tailoring business in Brooklyn and shined shoes in front of Broadway theaters. Eventually, he also did nine months in Leavenworth for drug trafficking and, despite being only 5 feet, 7 inches, a spell as an itinerant pro fighter. After meeting and marrying a nice Minnesota girl named Helen Barbara Kruger (who, as Bobbie Nudie, would be his lifelong business partner and muse), he headed back to New York, where he struck up a friendship with gangster Pretty Boy Floyd and opened Nudie's for Ladies in 1934, which specialized in G-strings for strippers. Finding New York hard going during the Depression, the couple moved to Minnesota to open a dry cleaner. Heading to Hollywood in 1939, the Cohns finally settled down and began successfully selling their own over-the-top take on cowboy clothes—culminating

Norwegians

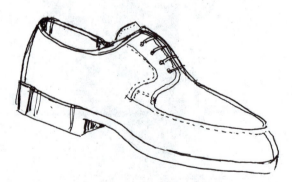

with the opening of Nudie's Rodeo Tailors in North Hollywood in 1947. The business logo was a naked cowgirl that Nudie claimed was inspired by the night that his wife appeared wearing nothing but cowboy boots, a hat, and a holster, and then asked him "When are you going to make the rest of the outfit?"

All the stars went to Nudie's. So did all the country singers. Then, eventually, so did all the rock stars. Over the years, his customers comprised Tony Curtis, Clint Eastwood, John Lennon, Buck Owens, Gram Parsons, ELVIS PRESLEY, Ronald Reagan, and Hank Williams. Roy Rogers was buried in a Nudie suit. Even after Cohn converted to Christianity in the mid-1960s and put clothes on his naked cowgirl logo, Cher, Jimi Hendrix, Elton John, Janis Joplin, Sly and the Family Stone, and other celebrity customers kept coming. Eye-blindingly bright, Nudie's clothes were covered with rhinestones, fringes, braids, and embroidery, and cost thousands of dollars, even back in the 1940s. Nudie also customized saddles for his clients. Beginning in the 1950s, he created a series of notorious "Nudiemobiles," which were usually huge customized Cadillac Eldorados or Pontiac Bonnevilles with tooled leather interiors, steer horn hood orna-

ments, silver dollar inlays, and silver-plated, six-shooter door handles. (The Bonneville he bestowed on Roy Rogers is now in the same Branson, Missouri, museum of Rogers memorabilia as Trigger, the horse.) A devoted player, Nudie also recorded an album of his mandolin music in 1974.

After his death in 1984, his wife and granddaughter continued the business for a few years, but, by the 21st century, original Nudies had become icons, collected and quoted by designers ranging from TOMMY HILFIGER to TOM FORD. In 2004, his granddaughter Jamie Lee Nudie published a biography called *Nudie the Rodeo Tailor*.

Nureyev, Rudolf   Born in Siberia in 1938, Rudolf Hametovich Nureyev was already a star of the Kirov Ballet when his defection to the West made headlines in 1961. Thereafter, he costumed himself in dramatic, androgynous, vaguely Eastern combinations of clothes that seemed designed to repudiate the reactionary rigor of Soviet Russia.

Half Bashkir and half Tatar (on his mother's side), he showed his razor-like cheekbones to advantage under a series of NEWSBOY and fishermen caps. Borrowing the

Nudie Cohn

habit of the rehearsal studio, he burrowed under layers of scarves and mufflers and turtleneck sweaters. He affected long TRENCH COATS made of leather. Or dark, floor-sweeping coats. Or silk robes appropriate to an oriental potentate. He wore thigh-high boots and extravagant furs with aplomb. As befit someone who often played a prince onstage and who reached world fame at approximately the same time as THE BEATLES, he kept his hair long and MOP-like through most of his life. In the days when such things were newsworthy, Nureyev became the first man admitted to the Manhattan restaurant "21" without a tie.

Although he sometimes wore designer clothes—especially early YVES SAINT LAURENT—Nureyev's basic look changed little in the last two decades of his life. He died in 1993. In 2006, an exhibition devoted to him at the Museum of Costume in Bath, England, was credited with influencing designers at Costume National, Louis Vuitton, and PRADA to quote his look in their runway presentations.

Nutter, Tommy   Born in Wales in 1943, Nutter abandoned what he variously claimed to be architecture studies or a plumbing apprenticeship to work for the London tailoring firm of Donaldson, Williamson & Ward. In 1969, he launched his own tailoring firm at 35A SAVILE Row, backed by singer Cilla Black, Peter Brown of Apple Records, and lawyer James Vallance White.

One of his own best models, the trim, sometimes mustachioed, very social Nutter was best known for jackets with a nipped waist, flaring SKIRT, and extraordinarily wide lapels. Later, he added strongly padded shoulders to this signature silhouette.

Nutter was widely credited with attracting younger customers to the then-stodgy precincts of Savile Row.

BEATLES John, Paul, and Ringo were customers (as were their wives), and all three wore Nutter clothes on the cover of the Abbey Road album. Nutter also created John Lennon and Yoko Ono's white wedding suits, as well as suits for Mick and Bianca Jagger, and Bill Wyman's suit for his wedding to Mandy Smith. Other prominent customers included Twiggy, Diana Ross, and Elton John. Timothy Everest, who would one day start his own tailoring firm and ready-to-wear line, worked briefly as Nutter's design assistant.

Nutter was made creative director of KILGOUR, FRENCH & STANBURY in 1974, and divorced himself from his own label by 1976, although it continued under his name for a few more years, maintained by business partner Edward Sexton. Nutter's later forays included costuming Jack Nicholson with the purple, peak-lapel, padded-shoulder jackets he wore as the Joker in *Batman*. Nutter died in 1992.

nylon   The synthetic fiber developed by Wallace Hume Carothers (who also developed NEOPRENE) at the DUPONT laboratories in Delaware in 1934, patented by that company in 1935, and announced to great fanfare at the World's Fair in 1938, when it was described as being "strong as steel, as fine as a spider's web." A long-chain polyamide billed as "synthetic silk," nylon first became popular for women's stockings (hence their designation as "nylons") and underwear, due to the polymer's strength, elasticity, and ability to retain dye. It moved to the men's market as a material for dress socks, where it was also prized for its resistance to abrasion and rot. Thereafter, nylon was and is featured as a component in textiles where added strength is required (e.g., wool/nylon blends for suits or sweaters). Synonym: POLYAMIDE (especially in European usage).

Ocean Pacific An iconic surf brand, this apparel maker traces its heritage to the California beach culture of the 1960s and its origins to the sporting goods distributorship, California Surfing Products, started by Jim Jenks in 1968. While delivering products, Jenks realized there was both a general interest in surfwear and a specific need for better-made BOARD SHORTS. After acquiring the name Ocean Pacific (Op) and finding backers, Jenks officially founded the company in 1972 with five styles of shorts and then placed his first ad in the December 1972 issue of *Surfer* magazine. He soon added tops modeled after HAWAIIAN SHIRTS, then corduroy walking shorts, later expanding to other activewear and sportswear and a range of labels—including Op Classic, Seven2, and Ocean Pacific—aimed at various market segments.

From the beginning, Op sponsored surfers and surfing events to stress its authenticity. For example: In 1974, it signed Larry Bertleman to head its pro team. (During the next decade Bertleman would rack up nine covers of *Surfing* and *Surfer* magazines and countless controversies.) In 1982, it started the spectator-oriented Op Pro Surfing Championships, at the legendary Huntington Beach Pier, drawing an audience of 35,000.

In 1985, Op-sponsored Tom Curren became World Champion, a feat he repeated in 1986 and 1990.

In the 21st century, the brand changed ownership several times, moving its operations to the East Coast in 2007.

Ocean's 11 The 1960 movie about a heist in Las Vegas, best known as a RAT PACK buddy pic and better remembered for its sharpie Hollywood/Las Vegas-style menswear than for its other merits. Directed by Lewis Milestone, it starred Frank SINATRA as Danny Ocean, with Dean Martin as Sam Harmon, Sammy Davis Jr. as

Ocean's 11

Josh Howard, Peter Lawford as Jimmy Foster, Joey Bishop as Mushy O'Connors, and longtime Sinatra collaborator Nelson Riddle supervising the soundtrack. Although Howard Shoup is credited with the costume design, most of the main characters—Sinatra in particular—seem to be wearing clothes from their own closets. For example, in one key scene Sinatra sports a hairy, V-neck sweater in his favorite shade of orange.

In 2001, it was remade as a buddy pic with George Clooney and Brad Pitt in the Sinatra and Martin roles and costumes designed by Jeffrey Kurland. In 2004, the sequel, *Ocean's 12* was released with costumes designed by Oscar-winner MILENA CANONERO. In 2007, yet another sequel, *Ocean's 13*, was released with costumes by Louise Frogley.

Oeko-Tex   A trademarked certification system that tests raw materials and textiles for the presence of substances known to be harmful to humans (such as certain dyes and FINISHING processes).

This product-labeling system grew out of a scheme developed in Austria (in the late 1980s) and another developed in Germany (in the 1990s) into what became, by the mid-1990s, the International Association for Research and Testing in the Field of Textile Ecology.

The Official Preppy Handbook   Edited by Lisa Birnbach and published as a best-selling trade paperback by Workman Publishing in 1980, this tongue-in-cheek guide to the mores and mannerisms of the PREPPY included an illustrated and exhaustively annotated chapter on "Dressing the Part," complete with lists of stores both extant and extinct, basic body types, diagrams of the J. PRESS pocket flap, and an authoritative section called "From Desk to Duck Blind: The Look for Men."

off-price   Any garment that is discounted or not sold at suggested retail price for whatever reason. Thus, an "off-price clothier" may be one who deals in factory seconds, remainders of other lines, or goods produced traditionally but not given their customary markup.

offshore   Jargon for goods produced outside the United States; usually indicates production in Asia.

off-the-peg   Jargon for any garment that is not custom-tailored or otherwise customized. A slightly more old-fashioned usage than OFF-THE-RACK.

off-the-rack   Jargon for what would be known as READY-TO-WEAR in women's wear: any garment that is not custom-tailored or otherwise customized. As in: "Instead of spending thousands commissioning a bespoke suit, he popped into the department store and bought an off-the-rack suit for a few hundred dollars."

oilcloth   Fabric varnished with oil—traditionally linseed oil—to make it waterproof. Predating the wide use of laminates (like GORE-TEX) and water-repellent finishes (like Teflon).

oilskin   Can be used as a synonym for OILCLOTH or for the apparel made from it. Commonly, a reference to "oilskins" is a reference to FOUL-WEATHER GEAR.

Old Spice   Probably the fragrance that has been most popular for the longest time with American men, the group of toiletries originally called Early American Old Spice was introduced by the Shulton Company in 1938 (following the 1937 debut of toiletries of the same name for women). To enhance the colonial connection, its distinctive milky-white glass packaging was based on an antique apothecary bottle with a metal stopper and featured a clipper ship and blue and red printing.

At certain points in the brand's history, different ships signified different Old Spice products: The Recovery was the ship on the cologne bottle; the Grand Turk was on the aftershave; the Mt. Vernon was on the talc. In various eras, other antique sailing ships also figured on its labels.

In 1990, the brand was purchased by Procter & Gamble, which changed its logo from an old-fashioned clipper ship to a streamlined sailing yacht in 1992.

oleophobic   A treatment, fabric, or fiber that repels oil.

olive *or* **olivet**   Reference, now obsolete, to a fancy closure (of a roughly olive shape), similar to a toggle closure: synonymous with a FROG or BRANDENBURG. Used most often in the 19th century.

ombré   Literally "shaded." Thus, a sweater or shirt with an ombré effect varies in color from top to bottom, changing from dark to light (or vice versa).

ombré stripe   A stripe that incorporates an OMBRÉ effect, usually in the body of the stripe itself and not in the background.

onesie   The all-in-one garment worn—especially for sleeping—by babies. Although the term is applied to sleeveless and legless, JUMPSUIT-like garments, by tradition the term was first identified with long sleeves and long pant legs, and snaps or buttons down the center front. It may also feature snaps or some similar access on

Old Spice

the inside of the legs to facilitate changing the baby's diaper. In older references, a onesie may also have attached "footies" that cover the baby's feet like slippers and mitts to cover the baby's hands—although more contemporary usage refers to a garment without the hand and foot covering.

one up, one down   The simplest possible style of weave, also called a PLAIN WEAVE.

Op   See OCEAN PACIFIC.

open-end   Technical jargon used most often when describing the construction of DENIM for JEANS. The term refers to the method in which yarn is spun before the denim is woven—the open-end method being quicker and cheaper, and resulting in yarn that is not as sturdy as RINGSPUN (the other most popular method of making yarn to be used for denim). Thus, open-end denim refers to products made from those particular yarns.

opera cape   A black cape, made with a collar but no hood and sometimes featuring a contrasting lining (e.g., bright red), worn over evening FORMALWEAR in place of a TOPCOAT; usually reserved for WHITE TIE.

opera hat   A collapsible TOP HAT; usually black or midnight blue, with a crown between 5 and 5½ inches in height. To avoid the creation of unsightly lines in the shiny silk when its spring mechanism collapses the hat, many opera hats are made from a matte silk. Synonym: GIBUS.

opera pumps   A style of lightweight, slipperlike shoe with a thin sole worn for formal occasions. Most often made of black PATENT LEATHER, opera pumps may also be made of unshiny, supple, good-quality black leather, but generally feature flat, decorative black bows on the instep, usually made of GROSGRAIN or similar material.

optical whiteners   Chemicals, usually fluorescent dyes, added to laundry bleaches, detergents, dyes, and finishing agents to make whites look brighter. Optical whiteners manipulate absorption of light so that a fabric looks slightly less yellow and more blue; they also enable a surface to reflect more light than is actually shining upon it, thereby creating the effect of a very bright white. Synonym: optical brighteners.

optima   Refers to a style of straw hat, most often a PANAMA hat, that sports a crease through the center of its crown like a sort of backbone.

Not to be confused with Optimo, maker and retailer of panama hats.

orders   Refers to decorations, awards, medals, and other honors; as in "wearing orders." Rules of etiquette vary according to the custom of the country awarding the honor, the circumstance and time (i.e., business dress or formal attire), and the occasion. For example, in most Western countries, a civilian who has been awarded a medal may wear it on a ribbon around his neck while in formal dress but, for everyday wear, indicate the honor only with a simple thread or bar of the appropriate color on the left lapel of his suit.

organic cotton   Refers to cotton plants grown organically, meaning that the plants are raised without chemical pesticides and certain fertilizers; or refers to the fiber, yarn, or fabric made from such plants.

Onesie

In some cases, the designation may also extend to the dyeing, weaving, knitting, finishing, sewing, and/or shipping of the products labeled as organic. In other cases, only the original plant fiber is certified as organic. Internationally, several accrediting organizations and certification systems exist and have slightly varying standards. In the United States, U.S. Department of Agriculture agents must annually inspect fields for compliance to the National Organic Program, which requires, among other things, a three-year conversion period (during which prohibited pesticides and fertilizers cannot be used) before the field is eligible for certification.

Orlon A brand of ACRYLIC fiber developed by DuPont in the 1940s as a substitute for wool. Touted as an improvement to sheep's wool because it was mothproof and washable, Orlon also took dye easily and did not provoke the allergic reactions of sheep's wool. The brand grew rapidly during the 1950s, and, by 1960, DuPont claimed that over 100 million Orlon sweaters were being sold each year.

orthotics Refers to corrective or supportive devices, similar to innersoles, which may be either custom-made or bought over the counter and are worn inside the shoe. Orthotics vary widely in price and may be either purchased directly in drugstores or shoe stores or made according to prescription from a medical doctor or podiatrist. They also vary in length and material: They may be rigid or composed of flexible material (such as leather); they may be as long as the foot or only cover the arch and heel.

Orvis The Manchester, Vermont-based sporting goods and apparel company that was founded as a specialist in fly-fishing equipment in 1856 by Charles F. Orvis and maintains the American Museum of Fly Fishing next to its flagship store on Route 7A.

In 1939, the Orvis family sold the company to Dudley Corkran, an avid sportsman. In 1965, Leigh Perkins bought the company and expanded it beyond fishing equipment, creating a catalog that carried the clothes and accoutrements of upper-class country life.

Opera cape and hat

orylag   A soft, dense fur made from specially bred rabbits originally developed in France at the end of the 20th century from a natural mutation of the Rex rabbit. Prized for its lightness and the fineness of its fiber (averaging 15 microns or less), the orylag has a fur that is denser than chinchilla but a leather that is far more workable and sturdy; at the same time, the hair does not shed like an ordinary rabbit pelt. In menswear, it appears most often as a trim or as a luxury fiber blended with other fibers (e.g., a woven coat material made of 95 percent cashmere and 5 percent orylag).

Osborn, Derrill Radcliff   Equally well-known for his influential tenure as a menswear buyer for luxury retailer Neiman Marcus and for his exaggeratedly exuberant personal style.

His long career in men's fashion included a decade at Saks Fifth Avenue, a year as general manager of Lew Ritter in Beverly Hills, and a total of 23 years at Neiman Marcus (six years as the buyer of men's clothing, followed by 17 years as vice president of men's tailored clothing). During that time, he was credited with hurrying the three-button suit back into fashion, as well as becoming the fervid champion of high-end Italian labels such as Brioni, Ermenegildo Zegna, and Kiton. He retired from the store in spring of 2003 and moved to his ranch in New Mexico to raise Hereford cattle.

Possessed of a bald head but a full beard, Osborn was regularly named to best-dressed lists even though most people considered his wardrobe eccentric. (For example, he delighted in slightly costumey or archaic accoutrements, was photographed wearing turbans and capes, and was rarely seen without a boutonnière.) A much-watched figure, he often changed costume several times a day—especially during days, such as in the midst of a Milan runway season, when he was apt to be photographed. His personal choice to wear a necktie—instead of a bow tie—with FORMALWEAR is credited with instigating that fad among fashionable men in the 1990s.

OshKosh B'Gosh   Workwear company founded in Oshkosh, Wisconsin, in 1895. Best known for its BIB OVERALLS, a franchise that it very successfully extended into the children's wear market during the late 20th century.

ostrich   An expensive leather made from the skin of the large bird. Prized for its distinctive pattern, which boasts large, round, pimply-looking protrusions on the skin (indicating where the ostrich feathers have been plucked—leather made from the unfeathered part of the bird does not have the distinctive grain). Also prized because, while soft and supple, the leather is extremely durable.

ottoman   A type of woven fabric, almost always silk or a blend made to imitate pure silk, that appears in menswear most often as a material for ties. Ottoman is

Derrill Osborn

distinguishable from other silks used for the same purpose because it has a prominent horizontal rib (whereas REPP, another common tie material, has a vertical rib). It also differs from FAILLE, another horizontally ribbed silk fabric used in menswear, by being denser and having a more prominent rib effect.

ounces   A measure of the heft of fabric, usually as the weight of a yard. (For fabric made outside the United States, the equivalent is GRAM WEIGHT.) In contemporary usage, most often quoted as a measurement of DENIM. For example, 6-ounce is a relatively lightweight denim, while 12-ounce denim is a heavyweight, COWBOY-style denim.

outerseam   As applied to pants, also known as OUTSEAM.

outerwear   Jargon for the coats used as the topmost layers of apparel to protect the wearer from weather conditions. In the garment industry, the term is generally reserved for nontailored garments. For example, a DUFFLE COAT would be classified as outerwear, but a CHESTERFIELD would not.

outseam   1. A measurement of the seam that runs on the outside of the leg, extending from the pants' waist to hem. By contrast, the INSEAM is the measurement of the seam that runs on the inside of the leg, from the crotch to the hem. Also known as an OUTERSEAM.   2. Reference to a type of seam in which the material's edges are turned outside, where they are visible, instead of inside, where they are normally hidden. For example, in menswear, DRIVING GLOVES are often made with outseams to enhance the close fit.

outsole   Jargon for what most people refer to as the sole of the SHOE: The bottom of the shoe that comes in contact with the ground. Industry specialists refer to it as outsole in order to distinguish it from other parts of the shoe's construction such as the unseen MIDSOLE and/or INSOLE. Synonym: TOP SOLE.

overalls   Any one of several types of apparel used for WORKWEAR. In contemporary usage, the word is sometimes a synonym for BIB OVERALLS and sometimes as a synonym for COVERALLS (meaning that they incorporate sleeves and cover the sides of the body). In usage before World War II, it is sometimes used interchangeably with what would later be called JEANS and CARPENTER'S PANTS.

overcheck   Refers to a pattern when a check (such a WINDOWPANE CHECK) looks superimposed over a ground pattern (such as a HERRINGBONE).

overcoat   Literally a coat worn over other coats or garments, used for warmth and/or protection from weather. Among traditionalists, the term connotes a garment that is equivalent to a GREATCOAT and heavier than a TOPCOAT.

overdyed   Refers to a fabric that is dyed again after being woven or assembled into apparel, usually to give it a special tint. For example, "black overdyed denim" would mean that DENIM woven of blue and white cotton yarns is dyed again after it is woven to lend a black tint to the blue.

overplaid   See OVERCHECK.

overshirt   A long-sleeved shirt that is used like a jacket or layering piece, a custom that dates back at least to the 1850s (as documented in Joan Severa's *Dressed for the Photographer*). As outerwear, the overshirt is made of heavy material, such as tweed or suede, and worn with the shirttails outside the pants. As a layering piece, the overshirt is often used like a sweater; its material is simply heavier than the T-shirt or sports shirt it is worn over, and shirttails may be worn out or tucked into the pants.

overshoes   Protective footwear worn over ordinary slippers or shoes, usually to prevent them—and the feet inside them—from becoming soaked by mud or wet weather. The practice is ancient, and examples range from PATTENS to more contemporary RUBBERS.

oxford   Refers to a general style of shoe that laces over the instep. Although the word had been applied to that style as early as the 18th century, it did not become common until the second quarter of the 19th century, and it was not until the 19th century turned into the 20th that the oxford style began to supplant high shoes and boots in the wardrobes of most men. (Some late-19th-century oxfords even fastened with buttons.) Hence, in early references to the style, especially before World War I, they may be described as LOW SHOES to distinguish them from boots.

The oxford differs from other laced shoes, such as the DERBY, by being a closed-lace shoe, meaning that the quarters go underneath the VAMP and not above it. Hence, it is the neat, clean-lined seam that starts at the sole (approximately under the arch of the foot) on one side and continues to the same point on the opposite side in an unbroken line that distinguishes the oxford from other laced styles.

Classically, the oxford style has four or more pairs of eyelets (traditionalists consider five ideal), a tongue, a heel counter, and either a straight toe cap or a curvaceous WINGTIP. (See SHOE diagram.) The most common ornamented variations on the oxford style include the full BROGUE and the semi-brogue (which both feature decorative punching).

Oxford bags   The style of outrageously baggy trousers, most often made of flannel, that originated among undergraduates at Oxford University and reached its peak of popularity around 1925. At a time when the bottom hem of a man's pants leg was almost always under 20 inches, Oxford bags sometimes measured 40 or more inches.

oxford cloth   A sturdy, PLAIN WEAVE of cotton (or some fiber intended to imitate it). The cloth and its name originated in Great Britain, probably in Scotland. For at least the last half century, oxford cloth has been the major material associated with BUTTON-DOWN SHIRTS. When it is made in pink, pale blue, or one of the other shades popular for shirts, the warp is usually colored and the weft is white (and may then be referred to as a CHAMBRAY oxford). A variation of the fabric used in the same contexts but made with a twill instead of a plain weave is known as HARVARD CLOTH.

Oxxford   The luxury tailored clothing label founded by Jacob and Lewis Weinberg in Chicago in 1916, renowned for traditional-looking readymade suits constructed with an extraordinarily high percentage of handwork and a customer list comprising Al Capone, CARY GRANT, and Lyndon Johnson.

In 1930, the brand started to be sold at Neiman Marcus, which, for many years, remained its best-known cus-

Oxford

tomer. Later in that decade, Oxxford moved its production to a four-story landmark building at 1220 West Van Buren near the University of Illinois. Oxxford also produces MADE-TO-MEASURE and, in the 1990s, added CUSTOM clothing. During the late 20th century, it was owned for seven years by LEVI STRAUSS & CO., then bought back and subsequently sold again. In 1998, it opened a flagship store in New York.

The brand prides itself on its American heritage, its selection of fabrics (chiefly from Italy and the United Kingdom), and its artisanal production (e.g., 45 pressings of each part of the suit during its assembly and approximately 5,500 handstitches per suit).

(Not to be confused with Oxford Industries, a much larger, publicly traded apparel maker that owns brands including Tommy Bahama and BEN SHERMAN and also produces private-label clothes for men, women, and children.)

oyster finish   Refers to a finish, used most often on woven cashmere, that gives the fabric a slightly mottled and undulating reflection of light, in a glistening pattern similar to an oyster's shell; found most often on solid-colored MUFFLERS. The effect is produced by steaming the fabric, raising the nap in wet form, and then pressing it flat.

ozone wash   Refers to a fabric finish, usually for JEANS or other BOTTOMWEIGHTS. Like many other methods of finishing DENIM, ozone is a way of stripping color from fabric and prematurely aging it.

Oxford bags

pachuco Refers to a Mexican-American subculture, especially from the 1930s to 1950s, and especially in Texas. In most mainstream references, the word is used interchangeably with ZOOT SUITER, because so many of the young men were associated with that style—notoriously as victims of the Zoot Suit Riots that began in Los Angeles in the summer of 1943.

Even when not in a zoot suit, the pachuco look was noted for full trousers, rolled shirtsleeves to show off prominent tattoos, and a DUCK'S ASS hairstyle with plenty of POMADE. By the 1960s, what had been known as *pachuquismo* (a.k.a., zoot suiters) evolved into what became known as *cholo* style.

pad stitching A traditional tailors' construction stitch, used to join layers of fabric by hand, which does not show in the finished garment. In menswear, the most important function of the pad stitch is to create the roll of the lapel and the roll of the collar on a jacket. The pad stitch is sized to its function on the garment—traditionally large and slanted on the lapel—and in a tension that ensures it does not create puckers in the finished garment. Stitches are aligned in vertical rows; one row may slant from lower left to upper right, while the next slants in the opposing direction, so that the final result looks like a misaligned herringbone.

paddock boots *or* **paddock shoes** A style of laced-front, ankle-high boots intended to be worn for chores in the barn or paddock, or for informal riding; usually in a black or dark brown, sturdy, undecorated leather; made with a sturdy sole and a slight heel (usually about one inch). Although they are often referred to as "shoes," the height remains the same even if the name changes.

painter's pants WORKWEAR, usually made of undyed cotton DUCK. Intended for housepainters and sold in hardware and painting supply stores. Painter's pants are wide-legged and have a zippered fly, two patch pockets in the back and two jeans-style pockets in the front. They may also have one or more tool loops or additional pockets on the legs, similar to BIB OVERALL styles. (This term is sometimes used interchangeably with CARPENTER'S PANTS, although carpenter's pants may also be made of other materials.)

During the 1970s, painter's pants became a crossover fad and were worn on college campuses by students of both genders.

paisley A curvilinear pattern distinguished by the teardrop-shaped motif known as a BOTEH or paisley.

Although paisley-like patterns can be traced back to pre-Roman times and also appeared on Byzantine robes, the design recognizable in contemporary Western apparel first appeared during the Mughal empire as a stylized flowering plant. Subsequently, it became even more stylized and flamelike in appearance, evolving into the shape found in Kashmir shawls imported to Europe in the 18th century. Originally a border element of those shawls, the paisley became their dominant pattern during the 19th century and, from there, was taken up by the men's market—primarily as an all-over pattern for silks.

pakol The round, cloth hat with a rolled brim and flat top associated with the Northern Alliance and Tajik tribesmen in the Hindu Kush region of Afghanistan and Pakistan.

palaka A precursor to the HAWAIIAN SHIRT, the palaka was originally worn by workers on the Hawaiian pineapple, sugar cane, and coffee plantations. Supposedly, the "palaka" (a word that may be a variation of "plaid") came to the islands as a traditional, brightly checked cotton shirt sometime in the late 19th century, and Hawaiians adapted it by cutting off its shirttails and long sleeves—creating the basic, boxy silhouette of the aloha shirt.

Today, palaka-checked material remains associated with pretourist Hawaii, and palaka shirts are often part of the traditional costume of the PANIOLO, Hawaii's cowboys.

paletôt A style of loose, hip-length outerwear, popular in the second and third quarters of the 19th century. A casual, workman's style, the paletôt was nonetheless used to top gentlemen's suits and city clothes, especially as a rain jacket. (In that sense, its closest contemporary equivalent would be the European custom of wearing a sporty style, like a PARKA or a VESTE FORESTIÈRE from ARNYS, over a suit.)

According to legend, the fashion originated in the 1830s when the COUNT D'ORSAY, then at the peak of his influence, got caught in the rain and improvised a raincoat by buying a jacket off the back of a sailor who happened to be passing by. The looseness of the style, its brevity, its crudity of execution, its comfort, and its lack of a waist seam provided a neat counterpoint to the careful, curved tailoring and the glossy materials that defined the dandy of the day.

By 1840, it had become ubiquitous on both sides of the English Channel, and, much like the contemporary parka, variations of it were sported by men of all classes: from the sailors and workmen who had first worn it to

Pakol

Paisley

students and apprentices. Many costume historians credit the popularity of the paletôt with the emergence of the loose, unfitted SACK SUIT later in the century.

pallium   The long strip of ornamented fabric that was worn over the tunic or robe in Byzantine and early medieval times. The pallium hung front and center and sometimes extended almost to the hem of the garment. Although Catholic archbishops are granted the right to wear the pallium, the garment is now more familiar from depictions of royalty and angels. Synonym: LORUM.

Palm Beach suit   Can be used as either a generic reference to describe a distinctive style and weight of suit or a specific reference to the clothing manufacturing firm that goes by the name of the Palm Beach Company. In neither case does it refer to suits or fabric manufactured in Palm Beach.

Most often, it refers to a type of lightweight summer suit that first appeared in the 1930s, when it was usually in an off-white, beige, or gray. Made from a distinctive, blended fabric produced by Goodall-Sanford, the classic Palm Beach suit was washable and less prone to wrinkling than the linen suit, a competitive style.

paludamentum   A large, heavy cloak worn by only the highest-ranking men in ancient Rome—usually reserved for emperors or generals.

pampooties   1. MOCCASIN-type footwear, often improvised from a single piece of untanned hide plus twine, worn with the hair side out and frequently soaked in water to keep the hide supple. Famously part of traditional dress on the Aran Islands, where they were worn well into the 20th century, the pampootie probably dates back to the Iron Age. Its twins or near-relatives in that part of the world include the "rivilin" or "rivelin" (in the islands off Scotland), "skin-sko" (in Iceland), and "cuaran" (usually a higher, more boot- or socklike style worn in other parts of Scotland and Ireland).   2. In Newfoundland and surrounding areas, the word usually refers to socks, slippers, or soft shoes.

panama   Refers to several styles of brimmed straw hat that actually originated in the coastal provinces of Ecuador—not Panama—in the 17th century.

The category is most associated with the broad-brimmed PLANTER'S HAT (also known as a JIPIJAPA), but can take virtually any form, from a COWBOY HAT to a FEDORA; all are created from very fine, pale TOQUILLA straw (which had apparently provided hats for the natives long before the Spanish invasion in the 16th century), and their production is extremely labor-intensive. For example, a MONTECRISTI *superfino* (one of the most prized varieties because of its extremely regular and small-scale weave) may have hundreds and hundreds of rows in its crown. Both the straw and the weaving styles contribute to the hat's much-touted pliability: By custom, a man could fold his hat in the center and roll it as though it were made of cloth (a custom that wise owners did not overemploy in dry climates). Other, less-pricey weaving styles include the *cuencas* and the *brisa* (a subcategory of *cuencas*).

pancake hood   A style of flat hood. Instead of having a vertical seam that divides the hood in half from the neck to the crown to shape the hood, a pancake hood is made with a horizontal seam across the crown, so that it lies flat like an envelope when not in use. In contemporary apparel, seen most often on DUFFLE COATS (e.g., those made by GLOVERALL).

Panerai Founded by Giovanni Panerai in Florence in 1860, Officine Panerai became an official supplier of precision instruments to the Royal Italian Navy at the end of the 19th century; best known for its DIVING WATCHES. During the 1930s, it developed a large, sturdy watch for use on submarines and, in 1938, produced the Radiomir, a model distinguished by an oversized face, luminous dial, domed case, and extra-long strap (so that it could be worn over uniforms or diving suits). In 1949, Panerai developed the Luminor and afterward began to produce watches for the Egyptian navy. In the 1990s, the company developed watches for actor Sylvester Stallone and, during the early 21st century, enjoyed a revived vogue when Panerai watches began to appear on the wrists of celebrities like Arnold Schwarzenegger and RALPH LAUREN.

paniolo The COWBOY of Hawaii. His claim to being the first American cowboy is based on the 1793 arrival of long-horned cattle in Hawaii, followed by the decade-later arrival of horses. In the early 1830s, *vacqueros* arrived in the islands to pass on their cattle-working skills, and the paniolo was established by about 1840. Up until World War II, the paniolo would drive herds from the ranches into the sea (sometimes losing a few to sharks), where the cattle would be hoisted aboard export ships.

The traditional paniolo costume includes "lauhala papale" (hat), often decorated with flowers or other greenery, lei (garland of flowers), PALAKA or ALOHA SHIRT, and BLUE JEANS.

panne velvet A VELVET in which the nap is all pressed in a single direction, so that instead of appearing matte like most velvet, it has a glossy or liquid appearance. Although it enjoyed a brief vogue in the late 1960s and 1970s, panne velvet is usually considered too drapey and fluid for menswear, and appears more often in women's wear.

pantaloons Connotes the very form-fitting pants, resembling modern leggings or stretch pants, that became popular from the 1790s.

Unlike BREECHES, which preceded them as the favored pants of the middle and upper classes, pantaloons were full-length. Unlike TROUSERS, then the full-length pants of the working man, they were intended to show off a shapely male leg, and, although a well-fit pair looked as though it might be made from modern stretch fabric, they were ingeniously constructed of knits or wovens. Keeping them from wrinkling and bagging was something of a fetish for well-dressed men (e.g., BEAU BRUMMELL), whose strategies for achieving that line ranged from tight ankle closures to STIRRUP PANTS with straps that fit under the sole of the boot or shoe. However, as the 19th century progressed, pantaloons became fuller and less revealing and PANTS became a more generic term.

pant Jargon for a pair of pants. (A FASHIONISTA would say a suit is made up of a jacket and a pant.) Rather than referring to a single pant leg, it is part of a speech pattern that tends to turn plurals singular: A similar usage is "trouser" for "trousers."

pants Derived from PANTALOONS (which had a very specific connotation in the days of dandies like BEAU BRUMMELL), "pants" has long since become a generic term. In industry usage the term encompasses most bottoms except for JEANS and shorts. In contemporary jargon, SLACKS connotes pants that are slightly dressier and TROUSERS connotes the very dressiest pants—especially those worn with tailored clothing and FORMALWEAR.

Pantone   A company based in Carlstadt, New Jersey, best known for its system of naming, standardizing, and matching colors—invented by Lawrence Herbert a year after he bought the company in 1963. Used by graphic designers, Pantone "color chips" provided clients with exact percentages of the black, cyan, magenta, and yellows inks needed to achieve a tone, and were also used by those in the fashion industry who needed a standard color reference to supply to various factories and freelancers.

paper   May refer to either fiber, yarn, or the fabric made from it. Most of the paper that finds its way into menswear is necessarily sturdier and more pliable than the product used for books and stationery, and it is most often derived from a CELLULOSIC source, such as ABACA. Its most common use in contemporary menswear is as a material for certain styles of COWBOY HATS, where it is known as SHANTUNG PANAMA.

paper-bag waist   A style of waistband for pants, popular during the 1980s, so called because it resembled a paper bag closed by a tight rubber band, with material extending up above the belt. Almost always a part of relatively baggy pants. Although the "paper-bag waist" sometimes extends above the belt by an inch or more, it is different from the earlier HOLLYWOOD WAIST, in which the material extending above the waist tends to be flat and not gathered.

parachute cloth   Lightweight woven cloth, usually silk, resembling the silk textiles used for old-fashioned parachutes. As might be expected, parachute cloth tends to catch air easily and is often used when a designer wants to enhance movement or create a ballooning effect.

pareo *or* **pareu**   A seamless rectangle of colorful and/or patterned cloth, which wraps around the body and remains in place by means of tying or tucking. The term comes from Tahiti and was originally used to describe the wraps worn by women; in contemporary usage, it applies to the wrap skirts used by both genders. It differs from a SARONG only in the design on the cloth: If the design is Tahitian, the cloth should be described as a pareo; if the design is BATIK or some other pattern traditionally associated with Indonesia, the cloth should be described as a sarong.

parka   A type of hooded outdoor jacket associated with cold weather and sports, particularly skiing and hiking. Adapted from Inuit dress, the contemporary parka has a full hood and long sleeves, and differs from an ANORAK (a pullover style) by having a front that can completely open from neck to hem—usually with a zipper.

In previous decades, the parka was often longer than it is in contemporary use (e.g., the parkas worn by the MODS during the 1950s and 1960s). In references older still (e.g., in descriptions of authentic Inuit parkas), the word may also be used to describe pullover styles made without a front closure.

parti-colored   Multicolored, especially to describe a garment divided into large blocks

Pantone Color System

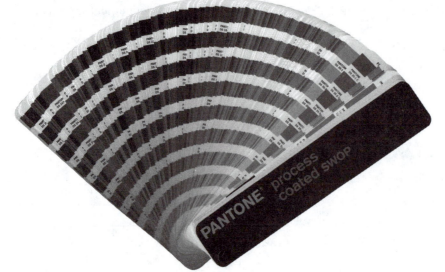

or "parts" of color. Used most often to describe apparel of the Middle Ages and Renaissance or fashions inspired by those eras.

pasguard   In ARMOR worn for jousting, the piece that protects the left elbow.

passementerie   A broad term for trimmings (e.g., cording, braid, tassels, decorative knots); in contemporary usage, the word is now more common in the home-decorating market.

paste   A mostly archaic term for fake jewels, applicable to both men's and women's jewelry and accessories. (For example, a fabulous pair of 18th-century shoe buckles might be dismissively referred to as paste, although they appear to be set with diamonds.) Much like contemporary costume jewelry, the best paste could be beautifully designed, elaborately made, and relatively expensive.

paste resist   Jargon for a method of applying dye to woven fabric. For example: In the Japanese dyeing technique called katazome, a paste made of rice is applied to the fabric with the aid of a stencil; afterward, the dye soaks in wherever the fabric is not protected by the paste.

Patagonia   The Ventura, California-based activewear manufacturing, catalog, and retail company founded by climber and adventurer Yvon Chouinard in 1972 as an outgrowth of Chouinard Equipment, which supplied hardware for rock climbers.

From its beginning, Patagonia gear reflected a sensibility that was Californian, colorful, and more offbeat

than the apparel customarily worn for outdoor sports, which tended to be tweedy and imitative of English hunting and fishing gear. The company also invested heavily in fabric development: During the late 1970s, it popularized the use of Malden Mills-made synthetic pile in the outdoors (later trademarked as Synchilla) and, in 1980, the use of BASE LAYERS made first of POLYPROPYLENE and then, in 1985, of a proprietary POLYESTER it called Capilene.

Patagonia was also the first company of its size to consistently emphasize environmental activism (e.g., printing its catalogs on recycled paper beginning in the 1980s and doing collections of Synchilla made from recycled soda bottles in the 1990s). In 2005, it received a National Design Award from the Smithsonian's Cooper-Hewitt Museum.

patch pocket   A pocket created by sewing an extra piece of material on the outside of the garment (as opposed to inserting the pocket in a slit or seam so that only the pocket opening is visible); almost always made of the same fabric as the main body of the garment. Generally, the term is reserved for flat pockets without bellows or pleats. For example, it would not be applied to CARGO POCKETS even though they appear on the exterior of the garment.

In extremely traditional men's tailoring, patch pockets often imply a slight informality, appearing on sports jackets and similar styles rather than BUSINESS SUITS or CERIMONIA.

patches   Artificial beauty marks applied to the face primarily by women, but also by men; attached with gum or a similarly sticky substance. The practice of wearing patches stretched all the way back to ancient Rome but was most prevalent among upper classes of

Patagonia

France and England in the 17th and 18th centuries—and was obsolete by the 19th century.

Mostly black in color, patches could be either simply geometric or elaborately ornamental in shape and might be made of either fabric (such as taffeta or velvet) or leather. Some writers mistakenly call the custom a way of hiding pockmarks or other skin flaws, but, although a few were undoubtedly advantageously placed, most applications were done for fashion and not concealment. During their heyday, an entire language of shape and placement evolved, and boxes to hold patches were executed by leading jewelers.

patchwork   A fabric purposely made up of smaller pieces of two or more fabrics, much in the manner of a patchwork quilt (as opposed to a "patched fabric," which would be a single material sporting surface patches for purposes of either repair or decoration). In contemporary use, patchwork MADRAS often features in PREPPY-style pants or sports jackets.

patent leather   Leather cured so that it has a highly glossed, impermeable finish. In menswear, it is has been used most often for evening shoes, e.g., PUMPS.

patio prints   Jargon for large-scale prints, usually featuring tropical foliage, that look as though they would be appropriate for wallpaper or patio furniture. Used particularly in the 1940s and 1950s for the type of casual shirt usually referred to as a HAWAIIAN SHIRT.

pattens   A sort of predecessor to platform shoes, worn from the Middle Ages onward, chiefly as OVERSHOES to elevate feet out of the muck and mud. A typical men's patten might have a thick wooden sole and attach to the foot with leather straps that resemble a modern SANDAL.

pattern maker   The person, especially in readymade apparel, who interprets the designer's sketch and creates a pattern from which the fabric will be cut; usually not the same person who designs the garment or eventually sews it.

pauldron   In plate ARMOR, a large piece that covers the shoulders, especially the gap where the arm meets the body.

Paul Stuart   The specialty store founded in New York in 1938 by Ralph Ostrove, who named it after his son Paul Stuart Ostrove. Known for traditional tailoring, occasionally quirky furnishings, and a general sense of whimsy symbolized by its "man on the fence" logo; the flagship store on Madison Avenue was followed by a branch on Michigan Avenue in Chicago and numerous licensed stores in Japan.

After World War II, Ralph Ostrove asked his son-in-law Clifford Grodd (a war hero who had married daughter Barbara Ostrove) to buy out his original partner. Thereafter, the business remained a family concern and Grodd was named president, although Paul remained involved in his namesake store until his death in 2004.

Despite being located on the stretch of Madison Avenue famous for stores selling the IVY LEAGUE LOOK in menswear (BROOKS BROTHERS is on the same block), Paul Stuart began to depart from the shapeless SACK SUIT in favor of a trimmer model. By the end of the 20th century, it was most strongly associated with an English-accented two-button suit with side vents and a TICKET POCKET. (Due to Grodd's personal distaste for belts, that suit was always made available with pants that sported adjustable side cinches instead of belt loops.) During the 1990s, the New York store was particularly noted for the fanciful window displays designed by then-creative director Tom Beebe.

PCR fleece   "Post consumer recycled" FLEECE, a PILE fabric manufactured from reused plastics, often including old soda bottles.

peachskin   A traditional woven fabric with a matte, slightly fuzzy surface that obscures the weave so that the material resembles a fresh peach. Lighter and usually made of finer yarn than a MOLESKIN.

peacoat   A style of double-breasted outerwear originally worn by sailors. The classic of the type is a hip-length, double-breasted style, with a large collar and wide lapels that fastened with six or eight large, flat buttons etched with an anchor emblem. It has two symmetrical handwarmer pockets placed as vertical slits on either side of its front, and is made of coarse, heavy wool in navy blue. The "pea" in its name is an English corruption of "pij," the Dutch name for the type of rough cloth associated with the original jackets. Synonyms: BRIDGE COAT (especially for a slightly longer version); pea jacket; pilot coat; REEFER (especially for a more tailored style that might be worn by a naval officer).

Peacock Alley   A 1960s-era slang reference to London's CARNABY STREET.

Peacock Revolution   A phrase coined to refer to the sea change in men's fashion during the 1960s; used especially in reference to London and especially to the men's fashions originating on CARNABY STREET and KING'S ROAD. Meant to imply that menswear went from conservative and drab to trendy and gaudy.

peak   The BILL of a cap, particularly in British usage. Synonyms: BEAK; bill; VISOR.

peak lapels   Refers to the style of jacket lapel that flares, or "peaks," upward, so that the NOTCH between LAPEL and COLLAR is narrowed (or, in some cases, virtually nonexistent); a common feature of—but not limited to—the styling of DOUBLE-BREASTED jackets.

pearl buttons   An abbreviated reference to MOTHER-OF-PEARL BUTTONS.

peascod   A distinctive, late-16th-century style of DOUBLET that purposely gave its wearer the appearance of a pot belly. A peascod concentrated its padding low over the abdomen and sloped from above the natural waistline in back to a defined point just over the genitals. Supposedly this silhouette recalled a peacock and gave rise to the name.

peccary   A type of LEATHER made from the hide of a wild pig. Favored for uses like gloves, in part because of its distinctive GRAIN that groups the bristle holes in threes.

Pee-wee Herman   A cartoonlike character developed in 1977 by actor Paul Reubens (b. 1952), who first played

Pee-wee Herman

Pee-wee onstage before eventually launching him on television (*The Pee-wee Herman Show* in 1981), the movies (especially 1985's *Pee-wee's Big Adventure* and 1988's *Big Top Pee-wee*), and Saturday morning children's television (*Pee-wee's Playhouse* on CBS, from 1986 to 1991). Pee-wee always wore an old-fashioned gray suit that was too small for him, a short-sleeved white shirt, and a skinny, red, clip-on bow tie. His voice was high, his laugh was obnoxious, his name was embarrassing, and his hair was unfashionably slicked back from a 1950s-style side part. In the early 21st century, when NERD chic appeared on designer runways and THOM BROWNE began receiving design awards, the Pee-wee character was widely cited by fashion writers as a style icon.

pegged pants   Pants that narrow abruptly at the bottom are said to be pegged, especially when the foot opening is so narrow that it becomes difficult to put them on. For a period in the mid-19th century and again before World War I, PEG TOPS were considered extremely trendy, although, perversely, they were narrow at their bottoms and not their tops (which were often extremely full at the waist and seat). A few decades later, they surfaced again in the ZOOT SUIT. Their opposite numbers would be FLARES or BELL-BOTTOMS.

peg tops   PEGGED PANTS.

pegs   1. A reference to PEGGED PANTS. 2. Tiny, tapered pieces—pegs—of hardwood used to reinforce the soles of workboots, COWBOY BOOTS, and the like. The pegs are pounded into the shank under the arch (usually in a row on either side), and the telltale holes are usually visible from the underside of the boot.

Pelham   EDWARD BULWER-LYTTON's 1828 novel, subtitled *The Adventures of a Gentleman*, which contemporaries called a manual for dandies because its narrator, dandy Henry Pelham, who was supposedly a fictionalized BEAU BRUMMELL, included an entire chapter on details of dress and frequently cited real people and places in London (such as tailor George Stultz), along with admonitions such as "Always remember that you dress to fascinate others, not yourself."

pen knife   A small, portable knife, with a name supposedly derived from its use sharpening pen quills. Today connotes a knife that is smaller and less complicated than many POCKET KNIVES. All pen knives are pocket knives, but not all pocket knives are pen knives.

pen pocket   A small pocket (usually less than an inch wide) in the lining of a man's jacket to accommodate a pen, usually on the left side.

pencil mustache   A style of very thin MUSTACHE, usually with a break in the center where the philtrum is shaved.

pencil stripe   A pattern with a stripe that is roughly the width of a carpenter's pencil mark (about $\frac{1}{16}$ of an inch). Wider than a PINSTRIPE, but narrower than a BENGAL STRIPE. Usually refers to shirt fabrics, rarely describes suit fabric.

Penguin   A brand of golfwear that uses a penguin logo, especially popular in the 1970s and revived in the early 21st century; produced by MUNSINGWEAR.

penny loafers   Refers to an informal style of leather slip-on shoe that featured a strap across the instep with a slit (into which a penny was sometimes inserted). Associated with collegiate wear from the 1930s through the early 1960s, and also with PREPPY style (e.g., the BASS WEEJUN).

perc   Slang for perchloroethylene, a common DRY CLEANING solvent.

perforated leather   In apparel, leather is usually perforated to create lightness and breathability. In shoemaking, it may be done for the same reasons or as part of the design (e.g., the perforations traditional to BROGUES).

performance fabrics and finishes   Jargon for fabrics that perform some special function (e.g., wicking perspiration away from the body) or that have some other added value (e.g., cotton that has been treated to remain wrinkle-free). Used from the late 20th century onward.

permanent press   Refers to fabrics, usually made of polyester or a blend that prominently features polyester, which are chemically treated (usually with methanol) to resist wrinkling.

perrotine print   A method of mechanically printing fabric invented by Louis-Jérome Perrot in France in 1834. Due to the restrictions of the technique, the design repeats had to remain quite small, no more than four colors could be accommodated, and the main figure still had to be a hand-carved wooden block or its equivalent.

Persian lamb   A synonym for ASTRAKHAN, the pelt of a newly born lamb; used more often as a description in the women's market.

petasos   A wide-brimmed, soft, low-crowned hat that tied under the chin. Worn by the ancient Greeks, it was later adopted by the Romans.

Peter the Great   Born in 1672, Peter is best known as the czar who forcibly Westernized Russia and founded the city of St. Petersburg.

Having toured Europe, Peter returned to Moscow in 1698 and promptly inveighed against the wearing of KAFTANS, encouraged the cutting of beards, and fostered the wearing of Western styles. Very tall (6 feet, 7 inches), he enjoyed wearing Western European military uniform whenever possible. In 1702, he commanded his court to follow French styles for their clothes and ornament. In 1705, he formally banned beards too. He died in 1725, and his wardrobe is now in the collection of the Hermitage in St. Petersburg, the city he created and made his capital.

petticoat breeches   BREECHES cut so full and so wide that they almost appear to be a skirt; similar in appearance to culottes later worn by women. A style popular in Western Europe during the third quarter of the 17th century, including the style known as RHINEGRAVES.

Peter the Great

Phat Farm   The successful line of HIP-HOP-inspired apparel, founded by entrepreneur Russell Simmons, cofounder of Def Jam Recordings, in 1992. In 2004, Simmons sold both Phat Farm and its offshoot brands (including the Baby Phat brand for women) to Kellwood Industries in a deal exceeding $140 million plus percentages.

Philbin, Regis   A television personality who became an unlikely trendsetter at age 68 when, in 2000, he gave his name to the widely copied fashion of wearing an exactly matching dress shirt and tie. During that year, Philbin, who was the host of a New York City-based late morning talk show called *Live! With Regis and Kathie Lee* and the three-times-a-week primetime game show called *Who Wants to Be a Millionaire?* almost always appeared to be dressed in shirts and ties of the same color.

That same year, manufacturer PHILLIPS-VAN HEUSEN launched a line of shirts and ties called Regis by Van Heusen and Philbin was honored at the Annual Neckwear Association of America Achievement Awards. Despite being widely reviled by the fashion elite, Philbin was lauded by the NAA's president as "the sultan of satin, the duke of deep tones." Within a year or two, the trend petered out and Philbin himself moved on to more traditional looks.

Phillips-Van Heusen   The corporation that officially became known as Phillips-Van Heusen in 1957 began in the early 20th century from the partnership of John M. Van Heusen (a native of Holland who had invented a new type of FOLD-OVER COLLAR) and Seymour Phillips (an American whose Polish immigrant father Moses had started peddling flannel shirts in Pottsville, Pennsylvania, in 1881 and, by 1907, built that business into the Phillips-Jones Corporation). Phillips acquired the patent for Van Heusen's collar in 1919 and began a heavy marketing push in the 1920s, thereby contributing to the demise of the previously fashionable DETACHABLE COLLAR. During the 1950s, it became renowned for dress shirt advertisements featuring the likes of Burt Lancaster, Anthony Quinn, and Ronald Reagan.

By the 21st century, P-VH, as it was popularly known, touted itself as the world's leading maker of dress shirts and had acquired the rights to one-time rival ARROW. In addition to its many licenses, P-VH had also become the parent company of brands including BASS, CALVIN KLEIN, and IZOD.

pick   Jargon for an individual WEFT yarn (the yarn that runs side to side on the loom). Its counterpart, the WARP yarn that runs vertically, would be an END. For example: When industry veterans are describing the construction and density of a fabric they might say "60 by 50," indicating the number of ends followed by the number of picks in a single inch of that fabric.

piccadilly   A style of large, starched standing collar popular during Elizabethan times; through its association with Elizabethan tailor ROBERT BAKER, it became the origin of the name for the London neighborhood known as Piccadilly.

Piccadilly weepers   A style of long, flowing SIDEBURNS that essentially resembled a flowing beard with the chin clean-shaven. In 19th-century England, virtually a synonym for the style of full SIDEWHISKERS known as NEWGATE KNOCKERS or DUNDREARIES.

piece-dyed   Dyeing the fabric after it has been knit or woven (e.g., GRAY GOODS) instead of dyeing the yarn before it goes into the fabric.

piece goods   Jargon that usually refers to a BOLT of cloth (i.e., "goods" sold by the length or "piece"). Traditionally, a piece runs around 60 yards. Synonym: YARD GOODS.

pied de coq   French or continental European usage for a particularly large or oversized version of the check pattern that Americans and Englishmen call a HOUNDSTOOTH. Literally, a "rooster's foot." In its smaller version, the same pattern would be referred to as a *PIED DE POULE* or "hen's foot."

pied de poule   French or continental European usage for the check pattern that Americans and Englishmen call HOUNDSTOOTH. Literally, a "hen's foot." In an oversized version, the same pattern would be referred to as a *PIED DE COQ,* or "rooster's foot."

pigache   A style of extremely long-toed shoe worn in Europe by both men and women during the late Middle Ages. Synonyms: crackowes; poulaines.

pigment-dyed   A method of dyeing fabric so that it purposely fades the more often it is washed. Popular, at various times, for JEANS and other materials used in bottoms.

pigskin   Exactly as it sounds, leather made from the skin of pigs. The same pitted surface and toughness that make it ideal for the construction of footballs also make it ideal for use in luggage, hiking boots, and the like. However, because the pitted surface of true pigskin (caused by the bristle holes in the animal's hide) is not particularly prized for the fashion industry, it tends to be seen more often as a SUEDE.

pile   Textile terminology for any fabric with a raised surface with loops that are cut (as in VELVET) or uncut (as in TERRY CLOTH). The difference between a fabric with a pile and a NAP is that a pile fabric is constructed to have a surface that imitates hair, whereas a napped fabric is constructed to be flat and then has any surface fibers raised by brushing or some other method.

pilling   A condition in which little balls of fuzz—"pills"—form on the surface of a fabric due to friction. Fabrics made of loosely spun threads are most prone to pilling, as are certain fibers (such as CASHMERE).

To test whether or not a fabric is predisposed to pilling, take the fabric and vigorously rub it against itself to see if loose fibers form on the surface.

pilot coat   Synonym for PEACOAT.

pima cotton   Depending upon the context, can refer to the plant, the fiber, or the fabric made from it.

Pima is a variety of LONG-STAPLE COTTON, *gossypium barbadense,* named for the Pima tribe of Native Americans who helped foster the variety on a U.S. Department of Agriculture station in Arizona at the beginning of the 20th century. Prior to World War I, known mainly as American-Egyptian cotton. Grown chiefly in the United States and Peru, it is considered a premium cotton (as opposed to the UPLAND COTTON more common in the United States), is prized for its silkiness and strength—and is priced accordingly. Within the category of pima cotton, several subvarieties exist (e.g., the TANGUIS cotton grown in Peru), some with longer fibers than others. In 1954, U.S. producers of pima founded SUPIMA, which is primarily a marketing organization to promote use of the American-grown fiber.

piña Pineapple fiber (and the fabric made from it). Piña is made from the leaves of special pineapples—not the kind found in American or European groceries—that have greens that can grow to a couple of feet.

Its best-known use in menswear is as material for the BARONG, the semisheer and often highly decorated dress shirt in Philippine traditional costume. Piña is also a component of JUSI, a traditional sheer fabric that uses piña as the WARP and SILK, COTTON, or ABACA as the filling.

pinafore An open-back garment with a solid front; worn as a protective garment as part of children's school clothes and play clothes; in the 19th century worn by both sexes, and later associated mainly with girls.

pince-nez A style of EYEGLASS FRAME that literally "pinches the nose." Unlike standard frames, the pince-nez has no side arms and is kept in place only by being perched on the bridge of the nose, sometimes with the help of a spring mechanism. Frequently, the glasses will be attached to a cord, which is usually mounted on the underside of the suit lapel so that the pince-nez can be stored in the jacket's chest pocket when not in use.

Pince-nez: Theodore Roosevelt

pinchback A style used on the back of sport coats that gathers fullness into a belt or MARTINGALE (instead of shaping them with DARTS).

pinchbeck A metal used as imitation gold in jewelry, usually made of a copper and zinc compound; used for watch chains, FOBS, and the like, especially in the 19th century.

pincheck A very small—pin-sized—squared check; appears most often on shirts and ties. Formed by weaving rather than printing. Usually limited to two colors. See color plates.

pindot A pattern of very small—literally pinhead-sized—POLKA DOTS, probably not visible unless you are within 3 feet of the fabric.

pinhead A pattern for woven suit fabric that resembles neatly aligned pindots; similar to, but smaller in scale than a BIRD'S EYE or a NAILHEAD.

pink, pinked, *or* **pinking** The practice of cutting fabric with PINKING SHEARS in order to produce patterned edges—usually in zigzag or scallop pattern—so that the fabric edge is both more decorative and less likely to unravel.

pink coat Slang for the scarlet coats worn by members of a hunt as part of FOXHUNTING ATTIRE; probably derived from a 19th-century tailor of that name. Theories that the term originated because scarlet coats became faded by the sun are certainly not correct and were not started by foxhunters (who never allow a badly faded coat on the field). Thus, the more current and correct term would be "scarlet coat."

Pinking

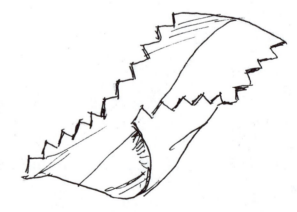

pinking shears   Heavy shears (which differ from scissors by having a longer blade and one handle larger than the other) with patterning on the blade edges that creates a PINKED edge on fabric.

pinstripe   A stripe that is width of a pin (less than 1/16 of an inch). Thinner than both a PENCIL STRIPE and a CHALK STRIPE. Used to describe both shirt and suit fabrics. See color plates.

pinto   A type of leather (or pattern made to imitate it) in two or more irregularly patterned colors. Primarily ponyskin with the hair left on, but sometimes used to describe cowhide (also retaining the hair).

pintucks   Very small, even tucks, equivalent to tiny, stitched-down pleats. In menswear, seen most often on shirtfronts intended to be worn with TUXEDOS.

pinwale   CORDUROY with WALES the width of a pin; usually twelve or more per inch. A pinwale might also be referred to as a NEEDLE-WALE (generally in British usage) or, more generically, as a "fine wale" or "thin wale." Its antitheses would be WIDE-WALE and no-wale.

piping   A narrow strip of BIAS fabric inserted into a seam as edging and/or decoration; when the seam is finished, generally only a small (less than a quarter of a inch) edge of piping is visible.

The piping used in menswear comes in two basic varieties. The first is essentially a piece of cord wrapped inside the bias fabric, which gives a three-dimensional edge used to outline lapel edges, yokes, jacket cuffs, and the like. The second has no cord and creates a small lip of fabric that is pressed flat; it may appear on the inside of a jacket to create a decorative edge between the LINING of a jacket and its FACING.

piqué   1. A woven fabric, usually cotton, distinguished by a subtly waffle-patterned surface; in traditional menswear, appears most often as the BIB FRONT of dress shirts accompanying FORMALWEAR or as the material of the white WAISTCOATS worn with WHITE TIE. Synonym (especially in British usage): MARCELLA.   2. A machine-knit fabric, usually cotton or cotton blend, that displays a subtly waffle-patterned surface, rather than the standard smooth knit used for T-shirts; in traditional menswear, appears most often in POLO SHIRTS like those made by LACOSTE.

pirate costume   1. Both Hollywood and Halloween costume designers tend to stereotype the pirate as wearing either a tattered white blouse or a horizontally striped sailor's jersey, together with a kerchief over his head, an eyepatch, at least one hoop earring, and either breeches or vertically striped pantaloons.

The stereotype for the captain of a pirate ship (e.g., the version of Captain Morgan depicted on that brand's rum bottles) is usually more formal and may include a long and elaborately decorated dress coat, an oversized TRICORNE or BICORNE, and a sword—plus a parrot as companion, accomplice, and accessory. In Halloween costumes and the like, the skull-and-crossbones flag flown by the pirate ship is expropriated to the pirate's clothes (e.g., appearing as a motif on his hat).

Piqué

Pink coats

2. A feature of the NEW ROMANTIC dressing of the late 1970s and early 1980s, which reached its apotheosis in the Pirate collection presented as VIVIENNE WESTWOOD's first runway show in 1981 and by the costumes worn by ADAM ANT during the same period. Although short-lived as a style, the historicism and romanticism of pirate dressing signaled a move away from PUNK.

pita   Cactus fiber. An extremely durable fiber, its best-known contemporary use is in the *cinto piteado*, the decorative belt that is part of the *TRAJE DE CHARRO* worn by MARIACHI musicians.

pith helmet   A lightweight, cloth-covered helmet with a rounded crown and a circular, sloping brim; made from the pith of the Indian spongewood tree. Used in the tropics by nonmilitary personnel to protect themselves from sunstroke. Synonyms: SOLA TOPEE; topee.

Pitti Uomo   A twice-yearly trade event for the menswear industry accompanied by fashion presentations, parties, and shows; held in Florence and timed to complement runway presentations in Milan.

PJs   Slang abbreviation for pajamas.

placement print   Synonym for an ENGINEERED PRINT, because it is "placed" to fall at a particular point on the final garment.

placket   An extra layer of fabric used to support or decorate the opening of a garment (which differs from a FLY, which is intended to cover closures such as a zipper or buttons). In menswear, most often encountered on shirts, which have a front placket down the center front opening and a sleeve placket above the cuff opening.

Traditionally, the placket is an extension of the shirt-front and not a separate piece: It is folded from the body of the garment with a thin INTERFACING added to give it an edge. Inclusion of a placket not only creates a becoming edge, it helps to support the button closure and prevent stretching or other distortion.

placket button   Synonym for the GAUNTLET BUTTON on the PLACKET of a DRESS SHIRT sleeve.

plaid   1. A pattern of two or more colors that is formed by horizontal and vertical lines intersecting at right angles. Originally, all plaids were woven into the fabric, but in the 19th century their distinctive look began to be imitated by printing. Synonym: CHECK.

The word is popularly identified with the style of TARTANS associated with Scotland, although tartan has a more specific meaning: Thus, all tartans are plaid, but not all plaids are tartans. However, the textile industry does use the same terminology for both genres: The pattern of lines is referred to as a SETT, and the background is the BASS.

2. In references to traditional Highland dress, the plaid is considered a garment as well as a pattern: a piece of heavy wool fabric worn as a wrap around the body. Originally the word was used for a length of cloth—from 5 yards on up—that the Highlander would pleat around himself to form an early, unsewn version of the KILT known as a "belted plaid." In contemporary use, it may refer to the length of fabric that is worn draped over the shoulder in conjunction with the pleated, sewn kilt.

plain front   Pants designed without any pleats or gathers in the waistband. Usually, the term is used to describe either sports SLACKS (like those worn for golfing) or pants that are part of a suit. The designation is not used for ACTIVEWEAR or JEANS.

Plain People   Refers to sects such as the AMISH, Hutterites, Old Order Mennonites, Church of the Brethren, and others who, for religious reasons, eschew modern fashion, especially in its decorative and attention-getting forms, and otherwise follow a plain lifestyle.

plain weave   The simplest weave known: One yarn meets another at a right angle, crossing over one row and under the next one. Row by row, the yarns alternate—in and out, up and down—which is why plain weave is also called ONE UP, ONE DOWN. Variations are made by altering the weight or color of the yarns, but not the simple way in which they interlace. Plain weaves still account for the majority of woven fabrics produced today, including most printed materials. Synonym: plain cloth (especially for woolens and/or suitweight fabrics).

plant fiber   See VEGETABLE FIBER.

plantation tie *or* **planter's tie**   The loop of dark ribbon worn in place of a NECKTIE, BOW TIE, or BOLO; associated with the southern United States. Unlike the bolo (which is a cord), the plantation tie is a ribbonlike material that is tied in a bow. Most familiar from images of Mark Twain and chicken entrepreneur Colonel Harland Sanders.

planter's hat   A style derived from the wide-brimmed, low-crowned hats favored by 19th-century Caribbean planters who needed to shield themselves from the sun, the planter's hat had become an established style at U.S. beaches and resorts by the 1930s and continued to be worn with sportswear and resortwear during the follow-

ing decades. By tradition, it was made from very light, almost white straw and featured either a black band or a colorful, pleated band (a PUGGAREE). Its uniform brim sported a very slight dip in the front and back so that the sides flared at a slightly rakish angle flattering to most faces. Synonym: JIPAJAPA.

pleat front   Jargon for pants with one or more pleats on either side of the fly. At various times in the history of menswear, pleated pants have been considered very fashionable (e.g., when FRED ASTAIRE sported them in the 1930s) or the complete opposite (e.g., when they were widely reviled by trendsetters in the 1990s). The opposite designation is PLAIN FRONT.

pleather   Fake leather. Plastic + leather = pleather. First used in the 1980s.

plimsoll   British reference for a traditional-looking SNEAKER, usually with lace-up ties and a rubber sole. In the first decade of the 20th century, the shipping term began to be used for sneakers because the join between the sole and upper supposedly resembled the Plimsoll mark (the loading line) on a ship's hull.

plissé   1. A simulation of SEERSUCKER in which the puckering and vertical stripes are created by chemicals instead of weaving. Plissé may look indistinguishable from seersucker—especially when it is brand-new—but the puckering effect is often changed by repeated laun-

Plissé

dering. Used most often as a shirt fabric.   2. In European-styled textiles, a simulation of seersucker in which the puckering and vertical stripes are created by the additional of extra threads, sometimes creating a ridge effect—which is permanent and not changed by laundering.

plus fours   A style of baggy pants cropped and gathered to just below the knee; worn for sports such as stalking and shooting; so-called because they extend 4 inches beyond the knee, hence the "plus." The style was especially favored by both EDWARD VII and grandson EDWARD VIII during their days as Princes of Wales. Synonym: KNICKERBOCKERS.

plus twenties   A style of full-length, very baggy pants used for hunting and shooting; literally an extension of PLUS FOURS—a nickname used by the set around EDWARD VIII when he was Prince of Wales. Synonym: STALKING TROUSERS.

plush   A woven PILE fabric that resembles VELVET but has a longer, more luxuriant—"plusher"—nap.

ply   1. Refers to the number of strands twisted together to make a single yarn. An "unplied" yarn has no twist (either because it has not been spun or because it is made by extrusion). A number is often assigned to ply to indicate the thickness of the resulting yarn or fabric: The higher the number, the thicker the yarn.   2. Refers, especially in traditional tailoring, to layers of fabric. For instance, a tailor may talk about building a SLEEVE HEADER out of two plies of fabric.

poacher's jacket   A piece of long-sleeved, collared outerwear usually worn for hunting or fishing, some-times used for workwear. The classic poacher's jacket style has big pockets on the sides and a huge (sometimes concealed) pocket across the back that is literally big enough to tote a dead duck—hence the "poacher" designation.

poacher's pockets   Very large, concealed pockets on a man's jacket or coat (usually big enough to hide a rabbit or duck).

pocketing   Fabric used to construct the interior of pockets (e.g., of pants or slit pockets in a jacket or coat). Never visible when the garment is being worn. SILESIA is sometimes used as a synonym for the bleached or undyed, mostly cotton fabric used.

pocket knife   A small knife that folds in on itself for safety and portability, used more often as a hand tool as opposed to an eating utensil. For that reason, the pocket knife often sports additions like corkscrews, nail files, and the like. The brands best known in America are probably the Genuine SWISS ARMY KNIFE manufactured by Wenger and the Original Swiss Army Knife made by Victorinox (which are both owned by the same company).

pocket protector   A flexible plastic or vinyl pouch placed inside the front pocket of a man's dress or sports shirt so that whatever pens or pencils he stores in that pocket will not stain his clothes. Pocket protectors were often used by engineers, sometimes carried advertising, and were thoroughly scorned by fashionable men.

pocket square   A fashionable rather than functional piece of fabric, usually between 12 and 18 inches square, worn in the breast pocket of a jacket as an accent.

Pocket squares were originally handkerchiefs, but today are purely decorative. Most often made of silk, pocket squares may match the shirt or tie, or be of contrasting material. White pocket squares, which hark back to their original use as handkerchiefs, are customarily made of very finely woven cotton or linen but, like their silk counterparts, usually sport ROLLED HEMS.

Several styles of folding pocket squares coexist. The most common are:

• The puffed style, in which roughly an inch of fabric curves beyond the edge of the pocket and no edges are visible; often favored as the easiest, since the square is simply stuffed into the pocket with its points down.

• The rectangular folded style (also known as the TV FOLD), in which roughly an inch of fabric is displayed above the pocket in a neat, symmetrical fold.

• The aligned four-point fold, in which all four points are visible in a neat row.

• The flamboyant three-point fold (also known as the peak fold), which calls for creasing the square so that its center is aimed downward inside the breast pocket and its three points extend about 2 inches above the pocket's edge.

poet's shirt   Refers to a style of long-sleeved shirt that is unfitted and blousey through the body and features full sleeves gathered into a tight (sometimes ruffled) cuff. Associated with romantics, pirates, and other iconoclasts, such a shirt may or may not be collarless, but it is usually in a pullover, rather than a button-front, construction.

point *or* **pointed blankets**   Usually refers to the distinctive blankets made by the Hudson's Bay Company, beginning in 1780, which were traded to Native Americans, who wore them as cold-weather wraps, and used by hunters, trappers, and soldiers as the basis of coat styles like the CAPOTE and the MACKINAW.

The word "point" derives from the French *empointer* and is an indirect reference to their size, not to the number of stripes on the blanket or their cost.

point to point   Nothing to do with the horse race of the same name. In tailors'

How to fold a pocket square

jargon, the phrase refers to the measurement of a man's shoulders, from the point of one shoulder to the other.

poke collar   A type of high, stiff standing collar (somewhat resembling an extra-high MANDARIN collar or CLERICAL COLLAR); usually reserved for evening wear and associated with very early 20th-century styles.

Polarfleece   A trademark of Lawrence, Massachusetts-based Malden Mills for the POLYESTER PILE fabric it invented in the 1970s, which was created to possess the thermal properties of wool without absorbing water or shrinking. Because Polarfleece is machine-washable and abrasion-resistant, it was widely adopted from the 1980s onward for outdoor and technical apparel. It can also be created from recycled polyester and/or from recycled materials like soda bottles.

Polarfleece comes in a range of standard weights. For example: 100 is 9.5 ounces per yard; 200 is 12.5 ounces per yard; and 300 is 16 ounces per yard. Other companies who produce polyester fleece follow a similar grading system for their fabrics, and may refer to their products as "polar fleece" in an attempt to get around trademark infringement. "Polartec" and "Polartek" are related and subsequent trademarks of Malden Mills.

poleyn   In ARMOR, the piece that protects the knee.

polka dots   A symmetrical pattern of circles in a solid color against a solid ground. In menswear, the pattern shows up most often in silks and similar materials used for ties, dressing gowns, and pajamas. Its name derives from a mid-19th-century craze for polka dancing.

polo   In lowercase, jargon for POLO SHIRT.

Polo   In uppercase, refers to the brand created by RALPH LAUREN in 1967; usually written as Polo/Ralph Lauren. Subsequent spinoffs and sub-brands include Polo Golf, Polo Jeans, Polo Roughwear, and Polo University.

polo coat   Refers to a casual and loose-fitting style of coat, originally made of CAMEL'S HAIR and worn by polo players in between chukkers. Early polo coats were often belted wrap styles, but the cut that became most identified with the term was the style of loosely fitted, double-breasted coat with patch pockets that BROOKS BROTHERS and other retailers began to offer in the United States before World War I. During the late 1920s, it became identified with prep schools and collegiate style, and later passed into the PREPPY canon. Synonyms: CAMEL'S HAIR COAT; WAIT COAT.

polo collar   1. In contemporary American usage, a polo collar usually indicates the kind of short, ribbed collar on a jersey shirt with a short, buttoned placket front—of the kind worn by polo players, tennis players, or many golfers. It is, in other words, the collar on a POLO SHIRT. 2. In Britain, a polo collar is what Americans call a TURTLENECK; more often called polo neck. 3. At BROOKS BROTHERS and especially in pre-World War II usage, a polo collar is a button-down collar, a reference to that style's origin among polo players in the late 19th century.

polo shirt   A short-sleeved, jersey shirt worn for sports or casual wear. It has a short, buttoned placket that extends no lower than the sternum and often features some kind of team or designer insignia over the chest on the upper left side over the heart.

Frequently worn for tennis, especially after its popularization by LACOSTE.

polo sweater   A TURTLENECK, usually British usage.

polyamide   NYLON, usually European usage.

polyester   A generic reference to man-made, petrochemically based fiber invented in 1941 in Great Britain (although DuPont chemist Wallace Carothers had almost developed it in the preceding decade, before concentrating his attentions on NYLON); it first appeared as TERYLENE and next, in the United States, as DACRON. Large-scale production began in the mid-1950s, and in the following decades, supply sometimes outstripped demand, contributing to its reputation for cheapness. By 1970, it was the world's most popular synthetic fiber—and virtually a synonym for bad taste (e.g., John Waters' 1981 movie *Polyester*).

Later in the 1980s, its reputation was somewhat rehabilitated by the development of expensive MICROFIBERS, chiefly in Japan. By the end of the century, textile companies had begun to routinely exploit polyester's ability to be engineered with a variety of performance properties (such as WICKING).

polynosic   A type of RAYON, known as "the expensive rayon" because its fiber was roughly twice as long as conventional rayon. Compared to other types of rayon, polynosic was easier to MERCERIZE, had more abrasion resistance, and allowed less shape distortion. For those reasons, it was popular for pants during the late 20th century; for environmental reasons, it is no longer produced.

polypro   Short for POLYPROPYLENE.

polypropylene   Petrochemically based, this man-made polymer was simultaneously "invented" in the 1950s in several laboratories and became one of the most popular multipurpose plastics. In apparel, it was particularly popular for its WICKING properties, strength, and resilience. Beginning in the 1980s, it began to replace SILK and COTTON as a fabric for BASE LAYERS (and, in turn, ceded some of its popularity to MERINO in the early 21st century).

pomade   1. A waxy hair dressing, in solid rather than liquid form; usually packaged in a jar or can. Older pomades tended to be highly scented, whereas contemporary products rarely are.   2. A highly scented, solid unguent.

pomatum   Old-fashioned synonym for POMADE.

pompadour   A hairstyle distinguished by flamboyant height in the front; most often with a forelock grown long and greased into a dramatic pouf that is swept straight up from the forehead; misnamed after a mistress of Louis XV (an 18th-century marquise who actually wore her hair in a small, neat style close to the skull). Usually coupled with hair combed into a DUCK'S ASS in back, associated with a variety of rebel subcultures, including GREASERS, PACHUCOS, ROCKERS, TEDDY BOYS, and ZOOT SUITERS. Synonym: QUIFF.

poncho   A simple, untailored piece of outerwear, derived from the garment worn in the Andes mountains of South America. The prototypical poncho is a blanket with a slit or hole in its center so the head can poke through; it is roughly hip-length, worn with one point forward covering the crotch, one point over each hand, and one point covering the buttocks.

poncy   Originally the adjective described, in British usage, someone who dressed like a pimp. In contemporary use, it has evolved to describe someone effete and overdressed.

pongee   1. A plainly woven—often roughly woven—SILK. Pongee, which is used for sports jackets and suits associated with hot-weather wear, is often left undyed, tends to contain slubs and nubs, and looks homemade (the English word derives from Chinese meaning "woven at home").   2. An imitation of that silk made from another fiber or blend.   3. A cotton fabric used for pajamas and the like; made of regular, evenly spun yarn and done on an industrial loom, its only similarity to the more familiar silk fabric is that the WEFT (horizontal) yarn is usually much thicker than the WARP (vertical).

ponyskin   Usually refers to hide or leather processed so that the hair is left on; a generic term that may refer to the hide of either ponies or horses. Like its bovine equivalent, COWSKIN (a term used most often to refer to a skin with the hair left intact), ponyskin is often prized for its pattern. Its smooth-textured, tanned, and hairless counterpart would usually be referred to as HORSEHIDE.

Poole   See HENRY POOLE.

poorboy   A style of SWEATER distinguished by thick, simple ribbing that covers the entire garment, instead of appearing only on the sweater's edges. At the beginning of the 20th century, these sweaters were loose-fitting and not especially fashionable. When poorboys were revived

in the 1960s, they were close-fitting, clingy, and often paired with BELL-BOTTOMS.

poplin   A plain, woven fabric that has WEFT or FILL yarns that are thicker than its WARP yarns. In menswear, it is often made of cotton and used primarily for dress shirts.

popover   A casual top, long- or short-sleeved, that "pops over" the head and is made from a woven instead of a knit material. As worn in the 1950s and 1960s, popovers were commonly short-sleeved, had a short button placket, and looked like a woven version of a POLO SHIRT. Later versions sometimes had crewnecks or V-necks. Reference to the same garment with a knit construction would be a PULLOVER.

porkpie   A style of hat with a round, flattened top, dished crown, and medium-length, softened brim; supposedly resembling a meat pie. A sportswear style; from the mid-20th century onward associated with jazz musicians.

Portobello Road   A traditional market area of London, known for both arcades full of antique dealers (near Notting Hill Gate) and outdoor stalls featuring start-up designers, cheap street fashion, and second-hand clothes (near Ladbroke Grove). Mention of a designer or stylist frequenting Portobello Road implies someone who collects vintage clothes.

pourpoint   Although some costume historians use the word as a synonym for the DOUBLET, others use it to refer to a short garment for the upper torso that preceded the doublet in the late Middle Ages in Western Europe: specifically to a style of padded shirt that sported laces (points) on the bottom, so that a man could attach his hose to the garment. Or going even farther back, to a garment related to the GAMBESON worn as or with armor and facilitating the attachment of defensive pieces. Synonym: jupon.

Prada   The brand that began in 1913 when Mario Prada, who had started making shoes and belts in the village of Levanelle, opened his luxury leathergoods store in the Galleria Vittorio Emanuele II in Milan. Under the design direction of Mario's granddaughter MIUCCIA PRADA (see following entry) and the business direction of her husband, Patrizio Bertelli, the marque would become an internationally celebrated lifestyle brand and fashion conglomerate.

Prada's first success came after World War I, when it won the custom of the local royalty for luggage executed in exotic leathers. However, the firm remained small until 1978, when Miuccia's mother persuaded her to abandon her studies as a mime and take over the store. Partially at the urging of Bertelli, a leather factory owner whom Prada had met in 1978 and married in 1987, she began expanding the line in the 1980s, changing its distribution and adding shoes in 1982. In 1985, she had her first big international hit: a line combining black leather with black nylon that went on to become a staple of the business. After gradually adding apparel items to its mix, Prada next launched a full line of women's ready-to-wear, another success, in 1989. In 1992, she launched menswear (for 1993 sales) and a secondary line named MIU MIU for women (adding Miu Miu menswear in 1998 for the 1999 selling season). In 1997, she added Prada Sport, a sports and activewear brand distinguished by its red rubber label, footwear with molded soles, and signature use of gray nylon.

By 2004, when former *Vogue* editorial assistant Lauren Weisberger wrote a roman à clef called *The Devil Wears Prada*, the brand had become a one-word synonym for expensive and much-coveted insider fashion.

Throughout the 1990s, Prada maintained an annual growth rate well into the double digits, emphasizing vertical integration by retaining shares or outright ownership in many of its manufacturing facilities. At a time when designer brands were being gobbled up by luxury conglomerates like LVMH, Prada went on the offensive and became the buyer instead of the bought. Chief Executive Officer Bertelli acquired all or part of Helmut Lang, Jil Sander, Azzedine Alaia, Church's Shoes, and other marques (only to sell off some of them less than a decade later). To finance his acquisitions, Bertelli planned much-publicized public offerings and then changed his mind—cancelling IPOs at least three times in three years.

Prada, Miuccia   Born in Italy in 1949, Prada attended the University of Milan, where she joined the Communist Party and eventually received a doctorate in political science. Thereafter, she enrolled at the Piccolo Teatro in Milan and trained as a mime, until her mother Luisa, who wanted to retire from running the luxury leathergoods business that had been founded by Miuccia's paternal grandfather Mario Prada in 1913, persuaded her to take over the firm in 1978.

Patrizio Bertelli and Miuccia Prada

Miuccia, despite having no formal training in design, became both manager and creative director, and, that same year, Prada met leather factory owner Patrizio Bertelli at a trade fair and negotiated a deal whereby he became exclusive manufacturer of Prada leather goods. They became a couple, married in 1987, and had two children: Lorenzo and Giulio.

Prada's true stardom began in 1985 with the international success of her bags combining black nylon and black leather, a line that thereafter remained a consistent bestseller for both sexes. Understated and practically logo-less, the Prada nylon bags were a radical departure from the glitzy fashion aesthetic of the 1980s and enjoyed a reverse chic among models and magazine editors. In 1989 she scored a similar hit, launching a line of women's ready-to-wear that was widely described as "dowdy" during a time when glamour and hype ruled the women's wear runways. As the company expanded in the 1990s, Prada retained her involvement in design. In 1992, she showed menswear of a similar sensibility for the 1993 season. That same year she also launched MIU MIU, a slightly lower-priced line aimed at a younger woman and based on her nickname. In 1997, she added Prada Sport. In 1998, she extended the Miu Miu franchise to men. By the turn of the century, Prada's intellectual past, feminist principles, and family involvement were often presented in the press as the polar opposite to the glitz and glamour of GUCCI, the archrival Italian brand that was, at the time, designed by TOM FORD.

In the 1990s, Prada also began seriously collecting contemporary art and leveraging her own notoriety to interest the general public in favored projects. For example: In 1995, she and her husband established Fondazione Prada, a space on the Via Spartaco in Milan; later they commissioned commercial spaces from architects such as Rem Koolhaas (for the Soho store that opened in New York City in 2001) an dHerzog & de Meuron (for a Tokyo store that opened in 2003).

premium denim   Early-21st-century jargon for pricey DENIM (usually jeans), worn for their fashion value rather than for their workwear function. For example: The $600 designer jeans worn with a tuxedo shirt and jacket would be considered premium denim; the jeans worn by a construction worker would not.

premium jeans   A synonym for PREMIUM DENIM.

premium sportswear   Early-21st-century jargon for SPORTSWEAR worn for its fashion value. Created to distinguish it from commodity sportswear, such as plain khaki pants, unbranded T-shirts, or unbranded sweaters.

preppy   A lifestyle, originally associated with students who attended elite East Coast prep schools (and who stuck to a similar dress code throughout college and their subsequent careers). Although icons of the preppy canon are periodically quoted by fashion designers, the style itself is the antithesis of fashion, since its elements vary little or not at all. By tradition, the spelling "preppie" is applied to women, while "preppy" is reserved for men.

A 20th-century term, preppy became most widely used after World War II (e.g., being famously addressed to the Harvard hero in the 1970 best seller *Love Story* and the movie made from it), and reached its apogee of fashion influence in 1980, when *Time* magazine published an article called "Here Comes the Preppie Look" and Lisa Birnbach edited THE OFFICIAL PREPPY HANDBOOK. In 2005, it temporarily overwhelmed the menswear runways again. Its distinguishing elements:

• A comfy, unfitted silhouette that is never sexy or revealing. Business attire follows the SACK SUIT and IVY LEAGUE models. Blazers are boxy. Shirts never taper.

• Natural fibers used in fabrics that are not expensive or especially luxurious to the touch. CAMEL'S HAIR, cotton CORDUROY, HARRIS TWEED-type fabrics, MADRAS, OXFORD CLOTH, SEERSUCKER, SHETLAND wools.

• Patronage of brands and emporia such as BROOKS BROTHERS, CHIPP, J. PRESS, L.L.BEAN, ORVIS, and—occasionally—POLO RALPH LAUREN.

• Liberal use of bright color, such as pink or candy-striped BUTTON-DOWN shirts, chrome yellow shetland crewneck sweaters, NANTUCKET RED pants, kelly green corduroys, pastel RIBBON BELTS, and golf UMBRELLAS in school or club colors.

• Indulgence in whimsical prints and patterns, such as LILLY PULITZER sports jackets in lime green and shocking pink, tennis rackets as a tie motif, golf clubs embroidered on a WEB BELT, Labrador retrievers prancing across a CUMMERBUND and matching bow tie for evening wear.

• Sportswear items such as LACOSTE "ALLIGATOR SHIRTS," BERMUDA SHORTS, CABLED and crewneck sweaters, KHAKI pants, SURCINGLE belts.

• Footwear such as BASS WEEJUNS, BELGIAN SHOES, white BUCKS, GUCCI LOAFERS, L.L.Bean DUCK BOOTS, and Sperry TOP-SIDER boating mocs.

preshrunk   Fabric (primarily cotton, linen, or wool) that has been washed or otherwise treated so that virtually all expected shrinkage takes place before it is made into a garment. (See also SANFORIZATION.) Once a garment has been preshrunk, its size is not expected to change by more than 2 percent.

Presley, Elvis   Born on January 8, 1935, in Tupelo, Mississippi, Elvis Aaron Presley moved with his parents

Elvis Presley

Vernon and Gladys to Memphis, Tennessee, in 1945, where he was exposed to gospel music at church and the Grand Ole Opry on the radio at home, as well as the music, costumes, and performance styles of the black musicians who had turned Memphis's Beale Street into a rhythm and blues mecca. He was also exposed to the custom tailoring offered at LANSKY BROTHERS MEN'S SHOP, a Beale Street clothier that catered to musicians, and where the clothes-obsessed Elvis began outfitting himself the minute he could afford it: Lansky's, which Elvis made world-famous, would create both his first and his last suit. Elvis amassed an offstage wardrobe full of Lansky's pink-piped clothes and pants with no back pockets.

From the start of his recording career in 1954, Elvis was almost as notorious for his clothes as for his moves and his music. He dyed his naturally brown hair a jet black and greased it into a POMPADOUR, darkening his eyebrows to match. In 1956, he spent the then-princely sum of $125 for a gold LAMÉ jacket from Lansky's. By the following year, he had progressed to spending $10,000 on a NUDIE creation that was essentially a solid-gold lamé tuxedo with collars and cuffs of rhinestone "diamonds" (worn for the cover of the 1957 album *50,000,000 Elvis Fans Can't Be Wrong*).

Although his early movies routinely costumed him in JEANS, the de rigueur rebel look of the 1950s, Elvis hated their associations with farming and poverty and avoided them until well into the 1970s. Despite his distaste, however, Elvis's seeming endorsement gave jeans an association with rock 'n' roll that they never lost.

After his two-year Army stint ended in 1960, Elvis continued to patronize Lansky's and Nudie, but also dressed both on and off camera in slick suits created by SY DEVORE. After Devore's death in 1966, Elvis's next major clothes collaboration did not come until BILL BELEW costumed him for the NBC "Comeback Special" in 1968. Thereafter he and Belew evolved style signatures such as the high collars, the outrageous belts, the capes, and the jeweled jumpsuits copied by generations of Elvis impersonators.

Elvis died on Aug. 16, 1977, leaving behind a huge collection of costumes—including more than 6,000 items in the museum made of his home in Graceland. He was buried wearing a white suit front that Lansky's hurriedly created for the occasion.

prêt   A shortened form of PRÊT-À-PORTER.

prêt-à-porter   Literally "ready to wear," meaning a collection of clothes shown to buyers so that they can make selections for their stores. A distinction that still applies more to women's fashion, where a designer's "prêt-à-porter" collections—and the RUNWAY shows that feature them—are distinct from haute couture collections, which are commissioned custom designs at much higher prices.

Price, Antony   The British designer, best known for the strong-shouldered suits he made for musician BRYAN FERRY in the 1970s, began designing for British label Stirling Cooper in 1968. In 1972, he opened his own shop in London, which attracted the likes of Ferry (who was then with Roxy Music) and women's wear designer Ossie Clark. Thereafter, customers for his big-shouldered, sharp-edged, untraditional tailoring included Mick Jagger, Annie Lenox, David Bowie, and members of Duran Duran. During the 1980s, he became better known for his glamorous women's wear. In 2002, he was featured in *When Shoulderpads Ruled the World*, a documentary for British television.

Prince Albert   A double-breasted style of FROCK COAT, often with silk-covered lapels, worn in the late 19th and early 20th centuries; usually as part of formal day wear. (The CUTAWAY and contemporary MORNING SUIT did not begin to replace it until World War I.)

Prince Albert slippers   A style of slip-on slippers with a lip of fabric that extends up over the instep, rather than being rounded and low-cut like most slippers. See ALBERT.

Prince of Wales   See under individual entries by the names of their eventual succession:

• For the Prince Regent, references to the Prince of Wales at the end of the 18th century or beginning of the 19th, the one-time patron of BEAU BRUMMELL, and Regency-era fashion influences, see GEORGE IV.

• For Queen Victoria and PRINCE ALBERT's eldest son, references to the Prince of Wales during the second half of the 19th century, Edwardian-era fashion influences, and the origin of the HOMBURG, NORFOLK JACKET, and SAILOR SUIT, see EDWARD VII.

• For the man who became known as the Duke of Windsor from 1937 onward, after his abdication of the throne in 1936 and his 1937 marriage to American divorcee Wallis Simpson, for Edward VII's grandson, and the origin of fashions such as the ENGLISH DRAPE, FAIR ISLE sweater, PRINCE OF WALES PLAID, see EDWARD VIII.

Because Edward VIII consciously emulated some of the styles and mannerisms affected by his grandfather, there can be considerable confusion when discussing which monarch is responsible for a particular fashion. For example, the pattern known as Prince of Wales plaid was created for Edward VII when he was prince, but was popularized by his grandson.

Prince of Wales plaid *or* **Prince of Wales check**   A pattern based on a black-and-white GLENURQUHART CHECK with a colored OVERCHECK. Most often the pattern annexes the glenurquhart and imposes a large WINDOWPANE plaid on top of it in a highly contrasting shade: Blue is popular, but the color of the overcheck varies according to the fashion of the season. Textile historians associate the pattern with EDWARD VII when he was Prince of Wales but acknowledge that it was popularized by his grandson EDWARD VIII during his own stint as Prince of Wales. Can be generically described as a GLEN CHECK.

Prince Valiant   The hairstyle worn by the popular cartoon character first drawn by Hal Foster for the King Features syndicate in 1937; the Arthurian-era hero sported the style that women usually call a "bob": It was worn straight to his jawline, completely covering his ears, and featured long straight bangs across his forehead.

prison stripes   A pattern of regular, extra-thick horizontal stripes in black and white. Originally, the pattern really was part of prison uniforms and a supposed deterrent to escapes, since it made prisoners easily identifiable— a practice that Michel Pastoureau, in *The Devil's Cloth: A History of Stripes*, traces back to the penal colonies in America during the 1760s and that lasted through the middle of the 20th century. Synonym: convict stripes.

proteinacious   A way to classify fiber composition, usually for purposes of DRY CLEANING, dyeing, and other chemical processing. Proteinacious means that the fiber derives from animals. For example: WOOL and SILK are proteinacious materials. The opposite classification for a nonsynthetic is CELLULOSIC, which refers to fibers that derive from plants.

prunella *or* **prunelle**   A type of twill fabric, usually WORSTED wool, commonly used for suits. Usually European usage.

PTU   Old-fashioned, especially British, slang for trouser cuffs. The abbreviation stands for "permanent TURN-UPS," meaning cuffs that were intended to be part of the trouser style.

pudding basin cut   A type of haircut in which the hair is trimmed to uniform length, as if a bowl had been upended on the man's head and any hair hanging below that bowl's edges cut off. (Costumers and illustrators often give medieval characters this type of haircut.) Synonyms include BASIN CUT or BOWL CUT.

puggaree   A cloth hatband, derived from a Hindi word indicating a small TURBAN. A puggaree is usually folded (if not pleated) and more substantial than the slim ribbon used as a HATBAND on stiff felt styles such as the FEDORA or HOMBURG. Most often it appears, sometimes in a colorfully printed material, as the ornament on a PANAMA or similar summertime style.

pull on   A hat style similar to a SKULLCAP, but usually longer and slightly less rounded in shape.

pull-on pants   Exactly what the name implies: pants that can be pulled on, without a fly, back lacing, or any other opening. Although DRAWSTRING pants may technically count as pull-on pants, the term is usually reserved for pants with an elastic waist.

pullover   A SWEATER that is "pulled over" the head when it is taken on or off, because it does not have a button or zipper opening. Its opposite would be a CARDIGAN. Its woven equivalent would be a POPOVER.

pumicing   1. In references to denim and jeans, a method of distressing the fabric by processing it with pumice stones.   2. In references to men's grooming, the use of a pumice stone (or something of similar consistency) to abrade the skin, usually for the purpose of removing calluses or rough patches (i.e., on the feet). In certain ancient and/or non-Western cultures (e.g., ancient Egypt), pumicing was also practiced for the purpose of hair removal.

pump   A style of lightweight, slipperlike shoe with a thin sole. Usually pumps have no laces or other fastening and stay in place because of their snug fit. Originally associated with the servant class, they evolved to be part of the formal or semiformal dress associated with court functions. For example, a man may wear OPERA PUMPS made of black PATENT LEATHER with flat, nonfunctional GROSGRAIN bows. Synonym: COURT SHOES (especially in British usage).

punk   A subculture that began in Britain in the 1970s and then spread worldwide. Inspired by bands like the Sex Pistols and egged on by designers like VIVIENNE WESTWOOD, the punk positioned himself as an avatar of alienation and anarchism. The punk adopted any aspect of dress that was deliberately unpretty and unmodish and, perversely, continued to influence high fashion for decades afterward. His hallmarks:

• Hair styled in a MOHAWK and/or dyed unnatural, discordant colors (e.g., the fluorescent shades sold by MANIC PANIC)

• Quotations from the fetish dress, especially rubber clothes and BONDAGE PANTS

• Razor blades and safety pins as both motifs and unorthodox ornamentation (e.g., a safety pin through the earlobe or lip)

• T-shirts with outrageous and obscene images and/or slogans

• Tattered hems, ripped clothes, paint-spattered surfaces, PILLED sweaters

puppytooth   A tiny HOUNDSTOOTH pattern. See color plates.

Puritan hat   Slang for the high-crowned style of hat properly known as the COPOTAIN; associated with illustrations of Puritan colonists.

purl   The stitch that is the opposite and balancing stitch to the KNIT stitch in knit fabrics, particularly those that are produced as flat pieces rather than shaped "in the round." A purl stitch inverts the customary action of the knit stitch: Instead of the yarn and needle passing through the back of a loop, they pass through its front. Technically, "purl" is a term of construction; nevertheless, people often refer to the "wrong" side or "rough" side of a knit as the purl side.

PVC   Polyvinyl chloride, a compound discovered in the 19th century and, after the 20th-century addition of plasticizers to create flexibility, used in apparel. Because PVC—particularly in versions that achieved a fabriclike consistency due to the addition of plasticizers—had been demonstrated to leach potentially destructive chemicals, its use in apparel was controversial by the end of the 20th century.

qiviut Fiber that comes from the soft undercoat on the underbelly of the musk ox, a long-haired arctic animal that has neither musk glands nor any relationship to domestic oxen. Fine (about 12 microns in diameter) and soft enough to be classified as a NOBLE FIBER, qiviut is prized because, like CASHMERE, it is lighter and warmer than sheep's wool. Variant spellings include qiviuk.

quality Jargon in the worlds of textiles and tailoring for a particular version or style of fabric. For example, when referring to a flannel, a tailor may say "that quality is 12 ounces and comes only in gray" in reference to a specific fabric.

quarters Jargon for the sides of a shoe that extend forward from the heel (covered by the counter) to the vamp (the section covering the instep of the foot). See SHOE illustration.

Queer Eye for the Straight Guy The reality television show conceived and produced by David Collins, which premiered on the Bravo network in July 2003 and starred five gay men, known as the "Fab Five," each with his own area of lifestyle expertise: Carson KRESSLEY, the fashion expert; Kyan Douglas, the grooming and fitness expert; Thom Felicia, the interior design expert; Ted Allen, the food and wine expert; and Jai Rodriguez, the expert on culture and conduct.

Initially filmed in the New York area, the show's premise involved the team swooping in on an unsuspecting straight man (usually at the instigation of his wife, girlfriend, or some family member), who had been deemed sadly unstylish but otherwise worthy. During the following hour, they would turn his house or apart-

Qiviut: Musk oxen

ment upside down, redecorate, reform his eating habits, and give him a new look. Kressley would raid the man's closet, rid it of everything unsuitable, then take the man shopping. During breaks, various team members would contribute quickie "hip tips" for the general audience. When the team's transformation of its subject was complete, the man's mastery of his new lifestyle and look would be tested via some event (e.g., a party for his friends) that he executed on his own while the Fab Five watched and commented on his performance.

A huge hit during its first season, the show was considered by many as proof of a new primacy of male style in mainstream American culture. In 2004, Crown Publishing brought out *Queer Eye for the Straight Guy: The Fab 5's Guide to Looking Better, Cooking Better, Dressing Better, Behaving Better, and Living Better*. The

show's success in the United States inspired local editions in Australia, Finland, France, Germany, Great Britain, Italy, and Spain. By its third season, however, its popularity waned markedly and the original premise was amended to include makeovers of women and worthy gay men while the show's title was shortened to *Queer Eye*. The series concluded in 2007.

Queue

queue   The term used most often to refer to a man's single braided pigtail, particularly a style of shaved forehead and long braid worn by Chinese men during the Qing dynasty (1644 to 1911).

In violation of previous practice and Confucian tradition that an adult male did not shave his head or cut his hair short, the queue had been imposed upon ethnic Han Chinese by Manchurian conquerors at the beginning of the Qing dynasty and, for over a decade during the 17th century, met with great resistance and concomitant retribution (including waves of execution for the estimated hundreds of thousands who refused to comply).

Ironically, refusal to cut the queue also met with resistance from 19th- and 20th-century Chinese immigrants to America, who were pressured to change hairstyle as a sign of assimilation and submission to Western culture; and also by conservatives at the start of the Republic in the 20th century, when cutting the queue symbolized acceptance of modernity and the new regime.

quiff   Most often a synonym for a POMPADOUR and worn with a DUCK'S ASS.

quilting   Stitching together two or more layers of fabric (usually a woven outer layer and a thinner, woven under layer with a layer of padding and/or insulation in between). Layers are anchored, via stitching, usually in a pattern, such as a grid.

quirk   On a traditionally made GLOVE, the name of the small gusset at the base of each FOURCHETTE (the larger gusset piece between each finger).

quizzing glass   Although often mistaken for a MONOCLE, which it resembles, the quizzing glass was a late 18th- through mid 19th-century affectation among fashionable men (e.g., the COUNT D'ORSAY) who wore this round magnifying glass suspended from a long ribbon, which usually attached to the waistcoat. Larger than a monocle (which must fit inside the eye socket), the quizzing glass was held in front of the face by a short handle, allowing the man to peer through it at the object of his interest. Its customary use is immortalized in the cartoon of dandy Eustace Tilley peering at a butterfly, drawn by Rea Irvin in 1925 as the first cover of *The New Yorker* magazine.

rabbit hair   A fiber, yarn, or fabric made from the hair of rabbits *except* for ANGORA rabbits or ORLAG. (For the purposes of producing textiles, these breeds are considered an elite of the rabbit world and are designated by name.)

ragg socks   Socks made of RAGG WOOL. Usually a thick sock in a plain STOCKINETTE stitch without any other patterning; most often used for hiking, hunting, camping, and similar outdoor pursuits.

ragg sweater   A sweater made of RAGG WOOL. Usually a thick sweater in a plain STOCKINETTE stitch in a PULLOVER or SHAWL COLLAR style; associated with utilitarian clothes favored for hiking, hunting, camping, and similar outdoor pursuits.

ragg wool   Originally a term that indicated a type of thick yarn made from recycled or waste wool—hence the reference to rags—now used to refer to thick wool or wool blend yarns (e.g., contemporary ragg wool may be 85 percent wool with 15 percent nylon blended for strength) that imitate the original look, feel, and weight of the yarn once made from rags; much prized for its heft, warmth, and sturdiness. Most often the yarn is a mixture of beige and off-white or gray and off-white, which produces a heather effect when knit into garments.

raglan cape *or* **raglan coat**   Refers to a loose style of cape or overcoat distinguished by a "shoulderless" sleeve seam that slants from the armpit to the neck on a diagonal line (as opposed to the more traditional set-in sleeve or a dropped shoulder). According to legend, the style originated during the Crimean War when Lord Raglan's troops were so cold that they cut a hole in their blankets and put them over their heads.

raglan sleeve   A sleeve seam, frequently used on sweaters, that slants in the manner of a RAGLAN COAT.

railroad vest   A four-pocket utility vest, made of dark, durable wool. WOOLRICH, the Pennsylvania mill that manufactured and marketed it for workers on nearby railroad lines, is credited with originating the style in the late 1800s.

rainshirt   Refers to a piece of hip-length outerwear, which can be either pullover in style or a full-button front. Meant to substitute for a raincoat, the fashion was promoted heavily in the 1970s, during the heyday of the LEISURE SUIT, which it closely resembled.

rain slicker   See SLICKER.

Rainey, Michael   Owner of the shop Hung on You, on KING'S ROAD in London's Chelsea, which influenced fashion during the 1960s, launching styles such as the SMARTIE SUIT.

Ralph Lauren   See under LAUREN, RALPH.

ramie   A strong CELLULOSIC fiber or fabric, produced from a plant of the same name, which is chiefly grown in southern and eastern Asia (and is sometimes called rhea or China grass). Used most often for shirt fabrics and blends, ramie is a BAST FIBER and is produced in much the same way that LINEN is produced from flax. Because it has a high resistance to rotting and bacteria, some apparel manufacturers tout it as a "naturally antibacterial" fabric.

Ramillies   A style of wig named for the Duke of Marlborough's great victory in May of 1706 in the village of Ramillies, in what is now Belgium, during the War of Spanish Succession. Like other styles of CAMPAIGN WIGS, the Ramillies was relatively no-nonsense: Hair was swept straight back from the forehead, kept in low puffs over each ear, to be gathered at the nape in a plaited pigtail tied with a (larger) black ribbon at its top and (smaller) black ribbon at its bottom. Early in that century, its simplicity gave it connotations of informality.

rank badges   The highly decorative, figurative, multi-colored badges worn as symbols of rank by Chinese officials, a custom that was codified at the end of the 14th century (building upon an extant practice of using similarly decorative badges as symbols of status) and continued at court until the end of the Qing dynasty and the imperial civil service in 1911.

Because the badges were worn on both the front and back of an outer robe, they are always in pairs, with the front split to accommodate the front opening of the robe. Badges indicating the rank of civil officials always depicted birds, whereas animals were reserved for the military—supposedly because birds, which can leave the earth, are higher in status than earthbound animals.

Thus, for civil officials, the nine orders of rank from highest to lowest were Manchurian crane; golden pheasant; Malay peacock; goose; silver pheasant; egret; mandarin duck; oriole, then (in the Qing dynasty) a quail; a quail, then (in the Qing dynasty) a paradise fly-catcher.

For military officials, the nine orders of rank from highest to lowest were: a lion, then (in the Qing dynasty) a qilin (a hooved chimera); lion; a tiger, then (in the Qing dynasty) a leopard; tiger; bear; panther; panther, then (in the Qing dynasty) a rhinoceros; a sea horse or a seal.

Beautifully designed and embroidered, rank badges were collected as *objets d'art* by Westerners even before the demise of the imperial system and were—then and now—most often seen detached from robes. Because the official's wife was also permitted to wear a mirroring badge, the direction that the bird or animal faced is crucial to knowing whether the badge was worn by a man or woman.

Rastafarian   The style associated with or inspired by the Rastafari religion, which originated in Jamaica in the second quarter of the 20th century. The distinctive dress of the Rastamen was exported to the rest of the world beginning in the 1970s, carried, in part, by the popularity of reggae music in general and Bob Marley's music in particular. Its distinguishing elements include:

• Uncut hair worn in long DREADLOCKS (a practice that the Rastamen say symbolizes the mane of the Lion of Judah and is supported by passages in the Old Testament books of Leviticus and Numbers)

• Green, gold, and red-themed garments (quoting the colors of the Ethiopian flag, associated with the deity of Emperor Haile Selassie, the original "Ras Tafari")

• The marijuana leaf as an emblem (symbolizing its use to attain spirituality)

• Enormously oversized, crocheted TAMS and caps to contain the dreadlocks (especially using the colors of green, gold, and red)

• Afrocentric fabrics, costume quotations, and motifs mixed with army surplus

Synonym: Rasta.

ratcatcher In the hunt field, a designation for the more informal version of FOXHUNTING ATTIRE, but one

Ratcatcher: Prince Edward

often borrowed for other riding events, such as horse shows. Traditionally, ratcatcher is worn during cubbing season and on "bye days" (additions to the club calendar) after the opening hunt. It is never worn to the large, formal meets (e.g., opening hunt, Thanksgiving, Christmas).

Nevertheless, ratcatcher is not considered totally dressed down, and comes with its own etiquette and a set list of personal appointments, which include:

• A black or brown BOWLER worn with a hat leash (or, depending on status and local rules, a hunt cap)

• A tailored, single-breasted, single-vented HACKING JACKET specifically designed for riding, in a subdued tweed or subtle pattern

• A lightly colored or patterned shirt worn with a STOCK TIE (in a muted color or pattern) pinned with a STOCK PIN; or, alternatively, a DRESS SHIRT worn with a necktie

• BREECHES in a muted shade (usually beige or tan but never a dark color)

• Brown FIELD BOOTS (although the black version is sometimes allowed)

• Brown or black gloves (either leather or STRING GLOVES)

As with the more formal foxhunting attire, most hunts and horse shows follow guidelines set by the Masters of Foxhounds Association of America, with a few local variations. For example, some masters allow NEWMARKET BOOTS as part of ratcatcher; some don't. Some accept POLO SHIRTS in warm weather; others would never dream of such informality. Boys under the age of 18 may be allowed to wear ratcatcher all year.

Ratcatcher never includes the FROCK COAT or SHADBELLY styles, nor does it encompass the scarlet PINK COAT or solid black coat, white stock tie, white breeches, or TOP HAT—all of which belong to formal attire, its opposite designation.

Rat Pack   The popular name for the gang consisting of FRANK SINATRA and his cronies Joey Bishop, Sammy Davis Jr., Peter Lawford, and Dean Martin during the late 1950s and early 1960s; especially in their stamping grounds of Las Vegas, Hollywood, and Palm Springs. (Although an earlier, Holmby Hills, California, version of the Rat Pack existed, which also included Sinatra but centered around nattily dressed Humphrey Bogart, its fashion statement was not as extreme as the later, Sinatra-centered version.)

Famously depicted in group shots in front of the Sands Hotel and Casino in Las Vegas where they frequently performed, the Rat Pack's style signatures included: crisply tailored suits made of SHARKSKIN or slightly shiny wool/MOHAIR blends in solid colors; skinny lapels; skinny ties; tight haircuts; plain-front pants made without cuffs; luxurious V-neck sweaters; and luxurious cotton shirts. Smooth and deceptively simple-looking, their clothes reflected their casual, ad-lib performance style onstage and their high-living, hard-partying lifestyle offstage.

During their heyday, they were famous for their lavish expenditures on clothes, for buying in multiples, and for becoming involved in the proportions and construction of their apparel down to the last line of the buttons and millimeter of the COLLAR STAND or lapel width. Their tailor of choice was SY DEVORE.

All five performed in the original 1960 version of OCEAN'S 11, the caper flick that became better known as a buddy pic and a fashion statement than a serious acting exercise. They reunited on-screen in 1962 for the somewhat less stylish *Sergeants 3*, but after Lawford was banished by Sinatra that same year, their group activities and their fashion influence waned.

During the late 1990s, when it became chic to cite old Hollywood tailors like Devore, designers and fashion editors often spoke of a Rat Pack revival, and, in 2001, *Ocean's 11* was remade as a buddy pic starring George Clooney and Brad Pitt.

raw denim   1. Denim that is noticeably stiff and dark because it has not been through either commercial or

Rat Pack

home laundering (and therefore still retains its SIZING). 2. In the early 21st century, denim that emulates the look of unlaundered denim but not its stiffness.

raw edge A cut fabric edge that is not finished by either trim (such as PIPING, RIBBING, seam binding, or a WELT) or by stitching.

rawhide As its name implies, an animal skin that has not been fully processed: The hide has been cleaned of its hair and limed but not tanned. In contemporary use, appears most often in shoelaces and straps.

raw silk Usually refers to SILK, with part of the natural silk gum still coating the fiber. It is heavier, stiffer, and darker in color (usually beige as opposed to white) than processed silk.

Ray-Ban Best known for creating the original AVIATOR sunglasses (in 1936) and the WAYFARER sunglasses (in 1953), the brand grew out of Bausch & Lomb's 1936 manufacture of sunglasses for high-altitude pilots in the U.S. military. The following year, 1937, B&L began selling that aviator style to the U.S. public through its newly created Ray-Ban brand, so called because the sunglasses "banned" high-altitude glare.

During World War II, Ray-Ban's aviator sunglasses were seen on military men up to and including General Douglas MacArthur. Postwar, the company became the first to popularize gradient mirror lenses and amber lenses, but ultimately became best known as the producer of the best-selling Wayfarer style, launched in 1953.

Since then, the Ray-Ban aviator and Wayfarer have been shorthand symbols of the cool American male. For example: The Wayfarer style was used in *The Blues Broth*-

ers (1980) and worn by Don Johnson in the television show *MIAMI VICE* (1984–1989), and the aviator style was a prominent feature of Tom Cruise's costuming in *Top Gun* (1985).

In 1997, a newer style, the Predator, was featured prominently in *Men in Black*. In 1999, the brand was acquired by Luxottica.

rayon Known as "artificial silk" (especially in the 1920s, when it first became widely used), rayon is produced from a range of plant materials, through chemical processing invented in the 19th century. Although several inventors worked on similar processes, modern rayon is most often associated with the fiber French chemist Count Hilaire de Chardonnet exhibited at the Paris Exhibition in 1889. However, the count did not build a plant to produce it for another two years, and rayon's commercial production in the United States did not begin until 1910. Supple and silky, it is classified as a CELLULOSIC FIBER, and its use in menswear is concentrated on linings, pajamas, and the like.

readymade Jargon for clothes that are sold already sized and tailored, as opposed to being MADE-TO-MEASURE, CUSTOM, or BESPOKE. Most menswear was not readymade until well after the Industrial Revolution. Synonyms: OFF-THE-PEG; OFF THE RACK.

ready-to-wear Jargon used, usually in the context of RUNWAY presentations, to designate a collection intended to be sold in stores. Borrowed from the women's market, where it is used to distinguish store lines from the haute couture designs that are available only by special order through the designer's salon. Abbreviated as RTW. A synonym (used more often for women's wear) is PRÊT-À-PORTER, sometimes shortened to PRÊT.

recovery   Jargon referring to the ability of fiber, fabric, or garment to return to its original shape. For example, a stretch JERSEY that slowly returns to shape, rather than snapping back immediately, may be said to have "delayed recovery." A wrinkled fabric that promptly returns to its original smooth appearance may be said to have "excellent recovery."

red carpet   Reference to the late-20th-century and early-21st-century press's passion for photographing celebrities on the red carpet as they enter and leave awards ceremonies, charity events, movie premieres, and other public functions. Apparel described as "red carpet" is photogenic and is usually FORMALWEAR.

red heels   A badge of nobility—*les talons rouges*—introduced by LOUIS XIV in the 1670s. Explanations of the symbolism vary. Some say the red heel was intended to show the blood of enemies beneath the heel of France. Some trace it to the preference of ancient Rome's patricians for red footwear. Others say it was simply a way of showing that the nobility never descended into the notoriously mucky streets of the time. In any case, the symbol spread to nobility throughout Europe, and vestiges of it survive in formal dress for pages at the British court. During the late 18th century in London, it also appeared in the dress of the famously overrefined MACARONIS, as yet another way to set themselves apart from the hoi polloi.

redingote   1. Originally, a French ellison of "riding coat," used in the late 18th century when ANGLOMANIA set so many fashions in Paris menswear. The redingote or "riding coat" was associated with the English passion for horses and the supposed simplicity of country clothes and country life. Unlike the stiff silk attire of the *ancien régime*, it was made of broadcloth in a modest color and relatively unornamented; it buttoned only to the waist (supposedly facilitating riding). As the style developed, it quickly came to recall the coat of a coachman rather than a rider (since it was long and closed in front and did not sport the CUTAWAY popular for wear in the saddle). Occasionally spelled "redinggote."   2. Inevitably, the French usage reentered the English language, becoming a synonym for a particular type of long (knee-length or below), plainly colored, large-collared overcoat with, in its English incarnation, buttons often extending below the waist.

reefer   1. A reference to a PEACOAT, in a dressier version of that style as it might be worn by an officer; especially one constructed of a better grade of fabric and made with brass buttons.   2. A reference to a style of slim-fitting TOP COAT or OVERCOAT, usually double-breasted (although the term is sometimes applied to single-breasted variations).

Regency stripes   Used to describe vertical stripes of equal width, most often in an historical context associated with Regency England. Like the shirt pattern known as BENGAL STRIPES, Regency stripes are often white alternating with another color, run vertically rather than horizontally, and can usually be classified as a BALANCED STRIPE. Unlike contemporary shirt stripes, however, Regency stripes are often rather oversized and may be as thick as an inch (or more).

regimental stripe   stripe (ranging from ⅓ of an inch to 1½ inches wide). Properly used to describe neckties only. Englishmen wear their ties so that the stripe slants from their left shoulder down toward the right of the belt buckle; Americans go the opposite direction.

This style of striped neckwear became popular in the early 20th century when decommissioned British officers continued to affect neckwear in their regimental colors after return to civilian life. Anglophile Americans imitated the style, but switched the direction of the stripes so they would not be accused of being parvenus. See also GUARD'S TIE.

regimental tie   See REGIMENTAL STRIPE.

relaxed fit   A designation, usually for jeans, indicating pants that are cut with extra room through the seat and leg.

repeat   Technical term that refers to the size of a pattern. A repeat is the size of a single complete pattern before it begins again. Thus, a tiny FOULARD may have a repeat that measures a half inch or less, and a particularly large, bold plaid may have a repeat of 8 or 9 inches. Because of the amount of tailoring in menswear and because of the convention that patterns should align at the seams, a larger repeat means that more fabric is required (and more is wasted).

rep *or* **repp**   Refers to the weave, not to the pattern. In apparel textiles, rep is often used as a synonym for rib—particularly one that runs vertically (i.e., warp-faced). REPP TIE refers to its material, not its pattern.

revers   Refers to the turned back portion of the LAPEL; the side that would normally be next to the body if the jacket was completely buttoned to the neck. In a TUXEDO, the FACING (e.g., black satin) is attached to the revers.

reversed twill   In menswear, used as a synonym for the HERRINGBONE weave and the resulting pattern.

revivers   Formulas used to improve or "revive" the appearance of worn fabrics or leathers, particularly during the 19th and early 20th centuries. As mentioned by novelist Charles Dickens, a reviver might be employed by a man of humble means who was attempting to mask the shabbiness of his clothes. The solution might contain dye as well as a DRY-CLEANING-type chemical. Also known as "patent revivers."

rhinegraves   A style of BREECHES most popular in Western Europe during the third quarter of the 17th century, in which the legs were so full and loose that the bifurcation was obscured and it looked as though a man was actually wearing a skirt. Synonym: PETTICOAT BREECHES.

ribbing   Any of dozens of knit patterns that varies stitches—usually between a KNIT stitch and a PURL stitch—to form vertical "ribs," which have more elasticity than a smooth knit; used at the edges of sweaters and other garments to improve the give of the garment and to prevent rippling.

ribbon belt   A staple of PREPPY style, the ribbon belt usually consists of a double-thick striped ribbon (usually about an inch wide) attached to brass rings or D-rings.

Richard James   Opened on SAVILE ROW in 1992, this business became noted for offering READY-TO-WEAR and MADE-TO-MEASURE alongside its BESPOKE tailoring, as well as staying open on Saturdays—all measures intended to attract younger customers. Cofounded by Richard James and Sean Dixon, its patrons have included Hugh Grant, Jude Law, Tom Cruise, and Prince Andrew.

Richmond-style   Refers to a mid-19th-century fashion for buttoning jackets only at the top, leaving other buttons undone and the belly and crotch fully exposed. This then evolved into jackets being cut so that their fronts curved away from the top—meaning that they couldn't have been buttoned at the waist, even if a man had wanted to try. Synonym, especially in 19th century America: ENGLISH-STYLE CLOSURE.

right-hand twill   Refers to a TWILL weave in which the diagonal runs from lower left toward upper right. For long periods of the 20th century, right-hand twill made of RINGSPUN yarn was the standard DENIM used in blue jeans. Its opposite: LEFT-HAND TWILL.

rigid   Jargon referring to stiff, like-new DENIM that has not been "washed" (particularly with special effects like and ACID WASH or ENZYME WASH), distressed, or otherwise broken in; for those reasons, associated with dark indigo color.

Riley   A style of dress shirt collar made popular in the 1990s by basketball coach Pat Riley. The Riley is a relatively low collar with a slight spread, with the points curving away from the tie knot rather than being in a straight line.

rimless glasses   EYEGLASSES that have no encircling metal or plastic rim around the lenses. Instead, the edge of lens is smoothly finished and both the nosepiece and the arms of the eyeglasses are attached directly to the lens—a style that appears more often in corrective, clear glasses (rather than sunglasses). Alternative eyeglass FRAMES include wire rims or tortoiseshells, which take their name from the material and color of the rim around the lenses.

ring-dyed   Textile jargon, usually for DENIM, indicating that only the outer portion of RINGSPUN yarn used to weave the denim has been dyed. Thus, as the fabric starts to wear, it reveals more of its white, undyed cotton core.

ringer T   A style of T-shirt in which the neck and arm edges are a contrasting color to the main part of the shirt.

ring ring   Textile jargon, usually for DENIM, indicating that the fabric is made, in both its WARP and WEFT, from RINGSPUN yarn.

ringspun   Textile jargon, almost always used in connection with DENIM, to describe the spinning process of the yarns used to make the fabric. Its opposite designation would be OPEN-END.

rise   The measure, in inches, from the crotch seam to the waistband. For example: Most men's jeans have a rise of about 12 to 13 inches, while a low-rise might be 9 inches, and an extremely low-rise 7 inches.

riser   The back YOKE on a pair of pants, a design that appears most often on JEANS and WESTERN WEAR.

robe de chambre   Usually a BANYAN or similar DRESSING GOWN-type garment. Used chiefly in references to clothes from the Renaissance through the mid-19th century, to indicate a garment worn in the house, but never outdoors or in town.

Rob Roy   The simplest of all TARTANS, also known as the MacGregor tartan; a symmetrical, two-color plaid that is evenly divided between red and black: forming pure red squares, pure black squares, and squares that are half red and half black. The same pattern, used on a slightly larger scale (and sometimes substituting another base color such as blue or yellow for the red), is known as a BUFFALO PLAID or BUFFALO CHECK.

Rocawear   The HIP-HOP apparel line founded in 1995 by music entrepreneurs Jay-Z (whose birth name is Shawn Carter), Damon Dash, and Kareem "Biggs" Burke, with a brand name inspired by the successful Roc-A-Fella record label.

Rocker   Synonym, especially in British usage, for the subculture Americans called a GREASER. See the entry under its antithesis: MOD.

rock of eye   British tailors' slang for relying on judgment and "eye," rather than elaborate measurements or a computerized template.

roll collar   1. Synonym for a TURTLENECK.   2. Synonym for a jacket with a SHAWL COLLAR.

rolled hems   See HAND-ROLLED HEMS.

roll line   On a jacket, the way that the material of the LAPEL folds back against the body. Because the lapel is part of the main body of the jacket and not a separate pattern piece, the fabric must be carefully rolled to the correct angle.

roll neck *or* **roll-over**   A generic reference to a style—usually of a sweater or knit shirt—with a collar that rolls down, rather than being folded, stitched, or shaped by stitching. A TURTLENECK is a roll-over, but not all roll-overs are turtlenecks.

Roman dress (ancient)   See individual entries for CAL-CEUS, DALMATICA, PALUDAMENTUM, PETASOS, SANDAL, TOGA, TYRIAN PURPLE.

Roman scarves   Reference to a general style of brightly colored, horizontally striped oblong silk scarves—approximately the size and shape of the contemporary MUFFLER—brought back from Rome and other Italian cities as souvenirs during the late 19th and early 20th centuries.

rope stitch   Jargon for a style of extra-heavy, mostly decorative stitching, chiefly used on JEANS.

roundabouts   Short, closely fitted jackets, especially as worn in the 19th century and especially for small boys.

Roundhead   A 17th-century nickname for Puritans, referring to their plain haircuts.

royal warrant   Refers to the Royal Warrant of Appointment awarded to tradesmen by members of the British royal family, based on the custom of royal charter, which

Rocawear: Jay-Z

dates back to Henry II's official recognition of a weaver in 1155.

Upon advice from the Lord Chamberlain, the royal grantor extends his grant, usually for five years, to the individual heading the particular company. The warrant holder is then allowed to display the royal coat of arms under a set of strictly proscribed conditions. Thereafter, the warrant, which may be withdrawn at any time, is reviewed at regular intervals.

Some firms hold multiple royal warrants, and some have held them continuously for a hundred years or more. Well-known makers of menswear include: AQUAS-CUTUM, BARBOUR, BERNARD WEATHERILL, BURBERRY, DAKS, GIEVES & HAWKES, HENRY POOLE, LOCK & CO., JOHN LOBB, and TURNBULL & ASSER.

rtw   Abbreviation for READY-TO-WEAR. Usually written in lowercase letters with no periods.

rubber   1. A flexible, slipper-shaped piece of rubber that fits over a shoe to protect it from wet weather. Although the term GALOSHES is sometimes used interchangeably with rubbers, galoshes are usually thicker, have a heavier sole with a more pronounced tread, and may follow a boot construction incorporating buckles and the like. Synonyms: OVERSHOE; GUM SHOE.   2. Slang for a condom.

ruff   Refers to one of a number of elaborate, face-framing collar styles, which evolved during the 15th century and were worn into the 17th-century as an accessory of dress by both men and women (and are probably best known today from portraiture of the Elizabethan period). At various times and in various Western European countries, ruffs were pleated, gathered, flat, supported by wires, open, or closed. Essentially an item of conspicuous consumption, they were a favored target of SUMPTUARY LAWS and sermons by Protestant clergy.

rug   Slightly derogatory slang for a TOUPEE.

rugby shirt   Shirts adapted from rugby uniforms worn in collegiate or other casual settings; part of the preppy canon.

Like the sport, the shirt style originated in the 19th century in Rugby, England. For contemporary apparel, the classic rugby shirt is long-sleeved and made of thick cotton jersey that sports a contrasting (usually white) collar and placket made of sturdy woven fabric, closing with flat rubber buttons (originally a safety feature on the playing field). Although it may be solid or have some other combination of stripes, it is most often composed of five or six thick, horizontal stripes (referred to as "hoops"). Synonyms: rugger shirt; rugby shirt.

rugger shirt   Variant for RUGBY SHIRT.

runway   1. The place, usually a long, elevated platform, where a live fashion show is held. (A synonym is CAT-WALK.) Although men frequently participated in women's fashion shows as cavaliers, the first "real" men's runway show was considered to have taken place in 1952 in Florence when Giovanbattista Giorgini invited BRIONI to show a full collection to international press and buyers at the Pitti Palace.   2. A style intended for presentation, but not for actual production. Usually a particularly extreme style that the designer uses to attract the press and/or express his creativity, but does not expect to sell to stores.

Rugby shirts

S-twist   A technical term that refers to one of the two directions that yarn can twist. Upon close inspection, an S-twist yarn shows a line from lower right to upper left. (Its opposite is the Z-TWIST, which twists in the opposite direction.) Weavers sometimes exploit the differences between S and Z—for example, variations in the way that each reflects light—to create effects in the finished fabric.

sabiro   See SEBIRO.

sablé   Solidly beaded material composed of small, grainlike beads, from the French word for sand. Used in the 18th century, mostly for accessories and more often for women's wear.

sack coat   Refers to a loosely tailored style of jacket that is not SUPPRESSED at the waist or otherwise shaped to the body; almost always made without a side or back vent.

The term, in use since the second quarter of the 19th century, often indicated a readymade garment and had connotations of quickly and inexpensively made apparel, often without the lining and interfacing associated with traditional tailoring. In addition, the sack was identified with lighter-weight materials and lighter colors. Although most often a short jacket, approximately the length of its contemporary counterparts, it sometimes reached almost to the knees during periods in the 19th century.

sack suit   1. A relatively loose-fitting style of suit, often with little or no shaping through the body and a NATU-RAL SHOULDER; in the contexts of the 20th and 21st centuries used often to describe the IVY LEAGUE style.   2. Used in the late 19th and early 20th centuries to describe a relatively casual style of loose-fitting suit with a shorter jacket, often in less formal materials, which resembles the contemporary American suit; worn in contrast to the more formal FROCK COAT in much the same context that a sports jacket would be worn in contrast to a business suit today. At that time, "sack" was applied to a style that did not have the waist seam and skirts of the frock coat.

sacque   1. A tunic-like garment worn by children, especially during the 19th century.   2. Reference to a SACK COAT or SACK SUIT.

saddle oxford *or* saddle shoe A style of laced OXFORD, usually made of white leather, with a contrasting dark color, usually black or dark-brown leather, forming a "saddle" over the instep and laces; often with a CREPE SOLE or red rubber sole. The saddle shoe evolved from racquet shoes in the early 20th century and remained an informal style, associated with collegiate fashion, and was never a dress shoe. It was particularly popular in the 1950s, when it was worn by students of both genders. Not to be confused with the dressier style known as a SPECTATOR (or as a CORRESPONDENT in England), another two-color style, which has a contrasting toe cap.

saddle shoulder A style of shoulder seam that combines characteristics of both a SET-IN SLEEVE and a RAGLAN; used almost exclusively on knits. The bottom portion of the sleeve is curved, as in the normal set-in sleeve. However, the top (i.e., the saddle), which would normally be the SLEEVEHEAD, is a long, straight piece that extends upward onto the shoulder and attaches straight to the collar.

saddle stitching Contrast stitching done in a large GAUGE with heavy thread, usually as much for fashion as function; so-called because of its resemblance to the stitching used on saddlery and harnesses.

safari jacket A pseudomilitary style of belted jacket, with two symmetrically placed chest pockets (usually button-flap PATCH POCKETS and/or BELLOWS POCKETS), two larger patch pockets (which may also be bellows style) symmetrically placed below the waistline, a buckled cloth belt of the same material as the body of the jacket, a shirt collar, and occasionally EPAULETTES; made of heavy cotton or cotton blend fabric, such as drill, in a KHAKI color; may be either long-sleeved or short-sleeved.

Established as sporting gear in the late 19th century—when it served as a sort of tropical counterpart to the Norfolk jacket—the safari jacket (then best known by the name BUSH JACKET), cycled in and out of fashion as casual sportswear but remained de rigueur attire for big-game hunter, gaining great glamour by its association with Ernest Hemingway and Hollywood depictions of Africa (e.g., Clark Gable in 1932's *Red Dust* and 1953's *Mogambo*). In 1968, the style gained street chic when it appeared on the runway as part of the "Saharienne" collection of YVES SAINT LAURENT, who was then at the apex of his fame. A decade later, it became a staple item in the original, tropically themed Banana Republic stores in California. Synonym: bush jacket.

safari shirt A style of SPORT SHIRT imitative of a SAFARI JACKET. Usually, a safari shirt has EPAULETTES,

Safari jacket: Grace Kelly and Clark Gable in *Mogambo*

Saddle shoulder

long sleeves, and two patch pockets (symmetrically placed, one over each pectoral), which either button close or have flap tops. The shirt may also have button tabs on the sleeves as an aid to keeping cuffs rolled up and off the forearms. In the 1990s, when the concept of big game hunting was no longer considered politically correct, alternative names—such as "trekking shirt"—began to be applied to the same style.

safety razor   Colloquial use for any style of razor with a guard or some other design intended to protect a man from slicing his skin as he shaves. (Its opposite would be the straight razor.)

Razors designed to be safer than the traditional straight razors were patented as early as the 1760s and continued to be refined throughout the 1800s (usually as "guards" or "guard razors"). The first American patent specifically named a "safety razor" was taken out in 1880. However, it was King Camp Gillette who became associated with safety razors, with his 1901 patent for a razor with flexible, disposable, double-edged blade, an invention that had taken years—and the intercession of William Nickerson—to put into production. The Gillette Safety Razor company was established in 1903 in South Boston, and, during World War I, all members of the U.S. military were issued safety razors as part of standard kit.

sailor collar   A large collar with no points in front, but forming a large square in the back. Its development is incorrectly attributed to the habit of sailors, in the late 18th and early 19th centuries, of wearing their hair in a tarred pigtail. The actual square collar became popular after the pigtails were no longer worn. Synonym: MIDDY.

sailor hat   1. A woven cloth cap, almost always white cotton, with a soft crown and a circular, turned-up brim reinforced by several lines of stitching.   2. Especially in the 19th century, refers to a broad-brimmed, flat-topped style, with a low to moderate crown; usually made of light-colored straw banded with a dark ribbon that is long enough to extend far over the brim. The version worn by small boys often included a chin strap and emphasized the streamers at the back.

sailor pants   Traditionally a high-waisted style that laces up the back and has a thirteen-button FALL closure in front, with BELL-BOTTOM legs; worn without belt or suspenders. (At various times in the history of the U.S. navy, the style has also sported as few as seven buttons and as many as fifteen.)

sailor suit   A style of children's wear based on traditional sailors' clothes, usually sported by boys before puberty and popular for middle-class and upper-class children from the mid-19th century through the early 20th century. The SAILOR COLLAR is always a prominent feature of the sailor suit and may or may not be attached to a MIDDY-style blouse, and accessorized with a kerchief or tie. BELL-BOTTOM trousers are a less frequent feature, since small boys were often in short pants. Synonym: MIDDY SUIT.

The style of dressing boys like small sailors was probably the first of the many, many fashions that were set by

Sailor suit

EDWARD VII when he was Prince of Wales: The practice dates from an outfit made for him in imitation of clothes worn by the crew on his mother Queen Victoria's yacht.

Saint Laurent, Yves   Born in 1936 in Oran, Algeria, to a French family, designer Yves Mathieu Saint Laurent first became famous for his success as a women's wear designer: going to work for Christian Dior, the most renowned women's wear designer of his day, in 1954, and then succeeding to the top spot upon Dior's death in 1957. In 1961, with the help of Pierre Bergé, his then romantic partner and his lifelong business partner, the slim and sensitive Saint Laurent established his own couture house.

Costume historians routinely cite Saint Laurent as being the first couture designer to recognize the power of street style, and loudly laud his clothes as contributions to the liberation of women, especially for the way he put women in "le smoking" (the TUXEDO pantsuits he first showed in 1966), safari looks (1968), blazers, TRENCH COATS, and the like. But his influence on menswear, while harder to quantify, was just as important. Both his professional life and his personal life went a long way toward blurring the borders between the sexes. Androgynous and fragile-looking, Saint Laurent wore his hair long, seemed to make no secret of being gay, and in 1971, posed nude for one of his own fragrance ads.

The first menswear for YSL—the routine industry reference to the house—came in 1969, concurrent with the designer's declaration that he couldn't find menswear he wanted to wear. And, although it was never as successful as the

women's wear, early YSL menswear got a lot of press through customers like RUDOLF NUREYEV, then at the peak of his notoriety. In 1974, YSL extended Rive Gauche, the ready-to-wear collection launched for women in 1966, into menswear.

In 1983, he became the first living designer to be the subject of a retrospective at the Metropolitan Museum's COSTUME INSTITUTE.

Despite all the acclaim, by the 1990s, a drop in demand for luxury goods in general and couture in particular meant that over three quarters of the YSL revenues came from beauty, and the house went through a number of investment deals. In early 1993, YSL was acquired by the pharmaceutical giant Elf Sanofi. In late 1999, as part of an industry trend to consolidate luxury brands, GUCCI bought Sanofi Beauté in order to acquire the rights to YSL. Afterward, Saint Laurent continued to design the couture collection, and TOM FORD was brought in to do the Rive Gauche line. Saint Laurent retired in 2002.

Saint Mark's Place   The main east–west thoroughfare in New York City's East Village and, as such, the city's closest equivalent to KING'S ROAD in London as a location of relatively inexpensive and ultra-trendy retailing—especially the head shops and HIPPIE boutiques of the late 1960s and the PUNK movement of the 1970s, decades when Saint Mark's benefited from its proximity to NYU and Cooper Union.

Yves Saint Laurent after retirement

Salon International de l'Habillement Masculin   See under SEHM, its usual acronym.

salwar kameez   See SHALWAR KAMEEZ.

Sam Browne belt   A thick, leather belt with an attached strap that crosses the body from the left front of the waist to the right shoulder, usually incorporating a sword or pistol holster. Supposedly derived from an adaptation for 19th-century British cavalry officer, later general, Sir Samuel J. Browne, who had lost his left arm during active service in India.

sandals   General reference to a type of footwear in which a full-length sole is secured to the foot by straps (or similar attachment) so that the foot is not fully covered; depending upon the design, either large parts of the foot may be exposed or only small portions. Because of that exposure, the sandal is associated with warm weather and/or warm climates. If the foot is fully covered, it is not a sandal, no matter how informal the style. For example: An ESPADRILLE or MOCCASIN is not a sandal.

Sandow, Eugen   A man best known for not wearing clothes. Born in Germany in 1867, Friedrich Wilhelm Mueller started out performing as a scantily clad strong man and soon became more famous for his physique, consciously posing in imitation of Greek and Roman statues and promoting himself as the "most perfectly developed man in the world." For that reason, he is sometimes hailed as the father of modern body building (a statue of Sandow is part of the Mr. Olympia trophy). He performed at the 1893 World's Fair in Chicago and in shows produced by Florenz Zeigfeld. He died in 1925.

sand wash   A finishing treatment, most often seen on jeans and silk shirts; in contemporary practice most often done with a material like aluminum oxide rather than actual silica sand. A method of purposely prematurely distressing fabric, sand washing—also known as sand blasting or sanding—usually results in an even finish, a slight removal of color, and a matte surface—similar to the effect of sandblasting on a piece of metal.

sandwich stripes   A nickname for a style of bold vertical stripes (usually about a half an inch wide). Used to describe sports jackets, pants, and outerwear; never used to describe shirts.

Sanforization   A trademarked name for "controlled compressive shrinkage," a preshrinking treatment for cotton and cotton blends invented by Sanford Cluett in TROY, NEW YORK, and registered by Cluett, Peabody & Co. in 1930. At that time, Sanforized underwear was such an innovation in the men's market that retailers began to use the term generically to refer to all preshrinking.

Sansabelt   Founded in the 1950s in France, where they were known as "New Belt" pants because the waistband was designed with inside elastic webbing that did not require the use of belt or suspenders to hold the pants up, and also did not roll when a man leaned forward. In 1957, the concept was licensed by JAYMAR-RUBY, an American company founded in 1915 that had specialized in slacks since the 1930s. Jaymar-Ruby renamed the pants Sansabelt, a French-English coinage that translates to "without a belt."

In 1959, Jaymar-Ruby began advertising its Sansabelt brand on *The Tonight Show* hosted by Jack Paar, whereupon they became tagged as "the slacks you see on NBC TV," a tradition that continued when Johnny Carson took over the show in 1962. At about that same time, Jaymar-Ruby bought the rights from the original owners. In 1967, the company became part of HARTMARX, but Sansabelt continued as a separate brand, with celebrity spokesmen over the following decades including football player and golfer John Brodie, football coach Mike Ditka, and baseball player Jim Palmer.

During the 1980s, the brand became identified with golfers and older men. In 1986, Sansabelt had an unsuccessful experiment with ladies' pants and, in 1988, had another when it offered pleated pants complete with belt loops.

sans culottes   A misleading term, usually mistranslated as "without pants," to describe working-class protestors and their sympathizers in the period immediately preceding and during the French Revolution. The term gained currency because peasants and other working men wore long TROUSERS, whereas the aristocrats wore KNEE BREECHES and the clergy wore CASSOCKS and robes. Thus, a more appropriate English translation would be "without breeches."

Santa Claus suit   Although Americans traditionally dress Santa Claus in a red suit and coordinating hat trimmed with white fur, he started life as Saint Nicholas, the 4th-century Bishop of Myra, in what is now Turkey, and therefore spent well over a thousand years dressed mainly in clerical costume. It was in Germanic countries that Saint Nick became known as Kris Kringle and took over some of the seasonal duties associated with Thor, the jolly, white-bearded god whose feast day had been celebrated in early winter and who was associated with the color red.

By the time New York-area residents Washington Irving and Clement C. Moore wrote their tales in the 19th century, Santa was established as a chubby, cheery, white-bearded man. Beginning in the early 1860s, Thomas Nast, a Bavarian-born illustrator who also created UNCLE SAM, began drawing him for *Harper's Weekly* in a fur jumpsuit (in reference to Moore's specification that "he was dressed all in fur from his head to his foot . . ."), a pointy cap rimmed with fur and adorned with a sprig of holly, and holding a long Dutch clay pipe. In 1862, R.H. Macy also introduced a Santa Claus into his New York store, and although he was recognizable as the bearded Saint Nick of the legend, his costume would vary in color and style for the next couple of decades.

By the end of the 19th century, however, Louis Prang, known as "the father of the American Christmas card," had standardized Santa in a red suit worn with a black belt and high boots, a costume reinforced by depictions

Santa Claus suit

such as J.C. LEYENDECKER's covers for the *Saturday Evening Post,* Macy's use of Santa as the grand marshal of its Thanksgiving Day parade (beginning in 1923), Haddon Sundblom's illustrations of Santa Claus advertising Coca-Cola (beginning in 1931), and actor Edmund Gwenn's portrayal in the 1947 movie *Miracle on 34th Street.*

sapeurs   Refers to a fashion-conscious subculture that evolved in 1970s in the Congo, spread to other French-speaking regions of sub-Saharan Western Africa, and later to French-speaking areas of Europe. *Sapeurs* were young men of limited means with an unlimited hunger for European designer fashion, particularly items with easily recognizable logos. In the face of dictator Mobuto Sese Seko's commands to wear authentic African styles, they opted for dressy, expensive European clothes.

Their name derives from "la SAPE," La Societé des Ambianceurs et des Personnes Élégantes (and not the *sapeurs* of the French civil defense corps). In 2004, the movement was the subject of a documentary called *The Importance of Being Elegant,* which included performances by musician Papa Wemba, the king of the movement.

sarong   A seamless rectangle of cloth, which wraps around the body and remains in place by means of tying or tucking. The term comes from Malay and applies to the wrap skirts used by both sexes. It differs from a PAREO only in the design on the cloth: If the design is Tahitian, the cloth should be described as a pareo; if the design is BATIK or some other pattern traditionally associated with Indonesia, the cloth should be described as a sarong.

Sartor Resartus   Thomas Carlyle's book-length condemnation of dandyism, famous for its author's coinage of the adjective "dandaical" in a usage akin to "maniacal," and its division of the British empire into Dandies and Drudges. Published serially by Fraser's magazine in London in 1833–1834, this prophecy of Victorian attitudes toward male fashion was then published as a book in the United States in 1836 and in the United Kingdom in 1838.

sartoria   An Italian word that roughly translates as "tailoring," hence its inclusion in labels, brands, and store names.

Sartorial Gazette   A monthly British trade journal, which began publishing in 1893 and ceased publication on the eve of World War II.

sash   1. A general term that can be used to refer to almost any long textile that is wrapped and tied or tucked around the waist.

Often a sash is intended as much or more to ornament the waist than for the simple function of holding up pants. (For example, the sashes worn by South Asian servants are thought to be the origin of the modern CUMMERBUND.) In contemporary usage, sashes tend to appear more in non-Western menswear or as part of military or court dress.

2. Reference to the belt component of a bathrobe, dressing gown, or similar garment.

3. Refers to the large ribbon component of a medal or decoration, even when that ribbon is fashioned into a bow or used to suspend the medal.

4. The band of cloth—often grosgrain—worn diagonally from the right shoulder to the left hip. It may be used to support medals or decorations (e.g., Boy Scout badges) or may be considered a signifier in and of itself.

sateen A lustrous fabric that uses a SATIN weave but is generally heavier and sturdier than a silk satin; most often made from cotton or cotton blend.

satin Technically, satin refers to a type of weave with long FLOATS so that the fabric's surface tends to appear glossy and smooth, especially when made of silk (or fibers meant to imitate silk, such as rayon or acetate). In menswear, satin fabrics are customarily confined to the edges of formalwear, or to accessories like ties, WAIST-COATS, and CUMMERBUNDS.

satin stripe A pattern of alternating shine and matte created by the fabric's weave. Popular for dress shirts made of fine cotton, a "satin stripe" may describe any width of stripe in any color or combination of colors, but it's usually a solid color (e.g., white on white) made by a DAMASK weave.

Saturday Night Fever The 1977 movie that starred John Travolta as Tony Manero, a Brooklynite reigning as king of his disco dance floor. In the costume design by Patrizia von Bradenstein, the hero's clothes were not meant to set fashion trends but rather to evoke Brooklyn and trends that were already mildly outdated by the time the movie was being made. Nevertheless, Travolta's white, three-piece suit (subsequently—and inaccurately—maligned as a LEISURE SUIT) became one of the iconic male costumes of movie history.

Savile Row An actual address as well as a symbol of British style. A short street in West London running parallel to nearby Regent Street, between Conduit Street and Burlington Gardens. Synonymous with the best of BESPOKE tailoring and the geographical and spiritual center, since the mid-19th century, of the best-known and best-regarded practitioners of that art.

The Row takes its name from Lady Dorothy Savile, who married Richard Boyle, the Earl of Burlington in the early 18th century. An ambitious land developer, Burlington created "Savile Street" in the second quarter of the 18th century. It remained a chiefly residential area—first for military officers and their families, then for physicians, then home to well-off theater people such as actor Charles Kemble and playwright Richard Brinsley Sheridan—until the first decade of the 19th century when tailors, who had already been congregating in the area, began to move their premises onto the row.

During the 19th and 20th centuries, Savile Row was the actual address of firms such as KILGOUR (at #8), H. Huntsman (at #11), HENRY POOLE (at #15), and ANDERSON & SHEPPARD (at #30), and attracted latecomers who aspired to similar status, such as Tommy NUTTER (at #19). However, at the beginning of the 21st century, zoning laws changed and rents on the Row skyrocketed, with many well-known firms (e.g., Anderson & Sheppard) remaining nearby, but finding it impossible to remain on the Row itself.

Savile Row Bespoke Code A voluntary code, instituted in the 21st century, loosely based on the rules issued by the Fédération de la Couture in France (which specify the amount of handwork that must be done on anything designated as a "couture" garment).

As subscribed to by ANDERSON & SHEPPARD, GIEVES & HAWKES, and other leading SAVILE Row tailors who are members of the lobbying and trade group called the Savile Row Bespoke Association, its rules specify that any suit advertised as bespoke must be handmade and take a minimum of 60 hours to complete. As with the making of couture gowns, no maximum is specified.

Savile Row

saxony   1. A style of soft tweed, especially as made with MERINO or some other especially fine and soft yarn.

Although the fabrics known as saxony originated in the British Isles, they take their name from the merino sheep traditionally raised in Saxony, a province in what is now Germany. Unlike their robust, crossbred English brethren, the saxony sheep produced a softer, finer yarn and, consequently, a softer and finer cloth. See color plates.

2. A reference to merino sheep raised in Germany, particularly in the 19th century before the merino was well established in Australia.

Scabal   The firm that began as a cloth merchant in Brussels in 1938, and then expanded into ready-to-wear and made-to-measure clothing. Founded by Otto Herz, Scabal is notorious for extremely expensive fabrics, sometimes costing thousands of dollars per yard, and has gone as far as incorporating 22-karat gold threads, crushed lapis lazuli, and crushed diamonds into its cloth. President George W. Bush wore a suit made of Scabal fabric during at least one State of the Union address.

scalplock   The lock of long hair left at the back of the head, especially in early Native American hairstyles and especially by men sporting a traditional MOHAWK (or those seeking to imitate them).

Scholte, Frederick   The famously irascible, red-headed, cigar-smoking Dutchman best known as principal tailor, from 1919 to 1959, of the Prince of Wales who later became EDWARD VIII and then Duke of Windsor; credited with the invention of the tailoring style variously known as the ENGLISH DRAPE or the LONDON CUT.

Before founding his own firm, Scholte worked at Johns & Pegg, a specialist in military tailoring. According to legend, as repeated in Richard Walker's 1988 *The Savile Row Story*, the prince appeared at Royal Ascot one day in a gray suit, a breach of formality that enraged his father the king. The prince repaired to Scholte, who cut a FROCK COAT on the spot and had someone stay up all night and stitch it together so that the prince would be suitably clad for Ascot the next morning.

Scholte's own style of tailoring, supposedly honed on military tunics (which demanded more freedom of movement than the civilian tailoring of the time), had great appeal for the comfort-loving prince, who would make Scholte's LOUNGE SUIT popular worldwide. The style spread still further since Swedish tailor Per Anderson, who trained under Scholte, had founded ANDERSON & SHEPPARD, still SAVILE ROW's most famous exponent of the draped silhouette.

Success, however, did nothing to temper Scholte temperament. The tailor became fanatically opposed to the big-shouldered, small-waisted extremes that his London cut eventually inspired: For example, when Captain Edward Metcalfe, the best man at Edward VIII's wedding to Wallis Simpson, asked for stronger shoulders in his jacket, Scholte refused him and flew into a rage. Connoisseurs considered Scholte's own products such masterworks that when the Duke of Windsor's wardrobe was auctioned in 1998, KITON paid $110,000 for 11 pieces.

school ring   See CLASS RING.

school tie   A NECKTIE or BOW TIE worn as part of the uniform of a private school; may also refer to a tie in the school colors worn by that school's graduate. Used in the same sense as club tie and therefore not necessarily a reference to a particular stripe, color, or pattern.

Schott Bros.   An East Coast outerwear company best known for its iconic MOTORCYCLE JACKETS, founded by brothers Irving and James Schott on New York City's Lower East Side in 1913. Two years later, inspired by Irving's favorite smoke, the brothers named one of their models the "Perfecto." During the 1920s, the company created its famous zippered motorcycle jackets; during the 1930s it created its leather bombers; and, during the World War II, supplied outerwear to the U.S. military. During the 1950s, it transferred the name "Perfecto" to its top-of-the-line motorcycle jacket. That same decade, Schott Bros. motorcycle jackets passed into legend when they were seen on the likes of James Dean and featured in the 1953 Marlon Brando movie THE WILD ONE.

Scotchgard   Any of the fabric treatments, manufactured and trademarked by St. Paul, Minnesota-based 3M, to repel water and/or oil.

Scotchgard originated in 1953 when a 3M scientist named Patsy Sherman, who was working on a new kind of rubber intended for the fuel lines of jets, accidentally splashed some latex onto a pair of tennis sneakers and noticed that the splashed canvas stayed clean while the rest of the sneaker soiled. Working with Sam Smith, Sherman perfected a way to apply the finish in textile mills and, in 1956, the first Scotchgard repellent for use on wool was announced. In 1959, a Scotchgard for wash-and-wear cotton was introduced. In 1963, Scotchgard was put in aerosol cans for consumer use.

screenprint   Trade jargon indicating that the pattern has been silk-screened on the fabric after the weaving or knitting process (as opposed to a JACQUARD, where the pattern is formed as the fabric is produced). A common example of a screenprint: A sweatshirt bearing a university or team logo.

scrubs   A shortened form of "scrub suit," refers to the loose pants and pullover-style top worn by doctors, nurses, orderlies, or others in hospital and clinic settings. Traditionally made of plain-weave cotton or a similarly stur-

dy, inexpensive material in order to withstand repeated harsh laundering. Traditionally done in industrial, solid colors (like green or blue), in the late 20th century scrubs began to be manufactured in colorful patterns—especially for medical workers dealing with children. Because they are cheap and unfitted, occasionally adopted by college students as a sort of anti-fashion statement.

scrub suit   See SCRUBS.

scye   The shortened slang form of ARMSCYE.

sea island cotton   Depending upon the context, can refer to the plant, the fiber, or the fabric made from it.

Sea island is a variety of LONG-STAPLE COTTON, *gossypium barbadense*, which takes its name from its primary habitat, in the Caribbean and the Sea Islands off the southeast coast of the United States. According to legend, Columbus carried this type of cotton back to Europe with him in 1492. In 1786, it was introduced to the United States from the Bahamas, and in 1790, William Elliott produced the first successful crop on Hilton Head Island in South Carolina. Cultivation thrived on low-country plantations both inshore and offshore until 1920, when boll weevils devastated the industry. Commercial cultivation was never successfully revived, particularly after the price of Sea Island's real estate rocketed.

Now a novelty, Sea Island is considered a premium cotton (as opposed to the UPLAND COTTON more common in the United States), sea island is prized for its silkiness and strength—and is priced accordingly.

seam allowance   The margin of fabric that falls outside the seam line; extra material so that the seam cannot pull apart or unravel when it is stressed by being worn. Generally around ⅝ inch and visible only on the "wrong" side of the garment.

seamless   Jargon for garments—usually socks, T-shirts, underwear, and the like—produced on circular knitting machines (like the ones originally made by Santoni or their modern equivalent) so that they have no chafing seams and also are less prone to split at weak points in the construction.

seam line *or* **seamline**   The actual line that the stitching follows.

seams   General reference to the ways of joining together pieces of textile—be it leather, knit, woven, or nonwoven.

seam binding   A very narrow, densely woven fabric—usually a twill tape—that is either sewn directly over a seam (to reinforce it) or over the raw edges of fabric (so that the fabric does not unravel and pull apart the seam). Appears only the "wrong" side of the garment, except when it is used for a special effect or deconstructed look.

Sean John   The menswear brand founded by SEAN JOHN COMBS—the music impresario known variously as Puff Daddy, Puffy, and P. Diddy—in 1998 as an urban (i.e., HIP-HOP) brand. In a move that he said was inspired by the AGNÈS B. merchandising, Combs began his brand by selling tens of thousands of black T-shirts and hats with his signature on them. By 2000, he had staged the first of his extravagant fashion shows and expanded into tailored clothing. By 2004, he had won the CFDA's award as Designer of the Year.

sebiro   A Japanese reference for a man's suit, supposedly derived from attempted pronunciation of SAVILE Row. The tailoring firm of HENRY POOLE takes credit for the coinage by virtue of being the first to create the first British-style suit for the Japanese ambassador to the court of Queen Victoria. Sometimes written as *SABIRO*.

secondhands   Industry jargon for the resale of fabric (usually GRAY GOODS).

Seditionaries   Opened by Malcolm McLaren and VIVIENNE WESTWOOD at 430 King's Road in the Chelsea section of London, this shop offered a depressing, industrialized take on PUNK fashion and succeeded SEX, the couple's previous shop at the same location, lasting roughly from 1976 to 1979. Its decor featured industrial gray paint, blow-ups of bomb-damaged Dresden and an upside-down Piccadilly Circus, and a hole smashed in the ceiling to make it look as if a bomb had dropped. A brass plaque outside announced: "Seditionaries: For soldiers, prostitutes, dykes and punks."

seersucker   A vertically striped fabric in which some of the stripes pucker, an effect created in the weaving process.

When making seersucker, selected WARP yarns (those running lengthwise, from top to bottom on the loom) are pulled tight and others are purposely left loose, thereby creating seersucker's distinctive crinkly texture. The first seersuckers were made of linen and came to Europe through India during the first quarter of the 18th century. (The English word is derived from a Hindi phrase meaning "milk and sugar," a reference to its texture.)

In PLISSÉ, a fabric often mistaken for seersucker, the same effect is created through application of a chemical coating rather than through weaving—an effect that sometimes wears off or washes out.

Seersucker is most often made of cotton, does not require ironing, launders easily, and has a pre-rumpled appearance that makes wrinkles less notable—all contributing factors to its popularity for summer suits.

seersucker suit Considered an American summertime classic, the SEERSUCKER suit established itself in the pre-air-conditioning era because it was lightweight, more or less wrinkle-proof, easy to wash, easy to tailor, and made of inexpensive material. Pre-World War I, it carried a connotation of being the poor man's substitute for a linen suit. After World War I, it became associated with college men (the origin of its entry into the PREPPY canon). After World War II, it became more generally accepted.

Throughout those decades, the style changed very little: The prototype was made of blue- or brown-and-white, vertically striped seersucker (or similarly conservative color combination). The jacket would be single-breasted, either unlined or lined with the lightest of materials, boxy in shape, and with natural shoulders. The pants would be loose and often PLAIN-FRONT.

SEHM A trade show for men's fashion, founded in 1960 with 80 exhibitors and formerly held twice yearly in Paris; credited with increasing the awareness of menswear trends at a time when traditional tailoring still dominated the market. The name was an acronym for the Salon International de l'Habillement Masculin, and was translated by the show organizers as "International Men's Apparel Show" until the late 1990s, when they changed the translation to "International Men's Fashion Show."

Like PITTI UOMO, its counterpart in Florence, SEHM concentrated on high-end and designer lines and its show dates were coordinated with Paris runway presentations so that buyers and fashion editors could attend both. During the last quarter of the 20th century, especially when runway shows for men's fashion were less common or less likely to be integrated with women's runway shows, SEHM virtually summarized Paris design of menswear (although it always included exhibitors from other countries, such as the United Kingdom). During the 1980s, its "Creators Club" was among the first to regularly stage menswear runway events. At one point in the late 1990s, it grew to a total of 700 exhibitors. In 2000, it was bought and merged into another trade fair, and the name became defunct.

self-besomed A WELTED edge created with the same fabric as the body of the garment. See BESOM.

self-fringed Means that the fabric or garment's fringe is formed by deliberate unraveling, rather than being sewn on as a separate component.

self-patterned Means that the pattern is integral to the fabric structure, rather than printed or added after the completion of weaving or knitting. For example: A JACQUARD is a self-patterned fabric.

self-striped Means that the stripe is integral to the fabric, rather than printed or added after weaving. For example: SEERSUCKER is a self-striped fabric.

self-tanner A cosmetic based on the active ingredient DHA (dihydroxyacetone), which reacts with the amino acids in skin to stain it orange-brown, producing an imitation tan that lasts for a few days.

The first well-known self-tanner was MAN-TAN, a product introduced in the 1950s and beloved by bodybuilders for decades afterward. Although various self-tanning products were introduced over the years, the category really took off after the American Cancer Society's 1988 warning that linked sun exposure to skin cancer and media warnings in the 1990s that sun exposure caused premature aging of the skin.

Standard formulations include gels, lotions, mousses, and spray liquids. Many companies also market different formulas for face and body, on the premise that facial skin contains more oil glands and has a faster cell turnover. Also known as "sunless tanners." (See also BRONZER.)

selham   See BURNOOSE.

sell-in   Industry jargon for what the manufacturer sells to the store.

sell-through   Industry jargon for what gets sold to the end user or average consumer. For example, a piece of fashion that sells promptly and does not have to be discounted is said to have "excellent sell-through."

selvedge *or* **selvage** *or* **selvege**   Woven textiles that are literally "self-edged" with a densely woven band on the vertical edges of the fabric to prevent unraveling.

In menswear, this term usually refers to a border that may be stamped with the name or trademark of the mill and/or may tout special properties of the cloth (e.g., super 120s wool). For this reason the selvedge is frequently in a lighter or contrasting color to the main body of the cloth. For example: Gray, suit-grade wool may have a bright yellow selvedge.

selvedge denim   Refers to denim that is produced on a shuttle loom, so that the material has a SELVEDGE. Because most denim intended for the JEANS market was produced on huge power looms beginning in the 1950s, selvedge denim is used as an indicator of age and/or artisanal production.

Selvedge denim is generally much narrower than run-of-the-mill denim, occasionally as narrow as 28 or 30 inches. The selvedge itself is usually thin and white. Unlike worsteds and other fabrics used in menswear, the selvedge is relatively small and rarely marked with the name of the manufacturer.

From about the 1990s onward, collectors began to prize jeans made of selvedge denim (which is only noticeable when the jeans are inside out or the cuffs are turned up) and selected mills began to re-create artisanal denim for the PREMIUM JEANS market. Perhaps the best-known example is the 10-ounce, 29-inch-wide, red selvedge denim that CONE MILLS began producing for LEVI STRAUSS in 1927.

semi-custom   MADE-TO-MEASURE tailoring.

semi-formal   Depending upon the time and place, the designation of semiformal dress may refer to either BLACK TIE (which is considered a step down in formality from full-on WHITE TIE) or, alternatively, to a BUSINESS SUIT or CERIMONIA. Sometimes used interchangeably with BLACK TIE OPTIONAL or CREATIVE BLACK TIE.

Selvedge

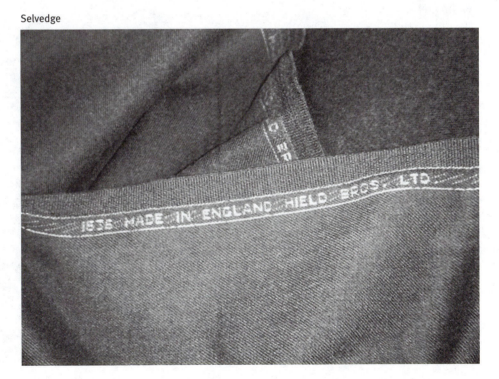

semi-ulster   A lighter version of the traditional ULSTER. Synonym: ULSTERETTE.

serging   1. The finishing of seams so that, on the wrong side, the SEAM ALLOWANCES appear neatly trimmed and encased in thread. The most common finishing for flat knit garments such as sweatshirts, polo shirts, etc., but also used on wovens to prevent unraveling. (Serging is never used with SELVEDGE fabrics, e.g., SELVEDGE DENIM, because it would be redundant.)

For knits both seam allowances are often bound together in a single edge; for wovens, the seam allowances may be finished separately.

Generally accomplished with a machine known as a serger.

2. The process of hand-sewing with an overcasting stitch also known as a serging stitch, also used on either unfinished edges of garments or raw seam allowances.

set-in sleeve   Refers to the standard method of tailoring a jacket or shirt sleeve; the sleeve is shaped as a separate piece that curves upward into a SLEEVEHEAD and then "set in" a shaped armhole on the body of the garment. Alternative styles include DROP SHOULDER, RAGLAN, and SADDLE SHOULDER.

sett   Refers to the pattern of a TARTAN, not to the actual fabric.

sett helmet   A tweed cap with a rounded, close-fitting crown and a narrow brim (so that the field of vision

is not impeded); traditionally worn for shooting, especially in Scotland.

seven-fold tie   Refers to a style of necktie made without a lining or interlining. Because of this construction, which must be done by hand, the tie material falls more freely and loosely down the shirtfront, invariably yields a less perfect and less rigid-looking knot, and, in general, recalls the contemporary necktie's family relationship to the 19th-century CRAVAT.

To create a "seven-fold," the material is laid on the bias and edges are folded back on themselves, with an extra fold at the end creating the uneven number; these folds are then hand-basted in place with a long, running stitch on the underside of the tie, so that the tie can accommodate movement without unfolding.

In addition to its hand production, a seven-fold tie uses much more silk than its lined counterpart—additional reasons for its higher price tag and its limited offering.

Seventh Avenue   Slang reference to the garment industry in New York, which grew from the concentration of women's wear manufacturers on Seventh Avenue, particularly in the midtown region in zip code 10018. For that reason, purists consider its use as a reference to the menswear industry to be incorrect.

Seven-fold tie

Seventh on Sixth   Semiannual runway shows of New York designers (hence the SEVENTH AVENUE reference) held in BRYANT PARK, the public park located behind the main branch of the New York Public Library at 42nd Street and Avenue of the Americas—originally named Sixth Avenue (hence the Sixth).

shad   Short for SHADBELLY.

shadbelly   A style of double-breasted TAILCOAT, now worn chiefly for dressage and show events. The shadbelly sports two rows of three buttons (all of which are worn buttoned) and is cut high enough so that the points of the vest worn beneath are clearly visible. Unlike the SWALLOWTAIL (the style that it has mostly replaced), the shadbelly does not have a strongly curved tail, but falls almost straight from the waistseam—giving the impression of frock coat tha-t is missing its front panels.

shades   Slang for sunglasses.

shadow plaid   Like the SHADOW STRIPE, this term usually describes a finer and/or fainter plaid running next to the main pattern.

Shaft: Richard Roundtree

shadow stripe   1. A vertical stripe, usually narrow, is bracketed or "shadowed" by lighter or smaller stripes on one or both sides. In the classic "shadow stripe," the shadow is a variation on the color of the main stripe. But it can also be a completely different color. Usually describes shirt fabric.   2. Used to describe a fabric that is self-striped (usually by alternating Z-TWIST and S-TWIST yarns in the structure of the fabric), so that the stripe becomes only visible only as it reflect light or falls into shadow.

Shaft   1. The 1971 movie starring Richard Roundtree as detective John Shaft and directed by Gordon Parks. Roundtree, a former football player and male model, sported an AFRO, a thick mustache, and exaggerated sideburns in his role as detective/sex god. His clothes—particularly the trademark dark turtleneck—were tight enough to leave no doubt that he was the movie's main attraction. Likewise, his lapels were wide enough—particularly on his beloved black leather coat—to get across the message that the movie's costumes were emphatically contemporary 1970s Harlem and not Harlem-via-Hollywood. Isaac Hayes' theme song, which began with the lyric "Who's the black private dick/that's a sex machine to all the chicks?/Shaft!/Ya damn right!" won the 1972 Oscar for best original song.

The movie was cited as spearheading the blaxploitation trend in 1970s cinema and was followed by 1972's *Shaft's Big Score* and 1973's *Shaft in Africa*.

2. The 2000 remake starring Samuel L. Jackson as John Shaft, nephew of the original detective (played by Roundtree in a cameo appearance), directed by John Singleton. In the costume design by Ruth Carter, Jackson sported a shaved head, a goatee, several pairs of futuristic, quasi *MATRIX*-style sunglasses, and an ARMANI

wardrobe heavy on hoodies, leather, turtlenecks, and long coats, winning that year's MTV Movie Award as Best-Dressed.

shag   A 1970s hairstyle that capitalized on layered, "feathered" hair and was worn by both men (teen idol David Cassidy in TV's *The Partridge Family*) and women (postergirl Farrah Fawcett-Majors at the height of her *Charlie's Angels* fame).

shagreen   1. The leather made from the skin of sharks or rays, distinguished by a round, nodule-like pattern on its surface. Because it is tough and generally not pliable, shagreen appears most often in menswear as a decorative accent on items such as cigarette cases. (Not to be confused with SHARKSKIN, the material used for suits.)   2. In very earlier references, may connote animal leather tanned to resemble the granular pattern found in the authentic fish skins.

shaker rib   A reversible ribbed knit stitch, often used for an entire sweater (as opposed to RIBBING that appears only on the edges of the garment). A variation of the stitch known as the fisherman's rib, the shaker is made by knitting alternating stitches into the stitch below, and it results in a relatively flat ribbing with long lines of single knit stitches. Synonym: shaker stitch.

shaker sweater   A sweater made primarily of SHAKER RIB, traditionally a simple style in a solid color and thick, usually unslubbed, yarn.

shako   A style of stiff, cylindrical hat with a flat top; unlike the FEZ, the shako does not taper toward the top, but often flares outward. It also has a short, attached visor and is almost always ornamented with a badge, braiding, and/or plume. The style originated in the first half of 19th century as military headwear and is now more familiar from band uniforms. Synonym: TARBUCK-ET (because of its shape).

shalwar kameez   A general style of loose, long tunic and pants, made of woven material, worn throughout Central and South Asia; used by both sexes. Generally, the "kameez," or chemise, is approximately knee-length and long-sleeved with a short placket opening that ends at mid-chest. It is unfitted, untailored, and its side seams are generally open from the hips down. Depending on local custom, the "shalwar," or drawstring pants, may be either very full, moderately full, PEGGED, or tight through the entire lower leg (i.e., CHURIDAR). The most common variant spelling is SALWAR KAMEEZ. Synonyms for the women's versions (which usually include a STOLE called a dupatta) include the Punjabi suit and salwar suit.

Shanghai tailors   From roughly 1900 until the Japanese occupation in the 1930s, Shanghai was widely reputed to have the world's best tailors outside Savile Row—or, at least, outside Europe. Historians of the trend attribute this to a confluence of factors, including: the European occupation of the city dating from 1842 and the number of businesses set up to cater to the British and French businessmen; the established Jewish community (and repeated waves of Jewish immigrants), who brought tailoring skills with them from Europe; the port city's ability to easily obtain high-quality materials; the city's traditional emphasis on the importance of style and appearance; and a ready supply of cheap, highly skilled labor that made repeated fittings and prodigious amounts of handwork easily available.

Although this tailoring tradition died out completely during World War II and the subsequent Communist regime, the resulting diaspora of Shanghai tailors was supposedly responsible for an increase in the quantity and quality of HONG KONG TAILORS. In the early 21st century, the best-known Shanghai tailoring firm became DAVE THE TAILOR, an establishment in the French Concession founded by Dave K.C. Sheung, a Taiwanese trained by a Shanghai tailor from the city's early-20th-century heyday.

shank 1. A piece of material inserted between the SOLE and INSOLE of a boot or shoe to lend it rigidity; its length and material determines the sole's flexibility. For example, a steel-shanked boot may be difficult for everyday walking, but excellent for climbing. MOCCASINS, SLIPPERS, and similar styles do not have shanks. 2. Refers to a connector on the underside of a button, usually a small loop of wire, elastic, or leather. (See SHANKED BUTTON.) If the button is not made with a shank, the person sewing a flat button to the garment may also form one out of thread. (This is often done with men's suits to enhance both the drape of the fabric and its wearer's ease of movement.) 3. Refers to what would otherwise be called the neck or shaft of a clothes hanger. For example, on a hanger intended to hold a jacket with a high collar, the shank may be extra long so that the collar is not compressed when the garment is stored. 4. Refers to the part of a ring that encircles the finger; does not include the setting and/or any stones. For example, on a man's SIGNET RING, the shank would be the metal circle but not the actual signet.

shanked button Refers to a button readymade with a small loop or tail underneath, so that the thread attaching the button to the garment is not visible from the top of the button. (Any button that does not feature piercing to allow the thread to pass through the top is, perforce, a shanked button.) From the side, a shanked button follows a T-shaped silhouette.

In menswear, shanked buttons are commonly used on BLAZERS (where the buttons may be brass and/or engraved) and in OUTERWEAR.

shantung 1. In menswear, the term refers to a simply woven silk made of irregular yarns so that SLUBS—or some similar unevenness—is evident on the fabric's surface; may also refer to a synthetic or blend made to imitate it. For men's tailored clothing, a synonym for the more frequently encountered DOUPPIONI. 2. For hats, particularly COWBOY styles, refers to a type of material called SHANTUNG PANAMA, which is actually rolled PAPER but resembles straw; sourced from ABACA.

shantung panama See SHANTUNG.

shark The tough leather made from the skin of the large fish is properly known as SHAGREEN.

sharkskin Refers to a woven material favored for suits, not, as one might guess, a leather. (The actual skin of the shark is usually called SHAGREEN.)

In the most classic sense of the word, sharkskin refers to crisp wool or wool blend composed of black and white threads that, put together in such close proximity, create a gray (hence the supposed resemblance to a shark's skin). However, the popularity of that material led to a more generic use of the word, meaning that other colors with the same finish, weight, and weave were also described as sharkskin. See color plates.

shatnes *or* **shatnez** *or* **shaatnez** Reference to a mixture of WOOL and LINEN, the wearing of which is prohibited, according to Jewish law, by all but priests.

shawl collar *or* **shawl lapel**   1. A long, rounded COL-
LAR with no notch, peaks, or sharp indents; used primarily on TUXEDOS, DINNER JACKETS, SMOKING JACKETS,
and similar formal and semi-FORMALWEAR during the
20th and 21st centuries; also a frequent feature of vests,
particularly double-breasted styles.

Technically, a "shawl lapel" is a misnomer, since the
style does not use a LAPEL (which is folded over from
the body of the suit) and is instead a separate, sewn-on
collar.

2. When used to describe a sweater, a shawl collar may
refer to a thick, gently rounded collar, generally aug-
menting a neck opening of some depth (e.g., anywhere
from just above the nipple line to the navel).

shearling   1. A SHEEPSKIN, particularly from a lamb,
that has been cured so that the fleece remains attached to
the leather, with that fleece "sheared" to a uniform
length. When the hide is taken from a MERINO sheep, it is
generally known as MOUTON.   2. A type of coat made
from such skins, especially a relatively untailored style
associated with rugged images of the American west
(e.g., the MARLBORO MAN).

shedded sheep   Sheep, usually MERINOS, raised in
sheds and sometimes wearing coats, to enhance the quality of their fleece. See SUPER 100S.

sheepskin   Usually
refers to a hide with
the fleece left on and
either untrimmed or
only partially trimmed.
The hide of a sheep or
lamb with the coat
left on but sheared to

a uniform length is known as SHEARLING (in general) or
MOUTON (for a MERINO sheep in particular).

shell buttons   A generic reference to buttons cut from
nacreous shells, up to and including MOTHER-OF-PEARL
buttons (which are considered the highest grade).

shell layer   In clothes for sports (or the clothes made
to look like them), a shell layer is usually the lightweight
layer worn over the BASE LAYER and any INSULATING
LAYER. Rather than warmth, it is intended primarily to
provide protection from wind and rain.

shepherd's check *or* **shephard's check**   Pattern
named after the simple plaid worn by herders working
on the border between Scotland and England, which was
originally six threads of black and six threads of white.

Sherlock Holmes   The fictional London-based detective created by Scottish-born doctor and author Sir
Arthur Conan Doyle (1859–1930) in 1887 and featured
in four novels and dozens of short stories thereafter, as
well as numerous portrayals on stage, screen (e.g., starring Basil Rathbone in a series of films beginning in the
late 1930s), and television (e.g., the series starring Jeremy
Brett in the 1980s and 1990s). The two items of dress
most associated with Holmes, the INVERNESS CAPE and

Shedded sheep

DEERSTALKER CAP, were not actually mentioned in the Doyle's work, but were the invention of Sidney Paget who illustrated the Holmes stories in the late 19th century.

sherryvallies   Similar to contemporary CHAPS, sherryvallies were worn by men on horseback as a protective covering over other pants. Popular in the last quarter of the 18th century and first quarter of the 19th century.

sherwani   Similar to the ACHKAN, the sherwani is a traditional style of high-collared, lapel-less, buttoned jacket worn in South Asia. However, unlike the plain-front achkan, the sherwani is often heavily embroidered and is considered formal dress (e.g., worn by the groom and other important participants in a wedding).

shetland   1. Due to the harsh conditions on the Shetland Islands, which are halfway to Norway off the north coast of Scotland, the small and hardy sheep there produce a sturdy, lightweight wool with a long STAPLE (which was traditionally plucked rather than shorn from the animal). That, in turn, was used to produce a sturdy fabric; particularly popular during the late 19th and early 20th centuries as a woven material for sportswear (e.g., KNICKERS, NORFOLK JACKETS, and the like). In contemporary use, a genuine woven shetland is relatively rare and appears mainly in SPORT COATS and outerwear.

2. Refers to a sweater knit from the type of sturdy wool associated with the Shetland Islands. Originally appeared (e.g., when imported to the United States by BROOKS BROTHERS in 1904) in the distinctive knitting patterns that had developed in the islands over centuries (and looked much more Norwegian than Scottish). Early and authentic shetlands were made of natural-colored wool.

However, as the 20th century developed, such patterns were often lumped together with FAIR ISLE knits and "shetland" came to mean something different: a reference to the style of wool rather than the style of knitting. By the mid-20th century, a shetland sweater usually indicated a simply styled sweater (often a plain crewneck or a cabled crewneck) that was sometimes in a bright color (like red or green) or sometimes in a simple, dark shade like navy blue. As such, the shetland sweater became a staple of PREPPY style.

shibori   Any one of several traditional Japanese resist-dyeing techniques that Westerners lump together under the crude general category of TIE-DYE. Cloth is gathered, shaped, or squeezed together and then dyed, the resulting pattern being prized for its organic quality and elements of randomness.

shield   A panel of INTERFACING, usually CANVAS or HYMO, especially one used to shape a jacket; never seen when the jacket is worn. See FRONT SHIELD and BACK SHIELD.

shillelagh   A sturdy, wooden CANE, rough and cudgel-like in its appearance; in the days when an etiquette of usage was attached to canes, considered appropriate for country use. In the late 19th and early 20th centuries, some people thought that a shillelagh should be made only of BLACKTHORN (and therefore used it as a synonym for blackthorn canes); others thought that it could also be made of oak or other sturdy woods (and therefore differentiated between a shillelagh and a blackthorn cane).

shirt   Although virtually every culture and historical period has had a garment that could be considered equivalent to a shirt, during most of menswear's history the shirt was relegated to the status of an undergarment. Prior to the 20th century, a man seen in a shirt without a jacket was still considered to be in a state of undress.

In contemporary use, reference to a "shirt" without additional specification (such as CAMP SHIRT, HAWAIIAN SHIRT, or POLO SHIRT) is understood to mean either a button-front DRESS SHIRT or SPORT SHIRT made of woven material with a FOLD-OVER COLLAR, SET-IN SLEEVES, and other traditional construction.

shirtfront   The portion of a shirt that covers the front torso. Its opposite is the shirtback.

shirting   Jargon for shirt fabrics. Refers to the fabric, never to the finished garment.

shirt points   The pointed edges of a turn-down collar on a shirt. As in: "A BUTTON-DOWN shirt is distinguished by its buttoning shirt points." In contemporary use, about 3 inches long. Synonym: COLLAR POINTS.

shirtsleeves   More often a synonym for taking off a jacket, rather than a reference to the actual sleeves—just as in the phrase "rolling up his shirtsleeves" is a synonym for getting down to work. Prior to the 20th century, considered a state of undress and therefore not acceptable in public, since the shirt itself was still categorized as underwear.

shirttail   The portion of a dress shirt or sports shirt that is normally not seen because it is tucked into pants; especially the rounded bottom of the shirt. In previous centuries, shirttails were sometimes extra long because they functioned as underwear in the absence of underpants.

In sportswear, a garment made with squared shirttails is normally interpreted as one not designed to be tucked in.

shirtweight   Jargon used to refer to fabric for shirts and tops. "Shirtweight" generally refers to wovens and indicates the fabric, never the finished garment. (See also TOPWEIGHT.)

shoe   For construction of a prototypical dress shoe, see diagram below.

shoe sizes   Shoes sizes are not standardized, either nationally or internationally; although sizes are loosely based on measurements, they change from manufacturer to manufacturer—easily varying an entire size between manufacturers. Here are rough equivalents between the four main sizing systems:

European size	Asian size	English size	U.S. size
39	24.5		
40	25		
41	25.5	6 to 6.5	7 to 7.5

Shoe

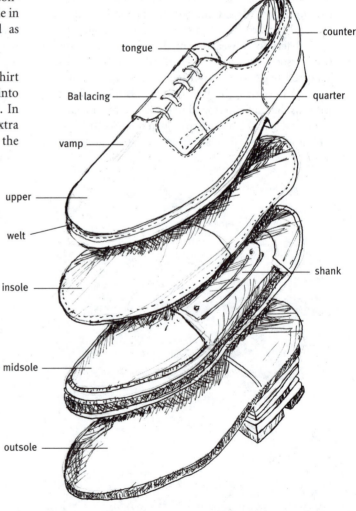

42	26	7.5 to 8	8 to 8.5
43	26.5 to 27	8.6 to 9	9 to 9.5
44	27.5	9.5 to 10	10 to 10.5
45	28	10.5 to 11	11 to 11.5
46		11.5 to 12	12 to 12.5
47		12.5	13 to 13.5
48			14 to 14.5
			15. to 15.5

shoestring tie   A thin necktie style, usually tied in a bow instead of a traditional FOUR-IN-HAND or other knot; named for its resemblance to a shoe lace; used especially when referring to the ties worn by TEDDY Boys, or in other British usage. Synonym: BOOTLACE TIE.

shoe trees   Devices intended to preserve the shape of the shoe when it is not being worn. The traditional shoe tree for an expensive bench-made shoe is a wooden tree expressly made to imitate the wearer's foot, but many other varieties exist, including inflatable models and spring-loaded plastic contraptions.

shooting stick   A type of CANE that also doubles as a folding chair. Used only by sports spectators—usually in field sports where no seating is available—a shooting stick usually has double handles at its top and a pointy end surrounded by a cup, so that it can be planted in the

Shoe tree

ground without completely sinking in. It is used like a walking stick until its owner wants to stop, at which point the handles unfold to provide an impromptu perch, usually leather in triangular or rectangular shape. In contemporary use, seen most often at events such as point-to-points or golf tournaments.

shot   Used to describe fabric woven with contrasting colors so that it appears to be one color from one angle and a different color from a different angle. As in "That solid-colored silk tie had a very handsome shot effect: It looked blue from the top and green from the side." Synonym: changeable.

shoulder bag   General reference to various styles of large tote bags (e.g., MESSENGER BAGS) carried by a long strap from the shoulder (or slung diagonally across the body). Used more often to refer to women's purses and accessories.

shoulder boards   The counterpart to EPAULETTES, shoulder boards are stiff and in a single piece (rather than the looped fabric used on TRENCH COATS, SAFARI JACKETS, and the like); more often a feature of uniforms rather than civilian dress.

shoulder pads   Part of the interior construction of a jacket or coat, especially in tailored clothing; used to enhance—and usually broaden—the shoulders and control the draping of the material covering the front torso; never visible when the garment is being worn. (Often a very lightweight and flexible shoulder pad is included in so-called "natural shoulder" and "unconstructed" garments.)

Customarily, the shoulder pad is made of cotton wadding, foam, or some combination, and is triangular or wedge-shaped, with the broad base of the triangle being aligned with the shoulder seam of the jacket and the apex of the triangle tapered toward the garment's neck opening.

sideboards   Another name for SIDEBURNS or side-whiskers, especially during the late 19th and early 20th centuries.

sideburns   1. Describes the part of the beard that meets the hairline in front of the ear; the equivalent of a demi-beard, designates whiskers that extend from the hairline downward toward the chin (but do not meet at or cover the chin, which would make them a beard). Fashionable during the 19th century—when they inspired coinages such as BURNSIDES, DUNDREARIES, PICCADILLY WEEPERS (a.k.a., NEWGATE KNOCKERS), and MUTTONCHOPS—they became trendy again in the late 1960s.   2. Also used, especially for preadolescents or women, to describe a lock of hair grown long so that it covers the front of the ear.

side-gussets   Synonym, especially in the 20th and 21st centuries, for the style of shoe that substitutes one or two elasticized gussets for the customary system of laces; better known in the 19th century as the BOSTON BOOT or CONGRESS GAITER.

side-tie shoes   A style of DRESS SHOE that is usually constructed as either a high-vamped SLIPPER or an OXFORD, but moves the lacing to the side of the shoe. Identified more with traditional British footwear and especially with high-end or custom cobbling.

A variation, the side-gusset shoe (which is directly descended from the CONGRESS GAITER of the 19th centu-ry), has essentially the same profile and is worn in the same situations but replaces the lacing with an elasticized gusset.

sidewalk shoes   Old-fashioned jargon for shoe styles that were somewhere between the dress shoes worn with full business regalia and the shoes used for sports. The closest modern equivalent might include today's rubber-soled MOCCASINS or PENNY LOAFERS. The term began to lose currency during the 1920s.

sidewhiskers   Slightly archaic synonym for what would probably be called SIDEBURNS. Like SIDEBOARDS, the term was used more often in the 19th and early 20th centuries, when it was a more accurate and more appropriate way of describing styles of facial hair, such as DUNDREARIES, that covered virtually all of a man's face except for his chin and upper lip.

signature item   Does not mean that the accessory or apparel bears a literal signature. Instead, a "signature item" is industry jargon for the item most easily identified with a designer or brand (which may or may not include an identifiable name or logo).

signet ring   A ring sporting an intaglio, either carved in stone or cast in precious metal, with a man's family crest, initial, personal motto, or similar symbolic token. Originally used for the practical purpose of leaving a signature impression on the sealing wax of letters and documents; its wear tended to connote land-holding gentry. In contemporary use, may be worn on either a man's ring finger or (more often in the United States) his pinkie finger.

Side-tie shoes

silent valet   A piece of furniture, rather than a person; more common in the days when bedrooms and dressing rooms were apt to feature armoires rather than closets. The silent valet is a stand, usually about 3½ feet high, featuring a thick, wooden hanger (or the equivalent, shoulder-width crossbar) on which a man is intended to hang his suit jacket, usually surmounting a rack where he can fold and hang his trousers. Use of the silent valet is supposed to preserve the suit by allowing it to air and allowing wrinkles to release without pressing. Sometimes called a valet's chair, especially when it incorporates a small seat.

silesia   A type of sturdy, traditionally cotton, fabric used for the insides of pockets. Once a reference to a specific fabric manufactured in the region of Germany known as Silesia. Synonym: POCKETING.

silhouette   Jargon for the shape or general outline of clothes. For example, someone watching a fashion show might comment, "The designer is moving toward a looser silhouette." For example: Well-known menswear silhouettes include the boxy IVY LEAGUE or the more body-conscious CONTINENTAL.

silk   May refer to either the fiber or the fabric made from it; prized for its resilience, luster, and brilliance when dyed. Most silk originates as filament spun by the *Bombyx mori*, usually known as the silkworm moth, when the caterpillars are constructing their cocoons; it is therefore classified as a PROTEINACIOUS fiber.

A single cocoon can yield a fine, strong filament hundreds of meters long. However, in order to process the fiber, the cocoons usually must be immersed in boiling water to kill the larvae inside, the filament unwound, and the gum that held the cocoon together rinsed away, until a white, shiny filament emerges. (Raw silk, which is darker, usually contains some of the original silk gum.)

Because of the fineness and shininess of the processed fiber, contemporary use of silk in menswear is usually confined to NECKWEAR; dressy apparel, accessories, and accents (e.g., silk satin FACINGS on a TUXEDO); blends with other fibers (e.g., JACKETINGS made of silk and linen); or LOUNGEWEAR. Although silk absorbs water, it dries faster than COTTON (hence its onetime popularity for long underwear).

silkies   Slang, particularly in the 1960s and 1970s, for HAWAIIAN SHIRTS.

silk knots   Usually refers to the knots of silk cord used as a substitute for CUFFLINKS, the *boutons de machettes en passementerie*, popularized in the 20th century by Denis Colban, the proprietor of CHARVET.

Sinatra, Frank   Born as the only child of a working class Italian family in Hoboken, New Jersey, in 1915, singer Francis Albert Sinatra was a clothes horse practically from birth. His mother Dolly costumed him in a TOP HAT and TAILS when he was still a toddler, and, before even entering high school, he had a dozen SPORT COATS, twice as many pairs of pants, and his own charge account at Geismar's, the local department store. As an adult, Sinatra would go on to compose a new American standard: a look of loosened ties, snazzy suits, and snap-brimmed hats.

Sinatra's look evolved through three distinct phases. The first, which began in the 1940s and coincided with his stardom as a crooner and bobby-soxers' heartthrob, was a BEBOP phase, when he sported SPANIEL TIES and strong-shouldered DRAPE suits. The second phase—and the one for which he is still celebrated—began around the time of his marriage to Ava Gardner in 1951 and continued through his winning of an Academy Award and signing with Columbia Records in 1953 into the RAT PACK years of the early 1960s. Having studied the Hollywood and Holmby Hills crowd centered around the notoriously natty Humphrey Bogart, Sinatra radically underplayed the shoulders and LAPELS of his suits. He employed a full-time valet, spent a fortune on clothes, and patronized both SAVILE ROW firms and SY DEVORE, but still managed to look completely casual. His hat would be tilted as a clue to his mood of the moment. His pinkie ring would be turned to the side, as if he'd forgotten it was there. His raincoat would be slung over his shoulder. As that style became more slick toward the end of the 1950s, he added luxurious V-neck sweaters (notably in orange, his favorite color) and shinier, mohair-blend suits.

By the time he announced his premature and short-lived retirement in 1971, Sinatra was well into his third and least distinguished phase. Although always impeccable, Sinatra now wore the blazers and cardigans seen on many other prosperous older men in Southern California. By the time Ronald Reagan ran for presi-

dent, the former Democrat had become a staunch Republican, the once skeletal singer had become portly, and his toupee and other methods of masking baldness were more obvious. He died of a heart attack in 1998.

single-breasted   Indicates a style of jacket that closes with a single row of buttons (usually two, three, or four of them), rather than the double row of buttons on a DOUBLE-BREASTED jacket. Jargon used most often in descriptions of items that are usually double-breasted, such as BLAZERS.

single cuff   Synonym for a BARREL CUFF (more common when describing women's and children's fashions). May also be called a BAND CUFF.

singlet   An UNDERSHIRT, particularly a TANK SHIRT and particularly in British usage.

siping   A pattern of thin slits cut into the sole of shoe or boot to increase traction. Common in TOP-SIDERS and other footwear designed for slippery surfaces.

siren suit   A JUMPSUIT or COVERALL, especially in British usage during World War II, when it was an effi-

Frank Sinatra

cient, no-nonsense way to get fully dressed at the fastest possible speed; its name refers to Nazi aircraft alarms rather than the temptresses of legend.

The garment is most associated with Winston Churchill, who had himself outfitted with a custom version that looked like an Eisenhower jacket from the waist up; he owned at least one model made from velvet and one made from pinstriped wool. One of Churchill's well-worn models brought £30,000 at auction in 2002. Synonym: boiler suit.

six-pack   Slang for abdominal muscles that are so well-toned that the ridges between them are visible. Popular from the 1980s onward especially when describing male models or swimwear. Its opposite, a flabby midsection, would be a "spare tire."

sizing   A compound (such as starch or gelatin) that is applied to thread or yarn during fabric production to make the weaving process easier—usually by making it more abrasion-resistant and less prone to unraveling. Sizing gives the garment a misleadingly stiff feel but is designed to wash out and return the fabric to its original hand, or unsized texture.

Skants   A style of underpants. Briefs made without a fly- or Y-front. Similar to a bikini swimsuit. Introduced by Jockey in the late 1950s.

skeleton suit   A late 18th- and early-19th-century fashion for boys, which featured a jacket buttoned to a pair of matching high-waisted trousers.

skew   Jargon to refer to the torque that takes place in a twill fabric after it comes off the loom. The shrinkage and skew must be figured into the pattern making of

jeans so they don't twist around the wearer's legs as they're being worn. Synonym: torque.

The retail term that is pronounced the same way, but has a totally different meaning, is spelled SKU.

ski mask   A knit cap that not only covers the head but can be rolled down over the face, leaving only small holes for the eyes, nostrils, and mouth; similar to a balaclava helmet.

skimmer   Mostly archaic synonym for a straw boater, implying both the style's association with casual dress and its shallow crown.

skinhead   A street style that originated in the late 1960s in Britain as a working-class response to the liberalism and look of the hippies. Because hippies wore their hair long, skinheads wore their heads shaved or in super-short, military styles. Likewise, as part of their anti-fashion statement: they favored Ben Sherman shirts or other button-downs, sometimes checked and/or short-sleeved, instead of hippie tunics and T-shirts; heavy workboots in place of sandals; suspenders in place of thickly decorated belts; and rolled-up, workman's blue jeans instead of long bell-bottoms.

skirt   Refers to the portion of a man's jacket from the waist to the hem. In a jacket that is nipped (i.e., suppressed) at the waist, the material may flare so that it resembles a woman's skirt.

Ski mask

skirt pockets   Usually an 18th- or 19th-century reference to pockets placed on the rear SKIRT of the coat or jacket; most often accessed through vertical flaps, which may or may not be buttoned.

skivvies   Slang for underwear, especially associated with the navy. Originally it referred only to an undershirt. But, by World War II, the meaning had grown to encompass underpants.

SKU   An abbreviation for "stockkeeping unit," usually written without periods and pronounced as "skew." A designer or manufacturer will sometimes refer to the number of SKUs in his line or collection as a way to indicate its size or the problems involved in financing and producing it. (See also ITEM.)

skull bucket   Slang for protective HARD HAT worn by workmen.

skullcap   A general reference to any circular soft cap with no brim, which may be knit, crocheted, or stitched together of woven material (usually in a pie-shaped, gore construction). Covers the crown of the head but does not extend to the forehead or the neck.

Slap sole

slacks   In industry jargon, slacks are full-length PANTS that are more casual than TROUSERS and more dressy than JEANS. The word is usually associated with SPORTSWEAR, whereas trousers are associated with tailored clothing.

slap soles   A style of footwear, usually high-heeled, worn in the 17th century; distinguished by a flat, protective sole that attached across the bottom extending from the top to the heel, so that it "slapped" against the shoe or boot's sole as the man walked.

slash pocket   A pocket entered through a slit in the outside of the garment (as opposed to a PATCH POCKET, which is positioned on the exterior). Usually used to describe a jacket or trouser pocket.

slashing   Describes the decorative rather than functional slitting of material. Small cuts are made in the surface of a garment not to ventilate the body but to form a pattern or to show off an undergarment (sometimes the surface is pulled through to form puffs, as in Hans Holbein's 1540 portrait of Henry VIII). Although the term can be used to describe contemporary fashion, slashing was more common in the 15th and 16th centuries.

sleepshirt   A long, knee- or calf-length shirt designed for sleeping. NIGHTSHIRT is an earlier and more general usage, usually associated with woven materials. If the garment is made of jersey or other knits, it is described as a "sleepshirt" and not a "nightshirt."

sleepwear   Industry classification for NIGHTSHIRTS, PAJAMAS, and coordinating pieces.

sleeve board   A padded board, resembling a mini ironing board, small enough to slip inside a sleeve to facilitate sewing or pressing.

sleeve cap *or* **sleevehead**   Refers to the topmost, rounded part of the sleeve. Thus, when viewed from the side, a sleevehead is the portion of the sleeve from the armpit to the shoulder.

When cutting traditional menswear, especially if it is made of wool, the sleevehead may be much larger than the corresponding ARMSCYE, allowing the tailor to shape and mold the fabric and allowing the wearer more ease of movement when the sleeve is completed.

sleeve garters   Elastic bands worn on shirt sleeves (but not jacket sleeves), in order to keep excess sleeve material from billowing around the cuff or dragging across a work surface; associated with the 19th and early 20th century when readymade shirts were often sized with one-length-fits-all sleeves.

sleeve header   Part of the unseen construction of a jacket, a sleeve header is a separate piece of fabric or wadding (e.g., a rectangular piece of lambswool) used to shape the SLEEVE CAP according to the particular style of the designer and/or tailor. It supports the top of the sleeve and disguises the impression of the seam allowance.

slicker   A utilitarian raincoat, untailored and capacious enough to be worn over regular clothes. In its best-known incarnation the slicker is made of yellow rubberized fabric with folding clasp closures and may be accessorized with a SOU'WESTER.

slides   An informal sandal or slipper that, like a woman's "mule," has no heel or toe. A slide is generally flat, and stays on by means of a band going across the instep. It differs from styles like a FLIP-FLOP because it has no thong between the big toe and second toe.

Slimane, Hedi   Born in 1967, the slim, fragile-looking designer began designing menswear for YVES SAINT LAURENT in 1997 and was so successful with his collections that he created crazes for very closely cut men's clothes and for waiflike models to wear them. Designer KARL LAGERFELD, who later became the famously shy Slimane's friend, is credited with saying that Slimane's narrow designs motivated his own tremendous weight loss. In 2001, at the height of his fame, Slimane switched to designing for DIOR HOMME, then left that label in 2007.

slim fit   Usually describes pants, particularly jeans, that are cut close to the body, especially through the thighs.

slip knot   Used as a synonym for the FOUR-IN-HAND knot for NECKTIES.

slip-ons   Shoes that do not tie or buckle. Considered more proper and more formal designation than LOAFERS, especially for dress shoes.

Hedi Slimane

slippers   Refers to lightweight footwear, generally meant to be worn indoors. In menswear the term also may be used to describe footwear intended for dances and/or evening events (e.g., certain styles worn with SMOKING JACKETS, DINNER JACKETS, and formalwear).

Not to be confused with SLIP-ONS, a term more often associated with shoes meant to be worn on the street. Thus, slippers may be—and often are—a slip-on style, but the two categories are not considered interchangeable.

Sloane   Short for "Sloane Ranger," slang for the British uppercrust (originally as it referred to those residing near Sloane Square in London). Like his American counterpart, the PREPPY, the Sloane favors traditional menswear and places a premium on sports attire. Although his clothing, shirts, and shoes may be custom-made in the environs of SAVILE ROW, he eschews fashion and avoids anything overly fitted to the body. Favored brands include BARBOUR, BURBERRY, and Husky. An unflattering synonym for an exemplar might be "Hooray Henry."

slops *or* **slopp** *or* **sloppe**   1. When it originated in the 16th century, the term referred to the baggy, rather long BREECHES favored by Dutch burghers.   2. By the 19th century, when the wearing of breeches during daytime had long since passed from fashion—it referred to ready-made clothes (as opposed to BESPOKE), and especially to simply constructed items worn for work.   3. A SMOCK.

slub   A lump or other noticeable irregularity in a yarn. Although sometimes considered a defect (since slubs can be caused by lint or other spinning problems), slubs are pur-posely added to certain yarns to produce a desired effect in the fabric (an effect known as engineered slubs). For example: Colored slubs are a characteristic of DONEGAL yarns and tweeds.

smalls   Abbreviation of SMALLCLOTHES.

smallclothes   1. Archaic reference to underwear, handkerchiefs, and the like.   2. Archaic reference to men's BREECHES, used mostly in the last quarter of the 18th century.

smartie suits   A mid-1960s fashion, which originated on the KING'S ROAD in London. Refers to suits done in the same pastels (pink, blue, and yellow) of the popular English candies called Smarties.

Smith, Paul   Born in 1946, British designer Sir Paul Smith's original hope to become a racing cyclist was derailed by an accident that left him hospital-bound for six months. Afterward, his father, a textile salesman, pressured him to take a menial job in an apparel warehouse. Smith started his own business with a tiny shop in his hometown of Nottingham, England, in 1970 and—after a stint studying tailoring in evening classes—launched his menswear label in 1974. Known for his witty juxtapositions of fabrics with traditional British cuts—he might pair a pink shirt with a pink-striped suit that was lined in a floral print—Smith's eclectic, slightly eccentric style was later copied by other labels. During

Paul Smith

the 1980s, in particular, he helped to create the crazes for boxer shorts, witty suspenders, and oddly colored sweaters.

Tall (6 feet, 4 inches), lanky, and universally liked, Smith opened his first London shop in 1976, stocking old toys and other quirky finds alongside his brilliantly colored sweaters, socks, and other offbeat accessories and apparel. Smith opened his first New York boutique on Lower Fifth Avenue in the late 1980s, pioneering the city's Flatiron District as a retail area. Likewise, in London, he was among the first to make Covent Garden a fashion district. He was knighted in 2000. Internationally distributed, Smith was particularly successful in Japan, where he partnered with Itochu, which bought a stake in his company in 2006.

smock   An oversized, long-sleeved style of blousey overshirt worn—usually for work—to protect clothes; often knee-length or longer. The traditional garment for workmen in certain areas of England often was made with SMOCKING stitches. Synonyms: smock-frock; SLOP.

smocking   Embroidery stitches used to secure pre-pleated material, usually in a decorative pattern. A distinguishing characteristic of the traditional SMOCKS worn by English workmen.

le smoking   A TUXEDO in French usage.

Smock

smoking cap   A soft cloth cap (typically a pillbox shape ornamented with a tassel in the center of the crown), worn during the 19th century as part of a man's at-home attire. Wearing a hat helped to prevent the man's hair from absorbing the odor of his cigar or pipe. Worn with a SMOKING JACKET.

smoking jacket   A jacket intended to be worn for entertaining or other semi-formal occasions at home, where it both looks and functions as a hybrid of DRESSING GOWN and DINNER JACKET; typically made of a dark shade of velvet, often ornamented by piping, silk braid, SOUTACHE, or lapels and cuffs of a contrasting material. Never worn on the street or to public events. In contemporary use, the three most common styles are a shawl-collared wrap style that looks like an abbreviated robe and is tied with a fringed sash; a double-breasted style with FROG closures, which may have a quilted lapel and cuffs; or a jacket that resembles a SHAWL-COLLARED tuxedo jacket except for its materials. None has a VENT.

Originally, smoking jackets, which became popular in the mid-19th century when the Crimean War made Turkish tobacco more available in England, served a function: Like SMOKING CAPS, they prevented smoke from penetrating a man's business clothes or formalwear.

Then, as now, the smoking jacket was traditionally accessorized in the same way as a dinner jacket: with a white shirt and black tie (or a contemporary substitute like a turtleneck), black trousers or striped tuxedo trousers, and slippers or pumps.

snakeskin   A leather made from the skin of any of several species of snakes (the most popular being python, boa, and anaconda—the last having a scale pattern so large it is sometimes mistaken for ALLIGATOR or LIZARD-

SKIN). Prized mainly for the decoration of its scale patterns and/or coloration.

snap brim   Refers to a hat style, usually a FEDORA, that is meant to have its brimmed turned down slightly in front—"snapped"—and slightly up at the back or sides. May be made of any material from straw to felt.

snap front   Sometimes a synonym for a Western shirt or cowboy-style shirt, in reference to their use of classic pearl-snap closures instead of buttons.

sneakers   Refers to rubber-soled shoes, particularly those intended for athletics. The usage was coined in the late 19th century in reference to the soundlessness of pliable, rubber soles (and hence their ability to "sneak up" on someone), although several shoe companies claim to have invented it in the 20th century.

sniper suit   A CAMOUFLAGE suit, originally used in hunting game, then identified with sniper activity. See GHILLIE SUIT.

S-numbers   A reference to "super 80s," "super 110s," and the like. See the entry and table for SUPER 100S.

soft goods   Retailers classify all menswear as soft goods, even though—as in the case of shoes or other accessories—they may not be particularly soft. The opposite designation, "hard goods," is used for appliances, electronics, furniture, and the like.

soft sew   Garment-trade slang for cloth that is easy to drape, cut, and sew. For example, WORSTED is a soft sew for a suit. BROCADE is not.

sola topee   A PITH HELMET.

sombrero   1. The hat with a high tapered crown and huge, curling brim that is associated with the folklore and tradition of Mexico (e.g., as worn with the *TRAJE DE CHARRO*); may be made of either straw (especially as worn by peasants) or felt (for the more formal and decorated versions). Synonym: Mexican hat.   2. Spanish for hat.

The Sorrows of Young Werther   The best-selling novel by German author and philosopher Johann Wolfgang Goethe (1749–1832), published in Leipzig in 1774, which influenced menswear because of its hero's preference for plain, English-style clothing (akin to the ANGLOMANIA then sweeping France).

soul patch   Refers to a style of beard. Usually the soul patch, a short tuft directly beneath the lower lip, is the only beard on an otherwise clean-shaven face.

sourcing   Jargon for finding fabrics and manufacturers. "Sourcing" can refer to anything from picking out the fabric at a mill, to finding a factory, to shipping the finished garments.

sou'wester *or* **southwester**   Refers to a style of protective headgear worn in foul weather, especially by sailors and commercial fishermen; usually ties under the chin so it does not blow away; made of rubberized cotton, vinyl, or a similarly pliable, waterproof textile, the hat has a round crown and a brim that is longer in back—giving it a resemblance to an upturned coal scuttle.

soutache   Flat, decorative trim, most often found on uniforms, SMOKING JACKETS, and the like.

soutane   See CASSOCK.

soybean Fiber or fabric made from soybean plants, usually from the waste of food production which was then processed through chemistry akin to that used to turn wood pulp into RAYON, by which mills were able to produce a very fine FILAMENT much prized for its silkiness and marketed as a "renewable resource."

space-dyed Yarn purposely dyed so that, instead of uniform saturation, the color varies across the length—usually at irregular intervals. When the yarn is subsequently knit or woven, this produces a variegated effect instead of the customary flat field of color. Used most often in sweaters or tops, where the irregularity can be exploited to imitate hand-production.

spandex Generic name for the stretch fiber derived from polyurethane (and therefore lowercased). LYCRA is a branded type of spandex (and therefore should be capitalized).

spaniel ties A style much longer than a traditional BOW TIE (but still shorter and narrower than a traditional NECKTIE), in which the tie was pulled into a big bow and allowed to flop down like the ears of a spaniel; a fashion identified with the hep cats of the 1940s, when it was affected by celebrities like FRANK SINATRA.

spats Now considered a charmingly ar-chaic garment, the spat is a shortened GAITER meant to cover only the instep and ankle (whereas a full gaiter might go to mid-calf or higher). Although the custom of wearing what were originally called "spatterdashers" began in the 18th century, by the 20th century they were considered more stylish than functional and were made of fabric or lightweight leather, often in a light shade that contrasted with the shoe, and were fastened on the outside with buttons or snaps. During the first half of the 20th century, frequently a feature of MORNING DRESS.

special order Among traditional clothiers, this usually refers to garments that are made from a standard pattern but are available with certain options, such as extra pockets or a particular range of fabrics.

specialty store Retail jargon for a store that positions itself at the high, or "specialist," end of the market, where it does not try to be all things to all people. Thus, the designation almost always connotes more expensive and

Sombrero: Emiliano Zapata

exclusive merchandise. In New York, for example, BAR-NEYS and Bergdorf Goodman would be considered specialty stores. Its antithetical retail classification would be MASS-MARKET.

spectator   A style of shoe that uses two contrasting shades of leather, most often white and black, white and navy, or white and brown; or a two-colored shoe, which may incorporate fabric, but is made to mimic that style. Usually constructed in an OXFORD style, the main body of the shoe is usually the lighter color, with parts such as the toe cap and QUARTERS in the darker, contrasting shade. Associated with warm-weather dressing. Known as a CORRESPONDENT in Britain.

Speedo   General reference to the style of skimpy, low-rise, revealing suits worn in swimming competition; derived from their longtime manufacture by the Australian company founded in 1914 and known since 1928 as Speedo.

spencer   Designation for an extremely short, skirtless jacket; now used more often to describe that garment in the women's market. The term originated around 1790 and is associated with George, the second earl of Spencer. According to various legends, he either accidentally burned off the tails of his tailcoat, ripped them when out riding, or hacked them off to see if he could get away with starting a fashion. Costume historians now consider all apocryphal.

Sperry Top-Sider   See TOP-SIDER.

spinner   A yarn producer. A "spinner" takes fiber from its production source (e.g., loose wool from the sheep farmer) and spins it into yarn, which then goes to a MILL

for the actual fabric production. Although a spinning operation may be aligned with a mill or knitter, it does not necessarily produce fabric.

spitalsfield   Used to describe a distinctive type of SELF-PATTERNED necktie silk. A spitalsfield has a discreet, usually nonfigurative, weave pattern with an average of two to four colors (looking more geometric than the FOULARD, which, in any case, is printed as opposed to woven). The name derives from a style of weaving practiced in east London, where Protestants driven from France helped to establish the British silk industry in the late 17th century.

In earlier references, when all ties with this type of pattern could be assumed to have originated in Spitalsfield, the word was capitalized. In contemporary usage, when ties of that type are just as likely to have originated in China or Italy, the word is lowercased.

The spitalfield differs from the MACCLESFIELD, a patterned black-and-white necktie silk of similar origin, by being larger in pattern and more varied in color.

splash   See *EAU FRAICHE*.

split yoke   Refers to a seam falling in the center of the shoulder blades, dividing the back YOKE of a shirt or jacket. On a shirt, almost always a hallmark of custom work—or of a pricey readymade that seeks to imitate it. By tradition, the split allows a tailor or shirtmaker to adjust his pattern so that differences between the two shoulders can be accommodated for the most personalized and flattering fit.

sponging   Refers to a method of cleaning, particularly associated with valet maintenance of traditional tailored clothing; done in between sending the suit to cleaners as a way to freshen the cloth. For example: After being worn, the suit may be brushed to remove loose dirt, then sponged to remove soil in specific areas.

sporran   The pouchlike purse worn with the KILT as part of full Highland regalia. By tradition, the sporran, which comes from the Gaelic word for purse, dangles from a chain around the waist and is worn front and center over the genitals. Its material and decoration may vary greatly—from leather to fur—depending upon the formality of the occasion and the finances of the wearer.

sport shirt   Usually connotes a button-front shirt that is less formal and slightly less stiff and constructed than a DRESS SHIRT. (For example, a sport shirt is rarely starched.) By custom, the sport shirt, which has a FOLD-OVER COLLAR and either short or long sleeves, may be made of a material considered inappropriate for business attire either because of its heft or brightness—anything from a psychedelically printed cotton to a dark-green flannel. The sport shirt is also worn in the widest variety of situations, paired with anything from JEANS to SPORTSWEAR such as a SPORTS JACKET and tie. It is also sized differently. Instead of a collar measurement and sleeve length being given in inches, as it is with a dress shirt size, the sport shirt is sized small, medium, large (sometimes through XXL).

sports jacket *or* **sport coat**   A 20th-century invention, the sports jacket indicates a jacket that is not—and never was—part of a suit, even though its tailoring may be virtually identical. It is always worn with unmatched pants and is, even when accessorized by a NECKTIE, considered a step down in dressiness and formality from the business suit. Depending upon the season and style, it may be made of a variety of materials and patterns, but the fab-rics used for it, usually categorized as JACKETINGS, are usually slightly heavier and slightly showier than suit fabrics.

Although men were already in the habit of wearing jackets unmatched to their pants at the end of the 19th century, most of those jackets were borrowed from a dark suit and simply worn with flannel pants (perhaps part of another suit). The sports jacket grew from this tradition, as well as the habit of wearing BLAZERS for spectator sports and NORFOLK JACKETS and HACKING JACKETS while engaging in sports. By the Roaring Twenties, however, items known as sports jackets—many of them strongly resembling Norfolk jackets—were being sold by menswear outfitters.

sports sandals   A hybrid of sneaker and sandal. Sports sandals usually have a sole that provides traction and/or cushioning, plus an open design to keep the foot ventilated.

sportswear   Refers to the general category of garments that encompasses SPORTS SHIRTS, KHAKI pants, SPORTS JACKETS, and the like—although, confusingly enough, it is no longer the apparel worn when actually partaking in sports (which is usually classified as ACTIVEWEAR, or in a more specific category such as golfwear). Thus, to traditionalists, sportswear is considered less dressy than TAILORED CLOTHING (suits and ties) and more dressy than activewear (sweatsuits and sneakers).

Contemporary men's sportswear evolved from the 19th-century sporting and shooting costumes worn by men such as EDWARD VII when he was Prince of Wales; these clothes were made of sturdier, less formal fabrics, were differently colored than the tailored clothing worn for business attire, were designed to allow more freedom of movement, and were considered more appropriate to country life.

spread collar   A style of shirt collar in which the points of the collar flare outward, rather than pointing downward (with an angle and the amount of open space left at the throat varying widely depending on the shirt-maker and the preference of the wearer). Found chiefly on DRESS SHIRTS, spread collars are associated with thicker NECKTIES and may be worn to accommodate the resulting wider knot, especially if a WINDSOR KNOT or HALF-WINDSOR KNOT is used.

stacked heels   Heels that continue a straight line from the back of the shoe or boot to form a thick, supportive base, especially in reference to heels between a half inch and 2 inches in height.

In men's footwear their opposite would be tapered or UNDERSLUNG heels (e.g., styles made with CUBAN HEELS or the classic COWBOY BOOT).

stain repellency   Refers to the ability of a fabric to repel food, grass, or other stains, usually by means of a topical treatment. The first well-known fabric treatment in the category was SCOTCHGARD, which was introduced for wool in 1956 and for other fabrics thereafter. Subsequent introductions, such as TEFLON, were also topical treatments with efficacy guaranteed for a finite number of cleanings or machine washings.

In the early 21st century, NANOTECHNOLOGY and fiber engineering meant that stain repellency could be incorporated in the actual structure of the fiber, making it less likely to change the feel of the fabric and more likely to last for the life of the garment.

stalking cap   See DEERSTALKER.

stalking trousers   A style of baggy trousers worn for sport, popularized by EDWARD VIII when he was Prince of Wales during the 1920s. Because they were basically a full-length version of PLUS FOURS, the prince called them PLUS TWENTIES (a pun on "plus fours," which are so named because they extend 4 inches below the break of the knee).

stance   A shortened reference to BUTTON STANCE.

stand   Jargon for the inside of a shirt collar, the piece that determines the collar's height and stiffness and lies directly next to the skin of the neck. When the stand is made of contrasting material, it is usually a signal that the shirt is intended to be worn with the collar unbuttoned. Most stands, especially in readymade shirts, measure between an inch and an inch and a half. Synonym: COLLAR STAND.

standing collar   General reference for any style of collar that stands up on the neck instead of folding down toward the torso. MANDARIN collars, NEHRU collars, and POKE collars are all styles of standing collars. BARRYMORE collars, SPREAD collars, and TAB collars are not. Antonym: FOLD-OVER COLLAR. Synonym: stand-up collar.

staple   Raw, unprocessed, unspun fiber; the most basic material of a yarn or fabric.

Most natural fibers are designated as being LONG-STAPLE or short-staple with a long-staple version of the fiber (e.g., PIMA COTTON) generally preferred for apparel because it requires less twisting to turn into a yarn; a yarn that is twisted fewer times is not as stiff and therefore makes fabric with a softer HAND.

steel-toed shoes *or* **steel-toed boots**   Footwear in which the cap or toe portion has been unobtrusively and invisibly reinforced with steel to protect the toes. Generally popular for workmen from 1925 onward.

steer hide   Synonym for COWHIDE, although made from neutered males rather than cows.

steinkirk, steenkerque, *or* **steenkerke**   A fashion of a semi-untied or casually tied CRAVAT worn in the late 17th and early 18th centuries; named for the 1692 Battle of Steinkirk (located in modern Belgium), where, according to legend, the encamped French soldiers were surprised by the attacking British, German, and Dutch allied forces at dawn—before the French had fully finished dressing. (Doubtless celebrated because the French managed to win the battle anyway.) Ergo, instead of a complicated knot, the steinkirk was pinned off to the side or pulled through a jacket buttonhole.

Stephen, John   A menswear merchant best known as the pioneer of trendy retailing on London's CARNABY STREET, and in particular for its 1960s reputation as PEACOCK ALLEY.

Steinkirk

Born in 1934, the handsome and high-living Stephen moved to London from Glasgow in 1952 at age 18, and opened his first boutique four years later, opening another on Carnaby Street—then a relative backwater—soon after. By that street's heyday in the 1960s, he owned multiple boutiques there and had outfitted a variety of pop icons (e.g., THE BEATLES, The Rolling Stones). He is credited with inventing fashions for flowered shirts and hip-slung pants and, in 1966, was in a *Time* magazine cover story on Swinging London. He died in 2004, and, the following year, the city of London dedicated a plaque on Carnaby Street commemorating his contributions to its history.

Stetson   The American brand founded by John B. Stetson in 1865, best known for the COWBOY HATS manufactured in its Garland, Texas, factory. Although the brand name is sometimes used as a generic reference for a Western hat, the company has always made other styles—including the distinctive hat that is part of the Canadian Mountie uniform.

stickpin   A sharp, straight pin, usually 2 to 3 inches long, with an ornament at its head (which may be either a simple pearl or a fanciful shape like a four-leaf clover). Worn—with its point downward and only the ornamental top visible—beneath the knot of a NECKTIE or ASCOT but above the GORGE of the jacket, supposedly as a means of keeping the ends of the tie from sliding around. Synonym: tiepin.

stirrup pants   Pants secured with a tab or elastic that fits under the arch of the foot, to discourage the trousers from riding up, bunching, or wrinkling. Several early-19th-century dandies claimed to have invented the style, which was of particular importance in the days when elegance was measured by a straight, tight-fitting PAN-TALOON leg.

stitch gauge   The measure of how many stitches are in an inch or centimeter of a knit. The higher the number, the "finer" the GAUGE. For example: Knits made from silky, thin yarns usually have a stitch gauge exceeding ten stitches per inch, whereas thick, coarse yarns usually result in a stitch gauge of five stitches or fewer per inch.

stockinette   The plainest and most commonly used pattern—sometimes referred to as a stitch—formed by knitting. Stockinette stitch is distinguished by flat, interlocking V shapes on its "right" or facing side, and nubbly, purl stitches on its "wrong" or interior side.

stocking cap   A style of soft cap, either knit or woven, that fits close to the head and then tapers to a long, often pointed tail (so that it is shaped much like a stocking pulled onto the head). The end of the tail, which may vary in length from a few inches to a foot or more, may be ornamented with a tassel or pompom. For instance, a stocking cap is the fur-trimmed style worn in traditional depictions of SANTA CLAUS.

stock service   Industry jargon for fabric or apparel that the wholesaler keeps in stock, so that it is available at any time. The term is sometimes used to distinguish standard items from seasonal collections. For example, someone who supplies fabric to tailors might have a series of fancy new stripes in his latest collection and keep his best-selling weights of gray flannel in his stock service.

stock pin   The horizontal pin, shaped like an oversized safety pin, used for securing the STOCK TIE in traditional English riding attire. A man's stock pin is traditionally plain gold or gold-colored and 3 inches long. (The women's version is shorter and often ornamented.)

stock tie   The NECKWEAR, akin to the NECK CLOTH of earlier eras, worn for horse shows and as FOXHUNTING ATTIRE. The stock, which vaguely resembles an ASCOT or an old-time CRAVAT, comes in two basic varieties:
  • The "shaped stock" comes in a single, long, presewn piece without folds and has a slit in its center back to facilitate tying.
  • The less common but more traditional "folded stock" is folded lengthwise and pressed but is not stitched, making its construction something like a four-fold version of the FIVE- or SEVEN-FOLD TIE.

Horsemen are fond of saying that a stock retains its utility in the field, since it can be used to improvise bandages, slings, and other bits of required jerry-rigging. Depending on the dress code (e.g., RATCATCHER or formal), the stock may be colored and patterned or may be snowy white. For the show ring or hunt field, the stock is ornamented with a STOCK PIN.

stole   An oblong-shaped, usually fabric or fur garment, made without obvious tailoring or shaping; similar to a long, rectangular shawl or enormously oversized muffler in shape and length. Unlike women's wear, where it usually indicates an item of light outerwear (e.g., a mink stole), the stole appears in menswear most often as part of an ecclesiastical or other ceremonial ensemble.

stone wash   A FINISH given to jeans to purposely make the DENIM appear prematurely aged. In a classic stone wash, the fabric is lighter, usually in a slightly

Stockinette: Front and back

uneven pattern, because it has been tumbled with pumice stones (which may or may not have themselves been soaked in bleach or some other agent intended to distress the fabric further).

storm flap   See THROAT LATCH.

stovepipes   Slim-lined, often tight-fitting pants. In the late 20th century, often worn by PUNKS. Because they taper at the ankle instead of flaring, their opposites would be BELL-BOTTOMS or FLARES. Synonym: DRAIN-PIPES.

stovepipe hat   A 19th-century style of TOP HAT with an extra-high crown so that it supposedly resembled a stovepipe; a style associated with Abraham Lincoln.

straights   Refers to shoes or slippers made with no differentiation between the left and right.

streetwear   An industry classification that evolved from HIP-HOP fashion (which itself evolved from URBAN fashion, another bit of retail jargon). The term passed into general usage around 1990, as the fashion movement linked to hip-hop culture, which began in New York in the 1970s, continued to grow beyond its original urban and ethnic base.

strié   A slight streaking incorporated in a fabric's design. Usually refers to a slim and purposely irregular effect.

striker   A junior CUTTER in a traditional tailoring firm; roughly the equivalent of a sous chef in a professional kitchen.

string decoration   Industry jargon referring to suit fabrics with a prominent, textured decoration. So called because some look as though a piece of string has been basted to their top.

string gloves   Gloves knotted or knit of string. Traditionally worn when riding or driving horses in wet weather, to make it easier to hold wet reins.

How to tie a stock tie

string tie   A length of cord used as a substitute for a NECKTIE and tied in a bow. Not to be confused with a BOLO. Sometimes used interchangeably with BOOTLACE TIE.

studs   Fasteners that substitute for buttons on the shirts worn with FORMALWEAR; unlike buttons, not attached to the garment itself. Usually sold in sets of four and sometimes structured like CUFFLINKS (with which they are sometimes paired in jewelry sets).

stylist   The person who dictates how apparel is worn, but does not design it. A stylist's involvement in a fashion or advertising shoot may include some or all of the following duties: choosing the clothes, selecting the models, hiring a collaborating crew (including GROOMING), dictating the choice of accessories, and deciding the mood or theme of the story. For a runway show, the stylist is usually hired to provide spin to a designer's collection, playing up—or sometimes creating—its theme.

A celebrity stylist usually works with a client by preselecting fashion (often capitalizing on personal relationships with designers and retailers to procure the clothes), particularly for important public appearances.

suede   Leather that is buffed on the flesh side of the skin. (NUBUCK, by contrast, is buffed on the outside of the skin.)

Sugarman, Arthur Bernard   The original name of the man who rechristened himself BEN SHERMAN and began that label.

Suiting: A similar style in two very different fabrics

suit length   Jargon for the amount of fabric required for a man's suit. Usually a little more than 3 yards.

suiting   Jargon for suit fabrics. This word refers to the fabric, never to the finished garment.

suit separates   A coordinating sports jacket and pants created to be worn together or used as separate pieces of sportswear. The jacket and pants are sold separately, rather than in a single unit as is usual with suits—a practice used by some retailers to accommodate customers who do not have the standard DROP (the chest-to-waist differential) used to size suits.

sulfur dye   A dyeing process used most often for JEANS or other pants. Usually, a sulfur-based dyestuff is applied to the basic yarn before or after the indigo blue (or whatever other main color is being featured) in order to control its CAST. For example: A green sulfur dye will be applied after the blue so that the resulting DENIM has a slight greenish tint.

Sulka *or* **A. Sulka & Co.**   Founded by Amos Sulka (a salesman from Johnstown, Pennsylvania) in 1895 in lower Manhattan in partnership with Leon Wormser (a shirtmaker from the Alsace-Lorraine), the store that began as a utilitarian uniform supplier became internationally renowned for its luxury goods, such as SMOKING JACKETS, silk DRESSING GOWNS, and custom shirts.

After the first decade of the 20th century, Sulka's reputation was such that it was able to challenge its European competitors—CHARVET in Paris and the shops on JERMYN STREET in London—on their own turf by opening a Paris branch in 1911 and a London store in 1924. Thereafter, its celebrity customers included statesmen such as Winston Churchill, assorted royalty up to and including EDWARD VIII, business titans such as Henry Ford, and Hollywood royalty such as Clark Gable. Along with its custom shirts (for which it even provided a special hand-laundering service), Sulka became identified with silk items such as neckties and dressing gowns, and with understated indulgences such as CASHMERE socks and VICUÑA robes.

During the last quarter of the 20th century, Sulka's fortunes declined as it passed through a variety of managements, at one time being owned by Syms, the New York-based discount clothing chain, and then by the Swiss-based Vendôme Group, which also owned Cartier. By 2001, it had shuttered its stores in Paris, London, and San Francisco; in 2002, the lease of its last remaining store, on Madison Avenue and East 69th Street, was taken over by GUCCI.

sumptuary laws Laws governing the wearing of apparel, accessories, and/or fabrics. At various times and in various countries, sumptuary laws were used to both suppress fashion and promote it. For instance, in pre-17th-century Europe, sumptuary laws forbade people of non-noble birth to wear certain luxurious fabrics or furs; it was equally common for laws encouraging local industry to ban the importation of certain fashions or fabrics.

sunless tanner Synonym for SELF-TANNER.

super 100s A designation to measure the fineness of the fiber in a wool cloth; the "super" stands for "superfine" and the number varies according to the MICRON count (i.e., the diameter), of the fiber used in the fabric; most super 100s are only a fifth (or less) the diameter of a human hair. The finer the fiber, the higher its S-NUMBER—and the higher its price tag.

The number derives from the worsted industry standard developed in Bradford, England, which set the number 64 as a benchmark for quality worsted wool—that number being the count that a good worsted would produce on a spinning machine. Hence, a super 100 would produce the number 100 on a spinning machine, a super 120 would produce the number 120 on a spinning machine, and so forth.

Although the system of super 100s was developed mainly by Australia's wool industry in the 1960s, it remained industry jargon until the end of the 1990s, when the super 100s designation began to be communicated to the consumer as a marketing ploy: Supposedly, a man would be willing to pay more money for a suit with a higher number, since a super 100s designation appealed to a male shopper's desire to quantify quality. The wool itself was produced mostly from MERINO sheep (a breed that already yielded a very fine micron-count fleece), who were then further protected by coats and raised mainly in special shed—hence their designation as SHEDDED SHEEP.

By the 21st century, S-numbers, generally ranging from "super 80s" all the way through the ultraexpensive "super 220s"—generally in increments of 10s and 20s—were being bandied about, even by discounters and even though it was impossible for even a fabric expert to tell whether or not a super 120s was really a 120 without resorting to a testing lab.

The ploy soon became so widely used and abused that a trade group called the International Wool Textile Organisation set up a standard for super 100s, which was then introduced in a 2006 U.S. bill amending the Wool Labeling Act of 1939. Thus, a manufacturer who misrepresents a super 100s fabric is liable for fines if his labeling does not conform to these designations:

Designation	Diameter (in microns)
Super 80s	19.75
Super 90s	19.25
Super 100s	18.75
Super 110s	18.25
Super 120s	17.75
Super 130s	17.25
Super 140s	16.75
Super 150s	16.25
Super 160s	15.75
Super 170s	15.25
Super 180s	14.75
Super 190s	14.25
Super 200s	13.75
Super 210s	13.25
Super 220s	12.75
Super 230s	12.25
Super 240s	11.75
Super 250s	11.25

supergaiters   A style of GAITERS, usually worn for outdoor pursuits like hiking, mountaineering, or skiing, that extends from the welt of the shoe to the knee, completely covering the shoe top, the ankle, and most of the lower leg, leaving only the sole of the shoe uncovered (unlike standard gaiters, which usually expose most of the shoe and seal mostly the join between the shoe and sock to prevent moisture from entering through the top of the boot). Usually insulated and worn in extreme weather.

Supima   The marketing and promotional organization funded by U.S. growers of PIMA, a LONG-STAPLE COTTON. Founded in 1954 in El Paso, Texas, its name is a contraction of "superior pima." Like COTTON INCORPORATED (which performs similar advertising, research, and promotional functions for growers of UPLAND COTTON), it does not manufacture yarn or fabric; instead, it advertises and promotes use of the fiber to foster more consumption of its members' product.

suppressed waist   Actually a term that enhances the waist rather than masks it, a "suppressed waist" refers to a jacket made with DARTS so that it has an indentation at the waist (as opposed to hanging straight from the shoulder like a SACK SUIT). In contemporary use, associated with British and Italian tailoring.

surcingle belt   A belt made mostly of the distinctive sturdy and striped (usually two-color) wool webbing employed for horses' surcingles and girths, sewn in its front to a traditional leather and metal buckle closure. Popular for riding, country wear, and PREPPY attire.

surf trunks   Usually a synonym for BOARD SHORTS.

surfwear   An industry designation dating from the 1970s and used for casual apparel intended to reflect the California surfer's lifestyle. Apparel items associated with the category include BOARD SHORTS, corduroy walking shorts, HAWAIIAN SHIRTS or SILKIES, RINGER T-SHIRTS, and FLIP-FLOPS. Brands associated with the category include HANG TEN, OCEAN PACIFIC, Quiksilver, and Stussy.

suri *or* **suri alpaca**   Fiber or fabric made from the CAMELID of that name; classified as a NOBLE FIBER because of its extreme fineness (at 17 microns or less, comparable to CASHMERE) and silkiness, the suri's coat is particularly prized for its LONG-STAPLE fiber (which makes it more resistant to PILLING than most noble fibers). The animal itself is one of the two types of ALPACA (the other, more common, type being known as the huacaya).

surplice   An extremely full overblouse, usually worn in an ecclesiastical context (e.g., by altar boys and choirboys). The main body of the surplice is most often plain white fabric and is sometimes banded at the bottom of the body and sleeves with lace. Untailored, its front and back gather into a band or drawstring collar. The garment may range from hip-length to ankle-length, but the shorter variation worn by choirboys is usually known as the COTTA (especially in the Anglican church).

surplice front   A garment with a wrap front or a front that crosses one side over the other as if it is wrapped; usually applied to untailored garments, such as sweaters.

surtout   1. An overcoat; usually 19th-century usage. A functional and protective garment, it was most often made of wool, had a rounded collar, and ended below the knee but above the ankle. Literally translated as "over all."   2. A long jacket worn as a predecessor to the modern suit jacket beginning in the late 17th century and continuing through the 18th century. Similar to a JUSTACORPS.

suspender buttons   Buttons sewn on the waistband of pants as a place for a man to fasten his suspenders (and, for that reason, rarely seen on the same garment as belt loops). A dominant feature on men's pants until well after World War I, when the use of belts became more widespread.

suspenders   An accessory used to hold up pants, which always has two straps in the front but may have a single strap (e.g., in a Y design) or double straps (e.g., in an X design) in the back. Most suspenders fasten to pants by means of grips or by attaching to SUSPENDER BUT-TONS sewn to the waistband. They may be plain or fancy, and are made of materials as various as the materials used for belts: woven webbing, ribbon, leather, or fabric. Most are adjustable by means of levers. Synonym (in British usage): BRACES.

sutler   A civilian, particularly in the 19th century, who sold supplies—including uniforms and other articles of clothing—at military posts and encampments. Beginning in the late 20th century, with the popularity of historical reenactments, the word was also applied to firms selling military and historical costume to reenactors.

swaddling   The ancient custom of binding babies in narrow strips of fabric to inhibit wriggling, a practice thought to protect soft bones. Familiar to most people from depictions of the Christ child wrapped in swaddling and lying in a manger, the custom persisted in England and the United States until the 1820s, with the French (despite the teachings of Jean-Jacques Rousseau) continuing into the 20th century.

swagger stick   Refers to a very short CANE or riding crop, usually carried under the arm (i.e., for "swagger" and appearance rather than function); associated with the military—most familiarly with General George Patton during World War II.

Swaine Adeney Brigg   Founded as Swaine Adeney in London in 1750 and best known for its small goods (such as whips, which occasioned its first royal warrant from George III). After 1943, when it merged with umbrella maker Brigg, the firm became better known for its UMBRELLAS, including models with crocodile and solid silver handles, and frames doubling as flasks.

Swakara   A trademarked name for ASTRAKHAN, pelts of newly born karakul lambs raised and harvested in Namibia.

swallowtail   A style of double-breasted TAILCOAT, now known mostly from its occasional appearance in dressage trials and horse shows. The swallowtail has two rows of three buttons each and is worn with all of them fully buttoned. The style is distinguished by the graceful rounding of its tails, which begin just beneath the row of buttons on either side of the front waist seam and curve to the back of the knees (whereas the SHADBELLY falls from the waistseam in a nearly straight line, forming a nearly right angle at its bottom edge).

swatch book   Fabric swatches from a particular fabric manufacturer grouped according to weight, color, and/or pattern. A tailor typically keeps several on hand, from which his customer selects the makings of his new clothing. Synonym: BUNCH (a more traditional term).

sweatband   1. A band on the inside of a hat, usually leather (or a material made to imitate it). The sweatband helps to stabilize the structure of the hat, acts as an aid to sizing, and literally absorbs sweat. Not visible when the hat is being worn.   2. A stretchy, usually TERRY CLOTH band worn over the forehead and around the head; usually for tennis, jogging, or similar activities.

sweater   1. A catchall category used for KNIT tops. Sweaters may be either very heavy (e.g., ARANS that double as outerwear) or relatively light (e.g., a fine-GAUGE cashmere TURTLENECK). However, when they are light enough to be worn as underwear or a base layer, they are generally referred to as knits or JERSEYS, rather than sweaters.

Like most knit apparel, they are shaped during production rather than CUT AND SEWN: In other words, the fabric is created at the same time as the garment rather than trimmed and stitched afterward. Therefore, the common jargon "knit sweater" is actually redundant.

The word sweater was not widely used until well into the 19th century, when the term grew from their association with athletes and others who wore jerseys, supposedly as "sweat-ers."

2. In 19th-century England, when the production of men's apparel was often contracted to workshops or ad hoc groups of semiskilled labor and piece workers, the "sweater" was the subcontractor who doled out the work or ran what would now be called sweatshops.

sweater vest   A VEST made of knit rather than woven material. A sweater vest may be either a PULLOVER style or have a button or zip front that extends from neckline to waist.

swelled seam   A method of attaching a piece of cloth—most often a patch pocket sewn to the outside of

Swiss Army Knife

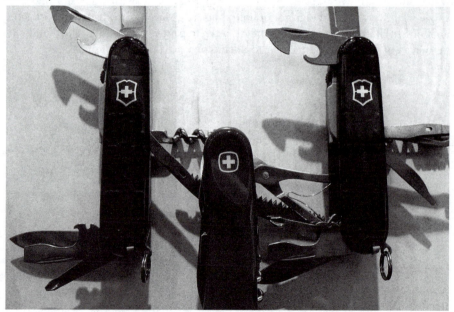

a jacket—so that a visible line of stitching appears about ⅛ inch to ¼ inch inside the actual edge. This method sometimes produces a slight swelling of the small edge of the fabric that is not stitched down, creating an outline effect.

Swiss Army Knife   Refers to a type of POCKET KNIFE pioneered by Karl Elsener in the 1890s, when the incensed inventor discovered that Switzerland's army used knives made in Germany. In Elsener's design, which incorporates a spring, blades can open from both sides of the handle, a feature that increases the available number of tools.

Elsener's company, VICTORINOX, supplied his design to the Swiss Army exclusively until 1908, when Wenger also began making and supplying the knives. Thereafter, the Genuine Swiss Army Knife became the one manufactured by Wenger and the Original Swiss Army Knife was the one made by Victorinox. In 2005, Victorinox bought its rival but continued to advertise the two brands separately.

synthetic   Most often a general term applied to any fiber or fabric that is not derived from plants, animals, or minerals. However, in the apparel business there is often some leeway about what is popularly considered a synthetic and what isn't—the label tends to be slapped soonest on fibers that are petrochemically derived. For example, ACRYLIC, NYLON, and POLYESTER are all synthetics. RAYON (and materials produced in a rayon-type process, such as SOY FIBER and BAMBOO) is usually not considered a synthetic, although it undergoes quite a bit of chemical processing.

T-400 A stretch fiber manufactured by Invista (the company formerly known as DuPont), and introduced in 2001. Initially aimed at the menswear market, T-400 featured a slightly slower RECOVERY, or "snap," than the elastic fibers then popular for women's wear, and was also more chlorine-resistant.

tab Traditional British tailors' jargon for a customer who is impossible to please.

tabard A simple, unshaped, sleeveless garment consisting of a front panel that covers the torso and a back panel of equal length, best known from monkish and medieval dress. Tabards could be joined under the arms by tabs of fabric, by a seam, by a pin, or left totally open. Their length varied according to the time and use; in general: They were short when worn by working men, grew longer as they were adopted in monasteries and used in more formal settings, then were worn over armor or used by servants as a sort of livery.

tab collar A style of FOLD-OVER shirt collar with a small tab of fabric uniting its two sides, so that the knot of the man's NECKTIE is then propped up by the tab. In this style, the collar tab takes the place of a COLLAR PIN. Used with a necktie tied with a FOUR-IN-HAND knot. Popularized by EDWARD VIII when he was Prince of Wales.

tabi Japanese socks, with a split between the big toe and other toes because they are designed to be worn with THONG-style footwear, such as ZORI or geta sandals. Worn by both men and women. Tabi with a light sole attached to the bottom are called "odori tabi."

tailclout Archaic reference for a diaper or for a diaper-like binding around a baby's bottom.

tailcoat 1. A style of tailed coat worn, in contemporary use, only on the most formal evening occasions; an essential part of WHITE TIE regalia. In front, the tailcoat is cropped to just below the waistline (so that its front points are just long enough to cover the white vest with which it is inevitably worn); in the rear, a split flap of material (i.e., the "tails") descend from the waistline to the back of the knee. The tailcoat is cut close and shaped to the body, but its buttons (usually three on either side of the front and an additional two placed in the back over the tails) are completely vestigial, since the two front sides never meet (but instead show off the vest and shirt-front beneath). LAPELS, which are often a PEAKED LAPEL style, are FACED with a contrasting material, most often black silk satin.

The tailcoat differs from the CUTAWAY, which is a tailed style worn on formal daytime occasions, by the dramatic abruptness of its cut in the front: Instead of tapering gradually toward the tails in the back as the cutaway does, the tailcoat emphasizes the crop of the jacket with two points that fall just below the waistline.

2. Generic reference to formal coats, including the tailed style worn for white tie but also the CUTAWAY, SHADBELLY, and SWALLOWTAIL.

tailleur 1. A French word to connote a structured suit or garment: usually what Americans would call a tailored suit. In contemporary usage, applied more often to women's wear. (The more common French reference for a man's suit is *costume*.) 2. The French word for tailor, which carries the implication of cutting that it does not have in English (where the word is more identified with the function of sewing).

tailor In everyday language, the word connotes someone who sews and has special expertise in fitted, "tailored" garments such as jackets and pants. However, in a traditional tailoring firm (e.g., on SAVILE ROW), a tailor is the person who does sewing only. The person who takes the measurements and has most of the other client contact is properly known as the CUTTER.

Tailor & Cutter The London-based trade magazine founded on Drury Lane in 1866 by Miss Angelica

Patience Fraser, a tiny Scotswoman who preached passionately against the sweatshop system that supported the men's apparel industry in London at that time (and who also founded Tailors Institute on Mill Street in 1885 as a sort of temperance and tailoring information exchange). Its emblem was Italian mannerist painter Giovanni Battista Moroni's 1560s "Il Tagliapanni," a portrait of a cutter posed with cloth and shears that hung in England's National Gallery.

Initially a weekly technical journal interspersed with invective against drunkenness and otherwise juvenile behavior, by the mid-20th century *Tailor & Cutter* had evolved into a lively monthly magazine: an arbiter of taste and quasi-official voice of SAVILE ROW that coined names for new fashions and conferred its "Dandy" awards on deserving firms. It ceased regular publication in November of 1972.

An unrelated American publication, *American Tailor and Cutter*, was published from 1880 until 1916, when it was absorbed into another trade magazine, the *Sartorial Art Journal*.

tailored clothing Industry jargon for tailored garments such as suits, topcoats, and the like. A SPORTS JACKET is tailored clothing. A BOMBER jacket is not. Synonym: CLOTHING.

tailor's chalk A special type of claylike chalk, usually in a disc shape, used by tailors to mark alterations on a garment—the idea being that, like the chalk erased from a blackboard, the marks can be brushed away when they are no longer needed.

Tailors Institute See *TAILOR & CUTTER*.

tailor's twist A special type of thread, usually silk,

used for hand-finishing—especially of BUTTONHOLES—on BESPOKE and other expensive, traditionally constructed garments.

tails   Shortened or slang reference to a formal TAIL-COAT.

tam *or* **tam o' shanter**   A flat, round, soft Highland hat (traditionally referred to as a "bonnet") that resembles an oversized BERET, named after a character in a poem by Robert Burns. A traditional style, the Highlanders' bonnet, was topped by a TOORIE (i.e., a pompom) on its center top.

tanga   Refers to a THONG-like style of underwear or swimsuit that has no coverage over the legs or buttocks; has been described as "a pouch connected to a string."

Tanguis   A variety of LONG-STAPLE PIMA COTTON, grown chiefly in Peru. Depending upon the context, may refer to the plant, the fiber, or the fabric made from it.

tank shirt   A sleeveless undershirt or athletic top made of knitted fabric. Synonym: A-SHIRT; ATHLETIC SHIRT.

tapa   A type of BARK CLOTH used for traditional apparel in Oceania. As opposed to other textiles incorporating fibers from the inner barks of trees, tapa is made by beating the tree fiber—and not spinning, weaving, or otherwise interlacing it. Known by various names, including "siapo" in Samoa and "kapa" in Hawaii.

tape measure   See MEASURING TAPE.

tarboosh   A FEZ, especially in Egyptian usage.

tarbucket   A SHAKO hat.

tartan   Refers to any of several distinctive and named checked patterns that are intrinsic to the fabric; clan tartans are identified with Scotland and its heritage, particularly as the traditional material of the KILT. The pattern of the tartan is known as a SETT, its background area is the BASS, its weave is a simple two-by-two TWILL made from solid-colored, unslubbed yarns. The original dyes came from vegetable colors and are now known as "ancient colors," while contemporary chemical dyes are known as "modern colors." Tartan should not be used interchangeably with PLAID, which, in Scottish tradition, implies a garment rather than a pattern.

Tartan-type patterns were identified with the Highlands and Islands of Scotland from early medieval times and reportedly go back to the ancient Celts. In the 18th century, they became political when, after the Jacobite uprising, Highland dress was suppressed by an act of Parliament. (The exception being the BLACK WATCH used for regimental dress.) The act was repealed in 1782, and due to a convergence of factors—including the popularity of Sir Walter Scott, the Romantic movement, and George IV's 1822 visit to Scotland—they soon became fashionable.

Although most people think of tartans as a form of strict clan identification, that came long after their origin. Formal association of family with tartan pattern was not really followed until Victorian times; claims that it is an ancient tradition are bunk. Often, tartans were known as "district setts," to identify a particular area (in the same way that ESTATE TWEEDS later developed). Additionally, a single clan might have several tartans. See color plates.

tattersall   Refers to a symmetrical, thin-lined pattern of checks—most often two colors of check (e.g., black and yellow) on a white or other plain-colored background. The name is derived from the horse blankets used by an auctioneer at Newmarket race course in England, which is why it is capitalized in most early usage. The London firm of CORDINGS claims that it popularized the check by copying it from horse blankets and putting it on shirt fabrics during the early 20th century. The original tattersall checks were fairly small—about half an inch—but now the term is applied to similar checks of almost any size. In light wools, the pattern has been popular for WAISTCOATS, and in cotton it has been a popular shirt fabric for country clothes (including RAT-CATCHER riding clothes). See color plates.

teasel *or* **teazle**   A slightly hairy or napped finish given to traditional woolen wovens, particularly in the United Kingdom (or cloth that aspires to look as though it has been produced there). Mills use the prickly, dried flower of a weed called the teasel to catch the fibers on the surface of the fabric. (Or, they use a machine mounted with wire brushes to imitate that effect.)

teck   A style of necktie (usually purchased pre-tied), popular in the late 19th and early 20th centuries; the teck used a traditional four-in-hand knot but had shortened aprons of equal width, which were often worn spread apart (as opposed to the contemporary custom of having a wide apron cover a slimmer apron). The style took its name from the Duke of Teck, Francis von Hohenstein (1837–1900), who became the father of Queen Mary, consort of England's George V, but in the United States, became particularly associated with the dress of the Old West.

Ted   Someone who follows TEDDY BOY fashion, as in "the Teds like BOOTLACE ties."

Teddy Boy   A post-World War II fashion movement that originated with the proletariat of South London who harked back to Edwardian—hence the "Ted"—looks. Although the Teds may have actually been copying the contemporary NEW EDWARDIAN style set by the toffs who patronized Savile Row, they took the longer jacket and styled hair and other elements of that style and made them so extreme as to be unrecognizable. Teds favored:
- Pointy-toed shoe styles like WINKLEPICKERS
- DUCK'S ASS and POMPADOUR-front hairstyles
- FROCK COATS with a high BUTTON STANCE (sometimes accessorized with a razor blade concealed under the lapel)
- BOOTLACE TIES in a neat bow
- Fancy WAISTCOATS
- Tight, structured apparel like DRAINPIPE pants

Although the style's heyday was the 1950s, Teddy boy fashion was endlessly revived, reliably reappearing in mainstream fashion at least once a decade. For example: In 1971, VIVIENNE WESTWOOD and Malcolm McLaren made it the basis of their Let It Rock shop in London, to signal a departure from the rich HIPPIE look that then dominated fashion.

Tencel   A fiber best known in the jeans and shirt markets, either as 100 percent Tencel or part of a blend. Owned by Lenzing, a company based in the town of that name in Austria, Tencel is the trademarked name for lyocell, a fiber processed primarily from wood pulp.

Teddy Boy

ten-gallon hat   A style of COWBOY HAT with an extra-high crown. The name supposedly derives from *galon*, a Spanish word for braid. (Even the largest "ten-gallon" holds less than a gallon of liquid.)

tennis tail   A shirt, usually a POLO SHIRT or similar activewear style, that has a split hem and is slightly longer in back than in front.

terry cloth   Usually made of cotton or a cotton blend, terry is a woven fabric with uncut loops on one or both sides. Because this structure increases its moisture absorbency, terry cloth is most often used in bathrobes and beachwear. Apparel makers also refer to this material as toweling. The plural is "terries."

When the fabric is called FRENCH TERRY, that indicates that its underlying structure is knit instead of woven. Used with its smooth, jersey side showing and its looped side facing the body, French terry and has become a popular material for sweats, warmups, and other casualwear.

Terylene   An early name for POLYESTER, especially in the United Kingdom.

Thinsulate   A brand of thin, nonabsorbent insulation composed primarily of microfibers, developed by 3M during the 1960s and introduced for apparel in 1978 and in 1983 for footwear; flexible, washable, and lightweight, and therefore popular for gloves, outerwear, and sports gear.

thistle—Refers to one of the common styles of BOW TIE. When untied, each end of the tie is shaped like a thistle bloom seen from the side; alternatively, some people describe it as an hourglass shape. When tied, this shaping helps to create a bow that flares out from the knot, like two triangles meeting in the center. (Its alternative number would be the BATWING bow tie, in which the tie ends are left unshaped.) Synonym: butterfly.

thob *or* **thobe**   The loose, long-sleeved, ankle-length body covering of traditional ARAB DRESS. Worn over pants, a thobe is usually white and made of lightweight fabric in hot weather, but may be other colors and made of heavy wool during cold weather.

thong   1. A style of sandal, which stays on the foot by means of a strap or straps bisecting the first and second toe.   2. A style of brief or bathing suit that has no rear covering for the seat, only a strap that bisects the buttocks.

thornproof tweed   Heavy TWEED, usually for hunting or shooting gear, that is so densely woven it literally resists snags or tears from thorns. Often highly water- and wind-resistant.

thread count   A number that connotes the amount of yarns, or threads, in an inch of fabric. Although a high thread count is assumed to be a finer, more expensive fabric, much depends on the way that the fabric is woven. For example: An industrial loom may be able to cram a great number of cotton threads into a square inch and thereby create a stiff, unattractive shirt fabric,

Thistle bow tie: Daniel Craig in *Casino Royale*

Thong sandal

whereas a lower thread count made of a higher-quality cotton may look and feel better to the touch.

thread shank   In imitation of a SHANKED BUTTON (which has a small loop on its underside), the person sewing on a flat button with a pierced surface may create a SHANK out of thread. In menswear, this is often done with suits to enhance both the drape of the fabric and its wearer's ease of movement.

Three on the Bund   The seven-story retail and restaurant complex that opened on the Bund in Shanghai in 2004, in an Italianate building originally erected in 1916 for the Union Assurance Company and renovated in the early 21st century by architect Michael Graves. Notable as the first foreign-owned building on the Bund, Three became the site of the local GIORGIO ARMANI flagship, as well as its own luxury-priced fashion stores, an art gallery, a full-fledged Evian Spa, and restaurants including chef Jean-Georges Vongerichten's four-star Jean George.

three-button   Refers to the single-breasted jacket silhouette with a three-button front closure (although in contemporary use the bottom button is almost always left unbuttoned and indeed may be cut in such a way that it will not close).

three-piece suit   Refers to a suit that includes a VEST along with the customary jacket and trousers.

three seams *or* **three seamer**   Slang for a style of jacket in which the side seams have been moved from underneath the arm to the back. Thus, in a rear view, the jacket shows three seams: the center seams and both side seams.

three-season suit   A designation used in opposite ways: either describes a suit made of a fabric that can be worn in all but the coldest winter weather (hence, three out of four seasons) or a suit made of fabric that can be worn in all but the most sultry summer weather. When in doubt, assume that it refers to fall/winter/spring and that it is constructed from MIDWEIGHT fabric.

thrifting   Slang for shopping in thrift stores (such as Salvation Army or Goodwill stores). In general use since the mid-1990s, when the craze for vintage fashion entered the mainstream.

throat   On the upper of a shoe, where the VAMP opens over the instep; the TONGUE emerges from the throat. See SHOE diagram.

throat latch   A strap or triangle of cloth attached to the underside of the collar on SPORTS JACKETS and outerwear. Usually made of leather or the same fabric as the rest of the garment and attached to the left side. When not in use, the throat latch remains unseen. When a man turns up his collar to protect his throat from the cold or other elements, the throat latch swings across and attaches to a corresponding button or buckle sewn on the collar's underside. Synonyms: KIDNEY; STORM FLAP.

Tibetan lamb   Reference to the variety of long, wavy sheepskin better known as MONGOLIAN LAMB.

ticket pocket   A small pocket located just above the regular pocket on the right side of a sports jacket, suit coat, or tailored coat, where it supposedly provides easy access to tickets and such; its shape, canting, and construction (e.g., flapped or not flapped) echoes the main pocket beneath it. Associated with traditional British menswear; especially a hallmark of HACKING JACKETS.

ticking   A sturdy, simply woven fabric (usually a TWILL or PLAIN WEAVE), best known as a covering for mattresses and pillows. Marked with distinctive vertical stripes known as TICKING STRIPES, the material was tightly woven to prevent the bedding or upholstery stuffing from escaping. Inexpensive and unpretentious, it was sometimes used in WORKWEAR (such as bib overalls), or apparel that wanted to quote those styles. Sometimes, more archaically, referred to as "tick."

ticking stripe   Any of several simple vertical stripe patterns, usually blue and white or black and white, that look like mattress TICKING. Popular for DENIM, canvas, and shirt fabrics. See color plates.

tick weave   Refers to a traditional suit fabric patterned in a small regular pattern; not to be confused with BIRD'S EYE or with a TICKING STRIPE. See color plates.

tie   Most often used as a shortened form of NECKTIE (rather than a BOW TIE), the notable exceptions being BLACK TIE and WHITE TIE, when the wearing of a bow tie is usually assumed.

tie bar   A piece of jewelry that is generally about 2 inches long, thin, and made of metal, used with a NECKTIE to secure the APRON of the tie to the PLACKET of the shirt beneath; worn more for fashion than function. Because the tie bar (like the TIE CLIP) depends on being fastened to the shirt, it is usually in fashion only at the same time as narrow neckties. Unlike the tie bar, it does not use a spring or grip mechanism but slides onto the fabrics like a paper clip. Synonym: TIE SLIDE.

tie chain   A piece of jewelry that is slightly wider than the NECKTIE it is worn with; worn more for fashion than function. The unseen part is a wire or thin bar with a hook in the middle that fastens to a button on the PLACKET of the dress shirt being worn beneath; the visible part is a thin chain that goes over the APRON of the tie, which is then threaded through the tie chain.

tie clasp   A TIE CLIP.

tie clip   A piece of jewelry that is generally about 2 inches long, thin, and made of metal, used with a NECKTIE to secure the APRON of the tie to the PLACKET of the shirt beneath; worn more for fashion than function. It resembles a TIE BAR and has essentially the same use, but differs by the inclusion of a simple grip or spring mechanism, resembling a clothespin, that allows it to snap onto the fabric. Synonym: TIE CLASP.

tie-dye   A pattern formed by bunching, tying, or squeezing cloth so that the dye does not fully penetrate. Or a pattern printed to look like tie-dye.

Because of its randomness and association with the hand-made, tie-dyeing became emblematic of the HIPPIE look in the late 1960s. In that fashion's simplest form, white T-shirts were bunched together with rubber bands and then dipped in a different dye baths. Since then, tie-dye has enjoyed periodic revivals, usually intended as a reference to the 1960s and 1970s.

As an ancient form of resist dyeing, more or less elaborate versions of tie-dye are known throughout the world, especially in the textile traditions of South Asia and Africa. In Japan, the group of traditional tie-dye techniques is known as SHIBORI.

Tielocken   The direct antecedent of the TRENCH COAT, developed by Thomas BURBERRY & Sons in 1895 and worn by British officers in the Boer War.

tiepin   A STICKPIN.

tie slide   A TIE BAR.

tie tack   A tack-shaped piece of jewelry worn in the center of the tie APRON, approximately halfway down the chest. Made in two parts, the front is a tack with an ornamental head and a short, protruding point that pierces the tie silk. The back, unseen part is a pinch clasp that blunts the point and keeps the tack in place. Most tie tacks also have a light chain attached to the back: This chain has a toggle at the end, which is meant to be slipped through the buttonhole of the dress shirt worn beneath as a method of lightly securing the tie to the shirt PLACKET.

Not to be confused with a STICKPIN, which has a much longer pin and is worn much higher and closer to the collar.

tightie whities   Slang for traditional, white, Y-FRONT briefs, such as JOCKEY SHORTS.

tin pants   Old-fashioned slang for a type of work pants made with sturdy, stiff, woven cloth; so called because they wore like metal and stood up on their own.

tipped   1. In apparel, jargon for a design that concentrates a color on the edges or "tips." For example: a T-shirt with a contrasting color of ribbing at its cuffs and neckline.   2. In textiles, jargon for dyeing or some other finishing that concentrates color on the ends of fur or pile.

T-neck   Jargon for a TURTLENECK.

toe box   The area of a shoe that covers and protects the toes; refers to the interior construction of the shoe (its exterior would be the TOE CAP). On workboots, the toe box may be reinforced with steel or other material to protect the toes from being crushed.

toe cap   The area of a shoe that covers and protects the toes; refers to the exterior (the interior is known as the TOE BOX). A CAP TOE is a style of boot or DRESS SHOE in which the toe cap is delineated by a seam or decoration.

toga   The distinguishing draped garment of the male citizens of ancient Rome; usually worn over a tunic and most often made of wool or a wool blend. Most togas were a huge piece of woven cloth that looked like half of a circle or half of an oval when unfolded and often had a band of decoration on the curved side.

A man wore the toga by draping it roughly in half over his left shoulder with the front point hanging down to his right calf. The back point was then lifted under his right arm and thrown over his left shoulder, leaving the right arm free and the left arm almost completely covered.

Several versions were worn and their etiquette grew more elaborate as the Roman Empire evolved. Originally it was a more common and probably more gender-neutral garment until, in the first century, its use was restricted to adult male citizens. The most commonly worn was the white version called the *toga pura*, but

Toga

striped versions were worn by augurs; purple-bordered togas were worn by adolescent nobility and by certain officials or priests; and dark colors were worn for mourning. The imperial toga was a larger, almost circular, piece of cloth that was folded over before being draped, thus creating more elaborate folds once it was worn.

toggle coat   Synonym for a DUFFEL COAT, because of that style's toggle closures.

tongue   The flap over the instep or VAMP or shoe, roughly shaped like a human tongue, that is fastened at its lower end (at what is called the THROAT of the shoe) and loose at its top end where the foot enters the shoe; under most styles of laced shoes, it is the part directly beneath the laces. See SHOE diagram.

tonsure   1. A style of shaving part of the head, primarily associated with monks and men preparing for the priesthood. The practice, which probably dates back to Roman times, was not officially abolished by the Roman Catholics until the 1970s. Tonsure styles varied according to religious order and local custom, but probably the best known is the practice of shaving the crown of the head and leaving the rest of the hair to form a circular fringe.   2. Refers to the section of shaved scalp in a tonsure style.

toorie   A pompom, especially when referring to Scottish dress (e.g., as the adornment on a GLENGARRY BONNET).

topcoat   Tailored outerwear, usually worn over a suit or some other business or formal attire. Its hem may be anywhere from slightly above the knee to slightly above the ankle. Among traditionalists, the term connotes a lighter style than an OVERCOAT or GREATCOAT. For example, a CHESTERFIELD is a style of topcoat.

top collar   The visible, or "right," side of a COLLAR, especially on a coat or jacket.

top grain   Slang for top quality, originally derived from leather terminology. In leather making, the "top grain" is the uppermost part of any hide.

top hat   The traditional accompaniment to formalwear; in contemporary use, most often black (for evening wear with tails and sometimes with a MORNING SUIT) although gray is still worn at Royal Ascot and with morning suits donned for equivalent events; noted for its high, cylindrical crown (usually about 5 to 5½ inches) and short, slightly curled brim.

Most costume historians say the style originated in Italy in the 1760s and was first worn in England by a Londoner named John Hetherington in 1797, a haberdasher who was promptly arrested for it. Customarily constructed of silk plush (a distinction at a time when most hats were made of fur felt), for nearly two centuries it was produced with the aid of a special shellac made from the droppings of insects found only in India. But versions were also made in everything from straw to various felts. Worldwide, the best-known maker was Spoorenberg of Einhoven in the Netherlands, which ceased production in 1975. Synonyms: high hat; silk hat; tall hat; TOPPER. The collapsible version is usually known as an OPERA HAT or GIBUS.

topper   1. Slang for a TOP HAT.   2. Slang for any traditional style of hat.

Top-Sider   A registered trademark for the type of boating MOCCASIN invented by yachtsman Paul Sperry in New Haven, Connecticut, in 1935, with a sole inspired by the bottom of his dog Prince's paws. The classic Sperry Top-Sider is a slip-on moccasin UPPER of brown leather with four eyelets, a rawhide tie, and a nonmarking, white rubber sole with SIPING (small slits in a zigzag pattern) to be non-skid.

Because of their relatively unchanging style and their association with sailing, Top-Siders have been a popular part of PREPPY casualwear for both sexes.

top sole   Synonym for the OUTSOLE of a SHOE.

topweight   Jargon used to refer to fabric for shirts and tops. "Topweight" may also include knits, whereas SHIRTWEIGHT generally refers to wovens. Refers to the fabric, never to the finished garment.

toque   1. The tall, cylindrical hat made of starched cotton worn by professional chefs (especially those working in the French tradition), or a style made in its imitation. In contemporary usage, a common height for a full-fledged professional may be about 10 inches (although a very eminent chef may claim an even taller tocque). Apprentices, butchers, and pastry chefs wear a lower *toque blanche*, about 5 or 6 inches in height. Many legends attach to the classical toque, including one that says it should have 100 pleats, symbolizing the chef's mastery of 100 different ways to cook an egg.   2. A general category of tall, brimless hat.

toquilla   Can refer to either the type of straw used in a PANAMA hat or to the resulting hat.

torque   A necklace that is usually constructed of a rigid band of metal (rather than flexible links or components that enable it to lie flat against the throat). Its construction may be closed or open. In the open version, the torque slides onto the throat via a narrow opening—in much the same way that a CUFF bracelet slides onto the wrist—and is usually worn with the opening facing the front of the throat. Many cultures, dating back to the Bronze Age, wore torque ornaments, but today the style is most often identified with the Celts. Synonym: NECK RING.

toupee   1. A small wig worn to mask baldness, usually intended to be unobtrusive.   2. A variant spelling of TOUPET.

toupet   1. Used to describe a hairstyle in which the hair at the front of the head is puffed and/or rolled (somewhat like an 18th-century antecedent to ELVIS PRESLEY's POMPADOUR). Used especially to describe styles of wigs or hairstyles worn in Western Europe and colonial America after the first quarter of the 1700s. From the French word for forelock. Synonym: FORETOP.   2. Used as a variant spelling for the style of small wig known as a TOUPEE.

Tout Beau Tout Propre   The "makeup for men" line launched by JEAN PAUL GAULTIER in France in 2003, which made its U.S. debut at Macy's in 2004. Along with the more usual grooming, skin care, and fragrance ancillaries (based on the designer's previously introduced "Le Male" cologne), Gaultier's line was the first widely publicized men's line to incorporate traditionally female products such as BRONZER, blusher, concealer, colored lip balms, and eyeliner.

toweling   Synonym for TERRY CLOTH.

tracht   Traditional German styles; usually refers to garments such as LODEN COATS and LEDERHOSEN.

trade cloth   Refers to a wide category of textiles, rather than a specific design. Most often, trade cloth was manufactured in Europe for export to colonies and was made to local, colonial taste. One example of trade cloth is the imitation BATIK printed in Europe for export to Indonesia during the 19th century.

trainers   Slang, usually British, for SNEAKERS.

le training   Slang, usually French, for a track suit.

traje de charro   The highly decorated "suit of the horseman" worn by MARIACHI musicians. Tradition dictates that it consist of a long-sleeved jacket that ends at the waist, a vest in matching material (usually wool, but occasionally suede in a reference to the suit's origin as riding apparel), plus slim-fitting pants that are long and tight over the ankles (and therefore must be worn with special ankle boots called *botines*). Rows of fancy gold buttons, called *botonaduras*, decorate the outside length of each leg—although sometimes they are replaced by leather decoration called *greco*.

The suit is worn with a short, full tie called a *MOÑO*, which resembles a cropped JABOT, and a decorative belt called a *cinto piteado*, made from PITA cactus fiber. Famously, the outfit is sometimes topped with the huge-brimmed hat known as the SOMBRERO.

Its many variations include the *traje chinaco*, which features pants that flare out

from the knee like a BELL-BOTTOM and has a different style of side decoration.

trapper hat   A style of warm, bulky, winter hat; so named because of its association with fur trappers. Often made of fur or fur-lined fabric, the hat covers the head completely and has flaps, designed to descend over the ears during extreme weather but be tied up the rest of the time (sometimes with a small bow or buckle directly over the top center of the hat). The front of the hat usually has a very short visor or cuff of the same material covering the forehead; the back is usually made to fully cover the neck (or has another flap which can be lowered over the neck).

trench   Jargon for TRENCH COAT.

trench coat   The belted outerwear style identified with World War I and derived from the TIELOCKEN manufactured by BURBERRY and worn during the Boer War, which became the traditional costume of flashers, foreign correspondents, and spies. Its distinguishing attributes are a DOUBLE-BREASTED front, a GUN FLAP, a belt, a collar of 2 or more inches, EPAULETTES, insert pockets, and sleeves that can be cinched at the cuff. Traditionally made of tan GABARDINE, the style is now translated to any of a variety of materials from leather to synthetics. Likewise, in its high-fashion incarnations, the coat can be stripped of almost any of its distinguishing attributes except the belt and still be called a trench.

trews   Legwear in traditional Highland dress; worn alone or under the PLAID or KILT, especially in winter or

Trench coat: Humphrey Bogart in *Sirocco*

for horseback riding; similar in their tight fit to contemporary leggings or the very tight PANTALOONS of the early 19th century.

In order to keep them clinging to the leg, trews were often cut on the BIAS. In their classic depiction, a Scotsman sporting trews has a diagonal, diamond-shaped pattern running up and down his legs (much in the manner of an ARGYLE) because he is wearing his TARTAN turned on its side.

tricorne   A three-cornered hat. The style developed in the late 17th century, when men began turning up the brims of the large, floppy-brimmed headgear that was fashionable at the time, and variations of the style persisted into the early 19th century. Specific use of the term tricorne (as opposed to the more generic COCKED HAT) implies a style that is even on all three sides. The tricorne is familiar to most Americans from depictions of the Revolutionary War. Synonyms: cocked hat; three-cornered hat.

trilby   A style of brimmed hat with a creased, low crown. Made of soft felt, tweed, or similar material, the trilby is associated with more informality than the HOMBURG (i.e., the country versus the city, or weekend wear versus business attire).

The style first became popular toward the end of the 19th century and got its name when a performer wore it in the stage production of the popular 1894 George du Maurier novel *Trilby*. During the 20th century, the trilby was associated with British actor Rex Harrison, who wore it on-screen in the 1964 film *My Fair Lady*, and was part of Sean Connery's costume in the 1989 *Indiana Jones and the Last Crusade*.

F.R. Tripler   A specialty store located on New York's Madison Avenue near BROOKS BROTHERS, PAUL STUART,

J. PRESS, and CHIPP from 1918 until 1994 (when its owner, HARTMARX, relocated it to a Wallach's store on Fifth Avenue). In its heyday, Tripler was a bastion of traditional business attire, including—for several decades—the two-button suit with a natural shoulder.

tropicals *or* **tropical weight**   Usually refers to the lightweight wools—less than 9 ounces per yard and sometimes much, much lighter—used for suits. Although traditional looking suits made of lighter weights were around for most of the 20th century, they were scorned by Savile Row and similarly traditionalist firms until well into the 1970s.

Trouble, Agnès   The real name of French designer AGNÈS B.

trousers   In industry jargon, trousers connote the PANTS that are worn with tailored clothing (whereas SLACKS are a less dressy designation).

However, in the late 1700s and early 1800s, when full-length pants were a relatively new fashion for upper-class men, the word connoted the loose, full-length trousers worn by working men (whereas the more form-fitting PANTALOONS were a favored fashion of beaus like BRUMMELL). As the 1800s wore on, the word assumed its present meaning.

trowsers   An archaic spelling of TROUSERS, especially in the 19th century and especially in England.

Troy, New York   The Rensselaer County town, directly north of New York City at the state's eastern edge, known as "Collar City," or as the DRESS SHIRT and DETACHABLE

Trilby: Rex Harrison in *My Fair Lady*

COLLAR capital of America, due mainly to the many manufacturers located there, but especially to ARROW, the Cluett, Peabody brand that dominated that industry for decades.

The town's claim to fame began in the 1820s, when the wife of a local blacksmith invented the detachable collar as a labor-saving device. Ironically, in 1864, it was also the site of the area's first female labor movement, the Collar Laundry Union, which addressed conditions stemming from the fact that the labor force of the local factories was predominantly female and their ownership predominantly male. Troy's prosperity peaked in the decades following the invention of the popular Arrow brand of shirts and collars in 1889, and the town was immortalized in 1923's "Helen of Troy," a Broadway musical about the mythical ARROW COLLAR MAN. At that time, Troy was the site of some 20 factories turning out a total of 1 million collars a day, and was estimated to produce over 90 percent of all the collars and dress shirts sold in the United States; the local industry employed approximately 15,000 workers, who were 87 percent female.

In 1930, it became the birthplace of SANFORIZATION, Cluett, Peabody's trademarked method of controlling cotton shrinkage for apparel manufacture. However, when the popularity of the detachable collar began to wane in the late 1920s, so did the fortunes of Troy. Cluett, Peabody, once the town's major employer, had phased out its collar production during the 1930s and began to produce elsewhere in the second half of the 20th century, finally relocating the remainder of its Arrow dress shirt business to Atlanta in 1989.

trunks   Originally a general description for ACTIVEWEAR bottoms (e.g., swim trunks, boxing trunks) that have an abbreviated leg like shorts; in contemporary use, the word is sometimes applied to underwear styles. The difference between trunks and other abbreviated bottoms is that trunks have a short inseam; BRIEFS do not.

trunkhose   Not HOSE in the modern sense, but a form of BREECHES; the term is associated with a general type of baggy, knee-revealing pants that evolved in the 16th century.

T-shirt   A pullover style of shirt with either a V-NECK or crewneck, made of lightweight knit material (originally cotton); originally with short sleeves (although the term was later applied to long sleeves).

Originally worn as underwear during the early 20th century, the T-shirt came into the open after World War II when returning soldiers, who had been issued T-shirts during the war and gotten into the habit of wearing them while doing casual labor, continued the practice in civilian life.

tube socks   Socks made without a heel, so that when not being worn, they are shaped like a tube instead of a human foot. Tube socks extend above the ankle, are primarily white (often sporting a stripe with the team color near their top), and are worn for athletic activity.

tuck   Old-fashioned slang for TUXEDO.

turban   A broad reference to any one of several styles of head covering that is created by wrapping a long band of cloth around the head (rather than being prefabricated in the manner of a hat or cap). Depending on the time, place, and tradition (as well as the width of the material being used), the length of the wrap may vary from a few feet to many, many yards.

Troy, New York

turkey red An old-fashioned term for a shade of bright red in which "turkey" refers to the country rather than the bird. Popular in printed textiles, especially calico and other cottons, from the 1780s through the 19th century, when specialists in the trade of turkey red were much sought after (since cotton was trickier to turn red than PROTEINACIOUS textiles). The modern legacy of the technique of dyeing with turkey red is the BANDANA, which used turkey red as its primary color during much of the 19th century.

turkey skin The leather made from the large birds, properly known as GALLAPAVA. A sort of poor man's version of OSTRICH, turkey features a similarly pimply surface indicating where the feathers have been plucked, but the grain is not as prominent and the skin is not as sturdy.

Turnbull & Asser The JERMYN STREET firm that traces its origin to an establishment of a furnishings shop known as "John Arthur Turnbull" on London's Church Place in 1885. In 1895, salesman and cofounder Ernest Asser's name was added to the shop. In 1903, the firm then known as Turnbull, Asser & Co. moved to larger premises on Jermyn Street, where it subsequently became famed for its BESPOKE shirts. For instance: Novelist F. Scott Fitzgerald, who put his own paean to shirting in 1925's *The Great Gatsby*, was a Turnbull & Asser customer, as were CARY GRANT, Winston Churchill, FRANK SINATRA, and assorted royalty (later including Prince Charles). During London's "Swinging Sixties," it also employed MICHAEL FISH, who turned Turnbull & Asser into Jermyn Street's top source of bright shirts and trendy wide ties before leaving to launch his own business.

turn-ups Trouser CUFFS; more common in British usage. Synonyms: cuffs; PTUs (in old-fashioned British slang).

turtleneck A style of SWEATER or top distinguished by a close-fitting, usually RIBBED collar that covers the entire throat and then folds back on itself, so that the neck is protected by a double layer of material. A turtleneck is usually integrated to the main body of the garment (as opposed to being buttoned on or otherwise attached separately); thus turtleneck tops must usually be pulled over the head and must usually be made of some kind of knit so that they expand to accommodate the head and then reduce in size to hug the neck. Its synonyms include POLO NECK (in British usage, but not American), T-NECK, and ROLL COLLAR or ROLL-OVER (however, calling it a ROLLED COLLAR is technically incorrect, since that term usually signifies cut-and-sewn collars). Similar-looking styles that feature a single layer and do not fold over are the FUNNEL NECK and MOCK TURTLE.

tussah A type of SILK (or the material made to resemble it) that is usually duller, less supple, and more filled with SLUBS than ordinary silks, since it is made from tussah silkworms or similar types of silkworms. Because it is also more difficult to dye, tussah often appears in its natural, beige-colored state—especially for menswear, where it may be used for DINNER JACKETS or suits.

tuta A simple, egalitarian style of belted OVERALL proposed as part of a dress reform movement by Florentine artists Ruggero Michahelles (known as Ram) and his brother Ernesto (known as Thayaht), who were inspired by Italian Futurism. Designed around 1919, the tuta was run up by French couturier Madeleine Vionnet (a family friend) and was similar to styles invented simultaneously by Russian Constructivists and other artists aiming to reform dress and society after World War I.

tuxedo   An evening suit with no tails. One step down in formality from WHITE TIE, the tuxedo is traditionally worn with a BLACK TIE—hence its nickname—although alternatives are acceptable and the suit has its own set of dress conventions.

The style was first created by the SAVILE ROW firm of HENRY POOLE in 1860 for EDWARD VII, then Prince of Wales. After watching the Prince wear his informal formalwear at Sandringham in 1886, American James Potter had the style copied by his own tailor and wore it to his club at home in Tuxedo Park (a wealthy suburb of New York). There, the style became so popular that it was virtually a club uniform and thereafter became known as a tuxedo. (Despite the wide currency of its alternate creation myth, it was most certainly *not* invented by Griswold Lorillard.)

By tradition, the tuxedo may be either black or midnight blue (a fashion furthered by Edward's grandsons and known as the KENT), and either single- or double-breasted. If single-breasted, it may be SHAWL-COLLARED, PEAK-LAPELED, or a traditional NOTCH. (If double-breasted, it is almost certainly peak-lapeled.) It is worn with matching trousers with a single stripe down the outseam in a material that matches the FACINGS of its lapels. Its other accompaniments vary, but usually include a CUMMERBUND, black bow tie (or tie of material matching the cummerbund) or a FOUR-IN-HAND of equivalent formality, a TUXEDO SHIRT, STUDS and CUFFLINKS, black PUMPS, and perhaps a BOUTONNIÈRE and POCKET SQUARE. Synonyms: black tie; dinner clothes; dinner suit; tux; *LE SMOKING*.

tuxedo shirt   A DRESS SHIRT specifically created to be worn with a TUXEDO, usually meaning that it has a pleated front, MARCELLA or PIQUÉ FRONT, or ruffled front; and/or that it accommodates the use of STUDS and CUFFLINKS instead of buttons; and/or that it sports a WING COLLAR, has an attachment for a DETACHABLE COLLAR, or sports some other collar style identified with relatively formal evening attire.

TV fold   Refers to a style of folding a POCKET SQUARE so that roughly an inch of fabric is displayed above the pocket in a neat, symmetrical fold.

tweed   A word referring to a category of rugged wool fabrics, which often look as though they are artisanally produced (and originally were); coined—probably by accident—in the 19th century as a mispronunciation of TWILL and continued through misunderstanding of the fabrics' association with the River Tweed in Scotland.

Tuxedo: Hal Sherman in "Hellz-a-Poppin"

twill   Refers to a weave pattern distinguished by its strong diagonal line, called the twill line. Simple to execute and sturdy, twill is (after a PLAIN

WEAVE) the most popular way of weaving fabric for menswear. Virtually all DENIM is twill. So are all TARTANS. A HERRINGBONE is a twill that reverses direction.

For example, in a "2/2 twill," two warp threads cross over two weft threads in staggered succession—thus creating the diagonal twill line. Other common twill patterns are 2/1, 3/1, and 4/1. The steepness of the twill line varies according to the weave—the higher the number of crossed yarns, the steeper the line. Thus a 4/1 will present a steeper diagonal line than a 2/1.

When the twill line slants to the right, it's called a right-hand twill. When it slants to the left, the fabric is known as a left-hand twill. Occasionally, the twill line may be purposely broken (as often happens in fashion denim) and the fabric is called a broken twill.

twill tape   A narrow, ribbonlike weight of sturdy tape (usually cotton or a cotton blend); used to reinforce seams; not intended to be visible from the right side of the garment. For example: A sports jacket constructed of a loosely woven silk or linen might have twill tape used on its interior construction so that the seams do not gape or lose shape while the jacket is being worn.

twist   Industry jargon—as in "high twist" or "low twist"—used to describe the structure of a yarn; the word twist being used as synonym for the visible turns created when a fiber is spun into yarn. For example: A high twist yarn might have dozens of twists, which tends to make the yarn somewhat stiffer when it is woven or knit into fabric. Yarns are further classified as Z-TWIST or S-TWIST to indicate the direction that they turn.

two-button   Jargon for a style of single-breasted suit jacket or sport coat that has only two buttons (as opposed to three or four) in its center front and, perforce, has a deeper, lower STANCE. In contemporary convention, only the topmost button is fastened when the garment is worn.

two-suiter   Reference to a piece of luggage rather than an ensemble. See WEEKENDER.

tyrian purple   An ancient and expensive dye, once worth much more than its weight in gold and therefore restricted to the robes of nobility and ceremonial garments (the origin of the phrase "born to the purple"). Commercially produced in the Middle East for thousands of years—from the Minoan times through the fall of Constantinople in the 15th century—its best-known center of production during Roman times was the city of Tyre (hence its name). Resulting in a color range that shades from burgundy through purple through violet blue, the dyes were also prized because they stayed true on wool and linen. Tyrian purple was made from a shelled sea creature (*murex brandaris*) and legend ascribed its discovery to Heracles.

Two-button jacket

U

ulster   1. A style of long, boxy OVERCOAT; named for the region in Northern Ireland and characterized by its heavy, rough material. The ulster resembled a TRENCH COAT in being double-breasted, having set-in sleeves, and having a large collar (which could be buttoned up in blustery weather), but it differed in rarely being worn with a belt and not having EPAULETTES, as well as being made of coarser material. Most popular from the Civil War to the beginning of World War II.   2. Heavy overcoat fabric with a flattened NAP, produced in Northern Ireland.

ulsterette   A lighter version of the ULSTER, which, despite being lighter than a traditional material, might still be rendered in a tweed or rough wool. Synonym: SEMI-ULSTER.

Ultrasuede   Trademarked name for the nonwoven fabric, made of POLYESTER and urethane, created by Toray Industries in 1970. Unlike suede, which it was cre-ated to resemble, Ultrasuede is colorfast, not prone to shrinking, and can usually be machine-washed. During the 1970s it became a high-fashion fabric, and was particularly associated with Halston, the American designer.

umbrella   In Western tradition, the umbrella is most often used as a portable, collapsible canopy protecting its user from adverse weather: most often from rain, but also from snow, bright sun, sleet, or hail. Usually round, it consists of an expanse of fabric or plastic, known as the "cover," seamed by "ribs," which are attached to the umbrella "shaft" by means of "runners." Its nicknames include BROLLY, BUMBERSHOOT, and GAMP.

In the English and American traditions, it did not come into wide use until the end of the 18th century and, up until that time, was considered a somewhat effete accessory. By contrast, in ancient and many Eastern traditions, an umbrella signified status, and appears in that context in many Moghul paintings.

Umbrella

unbranded apparel   Industry jargon for generic fashion that is usually produced at a relatively low cost so that it can be sold to a store or manufacturer who will then slap on its own brand.

Uncle Sam suit   A character named Uncle Sam had been used as a verbal reference to the personification of the United States as early as the early 19th century (according to legend, a TROY, NEW YORK meatpacker named Sam Wilson who supplied the U.S. Army with victuals during the War of 1812 inspired the name). But the character did not make his appearance in editorial cartoons until about two decades later and his association with the famous, flashy, flag-inspired red, white, and blue suit did not become codified until a series of *Harper's Weekly* cartoons drawn during the Civil War. Later still, Bavarian-illustrator Thomas Nast (the same man who created our images of Santa Claus, the Republican elephant, and the Democratic donkey), in his cartoons for that same publication, added a wispy white beard and forever fixed the white-bearded, top-hatted version in the popular imagination.

Uncle Sam's appearance was further codified by illustrator James Montgomery Flagg's 1917 recruiting poster—"I Want You"—and a succession of World War I posters that depicted Uncle Sam as a lean and vigorous, white-bearded but balding man, usually wearing a blue tailcoat, star-spangled waistcoat, red-and-white striped trousers, white shirt, red bow tie, and white top hat with a star-spangled hatband. The same attire and same character were used by illustrator J.C. LEYENDECKER when he featured Uncle Sam in a series July 4 covers during his four-decade-long association with *The Saturday Evening Post* magazine.

unconstructed   Jargon that usually indicates a suit, coat, or jacket that is unlined (or half-lined) and done with minimal amounts of traditional tailoring's structural elements, such as PAD STITCHING, SHOULDER PADS, CANVAS, and the like.

underarm shield   1. A removable pad or piece of cloth, which may be disposable or washable, worn on the inside of a jacket to prevent sweat stains.   2. Crescent-shaped piece of fabric, applied over the body of a jacket lining as an extra thickness; in contemporary use, often made of a fabric with WICKING or MOISTURE-MANAGEMENT properties.

underlay   Reinforcement, usually not visible on the "right" side of the garment; used in selected areas, such as button attachments or monogramming, where the fabric of the garment might be too weak to support the addition without a little help. For example: On a very fine and lightweight shirt, a small underlay of fabric may be added beneath the button (on the wrong side of the garment) so that, when it is tugged, the button does not pull through the fabric and create a hole.

undershirt   An undergarment worn for warmth or to protect the skin from the material of a shirt. The under-

Uncle Sam suit

shirt in its current form did not appear until well after World War I, when underwear began to be scantier and less constricting. Immediately preceding it, the all-in-one UNION SUIT was considered the latest innovation in undergarments.

The first garment recognizable as a modern undershirt was the ATHLETIC SHIRT, a tank style that became popular in the late 1920s. During the subsequent decade, advances in the production of cotton jersey helped the T-SHIRT, with either a crewneck or V-neck, to supplant the A-shirt in popularity. (Famously, Clark Gable supposedly caused a two-year setback to the rise of the undershirt by leaving one out of his wardrobe in 1934's *IT HAPPENED ONE NIGHT*.)

In contemporary use, the all-American undershirt is typified by a style like the white cotton Hanes T-shirt.

underslung   Usually refers to the heel of a shoe that tapers at a visible angle from the back of the shoe to in—"under"—the sole (instead of running straight down from the back of the shoe, which is referred to as a STACKED HEEL). For example, CUBAN HEELS are always underslung. In contemporary use, most often seen in COWBOY BOOTS.

Union-All   Supposedly suggested by Henry Lee's chauf-feur John Hemsley, manufactured by LEE in 1913, launched with an ad campaign in the *Saturday Evening Post*, adopted by the army in 1917, and later endorsed by Babe Ruth, the Union-All was a long-sleeved, collared WORKWEAR garment indistinguishable from today's OVERALLS.

union suit   Underwear in which the top and bottom are united into a single piece (a sort of next-to-the-skin jumpsuit) with a center front—usually buttoned—opening; most often indicates long-sleeved, long-legged underwear worn for warmth, although the term may also be applied to a shorts-and-tank combo.

unisex   A system of sizing clothes that usually extends from extra small (XS) to extra large (XL); applied to T-shirts, pajamas, and other garments that can be used by both sexes. Because it is based on traditional menswear sizing, there is usually no difference between a man's

Undershirt: Marlon Brando in *A Streetcar Named Desire*

large and a unisex large (whereas, with women's wear, a woman's large most often translates to a man's medium).

unmentionables   See INEXPRESSIBLES.

upholstery fabric   A fabric made to cover furniture that is occasionally used for jackets or outerwear. Upholstery fabric is usually heavier in weight, has a larger REPEAT, and is more decorative than traditional jacket materials.

upland cotton   Refers to *gossypium hirsutum*, the majority of the cotton grown in the United States. (For example, you can assume that anything with a COTTON INCORPORATED tag or label is made from this variety, since Cotton Inc. is the marketing company for U.S. upland cotton growers.) Upland cotton's four major varieties are Acala, Delta, Eastern, and Plains.

Originally, the word "upland" distinguished this type of hardy, snowy-colored cotton from silkier, LONG-STA-PLE varieties grown elsewhere, such as PIMA cotton, SEA ISLAND COTTON, and EGYPTIAN COTTON.

upper   Literally the upper part of the shoe; visible when the foot is on the ground. Depending upon the style, the upper (especially of a DRESS SHOE) can be further subdivided to include parts such as the VAMP, the QUARTERS, the back, the COUNTER, the TONGUE, and the TOE CAP. See SHOE diagram.

urban   Usually an industry synonym for HIP-HOP apparel or retailers' euphemism for the clothes preferred by young men who lived in cities, especially from the 1980s onward. "Urban" started as a description of baggy clothes associated with rap culture. In the 21st century, it became a broader and more general description of street styles, from ACTIVEWEAR up to and including TAILORED CLOTHING. Associated with brands including Ecko, Enyce, Fubu, PHAT FARM, ROCAWEAR, and SEAN JOHN.

V-neck A neckline shaped so that it descends to a point in the center front, forming the letter V underneath the face. A V-neck may be so high that it is only an inch or two below the Adam's apple, or it may be so low that it plunges practically to the navel. Most often, it covers the breasts and descends no lower than the clavicle. When used without additional description, "V-neck" usually describes a PULLOVER sweater with that neckline.

vambrace In ARMOR, the piece that covers the forearm.

vamp The portion of the shoe that covers the instep; the top, front area of the shoe. See SHOE diagram.

vamplate In ARMOR, the handguard for the lance.

Vandyke A small beard that includes a mustache but does not include sidewhiskers; always trimmed, often to a point. Named after the style of beard popular in the 17th century and associated with the portraiture of Flemish painter Sir Anthony Van Dyke (1599–1641), best known for his portraits of British royalty and for being appointed "painter to the king" by Charles I.

When referring to the beard, properly spelled as a single word, either upper- or lowercase.

When a similar beard is present but does not include a mustache, it is called a GOATEE; when the goatee does not extend below the chin or to the full width of the mouth, it is a SOUL PATCH.

Varvatos, John Born in 1954, Detroit-area native John Varvatos became best known for an understated, luxury ready-to-wear label for men that virtually ignored the costumey aspects and fashion extremes of the market.

The designer joined POLO RALPH LAUREN in 1983 and moved to CALVIN KLEIN in 1990 (where he headed menswear and then worked on the cK brand). In 1995,

Vandyke: John Legend

374

he moved back to Polo Ralph Lauren as head of menswear design. In 1999, aiming at the luxury end of men's ready-to-wear, he launched his first collection, for spring 2000, under the aegis of Nautica (a brand that was itself bought by VF Corporation a few years later). In June of 2000, he won the first of his multiple CFDA awards and, in the fall of that year, opened his first store under his own name.

vegetable dye   A designation used to distinguish dyes derived from plant rather than chemical sources. For example, true INDIGO is a vegetable dye and MADRAS fabric is dependent upon vegetable dyes.

vegetable fiber   A fiber or fabric derived from a plant, such as COTTON, LINEN, or RAMIE. A designation used to differentiate a fiber or fabric from PROTEINACIOUS fibers (such as WOOL), mineral fibers (such as asbestos), and SYNTHETICS (such as POLYESTER). In menswear, PLANT FIBER and CELLULOSIC are used as synonyms.

Velcro   Trademarked name for the fastening system patented by Swiss inventor George de Mestral in 1955 and manufactured by Velcro Industries. Velcro closures depend on two strips of fabric tape: One strip is covered with tiny hooks; the opposite strip is a thick PILE. To fasten, the strip of hooks is pressed into the strip of pile. To unfasten, the two strips are simply pulled apart.

According to de Mestral, one day during the summer of 1948, he and his dog returned home covered with burrs. Upon removing the annoying burrs and examining their tiny hooks under a microscope, he realized that the structure was ideally suited to fastening fabrics, whereupon he began working with a French textile maker to come up with an economically viable version. He coined the word Velcro as a hybrid of "velour" (velvet) and "crochet" (hook), the two sides of his invention.

velour   1. From the French word for VELVET, used to connote a velvetlike PILE fabric woven or knit from an unlikely fiber, such as wool or heavy cotton.   2. Velvet, in reference to French design.   3. A type of felt that resembles velvet.

velvet   A woven fabric with a cut PILE (long, uniform, hairlike protrusions from the surface); usually made of a fiber such as silk or rayon. Prized for its rich and sensual surface, velvet is made by several methods, all of which involve the creation of uniform loops on the surface of the cloth (usually from the WARP of the loom), which are then cut to create the pile.

velveteen   Usually describes a velvetlike woven fabric, with a shorter, often denser, PILE than velvet. Originally the word was applied only to velvets or velvetlike fabrics made from cotton; in contemporary usage, it implies sturdier, less dressy pile fabric and/or those created by cutting from the WEFT of the loom (as opposed to the traditional WARP construction of velvet).

venetian   1. In menswear, the word refers to a traditional, relatively untextured woven, almost always in a solid color of wool. See color plates.   2. In women's wear, the word tends to refer to a lustrous, smooth-faced fabric.

vent, single-vent, double-vent, *or* **ventless**   Refers to the vertical slit (or lack thereof) on the back of a jacket. Originally, the slit or slits were supposed to facilitate access to the back pants pockets and also keep the jacket from developing a bulging seat; in contemporary use

John Varvatos

their presence or absence is more dependent on the house style of the designer or tailor and/or the physique of the wearer.

In the United States, the most conventional choice may be the center single vent. Double vents are associated with double-breasted BLAZERS and shorter, British-cut jackets. The ventless jacket was originally considered a sportier, American style, but, over the decades, it became associated with designer wear (e.g., early ARMANI).

Versace, Donatella Born in 1955, the flamboyant blonde was best known as the younger sister and muse of designer GIANNI VERSACE until his abrupt death in 1997, when she took over as head designer.

She married (and later divorced) former model Paul Beck, who eventually ran the Versace menswear business, and had two children, Allegra (born in 1986) and Daniel (born in 1989).

Versace, Gianni Born in 1946 Reggio Calabria, a city in southern Italy surrounded by ancient ruins of many cultures, Giovanni Versace became best known for injecting huge doses of sex and rock 'n' roll into the then-staid world of Milan runways. He not only created vivid, flashy prints, he made it fashionable for men to be flam-

boyantly sexy. For his own fashion shows, he instituted the celebrity-stuffed front row and sparked the super-model movement of the 1980s. His company logo was the head of Medusa.

Versace first learned his trade from his mother Francesca, who was a successful dressmaker, and did not move to Milan to embark on a separate career until 1972, starting his own company with women's wear in 1978 and eventually employing his older brother Santo (who was in charge of finance), his younger sister Donatella (who designed the Versus line), Donatella's husband Paul Beck (who was in charge of menswear), and his own longtime companion Antonio D'Amico (in charge of Versace Sport). In 1989, he surprised the fashion world by adding a successful couture collection of women's wear. Spinoff collections eventually included Istante, Versus, Versace Jeans, Versace Sport, and a home furnishings line. Versace also designed costumes for opera and ballet, was credited with spurring the revitalization of Miami's South Beach neighborhood, and energetically collected art. His many friends and celebrity customers and friends included Elton John, Jon Bon Jovi, Princess Diana, Madonna, and Sting.

After successfully battling cancer in the early 1990s, Versace was murdered on the front steps of his villa in

Donatella Versace

Gianni Versace

Miami in 1997. Brother Santo inherited 30 percent of the business, Donatella inherited 20 percent and took over design duties, and Donatella's daughter Allegra inherited the remaining 50 percent.

vest   1. Synonym, especially in the United States, for a WAISTCOAT.   2. Synonym, especially in Britain, for the style of UNDERSHIRT that Americans would call a TANK.

vesta cases   Small, flat cases with closable lids for "vestas," i.e., matches, particularly in British usage. Often highly decorated and worn as a piece of jewelry attached to a watch chain, especially during the 19th century. Synonym: MATCHSAFES.

veste   The French word for jacket (not for vest). A frequent source of misunderstanding and mistranslation, when it is commonly mistaken to mean a WAISTCOAT. Similarly, the word *veston* also indicates a jacket (not a vest), and a *complet veston* is what most English speakers think of as a SACK SUIT.

Veste Forestière   A style of lapel-less jacket originated by ARNYS in Paris; usually worn in the context of a sports jacket. First made in 1947 for the architect Charles-Eduoard Jeanneret, better known as Le Corbusier, who was lecturing at the Sorbonne nearby and who needed a style that would both look modern and not ride up when he lifted his arms to write on the blackboard. The result, made by Léon Grimbert to Le Corbusier's specifications, included a sleeve design with a shortened SLEEVE CAP to allow more lift of the arm, PATCH POCKETS, and a band collar modeled on the traditional working jacket of the French forester, a sort of Gallic equivalent of the British

gamekeeper. In style, the jacket presaged the MANDARIN-COLLAR STYLES that would come into fashion a decade or two later. Rendered in various materials (from fine wool to colored corduroys), the Forestière was regularly reissued and went on to become the store's best seller.

Vibram   A registered trademark for the heavy rubber soles invented by Italian Alpine guide Vitale Bramani, who was inspired to create them after several of his friends died in a climbing accident that he attributed to their old-fashioned approach boots. Bramani experimented with various compounds in the Pirelli family's tire factory and brought his invention to market in 1937. Most Vibram soles are marked by the yellow logo set into either the back of the heel or the bottom of the sole.

vicuña   Refers to fiber (or the fabric made from it) sourced from the coat of a small and rare CAMELID called the vicuña; best known for being the most expensive material used in menswear.

A small animal, related to the LLAMA, GUANACO, and ALPACA, the vicuña (*Vicugna vicugna*) lives in the Andes, mostly in Peru, at an altitude of 12,000 to 16,000 feet, and its beige-blond or off-white coat yields a fiber—usually 12.5 MICRONS—finer than cashmere. Classified as a NOBLE FIBER and prized as the softest of the soft and rarest of the rare, the vicuña population was down to an estimated 15,000 animals by the late 1960s and was officially listed as an endangered species by the U.S. government in 1970. Thus, from 1970 until 2002, when it was officially downgraded to "threatened" status, importation of vicuña fiber or fabric was essentially outlawed in the United States.

Still classified as a protected species, the animal is now bred in captivity, and the local Peruvian population has

Vesta case

Vibram

been encouraged to see that it can make more money from protecting vicuña than hunting them. At the beginning of the 21st century, a number of luxury firms began promoting their limited editions of tailored clothing using vicuña or a vicuña blend, producing garments which used only 3 or 4 yards of the fabric and carried five- and six-figure price tags.

Victorinox   A lifestyle brand encompassing watches and outdoor gear, best known as original manufacturer of the SWISS ARMY KNIFE.

virgin wool   1. In the United States, "virgin" is any wool that does not reuse wool from a previously spun, knit, or woven wool yarn or fabric. The term was made official by the Wool Products Labeling Act of 1939 , a time when wool recycling was more widely practiced in the United States than it is today. The distinction was important because reprocessed wool has shorter fibers than "virgin" wool and is therefore considered less desirable for apparel. 2. In other countries, particularly Australia, "virgin" refers to wool from a sheep's maiden shearing.

viscose   Most often used as a synonym for RAYON. Supple and silky, viscose is classified as a CELLULOSIC FIBER, and appears in apparel where silk might be used, such as linings, pajamas, and underwear.

Technically the word viscose should refer only to a rayon produced by the particular chemistry called the "viscose process," which was first developed in 1892, although not widely applied until the 20th century.

visor   1. In a hat, the piece that protrudes from the front to shield the face; essentially a brim that only projects in one direction (e.g., on a BASEBALL CAP). Synonyms: BEAK; BILL; PEAK.   2. With a helmet or other similarly protective headgear, the movable piece that covers the eye area.   3. A piece of headgear worn to shield the eyes; essentially a visor attached to a headband, but with no cap to cover the crown of the head. When worn indoors, known as an EYESHADE.

Viyella   Trademarked name for the 55/45 wool/cotton blend twill fabric, first developed in 1891, in which LONG-STAPLE COTTON and MERINO wool are blended together *before* the yarn is spun. Resembling a light FLANNEL, Viyella is popular for shirts, particularly expensive SPORT SHIRTS, because it is machine-washable and shrink-resistant in addition to being soft. Although the fabric was developed by James and Robert Sissons at the start of the 1890s, the company for which they worked, Hollins, was actually founded in 1784 and is therefore the basis of the brand's claim to go all the way back to the 18th century.

E. Vogel   A New York City maker of bespoke boots and shoes, founded by German immigrant Egidius Vogel in 1879. Particularly well known for its custom, English-style riding boots.

voile   A crisp woven material, most often used for shirts. Extremely lightweight and translucent, voile uses yarns with a hard, smooth twist and then puts them in PLAIN WEAVE that is fairly open (meaning a low thread count per inch) so that the end effect is airy yet HARD-FINISHED. May be made of any fiber, but for men's shirts is most often a fine cotton.

vrillé   A type of fancy yarn, similar to BOUCLÉ, that is purposely spun so that it twists back upon itself and forms long nubs or lashes. Sometimes appears in novelty sweaters or the trim of knit accessories.

Vicuña

waist   1. A horizontal measurement of girth, generally taken at a point an inch below the navel.   2. In the shape of shoe's SOLE or bottom of a man's foot, the "waist" refers to the narrowing between the ball of the foot and the heel, specifically to the area on the bottom of the shoe that usually remains unworn, since it does not come in contact with the ground.   3. Jargon for the placement of the waistline, particularly on pants. Usually HIGH WAIST indicates above the natural waistline (a style particularly popular in the 1940s and 1950s). "Low waist," like the more commonly used term LOW-RISE, indicates pants that fall below the natural waist (usually determined as just beneath the navel).

waistcoat   The garment that most Americans refer to as a VEST; the third part of a "three-piece suit." In contemporary use, the waistcoat is almost always sleeveless, has a zippered or buttoned front (which may be either single- or double-breasted), and may or may not have its own lapels and/or collar. In industry jargon, the word generally connotes a more tailored, traditional garment. (Few retailers, for example, would refer to a "sweater waistcoat.")

The garment originated in the 17th century when CHARLES II introduced the ensemble that would evolve into the suit. At that time, and through the first half of the following century, the waistcoat was nearly as long as the jacket worn over it. However, by the late 18th century, it had become abbreviated, and, through most of the 19th century, ended at, or slightly below, the waist. In the darkest, drabbest days of 19th century, it was also the last bastion of male exhibitionism—a place to wear bright colors and fancy fabrics. In the 20th century, it was considered optional or old-fashioned with the rise of loosely fitted styles modeled on the SACK and sportier styles.

waist overall   A description for JEANS-like pants, usually made of DENIM, that predates wide use of the term "jeans."

wait coat   Early slang for a POLO COAT, from the days when polo was a more widely played sport and the coat was thrown on in between chukkers.

wale   The velvety, vertical rib created by weaving a pile fabric, especially in CORDUROY.

walking stick   Refers to a CANE used for fashion rather than function.

Wallabees   See CLARK WALLABEES.

Wallace Beery   Slang reference to a collarless, HENLEY-collar, long-sleeved undershirt because of its association with the 20th-century actor who wore that style on-screen.

wallpaper print   Jargon for a style of print that has a vertical emphasis—be it a stylized stripe or simply a vertically arranged pattern—and a fanciful or flowery decoration in the manner of old-fashioned wallpaper. Used to describe shirts.

walrus mustache   A style of exaggeratedly luxuriant mustache that droops below the bottom lip at each end (much fuller than the similarly drooping FU MANCHU mustache).

wamus   Equivalent to a suit coat in AMISH traditional dress. Usually black and made with no outside pockets. (The longer coat worn for more formal occasions is a MUTZE and resembles a FROCK COAT.)

warp   One of the two basic components of any woven fabric (the other is the WEFT). The warp is the yarn that runs up and down (i.e., vertically) and must be set up on the loom—which is then said to be "warped"—before any weaving can begin. Warp yarns must then remain at a uniform tension throughout the entire weaving process. Depending on the particular weave being produced, a fabric design may use multiple warps. Synonym for individual warp yarn: END.

warp-faced   Woven fabrics where the WARP threads (i.e., the ones running vertically, or from top to bottom when the fabric is on the loom) are more prominent than the WEFT yarns. Most DENIM, for example, would be called a "warp-faced twill," since its blue warp (versus its white FILL) usually dominates the fabric's appearance when it is worn. Synonym: warp-dominant.

warp-striped   Vertical stripes created by changing color or adding extra warp yarns (which run vertically on the loom). Most menswear stripes—PINSTRIPES, CHALK STRIPES, CANDY STRIPES, BENGAL STRIPES—are considered warp-striped.

watch cap   A close-fitting, RIBBED, knitted wool cap; traditionally worn by sailors outdoors (e.g., when "keeping watch"). The style is pulled down so that it hugs the head and covers the ears, usually covering most of the forehead as well. Like the PEACOAT, its functionality, cheapness, and availability in army surplus stores helped it cross over to the population at large.

watchfob   See FOB.

watch pocket   1. The small and shallow pocket (traditionally sized to accommodate a pocket watch), usually placed on the waist seam of pants on the right side.

2. A small and shallow pocket (sized to accommodate a pocket watch), placed on the right side of a vest.

Traditionally the pocket of equivalent size that appears on the outside of a jacket is called a TICKET POCKET and the small pocket built into the jacket's lining is referred to as a CASH POCKET.

water buffalo   A sturdy leather with a distinctive rough surface texture, sourced from the skin of both domesticated and wild water buffalo.

waulking   A now little-used term for the fabric finishing process usually known as FULLING or MILLING; an old word for purposely shrinking fabric—especially a wool fabric—to create a denser weave and narrow its width.

Originally, waulking was a labor-intensive process that involved the use of an agent like sheep's urine to turn textiles taken straight from the loom into sturdier, more weather-resistant fabrics, hence the genre of Celtic "waulking songs" sung by women to pass the time as they worked on the fabrics.

waxed cotton   A method of windproofing and waterproofing cotton used in the days before laminates (such as GORE-TEX) or resistant finishes (such as Teflon) were widely available. Special oils and waxes are applied to the surface and when, after extended use, the "waxing" begins to crack or wear thin, it can be "reproofed." In contemporary use, associated with BARBOUR and other traditional British sporting brands.

waxed thread   Thread that has been lightly coated, usually with beeswax, so that it is less prone to tangling. Used for hand sewing and hand finishing, particularly of BESPOKE garments.

wax resist   Refers to a general category of dyeing techniques—BATIK being the best-known example—in which wax is applied to protect the area of the fabric where no color change is desired (i.e., where it "resists" the dye). After dyeing, the wax is removed either by chemical means or application of heat. The process may then be repeated for multiple dye applications until the desired pattern is achieved.

Wayfarers   The iconic style of sunglasses launched by RAY-BAN in 1953, and that company's longtime best seller. The classic Wayfarer frame is squared at the temples and made of thick, black plastic that holds dark, opaque lenses. Featured prominently in music videos, television shows, and movies, especially *The Blues Brothers* in 1980 and the television show *MIAMI VICE* (1984–1989).

weave   1. Probably the most familiar form of textile construction: A loom is rigged with WARP yarns running from top to bottom, and then a WEFT yarn is inserted between them, crossing from side to side, thereby forming a solid fabric.   2. Jargon for a fabric, to distinguish it from alternative constructions, such as KNIT. Synonym: WOVEN.   3. Jargon referring to a particular type or subcategory of woven, used in conjunction with another modifier or identifier to distinguish one type from another. As in the usage: "Now the company is making its khakis in a twill weave; before, they used a plain weave."

web belt   1. A plain belt that uses webbing, rather than leather, for its construction and closes with adjustable rings, rather than a buckle.

In its decorative form, a staple of PREPPY style, where the web belt usually consists of a ribbon embroidered with a repeating motif (e.g., crossed tennis rackets),

Wayfarers: Dan Aykroyd and John Belushi on *Saturday Night Live*

which is stitched to a length of webbing and attached to brass rings or D-rings.

2. Reference to a SURCINGLE BELT, another staple of preppy style.

wedding bag   A small, usually highly decorated pouch. According to custom, worn after the ceremony to collect gifts of money from the wedding guests.

weejuns   Abbreviated reference to the style of shoe originally known as NORWEGIANS (from its country of origin); especially in reference to the styles made by BASS. (When referring to Bass Weejuns, the word should be capitalized. When making a general reference, it should be lowercased.)

weekender   Refers to a category of luggage, typically a bag between the size of a gym bag and a full-fledged suitcase—a bag just big enough to hold a weekend's worth of clothes. Its equivalent for a short business trip would be a TWO-SUITER, which is shaped like a sturdy, folded garment bag complete with hanger at one end.

weepers   Slang in the 19th century referring to extremely long SIDEWHISKERS, as in the style known as PICCADILLY WEEPERS.

weft   One of the two basic components of any woven fabric (the other is the WARP). In the creation of 99.9 percent of woven fabrics, the weft is the yarn that runs side to side (i.e., horizontally) once the loom is already set up or "warped," meaning that its (vertically positioned) warp yarns are already in place. (The rare exceptions are when a weft is used to form a curve or insert, something that tends to happen more in tapestry-style weaving.)

Because the tension is usually not as great on the weft yarn as on the warp (which must remain taut during its time on the loom and withstand the back-and-forth passage of a shuttle), weft yarns did not have to be as sturdy and/or tightly wound as warp yarns—hence the reference to them as "fill." DENIM, for example, is often described as having "a blue warp and a white fill."

Depending on the particular weave being produced, a fabric design may use multiple wefts.

Synonyms: FILL or filling. Synonym for individual weft yarn: PICK.

weft-faced   Woven fabrics where the WEFT threads (i.e., the ones running horizontally from SELVEDGE to selvedge, or from side to side when the fabric is on the loom) are more prominent than the warp yarns. Synonyms: filling faced; weft-dominant.

weft-striped   Fabric with horizontal stripes formed by changing the WEFT, which runs from side to side on the loom. Less common for men's apparel than WARP-STRIPED fabrics.

weight   Jargon used to classify menswear fabrics. As general designations, manufacturers and retailers may refer to SHIRTWEIGHTS, BOTTOMWEIGHTS, etc. Or they may be more specific, calling fabric a "10-ounce denim" or a "220-gram suitweight."

If the measurement is given in ounces it refers to a yard of fabric; if it is given in grams, it refers to a meter.

weighted silk   Refers to the days (generally before 1900) when silk was sold by weight, and compounds—usually metal salts—were added to make the material heavier (which often had the side effect of making otherwise cheap and lightweight silk easier to drape and sew).

In contemporary usage, notable because vintage garments originally made of weighted silk are more likely to irreparably shatter due to the effect of the additives upon silk fiber.

Weitz, John Born as Hans Werner Weitz in Berlin in 1923 into a Jewish family already successful in the apparel business, tall, dark, and handsome designer John Weitz sold clothes and accessories based in part on his own glamorously masculine lifestyle.

After a British public school education at St. Paul's and an apprenticeship at the Molyneux atelier in Paris, Weitz emigrated to the United States at the start of World War II and worked as a spy for the United States Office of Strategic Services (OSS) during the war. In peacetime, he got into the apparel business in New York and started his own label in 1954, concentrating on women's wear. During the 1950s, Weitz LICENSED his name widely, long before it was common practice among designers, implying that the practice gave him time for his many other interests (such as racing at Sebring). He expanded into the men's business in 1964, and soon became best known for menswear, winning a special COTY AWARD in 1974. In 1964 he also married Academy Award-nominated and Golden Globe-winning actress Susan Kohner (best known for 1959's *Imitation of Life*).

John Weitz

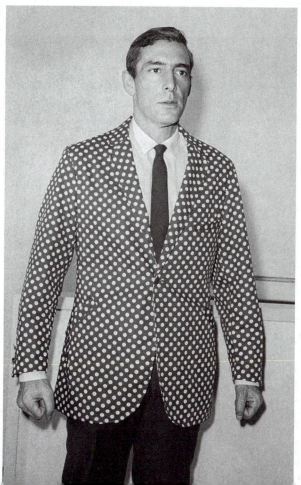

Weitz also designed sports cars, was a licensed race-car driver, was a member of the New York Yacht Club, entertained widely at his Park Avenue apartment, was an accomplished photographer, and wrote several books of history (mainly about World War II) as well as two books of fiction and a best-selling book of fashion advice, *Man in Charge*, published in 1974. Even when Weitz was less active as a designer, his name and face remained familiar to New Yorkers because of an extensive advertising campaign on city buses. He died in Bridgehampton in 2002.

wellies Slang for WELLINGTON boots or for any rain boots, especially in British usage.

Wellington *or* **Wellingtons** 1. In contemporary use, pull-on rubber rain boots that cover the calf, nicknamed "wellies." In England, the name is especially associated with a dark-green version. 2. In usage before the mid-20th century, may refer to any one of several garments (e.g., a 19th-century style of coat) named for Arthur Wellesley, Duke of Wellington, who helped the British defeat Napoleon at Waterloo and became prime minister in 1828. Clothes were one of Wellington's few indulgences and, as well as popularizing shaving, he hastened the century's trend toward TROUSERS by wearing them in preference to knee BREECHES.

welt Depending on the reference, may refer to either a garment detail, a type of seam, or a feature of shoe construction.

1. A style of creating an edge, especially around the slits made for pockets, using a flattened lip of fabric: The two lips, generally about a quarter of an inch deep, kiss around the opening. When used as the edging of a buttonhole, it replaces a handstitched or machine-stitched

edge. By tradition, the word welt is used more often for pants and the word BESOM for jackets and vests. When the same style of construction is used on a buttonhole, it is called a BOUND BUTTONHOLE.

2. A type of flattened, reinforced seam in which both SEAM ALLOWANCES are pressed to one side, with the bottom one being trimmed to a quarter of an inch; the top seam allowance is then pressed over it and stitched down so that it encases the bottom one. The method results in a strong, slim seam; but, because it requires the bottom seam allowance to be trimmed so closely, it can only be done with materials that do not easily unravel.

3. Refers to the method of attaching the UPPER of a shoe or boot to its SOLE, by stitching or glue. In the simplest construction, a strip of leather is placed on the outside of the shoe, with one side of that strip being joined to the upper and the other side being joined to the sole. Types of welts include: cemented, Goodyear, Littleway, and Norwegian.

welted edge   A slit opening, such as a pocket or buttonhole, trimmed with a WELT (as opposed to PIPING, a raw edge, handstitching, or machine stitching).

welted pockets   Usually indicates a split, slash, inserted pocket with no outer flap. Synonym (especially on a jacket): BESOM POCKET.

weskit   A slightly slangy synonym for WAISTCOAT—a word that is generally spelled more formally but often pronounced the same (particularly in British usage). Synonym: VEST.

western pocket   Refers to a style of trouser pocket in which the top of the pocket runs parallel to the waist seam (instead of slanting or being part of the pants' side seam). Never used in pleated pants.

Western wear   Industry category for COWBOY-styled clothes and accessories, including SNAP-FRONT shirts, COWBOY BOOTS, COWBOY HATS, BANDANAS, and Western-style tailored clothing (e.g., jackets made with front yokes and pants made with RISERS).

Vivienne Westwood   Agitator, appropriator, and agent provocateur, Vivienne Isabel Swire was born during World War II: on April 8, 1941, in Derbyshire's Peak District. Beginning in the 1970s, she would become best known as the main design mind behind a series of extremist styles (PUNK, NEW ROMANTICS) and accompanying retail ventures (Let It Rock, Sex, SEDITIONARIES, WORLDS END), which were co-opted by the fashion establishment with lightning rapidity. During the 1980s and 1990s, she was consistently copied by other designers in ways that made her influence on fashion vastly disproportionate to her modest financial success.

Both parents were avid ballroom dancers, and Vivienne, who learned to sew as a child, grew up with both the drab tweeds-and-wellies dressing of postwar England and the sequins-and-satins fantasy of 1940s and 1950s ballrooms. More germane to her development as a designer, Westwood also grew up in a world where the

Vivienne Westwood

working class let off steam through irony, dissidence, and poking fun at its social betters. A teenager when her family moved to London, she took a teacher training course then married tool shop apprentice Derek Westwood in 1962, giving birth to son Benjamin in 1963. By 1965, she met an art student named Malcolm Edwards, who would become better known as Malcolm McLaren. Unmarried, the couple had a son, Joe Corre (founder of the lingerie label Agent Provocateur), in 1967.

Sharing a house with McLaren and assorted other students preoccupied by the Situationists and Surrealists, Westwood began her fashion career by sewing, at McLaren's instigation, a pair of gigantically oversized workman's overalls in fluorescent yellow fabric. By 1971, the pair had opened a Teddy Boy shop called Let It Rock on the otherwise hippie-dominated King's Road. Bored with Teds, the two opened Too Fast to Live, Too Young to Die (prefiguring punk) in 1973, followed by Sex (a bondage and fetishwear specialist) in 1974. In 1976 they reopened the shop as Seditionaries, which became the epicenter of punk, but evolved into Worlds End (the epicenter of the New Romantic look) by 1979. From 1981, when their romantic partnership ended, Westwood began to take her own design more seriously. After 1983, she staged her runway shows wholly without McLaren's help.

As her technical prowess grew, she added more historicism in her clothes—quoting 18th-century tailoring and using traditional British fabrics like Harris tweed and tartan in perversely untraditional ways. She married her assistant Andreas Kronthaler in 1992. That same year, she was awarded an Order of the British Empire (where she famously displayed to photographers that she was wearing no panties beneath her pantyhose). She launched her "Man" line of menswear in 1996 and was named a Dame of the British Empire in 2006.

whiskering   Refers to a treatment applied to denim, especially jeans, to give the effect of aging. Typically, whiskering gives the effect of worn and/or bleached-out fine lines similar to the crease lines formed on very worn jeans. Sometimes called "cat whiskers."

white tie   Reference to the most formal evening wear; considered the nighttime counterpart to the morning suit and a step up in formality from black tie. Full-on white white-tie regalia traditionally consists of:

- A tailcoat
- Formal evening trousers made of cloth that matches the tailcoat. These traditionally feature two narrow ribbons outlining their outside leg seams and are usually supported by suspenders in order to be positioned appropriately high at the waist
- A formal dress shirt, which most often has a stiff collar and shirtfront (or, perhaps, a bib front) that must be fastened with studs
- A white waistcoat, usually made of cotton piqué and often cut with lapels (frequently designed so that it is backless)
- A white bow tie
- Opera pumps or equivalently formal footwear
- Accoutrements such as cufflinks, a pocket square, and a boutonnière

An exception to the rule that the tailcoat must match the material of the trousers is a hunt ball, or other fox-hunting-related formal events when members who are

White tie: George Murphy and Fred Astaire in *Broadway Melody of 1940*

entitled to wear a scarlet coat on the hunt field may wear a scarlet tailcoat with their evening trousers.

wicking   Refers to a fiber or fabric's ability to "wick" or draw moisture away from the body toward the outermost surface of the fabric, where it can more easily evaporate, thus keeping the wearer warmer and drier. For example, activewear or undergarments made of materials like POLYPROPYLENE or COOLMAX are usually touted for their wicking abilities. In industry jargon, this property may also be referred to as MOISTURE MANAGEMENT.

wideawake   A style of hat popular from 18th through the beginning of the 20th century (although some costume historians trace it even further back, linking the style to the broad-brimmed hats worn by the Quakers). Usually either straw or dark felt, the wideawake featured a deep, relatively rigid, brim and flattened crown (although the crown was sometimes creased by the wearer). To art lovers, it will be most familiar from Gilbert Stuart's 1782 portrait of William Grant, known as "The Skater."

wide-wale   Describes CORDUROY that has thick wales, usually six or fewer per inch.

wifebeater   Slang for white TANK undershirt.

wig bag   See BAG WIG.

wigan   A firmly woven BIAS fabric used primarily as INTERFACING in sleeve and jacket hems (to control shaping and distortion); can also be used to create a sleeve header in a sleeve cap. Named for the town of its original production in England. Never seen when the garment is being worn.

Wilde, Oscar   Born in Dublin in 1854, Anglo-Irish author Oscar Fingal O'Flahertie Wills Wilde became best known for the exaggeration of his personal dress (particularly during his espousal of AESTHETICISM), as well as witticisms on the subject of style (e.g., "It is only shallow people who do not judge by appearances") larded throughout works such as the 1891 novel *The Picture of Dorian Gray* and plays such as 1895's *The Importance of Being Earnest.*

His personal style went through three distinct phases: The first, which appeared when he left Trinity College in Dublin on a scholarship prize to attend Magdalen College from 1874 to 1878, was part of an Oxford student fashion that exaggerated aspects of English country style to the point of provocation, and was distinguished by loud checks (which looked particularly outrageous on Wilde's bulky, 6-foot, 3-inch body), loud colors, thick ties, thick fabrics, and too-small BOWLER hats (which looked especially absurd atop Wilde's long, fleshy face).

His second and most famous phase came when he moved to London and again adopted outrageous clothes as a route to personal publicity. In declaring his allegiance to Aestheticism, Wilde went the movement's most previously notorious figure, painter James McNeill Whistler, one better, by adopting knee breeches, longer locks, romantically inappropriate materials like velvet, cravats looped into droopy bows, poetic blouses, dramatic capes, and props like lilies and sunflowers. It was in just such a costume that Wilde sailed to New York in 1881 for a cross-country lecture tour that eventually

Oscar Wilde

comprised 140 talks and made him as renowned throughout the United States as he had become in London. However, Wilde's style was not widely imitated in either country, nor were many of his theories on men's dress (e.g., his urging that men wear brighter colors) as influential as his theories on interior design.

Later, after his marriage to Constance Lloyd in 1884, the birth of his sons Cyril and Vyvyan (in 1885 and 1886), and the success of his plays, Wilde settled into a more copied mode of attire. The extreme knee breeches were foregone in favor of full-length pants, the hair was somewhat shorter, the boutonnières still bizarre (green was a favored color) but proportionate, the overall outfit predominantly black. During this period he also created literature's most famously decadent dandies, such as Dorian Gray, who wore Parma violets in his buttonhole, and the overaged and overcultivated Lord Goring in 1895's *An Ideal Husband*.

After his public affair with Lord Alfred Douglas in the 1890s, his prosecution, and two years in jail, Wilde no longer had the means or motivation to affect attention-getting garb. He died in Paris in 1900.

The Wild One   The 1953 movie about motorcycle gangs starring Marlon Brando, which codified biker clothes as a uniform of youthful rebellion and inspired the sale of countless black leather MOTORCYCLE JACKETS for decades afterward. The main costume of narrator Johnny Stabler, as played by Brando, consists of heavy leather boots with thick soles; cuffed JEANS; a T-shirt; a

The Wild One: Marlon Brando

waist-length, SCHOTT BROTHERS black leather jacket with thick zipper closure, and a billed, captain's style cap.

Wilkes Bashford   The specialty stores founded by a man named WILKES BASHFORD in the summer of 1966, with a flagship on Sutter Street in San Francisco.

Using the tagline "menswear for the bold conservative," Bashford opened his 2,400-square-foot shop with pricey imports like BRIONI, which were relatively unknown in the United States at that time. As menswear became more influenced by designers, he expanded into designer lines, becoming an early and enthusiastic supporter of RALPH LAUREN in the late 1960s. He expanded into women's wear in 1978, by which time his store comprised 18,500 square feet.

Known for a level of service that included wet bars on every floor of the main store, the store expanded in the 1990s with a handful of WilkesSport shops throughout the tonier enclaves of the Bay Area.

windowpane plaid *or* windowpane check   A grid pattern using thin bars of color to outline a large blank area—in the same way that ribs of wood or steel outline the panes of glass in a window. Appears more spacious than other check patterns, since the ground color predominates. Often used as a pattern on top of another pattern (e.g., as an OVERCHECK on PLAIDS or HERRINGBONES).

In menswear, when a windowpane check is the fabric's chief design (and not used as an overcheck), the grid is sometimes subtly elongated so that what appears at first glance to be a pattern of perfect squares is actually a pattern of rectangles. In the final garment, these run vertically—in a windowpane shape—so that the rectangle is taller rather than wider (supposedly to give the wearer that same appearance).

wind shirt A very lightweight, pull-on style of long-sleeved shell, made to be worn as a top layer during sports (climbing, jogging, biking) for protection from the wind. May or may not also be water-resistant.

Windsor collar On a DRESS SHIRT, a variation of SPREAD COLLAR, so-called because it is made to accommodate a necktie with a WINDSOR KNOT.

Windsor knot Refers to a method of tying a NECKTIE so that it results in the largest knot, and of the three best-known methods (the other two being the FOUR-IN-HAND and the HALF-WINDSOR KNOT), the one that produces the fattest knot and uses up the most amount of tie (about 3 inches more than a four-in-hand knot).

Although the knot is named after EDWARD VIII when he was the Duke of Windsor, it is a misnomer: Despite the Duke's pronounced fondness for neckties and BOW TIES with a puffy, fat knot, he used a FOUR-IN-HAND knot on neckties that had been specifically made with a thicker lining (usually by HAWES & CURTIS) to create the style he favored. (He also, on more than one occasion, declared that he did not knot his tie with the method named after him and demonstrated his own method for *Vogue* in 1967.)

Because it results in a thick knot, the Windsor is associated with spread collars (or at least collars with enough of a spread to accommodate it) and is usually in fashion at the same time as medium or wide neckties. The half-Windsor knot is a variant resulting in a thinner knot. The traditional four-in-hand results in a knot that is smaller still.

wing collar A style of high, standing collar in which the front edges, for the sake of both comfort and style, are bent down to create "wings"; in the 20th and 21st centuries, most often associated with FORMALWEAR. When worn with a BOW TIE, convention dictates that the collar be positioned so that the wings are behind the bow.

wingtips Refers to a style of shoe with a toe cap that, instead of running across the foot in a straight line, comes to a point in its center and then sweeps dramatically back toward the instep in two curves, like the outline of angel wings or the shape made by the top of a valentine; most often a feature of BROGUES, where BROGUEING and GIMPING are used to accentuate the curves.

winklepickers British slang for a style of exaggeratedly pointy-toed shoes, associated with TEDDY BOYS. Synonyms: BEETLECRUSHERS; BROTHEL CREEPERS.

How to tie a Windsor knot

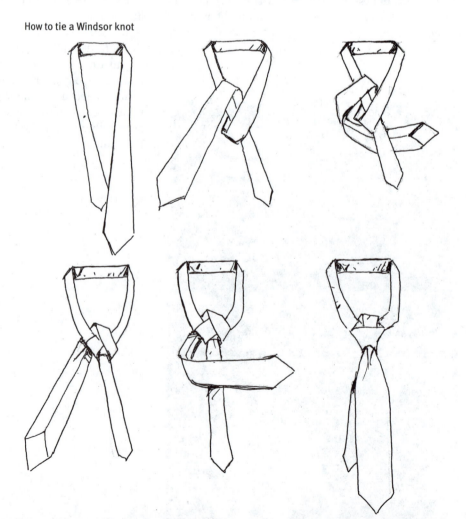

wire rims   A style of FRAMES for EYEGLASSES in which the lens is surrounded and supported with a thin strip of metal.

woad   See INDIGO.

wool   May refer to either the fiber or the fabric made from it. Wool is made by shearing the fleece from sheep, with different breeds of sheep yielding different qualities of wool. For example: MERINO sheep generally produce the finest wool (and are responsible for most of the fiber that goes into wool SUPER 100S), whereas Romney and Lincoln breeds produce a sturdy wool prized for carpets and upholstery. Classified as a PROTEINACIOUS fiber, wool dyes well and has excellent RECOVERY—being about four times as elastic as COTTON.

The properties inherent in the fiber make it the ideal material for tailored clothing, and it is no coincidence that England, which had a thriving wool industry, was also the place where the arts of cutting and tailoring developed. Whereas silk can be unrewarding in attempts to form it to the body, wool cloth responds well to the shaping techniques used in a traditional suit.

See also CRIMP; MERINO; MICRONS; SUPER 100S; WOOLEN; WOOL PRODUCER; WORSTED.

woolen   In menswear, the word has a specific meaning for a style of textile that has a wooly surface—whereas its smoother, differently processed counterpart is called WORSTED.

Technically, a woolen is produced by spinning and carding wool, whereas a worsted is produced by spinning and combing the wool. In general, a worsted is smooth and a woolen is not (which is why, to make matters more confusing, a fabric is occasionally called a woolen even if it is mostly made from another fiber). Or, to oversimplify

again, a worsted is traditional town wear and a woolen is traditional country wear.

In the United Kingdom and countries that copy its usage, the word is spelled "woollen" with a double *L*.

Woolmark Awards   Awards for men's fashion design sponsored by the Wool Bureau (a promotional division of the International Wool Secretariat) in conjunction with the MEN'S FASHION ASSOCIATION (MFA). In 1989, the Wool Bureau took over the awards, which had been known as the CUTTY SARK AWARDS and were founded in 1980. However, the Bureau discontinued them after the 1992 edition due to both lack of funds and competition from the CFDA awards.

wool producer   Refers to sheep farmers only. The maker of the actual fabric is known as a woolen producer, a worsted producer, or a mill.

Woolrich   America's oldest operating woolen mill, Woolrich was founded by English immigrant John Rich and his partner Daniel McCormick in Little Plum Run, Pennsylvania, in 1830. In 1843, Rich bought out his partner, then moved to the city that is now Woolrich, Pennsylvania, in 1845. The mill prospered during central Pennsylvania's logging boom and is still identified primarily with rugged, "lumberjack"-style plaids. The company is credited with the invention of the RAILROAD VEST, a sturdy, four-pocket wool utility vest popular with workers on the railroad, another local industry. In 1939, it helped to outfit Admiral Byrd's third expedition to Antarctica and, in the early 1960s, enjoyed a vogue among college men.

workboots   A general reference to sturdy footwear designed for utilitarian purposes such as construction or

Wingtips

farmwork (even though certain subgroups may adopt the same styles for fashion purposes). For the last century or two, workboots generally have been made of heavy leather in a LACE-UP design that extends over the ankle to cover and support the joint. Other characteristics: a thick, nonslip sole (sometimes reinforced with a steel SHANK) and a wide, square-shaped or round toe with a high TOE BOX (sometimes reinforced with steel to prevent crushed toes).

worked buttonhole   A general term for a BUTTON-HOLE that is finished (either by hand or machine), as opposed to being a mere slit in the fabric. Not to be confused with WORKING BUTTONHOLES.

working buttonholes   Used to describe BUTTON-HOLES that are functional rather than purely decorative. In practice, most frequently used to refer to the cuff buttonholes on a man's SUIT: On a less expensive suit, the cuff buttons are usually decorative; on a BESPOKE or expensive readymade suit, they are usually functional.

workshirt   A general reference to long-sleeved, button-front shirt, usually made of a sturdy fabric such as DENIM or CHAMBRAY—fabrics that literally make it a BLUE-COLLAR STYLE—and used for utilitarian purposes such as construction or farmwork (even though certain subgroups may adopt the same style for fashion purposes). Other characteristics: buttoning BARREL CUFFS, a small-ish collar, one or two PATCH POCKETS on the chest, and construction giving it the ability to withstand repeated machine launderings.

workwear   An industry designation for the sturdy clothes and utilitarian styles favored by BLUE COLLAR laborers, including construction and factory workers. Brands associated with this retail category include CARHARTT, Spiewack, Williamson-Dickie (better known as Dickies), and Wolverine. In the 1990s, workwear brands were also adopted as STREETWEAR by young men who favored their authenticity, their association with masculinity, and their loose fit.

Worlds End   The retail epicenter of the NEW ROMANTIC look, open roughly from 1979 to 1982 by Malcolm McLaren and VIVIENNE WESTWOOD at 430 King's Road in London's Chelsea (on the site of SEDITIONARIES, their previous venture). Store decor featured 13-hour clocks running backward, a tilted floor that evoked a storm-tossed pirate's ship, Lewis Carroll quotations, and an elaborately tarnished chandelier. In 1981, it served as the launching pad for "Pirates," Westwood's first runway collection.

worsted   The most common fabric of traditionally tailored men's suits, worsted refers to WOOL or wool blend that has a smooth surface and no nap, because it has been woven from smooth, neatly twisted yarns made from combed fiber. Because of this smooth surface, worsted is also prized for its ability to render patterns clearly and distinctly. By contrast, the term WOOLEN is used to imply a wool fabric with a "woolier," rougher surface.

wovens   Industry jargon for woven (as opposed to KNIT) fabrics. The term is used most often in describing shirts, as in "our new line of wovens, based on Italian shirtings, is outperforming our knit tops."

wraps *or* **wrap-arounds**   A style of sunglasses in which the lenses are integrated into what looks like a continuous, rounded frame without any angles, so that the frames "wrap" around the head. Fashionable, off and on, from the 1960s onward. (See FRAMES.)

wrap coat A style of coat that falls to the knees or below and is belted like a bathrobe. A wrap usually has no buttons or other closures in front (one method of dis-tinguishing it from a TRENCH COAT), and sartorial tradi-tion dictates that it never be worn with a suit and tie. In their heyday in the 1930s, wrap coats were often made of CAMEL'S HAIR. At that time, the POLO COAT was some-times a wrap coat, and the style was synonymous with casual chic—something a toff might toss over tennis togs or polo gear.

XLA A brand of stretch fiber introduced in the 21st century by Dow. Unlike SPANDEX stretch fibers, such as LYCRA, XLA was olefin-based and therefore had a chemistry that gave it greater toleration to heat, chlorine, and certain dyes.

yachting cap Refers to a quasi-naval style of flat, circular cloth cap (most often white, navy, or black) with a dark visor, usually with a crest or insignia placed front and center on the cap and decorated with gold braid where the visor joins the cap.

Traditionally it might be sported by the boat's captain or owner. (For example, a dark version was worn by the Skipper character played by Alan Hale Jr. in the 1964–67 TV series *Gilligan's Island*.)

Yamamoto, Yohji Born in Yokohama in 1943, Yamamoto graduated from fashion studies at the Bunka-fukuso Gakuin—better known as the Bunka Institute—

in Tokyo in 1969, and established his own company in 1972, rising to prominence in the West during the 1980s together with fellow Japanese designers Rei Kawakubo (a one-time personal partner), Matsuhiro Matsuda, and Issey MIYAKE.

After opening a Paris boutique in 1981, he became known for rethinking apparel conventions: His early men's collections featured draped silhouettes, unconventionally finished fabrics, and oddly augmented shirts (e.g., double bibs or collars). For example: At a 1986 Paris runway show, he offered tailored clothing made entirely of knits, alongside clothes with clashing patterns, and long, lapel-less jackets.

During the following decades, he became a regular participant in Paris ready-to-wear presentations, although his interpretations remained intellectual and idiosyncratic. In 1989, he became the subject of a full-length documentary, CARNET DE NOTES SUR VÊTEMENTS ET VILLES (*Notebook on Clothes and Cities*), by director Wim

Yachting cap: Alan Hale, Jr. on *Gilligan's Island*

Yohji Yamamoto

Wenders. In 1993, he opened a store on Paris's Left Bank designed by Yoshiki Matsui. In 2002, he published *Talking to Myself*, which he called "an illustrated notebook." In 2001, he debuted a successful sneaker collection for ADIDAS, called Y3, followed by apparel under that label in 2003.

yard goods As one might guess, refers to fabric that is sold by the yard. Hence, the material found in fabric shops is known as yard goods (and thereby distinguished from materials produced and sold directly to large manufacturers). Synonym: PIECE GOODS.

yarmulke Yiddish word for the small SKULLCAP worn by observant Jewish men, especially those in the Modern Orthodox tradition. Hundreds of variations on the size, construction, and wearing of the yarmulke exist—signifying everything from degree of religious observance, to age, to nationality. For example: In contemporary use in the United States, it may be a small circle that is flat, homemade (often crocheted), and kept in place with the help of one or more hair clips. Synonym: KIPPAH.

yarn In the apparel and textile industries refers to a continuous strand of FIBER or fibers that is then knitted, knotted, woven, or otherwise made into fabric. In this sense, yarn can be almost microscopically fine—what people outside the apparel industry would probably call thread—and is rarely as thick as the yarns sold for crafts (such as knitting yarns).

Yarns may have a Z-TWIST, an S-TWIST, or be in the form of a continuous FILAMENT with no twist at all. The factory that manufactures yarn is referred to as a SPINNER. The hierarchy of production is: fiber, yarn, fabric, apparel.

yarn-dye Jargon for any fabric in which the yarn is dyed before being woven or knit. Shirtmakers frequently tout this distinction because yarn-dyes give an intensity of color to a stripe or pattern that is rarely equaled by GRAY GOODS that, after their production, receive their patterning at a CONVERTER.

The Yellowplush Papers William Makepeace Thackeray's satire of dandyism and fashionable novels like BULWER-LYTTON's *PELHAM*. Published in London in 1837, its hero is a snobbish footman named Charles Yellowplush, who sets himself up as an authority on matters of style.

The Yellow Earl Born in 1857, Hugh Cecil Lowther was—even in a time and place noted for sportsmen and high rollers—famous for living life to the fullest. His nickname derives from the vivid canary yellow splashed so showily on his livery and his impressive fleet of carriages (and later on his even more impressive fleet of automobiles), as well as from his ownership of numerous yellow Labrador dogs (usages inspired by the gold color featured on the family crest).

The Yellow Earl also came of age at a time when, as evidenced by the use of "Yellow Nineties" as a synonym for *fin de siècle* decadence and "The Yellow Book" as the semiofficial journal of the AESTHETIC movement, the color was synonymous with saucy novels, displays of dandyism, and all things offensive to middle-class morality and normality.

Before acceding to the title as fifth Earl of Lonsdale in 1882 upon the death of his brother, Lowther had already run away to join the circus (in Switzerland) and become a cowboy, buffalo hunter, and rancher (in Wyoming). Notorious as a *bon vivant* and admirer of beautiful

The Yellow Earl (center, in cutaway)

women (lover of Lily Langtry, among many, many others), he frequently entertained royal friends like the Kaiser and the Prince of Wales, and lavished money on horses (serving as master of foxhounds of three of England's best hunts and establishing many of that sport's subsequent protocols, including those of dress for the field). When a scandal involving the actress Violet Cameron made it expedient for him to leave England, he undertook a 14-month expedition to the Arctic, returning in 1890 as a national hero. Having once decked heavyweight John L. Sullivan in a private bout, he used his influence to give regulations and respectability to the sport of boxing (giving his name to the Lonsdale Belt). An Edwardian through and through, he also smoked the type of outsized cigars that became known as Lonsdales, was a senior steward of the Jockey Club, a president of the National Sporting Club, and was first president of the Automobile Association.

As might be expected, his style of dress was consistent with his exuberant and extravagant style of living. Although always meticulously turned out for the hunt field, he set off for the Arctic in outrageous checks that occasioned as much press as the proposed expedition. He also pioneered the wearing of pink-and-white striped shirts that later came to be identified as JERMYN STREET style and was cited by EDWARD VIII as a stimulus for Edward's own predilection for pattern mixing.

His expenditures forced him to sell the family seat in 1921. He died in 1944. In 1965, he became the subject of Douglas Sutherland's biography *The Yellow Earl*.

yé-yé   Refers to French pop styles of the mid-1960s, supposedly derived from the French pronunciation of THE BEATLES' chorus "yeah, yeah, yeah." The older, less teenybopper-ish counterpart of the same period would be the *MINET*.

Y-fronts   A design for the fly of underpants, resembling an upside-down Y; invented in 1934 by the Cooper Company for its JOCKEY SHORTS. Today used as a generic name—especially in England—for any underwear in that style.

YKK   The world's largest producer of ZIPPERS. Founded as Yoshida Kogyo Kabushililaisha in Japan in 1934; abbreviated to YKK during the 1990s, and operative under that name in more than 50 countries.

yoke   In menswear construction, refers to a piece of fabric that runs across the front and/or back of a shirt or jacket, extending horizontally from shoulder to shoulder and starting vertically from the top shoulder seam to end in a point above the midline of the chest or shoulder blades. The large front and/or back pieces of the shirt or jacket are then attached to the yoke. (Less often, the term can also be applied to pants construction where the yoke falls around the waist instead of the neck and shoulders.)

In contemporary use, most tailored jackets are constructed without yokes. However, the front yoke is a prominent feature of Western-style shirts and JEAN JACKETS. The back yoke is a prominent feature of the NORFOLK jacket and most BUTTON-DOWN shirts. SPLIT-YOKE construction is also associated with old-fashioned, custom shirtmaking.

In a shirt, the fabric that falls from the back yoke may either be gathered into an inverted box pleat, a regular box pleat, or in two pleats (one placed over each shoulder blade).

yuzen   A Japanese dyeing process prized for its ability to translate the vividness and variation of color associated with painting into the permeability and flexibility required of wearable textiles. The method, which uses rice paste resist, takes its name from artist Yuzensai Miyazaki, who pioneered the technique in the 17th century.

Z-twist   A technical term that refers to one of the two directions that yarn can twist. Upon close inspection, a Z-twist yarn shows a line from lower left to upper right, in a direction imitative of writing the letter "Z." (Its counterpart is the S-TWIST, which indicates yarn twists in the opposite direction.) Weavers sometimes exploit the differences—for instance, the way that each reflects light—to create effects in the finished fabric.

zazou   France's counterpart to America's ZOOT SUITER, who flourished—particularly in Paris and particularly in its jazz clubs—during the Vichy regime. (According to legend, the word "zazou" was taken from the chorus of a 1942 Johnny Hess song.) During a time of fabric rationing, the zazou wore baggy jackets that extended to mid-thigh and used extravagant amounts of material. He espoused bebop long before it was fashionable in France. He flouted wartime sobriety with loud checks—particularly lumberjack styles. His pants were cinched at the waist, his ties were narrow, his collar was buttoned high and held together with a horizontal pin. He wore thick-soled, clunky shoes and long hair that was slightly poufed on top (occasionally with a thin mustache, à la jazz guitarist Django Reinhardt). After the war, the zazou culture began to integrate into the Left Bank jazz clubs around Saint Germain.

Zegna   See ERMENEGILDO ZEGNA.

zephyr   Jargon for either a particularly lightweight yarn or the fabric woven from it; in menswear, applied most often to cotton shirt fabric. The word is also applied to wovens made of other fibers (e.g., wool, silk, blends) but always indicates a PLAIN-WEAVE fabric that is exceptionally soft and lightweight—and usually pricey.

zibeline   Refers to a type of soft, woven fabric that is either exclusively made of animal hairs (such as alpaca, camel or mohair) or is a blend of one of those animal fibers with traditional sheep's wool. Particularly popular at the end of the 19th century.

zigzag   A type of machine stitch that follows a Z pattern and is often used on a fabric's edge or its underside (or "wrong" side) to prevent unraveling of the fabric's edge.

zip-out lining   A removable lining—most often made of quilted material, pile, or fur—that is added to a raincoat or shell for warmth. Not popular until after World War II, zip-out linings were supposed to increase a coat's efficiency and economy by making it wearable year-round. The ZIPPER on a zip-out extends down the front of the garment and sometimes around the neck, but almost never around hem or armhole. The lining portion is made to cover the wearer's torso but usually does not extend into the sleeves, so that, when removed, it looks like a long vest.

zipper   All zippers are constructed of "teeth" (aligned in parallel strips) plus a "slider" (the movable fastener that slides along the two tracks of teeth), which is usually manipulated by means of a tag called a "pull" or a "tab." At the top of the traditional zipper, there is a "top stop" on each side (which looks like extra-large teeth) to keep the slide from coming off track; on the opposite end, there is a single horizontal bar called the "bottom stop" to stop it from sliding off the bottom.

Although the zipper as we know it today was not patented until 1917 and did not become popular for fly-front pants until well into the 1930s, several inventors in the 19th century had tried to come up with faster and better methods of getting dressed and undressed. For example: In 1851, Elias Howe patented the "continuous clothing closure"; and, in the 1890s, Whitcomb Johnson invented the "clasp locker." Both look like a cross between the modern zipper and long strips of hook-and-eye closures.

It was Johnson who founded the Universal Fastener Company to perfect his invention, and it was an employee of that company, Gideon Sundback, who is credited with inventing the modern zipper in December of 1913 and patenting it as the "separable fastener" in 1917. Sundback's version improved on previous attempts by adding more teeth per inch. Sundback also invented machinery that made mass production of this new fastener cost-effective.

The name "Zipper" was coined by the B.F. Goodrich company when it used Sundback's invention to make rubber boots during the early 1920s. During the following decade, most men encountered zippers only on tobacco pouches and galoshes. As a clothing fastener, the zipper was promoted first for children's wear in the early 1930s and later for adult apparel. The zip fly did not appear on Savile Row until 1934 (when it was endorsed by Lord Louis Mountbatten and then by the future EDWARD VIII), and it was not widely used until the end of that decade.

Types of zippers also include the "two-ended" or "separating zipper," which separates completely, and the "invisible zipper," which uses teeth that are hidden inside the seam when the zipper is zipped (because it is appropriate for lighter-weight fabrics, the latter appears more often in women's wear). See also YKK.

Zoolander   The 2001 movie directed by and starring Ben Stiller as male supermodel Derek Zoolander. Tagline: "3 percent body fat. 1 percent brain activity."

During his career at Balls, the male modeling agency managed by Murray Ballstein (played by Jerry Stiller, Stiller's real-life father), Derek has perfected a knowledge of hair products and a pose he calls "Blue Steel." As the film progresses, his industry dominance is challenged by a newcomer named Hansel (played by Owen Wilson) who challenges him to a "walk-off," and he also unwittingly becomes the stooge of an evil designer (played by Will Ferrell) who makes him part of a plot to assassinate the prime minister of Malaysia.

zoot suit   Considered a statement of cultural identity as much as a costume, the zoot suit flourished in black and Latino communities at the end of the 1930s and beginning of the 1940s, reaching its peak of notoriety in 1943, when Cab Calloway wore similar styles in the movie *Stormy Weather*, when cartoonist Al Capp included a zoot-suited character in his popular L'il Abner

Zoolander

comic strip, and when the summer of civil unrest known as "the Zoot Suit Riots" began in Los Angeles and then spread to other cities.

The jacket of the suit so favored by sharpies and hep cats could be either double- or single-breasted, but invariably boasted padded shoulders that were enormous even by the standards of the 1940s, plus huge PEAK LAPELS, and a draped front; it tapered to a tiny, fitted waist and then flowed to the knees. The pants that went with it were hitched high above the natural waistline by SUSPENDERS, ballooned from a pleated waistband, and then abruptly pegged into extra-tight, cuffed ankles. In the slang of the day: "a killer-diller coat . . . a drapeshape . . . a stuff cuff . . . shoulders padded like a lunatic's cell."

Ideally, all this was worn with a PENCIL MUSTACHE and long, POMADED and POMPADOURED hair, and accessorized by an oversized, skinny bow tie made to look like an airplane propeller's blade, and pointy-toed, thick-soled shoes, preferably from Florsheim. The favored headgear was a felt hat with a broad brim, low crown, and extra-long feather on its side. A keychain might be attached to a belt loop and then droop past the knees before finding its way back to a trouser pocket. If CUF-FLINKS were used, they were enormous and flashy. PIN-STRIPES were greatly favored, but jazzier, showier variations were considered even better.

On June 11, 1943, the *New York Times* reported that the zoot suit currently cost anywhere from $18 to $75 in Harlem. The same story also repeated as gospel the claim that it had been invented in February of 1940 by a Gainesville, Georgia, busboy named Clyde Duncan who walked into Frierson-McEver's and ordered a suit with 37-inch-long jacket because he wanted to look like Clark Gable's Rhett Butler character in 1939's *Gone With the Wind*. Although widely repeated in the white press of the time, that claim was later considered apocryphal. Much

like the exaggeratedly baggy silhouette that would later be identified with HIP-HOP, the zoot suit is more likely to have originated in an urban, music-centered subculture: The JAZZ SUITS of the early 20th century had sported a similar silhouette, and fans of urban jazz had been using the word zoot as a synonym for extravagant style since the mid-1930s.

When the 1942 War Production Board's fabric rationing essentially banned further zoot suit manufacture, wearing the style became a red flag: In June of the following year, when sailors on shore leave in Los Angeles saw Mexican-American teenagers in zoot suits, they beat up the teenagers and stripped off the suits. Similar "zoot suit riots" erupted in other cities, with the black and Latino zoot suiters mostly unprotected by police. Thereafter, the zoot suit served, especially in Latino culture, as a reference to rebellion against the white, middle-class mainstream.

zori *or* **zori sandal** Japan's traditional flat-bottomed, simply styled THONG sandals, worn by both men and women. Although the thongs are usually fabric, the material of the bottoms may vary (e.g., tatami straw for casual wear, black lacquer or vinyl for more formal use). They differ from geta sandals (which have a similar thong top, but are made with a heel) and can be worn with TABI, which are socks with a split between the big toe and second toe.

Zouave The 19th-century French military units whose distinctive, ethnically inspired uniforms were perceived as particularly dashing and exotic and therefore were adapted as fashions for men, women, and children during the 19th century. The costume's key characteristics: baggy, gathered pants; a short, collarless jacket with a front opening that was curved at the bottom rather than squared; curving braid decoration on the jacket, often in a contrasting color; and a long waist sash. Frequently, a tasseled FEZ topped off the outfit.

The word derives from French pronunciation of the name of a Berber tribe, and the initial recruits in 1831 French army regiments were North African natives. Recruitment practices among the Zouave regiments of the French army changed repeatedly during subsequent decades, but the traditional of colorful battle dress remained in place until the trench tactics of World War I forced a change to khaki and relegated the romantic costume to non-battle dress. However, Zouave dress also appeared in other armies. For example: During the Civil War in the United States, both Union and Confederate fielded fighters in adapted Zouave uniforms (a Zouave being a recurring minor character in the novel *Gone With the Wind*).

Zucchelli, Italo   Born in 1965 in Italy, the designer, who became best known as designer of the menswear collections for CALVIN KLEIN, briefly studied architecture, then graduated from fashion college in Florence and, after various assistantships, designed for Romeo Gigli and Jil Sander, before joining Calvin Klein in 2000. In 2004, when Klein himself retired from his company, Zucchelli became creative director for menswear and thereafter became noted for runway shows integrating high-tech and unconventional materials into the brand's luxurious minimalism.

zucchetto   The small SKULLCAP, usually silk, worn by Roman Catholic clergy. Like the CASSOCK, which it matches, the zucchetto's color is dictated by rank: The pope wears white; cardinals wear red; bishops wear purple; priests wear black.

Zuleika Dobson   The 1910 satirical novel by MAX BEERBOHM, which uses a dandy-as-dunce duke as its male protagonist.

Selected Bibliography

Aav, Marianne, ed. *Marimekko: Fabrics, Fashion, Architecture.* New Haven, CT: Yale University Press, 2004.

Adler, Bill. *Fred Astaire: A Wonderful Life.* New York: Carroll & Graf, 1987.

Amaden-Crawford, Connie. *Guide to Fashion Sewing.* New York: Fairchild Publications, 2004.

Anquetil, Jacques. *La Soie en Occident.* Paris: Flammarion, 1997.

Astaire, Fred. *Steps in Time.* New York: Da Capo Press, 1979.

Balfour-Paul, Jenny. *Indigo.* London: British Museum Press, 1998.

Barr, Ann, and Peter York. *The Official Sloane Ranger Handbook.* New York: St. Martin's, 1983.

Batterberry, Michael and Ariane. *Mirror Mirror: A Social History of Fashion.* New York: Holt, Rinehart and Winston, 1977.

Beerbohm, Max. *Zuleika Dobson.* New York: Modern Library, 1998.

Bhushan, Jamila Brij. *The Costumes and Textiles of India.* Bombay: Taraporevala's, 1958.

Birnbach, Lisa, ed. *The Official Preppy Handbook.* New York: Workman Publishing, 1980.

Bliss, Debbie, ed. *Traditional Knitting from the Scottish and Irish Isles.* New York: Crown, 1991.

Bonafante, Larissa. *Etruscan Dress*. Baltimore: The Johns Hopkins University Press, 1975.

Boucher, François. *20,000 Years of Fashion: The History of Costume and Personal Adornment*. New York: Harry N. Abrams, 1987.

Braun & Schneider. *Historic Costume in Pictures*. New York: Dover, 1975.

Breward, Christopher, Edwina Ehrman, and Caroline Evans. *The London Look: Fashion from Street to Catwalk*. New Haven, CT: Yale University Press, 2004.

Brusatin, Manlio. *A History of Colors*. Boston: Shambala, 1991.

Buchet, Martine. *Panama: A Legendary Hat*. New York: Assouline, 2004.

Burnham, Dorothy K. *Warp and Weft: A Textile Terminology*. Toronto: Royal Ontario Museum, 1980.

Cabrera, Roberto, and Patricia Flaherty Meyers. *Classic Tailoring Techniques: A Construction Guide for Men's Wear*. New York: Fairchild Publications, 1983.

Calloway, Stephen. *Liberty of London: Masters of Style and Decoration*. Boston: Bullfinch Press, 1992.

Carlyle, Thomas. *Sartor Resartus*. Oxford: Oxford University Press, 1987.

Carr, Ian. *Miles Davis: The Definitive Biography*. New York: Thunder's Mouth Press, 1998.

Chaille, François. *La Grande Histoire de la Cravate*. Paris: Flammarion, 1994.

Chambers, Jack. *Milestones: The Music and Times of Miles Davis*. New York: Da Capo Press, 1998.

Chenoune, Farid. *A History of Men's Fashion*. Paris: Flammarion, 1993.

Chenoune, Farid. *Brioni*. New York: Universe Vendome, 1998.

Davis, Miles. *Miles: The Autobiography*. New York: Simon & Schuster, 1989.

Debray, Régis, and Patrice Hugues, eds. *Cultural Guide to Fabrics*. Paris: Babylone/Fayard, 2005.

De la Haye, Amy, and Cathie Dingwall. *Surfers, Soulies, Skinheads, and Skaters: Subcultural Style from the Forties to the Nineties.* Woodstock, NY: The Overlook Press, 1996.

Delamare, François, and Bernard Guineau. *Colors: The Story of Dyes and Pigments.* New York: Harry N. Abrams, 2000.

DeLano, Sharon. *Texas Boots.* New York: Penguin Books, 1981.

Delpierre, Madeleine. *Le Costume: Consulat/Empire.* Paris: Flammarion, 1990.

de Dillmont, Thérèse. *The Complete Encyclopedia of Needlework.* Philadelphia: Running Press, 1972.

Donaldson, Maureen. *An Affair to Remember: My Life with Cary Grant.* New York: Putnam, 1989.

Drake, Alicia. *The Beautiful Fall: Lagerfeld, Saint Laurent, and Glorious Excess in 1970s Paris.* New York: Little, Brown, 2006.

Edward, Duke of Windsor. *A King's Story: The Memoirs of the Duke of Windsor.* New York: G.P. Putnam's Sons, 1947.

Edwards, Isabel M. *Glove Making.* London: Sir Isaac Pitman & Sons, 1929.

Emery, Irene. *The Primary Structures of Fabrics: An Illustrated Classification.* Washington, D.C.: Watson-Guptill Publications/Whitney Library of Design, 1990.

Finlay, Victoria. *Color: A Natural History of the Palette.* New York: Random House, 2004.

Flusser, Alan. *Style and the Man: How and Where to Buy Fine Men's Clothes.* New York: HarperStyle, 1996.

Flusser, Alan. *Dressing the Man: Mastering the Art of Permanent Fashion.* New York: HarperCollins, 2002.

Foulkes, Nick. *Last of the Dandies: The Scandalous Life and Escapades of Count d'Orsay.* New York: St. Martin's Press, 2003.

Fountain, Charles. *Another Man's Poison: The Life and Writing of Columnist George Frazier.* Chester, CT: The Globe Pequot Press, 1984.

Gaines, Steven and Sharon Churcher. *Obsession: The Lives and Times of Calvin Klein.* New York: Birch Lane Press, 1994.

Garfield, Simon. *Mauve: How One Man Invented a Color That Changed the World.* New York: W. W. Norton, 2000.

Gavenas, Mary Lisa, *Color Stories.* New York: Simon & Schuster, 2002.

Giles, Sarah. *Fred Astaire: His Friends Talk.* New York: Doubleday, 1988.

Gillow, John and Nicholas Barnard. *Traditional Indian Textiles.* New York: Thames and Hudson, 1993.

Grimble, Ian. *Scottish Clans and Tartans.* Edison, NJ: Alva Press, 2002.

Gross, Michael. *Genuine Authentic: The Real Life of Ralph Lauren.* New York: HarperCollins, 2003.

Hall, Maggie. *Smocks.* Aylesbury, UK: Shire Publications, 1979.

Hamill, Pete. *Why Sinatra Matters.* New York: Little, Brown, 1998.

Hansen, Henny Harald. *Costumes and Styles.* New York: E. P. Dutton, 1956.

Harrison, E. P. *Scottish Estate Tweeds.* Newmill, Elgin, UK: Johnstons of Elgin, 1995.

Harvey, John. *Men in Black.* Chicago: The University of Chicago Press, 1995.

Head, Edith, and Paddy Calistro. *Edith Head's Hollywood.* New York: E. P. Dutton, 1983.

Holland, Merlin. *L'Album Wilde*, Paris: Anatolia, Editions du Rocher, 2000.

Hostetler, John A. *Amish Society.* Baltimore: Johns Hopkins University Press, 1980.

Houston, Mary G. *Ancient Greek, Roman, and Byzantine Costume and Decoration.* London: Adam & Charles Black, 1963.

Hua Mei. *Chinese Clothing.* Beijing: China Intercontinental Press, 2004.

Jacobs, George. *Mr. S: My Life with Frank Sinatra.* New York: HarperEntertainment, 2003.

Johnston, Lucy, with Marion Kite and Helen Persson. *Nineteenth-Century Fashion in Detail.* London: V&A Publications, 2005.

Join-Diéterle, Catherine and Françoise Tétart-Vittu. *La Mode et l'Enfant 1780–2000*. Paris: Musée Galliera, 2001.

Jones, Mablen, with Ellen Colon-Lugo. *Getting It On: The Clothing of Rock 'n' Roll*. New York: Abbeville Press, 1987.

Jump, Harriet Devine, gen. ed. *Silver Fork Novels, 1826–41*. London: Pickering & Chatto, 2005.

Kelly, Ian. *Beau Brummell: The Ultimate Dandy*. London: Hodder and Stoughton, 2005.

Kohler, Carl. *A History of Costume*. New York: Dover, 1963.

Kosa. *Dictionary of Fiber and Textile Technology*. Charlotte, NC: Kosa, 1999.

Koslin, Désirée G., and Janet E. Synder, eds. *Encountering Medieval Textiles and Dress*. New York: Palgrave Macmillan, 2002.

Kraybill, Donald B. *The Riddle of Amish Culture*. Baltimore: The Johns Hopkins University Press, 2001.

Laver, James. *Taste and Fashion: From the French Revolution to the Present Day*. London: George G. Harrap, 1937.

Laver, James. *The Book of Public School, Old Boys, University, Navy, Army, Air Force, and Club Ties*. London: Seeley Service, 1968.

Labovitch, Mark. *Clothes Through the Ages*. London: Quality Press, 1944.

Lester, Katherine Morris, and Bess Viola Oerke. *Accessories of Dress: An Illustrated History of the Frills and Furbelows of Fashion*. Peoria: The Manual Arts Press, 1940.

Lethuillier, Jean-Pierre, ed. *Des Habits et Nous Vêtir Nos Identités*. Rennes, France: Presses Universitaires de Rennes, 2007.

Levine, Joshua. *The Rise and Fall of the House of Barneys*. New York: William Morrow, 1999.

Lobenthal, Joel. *Radical Rags: Fashions of the Sixties*. New York: Abbeville Press, 1990.

Lytton, Edward Bulwer. *Pelham*. New York: Lincoln, 1972.

Madsen, Axel. *Living for Design: The Yves Saint Laurent Story.* New York: Delacorte Press, 1979.

Mansel, Philip. *Dressed to Rule: Royal and Court Costume from Louis XIV to Elizabeth II.* New Haven, CT: Yale University Press, 2005.

de Marinis, Fabrizio. *Velvet: History, Techniques, Fashions.* Milan: Idea Books, 1994.

de Marly, Diana. *Fashion for Men: An Illustrated History.* New York: Holmes & Meier, 1986.

Martin, Richard, and Harold Koda. *Jocks and Nerds: Men's Style in the 20th Century.* New York: Rizzoli, 1989.

Martin, Richard, and Harold Koda. *Splash! A History of Swimwear.* New York: Rizzoli, 1990.

Master Designer. *Modern Garment Design and Grading: Clothing for Men and Boys.* Chicago: The Master Designer, 1987.

McCann, Graham. *Cary Grant: A Class Apart.* New York: Columbia University Press, 1997.

McDowell, Colin. *The Man of Fashion: Peacock Males and Perfect Gentlemen.* New York: Thames and Hudson, 1997.

McInerney, Jay, Nick Foulkes, Neil Norman, and Nick Sullivan. *Dressed to Kill: James Bond, the Suited Hero.* Paris: Flammarion, 1996.

Meller, Susan, and Joost Elffers. *Textile Designs: Two Hundred Years of European and American Patterns.* New York: Harry N. Abrams, Inc., 2002.

Menkes, Suzy. *The Windsor Style.* Topsfield, MA: Salem House Publishers, 1988.

Moers, Ellen. *The Dandy.* New York: The Viking Press, 1960.

Molloy, John T. *New Dress for Success.* New York: Warner Books, 1988.

Moor, Jonathan. *Perry Ellis.* New York: St. Martin's Press, 1988.

Mulvagh, Jane. *Vivienne Westwood: An Unfashionable Life.* New York: HarperCollins, 1998.

Mundy, Julie in association with Graceland. *Elvis Fashion: From Memphis to Vegas.* New York: Universe, 2003.

Pastoureau, Michel. *The Devil's Cloth: A History of Stripes.* New York: Washington Square Press, 2001.

Pedorthic Footwear Association. *Professional Shoe Fitting*. New York: National Shoe Retailers Association, 2000.

Porcher, Richard Dwight, Sarah Fick. *The Story of Sea Island Cotton*, Charleston: Wyrick Co., 2005.

Ribeiro, Aileen. *Dress in Eighteenth Century Europe 1715–1789*. New York: Homes & Meier Publishers, 1984.

Ribeiro, Aileen. *The Art of Dress: Fashion in England and France 1750 to 1820*. New Haven, CT: Yale University Press, 1995.

Ribeiro, Aileen. *Fashion and Fiction: Dress in Art and Literature in Stuart England*. New Haven, CT: Yale University Press, 2005.

Rice, Charles S., and John B. Shenk. *Meet the Amish: A Pictorial Study of the Amish People*. New Brunswick, NJ: Rutgers University Press, 1947.

Roche, Daniel, trans. by Jean Birrell. *The Culture of Clothing: Dress and Fashion in the Ancien Regime*. Cambridge: Cambridge University Press, 1994.

Sandford, Christopher. *McQueen: The Biography*. New York: Taylor, 2003.

Schoeffler, O. E., and William Gale. *Esquire's Encyclopedia of 20th Century Men's Fashions*. New York: McGraw-Hill, 1973.

Severa, Joan L. *Dressed for the Photographer: Ordinary Americans and Fashion, 1840–1900*. Kent, OH: The Kent State University Press, 1995.

Sherwood, James. *The London Cut: Savile Row Bespoke Tailoring*. Florence: Marsilio/Fondazione Pitti Discovery, 2007.

Simon, Marie. *Les Métiers de l'Elégance*. Paris: Éditions du Chêne, 1996.

Starmore, Alice. *Alice Starmore's Book of Fair Isle Knitting*. Newtown, CT: Taunton, 1993.

Starmore, Alice. *Fishermen's Sweaters*. North Pomfret, UK: Trafalgar Square, 1993.

Summer, Anthony. *Sinatra: The Life*. New York: Alfred A. Knopf, 2003.

Terrill, Marshall. *Steve McQueen: Portrait of an American Rebel*. New York: D.I. Fine, 1993.

Thackeray, William Makepeace. *Works.* New York: AMS Press, 1968.

Thomson, David. *The New Biographical Dictionary of Film.* New York: Alfred A. Knopf, 2004.

Tortura, Phyllis G., ed., and Robert S. Merket, consulting ed. *Fairchild's Dictionary of Textiles.* 7th ed. New York: Fairchild Publications, 2005.

Trachtenberg, Jeffrey A. *Ralph Lauren: The Man Behind the Mystique.* Boston: Little, Brown, 1988.

Ulrich, Laurel Thatcher. *The Age of Homespun.* New York: Alfred A. Knopf, 2001.

Vass, Laszlo, and Magda Molnar. *Handmade Shoes for Men.* Cologne: Konemann, 1988.

Vermorel, Fred. *Fashion and Perversity: A Life of Vivienne Westwood.* London: Bloomsbury, 1996.

Versace, Gianni. *Men Without Ties.* New York: Abbeville Press, 1994.

Vigarello, Georges, trans. by Jean Birrell. *Concepts of Cleanliness: Changing Attitudes in France Since the Middle Ages.* Cambridge: Cambridge University Press, 1988.

Waisman, A., and Master Designer. *Modern Custom Tailoring for Men.* Chicago: Master Designer, 1986.

Walker, Barbara G. *A Treasury of Knitting Patterns.* New York: Charles Scribner's Sons, 1968.

———. *A Second Treasure of Knitting Patterns.* New York: Charles Scribner's Sons, 1970.

Walker, Richard. *The Savile Row Story: An Illustrated History.* London: Prion, 1988.

Walkley, Christina and Vanda Foster. *Crinolines and Crimping Irons, Victorian Clothes: How They Were Cleaned and Cared For.* London: Peter Owen, 1978.

Waugh, Norah. *The Cut of Men's Clothes 1600–1900.* New York: Theatre Arts Books, 1964.

Weston, Madeline. *Classic British Knits.* New York: Crown, 1986.

Wilde, Oscar. *The Picture of Dorian Gray.* New York: Dover, 1993.

Williams, Greg. *Bond on Set.* New York: Dorling Kindersley, 2006.

Zakim, Michael. *Ready-Made Democracy: A History of Men's Dress in the American Republic, 1760–1860.* Chicago: The University of Chicago Press, 2003.

Ziegler, Philip. *King Edward VIII.* New York: Alfred A. Knopf, 1991.

Credits

A

Abboud, Joseph, page 1, courtesy of Fairchild Publications, Inc.

Academic gowns, page 2, istockphoto.com

Achkan, page 3, United Press International/New York World-Telegram and the Sun Newspaper Photograph Collection/Library of Congress

Adinkra, page 4, © Margaret Courtney-Clarke/CORBIS

Aestheticism, page 5, Frederick Burr Opper/Library of Congress

Afro, page 6, © Michael Ochs Archives/Getty Images

After Six, page 7 (left), The Advertising Archives

Agnès b., page 7 (right), © Jean Francois Rault/Kipa/Corbis

American Gigolo, page 9, courtesy Everett Collection

Amish dress, page 10, © Robert W. Ginn/PhotoEdit Inc.

Ant, Adam, page 12, image by © Denis O'Regan/CORBIS

Argyle, page 16 (left), illustration by Don Morrison

Armani, Giorgio, page 16 (right), courtesy of Fairchild Publications, Inc.

Arnys, page 18, © Thomas Heydon/courtesy of Fairchild Publications, Inc.

The Arrow Collar Man, page 19, J. C. Leyendecker/Library of Congress

Ascot, page 20, illustration by Don Morrison

Astaire, Fred, page 21, © Michael Ochs Archives/Getty Images

Chlamys, page 89, courtesy of Fairchild Publications, Inc.

Collars, page 93, courtesy of Fairchild Publications, Inc.

Columbia Sportswear, page 95, courtesy of Columbia Sportswear

Combs, Sean, page 96 (left), courtesy of Fairchild Publications, Inc.

Concho belt, page 96 (right), Edward S. Curtis/Library of Congress

Converse high tops, page 98, © Mario Tama/Getty Images

Cotton, page 100, © David Nance/ Courtesy USDA

Cowboy boots, page 102, istockphoto.com

Cuban heel, page 105, courtesy of Fairchild Publications, Inc.

D

Dale of Norway, page 110 (left), courtesy of Dale of Norway

Dalmatica, page 110 (right), © Erich Lessing/Art Resource

Dashiki, page 111, © Lee Lockwood/Time Life Pictures/ Getty Images

Davis, Miles, page 112, Christian Rose/Dalle/Retna Ltd.

Deely-boppers, page 113, © Robert Daly/Getty Images

Deerstalker, page 114, © 20th Century-Fox Pictures/ Photofest

Derby (also, brogue), page 115, illustration by Don Morrison

Dhoti, page 116, © Keystone/Getty Images

DNR, page 118, courtesy of Fairchild Publications, Inc.

Dolce & Gabbana, page 119, © Davide Maestri/Courtesy of Fairchild Publications, Inc.

D'Orsay, page 120, © The Granger Collection, New York

Dreadlocks, page 124, © David Corio/Retna Ltd.

E

earmuff parade, page 129, courtesy of the U.S. Patent Office

Edward VII, page 130, Lea Brothers & Company/Library of Congress

Edward VIII, page 131, Library of Congress

Ellis, Perry, page 133, courtesy of Fairchild Publications, Inc.

Ermenegildo Zegna, page 135, courtesy of Fairchild Publications, Inc.

Etro, page 137, © Massimo Listri/CORBIS

F

Fall, page 140, illustration by Don Morrison

Ferry, Brian, page 142, © Pascal Baril/Kipa/Corbis

Fibula, page 143, courtesy of Fairchild Publications, Inc.

FIT, page 145, courtesy of Fairchild Publications, Inc.

Flip-flops, page 147, courtesy of Old Navy

Flusser, Alan, page 148, © Steve Eichner/Courtesy of Fairchild Publications, Inc.

Ford, Tom, page 149, courtesy of Fairchild Publications, Inc.

Four-in-hand, page 151, illustration by Don Morrison

Fu Manchu, page 155, courtesy Everett Collection

G

Galliano, John, page 157, © Jimi Celeste/Courtesy of Fairchild Publications, Inc.

Garment District, page 158, photo © Erin Fitzsimmons

Gaultier, Jean Paul, page 159, © George Chinsee/Courtesy of Fairchild Publications, Inc.

George IV, page 160, British Cartoon Prints Collection/Library of Congress

Girbaud, page 162, © Stephane Cardinale/People Avenue/Corbis

Grant, Cary, page 167, © Ernest Bachrach/Getty Images

Grunge, page 169, © S.I.N/Alamy

H

Hakama, page 174, © Eric Nathan/Alamy

Half-Windsor, page 175, illustration by Don Morrison

Half-zip, page 175, courtesy of Columbia Sportswear

Hawaiian shirts, page 179, © Dynamic Graphics Group/Creatas/Alamy

Hermès, page 181, Courtesy of Fairchild Publications, Inc.

Hilfiger, Tommy, page 182, © Craig Blankenhorn

Hippie, page 184, © Ted West/Central Press/Getty Images

I

Ice cream suit, page 189 (left), © Steve Eichner/Courtesy of Fairchild Publications, Inc.

Ikat, page 189 (right), © Richard Goodbody, Inc./The Jewish Museum/Art Resource

Incroyable, page 190, The Art Archive/Bibliothèque des Arts Décoratifs Paris/Dagli Orti

Intarsia, page 191, courtesy of Fairchild Publications, Inc.

Interfacing, page 192, © AP Photo/John Stanmeyer/VII

It Happened One Night, page 193, © COLUMBIA/THE KOBAL COLLECTION

J

Jacob the Jeweler, page 195, courtesy of Fairchild Publications, Inc.

Jockey, page 198, courtesy of Jockey

Julian, Alexander, page 199, courtesy of the author

K

Kafiyeh, page 201, © AP Photo

Kenosha Klosed Krotch, page 203, courtesy of the author

Kilt, page 205, istockphoto.com

Kiton, page 206, courtesy of Fairchild Publications, Inc.

Klein, Calvin, page 207, © David Turner/Courtesy of Fairchild Publications, Inc.

Kressley, Carson, page 208, © Giovanni Rufino/Bravo

Kurta, page 209, © photosindia/Getty Images

L

Lacoste, page 210, © AP Photo

Lagerfeld, Karl, page 211, courtesy of Fairchild Publications, Inc.

Lansky's, page 212 (left), © AP Photo/File

Lapel, page 212 (right), illustration by Don Morrison

Lauren, Ralph, page 213, © George Chinsee/Courtesy of Fairchild Publications, Inc.

Lederhosen, page 214, © Hulton-Deutsch Collection/CORBIS

Leisure suit, page 216, © Evening Standard/Getty Images

Levi Stauss & Co., page 217, courtesy of Levi Strauss & Co.

Liberace, page 218, © AP Photo/Mario Cabrera

Little Lord Fauntleroy, page 220, courtesy of Library of Congress

Loro Piana, page 223, courtesy of Fairchild Publications, Inc.

Louis XIV, page 224, Hyacinthe Rigaud/John Davis Batchelder Collection/Library of Congress

M

Macaroni, page 226, Mary Dorothy George/British Cartoon Prints Collection/Library of Congress

Mao Zedong, page 230, © AP Photo

Marimekko, page 231, courtesy of Fairchild Publications, Inc.

McQueen, Steve, page 233, © Horst P. Horst/Courtesy of Condé Nast Archives

Men's Vogue, page 235 (left), courtesy of Condé Nast

Merino, page 235 (right), courtesy of Icebreaker

Messenger bag, page 236, courtesy of Macy's Inc.

Missoni, page 238, courtesy of Fairchild Publications, Inc.

Miyake, Issey, page 239, courtesy of Fairchild Publications, Inc.

Mohawk, page 241, © Jeremy Gray/Alamy

Morrison, Jim, page 244, © Yale Joel/Time Life Pictures/ Getty Images

Mullet, page 247, © Redferns Music Picture Library/ Alamy

N

Nantucket Reds, page 250, courtesy of Nantucket Reds/Photo © Erin Fitzsimmons

Nehru jacket, page 252, © Zachary Freyman/Courtesy of Condé Nast Archives

Nightshirt, page 255, © Bettmann/CORBIS

Nike "Just Do It", page 256, PRNewsFoto/Nike, Inc.

Ninja, Willi, page 257 (left), © Off White Productions/ Courtesy Everett Collection.

Norfolk jacket, page 257 (right), © Hulton Archive/Getty Images

Norwegian, page 258, illustration by Don Morrison

Nudie (Cohn), page 259, © Jeff Albertson/CORBIS

Rat Pack, page 304, © CBS Photo Archive/Getty Images

Rocawear, page 309, courtesy of Fairchild Publications, Inc.

Rugby shirt, page 310, © AP Photo/Shizuo Kambayashi

S

Saddle shoulder, page 312 (left), illustration by Don Morrison

safari jacket, page 312 (right), courtesy Everett Collection

Sailor suit, page 313, George Grantham Bain Collection/Library of Congress

Saint Laurent, Yves, page 314, courtesy of Fairchild Publications, Inc.

Santa Claus, page 316, The Coca-Cola Company/Library of Congress

Savile Row, page 318, courtesy of Fairchild Publications, Inc.

Selvedge, page 323, courtesy of Fairchild Publications, Inc.

Seven-fold tie, page 324, courtesy of Fairchild Publications, Inc.

Shaft, page 325, © MGM/Photofest

Shedded sheep, page 328, © Stephanie Epiro/Courtesy of Fairchild Publications, Inc.

Shoe (oxford explosion), page 330, illustration by Don Morrison

Shoe trees, page 331, courtesy of Fairchild Publications, Inc.

Side-tie shoe, page 332, courtesy of Fairchild Publications, Inc.

Sinatra, Frank, page 334, © Murray Garrett/Getty Images

Ski mask, page 335, illustration by Don Morrison

Slap-sole, page 336, illustration by Don Morrison

Slimane, Hedi, page 337, courtesy of Fairchild Publications, Inc.

Smith, Paul, page 338, courtesy of Fairchild Publications, Inc.

Smock 339, page illustration by Don Morrison

Sombrero, page 341, George Grantham Bain Collection/Library of Congress

Steinkirk, page 345, illustration by Don Morrison

Stockinette swatch, page 346, Courtesy of Fairchild Publications, Inc.

Stock tie, page 347, illustration by Don Morrison

Suit separates, page 348, © Douglas Miller/Getty Images

Swiss Army Knife, page 352, AP Photo/Keystone, Eddy Risch

T

Teddy boy, page 357, © Joseph McKeown/Picture Post/Hulton Archive/Getty Images

Thistle bowtie, page 358 (left), © MGM/Columbia Pictures/Photofest

Thong sandal, page, 358 (right), illustration by Don Morrison

Toga, page 361, © Alinari/Art Resource

Trench coat, page, 364, courtesy Everett Collection

Trilby, page 365, courtesy Everett Collection

Troy, New York, page 366, Keystone View Company/Library of Congress

Tuxedo, page 368, © André Kertész/Courtesy of Condé Nast Archives

Two-button, page 369, © Jimi Celeste/Courtesy of Fairchild Publications, Inc.

U

Umbrella, page 370, istockphoto.com

Uncle Sam suit, page 371, courtesy of Library of Congress

Undershirt, page 372, © Warner Bros./Photofest

V

Vandyke, page 374, courtesy of Fairchild Publications, Inc.

Varvatos, John, page 375, © David Turner/Courtesy of Fairchild Publications, Inc.

Versace, Donatella, page 376 (left), © Steve Eichner/Courtesy of Fairchild Publications, Inc.

Versace, Gianni, page 376 (right), AP Photo

Vesta, page 377 (left), © Amoret Tanner/Alamy

Vibram, page 377 (right), courtesy of Vibram

Vicuña, page 378, © John and Lisa Merrill/Corbis

W

Wayfarers, page 381, © NBC/Photofest

Weitz, John, page 383, © AP Photo

Westwood, Vivienne, page 384, courtesy of Fairchild Publications, Inc.

White tie, page 385, © MGM/Photofest

Wilde, Oscar, page 386, courtesy of Library of Congress

The Wild One, page 387, © Columbia Pictures/Photofest

Windsor knot, page 388, illustration by Don Morrison

Wingtips, page 389, courtesy of Fairchild Publications, Inc.

Y

Yachting cap, page 392 (left), courtesy Everett Collection

Yamamoto, Yohji, page 392 (right), courtesy of Fairchild Publications, Inc.

Yellow Earl, page 393, © Topical Press Agency/Getty Images

Z

Zoolander, page 396, © Paramount Pictures/Photofest